LEGAL METHOD
AND **WRITING**

Aspen Coursebook Series

LEGAL METHOD
AND WRITING

SEVENTH EDITION

CHARLES R. CALLEROS
PROFESSOR OF LAW
ARIZONA STATE UNIVERSITY

Wolters Kluwer

Law & Business

Published by Wolters Kluwer Law & Business in New York.

Wolters Kluwer Law & Business serves customers worldwide with CCH, Aspen Publishers, and Kluwer Law International products. (www.wolterskluwerlb.com)

To contact Customer Service, e-mail customer.service@wolterskluwer.com, call 1-800-234-1660, fax 1-800-901-9075, or mail correspondence to:

Wolters Kluwer Law & Business
Attn: Order Department
PO Box 990
Frederick, MD 21705

Printed in the United States of America.

1 2 3 4 5 6 7 8 9 0

ISBN 978-1-4548-3099-3

Calleros, Charles R., author.
  Legal method and writing / Charles R. Calleros, Professor of Law, Arizona State University. -- Seventh Edition.
     pages cm
  Includes bibliographical references and index.
  ISBN 978-1-4548-3099-3 (alk. paper)
  1. Legal composition. 2. Law--United States--Methodology. I. Title.
  KF250.C345 2014
  808.06'634--dc23
                                                    2013049422

About Wolters Kluwer Law & Business

Wolters Kluwer Law & Business is a leading global provider of intelligent information and digital solutions for legal and business professionals in key specialty areas, and respected educational resources for professors and law students. Wolters Kluwer Law & Business connects legal and business professionals as well as those in the education market with timely, specialized authoritative content and information-enabled solutions to support success through productivity, accuracy and mobility.

Serving customers worldwide, Wolters Kluwer Law & Business products include those under the Aspen Publishers, CCH, Kluwer Law International, Loislaw, Best Case, ftwilliam.com and MediRegs family of products.

CCH products have been a trusted resource since 1913, and are highly regarded resources for legal, securities, antitrust and trade regulation, government contracting, banking, pension, payroll, employment and labor, and healthcare reimbursement and compliance professionals.

Aspen Publishers products provide essential information to attorneys, business professionals and law students. Written by preeminent authorities, the product line offers analytical and practical information in a range of specialty practice areas from securities law and intellectual property to mergers and acquisitions and pension/benefits. Aspen's trusted legal education resources provide professors and students with high-quality, up-to-date and effective resources for successful instruction and study in all areas of the law.

Kluwer Law International products provide the global business community with reliable international legal information in English. Legal practitioners, corporate counsel and business executives around the world rely on Kluwer Law journals, looseleafs, books, and electronic products for comprehensive information in many areas of international legal practice.

Loislaw is a comprehensive online legal research product providing legal content to law firm practitioners of various specializations. Loislaw provides attorneys with the ability to quickly and efficiently find the necessary legal information they need, when and where they need it, by facilitating access to primary law as well as state-specific law, records, forms and treatises.

ftwilliam.com offers employee benefits professionals the highest quality plan documents (retirement, welfare and non-qualified) and government forms (5500/PBGC, 1099 and IRS) software at highly competitive prices.

MediRegs products provide integrated health care compliance content and software solutions for professionals in healthcare, higher education and life sciences, including professionals in accounting, law and consulting.

Wolters Kluwer Law & Business, a division of Wolters Kluwer, is headquartered in New York. Wolters Kluwer is a market-leading global information services company focused on professionals.

Dedicated to our wonderful mother, Emily Calleros,
with love and gratitude

SUMMARY OF CONTENTS

CONTENTS

Contents

TABLE OF CHARTS AND SAMPLE DOCUMENTS

PREFACE

The activities of practicing attorneys speak volumes about the importance of legal writing classes in law school. Although analytic skills and a general knowledge of legal principles form the intellectual foundation of the practice of law, legal analysis is only as effective as the quality with which it is expressed. In your practice, you undoubtedly will devote a substantial proportion of your time and effort to drafting legal documents such as office memoranda, letters, pleadings, motions, briefs, contracts, and wills. Moreover, techniques of expression are closely linked to the underlying substantive analysis; indeed, problems in writing style often betray confusion in the analysis.

Unfortunately, as a first-semester law student, you may have difficulty seeing the relationship between your efforts in legal writing classes and your short-term objectives for success in law school. With this book, I hope to reassure you that the work in your first-year legal writing courses will directly contribute to your success with law school exams as well as with legal documents that you draft in a summer clerking position or in postgraduate employment. I attempt to achieve that objective in two ways. First, I hope to eliminate any mystery in the study of law by comprehensively examining the three critical components for success in law school: (1) briefing and synthesizing cases, (2) reorganizing and summarizing course materials in course outlines, and (3) analyzing and answering essay examinations. Second, I demonstrate in Parts I through V that the skills you develop in analyzing a client's legal problem and drafting an office memorandum are directly transferable to your task of analyzing an essay exam and writing the exam answer.

Additionally, this book examines techniques of advocacy and client representation that should appeal to a broad spectrum of readers: participants in a first-year moot-court program, students in an advanced writing seminar, student law clerks, and practicing attorneys. For example, Parts VI through VIII examine written advocacy in the context of pleadings, pretrial motions, and appellate briefs. Moreover, they thoroughly examine principles of writing and persuasion that apply generally to any litigation document. Part IX provides a step-by-step approach to drafting simple contracts, advice letters, and demand letters. Finally, the extensive citations in footnotes, most of which first-year law students can pass over, will provide attorneys with a valuable source of authorities.

Chapters 1, 12 through 14, and 17 of this book address matters of style. They use problems and examples to outline a general approach to style that focuses on the policies underlying conventions of composition. In these chapters, I encourage you to adopt the following philosophy: We should not memorize and mechanically apply rules of composition any more than we would mechanically apply "black letter" rules of law. Instead, we must understand the goals and purposes of the conventions of legal writing, and we should apply them flexibly to satisfy those goals and purposes.

Of course, this book reflects my own style quirks and biases: I freely split infinitives but always use the serial comma, and I dislike sexism in language. While writing this book, I encountered the problem of sexism in language most often in the form of personal pronouns in the third person. If I constantly resorted to an ostensibly generic pronoun normally associated with the male gender, such as "his" or "him," I would offend those readers who do not view the pronoun as gender generic and who believe that the increasing number of female attorneys and judges deserves specific recognition. On the other hand, the disjunctive phrase "his or her" often needlessly clutters already complex sentences, and plural pronouns such as "they" are not always consistent with content. As a provocative response to the problem, I have alternated between male and female pronouns, for example, by referring to an associate in a law firm with the pronoun "he" and to his assigning attorney with the pronoun "she." This approach may distract readers at one time or another, perhaps because it catches readers assuming that a judge or a senior partner is male. If so, perhaps the distraction is constructive: It may help us to envision a profession so well integrated that feminine pronouns and ethnic names will sound natural and commonplace.

The text is heavily footnoted with source material and with acknowledgments to others whose ideas inspired the text. Readers may find some of the additional information in the footnotes to be illuminating or to be helpful in practice as a starting point for research. Otherwise, however, busy students can focus on the text and skip the footnotes without missing any significant points.

Charles R. Calleros

January 2014

ACKNOWLEDGMENTS

My interest and enthusiasm for legal writing stem largely from the inspiration and training that I received as a court law clerk at the Office of Central Staff Attorneys for the United States Court of Appeals for the Ninth Circuit. In particular, I am grateful to United States Court of Appeals Judge Procter Hug, Jr., who sowed the seeds of my current views on flexible, policy-oriented approaches to legal writing.

Other attorneys, judges, and colleagues contributed to my first edition with their comments on early drafts. In particular, I thank the late Thomas Gordon, who was a staff attorney for the Arizona Court of Appeals, fellow legal writing instructor, and former classmate at the University of California at Davis School of Law. Mr. Gordon's keen analytic insights into the art of legal writing contributed greatly to this book. Other important contributors include the rigorous reviewers who strongly influenced the organization and content of the book, and Janet Wagner, an attorney who skillfully and artfully critiqued my writing style. Several colleagues contributed to selected portions of the book. They include Fred Cole, Amy Gittler, Mark Hielman, Susan E. Klemmer, Christopher Mason, William Monahan, Roger Perry, Frank Placenti, Thomas Quarelli, Jeffrey P. Travers, Paul Ulrich, Sherin Vitro, Judge Noel Fidel, and Professors Jane Aiken, Rebecca Berch (now Chief Justice of the Arizona Supreme Court), Paul Brand, Susan Chesler, Betsy Grey, Mark Hall, David Kader, Amy Langenfeld, Robert Misner, Cathy O'Grady, Mary Richards, Judy Stinson, Bonnie Tucker, James Weinstein, and Larry Winer.

The truly indispensable contributors to the early editions of this book, however, are the students and attorneys who accepted my instruction and used the early versions of the teaching materials from which this book is derived. I especially acknowledge the Phoenix law firm of Streich, Lang, Weeks & Cardon, now merged with Quarles & Brady, for its dedication to continuing education in legal writing during those years.

I also thank staff and student research assistants for their contributions to the seven editions, in the order of their participation over the years: Donna Blair, Gail Geer, Kay Winn, and Vera Hamer-Sonn provided word-processing assistance; Janice Fuller, Mark Burgoz, Michael Rutledge, Virginia Vasquez, Toby Schmich, Victoria Stevens, Jane Proctor, Lizzette M. Alameda, Brian M. Louisell, Lauren Elliott Stine, Robert Stultz, Jason Zasky, Ashley Stallings, Sarah White Mansfield, Nora Nuñez, and Natalya Ter-Grigoryan provided student research, cite-checking, and proofreading assistance. Ms. Ter-Grigoryan was especially conscientious and tireless in assisting me in preparing the much improved sixth edition after compositor's errors in the fifth edition had introduced errors in the files. Alyssa

Whetstine (class of 2015) provided excellent proofing, editing, and critiques for the seventh edition. I am also grateful to the law library staff at Arizona State University, and particularly to Alison Ewing, Beth Difelice, and Serene Rock. Finally, I am indebted to Arizona State University College of Law, and especially to Deans Paul Bender, Richard Morgan, Patricia White, Paul Berman, and Douglas Sylvester, who fully supported my efforts to produce the seven editions of this text.

Finally, I thank my mother, Emily, for her early guidance in grammar and for creating the drawings (one for the first three editions, and a new one in its place for the fourth edition, and an updated version appearing in the fifth and sixth editions) illustrating the discussion of restrictive and nonrestrictive clauses in Chapter 13.

Part I

Law School— Getting Started

Welcome to law school! For many of you, law school will present at least two new educational challenges. First, the instructor in your legal writing course may encourage you to adopt a legal writing style that differs from the writing style you displayed in undergraduate courses. Second, most of your law school courses will help you develop skills of legal analysis through the "case method," a teaching and study technique that complements your work in your legal writing course but that differs markedly from the simple lecture format used in many undergraduate courses.

Chapters 1 and 2 facilitate your orientation to law school by introducing you to some fundamental principles of legal writing style and the case method of study. Later, after you have a few weeks of legal education under your belt, you will examine legal writing style and the case method in much greater detail in Chapters 7 and 13.

Your first reading of each chapter in this book will provide essential guidance for your legal writing assignments and for success in law school generally. You likely will not be able to take full advantage of the book's lessons on first reading, however, because they will frequently address topics with which you do not yet have any concrete experience. As you gain experience throughout the first year of law school, you will find that chapters assigned earlier in the year will make even more sense to you on a second reading, because you can then connect the text to tasks that you have undertaken and to questions that have come to mind since your first reading. To get the full benefit of this book, therefore, read each chapter carefully when it is initially assigned, and then periodically review earlier reading assignments after you have gained experience and generated new questions. You will find that the assigned text is even more meaningful and informative on second reading, as it addresses issues that have only recently come into sharp focus in your studies.

To get started, turn to the next page, and have a fruitful journey.

Chapter 1

Introduction to Writing Style:
Policy, Purpose, and Audience

I. General Approach

Much of this book addresses matters of content or substance in legal writing, which are qualities relating to sound legal analysis and to the accuracy of statements on which courts and clients rely. As a matter of style, however, a substantively good analysis of facts or law will be effective only if expressed clearly and concisely.

The importance of clarity in legal writing should be obvious: Your legal memorandum will not enlighten, nor will your brief persuade, unless the reader can understand it. To appreciate the significance of concise writing, you need only consider the time pressures that a supervising attorney or a judge faces; neither has time to glean from 20 pages ideas that you could have clearly expressed in 10.[1]

---

1. *See, e.g.*, Westinghouse Elec. Corp. v. NLRB, 809 F.2d 419, 424-25 (7th Cir. 1987) (imposing $1,000 penalty on counsel for evading federal rule limiting the number of pages of its opening brief); Morgan v. S. Bend Cmty. Sch. Corp., 797 F.2d 471, 480 (7th Cir. 1986) ("A

The dual goals of clarity and concision are often compatible: Improving concision by omitting surplus words and by organizing your points more efficiently will also enhance clarity in most cases. After successive revisions, however, further concision may come only at the expense of clarity; in those circumstances, you must give priority to clarity.

II. The Perspective of the Legal Writer

Law students sometimes complain that the emphasis on clarity and concision in legal writing courses compels them to abandon the literary eloquence that they strove so hard to develop in college and to replace it with a dry, uniform style. They may overstate their complaints; effective legal writing reflects the application of principles of good writing generally. Nonetheless, as an inevitable consequence of the substance and purpose of legal documents, legal writing often does differ in both substance and style from other kinds of writing.

For example, consider how different writers might treat the subject of a male supervisor's sexual harassment of a female subordinate in the workplace. A poet might create an image of the pain and frustration of the harasser's victim, so vivid an image that readers who had never experienced sexual harassment could appreciate the victim's plight.[2] A writer for a political journal might describe the specific incident as a symptom of more general oppression within a sexist society. A novelist might describe the harassment in particularly dramatic prose, perhaps as a vehicle for character development or perhaps purely to engage or shock the reader.

On the other hand, an associate for the law firm representing the victim of the harassment is understandably preoccupied with the legal significance of the supervisor's actions. In preparing an office memorandum, the associate will analyze whether the harassment constituted "extreme and outrageous conduct," thus satisfying an element of a claim under the tort of intentional infliction of emotional distress. The extent of the injury suffered by the victim will interest the associate at least partly as an indication of the damages that the victim can recover. Moreover, the associate may discuss events or circumstances that other writers would ignore completely. For example, the associate may confirm the status of the harassing employee as an office supervisor, so that the institutional employer could more easily

---

[page] limitation induces the advocate to write tight prose, which helps his client's cause."); Reliance Ins. Co. v. Sweeney Corp., Md., 792 F.2d 1137, 1139 (D.C. Cir. 1986) ("this court encourages short, tightly argued briefs in all cases, regardless of their complexity").

2. *Cf.* Elisabeth W. Schneider, POEMS AND POETRY 3 (1964) (discussing the difficulty of transferring an "experience whole and alive into the mind, emotions, and sensations of another person").

be held liable for the supervisor's harassment under Title VII of the Civil Rights Act of 1964.[3]

The different perspectives of these writers necessarily influence their writing styles. The poet's meaning may be obscured in the interest of "avoiding dull exposition" and of gaining dramatic effect through rhythm and metaphor.[4] Similarly, the novelist may seek to entertain or stimulate the reader by resorting to elegant variation or other deliberate ambiguity.[5] But the legal writer can seldom afford to entertain at the expense of communicating clearly. On occasion, legal writers may have legitimate reasons for ambiguity, but deliberate ambiguity should be the exception, not the rule. A supervising attorney is not interested in dwelling on each sentence of an office memorandum to divine its meaning as he might dwell on each line of a poem. Similarly, a judge is not likely to be persuaded by a brief that she does not fully comprehend, even though it entertains her.

This does not mean that lawyers must always write from a legal perspective. If you desire to retain or develop literary eloquence, you may write poetry by night and easily adapt your writing style to the requirements of the law office by day.

Nor does it mean that legal writing must be dull, dry, and technical. Clear, concrete, concise legal writing can and should be active, vivid, and engaging. Indeed, you can enhance the persuasive effect of your writing with a telling metaphor, a dramatic phrase, or an engaging description of events that tells a client's story accurately but in a compelling fashion. In short, "law does have a poetic dimension,"[6] and the narrative techniques employed in a novel can play a role in legal advocacy.[7] If you can grab and hold the reader's rapt attention with clear, concise, engaging writing,[8] your memorandum or brief will drive your points home like a home run with the bases loaded.

Moreover, the legal perspective does not doom legal writers to a uniform writing style. The goals of clear communication or persuasion leave room

---

3. *See* Faragher v. City of Boca Raton, 524 U.S. 775, 802-09 (1998) (subject to some limitations and defenses, an employer is liable for supervisor's sexually harassing conduct under Title VII, 42 U.S.C. § 2000e-2(a)(1)(2006)).

4. Schneider, *supra* note 2, at 25-26.

5. *See* William Strunk, Jr. & E. B. White, THE ELEMENTS OF STYLE 79 (5th ed. 2009) ("There are occasions when obscurity serves a literary yearning, if not a literary purpose. . . .").

6. Gary Watt, EQUITY STIRRING: THE STORY OF JUSTICE BEYOND LAW 145 (2009); *see also* Stephen E. Smith, *The Poetry of Persuasion: Early Literary Theory and Its Advice to Legal Writers*, 6 J. ALWD 55, 56 (2009) ("The poem's aim of producing aesthetic pleasure may provide an avenue to persuasion that the legal writer should consider in drafting her own persuasive pieces.").

7. *See, e.g.*, Elizabeth Fajans & Mary R. Falk, *Untold Stories: Restoring Narrative to Pleading Practice*, 15 LEGAL WRITING: J. LEGAL WRITING INST. 3 (2009) (arguing for pleadings that tell a compelling story rather than merely meet the minimum requirements of modern notice pleading); Bret Rappaport, *Tapping the Human Adaptive Origins of Storytelling by Requiring Legal Writing Students to Read a Novel in Order to Appreciate How Character, Setting, Plot, Theme, and Tone (CSPTT) Are as Important as IRAC*, 25 T.M. COOLEY L. REV. 267 (2008) (storytelling is a powerful, persuasive tool that is part of the lawyer's tradition).

8. *See* Mark K. Osbeck, *What Is "Good Legal Writing" and Why Does It Matter?*, 4 DREXEL L. REV. 417 (2012).

for individuality. Indeed, you should approach rules of writing style in much the same way that you approach legal rules: You should extend the application of the rules no further than necessary to serve the policies that support the rules. Even seemingly inflexible conventions of punctuation or sentence structure may simply reflect a desire for clarity or proper emphasis, leaving room for writers' discretion about how best to achieve those objectives.

III. A Policy-Oriented Approach

Many rules of composition are nothing more than conventions that reflect generalities about the best way to achieve clear, concise writing with effective emphasis and flow. Even the traditional rule against splitting infinitives appears to have given way to a more flexible discretionary approach: "Some infinitives seem to improve on being split, just as a stick of round stove wood does."[9] You will do well to familiarize yourself with rules of composition, including the recommendations summarized in Chapter 13, as general guides to achieving the objectives of clarity and concision rather than as ends in themselves.

For example, many writers believe that they may never start a sentence with "However," because their teachers or editors strictly applied a rule against such placement. But it is difficult to justify an inflexible rule to that effect; instead, the placement of transitional words such as "however" should be influenced by considerations of emphasis and flow in the sentence. Those considerations often call for placement of "however" at a natural breaking point in midsentence, because it subordinates "however" as a parenthetic transition guide and permits more substantive parts of the sentence to enjoy the prominence of the position at the beginning of the sentence:

The statute of frauds does not apply, however, because Vasquez could have performed the contract within one year.

However, if you wish to draw immediate attention to a shift in position or perspective, such as from point to counterpoint, you can appropriately signal that shift at the beginning of the sentence, as in this one.

---

9. Strunk & White, *supra* note 5, at 78; *see also id*. at 58 (arguing against routine adherence to the traditional rule against splitting infinitives). A contemporary dictionary argues that the traditional rule against splitting infinitives was never well founded:

> Writers who long ago insisted that English could be modeled on Latin created the "rule" that the English infinitive must not be split: *to clearly state* violates this rule; one must say *to state clearly*. But the Latin infinitive is one word (e.g. amare, "to love") and cannot be split, so the rule is not firmly grounded, and treating two English words as one can lead to awkward, stilted sentences.

THE NEW OXFORD AMERICAN DESK DICTIONARY 1637 (2d ed. 2005).

The history of the debate about the "serial" comma rule further illustrates the benefits of understanding the justifications for rules or conventions of composition. According to the traditional rule, you should use a comma to separate each element of a series of three or more things, as in "meat, vegetables, and dairy products." During the "new English" and "new math" movements of the 1960s, elementary school teachers began teaching a discretionary trend to omit the last comma of the series on the ground that the conjunction "and" or "or" adequately separates the last two elements of the series. The trend never fully displaced the traditional rule: Strunk and White have never wavered in their support for the final comma,[10] and many elementary schools later returned to the traditional teachings. Unfortunately, many students in the meantime had adopted an inflexible practice of always omitting the final comma.

In fact, omitting the final comma may hamper clarity in a series in which some elements have multiple subelements. Consider, for example, the possible meanings of this clause: "imprisonment for a maximum of 30 days, a fine of $5,000 and community service for 90 days or probation for a maximum of five years." Depending on the location of a final comma, which would pinpoint the final element of the series, this clause could mean either:

1. [imprisonment for a maximum of 30 days], [a fine of $5,000 and community service for 90 days], or [probation for a maximum of five years];
   OR
2. [imprisonment for a maximum of 30 days], [a fine of $5,000], and [community service for 90 days or probation for a maximum of five years].

Subtle, temporary ambiguities in structure sometimes arise even if the series uses only the coordinating conjunction "and" and not the disjunctive conjunction "or."[11]

Armed with these insights, you can choose either of two approaches to the comma controversy, depending on the emphasis that you place on different policies of composition. If you value consistency as well as clarity, you could reasonably adopt a convention of always using the final comma, because you know that it will sometimes be necessary for clarity and will never cause confusion.[12] Alternatively, if you prefer to restrict punctuation to the necessary minimum, you could exercise stylistic discretion to insert the final comma when it is necessary for clarity and to omit it otherwise.

---

10. William Strunk, Jr. & E. B. White, THE ELEMENTS OF STYLE 1-2 (1st ed. 1959); *id.* at 2 (2d ed. 1972); *id.* at 2 (3d ed. 1979); *id.* at 2 (4th ed. 2000); *id.* at 2 (5th ed. 2009) (50th anniversary edition, reprinting the 4th edition text).

11. *See, e.g.,* Bryan A. Garner, THE ELEMENTS OF LEGAL STYLE 16 (2d ed. 2002) (providing illustrations).

12. Strunk & White, *supra* note 9, at 2 (5th ed. 2009) ("Always Use the Serial Comma"). This author adopts this approach.

IV. Purpose and Audience

In every legal document, you should adapt your writing style to achieve the purpose of the document and to suit the needs of your intended audience. Many of the chapters in this book thoroughly examine this feature of writing style in the context of essay examinations, office memoranda, briefs, and letters. An overview here will serve to introduce some fundamental principles.

A. Purpose

Many legal documents can be classified as having either of two essential purposes: (1) to communicate a balanced analysis or (2) to persuade. With few exceptions, essay examination answers, office memoranda, and advice letters to clients fall into the first category. Ordinarily, the purpose of each is to help your reader understand the strengths and the weaknesses of a legal claim or defense. Briefs to a court and demand letters to an opposing party, on the other hand, fall into the second category. The purpose of a brief is to persuade a judge or panel of judges to make a ruling that favors your client. The purpose of a demand letter is to persuade another party to take some practical action, such as pay a debt, drop a claim, or cease some activity that is causing injury to your client.

You should adapt the content and style of the writing in each of your documents to suit these distinct purposes. For example, in an office memorandum or an advice letter, you must communicate to your supervising attorney or your client the strengths as well as the weaknesses of your client's claims or defenses. Thus, if your client seeks to prove that her employer breached an employment contract by discharging her without good cause, you should candidly reveal to her and to your supervisor that the contract language is ambiguous on that point:

> Each of the five grounds for discharge specifically listed in section IX of the employment contract describes some kind of misconduct or unsatisfactory performance by the employee. However, the prefatory phrase "such as" suggests that the list is not exhaustive, but illustrative. If so, the employer may argue that he retained the right to fire an employee for any reason and that he listed only the most obvious reasons in the contract.
>
> To establish that the contract instead requires just cause for dismissal, we should . . . .

In contrast, in your brief to a court, you will attempt to persuade a judge or panel of judges to interpret the contract language in a way that limits grounds for discharge. Accordingly, you should adopt a writing style that reflects confidence in your client's position:

Section IX of the contract explicitly lists five types of employee misconduct or poor performance as grounds for discharge. Even if the five grounds listed in section IX are illustrative rather than exhaustive, as argued by the defendant, they all illustrate cases in which the employer has good cause for terminating the employment contract. Thus, section IX describes a limited category of grounds for discharge, one that does not justify the arbitrary discharge in this case. . . .

B. Audience

Even when you seek to achieve similar purposes with different documents, you may need to adapt your writing style to the needs of each audience. For example, in both an office memorandum and an advice letter, your purpose is to present a balanced analysis of your client's claims and defenses. The readers of these documents, however, may vary greatly in legal sophistication. The experienced attorney who reads your office memorandum will appreciate your use of fundamental legal terminology and legal authority, as in this excerpt from an analysis of a police officer's defense in a civil rights action:

If the district court denies Officer Tippett's motion for summary judgment on a question of law, Officer Tippett can file an interlocutory appeal on the issue of qualified immunity. *See Mitchell v. Forsyth*, 472 U.S. 511, 524-30 (1985).

On the other hand, your client, Officer Tippett, presumably has little or no legal training in pretrial and appellate civil procedure. Accordingly, in an advice letter to Officer Tippett on the same issue, you should explain your analysis in nonlegal terms:

Even if the trial court denies your request to dismiss the action against you before trial, you need not face a trial immediately. In many cases, you can immediately appeal the trial court's rejection of your immunity defense. In the meantime, the trial will be delayed while the appellate court determines whether your conduct was indeed sufficiently reasonable that you should be immune from liability for damages.

In some cases, your task is complicated by the presence of multiple purposes and audiences. You will explore these matters further in later chapters, in the context of particular documents.

V. Overview of the Process of Legal Writing

Chapter by chapter, this book introduces you to various steps in the process of analyzing a legal problem and expressing your analysis effectively in a legal document. The following overview provides a road map to what lies ahead.

A. Developing Skills of Legal Method and Analysis

First and foremost, you must have something to say. You cannot expect to communicate clearly or persuasively unless you have a clear understanding of the points you wish to express. Parts I through IV of this book provide you with the tools that you need to spot legal issues, analyze the issues, and develop legal arguments. Specifically, after the next chapter introduces you to the case method of study, Chapters 3 and 4 explore the roles of common law and legislation in our legal system. Chapters 5 and 6 introduce you to important legal concepts and tools of analysis: deference to prior case law and the application of deductive reasoning to legal problems. Chapters 7 through 9 build on the foundation laid in earlier chapters, exploring law school study and examination techniques. In addition, Chapters 7 through 9 serve as a bridge from the legal methods discussed in Parts I through IV to the expression of analysis in an office memorandum, addressed in Part V. Part IV also examines the application of inductive reasoning to legal problems, including the processes of analogy and distinction.

B. Researching the Law

Once you understand how the law operates, how to spot legal issues, and how to analyze a legal problem, you must find the legal authorities that state the applicable law. Unless your instructor or assigning attorney provides you with a file of legal authority, you must research the law in the library or online, a process described in Chapter 10.

C. Prewriting

As you draft a legal document, you will find that the process of putting your thoughts into writing will sharpen and deepen your understanding of the analysis, enabling you to improve your analysis throughout the drafting process. Nonetheless, you will produce a better final product, and will do so more efficiently, if you carefully plan your writing before you begin to write.

In its earliest and most tentative stages, this process of "prewriting" may take the form of refining the issues that you intend to research, taking your research notes in an organized manner, and developing your analysis of the law as your research proceeds. The most important stage of prewriting, however, is the process of organizing the points that you wish to express after you have completed your research. If you take this step seriously, you can develop an outline as a means of clarifying your analysis, allowing you to focus more of your attention on matters of composition when you begin writing.

To effectively organize your thoughts, you must have a general idea of the format of your document. Thus, Chapter 11 introduces the elements of an office memorandum of law, just as later chapters examine the formats of various kinds of briefs submitted to courts. The process of organizing your analysis, however, is introduced in Chapter 8, in the context of student course outlines, and is discussed further in chapters addressing essay exam answers and office memoranda.

D. Writing

If you have conscientiously researched and analyzed your problem and have carefully organized your thoughts in outline form, you will be better prepared to focus your attention on the process of writing your document in full, with effective citation to authority. The process of writing an objective analysis is examined thoroughly in Chapters 13 and 14, with further discussion of persuasive writing style appearing in later chapters.

An important thread, introduced in this chapter, runs through the discussion of writing style in Chapter 13: Good writers do not mechanically apply inflexible rules of composition, nor do they reflexively react without attention to goals or guiding principles. Instead, good writers consciously choose between alternatives, and they flexibly adapt conventions of composition to the needs of their audience and to the purpose of their document, all with the aim of achieving clearly identified goals, such as clarity, concision, and persuasiveness.

E. Revising Your Writing

The extent to which your document requires revision will depend partly on the care with which you engaged in the prewriting and writing processes. Nonetheless, regardless of the care with which you wrote and revised your document, you can nearly always improve a draft with additional revision. Strategies for revising your writing, as well as economic limitations on multiple revisions, are discussed in Chapter 13.

F. Revisiting Earlier Stages

This process of researching, analyzing, prewriting, writing, and revising may not proceed in a perfectly linear fashion because later stages of the process may reveal the need to "circle back" to previous stages. While prewriting or writing, for example, you may encounter gaps in your analysis that require you to supplement your research. During the writing stage, you may find problems with transitions between the sections of your document, leading you to return to your outline to reconsider the organization of your document. Thus, any stage of the thinking and writing process may pave the way for further progress on an earlier or later stage.

VI. Summary

Effective legal writing requires careful attention to the purpose of a document and to the needs of the intended audience. Rather than memorizing and dogmatically applying rules of composition, legal writers should flexibly adapt their writing to achieve their goals of communicating or advocating clearly and concisely.

VII. Proceeding with Purpose and Enthusiasm

This chapter and Chapters 12 through 16 develop and describe a method of approaching and resolving problems of composition, much as Chapters 3 through 6 describe a method of approaching legal problems.

Chapters 12 through 16 thoroughly examine problems of organization and writing style in the context of office memoranda and briefs. You may benefit by glancing at selected topics in those chapters as you work through Parts II through IV of the book. However, because problems in writing style are often closely linked with problems in legal method and analysis, you can profitably delay close examination of Chapters 12 through 16 until you have studied legal method and analysis in Parts II through IV.

As you proceed through the book and through your legal writing course, consider this reflection from a student who had just completed a first-year course in legal method and writing in 2013:

As I reflect on my year in legal methods, I know I have become a better student. I would like to talk about how my writing has improved, but I think this class has taught me much more than that. I learned how to manage my time, how to research, how to work with others, how to solve disputes, how to write persuasively, how to advocate, how to build personal relationships with my classmates, how to hold myself accountable, how to hold my partners accountable, and how to become a better overall law student. This was not a writing class for me. This class taught me how to excel in all of my classes, and I feel it is by far the most important class I have taken this semester. I understand that we are learning law in our other classes, and the interpretation of that law. However, this class is the foundation for everything else. Going into practice, I am confident that the education I received in this course has prepared me to excel. I do not think a single individual has received a better education, and the confidence that I have leaving this course is what I value the most.[13]

---

13. This quotation is taken from a student blog authored by 1L Richard Sgrignoli, in response to a reflection assignment from his Legal Methods professor, Anna Hemingway, Widener University School of Law.

Of course, reaping such rewards from a course requires dedication, hard work, and willingness to learn from constructive feedback. If you bring that commitment to your study of legal method and writing, you should greatly enhance your legal knowledge and your skills of analysis and expression.

Exercise 1-1

Examine your previous education and experiences relating to writing. Consider whether the special characteristics of legal writing require you to depart from writing styles that you have used successfully in other contexts. Use this self-examination to prepare for constructive criticism from your writing instructors.

To begin a dialogue with your writing instructor, write an essay in response to one or more of the questions posed at the end of the following problem, and discuss your response with your instructor. Do not feel compelled to identify a "correct answer" or to couch your response in any special legal format or style. Instead, simply develop an honest response based on your personal values and opinions, and express your response freely in a style that comes to you naturally and comfortably. Ask your writing instructor to assess the extent to which your natural writing style is consistent with or deviates from your instructor's view of effective legal writing.

Survival of the Fittest and the Common Law

Imagine that you are deciding cases in the nineteenth century as the chief justice of a state's highest appellate court. Your state has no criminal statutes; instead, the criminal law of the state is exclusively common law, a law fashioned by judges and based on custom, common sense, and community values.

Before you is an appeal from a murder conviction in the case of *State v. Blight*. After a full trial, the jury found that Fletcher Blight, the defendant and appellant, had killed Davie Jones by pushing him off a life raft and into the ocean.

The trial record shows that both men boarded the life raft after their vessel had sunk on the high seas. After days of drifting, and with no ship or land on the horizon, it became apparent that the water rations would not sustain both men until a rescue ship arrived. Blight, the stronger of the two, decided to (1) save the remaining water supply for himself; (2) stop administering water to Jones, who was too weak to move; and (3) allow Jones to die. Jones suffered great pain as he slowly died of dehydration. To end Jones's misery and to spare himself the emotional distress of watching Jones suffer, Blight tearfully pushed the helpless Jones into the sea, where Jones quickly died. When Blight was rescued by a passing ship a few days later, he was near death himself. Physicians testified at trial that both men undoubtedly would have died before the rescue ship arrived if Blight had continued sharing the water rations with Jones until the water was exhausted.

1. **Morally Judging Blight's Action.** Speaking as an individual with no connection to the case, do you think Blight's actions were morally justified? Why or why not?

2. **Should the Court Expand Legal Justifications?** Now, imagine that you are an attorney or a judge in the criminal prosecution of Blight in State X, which you can assume has jurisdiction. At the time of the prosecution, criminal law in State X is still a matter of "common law," developed by judges, and has not yet been codified into statutes by the State X legislature. In State X, the courts have defined the common law crime of murder as the "unlawful killing of a human being without justification." At the time of Blight's prosecution, the Supreme Court of State X had recognized only one justification for killing another person: self-defense in the face of a potentially deadly attack from the other person. Because Jones had not attacked Blight, Blight's actions were not justified under current law, and he was convicted at trial. On appeal, Blight asks the State X Supreme Court to expand the common law justifications to cover the circumstances of his case. In your view, should the law evolve to find justification in Blight's acts?

3. **Precisely what new common law rule or rules would justify Blight's deeds?** As Blight's attorney, draft Blight's proposed rule or rules in the form of proposed trial court instructions to the jury: "You must acquit the defendant of the charge of murder if he was justified in killing Jones. In this case, the defendant was justified in killing Jones if you find that . . . ." This will help to define the expanded justification that the Supreme Court is being asked to approve.

   a. As the Chief Justice of the State X Supreme Court, would you adopt the proposed rule? What reasons would you give for supporting or opposing an extension of the common law doctrine of justification that would result in Blight's acquittal?

   b. Would you support a new common law rule that would improve the law but would not necessarily result in acquittal for Blight? If so, describe the rule and explain your reasons for proposing it.

Chapter 2

Overview of the Case Method of Study

In your first-year contracts course, you probably will study the case of *Hadley and Another v. Baxendale and Others*.[1] By examining the history of this case now, you can become acquainted with the methods by which you will study law in most of your classes.

I. *Hadley v. Baxendale*: A Case Study

The dispute between the Hadleys and Baxendale began as a business transaction during an economic boom in the midst of England's industrial revolution. Operators of a flour mill in Gloucester entered into a contract with a carrier for the transportation of a broken engine shaft to a manufacturer in Greenwich, on the other side of England.

---

1. 9 Ex. 341, 156 Eng. Rep. 145 (1854).

The operators of the mill, the Hadleys, were anxious to transport the broken shaft to the manufacturer as quickly as possible; the failure of the shaft had halted the milling of corn, and the broken shaft would serve as a model for the manufacture of a new shaft. An employee of the carrier, Pickford and Co., promised that the shaft would be delivered to the manufacturer within two days after the date that the carrier took possession of the shaft. For this, the mill operators paid £2 4s. The carrier could have transported the shaft as promptly as promised had it immediately used available means of land transportation. Presumably to reduce costs, however, it held the shaft for several days in London before loading it onto a canal barge along with a shipment of iron that was bound for the same manufacturer. As a consequence, the carrier delivered the shaft to the manufacturer on the seventh day after the carrier received it, resulting in an additional delay of five days during which the mill was stopped.

The mill operators demanded that the carrier compensate for an estimated £300 in lost profits that the mill suffered because of the additional delay. The carrier refused, and the mill operators sued the carrier's managing director, Baxendale, in a trial court in Gloucester, claiming approximately £200 in damages. Although the carrier offered to settle the dispute for £25, the mill operators rejected the offer, and the case went to trial before a jury. The mill operators presented witnesses who testified to £120 in damages, and the jury awarded the mill operators £50 in a compromise verdict that became the judgment of the trial court.

The carrier appealed to the Court of Exchequer. The carrier ultimately persuaded a panel of three judges on this appellate court to reverse the judgment of the trial court and to grant a new trial on the ground that the trial judge had given the jury excessive latitude in awarding damages for lost profits.

In the appellate court's written opinion, the authoring judge explained that a jury may award only those damages that would flow naturally from the breach of such a contract or that would be reasonably within the contemplation of the parties because of special circumstances communicated at the time of contracting. The appellate judges assumed that the mill would ordinarily have spare shafts with which to keep running; consequently, they concluded that lost profits stemming from an idle mill would not be the natural consequence of the breach of the contract for prompt carriage. Whether the possibility of lost profits would nonetheless have been in the contemplation of the parties would depend on whether, at the time of contracting, the mill operators had communicated to the carrier the special circumstances that the broken shaft was the mill's only shaft and that the mill would be idle in its absence.

The appellate court concluded that the mill operators had informed the carrier only that they operated a mill and that the article to be transported was the broken shaft of a mill.[2] On this premise, the appellate court held that the trial judge should not have allowed the jury to consider any lost profits in its calculation of damages.

The case of *Hadley v. Baxendale* illustrates both how a case makes its way through the legal system and how you typically encounter the case only at the final destination in its legal journey. Reacting to a pressing commercial need, the mill operators entered into an agreement with the carrier to exchange money for certain services. Disappointed with the services rendered, the mill operators demanded compensation. Failing to secure the compensation through less formal means, they filed an action in a trial court to obtain a judgment compelling the carrier to pay compensation.

At trial, each party discovered that his claims or defenses were limited by his ability to present credible supporting evidence to the jury, to whom the court had delegated the task of finding facts. Hence, the mill operator's original demand dropped first from £300 to £200, and then to the £120 of losses for which it could produce evidence. Relying on centuries of development of law and custom, the court recognized the contractual relationship as one deserving the protection of the royal courts, and it permitted the jury to award damages for the carrier's breach of the contract. The jury awarded less in damages than the trial court's instructions and the evidence would have allowed, but more than the carrier thought the law should permit. Accordingly, the carrier took the dispute before a court of higher authority, which ordered a new trial and ruled that the mill operator should not be entitled to recover for lost profits in the new trial. The higher court explained its decision in a written judicial opinion.

---

2. Interestingly, this represents a departure from the summary of the trial proceedings prepared by the court reporter, who had reported at the beginning of the appellate opinion that the mill operators had informed the carrier that the mill was stopped. Richard Danzig & Geoffrey R. Watson, THE CAPABILITY PROBLEM IN CONTRACT LAW 62 (2d ed. 2004) (characterizing the finding of the Court of Exchequer as "remarkable").

II. The Litigation Pyramid

In only a tiny percentage of disputes do the parties complete this process of full trial followed by review of the trial court's judgment in one or more appellate courts. Countless people become entangled in disputes that could give rise to legal claims, yet they seldom take the formal step of filing lawsuits to test their claims. In even fewer cases do they fully litigate their disputes in the trial court. In most lawsuits, the parties manage to settle their disputes before trial by agreeing to a compromise, thus avoiding the expense and risks of full trial. In many others, a full trial of the facts is unnecessary to resolve the dispute, and the trial court grants judgment for one of the parties before trial.

In cases that result in judgment after a full trial, only a small percentage of losing parties seek review of the adverse judgment in an appellate court. Still fewer seek further review in a higher appellate court when available. Thus, the proportions of disputes that proceed to various levels of dispute resolution form a pyramid:

III. The Casebook Method of Study

Law school courses will direct your attention primarily to the decisions of the appellate courts. In nearly all first-year courses in law school, you will encounter the law in casebooks, each of which presents judicial opinions on various topics that relate to a general field of law such as property, contracts, crimes, procedure, or torts.

The cases in a casebook are the disputes that parties bring to courts for resolution. Most of the judicial opinions that analyze the cases are the opinions of appellate courts. The edited appellate opinions published in casebooks often summarize the facts of the dispute and the proceedings in lower courts as concisely as possible,[3] sometimes providing no more than a bare

---

3. Indeed, many of the details of *Hadley v. Baxendale* described in this book do not appear in the report of the Court of the Exchequer, much less in a casebook's edited version of that report. The source of this book's more detailed recounting of the case is Danzig & Watson, *supra* note 2, at 48-90.

outline of the human drama that has preceded the appellate litigation. Most appellate opinions focus instead on using the cases before them as vehicles for developing and articulating general legal rules or principles. In addition to resolving the dispute before the court, these rules also provide guidance to courts and litigants in future disputes of a similar nature, as well as to persons who desire to conform their actions to the law so as to avoid disputes.

Judicial opinions may mystify you in your first weeks at law school. They are peppered with legal terminology that will incrementally become part of your working vocabulary only after weeks and months of study. Even worse, some of the judicial language, particularly in the older cases, will be antiquated or overly formal and will have no place in your own writing; yet you must immerse yourself in the language to understand the opinions.

Moreover, the opinions assume that the reader is familiar with the legal system and the legal method that courts use when working within that system. For example, you might wonder how an early English decision such as *Hadley v. Baxendale* is relevant to your study of law in the United States. Also confusing to some new law students is the relationship between "common law" and "statutory law," both of which may be addressed in the same judicial opinion.

Parts II and III of this book answer these and many other questions by introducing you to our legal system and to fundamental principles of legal method. This foundation should better prepare you to develop skills in studying law in first-year courses, in analyzing legal problems in a law office or a judge's chambers, and in advocating a client's position to a court, all of which are discussed in Parts IV through VIII. Part II begins building the foundation with an introduction to the United States legal system.

You undoubtedly will be preparing case briefs for class discussion beginning with the first day of class. Accordingly, before your first week of classes, you may wish to glance through Chapter 7, which examines the process of briefing cases for class discussion. You will learn that your instructors discuss appellate opinions in a manner that suits their individual pedagogic preferences. Until you learn more about those preferences, or those of your legal writing professor, you may start with the following format in briefing cases:

1. Identification of the Case (state the case name and authoring court)
2. Facts (summarize the facts that led to the legal dispute)
3. Procedural History (summarize the judicial proceedings preceding this court's opinion)
4. Issue(s) and Holding(s) (state the questions addressed by the court, followed by the court's conclusion on each question)
5. Reasoning (explain the court's reasons for its conclusions)
6. Evaluation (explain your agreement or disagreement with the court's conclusions and reasoning)
7. Synthesis (explain how this opinion's holding and reasoning compare to those of other opinions that address the same issue)

After you complete Parts II and III of this book, you can study Chapters 7 through 9 more thoroughly to develop a comprehensive, three-point plan for success in your substantive courses: (1) briefing and synthesizing cases, (2) outlining course materials, and (3) applying effective examination techniques.

Part II

Introduction to the

Legal System

Chapter 3

Common Law

I. Overview—Sources of Lawmaking Powers

The United States Constitution allocates powers between the state and national governments and thus establishes the framework for our federal system of government. In turn, each state's constitution establishes the framework for that state's government. A fundamental tenet of these state and federal constitutions is the separation of powers between the legislative, judicial, and executive branches of government. Although lawmaking functions rest primarily with the legislative branch, all three branches exercise some form of lawmaking power.

A. Legislative and Executive Branches

The state and federal legislatures create law by enacting statutes within the authority granted to them by the state and federal constitutions. Although

23

the primary function of the executive branch is enforcement of laws, the executive branch may lead in policy development by proposing legislation to a legislature. Moreover, a legislature may delegate some of its lawmaking power to the executive branch by statutorily authorizing an executive agency to issue rules and regulations designed to help implement a statutory scheme.

For example, in the exercise of its federal constitutional authority to regulate commerce, the United States Congress has enacted comprehensive labor relations statutes, such as the National Labor Relations Act.[1] It has also created the National Labor Relations Board (NLRB), an agency of the United States, and has authorized the NLRB to issue administrative rules and regulations necessary to help the NLRB enforce the labor relations statutes.[2]

Legislatures cannot amend a constitution in the same way that they enact statutes. For example, Article V of the United States Constitution authorizes Congress to propose constitutional amendments, but such proposals do not become effective until ratified by the legislatures or constitutional conventions of three-fourths of the states. For convenience, this book uses the term "enacted law" to refer to both statutes and constitutions.

B. Judicial Branch

The judicial branch of government develops law in two ways, both of them in the context of particular disputes. First, state and federal courts contribute to the development of constitutional and statutory law by interpreting the necessarily general terms of such enacted law and applying those terms to the facts of disputes. Second, as offspring of the English judicial system, courts in the United States have adopted and continue to develop a substantial body of common law: judge-made law that applies to issues that constitutional or statutory law does not address. State courts are the primary source of common law, because federal courts no longer create and develop "federal general common law."[3] Nonetheless, the federal courts retain the power in a few restricted fields, such as admiralty law, to develop "specialized federal common law."[4]

---

1. 49 Stat. 449 (1935).

2. 29 U.S.C. §§ 153, 156 (2006); Am. Hosp. Ass'n v. NLRB, 499 U.S. 606, 609 (1991).

3. Erie R.R. v. Tompkins, 304 U.S. 64, 78 (1938).

4. Henry J. Friendly, *In Praise of* Erie—*And of the New Federal Common Law*, 39 N.Y.U. L. Rev. 383, 405 (1964).

C. Common Law as a Backdrop for Legislation

An example of the interplay between statutory law and common law is provided in your first-year contracts course. Many principles of contract law—such as consideration, offer and acceptance, performance and breach, and remedies—find their source in a substantial body of common law, developed by judges, first in England and later in the United States.

The common law of contracts forms a backdrop against which state legislatures have enacted statutes, which supersede some of the common law rules. In the resulting hybrid system, the statutes provide the rule of law on issues to which they apply, while common law applies to gaps within and between statutes, and to whole topics not addressed by statutes.

D. Local and Tribal Governments

These fundamental principles of state and federal lawmaking apply only in limited fashion to two other kinds of governments in the United States: (1) local governments, such as those of cities and counties, and (2) American Indian tribal governments.

Local governments come in a variety of models. Although many of them exercise legislative, executive, and judicial powers, they do not always practice the same degree of separation of these powers as do state and federal governments. A state's constitution and statutes may partially define the legal structure that a local government in the state can adopt and the powers that it can exercise. Typically, a municipality further defines its structure with a city or county charter that operates within limits set by state law.

More nearly autonomous are American Indian tribes. Although their powers may be limited by federal law, they are otherwise sovereign governments with inherent powers to exercise tribal authority. Not all of the tribes have chosen to adopt every fundamental tenet of the state and federal governments. For example, the Navajo Nation of the southwestern United States has no constitution, and it has not always recognized complete separation of legislative, judicial, and executive powers. Nonetheless, its legal system is similar to the state and federal systems in several important respects. Constituents elect the members of the Navajo Tribal Council, which enacts statutory law in the form of codes. The executive power rests primarily in the president, an elected official. Finally, the Navajo trial courts and the Navajo Supreme Court apply federal law and tribal codes, and they develop and apply a common law based on Navajo custom and cultural values or compatible state laws.

This book primarily addresses state and federal common law and statutes. The remainder of this chapter explores common law analysis. Chapter 4 examines statutory analysis before further addressing the relationship between legislation and the common law.

II. Common Law

A. Historical Roots

The common law that courts in the United States develop and apply has its roots in the English common law, which was dispensed in the courts of the English king or queen. This English law came to be known as the "common law" because it applied generally throughout medieval England. For many kinds of claims, the common law thus partially replaced a less uniform system of customary law dispensed in local courts and in the private courts of feudal lords. The English Court of Chancery supplemented the remedies of the early common law courts by developing and applying a form of "equity" that provided relief when common law remedies were inadequate.

Distinctions between common law and equitable claims, defenses, and remedies continue to have significance for some purposes, such as determining the right to a jury trial in some circumstances.[5] Most United States jurisdictions, however, have eliminated the dual court system and have largely merged law and equity procedure.[6] Accordingly, this book uses the term "common law" to refer generally to laws created and developed by the courts, regardless of whether the principles have their roots in early common law or equity law.

Oliver Wendell Holmes traced the origins of some English and United States common law to early Germanic and Roman law.[7] Other common law principles simply reflect judicial recognition of community needs, habits, or customs, and are "accounted for by their manifest good sense."[8] More generally, common law is "the embodiment of broad and comprehensive unwritten principles . . . inspired by natural reason and an innate sense of justice."[9]

---

5. *See, e.g.*, City of Monterey v. Del Monte Dunes at Monterey, 526 U.S. 687, 708-09 (1999) (discussing whether federal statutory claim was "legal" rather than "equitable," for purposes of applying the Seventh Amendment's guarantee of a jury trial to common law actions); Hutchinson v. Spanierman, 190 F.3d 815, 823 (7th Cir. 1999) (applying Indiana law and finding that stale claim was barred by the equitable doctrine of laches even though the legal statute of limitations had not expired); 1 Dan B. Dobbs, DOBBS LAW OF REMEDIES § 2.6(1), at 150-53 (2d ed. 1993) (discussing continuing limitations on equitable remedies, such as injunctive relief, that do not apply to legal remedy of money damages).

6. *See, e.g.*, FED. R. CIV. P. 2 ("There is one form of action—the civil action."); Ross v. Bernhard, 396 U.S. 531, 539-40 (1970) (discussing the procedural joinder of legal and equitable claims and remedies under rules of procedure for federal courts); Dobbs, *supra* note 5, at 149 ("In most states and in the federal system, there are no longer separate equity rules of procedure.").

7. Oliver Wendell Holmes, Jr., THE COMMON LAW 2, 18, 34, 340-44, 360 (Dover Publ. 1991) (1881).

8. *Id.* at 2, 337-39.

9. Stanley Mosk, *The Common Law and the Judicial Decision-Making Process*, 11 HARV. J.L. & PUB. POL'Y 35 (1988) (citing Rodriguez v. Bethlehem Steel Co., 525 P.2d 669, 682-83 (Cal. 1974)). Indeed, some scholars believe that humans have a biological predisposition to prefer some forms of legal order. *See generally, e.g.*, Richard D. Alexander, THE BIOLOGY OF MORAL SYSTEMS (1987); *cf.* John R. Alford, Carolyn L. Funk, & John R. Hibbing, *Are Political Orientations Genetically Transmitted?*, AM. POL. SCI. REV., May 2005, at 153-

The term "common" may be misleading when applied to common law in the United States: The courts in each state are free to develop the common law of that state in a manner that reflects local policies; therefore, variations in common law among the states are inevitable. Nonetheless, to a surprising degree, courts in different states share common views on general principles of law. For example, a federal appellate court has noted, "the principles of contract law do not differ greatly from one jurisdiction to another."[10] Perhaps more important for law students and practitioners, the method employed by courts in deciding disputes and developing common law does not vary substantially among the states.

B. Examples: Common Law Burglary and Murder

Although criminal law is now comprehensively addressed by statutes, it was once primarily within the domain of the common law. The early common law crime of burglary, which was punishable by death, illustrates the judicial development of common law rules to serve particular needs of the community. In imposing capital punishment for this crime, the common law courts sought to deter a serious invasion of the home during hours of darkness, when the inhabitants were most vulnerable to attack and the invader most likely to escape recognition. Efforts by the courts to narrowly address that evil are reflected in the general definition of common law burglary, which separates the crime into distinct elements: (1) the breaking and (2) entering (3) of the dwelling house (4) of another (5) in the night (6) with the intent to commit a felony.

In defining and applying these elements of common law burglary in the context of successive cases, the courts were reluctant to extend the crime beyond the minimum scope necessary to achieve the underlying purposes of the crime, probably because of the severity of punishment. For example, the courts viewed an intruder as less culpable if the occupant of a dwelling encouraged the intrusion by failing to properly secure the dwelling. Accordingly, many courts held that a trespasser who gained entry by further opening a partially open door or window had not committed the "breaking" necessary for a burglary.[11]

The history of another common law crime, murder, illustrates the manner in which courts gradually developed common law doctrine "over several centuries of time as a parade of cases, involving different fact situations, came before the judges for decision."[12] The common law decisions generally defined murder as the unlawful killing of another human being with malice aforethought. Early decisions defined "malice aforethought" narrowly by requiring proof of a premeditated intent to kill. Subsequent cases, however, presented unpremeditated or even unintentional killings that reflected suf-

---

67 (study supports conclusion that political attitudes and ideologies are partly shaped by genetics).

10. *E.g., In re* Cochise College Park, Inc., 703 F.2d 1339, 1348 n.4 (9th Cir. 1983).

11. Wayne R. LaFave, CRIMINAL LAW § 21.1(a), at 1070 (5th ed. 2010).

12. *Id.* § 14.1, at 725.

ficient culpability to warrant classification as murder. In those cases, courts effectively expanded the definition of "malice aforethought" by recognizing other circumstances that would justify conviction for murder: intentional but unpremeditated killing without sufficient provocation; unintentional killing during the commission of another felony; unintentional killing through conduct that reflects a reckless disregard for the lives of others; and killing while engaged in conduct with the intent to do serious bodily harm short of death.[13]

C. Common Law in Constant Change

This process of incremental development of the common law does not always proceed in an unbroken line. Courts sometimes abandon previously adopted lines of authority to chart new courses that better reflect current social, economic, and technological realities:

> The inherent capacity of the common law for growth and change is its most significant feature. It is constantly expanding and developing to keep up with the advancement of civilization and the new conditions and progress of society, and adapting itself to the gradual changes in trade, commerce, arts, inventions, and the needs of the country. . . . The vitality of the common law can flourish if the courts remain alert to their obligation and have the opportunity to change it when reason and equity so demand. The common law requires that each time a rule of law is applied, it must be carefully scrutinized to make sure that the conditions and needs of the times have not so changed as to make further application of the rule an instrument of injustice.[14]

A change in conditions is not the only possible inspiration for abandoning existing common law. A court will occasionally conclude that a previous decision was flawed from its inception. Hindsight may show that the previous court premised its decision on erroneous factual assumptions about conditions existing at that time. Alternatively, the current court, which itself may have changed in intellectual composition, may find intolerable flaws in the reasoning of the previous decision.[15] This process of evolution, however, is restricted by the doctrine of stare decisis, explored in Chapter 5.

III. Summary

Legislatures enact statutes within the authority granted to them by state and federal constitutions. Courts create case law in the context of individual disputes by (1) interpreting and applying the provisions of constitutions and statutes and (2) developing and applying a separate body of judge-made

---

13. *Id.* at 725-26.

14. Mosk, *supra* note 9, at 36.

15. *See generally* Geoffrey R. Stone, *Precedent, the Amendment Process, and Evolution in Constitutional Doctrine*, 11 HARV. J.L. & PUB. POL'Y 67, 71 (1988).

common law. The common law continually grows as new cases present the courts with opportunities to keep the common law current with social, economic, and technological developments.

Exercise 3-1

Wrongful Conception, Wrongful Life

In general, the common law of torts imposes civil liability on a physician who breaches a duty of care to a patient. By applying this general common law rule to new medical procedures, courts and juries necessarily refine the content of the rule. In the following problem, assume that the common law of the jurisdiction has not previously addressed the issues that are raised by the facts. You must decide how you would fashion the common law that applies to the issues if you were a judge approving instructions to a jury on the applicable legal rules. Specifically, you must decide to what extent you think the common law should impose liability on a physician for negligently permitting a child to be conceived.

Problem

When Sonia and her husband, Eddie, had their third child, they agreed that they desired no additional children and that Eddie should undergo sterilization. They consulted Dr. Leonard, who performed a vasectomy. Although Dr. Leonard pronounced the operation a success, he in fact performed the vasectomy carelessly and neglected to order routine follow-up tests. Eddie impregnated Sonia within six months after the failed sterilization procedure.

a. In the process of developing the state's common law of torts, should a state court permit Sonia and Eddie to sue Dr. Leonard on a negligence theory of "wrongful conception"? If so, should the damages include only the medical expenses and other costs associated with the childbirth, or should they more broadly include the costs of raising the fourth child?

b. Suppose that the fourth child was born with severe birth defects, but that the failed sterilization procedure did not contribute to the birth defects. Should these facts affect the court's evaluation of the parents' claims based on wrongful conception? Should the court recognize a cause of action on the behalf of the fourth child for "wrongful life," permitting the child herself to collect damages on the theory that she would have been better off had she not been conceived?

c. Should the analysis of any of these questions be affected by the fact that Sonia could have legally aborted her fetus soon after discovering her pregnancy?

Chapter 4

Legislation

I. Roles of Constitutional and Statutory Law

"The Constitution states the framework for all our law. Legislation is one great tool of legal change and readaptation."[1] As noted by a state supreme court, constitutional and statutory law reflect collective expressions of public policy: "As the expressions of our founders and those we have elected to our legislature, our state's constitution and statutes embody the public conscience of the people of this state."[2]

Of the three branches of government, the legislature is the paramount policymaking body. Consistent with that role, a legislature often enacts statutes to address problems that it concludes are not adequately addressed by the common law.

---

1. Karl N. Llewellyn, THE BRAMBLE BUSH 10 (10th prtg. 1996).
2. Wagenseller v. Scottsdale Mem'l Hosp., 710 P.2d 1025, 1033 (Ariz. 1985).

A. Example: Embezzlement

The early common law crime of theft was defined as a trespassory taking and carrying away of personal property of another with intent to steal.[3] The requirement of a trespassory taking was not satisfied by one who took possession of another's property lawfully, but who subsequently converted the property to his own use with the intent to permanently deprive the owner of it.

Legislators in England and the United States were aware that the common law did not impose criminal liability for the latter misappropriation, and they were determined to criminalize such conduct. Consequently, they created the statutory crime of embezzlement, generally defined as the fraudulent conversion of another's property by one who is already in lawful possession of it.[4] Had the legislatures not acted, the courts might have eventually achieved the same result through further development of the common law, but legislative action sometimes provides a quicker and more certain change of course.

B. Example: Consumer-Protection Legislation

A more contemporary example deals with the process of reaching a legally binding agreement through the process of offer and acceptance. Under the common law of contracts, a department store's newspaper advertisement typically amounts to an invitation to negotiate rather than an offer to enter into a binding contract; in most cases, a customer makes the first offer by entering the store and requesting to purchase the advertised goods. Under common law, the storeowner is free to reject the customer's offer without incurring any contractual liability.[5]

Unfortunately, this allocation of legal rights and obligations has encouraged some sellers to use bait-and-switch tactics: They lure customers into their stores with the "bait" of goods advertised at spectacularly reduced prices; then they "switch" goods by resisting the customer's desire to purchase the advertised goods and by persuading the customer to purchase a more expensive item. In response, state legislatures have promoted public policy favoring consumer protection by enacting legislation that restricts or prohibits such bait-and-switch tactics.[6] These statutes have altered rights and obligations as they were previously defined solely by the common law of contracts.

---

3. Wayne R. LaFave, CRIMINAL LAW § 19.2, at 971 (5th ed. 2010).

4. *Id.* § 8.6.

5. *See* 1 Arthur L. Corbin, CORBIN ON CONTRACTS § 25 (1963); John D. Calamari & Joseph M. Perillo, CONTRACTS § 2.6(d), at 32 (6th ed. 2009).

6. *See, e.g.*, David Adam Friedman, *Explaining "Bait-and-Switch" Regulation*, 4 WM. & MARY BUS. L. REV. 575 (2013); Note, *State Control of Bait Advertising*, 69 YALE L.J. 830 (1960).

Common Law of Contracts: If store's ad is not an offer, Customer makes first offer. Store can reject that offer and can "switch" Customer to more expensive item.	Consumer-Protection Legislation: Legislature concludes that common law is deficient and enacts protective legislation to address the "bait-and-switch" problem.

C. Increasing Significance of Legislation

Prior to the twentieth century, legislatures in England and the United States tended not to replace common law wholesale with a comprehensive system of statutes. Instead, they typically enacted statutes to correct specific defects or fill gaps in a well-developed body of common law. Statutory law thus assumed a role of secondary importance in the United States, inspiring one scholar to characterize them as "warts on the body of the common law."[7]

State and federal legislation, however, has so proliferated in recent history that "most American jurisdictions now are Code states."[8] Codes are collections of legislative enactments, organized by subject matter. This new prominence of statutory law in the United States warrants an examination of methods of statutory analysis.

II. Judicial Interpretation and Application of Statutes

A federal statute imposes liability on certain employers for discrimination against any individual in the "terms" or "conditions" of employment "because of such individual's . . . sex." Would the statute impose liability on an employer who fired your clients, lesbian and gay employees, because of their sexual orientation? Would it impose liability on an employer who made sexual advances toward only female employees, thus adversely affecting their working environment, but who did not withhold tangible job benefits in retaliation for the subordinate rejecting his advances? The answers to these questions depend on the intended meaning of the statutory language "because of . . . sex" and "terms" or "conditions" of employment.

A. Vagueness and Ambiguity

Questions such as these arise because statutory language sometimes is vague or ambiguous. A vague term is uncertain in its meaning and indefinite

---

7. Llewellyn, *supra* note 1, at 89; *see also* Roscoe Pound, *Common Law and Legislation*, 21 HARV. L. REV. 383 (1908).

8. Stanley Mosk, *The Common Law and the Judicial Decision-Making Process*, 11 HARV. J.L. & PUB. POL'Y 35 (1988).

in its scope, making it difficult to identify the meaning or meanings that it encompasses.[9] An ambiguous term has multiple meanings, although each of the meanings may be precise and all of the meanings may be easily identified.

As discussed more fully below, some statutes are necessarily vague because the legislature deliberately used general language, and some statutes are ambiguous because the legislature unintentionally used less precise language than it should have. Consequently, parties to a dispute frequently may reasonably disagree about the way in which statutory language applies to the facts of their dispute. Courts give greater specificity and precision to the vague or ambiguous statutory language by interpreting and applying the statute in the context of specific disputes.

According to one judge, legislatures should not be faulted for keeping judges so busy with cases requiring statutory interpretation,

> because however careful, wise and farseeing the Legislature, the abstract words of a statute often require fitting and tailoring when applied to real-life cases, which may be more bizarre than anyone could possibly have imagined. Fitting and tailoring are what judges do, and what they are supposed to do—they make judgments.[10]

On the other hand, a court does not engage in a wholly creative process when it interprets a vague or ambiguous statute. Rather, it seeks to determine and to give effect to the intent of the enacting legislature by analyzing the statutory language, the stated or apparent purpose of the statute, and the legislative activities related to enactment of the bill.[11]

This search for the intended meaning of a statute is governed by a separate layer of judicially developed rules of interpretation and construction. "Interpretation" refers to the process of determining legislative intent. "Construction" refers to the process of giving the statutory language a meaning that is consistent with general legislative and public policies, in the absence of conclusive evidence of legislative intent.

B. Intrinsic and Extrinsic Evidence of Legislative Intent

Evidence of legislative intent may be intrinsic to the statute, extrinsic to it, or both. Intrinsic evidence of legislative intent is the statutory text itself. This includes the statutory language in question and other portions of the statute that state or imply the statutory purpose or otherwise provide a context within which to interpret the language in question. Some statutes even include a section of defined terms, which may provide partial guidance even

---

9. *See generally* William Van Orman Quine, WORD AND OBJECT 85, 129 (1960).

10. Judith S. Kaye, *Things Judges Do: State Statutory Interpretation,* 13 TOURO L. REV. 595, 608 (1997).

11. *See, e.g.*, Jackson Transit Auth. v. Local Div. 1285, Amalgamated Transit Union, 457 U.S. 15, 22-29 (1982); Mohasco Corp. v. Silver, 447 U.S. 807, 815 (1980).

when it does not conclusively resolve a dispute over the proper interpretation of the language in question.

Extrinsic evidence of legislative intent includes other information about the social or legal context of the legislation in question. For example, case law may provide insights into the nature of the social problem that the statutory language in question was meant to address. Moreover, companion legislation may reveal the larger legislative context within which a statue operates:

> "[A] statute should be construed in conjunction with other statutes that relate to the same subject or purpose." . . . Our construction should harmonize related statutes together "as though they constituted one law." . . .[12]

When federal legislation applies to the dispute, an important source of extrinsic evidence of legislative intent is the legislative history of the statute in question. This includes the text of congressional debates, preliminary drafts of the legislation, and hearings or reports of congressional committees assigned to study the proposed legislation. Unfortunately, the history of state legislation in many states is less comprehensive and less accessible than federal legislative history.[13]

Courts in the United States have not settled on a uniform approach to statutory interpretation. Indeed, individual judges or justices on the same court may apply different approaches when determining the meaning of statutory language. For example, courts and judges differ in the extent to which they will determine meaning exclusively from the text of an arguably unambiguous term.

Under the "plain meaning" rule of interpretation, if the statutory language in question has a plain meaning on its face, a court will be reluctant to consider legislative purpose or legislative history supporting a less obvious interpretation.[14] However, many judges and scholars argue that the court is not precluded from doing so,[15] as when a state court of appeals gave effect to legislative purpose when it determined that the term "shall" in a statute did

---

12. Ariz. Dept. of Economic Sec. v. Lee, 264 P.3d 234, 236 (Ariz. App. 2011) (ellipses denote omission of citations).

13. Kaye, *supra* note 10, at 600.

14. *See, e.g.*, Hall Street Assoc. L.L.C. v. Mattel, Inc., 552 U.S. 576, 589 (2007) ("whatever the consequences of our holding, the statutory text gives us no business to expand the statutory grounds"); Connecticut Nat'l Bank v. Germain, 503 U.S. 249, 253-54 (1992) (giving priority to the plain language of the statute over legislative history and canons of construction); Ziotas v. Reardon Law Firm, P.C., 296 Conn. 579, 587, 997 A.2d 453, 457 (2010) (refusing to consider extrinsic evidence if the statutory text, considered in relationship to other statutes, is "plain and unambiguous and does not yield absurd or unworkable results"); Note, *Looking It Up: Dictionaries and Statutory Interpretation*, 107 HARV. L. REV. 1437, 1440-44 (1994) (tracing increasing use of the plain language rule, supported by dictionary definitions, in the United States Supreme Court).

15. *E.g.*, Maine v. Thiboutot, 448 U.S. 1, 13-14 (1980) (Powell, J., dissenting); Kent Greenawalt, LEGISLATION: STATUTORY INTERPRETATION: 20 QUESTIONS 57 (1999) (concluding that judges may have reason to depart from the "evident meaning" of statutory text in the case of an obvious "slip" in drafting and, "[s]omewhat more controversially," when "a straightforward reading of the text . . . is clearly at odds with underlying statutory purpose, is manifestly absurd, or is undoubtedly unjust").

not impose a mandatory duty,[16] or when a federal court of appeals engaged in an exhaustive analysis of legislative history and statutory policy to interpret the statutory term "or" to mean the conjunction "and," rather than the disjunctive "either/or."[17]

Unfortunately, misuse of legislative history may mislead more than enlighten. The search for legislative intent is an attempt to reconstruct the collective intent of numerous legislators whose views on the wisdom or scope of the statute may conflict. Opposing advocates often can draw on different portions of legislative history to support conflicting views about the proper interpretation of a statute: They simply invoke isolated statements of legislators taken out of the context of the complete debate on a bill. A court may then justify the result that it wants to reach by selectively drawing on portions of legislative history that support that result. These and other pitfalls have led United States Supreme Court Justice Scalia to decry the "level of unreality that our unrestrained use of legislative history has attained."[18] In his view, courts should give effect to the objective meaning of statutory text without inquiring into the subjective intent of legislators.[19]

Most judges, however, give priority to statutory text without slamming the door on other aids to interpretation. They start with the statutory text but seldom end with it. Of those courts that adopt the plain meaning rule, most also recognize exceptions to that rule, or they fairly readily find ambiguities that permit consideration of extrinsic evidence. As stated by Judge Learned Hand:

> Of course it is true that the words used, even in their literal sense, are the primary, and ordinarily the most reliable, source of interpreting the meaning of any writing: be it a statute, a contract, or anything else. But it is one of the surest indexes of a mature and developed jurisprudence not to make a fortress out of the dictionary; but to remember that statutes always have some purpose or object to accomplish, whose sympathetic and imaginative discovery is the surest guide to their meaning.[20]

C. Statutory Construction When Interpretation Fails

If a court cannot obtain clear evidence of legislative intent through intrinsic or extrinsic evidence, it may use other means to resolve vagueness or ambiguity in statutory language. For example, if an administrative agency

---

16. Ariz. Dept. of Economic Sec. v. Lee, 264 P.3d 234, 238-39 (Ariz. App. 2011).

17. Unification Church v. INS, 762 F.2d 1077, 1083-90 (D.C. Cir. 1985); *see also* Tomka v. Seiler Corp., 66 F.3d 1295, 1313-17 (2d Cir. 1995) (plain meaning of statute is not controlling in rare cases in which the literal meaning of statutory language clearly conflicts with legislative intent).

18. Blanchard v. Bergeron, 489 U.S. 87, 98 (1989) (Scalia, J., concurring). Perhaps due to Justice Scalia's influence, the Supreme Court's reliance on legislative history declined in the 1990s. Lori L. Outzs, *A Principled Use of Congressional Floor Speeches in Statutory Interpretation,* 28 COLUM. J.L. & SOC. PROBS. 297, 305-06 (1995).

19. Antonin Scalia & Bryan Garner, READING LAW 30 (2012).

20. Cabell v. Markham, 148 F.2d 737, 739 (2d Cir.), *aff'd,* 326 U.S. 404 (1945).

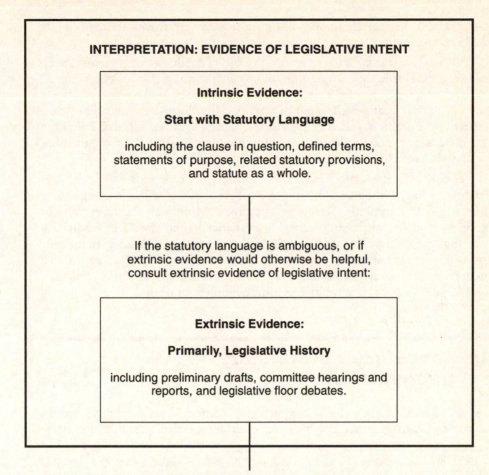

INTERPRETATION: EVIDENCE OF LEGISLATIVE INTENT

Intrinsic Evidence:

Start with Statutory Language

including the clause in question, defined terms, statements of purpose, related statutory provisions, and statute as a whole.

If the statutory language is ambiguous, or if extrinsic evidence would otherwise be helpful, consult extrinsic evidence of legislative intent:

Extrinsic Evidence:

Primarily, Legislative History

including preliminary drafts, committee hearings and reports, and legislative floor debates.

If legislative intent remains unclear, seek guidance from general rules of construction:

CONSTRUCTION: GENERALIZATIONS ABOUT PROBABLE LEGISLATIVE INTENT

Examples:

Construe criminal statutes narrowly, in favor of lenity.

Construe remedial statutes liberally to provide an adequate remedy for the full range of problems that inspired the legislation.

Avoid a construction that would render a statute invalid or a clause superfluous.

If a statute specifically lists some items for statutory treatment, the legislature likely intended to exclude other items that are not listed.

has developed expertise in administering the statute, the court may simply defer to that agency's interpretation of the statutory language.[21]

Otherwise, the court may resort to a judicial rule of construction, such as the general rule that ambiguities in criminal statutes "should be resolved in favor of lenity,"[22] or lenience, so that an act will result in a criminal charge only if the law clearly prohibited the act. Another longstanding rule of construction arguably saved the Affordable Health Care Act in 2012: "[I]f a statute has two possible meanings, one of which violates the Constitution, courts should adopt the meaning that does not do so."[23]

A rule of construction may reflect general policies with which the legislature is likely to agree, but it does not necessarily reflect the legislative purpose of the particular statute in question.[24] Moreover, statutory rules of construction are sufficiently varied and nuanced that advocates frequently can find opposing rules of construction that provide at least general support for different statutory meanings.[25] Accordingly, a court will resort to a general rule of construction only if a "statute's language, structure, purpose, and legislative history leave its meaning genuinely in doubt."[26]

III. Case Studies in Statutory Interpretation

In the following subsections, analyses of two kinds of uncertainty in statutory language provide vehicles for examining techniques that the courts

---

21. *See, e.g.*, Chevron U.S.A., Inc. v. Natural Res. Def. Council, Inc., 467 U.S. 837, 843 (1984); *cf.* United States v. Mead Corp., 533 U.S. 218 (2001) (describing circumstances in which an agency interpretation is entitled to deference only to the extent that it is affirmatively persuasive); Gonzales v. Oregon, 546 U.S. 243, 258-69 (2006) (U.S. Attorney General's interpretive rule was not entitled to special deference, but would be followed only if it was persuasive, because the rule exceeded the A.G.'s statutory rule-making authority).

22. Bell v. United States, 349 U.S. 81, 83 (1955); *accord,* State v. Tarango, 914 P.2d 1300, 1302 (Ariz. 1996); Johnson v. State, 602 So. 2d 1288, 1290 (Fla. 1992). Even a committed textualist such as Justice Scalia concedes that statutory meaning is partly the product of well-known rules of construction such as the rule of lenity, although they amount to rules of interpretation, rather than construction, in his view. Scalia & Garner, *supra* note 19, at 31.

23. Nat'l Fed'n of Indep. Bus. v. Sebelius, 132 S. Ct. 2566, 2593 (2012) (construing the Act's insurance mandate to be a tax, which offered an avenue for upholding its constitutionality). "[E]very reasonable construction must be resorted to, in order to save a statute from unconstitutionality." Hooper v. California, 155 U.S. 648, 657 (1895) (quoted in *Sebelius*, 132 S. Ct. at 2594).

24. *See, e.g.*, Bell v. United States, 349 U.S. 81, 83-84 (1955).

25. Karl N. Llewellyn, *Remarks on the Theory of Appellate Decision and the Rules or Canons about How Statutes Are to Be Construed*, 3 VAND. L. REV. 395, 401-06 (1950).

26. United States v. Otherson, 637 F.2d 1276, 1285 (9th Cir. 1980). Some commentators are more critical of established canons of statutory construction and would replace them wholesale with other means of resolving legislative ambiguities. *See, e.g.*, Richard A. Posner, *Statutory Interpretation—In the Classroom and in the Courtroom*, 50 U. CHI. L. REV. 800 (1983); *cf.* EEOC v. Arabian Am. Oil Co., 499 U.S. 244, 260-61 (1991) (Marshall, J., dissenting) (arguing that majority of the Court gave undue weight to a rule of construction disfavoring extraterritorial application of congressional legislation).

use to clarify the scope and effect of statutes. First, an analysis of ambiguous statutory language illustrates general rules of statutory interpretation and construction. Second, an analysis of vague statutory language illustrates the manner in which courts gradually give concrete meaning to abstract statutory language by applying general terms to particular disputes.

A. Illustration: Imprecision Leading to Ambiguity

Ambiguity may result from imprecision in the words or phrases selected by the drafter. The question concerning sexual orientation raised at the beginning of Section II above addresses the proper interpretation of a federal statute popularly known as Title VII of the Civil Rights Act of 1964. Section 703(a) of the Act prohibits certain kinds of employment discrimination:

> It shall be an unlawful employment practice for an employer . . . to discriminate against any individual with respect to his compensation, terms, conditions, or privileges of employment, because of such individual's race, color, religion, sex, or national origin . . . .[27]

1. The Problem

It is unclear from the quoted language whether section 703(a) prohibits an employer from discriminating against gay and lesbian employees because of their sexual orientation. Perhaps Title VII's reference to "sex" as a protected classification would prohibit such an employment policy. It would most clearly do so if Congress used the term "sex" to refer broadly to any sexual characteristic, including an individual's sexual identity, activities, preferences, or orientation, rather than only to the characteristic of being male or female.

2. Intrinsic Evidence

Judicial interpretation of a statute should start with the most direct intrinsic evidence of legislative intent: the statutory language in question.[28] An analysis of the language of section 703(a), however, reveals no single, plain meaning of the statutory term "sex." Dictionaries and common usage define "sex" as, among other things, either (1) the division of species between male and female or (2) more general sexual behavior and characteristics:

> 1: either of two divisions of organisms distinguished respectively as male or female 2: the sum of the structural, functional, and behavioral peculiarities of living beings that subserve reproduction by two interacting parents and

---

27. 42 U.S.C. § 2000e-2(a) (2006).

28. Laurence H. Tribe, *Judicial Interpretation of Statutes: Three Axioms,* 11 HARV. J.L. & PUB. POL'Y 51 (1988) ("Axiom one is: *Language first.*"); Unification Church v. INS, 762 F.2d 1077, 1083 (D.C. Cir. 1985).

distinguish males and females 3a: sexually motivated phenomena or behavior b: sexual intercourse.[29]

Thus, the statutory term "sex" is truly ambiguous, and the process of judicial interpretation will require an inquiry that goes beyond searching for a plain meaning in the term itself.

Other provisions of Title VII may provide intrinsic evidence of the intended meaning of "sex" in section 703(a). In a different subsection of the same legislative act, section 703(h), Congress probably used the term in the narrow sense of the division of species between male and female.[30] There it used "sex" in a reference to the Equal Pay Act of 1963, which more clearly prohibits only certain kinds of discrimination based on the status of an employee as male or female.[31] If Congress consciously used "sex" in that sense in section 703(h), the obvious virtues of consistency in statutory drafting suggest the likelihood, though not the certainty, that Congress used the term "sex" in the same way in section 703(a) of the same legislative act.

3. Extrinsic Evidence

Thus, intrinsic evidence of the intended meaning of the word "sex" in section 703(a) is helpful but inconclusive. Therefore, a court interpreting "sex" would likely seek guidance from extrinsic evidence, such as legislative history. The original House bill did not include "sex" as a prohibited basis of discrimination. Instead, Howard Smith, a southern Democrat and chair of the House Rules Committee, proposed the addition of "sex" as a protected classification in a last-minute amendment on the House floor. He apparently hoped that the amendment would spark sufficient controversy to cause the defeat of the entire bill.[32]

Smith's unsuccessful strategy left the courts with "little legislative history to guide us in interpreting the Act's prohibition against discrimination based on 'sex.'"[33] However, the few statements made on the House floor about the proposed amendment, both by Smith and by representatives who more sincerely favored equality of the sexes, suggest that the speakers interpreted "sex" to refer narrowly to the characteristic of being male or

---

29. WEBSTER'S SEVENTH NEW COLLEGIATE DICTIONARY 347 (1970), *as quoted in* Holloway v. Arthur Andersen & Co., 566 F.2d 659, 662 n.4 (9th Cir. 1977).

30. Section 703(h) incorporates a limitation set forth in the Equal Pay Act: "It shall not be . . . unlawful . . . to differentiate upon the basis of *sex* . . . if such differentiation is authorized by the provisions of [the Equal Pay Act]." 42 U.S.C. § 2000e-2(h) (2006) (emphasis added).

31. The Equal Pay Act refers to members of the "opposite sex": "No employer . . . shall discriminate . . . between employees on the basis of *sex* by paying wages to employees . . . at a rate less than the rate at which he pays wages to employees of the *opposite sex* . . . for equal work. . . ." 29 U.S.C. § 206(d) (2006) (emphasis added). The phrase "opposite sex" is commonly used to refer only to distinctions between males and females. Therefore, the Equal Pay Act is nearly unambiguous in its classifying only on the basis of employees being male or female.

32. Charles Whalen & Barbara Whalen, THE LONGEST DEBATE 84, 115-16 (1985).

33. Meritor Sav. Bank, FSB v. Vinson, 477 U.S. 57, 64 (1986).

female.[34] That interpretation is supported by post-enactment evidence of congressional intent. First, the House report on the 1972 Amendments to Title VII clearly shows that Congress was primarily concerned with putting women on equal economic footing with men. Second, successive congressional rejections of several bills proposing to amend Title VII by adding "sexual preference" as a protected classification suggest that members of Congress probably had never collectively intended the statutory term "sex" to encompass sexual preference.[35]

Relying on this legislative history, courts have interpreted the word "sex" in section 703(a) to refer only to male or female status and not also to sexual orientation.[36] Interpreted in that way, Title VII does not clearly prohibit an employer from discriminating against employees because of their homosexuality, provided that the employer applies the same policy to gay male employees as it does to lesbian female employees.[37]

Had the evidence of specific congressional intent been less convincing, the interpreting court might have applied the general rule of construction that "remedial" statutes should be liberally construed. Title VII is remedial in its purpose of redressing the pervasive social and economic problem of employment discrimination.[38] Therefore, the rule of construction would favor a liberal construction of the term "sex," which might encompass sexual orientation. However, this general rule of construction is subordinate to evidence of more specific congressional intent relating to the statute in question.[39]

B. Illustration: Generality Resulting in Vagueness

Even if the legislature chooses its words carefully, most statutory language is necessarily general, because almost all legislation addresses broad categories of activities or disputes rather than particular cases. Legislators simply do not possess the stamina and prescience required to consider every potential dispute within the scope of legislation and to provide a specific resolution for each. Instead, courts put the flesh on the bones of legislation by applying the general terms of the statute to the facts of particular disputes, thus adding precision to statutory language in much the same way

---

34. *See* Whalen & Whalen, *supra* note 32, at 116-17.

35. Holloway v. Arthur Andersen & Co., 566 F.2d 659, 662 (9th Cir. 1977).

36. *E.g., id.* at 662-63; Spearman v. Ford Motor Co., 231 F.3d 1080, 1084-85 (7th Cir. 2000).

37. *See, e.g.*, De Santis v. Pac. Tel. & Tel. Co., 608 F.2d 327 (9th Cir. 1979); Bibby v. Philadelphia Coca-Cola Bottling Co., 260 F.3d 257, 261-64 (3d Cir. 2001) (distinguishing between sexual orientation discrimination, which is not prohibited by Title VII, from same-sex gender discrimination, which is). *But cf.* Gay Law Students Ass'n v. Pac. Tel. & Tel. Co., 595 P.2d 592 (Cal. 1979) (different result under California constitutional and statutory law); Sam Marcosson, *Harassment on the Basis of Sexual Orientation: A Claim of Sex Discrimination Under Title VII,* 81 Geo. L.J. 1, 3-10 (1992) (critiquing *De Santis*).

38. Bell v. Brown, 557 F.2d 849, 853 (D.C. Cir. 1977).

39. *See* Mohasco Corp. v. Silver, 447 U.S. 807, 818-19 (1980) (Title VII is remedial legislation, but also is the product of legislative compromise).

that they develop common law—incrementally and in the context of successive disputes.

For example, section 703(a) of Title VII of the Civil Rights Act of 1964 prohibits discrimination only with respect to an individual's "compensation, terms, conditions, or privileges of employment."[40] That statutory phrase is necessarily general, because Congress could not practicably describe in more specific terms all of the possible kinds of discrimination that have a sufficient relationship to employment to trigger congressional concern about equal opportunity in the workplace. That generality results in a vagueness that promotes disputes over the interpretation and application of the statute in particular cases.

For instance, parties have reasonably disputed whether unwelcome sexual advances made by an employer's agent to an employee affect the employee's "terms, conditions, or privileges of employment" if the agent does not withhold tangible benefits of employment in retaliation for rejection of these advances.[41] Courts have given more specific meaning to the statutory phrase by adopting a more detailed legal standard for determining the circumstances in which the statute is satisfied: To give effect to Title VII's remedial purpose, courts have decided that sexual advances by an employer's agent may affect "terms, conditions, or privileges of employment" if they create "a substantially discriminatory work environment, regardless of whether the complaining employees lost any tangible job benefits as a result of the discrimination."[42]

Although the "discriminatory work environment" standard adds a judicial gloss to the statutory language, the judicial standard is itself abstract and suffers from its own problems of vagueness. True, the United States Supreme Court provided a small measure of guidance by approving liability only if the harassment is "sufficiently severe or pervasive 'to alter the conditions of . . . employment and create an abusive working environment.'"[43] Additionally, the Supreme Court later provided more detailed guidance by listing a number of factors that courts should consider in determining whether a working environment has become abusive.[44] Still, the precise parameters of the judicial standard, and thus of the statutory language that it seeks to effectuate, will take form only when courts repeatedly apply the standard to the facts of different disputes.

---

40. 42 U.S.C. § 2000e-2(a) (2006).

41. Such conduct constitutes sex discrimination if the harasser would not have engaged in the conduct but for the employee's status as a man or a woman; that requirement normally is satisfied in the case of a heterosexual or homosexual harasser, but not necessarily in the case of a bisexual harasser. *See* Barnes v. Costle, 561 F.2d 983, 990 n.55 (D.C. Cir. 1977). That analysis, however, does not answer the question whether the discrimination alters conditions of employment, as required by Title VII.

42. Bundy v. Jackson, 641 F.2d 934, 943-44 (D.C. Cir. 1981).

43. Meritor Sav. Bank, FSB v. Vinson, 477 U.S. 57, 67 (1986) (*quoting* Henson v. Dundee, 682 F.2d 897, 904 (11th Cir. 1982)).

44. Harris v. Forklift Sys., 510 U.S. 17, 23 (1993). The Supreme Court has also emphasized the value of employing "[c]ommon sense and an appropriate sensitivity to social context" in distinguishing "ordinary socializing in the workplace" from unlawful harassment. Oncale v. Sundowner Offshore Serv., Inc., 523 U.S. 75, 81-82 (1998).

In one case, for example, a federal trial court found that an employer's chief executive created a discriminatory work environment for an employee by giving her a pornographic magazine, leaving an article on her desk about extramarital affairs, and subjecting her to unwelcome sexual advances on at least seven occasions.[45] In contrast, in another case, a federal trial court found that a supervisor did not create a discriminatory work environment by displaying a condescending and impatient attitude toward an employee and by teasing her about her personal relationship with a coworker.[46] If you examine those and other decisions addressing the same issue in different factual contexts, you can gain a better understanding of the intended reach of the statute than is provided by the general statutory language, "terms, conditions, or privileges of employment," or even the more specific judicial interpretation, "discriminatory work environment."

Unfortunately, you should be prepared to encounter cases at the margin that add to your confusion rather than your understanding. For example, a federal appellate court held in two cases that supervisors and coworkers did not create a discriminatory work environment by subjecting employees to conduct and lewd comments that were relatively "isolated," even though the conduct included physical contact, such as a hand on an employee's shoulder or a slap on an employee's buttocks.[47] A federal trial court in a different geographic jurisdiction, however, found that a supervisor created a discriminatory work environment by subjecting an employee to a single slap on her buttocks and by threatening to repeat that conduct.[48] You could reasonably interpret such cases as reflecting disagreement among the courts about the proper interpretation and application of the legal standard, a phenomenon addressed in succeeding chapters in this book, particularly Chapter 7, Section II.B.7.

Exercise 4-1

1. Judicial Interpretation of Legislation

A statute of State *Y* provides without qualification that "any landlord of a residential unit may prohibit tenants from keeping pets in their units and may evict any tenant who violates such a prohibition and fails to cure the violation within one week of receiving notice of the violation." Does this statute permit a landlord

---

45. Ross v. Twenty-Four Collection, Inc., 681 F. Supp. 1547, 1551 (S.D. Fla. 1988), *aff'd*, 875 F.2d 873 (11th Cir. 1989).

46. Saxton v. Am. Tel. & Tel. Co., 785 F. Supp. 760, 765 (N.D. Ill. 1992).

47. Weiss v. Coca-Cola Bottling Co., 990 F.2d 333, 337 (7th Cir. 1993); Scott v. Sears, Roebuck & Co., 798 F.2d 210, 211-14 (7th Cir. 1986).

48. Campbell v. Kans. State Univ., 780 F. Supp. 755, 761-62 (D. Kan. 1991). This decision gains some support from the Supreme Court's subsequent dictum illustrating the importance of context, in Oncale v. Sundowner Offshore Serv., Inc., 523 U.S. 75, 81 (1998) (a coach may be acting abusively when smacking his secretary on the buttocks in the office, though not when smacking a football player on the buttocks as he heads out to the field).

of residential apartments in State *Y* to evict a tenant who refuses to get rid of a single goldfish that the tenant keeps in a two-gallon fish bowl in her apartment? You may assume that State *Y* has no helpful legislative history relating to this statute. Can opposing attorneys reasonably argue for and against application of the statute? Can different judges reasonably reach opposite conclusions on the proper interpretation and application of the statute in this case?[49]

2. Statutory Policy and Classification

The Highway Patrol of State *X* informed legislators of State *X* that motorists were causing accidents by consuming soft drinks while driving. The Highway Patrol was not overly concerned that drivers could keep only one hand on the wheel while consuming soft drinks. Instead, they were concerned that drivers often obstructed their own vision, and thus lost partial control of their automobiles, when they tilted their heads back and tipped their soft drink containers upward to consume the last of their soft drinks. In response, state legislators amended the State *X* Vehicle Code to make it a misdemeanor "to operate a motor vehicle while consuming any beverage from a can or bottle." If the concerns that motivated this bill are recorded in legislative history, should the new law apply to:

    a. a driver who tilts her head back to drink water from a paper cup?

    b. a driver who keeps his head level while he sips a soft drink through a straw from a bottle?

    c. a driver who eats a sandwich in a way that distracts her and obstructs her vision?

In addressing these cases, ask yourself to what extent a court should adhere to the strict terms of the statute, even if such an interpretation in a specific case is not perfectly consistent with the legislative purpose. To what extent should the court interpret the statutory language flexibly to more closely achieve the legislative purpose?

3. Legislative History

The current codification of a Reconstruction-era civil rights act prohibits certain kinds of discrimination:

> *All persons* within the jurisdiction of the United States shall have the same right in every State and Territory to make and enforce contracts . . . *as is enjoyed by white citizens* . . . .

42 U.S.C. § 1981(a) (2006) (emphasis added). The original predecessor to this statute contained similar language:

---

49. This problem is derived from a hypothetical case posed by Shirley Abrahamson, chief justice of the Wisconsin Supreme Court, and related by New York Court of Appeals Judge Judith S. Kaye in *Things Judges Do: State Statutory Interpretation*, 13 TOURO L. REV. 595, 606 (1997).

> [C]itizens of the United States . . . of every race and color, without regard to any previous condition of slavery or involuntary servitude, . . . shall have the same right, in every State and Territory in the United States, to make and enforce contracts . . . *as is enjoyed by white citizens* . . . .

Civil Rights Act of 1866 § 1, 14 Stat. 27 (1866) (emphasis added); *see also* Civil Rights Act of 1870 §§ 16, 18, 16 Stat. 144 (1870) (reenacting and adding to 1866 Act). The "immediate impetus" for the original statute was "the necessity for further relief of the constitutionally emancipated former Negro slaves."[50] However, to allay fears among some legislators that the proposed bill would favor nonwhites, proponents of the bill defended it at several stages of the legislative process as one that would protect *all* citizens.[51] More than a century after the initial enactment, the United States Supreme Court applied the modern version of this statute to prohibit private, commercially operated, nonsectarian schools from discriminating on the basis of race against African-Americans in admission to the schools.[52]

a. Should a court apply the statute to protect nonwhites other than African-Americans from race discrimination in contractual relations?

b. Should a court apply the statute to protect white citizens from race discrimination? *See McDonald v. Santa Fe Trail Transp. Co.*, 427 U.S. 273 (1976).

c. If the statute applies to protect racial groups other than African-Americans, how does one distinguish between different races for purposes of finding prohibited discrimination? Would the statute apply to prohibit discrimination against a person because he is Arab-American rather than Anglo-American? *See St. Francis College v. Al-Khazraji*, 481 U.S. 604 (1987) (looking to racial classifications recognized at time of enactment of predecessors to 42 U.S.C. § 1981). Would it apply to discrimination because one is Jewish? *See Shaare Tefila Congregation v. Cobb*, 481 U.S. 615 (1987) (analysis under companion statute, 42 U.S.C. § 1982).

IV. Legislative Enactment and Change

British law professor Gary Watt reminds us to constantly critique the current state of the law:

> We should acknowledge the present state of the law, but we should also acknowledge that it is only a starting point. It is important that we then use our imagination as the philosophers do . . . to imagine how we might move away from the worst errors of the present law. . . . We will not find Utopia there. Just humanity.[53]

---

50. McDonald v. Santa Fe Trail Transp. Co., 427 U.S. 273, 289 (1976).
51. *Id.* at 289-95.
52. Runyon v. McCrary, 427 U.S. 160 (1976).
53. Gary Watt, EQUITY STIRRING: THE STORY OF JUSTICE BEYOND LAW 247-48 (2009).

As a serious student of the law, or possibly a future legislator, or simply an engaged citizen, you should not be content to comprehend and interpret statutory law. You should also carefully evaluate the merits of current or proposed legislation.

When you encounter a social problem that you believe is not adequately addressed by current constitutional or common law, consider whether you would support legislation to address the problem. In light of questions of statutory interpretation explored in the previous sections, consider how you would draft legislation so that it achieves your statutory purpose with minimum ambiguity.

Of course, a legislature that has the power to enact legislation also has the power to repeal or amend it. A constant critique of current legislation helps to fuel the dynamic process of the growth and development of statutory law.

For example, the discussion in the previous section shows that Congress almost certainty intended Title VII's prohibition of sex discrimination to apply to discrimination on the basis of status as male or female but not on the basis of sexual orientation. In reaching that conclusion, however, some courts have suggested that sexual orientation discrimination, such as harassment on the basis of an employee's sexual orientation, warrants a remedy, though Title VII does not currently afford one:

> [H]arassment because of sexual orientation . . . is a noxious practice, deserving of censure and opprobrium. But we are called upon here to construe a statute . . . and we regard it as settled law that, as drafted and authoritatively construed, Title VII does not proscribe harassment simply because of sexual orientation.[54]

The first exercise below asks you to consider whether the policies underlying Title VII's current prohibitions apply as well to discrimination because of sexual orientation, and whether Congress should amend Title VII to prohibit such discrimination.

Exercise 4-2

1. Legislative Amendment: Invidious Discrimination

Thirty years after the 1963 civil rights march in Washington, D.C., for racial equality, hundreds of thousands of lesbian and gay Americans rallied in the nation's capital to demand freedom from discrimination.[55] President Bill Clinton later equated "the gay rights movement with the struggle for racial equality."[56]

---

54. Higgins v. New Balance Athletic Shoe, Inc., 194 F.3d 252, 259 (1st Cir. 1999), *quoted in* Rene v. MGM Grand Hotel, Inc., 243 F.2d 1206, 1209 (9th Cir. 2001).

55. Jeffrey Schmalz, *Gay Americans Throng Capital in Appeal for Rights,* N.Y. TIMES, Apr. 26, 1993, at A1.

56. Peter Baker, *Clinton Equates Gay Rights, Civil Rights,* WASH. POST, Nov. 9, 1997, at A18 (reporting on "the first speech by a sitting President to a gay rights organization"). In

Consider the bases of discrimination covered by Title VII of the Civil Rights Act of 1964: race, color, religion, sex, and national origin. Other federal statutes prohibit discrimination based on age or disability. Why is discrimination based on these classifications viewed as especially pernicious? Should Congress amend Title VII to prohibit discrimination on the basis of sexual orientation? Would you condition your support for the bill on a showing that sexual orientation is biologically determined,[57] or is that factor less important in light of the protected status under Title VII of one's religion, which is not an immutable characteristic?

Should your state legislature amend its marriage statutes to permit marriage between same-sex couples (or to ban it if your state now allows it)? Does this proposal raise different issues than does a proposal to prohibit employment discrimination on the basis of sexual orientation? Why or why not?

In formulating your support or opposition to such proposals, how do you define your role as legislator? Should you vote according to your best personal judgment on the ground that your constituents expressed confidence in your judgment and values by electing you to office? Or should you vote in a manner currently favored by most of your constituents, even if that differs from your personal convictions?

2. Enacting Mandatory Safety Rules

Do you support state legislation requiring a person to wear a protective helmet while driving or riding as a passenger on a motorcycle on a public street or highway? What policy arguments support or oppose such legislation?

3. Enacting Legislation Permitting Physician-Assisted Suicide

In 1997, the United States Supreme Court refused to recognize a constitutional right to physician-assisted suicide, and it left the matter of prohibition, regulation, or permission of physician-assisted suicide to be resolved in other legal arenas, such as state criminal legislation.[58] As a state legislator, what position would you take on this issue? Would you vote for a bill making it a crime for a physician to actively promote the death of any patient, regardless of the circumstances? Conversely, would you legislatively grant immunity to a physician who hastened the death of a terminally ill patient who requested such assistance? Would you permit

---

2000, a second rally in Washington, D.C., again drew hundreds of thousands. Robin Toner, *A Gay Rights Rally Over Gains and Goals*, N.Y. TIMES, May 1, 2000, at A14.

57. *Compare* E. Gary Spitko, *A Biologic Argument for Gay Essentialism-Determinism: Implications for Equal Protection and Substantive Due Process,* 18 U. HAW. L. REV. 571, 576-84 (1996) (reviewing studies tending to show a physiological or genetic basis for gay male sexual orientation) *with* Janet E. Halley, *Sexual Orientation and the Politics of Biology: A Critique of the Argument from Immutability,* 46 STAN. L. REV. 503 (1994) (arguing that immutability argument is divisive and is not necessary for advancing gay rights); *see also* Glenn Wilson & Qazi Rahman, BORN GAY 10 (2005) (concluding that sexual orientation in men is the product of genetic factors and hormonal activities in the womb).

58. Washington v. Glucksberg, 521 U.S. 702 (1997); Vacco v. Quill, 521 U.S. 793 (1997); *see also* Gonzales v. Oregon, 546 U.S. 243 (2006) (rejecting U.S. Attorney General's attempt to change this result through interpretive rulemaking that exceeded rulemaking authority under the federal Controlled Substances Act).

physician-assisted suicide, but regulate it by restricting it to certain circumstances? How would you draft your legislation?

4. Immigration Reform

How would you craft a federal bill that seeks to accomplish comprehensive immigration reform? If one of your goals is to gain complete control of our borders, what measures would you propose to achieve that result? What provisions would you include with respect to undocumented aliens who now reside and work in the United States? Would you include a path to citizenship? If so, on what conditions? Would you include any special provision for students whose parents brought them to the United States without documentation when they were children and are now successfully pursuing a college education in the United States?

5. Overruling Common Law

In August 1997, a North Carolina jury awarded $1 million to a jilted wife who sued her husband's secretary for committing adultery with her husband and breaking up their marriage.[59] The award was based partly on the common law tort of alienation of affection, defined as wrongful conduct that deprives a married person of the love and companionship of his or her spouse by interfering in a harmonious marriage.[60] Most states have legislatively abolished this and related torts, partly because the torts invite abusive legal tactics and are based on outdated notions about the nature of intimate relationships.[61] Indeed, the North Carolina Court of Appeals had judicially abandoned the common law tort of alienation of affection in 1984, but the North Carolina Supreme Court reversed on the ground that it had recognized the tort of alienation of affection in its own case law, which the court of appeals was not free to ignore.[62]

Do you believe such torts should be retained or abandoned? As a member of the state's highest court, would you abolish the tort of alienation of affection in the course of developing the state's common law, or would you view such a major policy change as one best left to the state legislature? As a state legislator, would you support or oppose a bill to abolish the common law tort of alienation of affection?

---

59. *See* Foon Rhee, *Jury Award Turns Attention to "Homewrecker" Law*, WASH. POST, Aug. 10, 1997, at A25.

60. *See, e.g.*, Fitch v. Valentine, 959 So. 2d 1012 (Miss. 2007).

61. *See, e.g.*, Susan L. Thomas, *Proof of Alienation of Affections*, 54 AM. JUR. 3D *Proof of Facts* § 135 (2009); Jill Jones, *Fanning an Old Flame: Alienation of Affections and Criminal Conversation Revisited*, 26 PEPP. L. REV. 61 (1999).

62. Cannon v. Miller, 322 S.E.2d 780 (N.C. Ct. App. 1984), *vacated*, 327 S.E.2d 888 (N.C. 1985).

V. Interplay Between Legislation and Common Law

A. Relationship Between Legislation and Common Law

1. Legislative Primacy

Although the legislature and the judiciary both exercise lawmaking powers, the legislature is the paramount lawmaking authority, and legislative enactments supersede inconsistent common law. The following United States Supreme Court statement about the federal system applies as well to the state governments:

> [W]e consistently have emphasized that the federal lawmaking power is vested in the legislative, not the judicial, branch of government; therefore, federal common law is "subject to the paramount authority of Congress."[63]

Accordingly, the legislature may enact statutes that modify, overrule, or codify existing common law.

2. Legislation as Guidance for Common Law

Even if no statute currently applies to a dispute, a court may decline to extend common law principles to the area if it concludes that the matter is better left to legislative action.[64] Moreover, if the court decides to develop and apply the common law, it nonetheless may look to statutory law for expressions of public policy that help the court formulate the common law rule. In one case, for example, a court drew guidance from an enacted, but not yet effective, commercial code to develop a common law doctrine of unconscionability in sales contracts.[65]

3. Common Law as Background for Legislation

Although statutory law supersedes common law, the common law at the time of a statute's enactment may provide a helpful context for analyzing

---

63. Northwest Airlines, Inc. v. Transport Workers Union, 451 U.S. 77, 95 (1981) (quoting New Jersey v. New York, 283 U.S. 336, 348 (1931)).

64. *See, e.g.*, City & County of S.F. v. United Ass'n of Journeymen etc. of U.S. & Can., 726 P.2d 538 (Cal. 1986); *see also* Raftopol v. Ramey, 299 Conn. 681, 710, 12 A.3d 783, 800 (2011) (stating this proposition but enforcing surrogacy agreement by interpreting ambiguous statute); Heard v. Stamford, 3 P. Wms. 409, 411 (1735) (in explaining why an English court of equity should not intervene, stating that "[i]f the law as it now stands be thought inconvenient, it will be good reason for the legislature to alter it, but till that is done, what is law at present, must take place") (as quoted in Gary Watt, EQUITY STIRRING: THE STORY OF JUSTICE BEYOND LAW 20 (2009)).

65. Williams v. Walker-Thomas Furniture Co., 350 F.2d 445 (D.C. Cir. 1965).

legislative intent.[66] If a statute overrules a common law rule or seeks to address a problem left untouched by the common law, a court can better understand the statute's intended scope if it appreciates the deficiencies of the common law to which the legislature responded.[67] Conversely, if a statute codifies existing common law, cases that developed the common law rule obviously will provide guidance in interpreting the statute.

Moreover, a statute often addresses only selected issues within the general subject matter touched by the statute, thereby creating gaps that common law may fill. In some cases, the statute itself provides for reference to common law, as in the Uniform Commercial Code:

> Unless displaced by the particular provisions of [the Uniform Commercial Code], the principles of law and equity, including the law merchant and the law relative to capacity to contract, principal and agent, estoppel, fraud, misrepresentation, duress, coercion, mistake, . . . and other validating or invalidating cause supplement its provisions.[68]

In other cases, statutes only implicitly incorporate common law principles. For example, a federal civil rights statute imposes liability for certain conduct without any express qualifications or limitations. Yet, courts have assumed that Congress intended the statute to implicitly incorporate common law defenses of immunity from liability for money damages:

> It is by now well settled that the tort liability created by [42 U.S.C.] § 1983 cannot be understood in a historical vacuum. In the Civil Rights Act of 1871, Congress created a federal remedy against a person who, acting under color of state law, deprives another of constitutional rights. . . . One important assumption underlying the Court's decisions in this area is that members of the 42d Congress were familiar with common-law principles, including defenses previously recognized in ordinary tort litigation, and that they likely intended these common-law principles to obtain, absent specific provisions to the contrary.[69]

B. Judicial Power and Limitations Regarding Legislation

Although legislatures can modify or overrule common law principles developed by courts, the courts retain an important role in the development of statutory law. Courts may review statutes for consistency with constitutional requirements and will refuse to enforce unconstitutional legislation.[70]

---

66. 2B Norman J. Singer, SUTHERLAND STATUTORY CONSTRUCTION §50.01 (6th ed. 2000); *see* Wayne R. LaFave, CRIMINAL LAW § 2.2(d), at 94-96 (5th ed. 2010) (discussing interpretation of criminal statutes in light of common law); City of Okla. City v. Tuttle, 471 U.S. 808, 835-38 (1985) (Stevens, J., dissenting).

67. *See, e.g.,* Heydon's Case, 76 Eng. Rep. 637, 638 (1584), *quoted in* Singer, *supra* note 66, § 45.05, at 25-26.

68. U.C.C. § 1-103(b) (2001).

69. City of Newport v. Fact Concerts, Inc., 453 U.S. 247, 258 (1981).

70. *See* Marbury v. Madison, 5 U.S. (1 Cranch) 137 (1803) (setting forth seminal dictum regarding judicial authority in the federal system); Dickerson v. United States, 530 U.S. 428

Additionally, as discussed in Section III above, courts determine the scope and effect of legislation by interpreting statutes and applying them to particular disputes.

Nonetheless, courts have less flexibility in interpreting statutory law than in developing common law. True, if a court finds good reason to abandon its previous analysis of legislative intent, it may overrule its earlier interpretation of a statute, just as it sometimes overrules its previous statement or application of a principle of common law.[71] However, the court may not ignore a statute or modify its terms to reflect judicial views that are inconsistent with legislative intent. In contrast, a court may directly reject the substance and reasoning of a common law principle that it had announced and applied in a prior decision: "[W]e have not hesitated to change the common law . . . where . . . such course was justified."[72]

Interestingly, some American Indian tribal court judges have boldly hinted that they may challenge the conventional hierarchy of laws in tribal governments. According to assumptions adopted by our state and federal systems, tribal codes should have priority over tribal common law, because the tribal council has adopted the codes, just as a federal or state legislature enacts statutes. However, even though tribal codes are formally enacted by tribal councils, many were conceived and drafted by Anglo-Americans and may reflect a poor understanding of tribal culture. In contrast, some tribal courts more consciously seek to promote tribal culture and policies when they develop and apply tribal common law.

This phenomenon may justify a departure from U.S. legal method in tribal courts. For example, the Navajo Supreme Court has hinted that it may refuse to give effect to outdated tribal code sections that fail to promote Navajo values or are inconsistent with longstanding Navajo custom. In gestures acknowledging the role of the legislative branch of government, the Navajo Supreme Court has explicitly recommended in its opinions that the Navajo Tribal Council amend tribal codes that do not promote Navajo culture and policies.[73] This kind of communication between branches of government is not foreign to the state and federal legal systems. However, not content to wait for action from its legislative branch, the Navajo Supreme Court has considered a more assertive legal method. When necessary to preserve important values of tribal culture or sovereignty, the Navajo Supreme Court has hinted at its willingness to elevate Navajo common law or custom above otherwise applicable tribal codes.[74]

(2000) (striking down congressional attempt to legislatively overrule the celebrated *Miranda* decision, which protected constitutional rights).

71. *See, e.g.*, Monell v. Dep't of Soc. Servs. of N.Y., 436 U.S. 658 (1978) (overruling the Court's previous decision that the term "person" in 42 U.S.C. § 1983 does not include municipalities); Wayne R. LaFave, CRIMINAL LAW § 2.2(m), at 107-08 (5th ed. 2010).

72. Kelley v. R.G. Indus., 497 A.2d 1143, 1150-51 (Md. 1985).

73. *E.g., In re* Validation of Marriage of Francisco, 16 INDIAN L. REP. 6113, 6115 (Navajo S. Ct. 1989).

74. *See id.* ("This court . . . does not rely on [the tribal code], but instead on Navajo custom.").

One scholarly judge supports similarly skeptical treatment of outdated state statutes.[75] Nonetheless, in the state and federal legal systems in the U.S., the conventional hierarchy of laws is firmly entrenched: A constitution defines the reach of statutory authority, and statutes can limit the application of common law.

VI. Summary

A state or federal legislature is the primary policymaking body within a jurisdiction, and it can modify or overrule common law by enacting a superseding statute. Nonetheless, courts review statutes for constitutionality, and they interpret and apply statutes in the context of particular disputes. In interpreting statutes, a court begins with the statutory language in question, viewed in the context of the statute as a whole. If that language is vague or ambiguous, the court may look to other evidence of legislative intent, including legislative purpose and legislative history. If evidence of legislative intent is inconclusive, the court may apply a rule of construction, which gives the statute a meaning that is consistent with general legislative and public policies.

For more problems and exercises related to the legal system, consult Appendix I.

---

75. *See* Guido Calabresi, A COMMON LAW FOR THE AGE OF STATUTES 163-66 (1999) (recommending that Anglo-American courts refuse to enforce outdated statutes unless reaffirmed by the legislature).

Part III

Legal Method

and Analysis

Chapter 5

The Role of Precedent: The Court System and Stare Decisis

I. Introduction to Stare Decisis

In the United States, previous court decisions may influence, or even dictate, the result in a dispute currently before a court. The legal effect of the previous decisions is governed by a complex set of conventions for which the Latin phrase "stare decisis" is often used as convenient shorthand.

"Stare decisis" means standing by what has been decided. Under the doctrine of stare decisis, a court endeavors to decide each case consistently with its own previous decisions, which are called its "precedent." Moreover, the deciding court ordinarily is strictly bound by the precedent of a higher court that reviews the decisions of the deciding court, if the precedent addressed essentially the same question currently before the deciding court.

Judicial adherence to the doctrine of stare decisis serves several significant goals:

- it promotes efficiency in judicial administration by relieving judges of the burden of revisiting settled legal questions in each case;
- it facilitates private and commercial transactions by ensuring a degree of certainty and predictability in the law that regulates such transactions; and
- it satisfies the common moral belief that persons in like circumstances should be treated alike.[1]

The strength of an authority as precedent depends in part on the relationship between the court that created the precedent and the court that may subsequently apply it. Therefore, our exploration should begin with an introduction to the court system.

II. The Court System

A. Structure of State, Federal, and Tribal Courts

1. State Courts

Most state court systems include courts of limited jurisdiction, which hear disputes on limited matters such as domestic relations, traffic violations, and civil suits with small amounts in controversy. All other disputes are tried in branches of a trial court of general jurisdiction, typically named "Superior Court," "Circuit Court," or "District Court."

In most states, final decisions of this trial court may be reviewed in appellate courts at two different levels: A disappointed litigant may appeal a trial court judgment to an intermediate court of appeals; further appeals are taken to a court of last resort, known as the "Supreme Court" in nearly all states. Some court systems, however, have no intermediate appellate court. Instead, a single state court of last resort hears appeals directly from judgments of the trial courts of general jurisdiction.[2] Under either model, a disappointed litigant in state court may seek further review on questions of federal law in the United States Supreme Court.[3]

---

1. *See* Edgar Bodenheimer, JURISPRUDENCE: THE PHILOSOPHY AND METHOD OF THE LAW 425-28 (rev. ed. 1974); Frederick Schauer, *Precedent*, 39 STAN. L. REV. 571, 595-602 (1987); *see also* Payne v. Tennessee, 501 U.S. 808, 827 (1991) (stare decisis "promotes the evenhanded, predictable, and consistent development of legal principles, fosters reliance on judicial decisions, and contributes to the actual and perceived integrity of the judicial process").

2. In 2013, those court systems included those of the District of Columbia and the following states: Delaware, Maine, Montana, Nevada, New Hampshire, Rhode Island, South Dakota, Vermont, West Virginia, and Wyoming. BNA'S DIRECTORY OF STATE AND FEDERAL COURTS, JUDGES, AND CLERKS xi-xiv (2013) [hereinafter, BNA'S DIRECTORY OF COURTS].

3. 28 U.S.C. § 1257 (2006).

The state court system in California is representative of those systems with two levels of appellate review:

California Supreme Court
State court of last resort

California Courts of Appeal		
1st App. District	3d App. District	5th App. District
2d App. District	4th App. District	6th App. District

California Superior Court
Primary trial court in 58 counties

Municipal and Justice Courts
Limited jurisdiction

In California, two courts of limited jurisdiction, Justice Courts and Municipal Courts, hear restricted classes of cases. The trial court of general jurisdiction is the Superior Court, which serves each of 58 counties throughout the state. The Superior Court hears appeals from the courts of limited jurisdiction, and it entertains original actions in a wide variety of civil and criminal cases. Disappointed litigants in a criminal or civil case may appeal from a judgment of the Superior Court to the California Court of Appeal. This intermediate appellate court is divided into six districts, each of which hears civil and criminal appeals from departments of the Superior Court in counties assigned to that district. A disappointed litigant in the Court of Appeal may appeal to the California Supreme Court in certain kinds of cases and may petition for discretionary review in others.[4]

For example, California's Second Appellate District includes the counties of Los Angeles, San Luis Obispo, Santa Barbara, and Ventura. The California Court of Appeal for the Second Appellate District would hear appeals from the decisions of the California Superior Court in those counties. A litigant disappointed by a decision of the Court of Appeal for the Second Appellate District could appeal to the California Supreme Court or petition it for discretionary review.

2. Federal Courts

The structure of the federal court system is similar to that of the California court system:

---

4. BNA'S DIRECTORY OF COURTS, *supra* note 2, at 90.

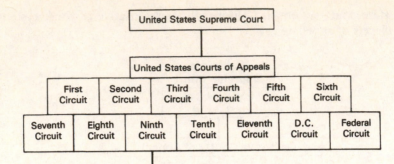

The primary federal trial courts are the United States District Courts. With few exceptions, disappointed litigants appeal from a judgment of a district court to the appropriate one of 13 "circuits" of the United States Courts of Appeals. Petitions for further review are taken to the United States Supreme Court. The chart above shows the line of review from judgments of the United States District Courts that serve the geographical area within the jurisdiction of the United States Court of Appeals for the Ninth Circuit.

The Ninth Circuit encompasses a large portion of the United States. Although Congress has repeatedly considered proposals to split this circuit into two circuits, the Ninth Circuit still includes the states and territories of Alaska, Arizona, California, Guam, Hawaii, Idaho, Montana, Nevada, the Northern Mariana Islands, Oregon, and Washington. Each of those states and territories has at least one district court; California and Washington have more. For example, California is divided into four district courts: the United States District Courts for the Central, Eastern, Northern, and Southern Districts of California.

3. Tribal Courts

Tribal communities in the United States typically employ a two-level court system, with a trial court and a single appellate court, as illustrated by the judicial system of the Navajo Nation:

The Navajo Judicial Branch alternatively offers the opportunity to resolve disputes in the Navajo Peacemaker Court. Rooted in traditional Navajo culture, the Peacemaking Program seeks to restore harmony in disrupted relationships through engagement, healing, and consensus.[5]

Some tribes are sufficiently small that they join with others to share a single court system. For example, 12 tribes in San Diego County have formed a judicial consortium, the Inter-Tribal Court of Southern California.[6]

B. Court Structure and Stare Decisis

Precedent has only limited stare decisis effect on the decision-making of the court that created the precedent: Although a court will do so only in unusual circumstances, it can depart from its own prior rulings. For lower courts within the same court system, stare decisis is less flexible: With very limited exceptions, precedent on the same issue is binding on the lower courts for which the precedent-creating court acts as a court of review.[7] The California Court of Appeal, for example, is bound by decisions of the California Supreme Court. As discussed further in Section III below, the lower court must either distinguish the reviewing court's precedent or apply it as controlling authority.

Stare decisis generally does not require a court to follow the precedent of coequal, autonomous courts, of lower courts within the same court system, or of any courts outside that system. For example, the Florida Supreme Court is not bound by the decisions of the other Florida courts or by those of the California Supreme Court. Similarly, the United States Court of Appeals for the First Circuit is not bound by the decisions of either the United States Court of Appeals for the Second Circuit or any United States District Court. Nonetheless, even if the precedent of another court is not binding on the deciding court, the deciding court is free to consider the nonbinding precedent as persuasive authority and to follow its reasoning as a matter of choice.

In some courts, a judicial unit of fewer than all members of the court may create precedent for the entire court. For example, the United States Court of Appeals for the Ninth Circuit has more than two dozen judges,

---

5. For more information about this program, see http://www.navajocourts.org/indexpeacemaking.htm.

6. This consortium is described as part of tribal and state programs in California at http://www.courts.ca.gov/14902.htm. For more information on tribal courts, see http://www.tribal-institute.org/lists/justice.htm.

7. *See* State Oil Co. v. Khan, 522 U.S. 3, 20 (1997) ("The Court of Appeals was correct in applying [Supreme Court precedent] despite its disagreement with [it], for it is this Court's prerogative alone to overrule one of its precedents."). In limited circumstances, a trial court may be compelled to depart from precedent of the intermediate court of appeals in its system. *E.g.*, Miller v. Gammie, 335 F.3d 889, 899-900 (9th Cir. 2003) (en banc) (federal district court could disregard precedent of court of appeals that reviews its decisions, if a decision of a yet higher authority, the United States Supreme Court, even though not precisely on point, has undermined the theory or reasoning underlying the court of appeals precedent); Auto Equity Sales, Inc. v. Super. Ct. of Santa Clara County, 369 P.2d 937, 940 (Cal. 1962) (if trial court is faced with conflicting decisions of two coequal panels or divisions of its reviewing court, it cannot follow them both but must choose between the two).

but most appeals in the circuit are heard by panels of three judges each. Each three-judge panel creates precedent that must be followed by all other three-judge panels in the circuit. Within the circuit, a decision of a three-judge panel can be overruled only by an "en banc" panel of 11 members of the court.[8]

III. Scope and Application of Stare Decisis

A. Building a Wall of Case Law, Brick by Brick

Courts add to existing common law or statutory interpretations incrementally, as they decide individual disputes on specific facts. Each resolution of a dispute, when published as a written opinion, adds one more "brick" of precedent to a wall of case law. When courts adhere to precedent under stare decisis, they build on the foundation created by the precedent of judicial "bricks" laid in previous decisions.

Some form of stare decisis is justified in any society that values efficiency, certainty, and at least those notions of fairness predicated on equal treatment for similarly situated parties. On the other hand, unquestioning adherence to precedent may inappropriately extend the rule of previous decisions beyond the rationale and policy of the original decision, or it may retain outdated or otherwise unsound precedent. A wall that rises ever higher on a flawed or outdated foundation will eventually fall.

Two limits to stare decisis help to avoid rigidity in the law while maintaining consistency:

(1) A court may *distinguish* a prior decision if it concludes that the prior decision addressed a significantly different dispute from the one now before the court. If so, even if the prior decision was issued by the same court or by a higher court within the jurisdiction, the prior decision does not control the result in the case now before the court. Of course, if the prior decision was issued by a lower court or by a court from another jurisdiction, it would never be *binding* on the current court. Moreover, if such a prior decision is distinguishable from the current case, the prior decision may lose even the persuasive value that it might otherwise have had.

(2) Alternatively, a court's own precedent may be indistinguishable from the dispute currently before the court. If so, the court normally would be

---

8. *See, e.g.*, United States v. McLennan, 563 F.2d 943, 948 (9th Cir. 1977); 9th CIR. R. 35-3.

bound under the doctrine of stare decisis to follow its precedent. Nonetheless, the doctrine of stare decisis is grounded in policy rather than inexorable mandate. In special circumstances, the court may depart from the normal dictates of stare decisis and reject its own precedent as authority for the present dispute.

The following sections thoroughly examine each of these limits on stare decisis. Section B explores means of determining whether a prior decision is sufficiently analogous that it creates precedent on the issue now before the court, or whether the prior decision instead is distinguishable. Section C assumes that a court's own prior decision is not distinguishable and therefore creates precedent that normally would be controlling in the current dispute. It then discusses the special circumstances in which a court may depart from such precedent.

B. Analogizing and Distinguishing Precedent

1. An Inexact Science with Ample Room for Argument

Few disputes are so similar in their facts and legal issues that resolution of the first dispute provides a clear basis for resolving the second. In those relatively rare cases, the prior decision is clearly "controlling" precedent in the same court or a lower court within the jurisdiction. Such controlling precedent normally dictates the result of the subsequent case under stare decisis.[9]

More often, differences between two cases in the facts or in the nature of the legal claims and defenses raised by the litigants are sufficiently substantial that the prior decision does not clearly dictate the resolution of the second. Whether the differences meet this standard often is a question of degree on which reasonable lawyers may disagree.[10]

Assuming that the precedent is not nearly identical to the current dispute and thus is not strictly controlling, it may still be sufficiently analogous to provide a strong basis for deciding the current dispute. Whether the prior decision is analogous or distinguishable is a matter of judgment and analysis, which provides opposing attorneys with plenty of room for argument.

In analyzing the precedential value of arguably distinguishable authority, you should pay attention to the rationale underlying the prior decision. Differences between the cases may be such that the reasons for the result in the prior decision do not apply to the current case. If so, the distinctions between the two cases justify a different result in the current case, or at least an analysis free of deference to the prior decision. Conversely, even though a prior decision does not provide a clear resolution of the current case because of differences between the two cases, many of the reasons for the legal result in the prior decision may apply equally to the current case. If so, the prior

---

9. *See generally* Hutto v. Davis, 454 U.S. 370 (1982).

10. *Compare id.* at 372-75 (majority opinion), *and id.* at 375-81 (Powell, J., concurring), *with id.* at 381-88 (Brennan, J., dissenting).

case—although not clearly controlling—is *analogous* to the current case in a way that may justify the same legal result in both.

Of course, this process of either restricting or extending the application of precedent in relation to a new dispute is far from an exact science. The determination whether a prior decision supports a proposed outcome in a new case may implicate the most deeply held values of those who must interpret and apply the precedent:

> Like the antebellum judges who denied relief to fugitive slaves . . . the Court today claims that its decision, however harsh, is compelled by existing legal doctrine. On the contrary, the question presented by this case is an open one, and our Fourteenth Amendment precedents may be read more broadly or narrowly depending upon how one chooses to read them. Faced with the choice, I would adopt a "sympathetic" reading, one which comports with dictates of fundamental justice and recognizes that compassion need not be exiled from the province of judging.[11]

Although uncertainty about the reasons for a prior decision often complicates the analysis, courts regularly engage in the processes of distinction and analogy to limit, extend, refine, and clarify the rules of prior decisions. Indeed, the precise parameters of the rule of a decision typically do not become clear until courts analyze the decision in subsequent decisions in the context of other disputes. This inquiry is largely one of defining, limiting, and extending the holdings of prior decisions; you will revisit it when you study techniques of briefing cases in Chapter 7.

2. Gaining Comfort with Legal Uncertainty

This "ample room for argument" retained in a flexible doctrine of stare decisis is illustrative of a more general characteristic of uncertainty or indeterminacy in our legal system. New law students are often eager to write down the "answer" to every legal question posed by their professors. But, as periodically pointed out in this book, the most interesting legal questions— the ones that are fully litigated and appealed—are ones to which the answer is uncertain prior to the final judicial determination. If the resolution of the legal dispute were perfectly certain, the parties likely would have settled the dispute well short of full litigation. And if the answer were certain during litigation, why would parties and attorneys wait with great anticipation for the jury's verdict on the evidence, and why would so many appellate decisions be decided on a split vote of learned judges or justices, who frequently disagree on the merits of the appeal?

British Professor Gary Watt describes the uncertainty in the outcome of legal disputes in a particularly colorful manner:

> There is never only one answer to a legal dispute; indeed it is a rare case that has only one right answer. As Lord Macmillan admitted: "in almost every case except the very plainest, it would be possible to decide the issue

---

11. DeShaney v. Winnebago County Dep't of Soc. Serv., 489 U.S. 189, 212-13 (1989) (Blackmun, J., dissenting).

either way with reasonable legal justification." Ronald Dworkin fantasizes that there is always one right answer to every case and that a hypothetical Herculean judge could find it. Perhaps Hercules might, but then perhaps Zeus would find another answer on appeal. . . . [T]he outcome often turns in large part on the purely practical contingency of running out of courts. The nature of the law in such a system is less like a scientific experiment and more like a wheel of fortune: the nature of the legal outcome is determined at the point the wheel stops spinning, and would have [been] determined earlier if the litigants had been at any stage unwilling, or financially unable, to give it an extra push. From the judges' perspective it is a living conversation across a range of reasonable alternative possibilities, and it just happens that the conversation must stop sometime.[12]

The example in the next subsection illustrates Professor Watt's metaphor of a roulette wheel signifying the outcome of a dispute by stopping its spinning and "running out of courts." It reminds us that the main task of law students and attorneys alike is not to know or discover the "right answer" to a novel legal question. Your main task instead is to identify issues—matters that are reasonably in dispute on the facts and the existing law—and to recognize or develop the arguments that can be persuasively advanced on either side of the dispute.

3. Example: Warrantless Searches of Cars, Houses, and Mobile Homes

Supreme Court decisions interpreting and applying the Fourth Amendment to the United States Constitution[13] illustrate the techniques of analogy and distinction as well as the difficulty of predicting legal outcomes. In *Carroll v. United States*,[14] the Supreme Court held that the Fourth Amendment permitted federal officers to search an automobile without first obtaining a warrant. The Court reasoned that, although a suspect may have privacy interests in the contents of an automobile, the ready mobility of the automobile makes it impracticable for officers to obtain a warrant before searching.[15] Seven months later, in *Agnello v. United States*,[16] the Supreme Court

---

12. Gary Watt, EQUITY STIRRING: THE STORY OF JUSTICE BEYOND LAW 12-13 (2009) (footnotes with citations are omitted from the quoted text).

13. The Fourth Amendment to the United States Constitution prohibits unreasonable searches and seizures by government officials:

The right of the people to be secure in their persons, houses, papers, and effects, against unreasonable searches and seizures, shall not be violated, and no Warrants shall issue, but upon probable cause, supported by Oath or affirmation, and particularly describing the place to be searched, and the persons or things to be seized.

14. 267 U.S. 132 (1925).

15. *Id.* at 153; California v. Carney, 471 U.S. 386, 390 (1985) (quoting and interpreting *Carroll*). Under *Carroll*, even if a warrant is not required, the searching officers must have probable cause to believe that the car contains contraband before they can search it. *Carroll*, 267 U.S. at 153-62. Discussion of the issue of probable cause, however, is not necessary to the analysis in the text above.

16. 269 U.S. 20 (1925), *overruled in part*, United States v. Havens, 446 U.S. 620 (1980).

held that the Fourth Amendment prohibited the warrantless search of the home of a suspect who had been arrested in another location.[17] In disapproving the warrantless search, the *Agnello* Court distinguished *Carroll* on the bases of the immobility of the house and the particularly great privacy interests the owner has in the contents of a house.[18]

Sixty years after *Carroll* and *Agnello*, in *California v. Carney*,[19] the Court considered whether the Fourth Amendment prohibited law enforcement officers from engaging in a warrantless search of a fully mobile motor home. Neither *Carroll* nor *Agnello* clearly controlled, because a motor home arguably combines the mobility of an automobile and the privacy interests associated with a house.[20] Consequently, the result in *Carney* under the doctrine of stare decisis depended on whether the Court found the facts of the case to be more nearly analogous to those of *Carroll* or to those of *Agnello*, as the next step in the Court's continuing interpretation of the Fourth Amendment.

On a vote of eight to one, the California Supreme Court had disapproved the search on two grounds. First, it had analogized *Carney* to cases like *Agnello*, reasoning that the nature of the contents of the motor home, in which the defendant was residing, created similarly high expectations of privacy in those contents as the privacy expectations that one has in the

---

17. Long before Carroll v. United States, the Supreme Court had assumed that police generally could not search a house without a warrant, unless the search was incidental to a lawful arrest in the house. *Agnello*, 269 U.S. at 32 (interpreting Boyd v. United States, 116 U.S. 616 (1886)). The Court did not directly decide that question, however, until *Agnello*, a few months after *Carroll*. *Agnello*, 269 U.S. at 32.

18. *Agnello*, 269 U.S. at 31-33; *see also* Payton v. New York, 445 U.S. 573, 585-90 (1980).

19. 471 U.S. 386 (1985).

20. *See id.* at 395 (Stevens, J., dissenting).

contents of a house. Second, it had distinguished *Carroll* on the basis of the comparatively low expectation of privacy that an owner has in the contents of an automobile.[21]

On review, the United States Supreme Court voted six to three to reverse the decision of the California Supreme Court and to approve the warrantless search. It analogized the case to *Carroll*, reasoning that an automobile and a motor home are not only similarly mobile but are similar in the reduced expectations of privacy in their contents. The expectations of privacy in a motor home are low partly because of the pervasive governmental regulation applicable to all licensed motor vehicles.[22]

The majorities in the state and federal Supreme Courts applied the precedent differently because they differed in their analyses, primarily factual, of the expectations of privacy that one has in the contents of a motor home. The United States Supreme Court's decision to approve the warrantless search was not unanimous and it was not the only "correct" or reasonable decision open to it. Indeed, if you count up the combined votes of the justices in both the California and United States Supreme Courts, you will find that a total of eleven state and federal justices voted to require a warrant in the case, while only seven voted to approve the warrantless search. Because the United States Supreme Court is the highest court in the land, however, so that no further appeals are possible, our society accepts as final the decision of a majority of its justices.

C. Overruling Precedent

1. Standards for Departing from Normal Application of Stare Decisis

A court's own precedent, or that of a higher court within the same jurisdiction, normally is controlling if it is materially indistinguishable from the dispute now before the court. Ordinarily, a lower court is absolutely bound by the controlling precedent of the appellate courts that review its decisions.[23] However, the doctrine of stare decisis is more flexible in the courts that created the precedent.[24] In exceptional circumstances, a court may depart from a strict application of stare decisis and refuse to follow its own, otherwise controlling precedent. In so doing, it overrules the prior decision and substitutes new precedent in its place.

To return to our metaphor of a wall of precedents, a court may change the direction of its own brickwork, if it has a very good reason to do so.

---

21. People v. Carney, 668 P.2d 807, 810-14 (Cal. 1983).

22. California v. Carney, 471 U.S. 386, 390-94 (1985); *see also* New York v. Class, 475 U.S. 106 (1986).

23. *See, e.g.*, Hutto v. Davis, 454 U.S. 370, 375 (1982); *see also supra* note 7 (identifying rare exceptions).

24. *See, e.g.*, Jaffree v. Wallace, 705 F.2d 1526, 1532 (11th Cir. 1983), *aff'd*, 472 U.S. 38 (1985).

An early decision of the United States Supreme Court was surprisingly liberal in its approval of such departures from stare decisis:

> The rule of stare decisis, though one tending to consistency and uniformity of decision, is not inflexible. Whether it shall be followed or departed from is a question entirely within the discretion of the court, which is again called upon to consider a question once decided.[25]

A statement of the Supreme Court in 2010 is more cautious: "Our precedent is to be respected unless the most convincing of reasons demonstrates that adherence to it puts us on a course that is sure error."[26] More specifically, "informed by a series of prudential and pragmatic considerations," the Supreme Court may feel justified in overruling its prior decision if that decision is outdated in light of intervening changes in law and society or if the prior decision has otherwise come to be viewed as hopelessly flawed, such as in any of the following four special circumstances:

1. "related principles of law have so far developed as to have left the old rule no more than a remnant of abandoned doctrine"; or
2. "facts have so changed or come to be seen so differently, as to have robbed the old rule of significant application or justification"; or
3. "a prior judicial ruling should come to be seen so clearly as error that its enforcement was for that very reason doomed"; or
4. "the rule has proved to be intolerable simply in defying practical workability."[27]

2. Changes in Social and Legal Context

In accordance with the first two justifications, a court may overrule a previous decision that was sensible in light of its original social, economic, technological, and legal context but that fails to serve important policies in current conditions. In one case, for example, a court overruled its own precedent when it recognized a legal right on behalf of a deceased fetus under

---

25. Hertz v. Woodman, 218 U.S. 205, 212 (1910).

26. Citizens United v. Federal Elections Comm'n, 130 S. Ct. 876, 911-12 (2010); *see also* Arizona v. Rumsey, 467 U.S. 203, 212 (1984) (departure from precedent requires "special justification").

27. Planned Parenthood of S.E. Pa. v. Casey, 505 U.S. 833, 854-55 (1992); *see also* Montejo v. Louisiana, 129 S. Ct. 2079, 2088-89 (2009) ("Beyond workability, the relevant factors in deciding whether to adhere to the principle of *stare decisis* include the antiquity of the precedent, the reliance interests at stake, and of course whether the decision was well reasoned.").

wrongful death and survival statutes.[28] The court justified its departure from precedent partly on the basis of intervening advances in medical knowledge and on changes in the laws of other states.[29] Although some precedents retain their force for centuries, "it must be true that most cases will eventually become obsolete because society as a whole does not stand still."[30]

3. Abandonment of Erroneous or Unworkable Precedent

Even absent an intervening change in conditions, a court may overrule a prior decision simply because it thinks that the prior decision was poorly reasoned at the outset or has proved to be unworkable in light of experience.[31] In 2013, for example, the California Supreme Court overruled its own decision issued in 1935, on the grounds that the precedent had misconstrued both statutory and case law on point, was out of step with prevailing views of the law, and had proven difficult to apply.[32]

In a notable departure from a strict application of stare decisis, the United States Supreme Court twice overruled precedent on the same issue in the space of 17 years. In 1985, it overruled a decision it had issued in 1976 on a question of state sovereignty under the Tenth Amendment,[33] even though that precedent had itself overruled another decision that the Supreme Court had issued in 1968.[34] In the last of these three decisions the Court explained:

> We do not lightly overrule recent precedent. We have not hesitated, however, when it has become apparent that a prior decision has departed from a proper understanding of congressional power under the Commerce Clause.[35]

4. Flexible Application of Stare Decisis to Constitutional Issues

The Supreme Court's double reverse on the proper interpretation of the Tenth Amendment in the space of 17 years may exemplify a more general

---

28. Amadio v. Levin, 501 A.2d 1085 (Pa. 1985).

29. *Id.* at 1094-97.

30. Gary Watt, EQUITY STIRRING: THE STORY OF JUSTICE BEYOND LAW 77 (2009).

31. *See* Geoffrey R. Stone, *Precedent, the Amendment Process, and Evolution in Constitutional Doctrine*, 11 HARV. J.L. & PUB. POL'Y 67, 71 (1988).

32. Riverisland Cold Storage, Inc. v. Fresno-Madera Production Credit Ass'n, 55 Cal. 4th 1169, 291 P.3d 316 (2013).

33. The Tenth Amendment to the United States Constitution reserves power to the states:

> The powers not delegated to the United States by the Constitution, nor prohibited by it to the States, are reserved to the States respectively, or to the people.

34. Garcia v. San Antonio Metro. Transit Auth., 469 U.S. 528 (1985), *overruling* Nat'l League of Cities v. Usery, 426 U.S. 833, 854-55 (1976) (which itself had overruled Maryland v. Wirtz, 392 U.S. 183, 198 (1968), on the ground that *Wirtz* had relied on "simply wrong" dicta in United States v. California, 297 U.S. 175, 184-85 (1936)).

35. *Garcia*, 469 U.S. at 557.

relationship between the Supreme Court and the United States Constitution. Stare decisis can safely apply with full force in cases of federal statutory interpretation, because Congress can correct judicial mistakes in statutory analysis by passing new legislation.[36] In contrast, Article V of the Constitution provides that an amendment to the Constitution is not effective unless approved by two-thirds of each house of Congress and ratified by three-fourths of the states. Thus, Congress cannot easily amend the Constitution to reflect changing social or economic conditions or to overrule judicial interpretations of the Constitution with which Congress disagrees.[37] Consequently, some scholars and judges believe that the Supreme Court should "keep [constitutional] law in accord with the dynamic flow of the social order," with less than the normal restraints of stare decisis.[38]

Nonetheless, countervailing considerations may justify adherence to stare decisis in some cases, even when they address challenges to previous interpretations of the Constitution. First, people may have so substantially relied on an established proposition of law that overruling the prior decision would result in "special hardship" and "inequity."[39] Second, an extraordinarily divisive issue may call for a ruling that is sufficiently durable to erase all doubts about its vulnerability to continuing political pressures. This second consideration is present

> whenever the Court's interpretation of the Constitution calls the contending sides of a national controversy to end their national division by accepting a common mandate rooted in the Constitution.
>
> The Court is not asked to do this very often . . . . But when the Court does act in this way, its decision requires an equally rare precedential force to counter the inevitable efforts to overturn it and to thwart its implementation. . . . [O]nly the most convincing justification under accepted standards of precedent could suffice to demonstrate that a later decision overruling the first was anything but a surrender to political pressure and an unjustified repudiation of the principle on which the Court staked its authority in the first instance.[40]

In *Planned Parenthood of Southeastern Pennsylvania v. Casey*,[41] the Supreme Court invoked both of these considerations in declining to abandon the

---

36. *See* Pearson v. Callahan, 555 U.S. 223, 233 (2009); Edelman v. Jordan, 415 U.S. 651, 671 & n.14 (1974).

37. In an exceptional reaction to a particular ruling of the Supreme Court, Congress proposed, and the states ratified, the Eleventh Amendment as a way of overruling Chisholm v. Georgia, 2 U.S. (2 Dall.) 419 (1793).

38. Edgar Bodenheimer, JURISPRUDENCE: THE PHILOSOPHY AND METHOD OF THE LAW 430 (rev. ed. 1974); *see also* Seminole Tribe of Fla. v. Florida, 517 U.S. 44, 63 (1996) (adopting flexible approach to stare decisis in abandoning Supreme Court precedent interpreting the Eleventh Amendment). *But cf.* Arizona v. Rumsey, 467 U.S. 203, 212 (1984) (even though stare decisis may be relaxed in constitutional cases, departure from precedent still "demands special justification").

39. Planned Parenthood of S.E. Pa. v. Casey, 505 U.S. 833, 854 (1992); *see also* Dickerson v. United States, 530 U.S. 428 (2000) (invoking stare decisis in declining to overrule Miranda v. Arizona, 384 U.S. 436 (1966), which spawned the *Miranda* warnings and which in turn "have become part of our national culture").

40. *Casey*, 505 U.S. at 867.

41. 505 U.S. 833 (1992).

central rule of *Roe v. Wade*,[42] which established a woman's limited constitutional right to terminate a pregnancy.

The Court conceded that the reliance factor weighs most heavily in commercial contexts, "where advance planning of great precision is most obviously a necessity."[43] However, even in the noncommercial contexts of reproduction and sexual equality, reliance could not be discounted:

> [F]or two decades of economic and social developments, people have organized intimate relationships and made choices that define their views of themselves and their places in society, in reliance on the availability of abortion in the event that contraception should fail. The ability of women to participate equally in the economic and social life of the Nation has been facilitated by their ability to control their reproductive lives. . . . The Constitution serves human values, and while the effect of reliance on Roe cannot be exactly measured, neither can the certain cost of overruling Roe for people who have ordered their thinking and living around that case be dismissed.[44]

Indeed, in the context of extraordinary national division over abortion rights, a dramatic change in the course of constitutional law might fan the flames of controversy by suggesting that continued strife could inspire further changes in course:

> The Court's duty in the present case is clear. In 1973, it confronted the already-divisive issue of governmental power to limit personal choice to undergo abortion, for which it provided a new resolution based on the due process guaranteed by the Fourteenth Amendment. Whether or not a new social consensus is developing on that issue, its divisiveness is no less today than in 1973, and pressure to overrule the decision, like pressure to retain it, has grown only more intense. A decision to overrule Roe's essential holding under the existing circumstances would address error, if error there was, at the cost of both profound and unnecessary damage to the Court's legitimacy, and to the Nation's commitment to the rule of law.[45]

Moreover, the central rule of *Roe* had not proved unworkable and had not been eroded by changes in facts or in related principles of law. Accordingly, although the Court departed from *Roe* in other respects, it reaffirmed *Roe*'s "essential holding,"[46] staying substantially within the boundaries dictated by stare decisis.

IV. Summary

Under the doctrine of stare decisis, a court endeavors to decide each case consistently with its prior decisions. Even so, a court may depart from

---

42. 410 U.S. 113 (1973).
43. *Casey*, 505 U.S. at 855-56.
44. *Id.* at 856.
45. *Id.* at 868-69.
46. *Id.* at 846.

its prior decisions, or precedent, if those decisions are distinguishable from the current dispute. Even if a prior decision is not distinguishable, a court may overrule its own precedent in special circumstances.

Stare decisis is less flexible with respect to the precedent of a higher court in the same jurisdiction: A trial court or intermediate court of appeals must distinguish or apply the precedent of a court that reviews its decisions. A court is never bound to apply the precedent of a lower court or any court in another jurisdiction, although it may treat such decisions as persuasive authority.

Exercise 5-1

Analyze the following problems based on decisions of the fictitious Calzona Supreme Court. For further practice in analyzing precedent, perform Problem 1 in Appendix II.

Precedent: *Smith v. Collier*, 47 CALZ. 78 (1891)

On February 1, Smith and Collier agreed to marry before the end of the year. They later announced a wedding date of December 1. In November, Smith complained about Collier's habit of playing poker on Saturday nights. In retaliation, Collier broke off the engagement. Smith sued Collier for breach of contract, requesting compensatory and punitive damages. Smith did not allege that Collier committed a tort.

The opinion of the Calzona Supreme Court includes the following excerpt:

> We affirm the trial court's factual findings that Collier breached the marriage contract with the malicious intent to cause Smith injury. Although the courts of this state recognize a general rule against punitive damages for breach of contract, the trial court correctly instructed the jury that it could award punitive damages as well as compensatory damages in this case. Unlike breach of an obligation to deliver coal or repair a carriage, Collier's callous decision to break his commitment to Smith caused such grave injury to her sensibilities and honor, and to the expectations of the community, as to justify vesting the jury with discretion to voice the full measure of its disapproval.

1. Distinguishing *Smith v. Collier*

In the following cases, you represent the defendant. Identify the facts in *Smith v. Collier* that appear to have motivated the court to permit an award of punitive damages. Identify factual differences in your case that might motivate the Calzona Supreme Court to distinguish *Smith v. Collier* and to rule that punitive damages cannot be awarded against your client. Explain why those factual differences justify a different result from the ruling in *Smith v. Collier*. Identify any factual similarities between your case and *Smith v. Collier*. Explain why those similarities do not justify the same result as in *Smith v. Collier*. Which of the following cases is easiest to distinguish from *Smith v. Collier*?

a. *White v. Strunk* (1955)

White agreed to pay Strunk $25,000 for construction of a house on White's property. Strunk agreed to complete construction by August 1, regardless of weather or labor conditions. Unfortunately, abnormally frequent rainfall and faulty workmanship by subcontractors delayed Strunk's work. Despite Strunk's best efforts, he breached the contract by failing to complete construction by August 1, causing White to suffer economic losses.

b. *Roget v. Webster* (1966)

Roget agreed to pay Webster $100,000 in exchange for Webster's promise to construct a retail store on Roget's property. Before either Roget or Webster began performance, Ballentine offered to pay Webster $150,000 to build an office building on Ballentine's property. Because he could not perform both jobs at once, and because a contract with Ballentine was more profitable, Webster committed a total breach of contract by repudiating his contract with Roget and accepting Ballentine's offer, causing Roget to suffer damages.

c. *White v. Benkowski* (1974)

White's property had no water supply. White agreed to pay Benkowski a monthly fee in exchange for fresh water supplied through pipes from Benkowski's well. After personal animosity developed between White and Benkowski, Benkowski maliciously breached the contract by shutting off the water supply to White's property, causing White to suffer damages.

2. Overruling *Smith v. Collier*

You represent the defendant in *Statler v. Corbin,* a contemporary case that is factually and procedurally indistinguishable from *Smith v. Collier*. Explain why the Calzona Supreme Court should overrule *Smith v. Collier* and disallow punitive damages for breach of a marriage agreement.

3. Distinguishing *Statler v. Corbin* (2013)

In *Statler v. Corbin*, the Calzona Supreme Court overruled *Smith v. Collier* and held that punitive damages are not available to remedy even a malicious breach of a marriage contract. In the following case, *Jones v. Marsh*, you represent the plaintiff. Identify factual or procedural differences between *Statler v. Corbin* and your case, and explain why those differences justify an award of punitive damages in your case.

Jones v. Marsh—In July, Jones and Marsh agreed to marry on November 1. At a family reunion in August, Marsh broke off the engagement in a public statement in which he maliciously and cruelly humiliated Jones. In addition to proving breach of contract, you have alleged and proved that Marsh intentionally inflicted emotional distress on Jones, conduct that is actionable as a tort in Calzona. In opposing Jones's request for punitive damages, Marsh relies on *Statler v. Corbin*.

Exercise 5-2

In his State of the Union address in January 2010, President Obama criticized a Supreme Court decision issued less than a week earlier, prompting one of the Justices attending the address to react momentarily in apparent disagreement. The decision was *Citizens United v. Federal Election Commission*, 130 S. Ct. 876 (2010), in which a nonprofit corporation challenged the constitutionality of federal legislation that arguably prohibited it from using its general treasury funds to broadcast a movie critical of Hillary Clinton within 30 days of the 2008 Democratic presidential primary election. The Supreme Court held in a 5 to 4 decision that the federal statute could not be enforced because it violated the corporation's free speech rights guaranteed by the First Amendment. Because the *Citizens United* decision required rejection of principles embraced by previous Supreme Court decisions, the lengthy combination of majority, concurring, and dissenting opinions includes a remarkable debate among the justices about the application of stare decisis to the case.

For an advanced exploration of stare decisis, read the excerpts of the *Citizens United* opinions below, and ponder the following questions:

1. **The Debate.** In what way do the dissenting Justices differ in their views about application of stare decisis from the Justices who joined the majority and concurring opinions?

2. **Is the Test Changing?** Is the majority signaling that it is embracing a newly relaxed test for stare decisis, such as one that permits the Supreme Court to accord less deference to a precedent if the precedent has remained controversial within a divided Court since it was decided, or if the party seeking to retain a precedent relies on a supporting rationale other than the one originally adopted in the precedent? Or one that minimizes the significance of legislative reliance on precedent, as contrasted with citizen reliance? Or does the Court's analysis of stare decisis fit comfortably within standards previously announced?

3. **Opinions as Advocacy.** How do you rate each opinion as persuasive writing? Do the majority and concurring opinions persuade you that the Court can overrule precedent in this case without offending or relaxing the doctrine of stare decisis? If so, does the dissenting opinion then cause you to reconsider?

4. **Judging Stare Decisis.** After considering this debate about the application of stare decisis in a particular case, what is your view of stare decisis

generally? Does it perform an important function of facilitating orderly development of the law, yet leaving ample opportunity to correct serious mistakes? Or does it unwisely encourage retention of outdated or ill-advised judicial decisions? Alternatively, do you view stare decisis as an overly flexible doctrine that is easily manipulated so that it allows a majority of the Court to accept or reject a precedent at its will depending on how it views the merits of the precedent?

CITIZENS UNITED v. FEDERAL ELECTION COMMISSION
Supreme Court of the United States
558 U.S. 310 (2010)
[Footnotes and parallel citations omitted.]

Justice KENNEDY delivered the opinion of the Court [joined by Justices ROBERTS, SCALIA, and ALITO, and by Justice THOMAS except with respect to Section IV].

Federal law prohibits corporations and unions from using their general treasury funds to make independent expenditures for speech defined as an "electioneering communication" or for speech expressly advocating the election or defeat of a candidate. 2 U.S.C. § 441b. Limits on electioneering communications were upheld in *McConnell v. Federal Election Comm'n*, 540 U.S. 93, 203-209 (2003). The holding of *McConnell* rested to a large extent on an earlier case, *Austin v. Michigan Chamber of Commerce*, 494 U.S. 652 (1990). *Austin* had held that political speech may be banned based on the speaker's corporate identity.

In this case we are asked to reconsider *Austin* and, in effect, *McConnell*. We . . . hold that *stare decisis* does not compel the continued acceptance of *Austin*. The Government may regulate corporate political speech through disclaimer and disclosure requirements, but it may not suppress that speech altogether. We turn to the case now before us.

. . . .

III

. . . .

C

Our precedent is to be respected unless the most convincing of reasons demonstrates that adherence to it puts us on a course that is sure error. "Beyond workability, the relevant factors in deciding whether to adhere to the principle of *stare decisis* include the antiquity of the precedent, the reliance interests at stake, and of course whether the decision was well reasoned." *Montejo v. Louisiana*, [129 S. Ct. 2079, 2088-89 (2009)] (overruling *Michigan v. Jackson*, 475 U.S. 625 (1986)). We have also examined whether "experience has pointed up the precedent's shortcomings." *Pearson v. Callahan*, [555 U.S. 223, 233 (2009)] (overruling *Saucier v. Katz*, 533 U.S. 194 (2001)).

These considerations counsel in favor of rejecting *Austin*, which itself contravened this Court's earlier precedents in *Buckley* and *Bellotti*. "This Court has not hesitated to overrule decisions offensive to the First Amendment." *WRTL*, 551 U.S., at 500 (opinion of SCALIA, J.). "*[S]tare decisis* is a principle of policy and not a mechanical formula of adherence to the latest decision." *Helvering v. Hallock*, 309 U.S. 106, 119 (1940).

... [I]t must be concluded that *Austin* was not well reasoned. The Government defends *Austin*, relying almost entirely on "the quid pro quo interest, the corruption interest or the shareholder interest," and not *Austin*'s expressed antidistortion rationale. . . . When neither party defends the reasoning of a precedent, the principle of adhering to that precedent through *stare decisis* is diminished. . . .

Austin is undermined by experience since its announcement. Political speech is so ingrained in our culture that speakers find ways to circumvent campaign finance laws. . . . Our Nation's speech dynamic is changing, and informative voices should not have to circumvent onerous restrictions to exercise their First Amendment rights. Speakers have become adept at presenting citizens with sound bites, talking points, and scripted messages that dominate the 24-hour news cycle. Corporations, like individuals, do not have monolithic views. On certain topics corporations may possess valuable expertise, leaving them the best equipped to point out errors or fallacies in speech of all sorts, including the speech of candidates and elected officials.

    . . . .

No serious reliance interests are at stake. As the Court stated in *Payne v. Tennessee*, 501 U.S. 808, 828 (1991), reliance interests are important considerations in property and contract cases, where parties may have acted in conformance with existing legal rules in order to conduct transactions. Here, though, parties have been prevented from acting—corporations have been banned from making independent expenditures. Legislatures may have enacted bans on corporate expenditures believing that those bans were constitutional. This is not a compelling interest for *stare decisis*. If it were, legislative acts could prevent us from overruling our own precedents, thereby interfering with our duty "to say what the law is." *Marbury v. Madison*, 1 Cranch 137, 177 (1803).

Due consideration leads to this conclusion: *Austin*, 494 50 U.S. 652, should be and now is overruled. We return to the principle established in *Buckley* and *Bellotti* that the Government may not suppress political speech on the basis of the speaker's corporate identity. No sufficient governmental interest justifies limits on the political speech of nonprofit or for-profit corporations.

D

Austin is overruled, so it provides no basis for allowing the Government to limit corporate independent expenditures. . . .

... The *McConnell* Court relied on the antidistortion interest recognized in *Austin* to uphold a greater restriction on speech than the restriction upheld in *Austin*, . . . and we have found this interest unconvincing and insufficient. This part of *McConnell* is now overruled.

    . . . .

Chief Justice ROBERTS, with whom Justice ALITO joins, concurring.

. . . .

II

. . . .

A

Fidelity to precedent—the policy of *stare decisis*—is vital to the proper exercise of the judicial function. "*Stare decisis* is the preferred course because it promotes the evenhanded, predictable, and consistent development of legal principles, fosters reliance on judicial decisions, and contributes to the actual and perceived integrity of the judicial process." *Payne v. Tennessee*, 501 U.S. 808, 827 (1991). For these reasons, we have long recognized that departures from precedent are inappropriate in the absence of a "special justification." *Arizona v. Rumsey*, 467 U.S. 203, 212 (1984).

At the same time, *stare decisis* is neither an "inexorable command," *Lawrence v. Texas*, 539 U.S. 558, 577 (2003), nor "a mechanical formula of adherence to the latest decision," *Helvering v. Hallock*, 309 U.S. 106, 119 (1940), especially in constitutional cases, *see United States v. Scott*, 437 U.S. 82, 101 (1978). If it were, segregation would be legal, minimum wage laws would be unconstitutional, and the Government could wiretap ordinary criminal suspects without first obtaining warrants. . . .

Stare decisis is instead a "principle of policy." *Helvering, supra*, at 119. . . .

. . . [W]e must keep in mind that *stare decisis* is not an end in itself. It is instead "the means by which we ensure that the law will not merely change erratically, but will develop in a principled and intelligible fashion." *Vasquez v. Hillery*, 474 U.S. 254, 265 (1986). Its greatest purpose is to serve a constitutional ideal—the rule of law. It follows that in the unusual circumstance when fidelity to any particular precedent does more to damage this constitutional ideal than to advance it, we must be more willing to depart from that precedent.

Thus, for example, if the precedent under consideration itself departed from the Court's jurisprudence, returning to the " 'intrinsically sounder' doctrine established in prior cases" may "better serv[e] the values of *stare decisis* than would following [the] more recently decided case inconsistent with the decisions that came before it." *Adarand Constructors, Inc. v. Peña*, 515 U.S. 200, 231 (1995) . . . . Abrogating the errant precedent, rather than reaffirming or extending it, might better preserve the law's coherence and curtail the precedent's disruptive effects.

Likewise, if adherence to a precedent actually impedes the stable and orderly adjudication of future cases, its *stare decisis* effect is also diminished. This can happen in a number of circumstances, such as when the precedent's validity is so hotly contested that it cannot reliably function as a basis for decision in future cases, when its rationale threatens to upend our settled jurisprudence in related areas of law, and when the precedent's underlying reasoning has become so discredited that the Court cannot keep the precedent alive without jury-rigging new and different justifications to shore up the original mistake. *See, e.g., Pearson v. Callahan*, [555 U.S. 223, 234-35 (2009)]; *Montejo v. Louisiana*, [556 U.S. 778, 792 (2009)] (stare decisis does not control when adherence to the prior decision requires "fundamentally revising its theoretical basis").

B

These considerations weigh against retaining our decision in *Austin*. . . . *Austin*'s reasoning was—and remains—inconsistent with *Buckley*'s explicit repudiation of any government interest in "equalizing the relative ability of individuals and groups to influence the outcome of elections." 424 U.S., at 48-49. *Austin* was also inconsistent with *Bellotti*'s clear rejection of the idea that "speech that otherwise would be within the protection of the First Amendment loses that protection simply because its source is a corporation." 435 U.S., at 784. . . .

Second, the validity of *Austin*'s rationale . . . has proved to be the consistent subject of dispute among Members of this Court ever since. . . . The simple fact that one of our decisions remains controversial is, of course, insufficient to justify overruling it. But it does undermine the precedent's ability to contribute to the stable and orderly development of the law. In such circumstances, it is entirely appropriate for the Court—which in this case is squarely asked to reconsider *Austin*'s validity for the first time—to address the matter with a greater willingness to consider new approaches capable of restoring our doctrine to sounder footing.

Third, the *Austin* decision is uniquely destabilizing because it threatens to subvert our Court's decisions even outside the particular context of corporate express advocacy. The First Amendment theory underlying *Austin*'s holding is extraordinarily broad. *Austin*'s logic would authorize government prohibition of political speech by a category of speakers in the name of equality—a point that most scholars acknowledge (and many celebrate), but that the dissent denies. . . .

. . . .

These readings of *Austin* do no more than carry that decision's reasoning to its logical endpoint. In doing so, they highlight the threat *Austin* poses to First Amendment rights generally, even outside its specific factual context of corporate express advocacy. Because *Austin* is so difficult to confine to its facts—and because its logic threatens to undermine our First Amendment jurisprudence and the nature of public discourse more broadly—the costs of giving it *stare decisis* effect are unusually high.

Finally and most importantly, the Government's own effort to defend *Austin*—or, more accurately, to defend something that is not quite *Austin*—underscores its weakness as a precedent of the Court. . . . .

Instead of endorsing *Austin* on its own terms, the Government urges us to reaffirm *Austin*'s specific holding on the basis of two new and potentially expansive interests—the need to prevent actual or apparent quid pro quo corruption, and the need to protect corporate shareholders. *See* Supp. Brief for Appellee 8-10, 12-13. Those interests may or may not support the result in *Austin*, but they were plainly not part of the reasoning on which *Austin* relied.

. . . .

To the extent that the Government's case for reaffirming *Austin* depends on radically reconceptualizing its reasoning, that argument is at odds with itself. *Stare decisis* is a doctrine of preservation, not transformation. It counsels deference to past mistakes, but provides no justification for making new ones. There is therefore no basis for the Court to give precedential sway to reasoning that it has never accepted, simply because that reasoning happens to support a conclusion reached on different grounds that have since been abandoned or discredited.

Doing so would undermine the rule-of-law values that justify *stare decisis* in the first place. It would effectively license the Court to invent and adopt new principles of constitutional law solely for the purpose of rationalizing its past errors, without a proper analysis of whether those principles have merit on their own. This approach would allow the Court's past missteps to spawn future mistakes, undercutting the very rule-of-law values that *stare decisis* is designed to protect.

[T]he Government's new arguments must stand or fall on their own; they are not entitled to receive the special deference we accord to precedent. . . .

Because continued adherence to *Austin* threatens to subvert the "principled and intelligible" development of our First Amendment jurisprudence, *Vasquez*, 474 U.S., at 265, I support the Court's determination to overrule that decision.

* * *

. . . Congress violates the First Amendment when it decrees that some speakers may not engage in political speech at election time, when it matters most.

Justice STEVENS, with whom Justice GINSBURG, Justice BREYER, and Justice SOTOMAYOR join, concurring in part and dissenting in part.

The real issue in this case concerns how, not if, the appellant may finance its electioneering. Citizens United is a wealthy nonprofit corporation that runs a political action committee (PAC) with millions of dollars in assets. Under the Bipartisan Campaign Reform Act of 2002 (BCRA), it could have used those assets to televise and promote *Hillary: The Movie* wherever and whenever it wanted to. It also could have spent unrestricted sums to broadcast *Hillary* at any time other than the 30 days before the last primary election. Neither Citizens United's nor any other corporation's speech has been "banned," *ante*, at 886. All that the parties dispute is whether Citizens United had a right to use the funds in its general treasury to pay for broadcasts during the 30-day period. The notion that the First Amendment dictates an affirmative answer to that question is, in my judgment, profoundly misguided. Even more misguided is the notion that the Court must rewrite the law relating to campaign expenditures by for-profit corporations and unions to decide this case.

. . . .

The majority's approach to corporate electioneering marks a dramatic break from our past. Congress has placed special limitations on campaign spending by corporations ever since the passage of the Tillman Act in 1907, ch. 420, 34 Stat. 864. We have unanimously concluded that this "reflects a permissible assessment of the dangers posed by those entities to the electoral process," *FEC v. National*

Right to Work Comm., 459 U.S. 197, 209 (1982) (NRWC), and have accepted the "legislative judgment that the special characteristics of the corporate structure require particularly careful regulation," *id.*, at 209-210. The Court today rejects a century of history when it treats the distinction between corporate and individual campaign spending as an invidious novelty born of *Austin v. Michigan Chamber of Commerce*, 494 U.S. 652 (1990).

. . . .

II

The final principle of judicial process that the majority violates is the most transparent: *stare decisis*. I am not an absolutist when it comes to *stare decisis*, in the campaign finance area or in any other. No one is. But if this principle is to do any meaningful work in supporting the rule of law, it must at least demand a significant justification, beyond the preferences of five Justices, for overturning settled doctrine. "[A] decision to overrule should rest on some special reason over and above the belief that a prior case was wrongly decided." *Planned Parenthood of Southeastern Pa. v. Casey*, 505 U.S. 833, 864 (1992). No such justification exists in this case, and to the contrary there are powerful prudential reasons to keep faith with our precedents. The Court's central argument for why *stare decisis* ought to be trumped is that it does not like *Austin*. The opinion "was not well reasoned," our colleagues assert, and it conflicts with First Amendment principles. *Ante*, at 47-48. This, of course, is the Court's merits argument, the many defects in which we will soon consider. I am perfectly willing to concede that if one of our precedents were dead wrong in its reasoning or irreconcilable with the rest of our doctrine, there would be a compelling basis for revisiting it. But neither is true of *Austin*, as I explain at length in Parts III and IV, *infra*, at 23-89, and restating a merits argument with additional vigor does not give it extra weight in the *stare decisis* calculus.

. . . .

The majority also contends that the Government's hesitation to rely on *Austin*'s antidistortion rationale "diminishe[s]" "the principle of adhering to that precedent." *Ante*, at 48; . . . . Why it diminishes the value of *stare decisis* is left unexplained. We have never thought fit to overrule a precedent because a litigant has taken any particular tack. Nor should we. Our decisions can often be defended on multiple grounds, and a litigant may have strategic or case-specific reasons for emphasizing only a subset of them. Members of the public, moreover, often rely on our bottom-line holdings far more than our precise legal arguments; surely this is true for the legislatures that have been regulating corporate electioneering since *Austin*. The task of evaluating the continued viability of precedents falls to this Court, not to the parties.

Although the majority opinion spends several pages making these surprising arguments, it says almost nothing about the standard considerations we have used to determine *stare decisis* value, such as the antiquity of the precedent, the workability of its legal rule, and the reliance interests at stake. It is also conspicuously silent about *McConnell*, even though the *McConnell* Court's decision to uphold BCRA §203 relied not only on the antidistortion logic of *Austin* but also on the statute's historical pedigree, *see, e.g.,* 540 U. S., at 115-132, 223-224, and the need to preserve the integrity of federal campaigns, *see id.,* at 126-129, 205-208, and n. 88.

We have recognized that "*[s]tare decisis* has special force when legislators or citizens 'have acted in reliance on a previous decision, for in this instance overruling the decision would dislodge settled rights and expectations or require an extensive legislative response.'" *Hubbard v. United States,* 514 U.S. 695, 714 (1995) (quoting *Hilton v. South Carolina Public Railways Comm'n,* 502 U.S. 197, 202 (1991)). *Stare decisis* protects not only personal rights involving property or contract but also the ability of the elected branches to shape their laws in an effective and coherent fashion. Today's decision takes away a power that we have long permitted these branches to exercise. State legislatures have relied on their authority to regulate corporate electioneering, confirmed in *Austin,* for more than a century. The Federal Congress has relied on this authority for a comparable stretch of time, and it specifically relied on *Austin* throughout the years it spent developing and debating BCRA. The total record it compiled was 100,000 pages long. Pulling out the rug beneath Congress after affirming the constitutionality of § 203 six years ago shows great disrespect for a coequal branch.

By removing one of its central components, today's ruling makes a hash out of BCRA's "delicate and interconnected regulatory scheme." *McConnell,* 540 U.S., at 172. . . .

Beyond the reliance interests at stake, the other *stare decisis* factors also cut against the Court. Considerations of antiquity are significant for similar reasons. *McConnell* is only six years old, but *Austin* has been on the books for two decades, and many of the statutes called into question by today's opinion have been on the books for a half century or more. The Court points to no intervening change in circumstances that warrants revisiting *Austin.* Certainly nothing relevant has changed since we decided *WRTL* two Terms ago. And the Court gives no reason to think that *Austin* and *McConnell* are unworkable.

In fact, no one has argued to us that *Austin's* rule has proved impracticable . . . . In the end, the Court's rejection of *Austin* and *McConnell* comes down to nothing more than its disagreement with their results. Virtually every one of its arguments was made and rejected in those cases, and the majority opinion is essentially an amalgamation of resuscitated dissents. The only relevant thing that has changed since *Austin* and *McConnell* is the composition of this Court. Today's ruling thus strikes at the vitals of *stare decisis,* "the means by which we ensure that the law will not merely change erratically, but will develop in a principled and intelligible fashion" that "permits society to presume that bedrock principles are founded in the law rather than in the proclivities of individuals." *Vasquez v. Hillery,* 474 U.S. 254, 265 (1986).

. . . .

V

. . . .

. . . At bottom, the Court's opinion is thus a rejection of the common sense of the American people, who have recognized a need to prevent corporations from undermining self-government since the founding, and who have fought against the distinctive corrupting potential of corporate electioneering since the days of Theodore Roosevelt. It is a strange time to repudiate that common sense. While American democracy is imperfect, few outside the majority of this Court would have thought its flaws included a dearth of corporate money in politics.

I would affirm the judgment of the District Court.

Chapter 6

Deductive Reasoning and IRAC—
Introduction to Legal Analysis

I. Overview—Solving Legal Problems

Attorneys perform many tasks for clients that may not directly relate to litigation of legal disputes, including estate and tax planning, business counseling, and legislative lobbying. Even these tasks, however, may be inspired partly by the desire to avoid or influence future litigation. Moreover, many people consult an attorney only after they have become embroiled in a legal dispute in which litigation has commenced or is imminent. With a little luck and skill, the parties or their attorneys may still avoid formal litigation in court by using alternative dispute resolution (ADR) such as negotiation, mediation, or informal arbitration.[1] However, at least some of these methods

---

1. *See, e.g.*, Leonard L. Riskin, James E. Westbrook, Chris Guthrie, Richard C. Reuben, Jennifer K. Robbennolt, & Nancy A. Welsh, DISPUTE RESOLUTION AND LAWYERS (4th ed. 2009); Stephen B. Goldberg, Frank E.A. Sander, Nancy H. Rogers, & Sarah Rudolph Cole, DISPUTE RESOLUTION: NEGOTIATION, MEDIATION & OTHER PROCESSES (6th ed. 2012); Stephen J. Ware, PRINCIPLES OF ALTERNATIVE DISPUTE RESOLUTION (2d ed. 2007).

of ADR require the parties to evaluate or present their cases within a general legal framework. Consequently, legal method relating to litigation of legal disputes is an important component of nearly every attorney's practice.

As explored in detail in Chapter 18, a lawsuit is formally commenced with the filing of "pleadings": The plaintiff brings suit by filing a "complaint" against the defendant, and the defendant responds by filing an "answer." If you represent a party in the early stages of such litigation, you must assess the strengths and weaknesses of your client's claims or defenses to help you prepare for various stages of advocacy, from the pleadings and settlement negotiations to trial and appeal.

In a large or medium-sized law firm, you often will communicate your evaluation to other members of the firm in an office memorandum of law, discussed in detail in Part V of this book. The principal means of persuading a judge or other adjudicatory body to accept your client's legal claims or defenses is a written brief, discussed in detail in Parts VI through VIII. To prepare either kind of document, you must apply fundamental skills of legal method and analysis that you develop in the first year of law school, as discussed in Parts II through IV.

This chapter examines methods of solving legal problems in the context of litigation of legal disputes. It builds on the groundwork laid in Chapters 3 through 5, and it provides an overview for more detailed discussions of legal method and analysis found throughout the remaining chapters.

II. Overview of Deductive Reasoning and IRAC

A. Deductive Reasoning in the Law—Uses and Limitations

1. The Legal Syllogism

Most essay examinations, office memoranda, and briefs require more than purely abstract legal analysis: They require you to apply legal standards to specific facts to reach a conclusion. In many cases, the analysis follows a pattern of deductive reasoning known as the "syllogism," which derives a conclusion from a major premise and a minor premise:

Major Premise:	All humans are mortal.
Minor Premise:	Socrates is human.
Conclusion:	Therefore, Socrates is mortal.[2]

In a legal argument, the major premise is a legal rule that helps resolve the issue raised by the parties to the dispute. It may represent the terms of a statute, the holding of a single judicial decision that acts as precedent, or

---

2. *See* Irving M. Gopi, INTRODUCTION TO LOGIC § 1.4, at 12-15 (12th ed. 2005).

a general principle derived from a series of previous decisions. The minor premise of a legal argument generally is a set of facts taken from the dispute that you are analyzing. The conclusion represents your answer to the question of whether the facts stated in the minor premise satisfy the legal standard stated in the major premise.

2. Validity and Correctness of Legal Syllogisms

A deductive argument is *valid* if its conclusion follows necessarily from its premises, but the *correctness* or *truth* of the conclusion of a valid argument depends on the truth of its premises.[3] For example, the Fourth Amendment to the United States Constitution ordinarily requires a police officer to obtain a search warrant from a judicial officer before searching an enclosed structure such as a house. Under the automobile exception, however, an officer may search an automobile without a warrant if she has probable cause to believe that it contains evidence of a crime. Suppose that a police officer searched Jack Greenberg's motor home without a warrant and found illegal drugs. In the state's criminal prosecution of Greenberg for possession of the illegal drugs, the state might advance the following valid deductive argument:

Major Premise:	The automobile exception to the Fourth Amendment's warrant requirement applies to all vehicles with mobility similar to that of an automobile on a street or highway.
Minor Premise:	Even while parked in Greenberg's backyard, Greenberg's motor home was a vehicle with mobility similar to that of an automobile on a street or highway.
Conclusion:	The automobile exception to the Fourth Amendment's warrant requirement applied to Greenberg's motor home while it was parked in Greenberg's backyard.

Although the conclusion of this valid argument follows necessarily from the premises, the conclusion is not true if either of the premises is untrue. The attorney for each party will attempt to persuade the judge to reach a certain conclusion by inviting the judge to accept particular formulations of the major and minor premises and by rejecting others. For example, Greenberg's attorney could raise the Fourth Amendment issue by asking the judge to exclude the evidence obtained in the warrantless search of Greenberg's motor home. In response, the state prosecutor would advance the deductive argument above to demonstrate that the Fourth Amendment did not require the police to obtain a warrant to search Greenberg's motor home. Greenberg's attorney could attack this argument either by arguing as a matter of law that the prosecutor's major premise exaggerates the scope of the

---

3. *See id.* at 13.

automobile exception or by establishing as a matter of fact that the prosecutor's minor premise exaggerates the mobility of the motor home parked in Greenberg's backyard.

A deductive argument is not valid if its conclusion does not follow necessarily from its premises. For example, if Greenberg's attorney proved that Greenberg's motor home was significantly less mobile than an automobile on the street or highway, the judge would undoubtedly replace the prosecutor's untrue minor premise with the minor premise established by Greenberg's attorney. As reconstructed, the deductive argument would no longer be valid, because the prosecutor's conclusion would not follow from the original major premise and the new minor premise.

3. Limitations of the Legal Syllogism

Deductive reasoning provides at least a rough organizational framework for most legal analyses in office memoranda, answers to essay examinations, and briefs. The usefulness of the syllogism in legal reasoning, however, is limited by the flexibility and uncertainty inherent in legal analysis. For example, to establish the major premise of your argument, you may state your interpretation of the holding of a previous decision or your synthesis of the holdings of a series of decisions. Until a judge expresses his opinion on the matter, however, you cannot be certain whether he will agree with your interpretation of previous decisions and thus with your statement of the major premise.

Indeed, the dominant description of legal method since the twentieth century, known as "legal realism," rejects the notion that the law is external to the judges and other officials who apply and enforce it. Instead, the law is simply a prediction about what such officials will do in the face of a dispute. Moreover, their decisions will take into account the social consequences of their actions and will be based on a complex set of motivations, including personal values and judicial approaches not explicitly accounted for in the formal abstract rule of law. Thus, judges or juries can take advantage of uncertainty in law or facts by shaping them to support results that they reach on other than purely logical grounds.[4]

---

4. *See* J. W. Harris, Legal Philosophies 98-103 (2d ed. 1997). The Critical Legal Studies movement goes beyond legal realism to broadly attack traditional legal method, scholarship, and education as a system that legitimizes and perpetuates an oppressive socioeconomic order. *See generally* Roberto M. Unger, The Critical Legal Studies Movement (1986); Mark Kelman, A Guide to Critical Legal Studies (1987); *Critical Legal Studies Symposium*, 36 Stan. L. Rev. 1 (1984). Scholars of Critical Race Theory and Feminist Jurisprudence more specifically charge that traditional legal reasoning is grounded in and helps to perpetuate racist and sexist institutions and attitudes. *See generally* Frances Schmid Holland, Feminist Jurisprudence (1996); Richard Delgado and Jean Stefancic, Critical Race Theory: An Introduction (2001). Latino and Latina scholars have developed a new branch of Critical Race Theory, popularly known as "LatCrit" theory. *See, e.g.*, Jean Stefancic, *Latino and Latina Critical Theory: An Annotated Bibliography*, 85 Cal. L. Rev. 1509 (1997); Keith Aoki & Kevin R. Johnson, *An Assessment of LatCrit Theory Ten Years After*, 83 Ind. L.J. 1151 (2008). Some scholars have argued that courts are retreating from legal realism and are returning to a more traditional and mechanical legal "formalism." *See, e.g.*, John E. Murray, Jr., *Contract Theories and the Rise of Neoformalism*, 71 Fordham L. Rev. 869 (2002).

In short, legal disputes cannot be analyzed with mathematical certainty:

> The life of the law has not been logic: it has been experience. The felt necessities of the time, the prevalent moral and political theories, intuitions of public policy, avowed or unconscious, even the prejudices which judges share with their fellow-men, have had a good deal more to do than the syllogism in determining the rules by which men should be governed.[5]

Nonetheless, the syllogism provides a useful starting point for discussing general techniques of presenting legal analyses.

B. IRAC

Most law students use the acronym "IRAC" to help them remember the elements of deductive reasoning. IRAC stands for Issue, Rule, Application, and Conclusion. Thus,

1. after identifying an **I**ssue, you should
2. state the legal **R**ule that will help resolve the issue,
3. **A**pply the rule to the relevant facts, and
4. reach a **C**onclusion on the question of whether the facts satisfy the legal rule.

For example, the following excerpt from an essay examination answer discusses the availability of punitive damages in a tort action. Although the examination answer itself should not explicitly refer to IRAC, the margin notes below represent the elements that a student should keep in mind when formulating a complete response. In this example, after raising an issue about punitive damages, the student has summarized general legal rules regarding the availability of punitive damages, has applied them to the facts of the examination, and has reached a conclusion.

Punitive Damages—In addition to demanding compensation for his actual losses, Ling may request punitive damages, designed to punish the tortfeasor and to deter others from engaging in similar wrongdoing.	Issue
A jury has the discretion to award punitive damages if the tortfeasor acted with the malicious intent to cause harm. In most states, punitive damages are also permitted if the tortfeasor acted with reckless disregard for the risk of harm to others.	Rules

5. Oliver Wendell Holmes, Jr., THE COMMON LAW 1 (Dover Publ. 1991) (1881); *see also id.* at 312 ("The distinctions of the law are founded on experience, not on logic. It therefore does not make the dealings of men dependent on a mathematical accuracy."); Neil MacCormick, LEGAL REASONING AND LEGAL THEORY 65-72 (1978) (discussing "the limits of deductive justification").

Application to Facts

Unless exceptional circumstances justify the risky conduct, a person acts recklessly if he consciously engages in conduct that he knows or should know poses a great risk of harm to others.

In this case, Con Motor Co. did not maliciously intend to cause injury when it designed its Backfire sports car. In fact, the discussion at the May meeting shows that the board of directors genuinely hoped that the risky design would not cause accidents. However, Con's chief engineer informed the board of directors of her opinion that placement of the gas tank near the rear exterior of the car would create a risk of deadly explosion in even minor rear-end collisions. Yet, the directors approved that design solely because it would save production costs of $200 per car, a trivial sum when compared to the $40,000 price of the car. In so doing, Con's directors knowingly created a great risk of death or terrible injury to consumers without any socially significant justification.

Conclusion

Con Motor Co. thus acted recklessly, permitting a jury in many jurisdictions to assess punitive damages against it. Indeed, in a jurisdiction that requires proof of malicious intent to injure, this would be a good case for a liberalization of the standards to include recklessness as a basis for an award of punitive damages.

To help you avoid the oversimplification that may result from an excessively mechanical application of IRAC, later chapters of this book explore some sophisticated techniques of analysis that build on the general framework of deductive reasoning. Chapter 8, Section II introduces two variations of inductive reasoning, and Chapter 12, Section III.D tackles problems of organization that arise when an issue or subissue presents different layers or levels of syllogisms.

In the meantime, the remainder of this chapter thoroughly examines each of the elements of IRAC. In the next four sections, you will learn more about identifying Issues, formulating Rules, Applying rules to facts, and reaching Conclusions.

III. "*I*"—Identifying Issues for Analysis

A. Defining Issues

A legal issue is a question that a judge, jury, agency hearing officer, arbitrator, or other adjudicator must resolve to determine the outcome of a legal dispute. Whenever an event creates the conditions for a legal dispute, you can identify potential legal issues immediately after the event, even though no party has yet begun to litigate a claim or has even made any demands on another.

Constitutions, statutes, agency regulations, case law, and perhaps even the private law of an agreement between the parties impose duties on some parties and correlative rights on others in the context of the event. Armed with at least a general knowledge of the law and of the facts of the event, you can address the question of whether any party is liable to another for breach of a legal duty. If the law and its application to the facts are clearly governed by settled law, the question of liability may be easily answered and is more likely to be addressed in a settlement between the parties than in litigation. In a surprising proportion of cases, however, uncertainty in the content of the law or in the application of the law to novel facts will block your efforts to supply a definite resolution to a legal dispute. In those cases, you can advance arguments in support of either a potentially wronged victim or a potentially liable party. If the arguments for both parties have potential merit, you have identified a legal issue that merits full discussion.

1. Issues and Subissues

A general issue may encompass discrete subissues. For example, case law establishes that a defendant generally will be liable to the plaintiff for damages caused by breach of contract if (A) the parties formed an enforceable contract and (B) the defendant failed to perform his contractual promises, thus breaching the contract. At the broadest level, the facts of a dispute might raise the general issue of whether the defendant is liable for breach of contract for failing to perform her contractual obligations by March 1. More specifically, the facts may raise separate subissues about (A) contract formation and (B) performance and breach.

You may want to further subdivide these subissues to recognize multiple legal elements associated with each. For example, case law establishes two primary requirements for contract formation: (1) an agreement reached through a process of offer and acceptance and (2) "consideration" in the form of a mutually induced exchange. These elements are distinct, because parties are capable of agreeing to a transaction that does not satisfy the consideration requirement. Thus, within the subissue of contract formation, the law and the facts may raise a second level of subissues regarding (1) offer and acceptance and (2) consideration. Similarly, within the subissue of performance and breach, the law and the facts may raise a second level of subissues regarding, for example, (1) interpretation of the defendant's contractual promises and (2) possible discharge of the defendant's obligations because unforeseen circumstances made his performance impossible. The law and facts may raise further issues regarding remedies for breach.

Without yet making the issues more specific by referring to critical facts, you can state these issues and subissues in outline form:

Is D liable to P for breach of contract by failing to perform by March 1?

    I. Did D and P form a valid contract?

      A. Did P accept D's offer?

      B. If so, is the agreement between D and P supported by consideration?

   II. Assuming a valid contract between D and P, is D liable to P for failing to deliver by March 1?

      A. Does the contract require D to perform by March 1?

      B. Did unforeseen circumstances for which D did not assume the risk excuse D from performing by March 1?

  III. Assuming D breached a valid contract with P, to what damages or other remedies is P entitled?

2. Continuing Development of Issues

At the inception of a dispute, incomplete knowledge of the facts and vagueness or ambiguity in the arguably applicable legal rules make the eventual outcome of the dispute particularly uncertain. At that stage, you can identify the issues only tentatively. As the dispute proceeds through stages of litigation, the issues will become increasingly well defined.

For example, a demand letter or complaint may reveal which of numerous potential legal claims a claimant has decided to advance, thus raising some questions of liability and eliminating others. Under modern rules of civil procedure, each party to a civil lawsuit must disclose some kinds of information to the opposing party, and each party may use various "discovery" devices to obtain certain other kinds of information from witnesses and from the opposing party.[6] This court-supervised discovery and disclosure process or other investigation may reveal that some claims or defenses are meritless and may raise new questions about others. Moreover, as explored in Chapters 19 and 20, a litigant may request that the court help define the issues by ruling before trial that certain evidence will be excluded from trial or even that the litigant is entitled to judgment without trial on one or more issues. In turn, these pretrial motions may raise separate issues under applicable rules of evidence or procedure concerning the admissibility of evidence or the proper application of standards for summary disposition. Finally, if the dispute goes to trial, the nature of the disposition in the trial court and the factual record developed in the trial court will help determine which issues the losing party might reasonably raise on appeal.

As illustrated by these examples, the parties help to define the issues by making strategic decisions about what claims and defenses to assert and about which procedural vehicles should be used to assert them. With few

---

6. *See* Fed. R. Civ. P. 26-37.

exceptions, courts will decline to address questions that are not raised by either party to a dispute.[7]

3. Materiality

Not every potential disagreement about the facts or the law amounts to a legal issue. Even a hotly disputed question of fact or law would not be "in issue" if it were immaterial. A disputed point is immaterial if it could not affect the outcome of the lawsuit in light of other facts and rules of law.

To take an obvious example, suppose evidence shows that the defendant drove his car through an intersection and struck the plaintiff in a pedestrian crosswalk. The defendant's liability for negligence would not be affected by even a heated disagreement over the color of the socks that the defendant wore that day. Assuming that the identity of the driver of the car is conclusively established through some means other than the color of the socks he wore, the issues of law and fact would instead include such material questions as the following:

1. Which party had the green light?
2. What injuries did the plaintiff sustain?
3. Does the law permit the jury to reduce the plaintiff's recovery if his own negligence combined with that of the defendant to cause his injuries?

Of course, many cases raise closer questions of materiality than that in the example above. As discussed in the next section, some questions of materiality may be a matter of degree requiring the exercise of judgment in selecting issues for discussion or argument in a legal document.

---

7. *See, e.g.*, Yee v. Escondido, 503 U.S. 519, 533 (1992) (Supreme Court "has, with very rare exceptions, refused to consider petitioners' claims that were not raised or addressed below."); Amcel Corp. v. Int'l Exec. Sales, Inc., 170 F.3d 32 (1st Cir. 1999) (discussing reasons for not addressing claims or legal theories that party neglected to raise in the trial court); Hershinow v. Bonamarte, 735 F.2d 264, 266 (7th Cir. 1984) (waiver of claim presented to appellate court in perfunctory manner); State v. Santana-Lopez, 613 N.W.2d 918, 921 n.3, 922 n.4 (Wis. Ct. App. 2000) (waiver of one argument not presented on appeal and of another argument presented only in a footnote in an appellate brief). *But cf. Yee*, 503 U.S. at 534-35 (if claim was properly presented below, appellate court will entertain a new *argument* in support of that claim); Giannakos v. M/V Bravo Trader, 762 F.2d 1295, 1297 (5th Cir. 1985) (federal trial and appellate courts must address questions of federal subject-matter jurisdiction on their own motions); *In re* Pizza of Haw. Inc., 761 F.2d 1374, 1377-78 (9th Cir. 1985) (appellate court must determine appellate jurisdiction on its own motion); *In re* Pac. Trencher & Equip., Inc., 735 F.2d 362, 364 (9th Cir. 1984) (discretionary appellate consideration of pure question of law not raised in the trial court).

Exercise 6-1

Although United States jurisdictions have enacted criminal codes that largely supersede the early criminal common law, imagine a state that still applies the common law definition of burglary: the breaking and entering of a dwelling of another at night with the intent to commit a felony. As stated in Chapter 3, the law relating to this crime reflected a concern about a serious invasion of the right of habitation during hours of darkness, when the inhabitants were most vulnerable to attack and the invader most likely to escape recognition. The element of a "breaking" does not require damage or destruction; it requires only the opening of a barrier to entry.

Armed only with this general knowledge of the law, identify the issues relating to the common law crime of burglary raised by the following facts:

> In June, Leova Rosales left her San Francisco apartment and drove her VW bus down the coast for a three-week vacation near Monterey Bay. Although she occasionally ate at restaurants or stayed with friends, she mostly slept in the back of the bus and prepared simple meals in the bus with groceries that she purchased at local stores.
>
> On the evening of June 20, Leova parked her bus in an overnight recreational-vehicle parking space at Seacliff State Beach. She prepared dinner from an ice chest in the back of the bus. At 11:00 P.M., she fell asleep in the back of her bus, leaving the driver's door closed but unlocked, with an iPod and a set of portable stereo speakers sitting on the driver's seat. A curtain separated the sleeping area of the bus from the driver's cab; other curtains blocked light from the windows in the back of the van, enabling Leova to sleep late in the morning.
>
> At 5:15 A.M., just as the first hints of a sunrise glowed from the hilltops opposite the ocean, Robert Glass approached Leova's van. Through the closed window next to the driver's seat, Robert spied the music equipment lying on the seat. Hoping to add it permanently to his own home system, Robert opened the closed but unlocked driver's door and placed his hand on the stereo speakers. At that moment, a patrolling police officer drove up to Leova's VW bus and arrested Robert for burglary and attempted larceny. Leova awoke only when the officer knocked on her bus after the arrest.

You may assume that theft of the stereo equipment would constitute felony larceny in the jurisdiction. In the prosecution of Robert Glass on the burglary charge, what elements of the common law crime of burglary would the prosecutor and defense attorney likely dispute? What elements of burglary are not reasonably in dispute? Would further facts help define or resolve the issues? Would case law that refines the law of burglary help define or resolve the issues? If you were assigned the task of preparing an office memorandum on this problem, what facts or law would you desire to investigate further?

B. Scope of Analysis

Any dispute of at least moderate complexity presents a range of potential legal theories and arguments that you might raise in litigation. At the near end of the spectrum are persuasive and conventional legal theories or arguments that a court would almost certainly address in analyzing the dispute. At the far end are legal theories or factual analogies of such doubtful merit or applicability that a court might view them as frivolous or immaterial to the outcome of the dispute.

The extent to which you discuss topics toward the far end of the spectrum is a question of "scope of analysis" and depends partly on the nature of your document. The scope of analysis typically is quite broad in a law school essay examination answer, somewhat narrower in an office memorandum addressed to a supervising attorney, and narrower still in a good brief addressed to a judge.

1. Examination Answers

You will often touch on a broad range of issues in an examination answer because most law professors are specifically testing your ability to spot issues. Indeed, on many examinations, you will maximize your grade if you identify and briefly discuss all plausible issues, including the less obvious ones.

2. Office Memoranda

In comparison, your supervising attorney may expect a slightly narrower scope of analysis in your office memorandum. She probably will want detailed discussion of significant issues and will generally encourage creative and aggressive analysis, but she may not have time to thoroughly examine more exotic theories or approaches if they are unlikely to have an effect on the outcome of the dispute. Unfortunately, you may be tempted to impress your supervisor with the long hours that you spent in the library by describing in detail every legal theory or authority that made its way into your library notes. Your supervisor will not be impressed. She realizes that you will regularly investigate leads that bear no useful fruit, and she expects the final draft of your memorandum to shield her from the burden of retracing your steps down paths that led only to distracting tangents.

On the other hand, the materiality of a fact or theory may be difficult to assess in the early stages of litigation and fact investigation. Accordingly, if you draft an office memorandum at the early stages of a dispute, you should consider discussing the appropriate scope of analysis with your supervising attorney before beginning to write. Absent specific direction from your supervisor, you probably should at least mention any argument of potential significance, even if only in a sentence or two. You can distinguish between a major theory and a less significant one in the depth of your analysis of each. Then, if later developments in the litigation establish the significance of an issue of previously questionable importance, you can analyze that issue in greater depth in a supplemental memorandum.

3. Briefs

When drafting a brief, you often must exercise even stricter control on the scope of analysis. Although creative and novel arguments often win appeals by inspiring changes in the law, some arguments are so clearly marginal that they may detract from the cumulative persuasiveness of the entire brief. If you add a nearly frivolous argument to one with greater merit, you reduce the number of pages within the maximum page limit that you can devote to the meritorious argument. Even worse, you may lose credibility on the whole brief.

This general advice about limiting the scope of briefs may apply with less force in criminal cases, in which a party's liberty, or even life, is at stake. In such cases, defense counsel may be reluctant to waive any argument that might possibly gain relief for her client, and she can realistically hope that some courts will carefully consider all plausible arguments.

IV. *"R"*—Formulating the Legal Rule

Consistent with the general pattern of deductive reasoning, your first step in discussing a legal issue is to identify and analyze applicable legal rules. You will seldom find these rules clearly set forth in a single source of authority. The law that an adjudicator applies to resolve a legal issue may be a combination of rules, any one of which may represent a synthesis of several sources of law.

A. Types of Rules: Elements, Factors, and Balancing Tests

Legal rules come in a variety of types. Many statutory or common law rules have multiple mandatory elements, each of which must be met to satisfy the rule. For example, a statutory crime may consist of four elements, all of which the prosecution must prove to establish the guilt of the defendant.

In contrast, some legal rules set forth a more general standard and then identify factors that a court should consider in determining whether the facts satisfy the standard. Such a test will not require satisfaction of all of the factors, and the list of factors may not be exclusive. For example, a common law rule provides that an owner may cancel a construction contract if the contractor has committed an uncured "material breach" of the contract. The determination of materiality of a breach is influenced by a number of factors that serve as general guidelines to a court or jury.[8]

---

8. *See, e.g.*, Frazier v. Mellowitz, 804 N.E. 2d 796 (Ind. App. 2004) (quoting six factors relating to material breach under the Restatement (First) of Contracts and then applying the five slightly different "circumstances" listed in the Restatement (Second) of Contracts, as well as other factors).

Still other tests may require the balancing of two or more opposing factors or values. For example, the reasonableness of a search under the Fourth Amendment often requires balancing (1) the constitutional interest in protecting people from intrusions into their privacy against (2) the legitimate needs of law enforcement in protecting the security of the community.[9]

Chapter 16 presents sample arguments that further illustrate the difference between a rule with mandatory elements and a standard with factors that serve as guidelines. At this point, however, you will gain more by examining the relative strength of different kinds of authorities that help to establish and define the legal rule.

B. Sources of Authority

The relative importance of legal authorities to your analysis of the issue depends on such factors as

1. the primary or secondary nature of the authority;
2. the jurisdiction, in the sense of the political or geographical body, in which primary authority is controlling; and
3. if the primary authority is case law, the strength of the case law as precedent.

1. Primary and Secondary Authority

So far, this book has addressed only primary legal authority: direct statements of law issued by lawmaking bodies. Primary authority includes constitutions, treaties, statutes and local ordinances, administrative rules and regulations, and judicial opinions. Subject to limitations discussed in Sections 2 and 3 below, a primary authority or combination of primary authorities will supply the applicable rule in any legal dispute.

Secondary authorities, such as treatises, restatements of the law, and law review articles, do not directly supply the rule of law in a legal dispute. Instead, they express a commentator's explanation of the law or her opinions about what the law should be. A secondary authority has persuasive value only. It may influence a court or legislature to act in a particular way, but it has no mandatory or binding effect.

An example of a popular treatise is PROSSER AND KEETON ON TORTS. This secondary authority generally describes tort law in United States jurisdictions and examines the relevant policies supporting competing approaches in the tort law of different states.

Another frequently cited example of secondary authority is the collection of Restatements of Law issued by the American Law Institute (ALI). The ALI has drafted two Restatements of Contracts, the Restatement (First)

---

9. *See, e.g.*, Safford Unified Sch. Dist. No. 1 v. Redding, 557 U.S. 364, 371-77 (2009) (content of suspicion regarding possession of prescription strength ibuprofen did not justify strip search of middle school student).

of Contracts (1932) and the Restatement (Second) of Contracts (1981). Each of these is divided into numerous sections and subsections, most of which attempt to summarize rules of the common law of contracts generally accepted when the Restatement was drafted. A few sections, however, are meant to influence the law by promoting trends that had not yet been widely accepted at the time of drafting. Section 90 of the First Restatement, for example, represented a relatively innovative view of a theory of recovery based on reliance, commonly known as "promissory estoppel." Although no court is required to follow the approach of either Restatement, section 90 has influenced many courts. Beyond that, more than a few courts have adopted the precise language of section 90 of the First or Second Restatement, thus incorporating it into their own case law and giving it the force of primary authority.[10] Further still, some courts have adopted a general policy of following the latest Restatement rules on certain kinds of issues if no statute or case law addresses the point.[11]

Unless a court has adopted such a policy, however, or has already incorporated the content of a secondary authority into its primary authority, you should use secondary authority only as a starting point in your analysis. You may use secondary authorities to help you locate and understand primary authority or to help develop an argument not fully addressed or supported by primary authority. However, you should not base your legal analysis or argument on a secondary authority when helpful primary authority is available.

2. Jurisdiction in Which Primary Authority Controls

Some federal constitutional, statutory, and special common laws apply broadly to all domestic jurisdictions. For example, the Thirteenth Amendment to the United States Constitution abolishes the institution of slavery within the United States, whether practiced by a government or a private entity.

In contrast, the constitutional, statutory, and common laws of a state are mandatory only within that state. For example, the Civil Code of California and the case law of the California courts interpreting that code do not have any binding effect on the law of torts, contracts, or property in New York. Similarly, the courts of one state are free to develop the common law of that

---

10. *See, e.g.*, Bank of Marion v. Robert "Chick" Fritz, Inc., 57 Ill. 2d 120, 311 N.E.2d 138 (1974); Vigoda v. Denver Urban Renewal Auth., 646 P.2d 900, 905 (Colo. 1982); *see also* Corbit v. J. I. Case Co., 424 P.2d 290, 300-01 (Wash. 1967) (en banc) (quoting § 90 as a "useful guideline").

11. *See, e.g.*, Smith v. Normart, 75 P.2d 38, 42 (Ariz. 1938) ("We have . . . announced that we would follow the Restatement of the Law where we are not bound by the previous decisions of this court or by legislative enactment . . . ."). *But cf.* Reed v. Real Detective Publ'g. Co., 162 P.2d 133, 138 (Ariz. 1945) ("We think it would be unwise to follow this rule blindly, particularly when to do so would result in the recognition of a new cause of action in this jurisdiction."); Ramirez v. Health Partners of So. Ariz., 972 P.2d 658, 665 (Ariz. Ct. App. 1999) ("Rather, we must consider whether the Restatement position, as applied to a particular claim, is logical, furthers the interests of justice, is consistent with Arizona law and policy, and has been generally acknowledged elsewhere.").

state independently of the judicial development of common law in other states.

Even though the laws of one state do not directly apply to activities in another state, in some circumstances those laws may have at least persuasive influence in the other state. For example, in recognizing a common law tort of wrongful discharge of an employee, the Arizona Supreme Court drew guidance from the emerging common law of California and of other states.[12]

Indeed, even case law from one state interpreting a statute of that state could be persuasive in the interpretation and application of a statute of a different state, if the statutes in both states have similar or identical language and purposes. For example, the New York and New Hampshire legislatures have adopted identical versions of Uniform Commercial Code section 2-302, which authorizes a court to deny enforcement of a contract provision that is "unconscionable."[13] A New York trial court interpreting section 2-302 of New York's commercial code drew support from, even though it was not bound by, a decision of the New Hampshire Supreme Court interpreting the identical language in section 2-302 of New Hampshire's commercial code.[14]

3. Hierarchy of Constitutional, Legislative, and Common Law Authority

Within a relevant jurisdiction, constitutional law can strike down or limit the reach of statutory law, and statutory law can modify or replace common law rules. Accordingly, even though your first-year courses may focus your attention largely on common law, do not neglect the possibility that a legal question is governed by one or more constitutional provisions, statutes, or administrative regulations that help to implement a statutory scheme.

On the other hand, courts interpret constitutional and statutory law, so interpretative case law helps to define the constitutional or statutory rule. Consequently, even when constitutional or statutory provisions apply, interpretive case law will frequently dominate the legal analysis.

Section C.2 illustrates the hierarchy of authority with an excerpt from a legal memorandum that addresses several kinds of legal authority. The remaining subsections of this section, however, focus on analysis of case law.

4. Strength of Case Law as Precedent

As discussed in Chapter 5, the controlling or persuasive force of case law will depend on its strength as precedent under the doctrine of stare decisis.

---

12. Wagenseller v. Scottsdale Mem'l Hosp., 710 P.2d 1025, 1030-31 (Ariz. 1985). This Arizona common law was later superseded by state legislation. ARIZ. REV. STAT. ANN. § 23-1501(3)(b) (West Supp. 2009).

13. N.H. REV. STAT. ANN. § 382-A: 2-302 (1961); N.Y. U.C.C. LAW § 2-302 (McKinney 1964).

14. Jones v. Star Credit Corp., 59 Misc. 2d 189, 298 N.Y.S.2d 264 (N.Y. Sup. Ct. 1969) (citing American Home Improvement, Inc. v. MacIver, 201 A.2d 886 (N.H. 1964), for the proposition that § 2-302 applied to "price unconscionability").

Section 2 above further examined one element of this relationship: the relationship of the authority to the forum jurisdiction. The strength of case law as precedent also depends on

1. the relative levels of the court that created the precedent and the one applying it, and
2. the degree to which the precedent is directly controlling, rather than merely analogous, to the current dispute.

a. Level of Court

To summarize some of the lessons of Chapter 5, a trial court or intermediate court of appeals is strictly bound by squarely applicable precedent of a higher court that reviews its decisions. Moreover, although a court can overrule its own precedent, it will do so only in special circumstances warranting departure from the normal mandates of stare decisis. On the other hand, the court need not defer to the decisions of a lower court within the same system or decisions of courts from other systems; at most, those decisions would have persuasive effect.

Thus, whenever possible, you obviously should support your analyses or arguments with case law from an appellate court in your jurisdiction that is higher than the court in which your dispute is currently being adjudicated. The basis for a helpful illustration is provided by the description of the United States Courts of Appeals for the Ninth Circuit in Section II.A of Chapter 5. When writing a brief to that court of appeals, you should try to support your argument with United States Supreme Court precedent, which is binding on the court of appeals. If no Supreme Court authority applies, you can strongly support your argument with a previous decision of the Ninth Circuit Court of Appeals itself. Only a special 11-member panel of the Ninth Circuit can overrule such precedent. If no higher authority is available, you can derive some support for your argument from a published decision of the United States District Court for the Northern District of California, a federal trial court. However, because decisions of the district court have only persuasive value in the court of appeals, you will then assume the burden of persuading the court of appeals that the district court's decision represents the best legal approach—the approach that the court of appeals should adopt as its own. You might more strongly support your argument with a decision from the United States Court of Appeals for the Tenth Circuit, but that decision too would have only persuasive value.

b. Controlling, Analogous, and Distinguishable Authority

To once again summarize a portion of Chapter 5, the strength of case law as binding or persuasive authority also depends on the degree to which it squarely applies to the current dispute. Even precedent of a higher court within the same court system will not control the outcome of the dispute if it is distinguishable. The more significant the distinctions between the precedent and the current dispute, the less nearly analogous is the precedent, thus decreasing the likelihood that the precedent from a higher court will control or even influence the outcome of the current dispute. Similarly, the persuasiveness of nonbinding authority from lower courts within the jurisdiction or from courts of other jurisdictions will depend in part on the degree of similarity between the precedent and the current dispute.

When evaluating the legally significant similarities or distinctions between precedent and the current dispute, you should resist the temptation to overemphasize superficial factual similarities that appear in legally distinct contexts. Consider, for example, a current dispute in which the plaintiff's new television set spontaneously generated an electrical fire, causing major damage to the plaintiff's home. In this dispute, the parties may raise the issue of whether the retailer is liable to the plaintiff on a claim of breach of the warranty of merchantability implied in the sales contract under the state's version of the Uniform Commercial Code (UCC).[15] Suppose further that an appellate opinion in the state, issued in 1957, addresses another case in which a television set spontaneously burst into flames, setting fire to the plaintiff's home. The 1957 opinion, however, holds only that the plaintiff in that action, a consumer, failed to file his complaint within the time prescribed by the state's statute of limitations, so that his action for negligent manufacture of the television set was barred.

At first glance, the prior decision might appear significant because of the factual similarities of the events giving rise to the actions. In fact, however, the prior decision may be completely inapplicable. It does not interpret the UCC's warranty of merchantability in a contract for a sale of goods because it addresses a legally distinct cause of action in tort for negligence; indeed, the prior decision was issued before state enactment of the UCC and before the widespread adoption of more contemporary tort doctrines of products liability. Most important, the prior decision discusses only the statute of limitations; it does not directly address the elements of any claim for relief other than timely filing. More helpful to the current dispute would be analogous precedent that addresses the scope of the warranty of merchantability, even if in the context of different goods causing different kinds of accidents and injuries.

5. Summary

Only primary authority within the forum jurisdiction is mandatory and potentially controlling. Primary authority from other jurisdictions and all secondary authority are persuasive only.

If the primary authority is case law within the forum jurisdiction, its strength as precedent will depend partly on the relative levels of the court that created the precedent and the court that will apply it. It will depend also on how closely analogous the precedent is to the current dispute.

---

15. The UCC's warranty of merchantability implies a promise on the part of a merchant that goods are fit for their ordinary purposes, among other things. U.C.C. § 2-314 (2002).

Professor Mary Dunnewold illustrates the relative strength of precedent with issue and authority dartboards,[16] which this text has combined into a single archery target to the right. A bull's-eye represents a precedent of the highest court within the relevant jurisdiction that decided the same issue on facts nearly identical to the facts in the current case. Just outside the bull's-eye, an appellate court decision within the same jurisdiction with facts that can be analogized to those in the current case might be highly persuasive, thus hitting one of the inner rings of the target. Precedent of a court from another jurisdiction—especially one whose issue and facts are only arguably analogous to those in the current case— might be useful, but it would have less persuasive value, thus hitting one of the outer rings. Of course, a precedent that has no relationship to the facts, issues, reasoning, and policies implicated in the current dispute would miss the target altogether and have no persuasive value.

In practice, it is exceedingly rare to find precedent that scores a bull's-eye. More often, an advocate must explain why a previous case is analogous to the current one, or why a decision on the same issue from another jurisdiction is so persuasive in its reasoning that it should be followed in the current forum. Conversely, the advocate must try to distinguish or undermine the soundness of precedent that is advanced as persuasive authority by opposing counsel.

Exercise 6-2

The Hazardous Materials Transportation Act (HMTA) of State X makes it a criminal offense to transport certain hazardous materials, such as toxic chemicals, except with statutorily specified safeguards. For example, the statute requires a transporter of regulated materials to first confine the materials in steel drums and then secure the drums within a cargo bay that is enclosed on the top and on all sides with material of specified strength. Leek Chemical Co. violated the HMTA by transporting highly toxic chemicals in steel drums secured to an open flatbed truck. The truck overturned on a slick highway, causing several of the barrels to roll across lanes of oncoming traffic. An automobile driven by Daniel Stein collided with one of the barrels, bursting the barrel and spreading the toxic chemical onto and into Stein's automobile. Stein was not seriously injured by the initial impact with the barrel; however, he was permanently injured by contact with the toxic chemical.

Stein sues Leek Chemical Co. in tort for damages, alleging both (1) strict liability for causing injury while engaged in an abnormally dangerous activity and (2) negligent transportation of the toxic chemicals. In State X, Leek Chemical Co.

16. Mary Dunnewold, *How Many Cases Do I Need?*, 10 PERSPECTIVES 10-11 (Fall 2001). Credit for the graphic in the text above goes to my colleague, Amy Langenfeld, who developed a more sophisticated version of the graphic for a classroom presentation.

will be liable on the second claim for negligence if it engaged in a negligent act or omission through breach of a duty of care owed to Stein, causing Stein to suffer injury. Stein hopes to establish the element of negligent act through the doctrine of "negligence per se," which other states recognize but which the Supreme Court of State X has never squarely adopted. Under the strongest version of the doctrine of negligence per se, proof of Leek Chemical Co.'s violation of the HMTA, a safety statute, would conclusively establish the element of negligent act, without any further showing of a breach of a duty of care.

To help her evaluate proposed jury instructions at the close of the trial in Stein's lawsuit, the trial judge requests briefing and oral argument on the question of whether State X recognizes the doctrine of negligence per se. Stein has the following authority at his disposal:

1. abundant case law from other states recognizing the doctrine of negligence per se in a variety of contexts;

2. an opinion from the highest appellate court of neighboring State Y approving application of the doctrine of negligence per se to a violation of a similar hazardous materials transportation statute in State Y;

3. an opinion of the State X intermediate court of appeals holding that evidence of violation of the State X speed limit laws, proximately causing injury, supported a jury verdict of negligence, even in the absence of any other evidence of lack of due care; and

4. an opinion of the Supreme Court of State X holding that a transporter of regulated hazardous materials may be criminally liable under the HMTA for intentional violations of that act's criminal provisions, even if the illegal transportation does not result in any accident or injury.

Discuss the relative strength of these authorities to Stein's position. How should Stein's attorney use each authority, if at all?

C. Analysis of Legal Standards

1. Depth of Analysis

In some legal disputes, formulation of the applicable legal rules is a simple task: The applicable laws are easily identified and their general content is clear, at least in the abstract. For example, a dispute over the jury's authority to grant punitive damages in a tort action may be governed by clearly defined rules in the forum state's case law. If so, you could summarize those rules directly and concisely in an office memorandum:

In this state, a jury may award punitive damages against a person who has committed a tort with either (1) intent to cause injury or (2) reckless disregard for the risk of harm to others. *Ray v. Bradbury* .... Unless exceptional circumstances justify the risky conduct, a person acts recklessly if he consciously engages in conduct that he knows poses a great risk of harm to others. *Id.* at 327.

In such a dispute, once the facts are found, any significant uncertainty about the outcome of the dispute typically derives from a mixed question of fact and law: Do the particular facts of the case satisfy the legal rule? Although analysis of such a mixed question necessarily involves refinement of the content of the legal rule, it also requires careful evaluation of the facts. Thus, assuming that *Ray v. Bradbury* reflects current policy in the jurisdiction, the alleged tortfeasor will not likely dispute the abstract rule governing the availability of punitive damages. Instead, the central issue is a mixed question of fact and law: Do the facts of the case satisfy the legal rule by reflecting recklessness or an intent to injure?

In other disputes, however, the parties may raise substantial issues about the fundamental content of applicable legal rules, such as the issue discussed in Chapter 4 of whether the word "sex" in Title VII of the Civil Rights Act of 1964 refers narrowly to gender or more broadly to sexual identity, activities, and orientation. Compared to the dispute described in the preceding paragraph, resolution of this question required less comprehensive fact analysis and more thorough analysis of the content of the rule at a fairly abstract level. An even more extreme example is provided by the question of whether a court should change the course of the common law by adopting a new theory of tort liability for wrongful discharge of an employee. Although such a question would arise in the context of the facts of a particular dispute, the question of whether to adopt a new common law theory of liability would be analyzed as a nearly pure question of law.

If an issue in a brief, office memorandum, or answer to a law school essay examination raises a question about the fundamental content of a legal rule at a general level, you should analyze the legal rule thoroughly, or "in depth," before engaging in substantial fact analysis. The discussions of common law and statutory law in Chapters 3 and 4 provide a foundation for the development of techniques of legal analysis. Four considerations are particularly important:

1. the hierarchical nature of authority,
2. policy analysis,
3. synthesis of incremental authority, and
4. recognizing arguments for both sides.

2. Hierarchy of Authority: Start with Constitutional or Statutory Text

Constitutional, statutory, and common laws form a hierarchy in descending order of priority: Assuming that the applicable state or federal constitution authorizes the exercise of state or federal power, a legislature can overrule or modify the common law by enacting statutory law. Accordingly, you should not assume that an issue is governed by common law; instead, you should first consider the possible applicability of constitutional or statutory law.

If a statute applies, you should begin your research and analysis with the relevant language of the statute, even though it may be insufficiently narrow to clearly resolve the issue by itself. Only after you have studied the letter of the statute and its context within an act or a code system can you fully appreciate interpretive case law on the matter. The following passage from an office memorandum illustrates the hierarchy of authority and the focus on statutory language.

The Arizona Constitution grants municipalities the right to engage in industrial activities: "The State of Arizona and each municipal corporation within the State of Arizona shall have the right to engage in industrial pursuits." Ariz. Const. art. II, § 34. The Arizona Public Utilities statute more specifically grants municipal corporations the power to acquire water utility corporations either within or without their corporate limits":

    A municipal corporation may engage in any business or enterprise which may be engaged in by persons by virtue of a franchise from the municipal corporation, and may construct, purchase, acquire, own and maintain within or without its corporate limits any such business or enterprise. . . .

Ariz. Rev. Stat. Ann. § 9-511(A) (2005). The statutory reference to corporate limits appears without qualification to permit a municipal corporation to acquire utilities that provide service outside the municipality's corporate limits. Arizona case law, however, hints at a narrower interpretation of the statute that recognizes two limitations on the acquisition power.

First, it is unclear whether a city may acquire a water company's property outside the city corporate limits unless the city has shown that it genuinely and reasonably anticipates future growth into that area. *See Sende Vista Water Co. v. City of Phoenix*, 617 P.2d 1158 (Ariz. Ct. App. 1980). In *Sende* . . . .

Constitution

Statute

Case Law

In theory, the principle of analyzing statutory language before turning to interpretive case law also applies to constitutional provisions, as illustrated in the example above. As a practical matter, however, some constitutional provisions are so general that their actual language may provide quite limited guidance, and interpretive case law takes on special significance. For example, the reference to "equal protection" in the Fourteenth Amendment to the United States Constitution is purposefully vague; its generality invites the courts to shape its contours in a way that best satisfies its underlying policies. The mass of case law interpreting the Equal Protection Clause has embellished this simple clause with rich detail. Accordingly, when researching and analyzing an equal protection problem, you should not begin with a grammatical analysis of the words "equal protection." Instead, after identifying the Fourteenth Amendment as the source of the clause, you could appropriately turn immediately to interpretive case law.

3. Policy Analysis

Almost by definition, policy analysis lies at the heart of most lawmaking. A legislature pronounces public policy when it enacts public legislation within the framework of applicable constitutions. Any such enactment represents elected officials' choice among alternative means to address the socioeconomic needs of the jurisdiction. Not surprisingly, the search for legislative intent typically does not end with a conclusive grammatical analysis of language or with a reference to specific and definitive legislative history. Instead, statutory interpretation most often takes the form of a multifaceted analysis reconciling the statutory language, legislative history, and general rules of construction with the apparent policies or purposes on which the legislation is based. Constitutions are less specific than most statutes and are not so easily amended; consequently, analysis of policy and general purpose often is even more important in constitutional interpretation.

Similarly, because common law rules are largely a reflection of judicial recognition of community needs, habits, or customs, they constitute the judiciary's pronouncement of public policy within the framework of constitutional and statutory law. Any question about further development of the common law, such as adoption of a new theory of common law liability or elimination of a common law basis for damages, necessarily raises policy questions about the effect that the new rule will have on the community and about the relationship of the new rule to legislative policies.

The arguments and conclusions that you develop in response to a policy question depend in part on the values that you apply to the problem. A policy argument may be based on moral, economic, political, institutional, or other social values.[17] When developing or evaluating a legal argument, you should identify the values underlying the legislative purpose or judicial policy of each applicable authority, and you should determine which policy arguments would best advance your client's position.[18]

---

17. *See* P. S. Atiyah & Robert S. Summers, FORM AND SUBSTANCE IN ANGLO-AMERICAN LAW 5 (1987) (defining "substantive reasons" for legal decisions); *see also* Robert S. Summers, *Two Types of Substantive Reasons: The Core of a Theory of Common-Law Justification*, 63 CORNELL L. REV. 707 (1978).

18. *See generally* J. M. Balkin, *The Crystalline Structure of Legal Thought*, 39 RUTGERS L. REV. 1 (1986).

Exercise 6-3

Policy Analysis—Surrogate Motherhood and Baby Selling

State *X* has a criminal "baby selling" statute, enacted in 1932, making it a felony "to relinquish custody of one's child to another for payment, or to pay or offer to pay another to relinquish custody of the other's child." What is the likely policy behind this statute, and what kind of conduct should be its primary concern? In light of your understanding of the statutory policy, should a court interpret the statute to prohibit a surrogate mother from charging a fee for carrying the fertilized ovum of another couple to full term and surrendering custody of the child to the couple after birth? Does the analysis change if the one charging the fee agrees to artificial insemination of her own ovum, thus making her the biological mother? Should the state enact new legislation more specifically addressing surrogate mother contracts?

---

4. Synthesis of Incremental Law

In few research problems is the legal standard set forth in a single, clearly controlling authority. More often, the legal rules that apply to a dispute are the products of a synthesis of multiple authorities. For example, a Reconstruction-era civil rights statute imposes liability for racial discrimination in private contractual relations,[19] but its application is tempered by constitutional interests in privacy and free association.[20] Thus, the true reach of the statute is defined both by the language of the statute and by values reflected in the First Amendment to the United States Constitution.

Synthesis of authority is particularly important in analysis of case law. Whether judicial opinions interpret statutory or constitutional law or develop common law, the resulting case law is inherently incremental. Courts express their legal analyses in the context of individual controversies, and a holding in a single judicial opinion is often too limited to support an accurate prediction about how the decision will influence subsequent cases. Instead, as discussed further in Chapters 7 and 8, a series of cases addressing the same topic in a variety of factual contexts will support a generalization about the case law. The generalization, or synthesis of the cases, can then be applied more broadly to a wide range of cases.

5. Recognizing Arguments for Both Sides

With few exceptions, essay examinations and office memorandum assignments call on you to present a balanced discussion of legal issues. Although

---

19. 42 U.S.C. § 1981 (2012).

20. *See generally* Runyon v. McCrary, 427 U.S. 160 (1976) (addressing, but rejecting, First Amendment challenges to application of § 1981 to racial discrimination in a private school).

one party may be identified as your client, your professor or supervising attorney expects you to explore the weaknesses of the client's claims and defenses as well as the strengths.

When writing a brief, you should not take such a balanced approach; instead, you must advocate your client's position and discredit your opponent's arguments. Nonetheless, to maximize your own advocacy, you must anticipate and evaluate the arguments of your opponent before your write your brief. You might express that more balanced analysis in an office memorandum, or you might simply contemplate it as you outline the arguments for your brief.

Thus, to analyze a legal dispute effectively, you must identify arguments for both sides of the dispute. In synthesizing case law, you should consider alternative formulations of the general principles that emerge from a series of holdings. Similarly, in analyzing statutory language, you should consider intrinsic and extrinsic aids that support alternative interpretations.

For example, the common law of negligence imposes tort liability on a person who proximately causes injury to another by breaching a duty of care owed to the injured person. As a specific application of this tort law, physicians in most circumstances are liable for injuries caused by their failure to exercise reasonable skill and care in their practices. Suppose that the courts of the fictitious State of New Maine have developed an additional common law doctrine of strict liability, which does not require proof of negligence, for injuries resulting from abnormally dangerous activities. The courts, however, have refused to apply this common law doctrine to medical practices, even risky or experimental ones. Against this background of common law, New Maine has enacted a statute that makes any "commercial enterprise strictly liable" for injuries caused by its use "of any toxic material."

Now suppose that a medical patient in New Maine died from a reaction to general anesthesia triggered by the patient's rare disorder of the nervous system. Much of the legal dispute in a malpractice action brought by the deceased patient's estate and surviving family members might center on the applicability of the statute. Assuming that anesthesiology is "a commercial enterprise," if the anesthetic is "a toxic material" within the meaning of the statute, the anesthesiologist or her employer would be statutorily liable without regard to the care that she exercised. In contrast, a companion claim based on common law negligence would require an inquiry into the duty of care that the anesthesiologist owed and the degree of care she actually exercised.

In preparing for advocacy, counsel for either side of this dispute would want to evaluate arguments for both sides on the question of the applicability of the statute. For example, without going beyond the face of the statute, counsel for the deceased patient's estate and survivors could argue that the statutory requirement of "toxic materials" is satisfied in this case because the ordinary meaning of "toxic" is "poisonous," and the anesthetic acted like a poison on the nervous system of the patient. Counsel for the estate and the survivors would also want to anticipate a strong counterargument: It is doubtful that the legislature intended to inhibit physicians' use of substances that produce medically beneficial results in almost all cases in which they are administered; rather, the statutory term "toxic materials" is likely intended to apply only to materials that are generally harmful to all persons, such as potent acids or pesticides. After formulating and evaluating the anesthesiologist's probable counterargument, counsel for the estate and the survivors should try to present their argument in a way that will reduce the impact of the counterargument.

Exercise 6-4

Review your responses to Exercise 6-3 above. Did you explore arguments for both sides on the question of interpretation? Summarize and list the opposing arguments for application of the criminal statute to the case of a "surrogate" mother who in fact is the biological mother. If you did not explore arguments on both sides of each of these issues, do so now.

V. "A"—Application of Law to Facts

A. Basic Patterns

At trial, the critical issues often are questions of purely historical fact. For example, the plaintiff in an employment discrimination suit might assume the burden of proving that an employer in fact exclaimed, "Women can't perform this job!" when he rejected the plaintiff's application for employment.

As explored in later chapters, appellate courts will defer to some degree to the factual findings of a jury or trial judge; therefore, issues on appeal inevitably contain a more substantial element of law. However, even nearly pure questions of law are developed in the context of particular disputes and with an appreciation for the probable facts of future disputes. Moreover, most disputes present nontrivial questions about whether the facts satisfy the applicable legal standards, such as whether certain acts of preparation leading up to a murder satisfy the premeditation requirement of a first-degree murder statute.

A pattern should emerge from your treatment of facts in an office memorandum or brief. First, you will state all the important facts of the dispute at or near the beginning of the document. Second, in the discussion section of a memorandum or the argument section of a brief, after you have explained the legal rule applicable to a particular issue, you will discuss or argue whether the relevant facts satisfy the legal rule. You and your professor will follow a similar pattern in an essay examination: Your professor will state all the facts in the essay question, and—after you have identified an issue and supplied a rule—you will analyze the subset of facts that are relevant to that issue.

If your assignment does not call for great depth of analysis, you might directly explain why particular facts support or undermine the application of a legal rule. Suppose, for example, that you are writing an office memorandum analyzing the claims of a client seeking punitive damages, as introduced in a previous example in this chapter. After stating the legal rule that a malicious or reckless tortfeasor may be liable for punitive damages, you could identify the facts relevant to this issue and explain how each supports or defeats application of the legal rule:

Facts showing no intent	We have no evidence that Con Motor Co. maliciously intended to cause injury when it designed the Backfire sports car. In fact, our notes of the May meeting of the board of directors show that the board members genuinely hoped that the risky design would not cause accidents.
Facts showing recklessness	However, we do have evidence of recklessness. Con's chief engineer informed the board of directors of her opinion that placement of the gas tank near the rear exterior of the car would create a risk of deadly explosion in even minor rear-end collisions. Yet, the directors approved that design solely because it would save production costs of $200 per car, a trivial sum when compared to the $40,000 price of the car. In so doing, Con's directors knowingly created a great risk of death or terrible injury to consumers without any socially significant justification.

B. Developing Arguments for Both Sides

As with your analysis of more abstract legal rules, your fact analysis in an essay examination answer or office memorandum ought to explore arguments for both sides of the dispute. Similarly, when writing a brief, you should consider your opponent's factual arguments as you develop your own. In the typical dispute, some facts will support application of the legal rule and others will suggest that the legal rule is not satisfied. Still other facts may be used in different ways to support both positions. By balancing and weighing the facts, you can reach at least a qualified conclusion about whether the legal rule is satisfied.

This can be illustrated by extending one of the examples in the previous section on analysis of legal rules. If the parties dispute an anesthesiologist's liability on a claim of common law negligence, an office memorandum might call for analysis of the following facts:

1. The anesthesiologist informed a patient scheduled for foot surgery of the advantages and risks associated with the three most appropri-

ate anesthetics. On the basis of relative costs, the patient rejected the safest anesthetic in favor of a generally safe and more widely used anesthetic.

2. The anesthesiologist administered general anesthesia without assistance, before the surgical team had arrived and while the circulating nurse was occupied with another patient.

3. While administering general anesthesia, the anesthesiologist concentrated intensely on gauges on her equipment that measured the patient's intake of the anesthetic.

4. The anesthesiologist did not maintain visual contact with the patient or with equipment monitoring the patient's vital signs; as a consequence, she failed to terminate the intake of anesthetic until 10 seconds after the first visible signs of an adverse reaction.

5. The patient suffered from a rare disorder of the nervous system that produced the fatal reaction to the anesthetic.

6. The patient died within a minute of the administration of general anesthesia.

The facts in the first paragraph suggest that the anesthesiologist followed a reasonable procedure in prescribing the anesthetic. Indeed, the facts in item 5 suggest that the patient's unusual disorder, rather than the anesthesiologist's conduct, precipitated the fatal reaction. Moreover, the facts in item 3 support an argument that the anesthesiologist used at least reasonable care in administering the anesthetic, because she concentrated intensely on an obviously important function.

In addition to providing some support for a finding that the anesthesiologist was not at fault, however, the facts of item 5 emphasize the need for special care in administering the anesthetic. Moreover, the facts in item 2 support an argument that the anesthesiologist breached a duty of care in administering the anesthetic without assistance, and the facts in item 3 raise a question about the appropriate focus of the anesthesiologist's attention. Finally, the facts in item 4 support an argument that the anesthesiologist acted carelessly in failing to monitor the patient and equipment measuring vital signs.

To complete your deductive reasoning in an office memorandum, you must discuss whether the facts establish a breach of a physician's duty of care, thus satisfying the legal rule that defines an element of the cause of action. Because the facts in this case support opposing arguments, different legal analysts might reasonably reach different conclusions, depending on the significance the analysts assign to particular facts. Regardless of the author's conclusion, however, the office memorandum should present the best factual arguments for both sides of the dispute. Of course, an advocate writing a brief would emphasize the facts supporting her argument and would develop her argument in a way that lessened the impact of anticipated counterarguments.

Exercise 6-5

Review your response to Exercise 6-1 at the end of Section III.A. For each issue that you identified in that exercise, discuss whether the relevant facts satisfy the applicable rule relating to the element of burglary that is in issue. Argue both sides of the facts whenever possible, but argue only the facts that help to resolve each issue.

For more practice in evaluating policy considerations and in applying law to facts, perform Problem 2 in Appendix II.

VI. "C"—Reaching Conclusions

The final element of deductive reasoning is a conclusion derived from the law of your major premise and the facts of your minor premise. When writing a brief, you obviously must state a firm conclusion for each argument that you present. Your conclusions represent the critical points that the court must accept before granting your client relief.

You may hesitate to state conclusions in the more nearly neutral analysis of an office memorandum or essay examination answer, particularly if the dispute presents close questions. Nonetheless, most supervising attorneys and professors will want you to take a position and to reveal your best judgment about the probable outcome of each issue. If necessary, you may hedge your conclusions with qualifiers such as "probably," but you should remember to complete your deductive reasoning by stating a conclusion for each issue:

On these facts, a jury likely will find that Con Motor Co. acted recklessly, permitting the jury to award punitive damages.

In some cases, you may find it appropriate to make your conclusion contingent on your ability to establish critical facts or law:

Assuming that we can prove that most hospitals require a team of at least two personnel to administer anesthesia, a jury will almost certainly find that Humana Hospital was negligent in this case.

VII. Summary

To analyze a legal problem, you should

1. identify the Issue,
2. state the legal Rule or rules that will help you resolve the issue,

3. Apply the rule to the relevant facts, and

4. reach a Conclusion on the question of whether the facts satisfy the legal rule.

A single dispute between two parties may present several issues. To achieve an appropriate scope of analysis, you must judge which issues and subissues are sufficiently significant and material to warrant discussion and which are sufficiently tangential to warrant exclusion or summary treatment.

Whenever the law or fact analysis is in doubt, you must evaluate arguments for both sides of the dispute. To evaluate arguments about the applicable legal rules and their application to the facts, you should consider

- the hierarchy of authority,
- synthesis of multiple authorities,
- the relative strength of different kinds of case law as precedent,
- policy analysis, and
- the ways in which each side might argue that relevant facts either satisfy or fail to satisfy the applicable legal rules.

Always state a conclusion for each issue, even in the analysis in an office memorandum or examination answer, and even if you have explained that the answer is uncertain.

You will find much more information, advice, and illustration relating to the construction of legal arguments when you reach Chapter 16.

Exercise 6-6

Gaining Comfort and Experience with Uncertainty in the Law and with Making Arguments for Both Sides. The following exercise is set in a nonlegal context but effectively illustrates some fundamental features of common law analysis.[21]

Pat is the mostly absentee owner of a small grocery store sitting adjacent to a busy downtown sidewalk. Pat made a rare appearance at the store one day to post a new rule on the employees' bulletin board. The posted rule instructed employees to place fresh produce in the window display case if the produce would attract pedestrians who had not previously planned to visit the store. The posting explained that the rule was designed to draw impulse shoppers into the store, because they might then buy several items and possibly become regular customers. According to the posting, if the produce did not meet this standard of attracting impulse shoppers, it should be placed in the appropriate section in the middle of the store.

---

21. This exercise is adapted and expanded from one developed by Professor Elisabeth Keller at Boston College Law School. *See* Jane Gionfriddo, *Using Fruit to Teach Analogy*, THE SECOND DRAFT: BULLETIN OF THE LEGAL WRITING INSTITUTE, Nov. 1997, at 4.

Kim, the store manager, has applied this written rule in two cases. In the first case, she arranged a crate of clean, shiny, round, red apples in the window display case. In the second case, she placed a crate of unwashed, unpeeled carrots in the produce section in the interior of the store.

On Monday at noon, Kim left to attend to family business for the remainder of the day. She instructed employees to promptly display any goods that arrived in her absence. On Monday afternoon, a crate of clean, shiny, nicely shaped red bell peppers arrived. Where should the employees place the bell peppers? In analyzing this problem, consider the following:

a. In the abstract, one may not be able to identify a single correct answer to this question. In practical terms, the "answer" is the location that will most please Kim when she returns, but that is the "answer" only because Kim is the employees' supervisor and has taken the lead in interpreting the new rule, and not because reasonable minds could reach only one conclusion on the best location for the red bell peppers under Pat's general standard. Moreover, in the meantime, employees must display the bell peppers in Kim's absence and so must predict where she would place them.

b. To better predict where Kim would place the red bell peppers, employees might wish to explore her apparent reasoning in the previous two cases. They might ask two questions: (1) On what basis did Kim conclude that the apples satisfied Pat's general standard of placing produce in the window only if it would attract customers into the store? (2) Does that rationale also explain why Kim concluded that the carrots did not satisfy that standard? If the employees can identify a rationale that explains both of the previous cases as a consistent application of Pat's general standard, then perhaps the employees could apply the same rationale to the red bell peppers. In that way, they might be able to better predict whether Kim would conclude that the bell peppers satisfied the standard of attracting customers into the store. Assuming that Kim did not explain her reasoning in the previous two cases to her employees, the employees may need to speculate on possible rationales.

c. Are the previous two cases potentially explainable on the basis of two or more equally plausible rationales? Do competing rationales sometimes point to different conclusions about where the employees should place the red bell peppers? Does this explain why reasonable judges and attorneys can disagree about the application of a general rule to new facts and about the interpretation of previous judicial decisions? Even with the posted rule (which you might compare to a statute) and with Kim's two applications of the rule (similar to judicial interpretations of a statute) it may be uncertain how Kim would apply the rule to new facts.

Accordingly, maybe your professors are not playing "hide the ball" when they raise legal questions and state that they have no answers to the questions. Perhaps your task is not to look for a single correct answer, but to identify issues, analyze the facts and the law, recognize arguments for both sides of the dispute, and either advocate for one party or make a prediction about the outcome. After all, cases are litigated precisely because the outcome is uncertain and the parties cannot predict with certainty how a judge or jury will view the dispute. An appellate court in the jurisdiction may eventually issue a definitive ruling in the dispute, providing its authoritative version of the answer. In the meantime, however, the dispute presents an opportunity for each party to work with law, facts, and policy in an effort to influence the judge, jury, or appellate panel in reaching a conclusion.

Part IV

Stepping Stones to Legal Memoranda—Case Briefs, Outlines, and Essay Exams

Chapter 7

Case Briefs

I. Study of Cases

When preparing for law school classes or researching an office memo-randum, you must analyze cases: judicial decisions, mostly appellate, that resolve particular disputes. Although you will encounter case law differently in a law firm than in law school, you ultimately will perform similar analytic functions in either context.

In a law firm, your supervising attorney will often request a formal memorandum or less formal report that addresses the rights and liabilities of parties to a pending dispute, and you will research and analyze case law with that dispute in mind. The reported judicial decisions that you find in the library are unedited opinions that often address multiple issues, some of which may be irrelevant to the pending dispute.

In law school your task is usually simpler. Rather than searching for unedited judicial opinions in the library, the opinions you read in assigned

115

casebooks will be grouped in logical fashion and edited to isolate selected issues.

In a law firm, you typically will analyze case law to determine its applicability to a dispute presented by a client. Similarly, when you analyze case law in law school, you should reflect on how it might apply to the next dispute that might arise. In other words, you should strive to appreciate the way in which the legal principles in a judicial opinion might apply to facts other than those presented in the opinion itself. Your professors will provide many opportunities for application of legal rules to new facts in classroom hypotheticals and essay examinations.

II. Preparing a Case Brief

A. General Approach and Format

Whether researching a memorandum problem or preparing for class, you should prepare "case briefs": written analytic summaries of appellate opinions. Although you will eventually develop shorthand techniques for taking notes on cases, during your first semester you should prepare formal, thorough case briefs to ensure that you develop skills of case analysis.

You should not be troubled if your instructors and textbooks recommend different formats for case briefs. All the formats include essentially the same information; they vary chiefly in emphasis and organization. Below are outlines of two sample formats. If necessary, you can modify them to suit the requirements of a classroom instructor who asks students to recite parts of a case in a different order.

A	B
1. Identification	1. Identification
2. Issue(s) and Holding(s)	2. Facts
3. Facts	3. Procedural History
4. Procedural History	4. Issue(s) and Holding(s)
5. Reasoning	5. Reasoning
6. Evaluation	6. Evaluation
7. Synthesis	7. Synthesis

Although format B may be more popular, format A has the advantage of forcing you to frame the legal issue before stating the facts, thus ensuring that you state the facts with an appreciation for their legal significance. The issue and holding also provide an effective overview of the case brief.

Whichever format you select, your first step is to read the case completely before beginning to write. To state some elements of a case brief, you must first understand other elements; moreover, the organization of an appellate opinion may differ from that of either case brief format outlined above. Indeed, some elements of the case brief may not appear explicitly anywhere in the opinion. For example, the precise issue and holding of a decision may be only implicit in the court's statement of the facts, legal reasoning, and disposition. Consequently, before briefing a case, you should read and reread the entire opinion until you understand all its elements.

B. Elements of a Case Brief

1. Identification of the Case

In preparing a case for class, you should begin your case brief with

1. the name of the case, which is usually taken from the names of two adversary parties;[1]
2. the jurisdiction, in the sense of the geographical and political body, within which the court sits;
3. the level of the deciding court;
4. the date of decision; and
5. the page on which the case appears in the casebook ("CB"), which facilitates quick cross-reference between notes and casebook.

For example, the following notes identify a 1904 decision of the Supreme Court of Rhode Island, which appears in the student casebook at page 387:

Davis v. Smith, Rhode Island Supreme Court (1904), CB 387

To develop familiarity with citation form, you may also wish to record the full citation to the reporters in the library in which the opinion appears, if that citation is presented in your casebook. The following example includes such a full citation, along with an additional reference to the page on which the edited opinion begins in the student casebook:

Davis v. Smith, 26 R.I. 129, 58 A. 630 (1904), CB 387

By citing to the official Rhode Island Reporter, "R.I.," you have referred to the Rhode Island Supreme Court under commonly accepted citation form. Consequently, both examples above identify the authoring court in *Davis v. Smith* as the court of last resort in Rhode Island. That information

---

1. In some *in rem* actions, a named party may be an object, such as money, a plot of land, or a ship. *E.g.*, United States v. $129,374 in U.S. Currency, 769 F.2d 583 (9th Cir. 1985); Winooski Hydroelectric Co. v. Five Acres of Land, 769 F.2d 79 (2d Cir. 1985); Giannakos v. M/V Bravo Trader, 762 F.2d 1295 (5th Cir. 1985); *see* Oliver Wendell Holmes, Jr., THE COMMON LAW 28-30 (Dover Publ. 1991) (1881). In other cases, the case name will refer not to adversary parties but to events, relationships, or other subjects of proceedings. *E.g.*, *In re* Garland Corp., 6 Bankr. 456 (Bankr. 1st Cir. 1980) (bankruptcy proceeding); *In re* Validation of Marriage of Francisco, 16 Indian L. Rep. 6113 (Navajo S. Ct. 1989) (marriage validation proceeding).

is significant: It shows that the court is not bound by lower court decisions within Rhode Island or by decisions in other states, although such decisions might provide persuasive authority.

The early date of the *Davis v. Smith* decision, 1904, helps identify the decision's place in Rhode Island law. This decision adhered to nineteenth century legal principles that minimized a landlord's duties and liability to a tenant's infant son for unsafe conditions, partly because the infant son was not, and could not be, a party to the lease. As discussed in Chapter 5, any aging decision may lose force or relevance over the years in light of growth in the economy, technological advances, and changes in social attitudes and legal context. Such changes prompted the Rhode Island Supreme Court to overrule *Davis v. Smith* in 1967, stating that "[we] can perceive no reason to abide by a rule of law promulgated over a half century ago and leave unchanged a principle which in our opinion no longer serves a useful purpose in today's times."[2]

The name of a case does not always clearly identify the original parties to the underlying dispute. A named party may be a representative of one of the original disputants or an assignee of its rights and obligations. For example, the dispute in *Hamer v. Sidway*[3] concerned the contract rights and obligations of William E. Story, Sr., and his nephew, William E. Story, II. The case name is taken from the parties to the lawsuit: (1) the executor of the senior Story's estate and (2) a person who acquired the nephew's contract rights through assignment.

Identifying the court may be problematic as well. Most court systems use "Court of Appeals" to refer to the intermediate appellate court and "Supreme Court" to refer to the court of last resort. In the New York state court system, however, the trial courts of general jurisdiction are the Supreme Court and the County Court; the intermediate appellate courts are the appellate divisions of the Supreme Court and the appellate terms of the Supreme Court; and the court of last resort is the Court of Appeals.[4]

2. Issue and Holding

a. Issue

An "issue" is a material question of fact or law that arises from the claims, defenses, and arguments of the parties. An issue may be a question of law, such as whether Congress intended the term "sex" to encompass sexual orientation as well as gender in section 703(a) of Title VII of the Civil Rights Act of 1964. Except at the trial level, an issue rarely presents only a question of fact, such as whether the evidence shows that an employer exclaimed "Women can't perform this job!" when he rejected a woman's application for employment.

---

2. Rampone v. Wanskuck Bldgs., Inc., 102 R.I. 30, 34, 227 A.2d 586, 588 (R.I. 1967) (allowing employee of tenant to sue landlord in tort after she stepped in a hole in the floor, when the landlord had undertaken a contractual obligation to the tenant to make repairs).
3. 27 N.E. 256 (N.Y. 1891).
4. BNA's DIRECTORY OF STATE AND FEDERAL COURTS, JUDGES, AND CLERKS 347 (2013).

Most commonly, the issue before a trial or appellate court requires a combination of legal and factual analysis in the determination of whether the facts of a dispute satisfy a general legal rule. An example of such a question is whether certain conduct by an employer in fact created a discriminatory work environment, thus satisfying Title VII's rule regarding discrimination in "conditions . . . of employment." By applying the rule to the facts and reaching a conclusion, the court not only resolves the immediate dispute before it, but it also refines the rule by adding more concrete substance to its abstract terms.

If you look for a concise statement of the issues in an appellate opinion, you may find only frustration. Courts do not always state the issues in simple terms before resolving them. When a court does formally state the issues, it may not state them with the narrowness and specificity to which you should aspire if you seek to maximize the development of your analytic skills. You may find clues to the precise question addressed by the court in the court's description of the trial court decision that it is reviewing, in its summary of the parties' arguments on appeal, in the emphasis it places on particular facts, and in its discussion of the law.

At a minimum, your statement of an issue should identify a substantive legal question that distinguishes the case from the bulk of case law in the casebook. In addition, you should specifically incorporate the facts of the case that are critical to the court's analysis and that therefore help to define the precedential effect of its decision.

For example, consider the following case summary, which is loosely based on the procedural history and appellate disposition of a tort claim in *Wagenseller v. Scottsdale Memorial Hospital.*[5]

> Catherine Wagenseller (the employee) worked for Scottsdale Memorial Hospital (the employer) as a staff nurse under an employment contract of indefinite term. She alleged that her supervisor discharged her partly because she refused to participate in a humorous skit in which the participants "mooned" fellow hospital employees. The trial court found that the parties did not dispute any material facts and that the employer was entitled to summary judgment, which is judgment before trial, because the indefinite term of the employment contract made it terminable at the will of either party. Such a contract is terminable at any time and for any reason, or for no reason at all. The intermediate court of appeals affirmed.
>
> The state supreme court reversed and remanded to the trial court, deciding that an employer is liable in tort to an employee if it discharges the employee for a reason that contravenes a clear mandate of public policy. The state supreme court found such a mandate in a state criminal statute that prohibited certain acts of "indecent exposure." In discussing the sources of public policy, the court compared criminal statutes to other sources, such as common law: "Although we do not limit our recognition of the public policy exception to cases involving a violation of a criminal statute, we do

---

5. 710 P.2d 1025 (Ariz. 1985). Some of the pronouncements of common law in *Wagenseller* were later superseded by state legislation. ARIZ. REV. STAT. ANN. § 23-1501(3)(b) (Supp. 2009). The discussion in the text, however, assumes that a student is briefing the case when it still presents applicable common law and that the student is interested in ways in which the authoring court will continue to develop the common law doctrine of *Wagenseller*.

believe that our duty will seldom be clearer than when such a violation is involved."

The following statement of the issue in *Wagenseller* obviously is too general:

Did the trial court correctly grant summary judgment for the defendant?

This issue statement describes the trial court's disposition and the stage of the proceedings at which it made the disposition. Unfortunately, if your statement of the issue does no more than identify elements of the procedural history, you will not distinguish the case from hundreds of others in first-year casebooks. The procedural facts will certainly help you understand the decision. Moreover, the standards for summary judgment may even be the central issue in a case raising a dispute about rules of civil procedure. However, this case presents substantive questions of tort and perhaps contract law, and the issue statement should identify them.

The following statement of the issue is an improvement, because it identifies a substantive legal dispute:

Is an employer liable in tort for discharging an at-will employee for a reason that violates public policy?

This statement of the issue identifies (1) a legally significant relationship between the parties (employer/employee), (2) the nature of the claim (tort), (3) the basis for the claim (public policy), and (4) the obstacle to relief on a contract claim (the at-will nature of the employment contract).

Though the second statement of the issue is much more informative, it still leaves room for improvement. Your issue statement will better define the effect of the decision as precedent if you more specifically refer to the critical facts of the case.

For example, the court discusses the sources of public policy. That discussion suggests that a subsequent case may raise the question of the legal significance of public policy that is expressed in a judicial opinion analyzing common law, rather than in a criminal statute. To help determine whether *Wagenseller* would be controlling on, distinguishable from, or persuasively analogous to the subsequent dispute, your statement of the issue in *Wagenseller* could incorporate material facts that provide a potential basis for analogy and distinction:

Is the employer liable in tort for discharging an at-will employee because of her refusal to participate in a public "mooning," a discharge that contravened the public policy against indecent exposure reflected in a criminal statute?

This statement of the issue identifies the source of public policy, and it gives sufficient factual details to permit an assessment of the importance of that policy.

The point at which the disadvantages of increased complexity begin to outweigh the benefits of enhanced specificity in the issue statement is a matter of judgment and personal style. As discussed in the next subsection, you can reduce the complexity of the issue statement by transferring some of the critical information to the statement of the holding.

Finally, although you should incorporate facts into your issue statement, your fact statement should not include factual conclusions on matters that are in dispute and thus are themselves issues considered by the court. For example, the previous statement of the issue assumes that (1) the employment contract was terminable at will and (2) the criminal statute reflected a public policy against compelled "mooning" and therefore against an employer's discharging an at-will employee for refusing to engage in "mooning." The statement questions only whether state law recognizes a claim in tort for such retaliation against an at-will employee. Suppose instead that the employee had alleged breach of contract and had disputed that the employment contract was terminable at will. In that case, you would not state in your facts that the contract was terminable at will. Instead, you would state the underlying facts about the contract that would help a court determine whether the contract was terminable at will. Suppose further that the employer had disputed that the criminal statute reflected a public policy against compelled "mooning." In light of these additional disputes, you should add an issue relating to contract law and should divide the tort issue into two subissues:

1. Did the employee establish a genuine factual dispute on the question of whether the employer made a binding promise in its personnel manual to give the employee job security, thus entitling the employee to a trial on her contract claim?
2. Even if the employment contract was terminable at will, is the employer liable to the employee for discharging her for a reason that violates public policy?
   a. Should the court recognize a new cause of action by imposing tort liability for such a discharge?
   b. Does a state criminal statute prohibiting public exposure of one's anus or genitalia reflect a public policy against compelled public exposure of bare buttocks?[6]

Issue #1 achieves specificity in procedural facts by identifying the employee's burden on a motion for summary judgment. It also incorporates a material historical fact, sometimes known as an "operative fact," by referring to the personnel manual, thus providing a specific context for the question of whether the employer has stated a promise of job security.

---

6. *See Wagenseller*, 710 P.2d at 1035 n.5 (admitting to "little expertise in the techniques of mooning").

b. Holding

The "holding" is simply the court's answer to the question presented in the issue. If you state the issue so that it is sufficiently narrow and specific to provide a basis for evaluating the effect of the decision as precedent, you may state the holding with a simple "yes" or "no." Of course, if a professor asks you during class discussion for the holding of a case without first asking for the issue, she expects you to offer more than "yes" or "no." In those circumstances, you should transform the issue into a detailed holding in the form of a statement:

The employee was entitled to a trial on her contract claim because she established a genuine factual dispute on the question of whether the employer made a binding promise in its personnel manual to give the employee job security.

Even when pairing the holding with a detailed statement of the issue, you may wish the holding to convey further information than "yes" or "no." For example, if a fully descriptive statement of the issue would be unwieldy, you can move some of the critical information to the holding:

Issue: Did the employer discharge the employee for a reason that violates public policy, thus rendering the employer liable in tort for wrongful discharge?

Holding: Yes. By discharging the employee because she refused to participate in public "mooning," the employer violated public policy reflected in a criminal statute prohibiting indecent exposure.

The holding and the issue are simply the opposite sides of the same coin. Therefore, the following examination of the appropriate scope of statements of *holdings* is simply a continuation and refinement of the preceding discussion of narrowness and specificity in *issues*.

Because narrowly drafted statements of the issue and holding represent an attempt to identify the effect of the decision under stare decisis, from a practical standpoint the precise contours of the issue and holding may not become clear until subsequent decisions interpret and apply them as precedent. Through that process of determining whether the prior decision is controlling, analogous, or distinguishable, subsequent decisions help explain—or may even redefine—the relative importance that various facts and policies played in the prior decision. In turn, this process helps the court explain the relative importance of various facts and policies to the resolution of subsequent disputes.

For example, in *Monge v. Beebe Rubber Co.*[7] the New Hampshire Supreme Court held an employer liable for breach of contract for discharging a female employee in retaliation for her refusing his sexual advances. The court's

---

7. 114 N.H. 130, 316 A.2d 549 (1974).

own statement of its holding is reasonably consistent with a broad theory of liability that encompasses a wide range of employer actions:

> We hold that a termination by the employer of a contract of employment at will which is motivated by bad faith or malice or based on retaliation is not in the best interest of the economic system or the public good and constitutes a breach of the employment contract.[8]

Six years later, in *Howard v. Dorr Woolen Co.*,[9] however, the same court adopted one of the narrowest of the possible interpretations of *Monge*'s holding. The *Howard* court clearly required (1) a link to public policy beyond a general interest in good faith and fair play in a private employment relationship and (2) retaliation by the employer for a specific act or refusal to act by the employee:

> We construe Monge to apply only to a situation where an employee is discharged because he performed an act that public policy would encourage, or refused to do that which public policy would condemn.[10]

The *Howard* court applied its view of the holding in *Monge* to refuse to impose liability for an employer discharging an employee because of the employee's sickness and age.[11]

This process of refining the holding of a prior decision may permit a court to interpret precedent in a way that was not intended by the court establishing that precedent. In most subsequent decisions, however, if courts do not explicitly overrule their precedent, they faithfully attempt to identify the considerations that were essential to a decision that acts as precedent and to evaluate the precedent's effect on the subsequent disputes.

If the holding of a decision is thus defined in terms of the way in which courts will make use of the decision as precedent in subsequent cases, the issue and holding of the decision cannot be identified with perfect certainty when analyzing that decision in isolation. Rather, each decision presents a range of possible statements of the issue and a holding.[12] When preparing for class, you should try to state an issue and a holding that fall somewhere within a plausible range. Try also to appreciate how other statements nearer to either end of the plausible range would aid in the advocacy of either side of a subsequent dispute.

For example, if you had argued on behalf of one of the parties in the *Howard* case, you would have addressed the holding of *Monge*, a previous decision of the state court of last resort in the forum jurisdiction. If you had represented the plaintiff employee in *Howard*, you might have argued for the broadest plausible interpretation of the *Monge* precedent, so that it would strongly support recovery for your client. Specifically, you might have

---

8. *Id.* at 133, 316 A.2d at 551 (the unofficial reporter, "A.2d," omits the word "in" in the quoted passage).

9. 414 A.2d 1273 (N.H. 1980).

10. *Id.* at 1274; *see also* Arizona v. Gant, 129 S. Ct. 1710 (2009) (providing a restrictive interpretation of its precedent on searching an automobile incident to arrest).

11. *Howard*, 414 A.2d at 1274, *interpreted in Wagenseller*, 710 P.2d at 1032 n.3.

12. *See* Karl N. Llewellyn, THE BRAMBLE BUSH 75-76 (10th prtg. 1996).

interpreted *Monge* to approve tort liability whenever an employer discharges an employee for a reason that would be viewed by the average person as grossly unfair, partly because such a discharge would be harmful to the morale and productivity of all employees and thus not in the best economic interest of the community. Conversely, if you had represented the employer in *Howard*, you would have argued for a narrower interpretation of *Monge*, so that you could more easily distinguish it from the *Howard* case. Specifically, you might have sought to limit *Monge* to its factual context of sexual harassment, interpreting it to impose liability only if an employer discharges an employee in retaliation for resisting a demand specifically prohibited by a civil rights statute, a strong source of public policy.

Finally, as a student analyzing *Monge* without the benefit of the appellate decision in *Howard*, you should formulate some reasonable statement of the *Monge* holding within the range defined by plausible arguments of advocates. You should also be prepared to play the role of advocate and discuss the narrowest and broadest plausible interpretations of *Monge*. Of course, the *Howard* court adopted a quite narrow interpretation of the holding in *Monge*. Such an interpretation was not inevitable, however, and you could reasonably have interpreted the holding of *Monge* more broadly until *Howard* came to your attention.

3. Facts

a. Significance of Facts

Pressed for time, you may be tempted to skim over the facts of a case and rush to the middle of the opinion, searching for succinct statements of law that you can preserve in your notes. In the final analysis, however, legal rules are nothing more than statements of the legal consequences of particular facts:

> Wherever the law gives special rights to one, or imposes special burdens on another, it does so on the ground that certain special facts are true of those individuals. In all such cases, therefore, there is a twofold task. First, to determine what are the facts to which the special consequences are attached; second, to ascertain the consequences. The first is the main field of legal argument.[13]

Whether case law is based on statutory interpretation or common law, it generally develops gradually, with each new opinion adding refinements in the law through its application of legal standards to the facts of a new dispute. A court's statements about the law are fully meaningful only when read in light of the facts of the dispute that the court resolves. Consequently, you should master the facts of a case with the same intensity that you devote to appreciating the court's discussion of legal principles.

---

13. Oliver Wendell Holmes, Jr., THE COMMON LAW 289 (Dover Publ. 1991) (1881).

b. Selecting Facts for Your Fact Statement

Your statement of facts should include all "material" facts, which are facts that have legal significance and therefore directly influence the court's holding and reasoning. Identification of material facts is not an exact science; rather, it is a matter of judgment that requires an appreciation of the factors that the court considered in reaching its decision. In your statement of facts, you may also refer in general terms to any additional background facts that are helpful to a full understanding of the dispute. At the least, your statement of facts should identify

1. the principal parties to the underlying dispute that gave rise to the legal proceedings,
2. the relationships between those parties, and
3. the events that led to the dispute.

You may wish to refer to such facts as "historical facts" to distinguish them from "procedural facts," which are discussed in Subsection 4 below.

For purposes of general discussion, this book often uses the procedural term "plaintiff" to refer to the party who initiates a lawsuit and the term "defendant" to refer to the one against whom suit is brought. You can create a more concrete image of the underlying dispute, however, if you identify the parties with their more specific, formal names.

In addition, you should consider supplementing the formal names with labels that have substantive, rather than merely procedural, significance. Because statutes generally address broad categories of activities rather than individual cases, they often create rights and obligations in broad but carefully defined classifications of persons, such as "employers" and "employees" or "buyers" and "sellers."[14] Similarly, although courts interpret statutes and develop common law in the context of individual disputes, a series of judicial decisions on closely related points may create case law that allocates rights and obligations according to membership within general classes of persons, such as "landowners" and "trespassers."[15] Therefore, you can more clearly reveal the legal significance of material facts in your case brief if you identify the named parties or other important actors with labels that reflect undisputed and legally significant classifications, such as employer, buyer, seller, merchant, landlord, tenant, landowner, or invitee.

When you assign a label to a party or otherwise characterize a factual matter, do not prematurely state a conclusion on an issue that is disputed by the parties and that is later analyzed in the opinion. For example, your statement of facts should not refer to a seller as a "merchant" if the parties dispute whether the seller is a merchant for purposes of determining

---

14. *See, e.g.*, Title VII of the Civil Rights Act of 1964, 42 U.S.C. §§ 2000e(b), 2000e-2(a) (2006) (defining and imposing obligations on "employers").

15. *See, e.g.*, W. Page Keeton et al., PROSSER AND KEETON ON THE LAW OF TORTS § 58, at 393 (5th ed. 1984) (duties owed by landowner to trespassers, licensees, and invitees).

the seller's warranty obligations under the Uniform Commercial Code.[16] Similarly, your statement of facts should not state that the defendant in a criminal burglary prosecution "broke into" a "dwelling" if "breaking" and "dwelling" are elements of the charged offense and if the parties dispute those elements.[17]

Rather than stating disputed legal conclusions in your statement of facts, summarize the subsidiary facts that the court analyzes in reaching its conclusion. For example, in the first case in the preceding paragraph, you might state that the seller of a computer system did not normally buy or sell goods, and that his sale of the computer system was an isolated transaction, but that the seller's occupation as a computer repair person led the buyer to believe that the seller had special knowledge of the performance capabilities of different computer systems. In other parts of your case brief, you can discuss whether those subsidiary facts satisfy the legal definition of "merchant," a matter that the parties dispute.[18]

c. Mastering the Facts

In most cases, the appellate judge who wrote the opinion has already sifted and condensed the facts that were presented to the trial court. Nonetheless, you should try to be even more discriminating in your identification of material facts and helpful background facts, and you should try to summarize them further. You should also reorganize the opinion's facts if its organization is not satisfactory; chronological order is often the most logical.

To truly master the facts, however, you must go beyond simply summarizing or reorganizing the opinion's fact statement. Otherwise, you may find yourself simply transferring words and phrases from the casebook to your case brief without truly comprehending their meaning. Instead, seek a conceptual understanding of the facts, one that creates concrete images of the parties and transactions. If necessary, prepare charts, timelines, or other graphics that vividly represent the relationships between multiple parties and events.

To fully appreciate this point, return briefly to the discussion of *Hadley v. Baxendale* at the beginning of Chapter 2. Notice how the charts summarize the transactions and legal proceedings in a rough timeline. Did those charts help you form a vivid image of the events? If so, imagine how your own charts or other graphics can help you visualize complex transactions or relationships among parties.

---

16. *See* U.C.C. § 2-314 (2002) (implying a warranty of merchantability in a contract for the sale of goods "if the seller is a merchant with respect to goods of that kind").

17. *See* Wayne R. LaFave, CRIMINAL LAW § 21.1 (4th ed. 2003).

18. The UCC definition focuses on regular practices and on representations of expertise:

> Merchant means a person who deals in goods of the kind or otherwise by his occupation holds himself out as having knowledge or skill peculiar to the practices or goods involved in the transaction. . . .

U.C.C. § 2-104 (2002).

As a practical matter, moreover, preparing graphics will enhance your class performance in at least three ways. First, you will force yourself to thoroughly study and comprehend the facts, because you will not be able to represent the facts in a graphic form unless you truly understand what happened in the case. Second, by glancing at your graphic representation in class, you can quickly recall the facts. Third, by relying primarily on such a representation in your class recital of the facts, you will tend to describe the facts more naturally and spontaneously than if you mechanically read your summary of the facts verbatim from your notes.

4. Procedural History

a. Elements of Procedural History

In your statement of the procedural history of a case on appeal, you should identify

1. which party or parties originally brought legal action against which others,
2. the legal claims and defenses and the relief sought in that action,
3. the trial court's disposition along with the stage of the proceedings at which the trial court rendered its decision,
4. the dispositions of any intermediate appellate courts below the authoring court, and
5. the authoring court's disposition.

In some cases, it may also be helpful to summarize the arguments that the parties made to the trial or appellate courts.

The case name on appeal does not always reveal which party initiated the legal action in the trial court. In the trial court the case name begins with the plaintiff's name. In some appellate courts, however, the case name begins with the name of the party who is dissatisfied with the trial court's decision and has thus appealed (the "appellant") or petitioned for review (the "petitioner").[19]

As with the statement of facts, you should not reach a premature conclusion in your statement of the procedural history regarding the nature of a legal claim if that is one of the issues disputed by the parties and analyzed by the court. For example, the parties may dispute whether a claim is properly classified as tort or contract, because that classification may determine the applicable statute of limitations or the availability of punitive damages.[20] In

---

19. *See, e.g.,* Fiege v. Boehm, 123 A.2d 316 (Md. 1956) (Hilda Boehm had successfully sued Louis Fiege in the trial court, and Louis appealed).

20. *See, e.g.,* Woodward v. Chirco Constr. Co., 687 P.2d 1275, 1278 (Ariz. Ct. App.), *approved as supplemented,* 687 P.2d 1269 (Ariz. 1984) (en banc) (implied warranty claim arose out of a written contract and therefore was governed by six-year limitations period rather than by shorter limitations period for tort claims); Gates v. Life of Mont. Ins. Co., 668 P.2d 213, 215 (Mont. 1983) (breach of implied duty of good faith and fair dealing in employment contract gives rise to a tort, thus permitting award of punitive damages).

many cases, however, the nature of the legal claim will be undisputed and easily identifiable.

b. Significance of Procedural History

The nature of the plaintiff's legal claim and request for relief in the trial court may provide a key to the appellate court's analysis. For example, classification of a plaintiff's legal claim as one in tort rather than in contract may determine whether the claim is barred by a statute of limitations[21] or whether the plaintiff is entitled to punitive damages.[22] Similarly, whether a contract is sufficiently definite to enforce may depend on whether the plaintiff seeks enforcement through an award of damages or through injunctive relief granting specific enforcement.[23]

Moreover, by stating the dispositions of all the courts that rendered decisions in the case, you can identify precisely the ruling that the authoring court has reviewed. The "disposition" is the practical, procedural effect of the court's holding on the litigation. In an opinion of a trial court, it might be "action dismissed," "summary judgment for the plaintiff," or "judgment on the jury verdict for the defendant." In an opinion of an appellate court, it might be "affirmed," "reversed," or "reversed and remanded for further proceedings."

In stating the trial court's disposition, try to identify the stage of the proceedings at which the trial court rendered judgment. An appellate court gives varying degrees of deference to different kinds of trial court decisions. Therefore, the likelihood of reversal by an appellate court depends partly on the stage of the proceedings at which judgment is rendered and, in some cases, on the classification of critical issues as ones of fact or law.[24]

For example, although appellate courts review without restriction the legal rules formulated by trial courts, they restrict their review of the factual findings made by a trial judge or jury after a full trial, overturning such findings only in unusual circumstances.[25] On the other hand, a trial judge does not resolve disputes of fact when he uses summary judgment to dispose of claims before trial, and an appellate court will reverse summary judgment if it determines, without deference to the analysis of the trial court, that the parties genuinely dispute material facts.[26] Further, on a motion to dismiss an action for failure of the complaint to state a claim for relief, both the trial

---

21. *See, e.g.*, Salmon Rivers Sportsman Camps, Inc. v. Cessna Aircraft Co., 544 P.2d 306, 310 (Idaho 1975).

22. *See* John D. Calamari & Joseph M. Perillo, CALAMARI AND PERILLO ON CONTRACTS § 14.3 (6th ed. 2009).

23. *See* E. Allan Farnsworth, CONTRACTS § 3.28 (4th ed. 2004).

24. *See infra* Chapter 21, Section II.

25. *See, e.g.*, FED. R. CIV. P. 52(a)(6) (federal appellate court may set aside trial judge's findings of fact only if the findings are "clearly erroneous"); Aetna Life Ins. Co. v. Kepler, 116 F.2d 1, 4 & n.1 (8th Cir. 1941) (reviewing court will overturn the fact findings of a jury only if they are not supported by substantial evidence).

26. *See* FED. R. CIV. P. 56(a) (summary judgment standards); Heiniger v. City of Phoenix, 625 F.2d 842, 843-44 (9th Cir. 1980) (standards for appellate review of summary judgment).

and appellate courts simply assume the truth of the allegations of fact in the complaint and analyze the legal significance of those allegations.[27]

5. Reasoning

a. Rule and Rationale

In part, published appellate judicial decisions serve the function of ensuring the "correct" result in a particular case. However, their primary purpose is to serve the "institutional function" of "developing and declaring legal principles that will have application beyond the case that serves as the vehicle for expression of the principles."[28] The reasoning set forth in a judicial opinion should guide others in predicting how the court will apply its decision to subsequent, analogous cases.

By carefully studying the reasoning of opinions, you will gradually develop a feel for the way in which judges decide cases. With that acquired knowledge, you can develop the ability not only to analyze a legal dispute and offer a reasonable prediction of its outcome in court, but also to persuade a court to reach a conclusion favorable to your client.

Unfortunately, published opinions provide only an imperfect guide to the decision-making process. For example, the published opinion may exclude some of the more pragmatic reasons privately expressed by panel members to one another and may focus instead on more conventional legal analysis. Because an opinion thus communicates a court's actual reasoning imperfectly, do not hesitate to read between the lines and to offer facts or policy considerations that you believe may have contributed to the court's decision, even though the court did not expressly identify them as critical factors.

On the most fundamental level, when stating a court's reasoning, note whether the court is interpreting and applying a constitution or statute or is developing common law. Many judicial opinions rely on two or more sources of law, sometimes in combination and sometimes applied to different issues. Beyond that, you should summarize the court's reliance on precedent, its analysis of policy considerations, its explanation of the significance of critical facts, and its adoption or recognition of a legal rule of general application.

Some opinions do not formulate or restate a general legal rule that controls the analysis. Instead, they simply define a dispute on particular facts, reach a decision, and provide a justification that is fairly narrowly tailored to the dispute before the court. Such an opinion leaves you only with a "holding" in the narrowest sense. Using techniques described in the next chapter, however, you can synthesize several such cases addressing similar issues and derive your own rule of general application.

---

27. *See, e.g.*, Experimental Eng'g, Inc. v. United Techs. Corp., 614 F.2d 1244, 1246 (9th Cir. 1980) (dismissal is appropriate only if court is convinced that the plaintiff can prove no set of facts in support of a claim that would warrant relief).

28. Charles Richard Calleros, *Title VII and Rule 52(a): Standards of Appellate Review in Disparate Treatment Cases—Limiting the Reach of* Pullman-Standard v. Swint, 58 TUL. L. REV. 403, 420-21 (1983).

b. Holding and Dictum

One of your most challenging tasks is to distinguish the holding of a decision from dictum. Narrowly defined, a "holding" is the court's resolution of an issue before it, limited to the material facts of that dispute. It does not include statements in the opinion about the probable outcome of disputes not before the court.

"Dictum," on the other hand, is a statement in the opinion that helps explain the court's reasoning by addressing questions not squarely presented in the dispute before the court. Courts make and apply law in the context of individual disputes. As a natural consequence of the uniformity of treatment demanded by stare decisis, however, courts have developed general rules that apply to whole categories of disputes.[29] As a means of explaining the reasons supporting its holding, a court may in dicta compare its rule of decision with other rules that it does not apply to the dispute, or it may discuss in dicta how its rule of decision would apply to facts other than those presented in the dispute before it.

As illustrated by the following excerpt, the issue and holding of a previous decision limits its effect as precedent under stare decisis. Even a lower court that is absolutely bound by the holdings of the previous decision may choose not to follow the dicta of the decision. In this example from civil rights litigation, a United States court of appeals extended the same immunity defense to judges of limited jurisdiction state courts, such as traffic courts, as had been applied to judges of general jurisdiction state courts, such as general trial courts. In doing so, it departed from United States Supreme Court dicta:

> The district court held that judges of courts of limited jurisdiction may be sued for judicial acts done merely in excess of jurisdiction. . . . Although the Supreme Court cases relied upon by the district court contain language supporting such a view, . . . we hold that judges of courts of limited jurisdiction are entitled to absolute immunity for their judicial acts unless they act in the clear absence of all jurisdiction.
>
> First, we emphasize that since the [Supreme Court] cases involved suits against judges of courts having general jurisdiction, any statements made by the Supreme Court about judges of courts having only limited or inferior jurisdiction were *dicta*.[30]

Dictum in an opinion is not meaningless; it may have considerable persuasive value, particularly if it represents a higher court's response to an argument raised by counsel in the previous case.[31] Nonetheless, because dictum does not carry the full weight of a holding, you should take care to read all of the court's reasoning in light of its narrow, fact-specific holding. Do not confuse what a court says, or even what it says it is doing, with what it actually does in a case.

---

29. *See generally* Karl N. Llewellyn, THE BRAMBLE BUSH 40-41 (10th prtg. 1996).
30. King v. Love, 766 F.2d 962, 966 (6th Cir. 1985).
31. *See* Nudell v. Forest Pres. Cook County, 799 N.E.2d 260, 264 (Ill. 2003) (stating that such "judicial *dictum* is entitled to much weight, and should be followed unless found to be erroneous").

6. Evaluation

You should resist any tendency to defer to the reasoning of a judicial decision as the expression of the single "correct" analysis of a dispute. Many disputes present close questions that are reasonably susceptible to alternative, inconsistent resolutions. You should read a decision critically to determine whether you agree with the result and the reasoning. Constant practice in critically examining judicial opinions will help you develop the ability later to persuade a court to adopt or reject the rule or reasoning of nonbinding authority.

On one level, you should examine an opinion for doctrinal integrity by asking questions such as these:

1. Does the court analogize or distinguish precedent in a convincing manner?
2. Does it apply the appropriate standard of review?
3. Does it analyze a statute under accepted principles of statutory interpretation and construction?
4. Does the court place excessive emphasis on certainty in a general rule at the expense of equitable considerations in the context of peculiar facts?

On another, closely related level, you should examine the policy and practical implications of an opinion. For example, you might ask:

1. Does a decision that promotes economic security for employees unwisely reduce economic efficiency at the expense of producers and consumers?
2. Does a court-developed tort standard allocate risks among parties in a way that encourages them to conduct themselves in a manner that avoids harm to others yet encourages socially productive ventures?

7. Synthesis

a. A Bridge Between Case Briefs and Outlines

Perhaps the most important and the most challenging element of a case brief is the "synthesis," in which you explore the relationships between two or more cases that address the same issue or closely related ones. After comparing the critical elements of each in a series of cases, you can refine your view of the holding of each case in the series. With synthesis, you can either (1) formulate a general principle that explains all the decisions or (2) compare and evaluate the inconsistent approaches of different courts or of the same court over time. By synthesizing cases, you take a critical step in legal analysis that will have special significance when you look ahead to final examinations: Synthesis forms a bridge between daily briefing of isolated cases and periodic preparation of course outlines.

The process of synthesizing cases reveals that the study of case law is analogous in some ways to the study of a foreign language. After a brief introduction to the basic structure of a language and its rules of pronunciation, you typically proceed to study the language by gaining familiarity with a succession of words and phrases that gradually grow into a working vocabulary. The learning process is complicated by the relationship of parts to the whole: You cannot fully appreciate the nuances of meaning of a word or phrase without a working knowledge of its role in a larger body of the language; yet you cannot attain a working knowledge of the larger body of the language without first gaining at least a preliminary understanding of individual words and phrases. As you gradually add to your vocabulary and to your understanding of the relationship of words and phrases to one another, you continually refine your understanding of the individual words and phrases that you studied earlier, and you come closer to attaining fluency in the whole language.

Similarly, when studying law, you cannot fully appreciate the legal significance of a single judicial decision without examining its role within a larger body of case law; yet you cannot master the larger body of case law without first gaining at least an imperfect grasp of its parts, first one case in isolation and then a growing group of cases. As you brief a series of cases, you gain new insights by examining the cases' relationships to one another. Those insights may cause you to modify your early, less sophisticated understanding of a case standing alone or standing with fewer cases in the series. Additionally, they may enable you to identify a general legal principle, or at least a set of accepted criteria, that helps to explain the decisions.

b. Reconciling Disparate Results

The first step in synthesizing cases is to compare the cases' substantive results as conveyed by their holdings, regardless of the procedural dispositions of the appellate courts. For example, assume that two appellate decisions from different jurisdictions, States X and Y, have addressed the question of whether a particular newspaper advertisement amounts to an "offer," defined at common law as an expression of willingness to enter into a contract that empowers the offeree to create a contract by accepting the offer. In Case A, an appellate court of State X affirmed a trial court judgment that a particular newspaper advertisement amounted to an offer to sell the advertised goods. In Case B, an appellate court of State Y affirmed a trial court judgment that another newspaper advertisement communicated only an invitation to negotiate rather than an offer to sell.[32] If you are not yet prepared to abandon hope of finding at least limited uniformity among the states in their formulation and application of common law, you should be curious about the reasons for the difference in results.

---

32. *Compare* Lefkowitz v. Great Minneapolis Surplus Store, 86 N.W.2d 689 (Minn. 1957) (offer) *with* Craft v. Elder & Johnston Co., 38 N.E.2d 416 (Ohio Ct. App. 1941) (no offer).

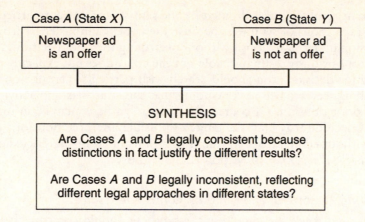

In the next step of the synthesis, you should determine whether Cases *A* and *B* are materially distinguishable and therefore warrant different results on application of the same legal principles, or whether they are legally inconsistent and simply represent different views of the law adopted by courts in different states. As a general approach, you should first attempt to reconcile the cases by searching for distinctions in facts, procedure, or both that support a conclusion that the cases are legally consistent. For example, unusually specific and detailed language of commitment in the advertisement in Case *A* might clearly communicate a willingness to conclude a contract for sale on a customer's assent. In contrast, more general language in the advertisement in Case *B* might leave important terms of sale unaddressed, suggesting a need for further bargaining before the advertiser is willing to commit to a contract for sale.

In these circumstances, you could compose a single legal rule that is consistent with the reasoning of both cases and that appropriately produces different results on application to the contrasting facts of the cases:

A newspaper advertisement is an offer only if it expresses definite commitment, leaving no important detail for future negotiation.

With such a synthesis, you will better understand the holdings of Cases *A* and *B*, more firmly grasp otherwise abstract legal principles, and improve your ability to predict the outcome of a new case that presents the same issue on new facts.

If you fail to find material distinctions in facts or procedure between Cases *A* and *B*, you can safely conclude that the appellate decisions are legally inconsistent. In that event, you should analyze the reasons for the different views of the law. Perhaps States *X* and *Y* apply different legal approaches because they emphasize different policies. Such a synthesis helps you to put conflicting case law into perspective and to develop the ability to persuade a court in a future case to adopt one line of conflicting authority over another.

Different results in cases decided by the same court present particularly interesting questions of synthesis, because the court cannot depart from its prior decision under stare decisis without overruling the prior decision. If the cases are not obviously distinguishable but the court does not explicitly overrule the prior decision, you should search with particular care for possible distinguishing features before concluding that the court has implicitly overruled the prior decision. Of course, the proper synthesis may lie in middle ground: A decision may limit the range of possible interpretations of a prior holding without completely overruling it, as illustrated in the discussion of *Monge v. Beebe Rubber Co.* in Section II.B.2.b above.

c. Comparing Reasons for and Limits on Consistent Results

If two cases reach the same result, a synthesis should compare the facts and reasoning of the two cases to determine whether the courts were influenced by similar factors. For example, suppose that in Case *A* a court in State *X* held that a particular newspaper advertisement constituted an offer to sell the advertised goods. Suppose further that in Case *C* a court in State *Z* found a different newspaper advertisement to constitute an offer. Although both decisions find offers, a comparison of the facts may suggest that Case *C* represents a significant extension of the holding of Case *A*. Similarly, the reasoning of Case *A* might suggest that the court in State *X* would not have reached the same result if presented with the facts on which the court in State *Z* found an offer in Case *C*.

d. Limited Utility of a Case Viewed in Isolation

When you synthesize, you compare two or more cases. Therefore, when you prepare a single case brief in isolation, you will not include a synthesis, except perhaps in the form of a prediction of the questions that may arise later from uncertainty in the breadth of the holding of the case. The late Professor Karl Llewellyn may be forgiven for overstatement when he asserted that a case read by itself is meaningless, is nil, is blank, is blah. Briefing should begin at the earliest with the second case of an assignment. Only after you have read the second case have you any idea what to do with the first.[33]

Thus, in a perfect world, you would read all opinions in a series of cases relating to a particular problem area before briefing any of them. You would then brief each case with an eye to the problems raised in the others, and finally prepare a single synthesis of the entire series of cases.

Unfortunately, class assignments and library research techniques seldom permit that luxury. As a more practical procedure, you should prepare a synthesis for each case brief in a series beginning with the second case. Each succeeding synthesis will reflect the addition of a case to the group of cases among which you can make comparisons, thus adding new insights to previous syntheses.

III. Summary

In preparing a case brief, follow these steps:

1. Thoroughly read the entire case at least once.
2. Identify the case. Include details that help identify the case's place in the overall case law of the jurisdiction and the case's value as precedent.
3. State the issue and the holding as narrowly as possible without making your question cumbersome and unwieldy; tailor your statement of the issue to the facts.
4. Summarize the material facts and the helpful background facts.
5. Summarize the procedural history, including the dispositions in the trial court and on appeal.
6. Summarize the reasoning of the court. Distinguish holding from dictum. Identify general rules recognized by the court and pay particular attention to the authority, policy analysis, and logic on which the court relies.
7. Critically evaluate the court's holding and reasoning.
8. Synthesize the case with others that present the same or a similar issue. Attempt to explain apparently conflicting results among the cases.

---

33. Karl N. Llewellyn, THE BRAMBLE BUSH 55 (10th prtg. 1996).

Exercise 7-1

1. Case Brief

Using the techniques described in this chapter, read the following excerpt of the appellate opinion in *White v. Benkowski* and prepare a case brief. The footnotes in this excerpt are taken from the opinion without revision and do not reflect current uniform citation style, so please do not emulate the opinion's citation form in your office memoranda. Additionally, do not be satisfied with the court's statement of the issue; try to improve it. Critically evaluate the court's holding and dicta regarding the availability of punitive damages; ask yourself whether you can defend the court's views on the grounds of economic efficiency, certainty in legal rules, equity in individual cases, the proper roles of compensation and deterrence, or any other policy considerations. You should not yet attempt to synthesize this case with any others, although you may comment on possible extensions or limitations to its holding that subsequent cases could introduce. After completing your case brief, compare it with the sample set forth in Exercise 7-1.2 below.

WHITE v. BENKOWSKI
Supreme Court of Wisconsin
37 Wis. 2d 285, 155 N.W.2d 74 (1967)

This case involves a neighborhood squabble between two adjacent property owners.

Prior to November 28, 1962, Virgil and Gwynneth White, the plaintiffs, were desirous of purchasing a home in Oak Creek. Unfortunately, the particular home that the Whites were interested in was without a water supply. Despite this fact, the Whites purchased the home.

The adjacent home was owned and occupied by Paul and Ruth Benkowski, the defendants. The Benkowskis had a well in their yard which had piping that connected with the Whites' home.

On November 28, 1962, the Whites and Benkowskis entered into a written agreement wherein the Benkowskis promised to supply water to the Whites' home for 10 years or until an earlier date when either water was supplied by the municipality, the well became inadequate, or the Whites drilled their own well. The Whites promised to pay $3 a month for the water and one-half the cost of any future repairs or maintenance that the Benkowski well might require. As part of the transaction, but not included in the written agreement, the Whites gave the Benkowskis $400 which was used to purchase and install a new pump and an additional tank that would increase the capacity of the well.

Initially, the relationship between the new neighbors was friendly. With the passing of time, however, their friendship deteriorated and the neighbors actually became hostile. In 1964, the water supply, which was controlled by the Benkowskis, was intermittently shut off. Mrs. White kept a record of the dates and durations that her water supply was not operative. Her record showed that the water was shut off on the following occasions:

(1) March 5, 1964, from 7:10 P.M. to 7:25 p.m.
(2) March 9, 1964, from 3:40 P.M. to 4:00 p.m.
(3) March 11, 1964, from 6:00 P.M. to 6:15 p.m.
(4) June 10, 1964, from 6:20 P.M. to 7:03 p.m.

The record also discloses that the water was shut off completely or partially for varying lengths of time on July 1, 6, 7, and 17, 1964, and on November 25, 1964.

Mr. Benkowski claimed that the water was shut off either to allow accumulated sand in the pipes to settle or to remind the Whites that their use of the water was excessive. Mr. White claimed that the Benkowskis breached their contract by shutting off the water.

Following the date when the water was last shut off (November 25, 1964), the Whites commenced an action to recover compensatory and punitive damages for an alleged violation of the agreement to supply water. . . .

The jury returned a verdict which found that the Benkowskis maliciously shut off the Whites' water supply for harassment purposes. Compensatory damages were set at $10 and punitive damages at $2,000. On motions after verdict, the court reduced the compensatory award to $1 and granted defendants' motion to strike the punitive-damage question and answer.

Judgment for plaintiffs of $1 was entered and they appeal.

WILKIE, Justice.

Two issues are raised on this appeal. . . .

2. Are punitive damages available in actions for breach of contract?

. . . .

Punitive Damages

"If a man shall steal an ox, or a sheep, and kill it, or sell it; he shall restore five oxen for an ox, and four sheep for a sheep."[3]

Over one hundred years ago this court held that, under proper circumstances, a plaintiff was entitled to recover . . . punitive damages.[4]

Kink v. Combs[5] is the most recent case in this state which deals with the practice of permitting punitive damages. In *Kink* the court relied on *Fuchs v. Kupper*[6] and reaffirmed its adherence to the rule of punitive damages.

3. Exodus 22:1.
4. McWilliams v. Bragg (1854), 3 Wis. 377 (*424).
5. (1965), 28 Wis. 2d 65, 135 N.W.2d 789.
6. (1963), 22 Wis. 2d 107, 125 N.W.2d 360.

In Wisconsin compensatory damages are given to make whole the damage or injury suffered by the injured party.[7] On the other hand, punitive damages are given

> . . . on the basis of punishment to the injured party not because he has been injured, which injury has been compensated with compensatory damages, but to punish the wrongdoer for his malice and to deter others from like conduct.[8]

Thus we reach the question of whether the plaintiffs are entitled to punitive damages for a breach of the water agreement. The overwhelming weight of authority supports the proposition that punitive damages are not recoverable in actions for breach of contract.[9] In *Chitty on Contracts*, the author states that the right to receive punitive damages for breach of contract is now confined to the single case of damages for breach of a promise to marry.[10]

Simpson states:

> Although damages in excess of compensation for loss are in some instances permitted in tort actions by way of punishment . . . in contract actions the damages recoverable are limited to compensation for pecuniary loss sustained by the breach.[11]

Corbin states that as a general rule punitive damages are not recoverable for breach of contract.[12]

In Wisconsin, the early case of Gordon v. Brewster[13] involved the breach of an employment contract. The trial court instructed the jury that if the nonperformance of the contract was attributable to the defendant's wrongful act of discharging the plaintiff, then that would go to increase the damages sustained. On appeal, this court said that the instruction was unfortunate and might have led the jurors to suppose that they could give something more than actual compensation in a breach of contract case. We find no Wisconsin case in which breach of contract (other than breach of promise to marry)[14] has led to the award of punitive damages.

Persuasive authority from other jurisdictions supports the proposition (without exception) that punitive damages are not available in breach of contract actions.[15] This is true even if the breach, as in the instant case, is willful.[16]

---

7. Malco, Inc. v. Midwest Aluminum Sales (1961), 14 Wis. 2d 57, 66, 109 N.W.2d 516, 521.

8. *Id.*

9. Annot. (1933), 84 A.L.R. 1345, 1346.

10. 1 Chitty, Contracts (22d ed. 1961), p.1339.

11. Simpson, Contracts (2d ed. hornbook series), p.394, sec. 195.

12. 5 Corbin, Contracts, p.438, sec. 1077.

13. (1858), 7 Wis. 309 (*355).

14. Simpson v. Black (1870), 27 Wis. 206.

15. White, Inc. v. Metropolitan Merchandise Mart (1954), 48 Del. 526, 9 Terry 526, 107 A.2d 892; Thompson v. Mutual Ben. Health & Acc. Ass'n of Omaha, Neb. (D.C. Iowa 1949), 83 F. Supp. 656; Cain v. Tuten (1950), 82 Ga. App. 102, 60 S.E.2d 485; Mabery v. Western Casualty & Surety Co. (1952), 173 Kan. 586, 250 P.2d 824; Bland v. Smith (1955), 197 Tenn. 683, 277 S.W.2d 377; 49 A.L.R.2d 1212.

16. McDonough v. Zamora (Tex. Civ. App. 1960), 338 S.W.2d 507; Holt v. Holt (Tex. Civ. App. 1954), 271 S.W.2d 477; Chelini v. Nieri (Cal. App. 1948), 188 P.2d 564.

Although it is well recognized that breach of a contractual duty may be a tort,[17] in such situations the contract creates the relation out of which grows the duty to use care in the performance of a responsibility prescribed by the contract.[18] Not so here. No tort was pleaded or proved.

Reversed in part by reinstating the jury verdict relating to compensatory damages and otherwise affirmed.

2. Sample Case Brief

Compare the case brief that you prepared in Exercise 7-1.1 with the following sample. Remember that the sample is only an example of a reasonable reaction to the opinion; it is not necessarily the best interpretation and evaluation of the opinion, and it certainly is not the only reasonable one. In particular, the "evaluation" is a matter of individual opinion.

White v. Benkowski, 37 Wis. 2d 285, 155 N.W.2d 74 (1967), CB 12.

Issue and Holding: Is Buyer entitled to an award of punitive damages for Supplier's malicious breach of a contract to supply water, even though Buyer established no independent tort? No.

Facts: The Whites (Buyer) and Benkowskis (Supplier) are neighbors. By written agreement Supplier promised to supply Buyer's house with water from Supplier's well for 10 years, unless the well became inadequate or unnecessary. The relationship deteriorated, and Supplier maliciously shut off Buyer's water supply partially or completely on nine occasions for the purpose of harassing Buyer.

Procedural History: Buyer sued Supplier for compensatory and punitive damages, alleging only breach of contract. On a finding of malicious breach of contract, the jury awarded Buyer $10 in compensatory damages and $2,000 in punitive damages. On motions after verdict, the trial court disallowed punitive damages and reduced the compensatory damage award from $10 to $1. Buyer appealed. The appellate court reversed the trial court's reduction of the award for compensatory damages, but it affirmed the trial court's elimination of the award for punitive damages.

Reasoning: Prior Wisconsin case law, persuasive authority from other jurisdictions, and the views of commentators support the following common law principle: Even an intentional and malicious breach of contract will not support an award of punitive damages. In dictum, the court suggests that punitive damages could be awarded if the breach of contract also constituted an independent tort; however, Buyer failed to plead and prove an independent tort. The court did not explicitly overrule a nineteenth century decision in which it had approved punitive damages for breach of a marriage contract, thus leaving open the question of whether the court will retain that exception and distinguish it from breaches of more ordinary contracts.

---

17. Colton v. Foulkes (1951), 259 Wis. 142, 47 N.W. 2d 901; Presser v. Siesel Construction Co. (1963), 19 Wis. 2d 54, 119 N.W. 2d 405; Peterson v. Sinclair Refining Co. (1963), 20 Wis. 2d 576, 123 N.W. 2d 479.

18. 38 Am. Jur., Negligence, p. 661, sec. 20.

Evaluation: In light of the maliciousness of Supplier's behavior, I think this decision is too restrictive. To deter such egregious conduct, I would allow punitive damages on a contract claim if the breaching party breached for the purpose of maliciously injuring the other party rather than to reallocate its resources to a more profitable and efficient use.

3. Case Briefs with Synthesis

Contracts are formed through a process of offer and acceptance. An offer is an expression of a willingness to enter into a contract. It gives to the party to whom it is addressed, the "offeree," the power to create the contract by assenting to the offer in a manner authorized by the offer. To constitute an offer, an expression must lead a reasonable person in the position of the offeree to understand that she has such power.

With that background, prepare a case brief for each of the following two cases. End the second case brief with a synthesis of the two cases. As with Exercise 7-1.1 above, do not assume that all the citations in these opinions are consistent with the current uniform citation style that you should use in your office memoranda.

For additional practice in synthesizing cases, perform Assignment 1 in Appendix III.

CRAFT v. ELDER & JOHNSTON CO.
Ohio Court of Appeals
38 N.E.2d 416 (Ohio Ct. App. 1941)

Barnes, Judge. . . .

. . . On or about January 31, 1940, the defendant, the Elder & Johnston Company, carried an advertisement in the Dayton Shopping News, an offer for sale of a certain all electric sewing machine for the sum of $26 as a "Thursday Only Special." Plaintiff . . . alleges that the above publication is an advertising paper distributed in Montgomery County and throughout the city of Dayton; that on Thursday, February 1, 1940, she tendered to the defendant company $26 in payment for one of the machines offered in the advertisement, but that defendant refused to fulfill the offer and has continued to so refuse. The petition further alleges that the value of the machine offered was $175 and she asks damages in the sum of $149 plus interest from February 1, 1940. . . .

The trial court dismissed plaintiff's petition as evidenced by a journal entry, the pertinent portion of which reads as follows: "Upon consideration the court finds that said advertisement was not an offer which could be accepted by plaintiff to form a contract, and this case is therefore dismissed with prejudice to a new action, at costs of plaintiff." . . .

We will now briefly make reference to some of the authorities. "It is clear that in the absence of special circumstances an ordinary newspaper advertisement is not an offer, but is an offer to negotiate—an offer to receive offers—or, as it is sometimes called, an offer to chaffer." Restatement of the Law of Contracts, Par. 25, Page 31.

Under the above paragraph the following illustration is given, "'A,' a clothing merchant, advertises overcoats of a certain kind for sale at $50. This is not an offer but an invitation to the public to come and purchase."

"Thus, if goods are advertised for sale at a certain price, it is not an offer and no contract is formed by the statement of an intending purchaser that he will take a specified quantity of the goods at that price. The construction is rather favored that such an advertisement is a mere invitation to enter into a bargain rather than an offer. So a published price list is not an offer to sell the goods listed at the published price." Williston on Contracts, Revised Edition, Vol. 1, Par. 27, Page 54.

"The commonest example of offers meant to open negotiations and to call forth offers in the technical sense are advertisements, circulars and trade letters sent out by business houses. While it is possible that the offers made by such means may be in such form as to become contracts, they are often merely expressions of a willingness to negotiate." Page on the Law of Contracts, 2d Ed., Vol. 1, Page 112, Par. 84. . . .

"But generally a newspaper advertisement or circular couched in general language and proper to be sent to all persons interested in a particular trade or business, or a prospectus of a general and descriptive nature, will be construed as an invitation to make an offer." 17 Corpus Juris Secundum, Contracts, Page 389, §46, Column 2. . . .

We are constrained to the view that the trial court committed no prejudicial error in dismissing plaintiff's petition.

The judgment of the trial court will be affirmed and costs adjudged against the plaintiff-appellant.

Entry may be prepared in accordance with this opinion.

Geiger, P.J., and Hornbeck, J., concur.

LEFKOWITZ v. GREAT MINNEAPOLIS SURPLUS STORE
Minnesota Supreme Court
251 Minn. 188, 86 N.W.2d 689 (1957)

Murphy, Justice

This is an appeal from an order of the Municipal Court of Minneapolis. . . . The order for judgment awarded the plaintiff the sum of $138.50 as damages for breach of contract.

This case grows out of the alleged refusal of the defendant to sell to the plaintiff a certain fur piece which it had offered for sale in a newspaper advertisement. It appears from the record that . . . the defendant published the following advertisement in a Minneapolis newspaper:

. . . .

Saturday 9 A.M.

. . . .

1 Black Lapin Stole
Beautiful,
worth $139.50 . . . $1.00
First Come
First Served

The record supports the findings of the court that on . . . the Saturday[ ] following the publication of the above-described ad[ ] the plaintiff was the first to present himself at the appropriate counter in the defendant's store and . . . demanded the . . . stole so advertised and indicated his readiness to pay the sale price of $1. . . . [T]he defendant refused to sell the merchandise to the plaintiff. . . .

The defendant relies principally on *Craft v. Elder & Johnston Co.* . . . On the facts before us we are concerned with whether the advertisement constituted an offer, and, if so, whether the plaintiff's conduct constituted an acceptance.

There are numerous authorities which hold that a particular advertisement in a newspaper or circular letter relating to a sale of articles may be construed by the court as constituting an offer, acceptance of which would complete a contract. [citations omitted]. . . .

The authorities above cited emphasize that, where the offer is clear, definite, and explicit, and leaves nothing open for negotiation, it constitutes an offer, acceptance of which will complete the contract. The most recent case on the subject is *Johnson v. Capital City Ford Co.*, La. App., 85 So. 2d 75, in which the court pointed out that a newspaper advertisement relating to the purchase and sale of automobiles may constitute an offer, acceptance of which will consummate a contract and create an obligation in the offeror to perform according to the terms of the published offer.

Whether in any individual instance a newspaper advertisement is an offer rather than an invitation to make an offer depends on the legal intention of the parties and the surrounding circumstances. Annotation, 157 A.L.R. 744, 751; 77 C.J.S., Sales, §25b; 17 C.J.S., Contracts, §389. We are of the view on the facts before us that the offer by the defendant of the sale of the Lapin fur was clear, definite, and explicit, and left nothing open for negotiation. The plaintiff having successfully managed to be the first one to appear at the seller's place of business to be served, as requested by the advertisement, and having offered the stated purchase price of the article, he was entitled to performance on the part of the defendant. . . .

Affirmed.

Chapter 8

Reorganization, Summary, and Inductive Reasoning in Outline Form

I. Reorganization—Mapping the Forest

Whether preparing for final examinations or preparing to write a legal memorandum, a law student or an attorney must make a significant transition from analysis of individual cases to the final expression of a completed legal analysis. In making that transition, the student or attorney begins by synthesizing the cases, as discussed in Chapter 7. She continues the transition by further analyzing and reorganizing the information in her library or class notes, eventually producing an outline that is organized around issues and legal principles rather than around individual cases.

An attorney or summer associate researching and analyzing a simple problem may not need to reorganize her modest library notes before expressing her analysis in a short memorandum or brief. On the other hand, long hours of researching a complex, multiple-issue problem may produce a mass of disorganized notes dealing with several issues and lines of authority. In those circumstances, the researching attorney may need to summarize and

143

reorganize her notes before writing or even outlining the memorandum, and perhaps even before completely analyzing the problem.

Attorneys increasingly type their research notes on computers or hand-held electronic devices, supplemented by copying and pasting text from electronic sources. Nonetheless, simple graphics showing a more traditional form of note taking can serve to illustrate the process of reorganization. Let's begin by assuming that an attorney is taking library notes by hand on note cards and is limiting the notes on each card to discussion of a single statute, case, or other authority. Indeed, if a single case separately discusses more than one issue relating to the assignment, our hypothetical researcher is noting the discussion of each issue on a separate note card:

The researching attorney can use these cards to help her prepare an outline of the fruits of her research. As an initial step, she can devise categories for the note cards that identify distinct legal issues and can assign each card to one of the groups:

If the attorney has used a note pad or a word processing file, rather than note cards, she may wish to prepare an index of the cases, and perhaps even of distinct issues within a case, by assigning consecutive numbers to her case briefs:

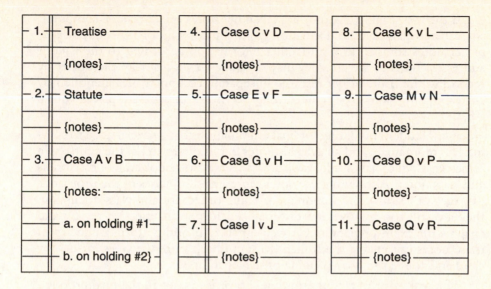

When reorganizing the product of her research in an outline, she can refer to her notes on a case or other authority by its number on the note pad or word processing file:

With either technique, the associate can more easily analyze her notes because she has divided them into manageable portions, each of which relates to a distinct legal problem. Moreover, the graphics above illustrate a theme of reorganization that runs throughout this chapter and sections of this book on case synthesis: Although you may initially digest the law of a dispute in the context of individual cases, encountered one at a time, your final analysis should be organized around issues, topics, themes, and syntheses of groups of cases, rather than around individual cases.

If the researching attorney has taken her notes on a portable computer, she can reorganize the information easily, by copying or moving passages in her notes so as to group together information according to the issue it addresses. Indeed, the attorney may organize her notes from the outset by recording the fruits of her research in separate computer files identified by corresponding issues, or by recording her notes in separate places within a file.

A law student preparing for final examinations has a special need to summarize, reorganize, and analyze his notes in outline form. In the course of a semester, a typical law student will amass several notebooks full of case briefs and class notes. Although these notes represent summaries of the thousands of pages of reading and hundreds of hours of lecture and class discussion, they are still too massive and disorganized to permit effective review and analysis for exam preparation. A well-organized, outline-form summary of these notes can enable the student to stand back from the trees formed by cases and to see the broad outline of the legal forest.

The real value of a course outline, however, is not in the final product, but in the processes of reviewing and synthesizing material and of drafting the outline. These tasks develop important skills of organization, analysis, and expression. A method of reasoning essential to the entire process of outlining is inductive reasoning.

II. Inductive Reasoning

Through two variations of inductive reasoning, you can use information from a series of specific cases to reach a conclusion about either

1. the outcome of another specific case, or
2. the likelihood of the truth of a general proposition.[1]

A. Analogy

Analogizing is the process of using inductive reasoning to predict the outcome of a specific case by comparing it to other cases. For example, a series of cases has permitted warrantless searches of automobiles and similar vehicles, if the searches were supported by probable cause, because (1) the mobility of the vehicles created exigent circumstances that made it impracticable to obtain a warrant before searching, and (2) the owner of each vehicle had only limited expectations of privacy in its contents because the vehicle was subject to extensive administrative regulation. From those cases, you could use inductive reasoning to argue that police may search a motor home without a warrant because (1) the motor home is similar in mobility to the vehicles that were the subjects of the prior cases, and (2) government

---

1. *See, e.g.*, Irving M. Copi, INTRODUCTION TO LOGIC 12-15, 442-47 (12th ed. 2005).

regulation of all licensed motor vehicles gives the owner of the motor home reduced expectations of privacy similar to those of the owners of the vehicles in the prior cases:

Four cases permitted warrantless searches of the following kinds of vehicles, because each vehicle was mobile and subject to administrative regulation:

Case #1:   car on highway
Case #2:   delivery truck in a private driveway
Case #3:   family van in a shopping center parking lot
Case #4:   four-wheel drive truck on unpaved desert

One reasonable conclusion from the prior cases:

In Case #5, a warrant should not be required to search a motor home parked on the street in a residential neighborhood, because it is mobile and subject to administrative regulation, as were the vehicles in Cases 1-4.

As with all inductive reasoning, this conclusion about the motor home does not necessarily follow from the outcomes of the previous cases. Rather, the strength of the supporting cases simply makes the truth of the conclusion more or less likely. Indeed, opposing counsel might argue that government regulation of licensed vehicles is less significant to the scope of privacy expectations than is the range and nature of activities for which a vehicle is designed. If that argument were accepted, she might use inductive reasoning to draw an analogy to a different series of cases, each of which held that police could not search a house, apartment, or other dwelling without a warrant even if they had probable cause to search. From those cases, a court could conclude that the occupant of a motor home would enjoy protection from warrantless searches similar to that enjoyed by the occupant of a house, because each structure is designed for residential uses such as sleeping, eating, and storing personal effects:

Four cases required a warrant to search the following kinds of dwellings, partly because the expectation of privacy in the contents of dwellings is so high:

Case #1:   unattached house on its own lot
Case #2:   rented unit of apartment complex
Case #3:   weekend cabin in the mountains
Case #4:   natural cave on private land used as a dwelling

One reasonable conclusion from the prior cases:

In Case #5, a warrant should be required to search a motor home parked on the street in a residential neighborhood, because it is used as a dwelling during vacation travel and contains the kinds of personal items normally stored in a fixed dwelling.

Thus, depending on the relative weight that a court assigned to competing factors and values, it would find one of the two competing lines of authority to present the stronger analogy to the current case. This flexibility in inductive reasoning explains why judges can reasonably differ on the proper application and extension of precedent.[2]

B. Generalizing from Particulars

The second variation of inductive reasoning allows you to construct a general proposition from specific cases. By using this process to prepare a course outline, you can begin making the transition from daily briefing of cases to solving problems on a final examination. With this type of reasoning, you attempt to construct a general rule that is consistent with the facts and outcomes of past cases. You can then apply the general rule to other cases with similar facts.

For example, you may have briefed four cases in which courts denied punitive damages on claims for various breaches of contract: innocent breach of a construction contract, intentional breach of a contract for the sale of real estate, malicious breach of a contract to supply water from a private well, and intentional breach of a lease. Although a universal rule would not necessarily follow from the cases, you could reasonably induce a general rule that punitive damages are not available for breach of contract. You could then apply that rule to a new case, such as the intentional breach of the confidentiality obligations in a settlement agreement. The new case is not identical to any of the prior cases but is nonetheless encompassed by the general rule derived from the prior cases through inductive reasoning:

Four cases denied punitive damages for the following kinds of breach of contract:

Case #1: innocent breach of a construction contract
Case #2: intentional breach of a realty contract
Case #3: malicious breach of a water-supply contract
Case #4: intentional breach of a lease

General rule derived from the prior cases:

Punitive damages are not available for breach of contract, regardless of the breaching party's state of mind.

Application of general rule to new case:

In Case #5, punitive damages will not be available for intentional breach of the confidentiality clause of a settlement contract.

---

2. *See, e.g.*, California v. Carney, 471 U.S. 386 (1985) (disagreeing with the California Supreme Court's conclusion that a warrant was required to search a motor home).

The degree of confidence that you have in the general rule will depend on the strength of the supporting cases. If one of the previous decisions had awarded punitive damages for breach of a marriage contract, the general rule stated above would be a less reliable guide, and you would apply the rule with caution. You could improve the reliability of the rule by modifying it to achieve consistency with all the previous cases: Punitive damages are not available for breach of contract, except for breach of marriage contracts.

Alternatively, the case law might present a consistent pattern under the common law but could be subject to legislation that permits an award of treble damages for an employer's bad faith withholding of wages earned by an employee or for a landlord's bad faith refusal to return a tenant's security deposit. In that event, your common law rule could be stated with some certainty, but with statutory exceptions: Punitive damages are not available for breach contract, except for statutory treble damages for bad faith breach of contractual obligations to pay wages earned by an employee or to return a tenant's security deposit.

Exercise 8-1

Imagine that a parent, Katherine, is developing rules governing the social activities of her teenage daughter, Lina, who is a senior in high school. Katherine has not articulated a comprehensive set of rules in the style of a statute or set of administrative regulations. Instead, Katherine provides guidance by admonishing Lina when she disapproves of Lina's actions and by expressing satisfaction when she approves, just as a court might develop the law incrementally by deciding disputes one case at a time.

In each of the following four "cases," put yourself in Lina's place by examining the facts, Katherine's statements, and Katherine's apparent or stated concerns. Then identify one or more reasonable interpretations of the "holding" of each case and translate it into a rule or set of rules that will govern Lina's future behavior.

Specifically, first determine the "ruling" in each case by determining whether Lina has apparently met or disappointed Katherine's expectations. Then, try to determine the "holding" of each case by identifying the facts that seem to be important to Katherine's ruling. Finally, engage in an ongoing process of "synthesis," by comparing each new holding to previous ones. Through this comparison, and by using inductive reasoning to generalize from specific cases, try to infer a rule or set of rules that will apply to Lina's future actions. This rule should evolve as more cases are added to your ongoing synthesis.

Is the first case ambiguous, inviting a number of reasonable arguments about the factual basis for Katherine's disapproval? If so, does its holding become clearer as you synthesize it with the second case? How does the third case add a second rule, or a second branch to the rule? How do you reconcile the fourth case with the previous ones?

1. Case #1: The Pizza Hideout

On the first Friday night of the school year, Lina and Lynn, two seniors in high school, went to JJ's Pizza after their school's first football game of the season. They ate and talked until 11 P.M.; indeed, Lina was so engaged in conversation that she didn't answer a call to her cell phone from her mother, Katherine. When Lina walked into her house shortly after 11 P.M., she and Katherine had the following exchange:

Katherine:	"Lina, where have you been? The game ended at 9:30, and you're coming home after 11."
Lina:	"Well, some of us went to JJ's afterwards for pizza."
Katherine:	"So you were at JJ's! And you didn't answer your cell phone!"
Lina:	"Sorry."
Katherine:	"Well, being sorry is not good enough. You're not going out for the rest of the weekend."

2. Case #2: Pizza Reprise

On the second Friday night of the school year, Lina attended the second football game and again went to JJ's afterwards for pizza. Before entering JJ's, Lina called her mother, Katherine, from the parking lot and informed Katherine of her plans. In response, Katherine wished Lina a good time and reminded her to drive carefully. When Lina entered her home shortly after 11 P.M., she had the following exchange with Katherine:

Katherine:	"Did you have a good time?"
Lina:	"We lost the football game, but the pizza was good."
Katherine:	{hugging Lina} "Good. Well, goodnight."

3. Case #3: Closing Out JJ's

On the third Friday night of the school year, Lina attended the football game with Lynn and watched her school's team win for the first time this season. After Lina notified Katherine by cell phone that she planned to go to JJ's for pizza, Lina and Lynn celebrated by eating and talking at JJ's until JJ's closed at midnight. When Lina entered her home shortly after midnight, she and Katherine had the following exchange:

Katherine:	{angrily} "Lina, it's after midnight!"
Lina:	"I told you we were going to JJ's afterwards."
Katherine:	{firmly} "It's good that you called me, but it's after midnight now. I need to draw the line somewhere."
Lina:	"So you mean I can't stay out past midnight? Why? Why do you care? Why do we have to set rules and limits like this? I always do my homework, and I get straight As."

Katherine: "Yes, I'm really proud of you. But I care what you do at night. I worry about your safety, and I want you to get enough sleep and stay healthy. That's why I have rules. Now goodnight."

4. Case #4: The Obligatory Wedding Reception

On the Saturday night of the fourth week of the school year, Lina accompanied her mother to a relative's wedding and reception. When they entered the house after midnight, they had the following exchange:

Lina: {wearily} "I can't believe you made me stay at your nephew's wedding all night; I was so bored."

Katherine: "Hey, John is your cousin, too. And we had a blast on the dance floor, dancing to those old tunes."

Lina: {complaining} "Yeah, I know. You even talked to everybody after the band stopped playing. And it's after midnight! We have to go to church tomorrow morning."

Katherine: "Yes, I know, but this was an important family event. Thank you for staying up late with me."

C. Relationship to Deductive Reasoning

Both forms of inductive reasoning described in Sections I.A and I.B above can be applied to the broad framework of deductive reasoning described in Chapter 6. In that framework, after identifying an issue, you state the applicable rule and apply it to the relevant facts to reach a conclusion:

Issue
Rule   {Major Premise}
Application to Facts   {Minor Premise}
Conclusion

1. Formulating the Rule

The process of synthesizing cases was introduced in Chapter 7, Section II.B.7. Further, the discussion of inductive reasoning that immediately precedes this section provides a fuller explanation and extension of one form of synthesis. You can use inductive reasoning to construct a general rule from a series of cases; in turn, you can use that rule to form the major premise of your deductive analysis, as discussed in Chapter 6. In an office memorandum or a brief, you could represent this process comprehensively in several paragraphs or pages of in-depth analysis of case law that shows how you arrived at your understanding of the current form of a developing legal principle. The discussion of law in the first sample memorandum toward the end of Chapter 11 illustrates moderately in-depth analysis.

Alternatively, you could state the rule as a simple proposition in a single sentence, followed by citation to the authority or authorities from which you derived the rule:

A purported promise does not satisfy the consideration requirement if it allows the promisor to refrain from performing at his unfettered whim or discretion. *See Strong v. Sheffield*, 144 N.Y. 392, 39 N.E. 330 (1895).

Because of time limitations and other constraints, when you state a rule in an examination answer, you will tend toward this simpler example in most classes, citing to authority only if your professor expects citations in exam answers and awards points for it.

2. Applying the Rule to the Facts

To help you apply the legal rule to the facts of your dispute, you can invoke the inductive process of analogizing between the facts of previous cases and the facts of your own case. In an office memorandum or brief, you may represent this process comprehensively in several paragraphs or pages in which you compare the facts and reasoning of previous cases to the facts of your own case. Again, the fact analysis in the first sample memorandum toward the end of Chapter 11 illustrates such explicit analogy and distinction.

Alternatively, you could analyze the facts more simply by directly explaining why the facts of your case do not satisfy the legal rule:

In this case, the lender's promise to forbear until he "needs" the money appears to condition the length of his forbearance on financial events that are at least partly outside his control. As long as his income and expenses create no need for the money, the lender arguably has committed to forbear from demanding payment. If so, the lender's promise satisfies the consideration requirement, and the guarantor's promise is enforceable.

As with the statement of the legal rule, your fact analysis in an exam answer will often tend toward this simpler example, although supplemented with factual arguments for the other side whenever possible. In developing even a simple fact analysis, however, you often will mentally compare the facts of your case with the facts and reasoning of the cases that you have earlier analyzed. Thus, although you will not always have time during an examination to express the details of your comparison, the inductive process of analogizing and distinguishing cases nonetheless informs your fact analysis.

3. Role of the Course Outline

By preparing a course outline, you can use inductive reasoning to derive general rules from particular cases and to compare and contrast the facts of those cases. This process will help bridge the gap between your case briefs and the deductive analysis called for in a law school examination.

As discussed more fully below, your outline should be organized around general legal rules, some of which you have constructed through inductive reasoning from groups of cases. These are rules that you can later recall and restate in an examination answer.

Moreover, your outline should illustrate these rules with brief summaries of the cases from which you derived the rules. Your familiarity with the facts and reasoning of these cases will help you apply the general rules to the facts of your examination questions, even if you do not always have time during the examination to fully express your process of analogizing and distinguishing cases.

III. Techniques of Outlining Course Materials

To transform your case briefs and class notes to a useful outline, you must reorganize, analyze, and summarize. The finished product will be an infinitely more useful study guide than your original notes, but the real value of a course outline is in the process of constructing it. Expressing your understanding of the law in outline form forces you to identify and resolve lingering areas of confusion that a less rigorous form of review might conceal. Moreover, outlining develops skills of organization and expression that you must summon and apply in the examination room and the law office. A commercial outline might contain information that you can understand and even remember, but it does not provide an effective means of developing critical skills, and it will not be tailored to your professor's choices regarding coverage and emphasis.

A. Fundamental Principles of Outlining

The format for a course outline is largely a matter of personal style. The techniques described in this chapter are not the only ones that you might find helpful. These techniques, however, will help you develop skills that can be readily employed in drafting office memoranda and briefs, as well as exam answers. These outlining techniques require you to

1. classify cases to facilitate a reorganization around general legal principles rather than individual cases, and
2. display the proper relationships among points in the outline.

1. Classification

Your course outline should not simply present a series of case brief summaries. Instead, it should emphasize general rules of law and should subordinate the cases to the role of illustrating the rules.

a. Topics and Subtopics

The first step in organizing a course outline is to classify the kinds of problems or rules addressed in the case briefs and class notes and to recognize which kinds of problems are subsets of more general topics. Depending on the volume and complexity of the material, you may identify several levels of problem areas or principles. If so, the most logical way to proceed is first to identify the classifications that have the broadest scope, and then to identify the subsidiary classifications that form subsets of the major classifications.

For example, an outline of legal remedies might encompass two broad categories of relief: (1) specific relief, in the form of an injunction to require a party to engage in, or refrain from, an act, and (2) substitutional relief, or money damages. Within each of those two major topics, the course material would undoubtedly present subsidiary problem areas, each of which encompasses another set of subsidiary problem areas, and so on. The following sequence of headings traces a single, descending line of such classifications leading to the topic of the availability of punitive damages in tort and contract actions.

I. Specific Relief
• • • •

II. Substitutional Relief—Money Damages
   A. Nominal Damages
   • • • •
   B. Compensatory Damages
   • • • •
   C. Punitive Damages
      1. Purpose and Measure
      • • • •
      2. Availability
         a. Torts
      • • • •
         b. Contracts
   • • • •

Each of the classifications in this outline identifies a subset of the area of law encompassed by the subject of remedies and identifies the subject matter of disputes that have required the application of legal rules to facts. Moreover, each major classification in the outline first addresses a topic at the most general level and then separately examines more specific problems within the topic.

b. Transitions and Overviews

To clearly signal the organizational procession from the general to the specific, you may wish to begin each significant section and subsection with a brief paragraph or a separate introductory section that presents an overview of the subsections that follow:

I. Overview

   A successful claimant may be entitled to either or both of two kinds
of relief: (1) specific relief, in the form of an injunction that orders the
defendant to take, or refrain from taking, some action; (2) substitutional
relief, in the form of an award of money damages.

II. Specific/Injunctive Relief
• • • •

III. Substitutional Relief

   Depending on the circumstances, courts may award any of three
kinds of money damages: nominal, compensatory, or punitive.

A. Nominal Damages
• • • •

B. Compensatory Damages
• • • •

C. Punitive Damages
• • • •

c. Revealing Comprehension or Confusion About Relationships Between Points

By displaying the proper relationships between points in your outline,
you demonstrate a full understanding of its analytic content. For example,
the excerpts presented above accurately identify some topics as subsets of
more general topics.

Conversely, the topic and subtopic headings of an outline may reveal
confusion that the author will need to clear up. For example, the following outline erroneously classifies compensatory damages as an element of
specific relief. It also misleadingly suggests that the topics of the availability
and measure of punitive damages are no more closely related to one another
than either is to questions about nominal damages:

I. Specific Relief
   A. Compensatory Damages
   • • • •
II. Substitutional Relief—Money Damages
   A. Nominal Damages
   • • • •
   B. Availability of Punitive Damages
   • • • •
   C. Measure of Punitive Damages
   • • • •

If you are not sure whether your outline headings reflect a solid grasp
of the course material, you might ask a classmate or classroom instructor to
glance at them and provide you with a quick evaluation.

2. Getting Started

a. Working from a Disorganized "Laundry List"

If you have trouble starting your outline, you might set organizational considerations aside until you clearly identify the points that you later will display in logical structure. For example, you might start by glancing through your notes and the table of contents of your coursebook and by making a "laundry list" of rules or problem areas that the cases have presented:

> injunctions
> expectation interest
> nominal damages
> adequacy of remedy at law
> compensatory damages
> mitigation of damages
> punitive damages
> unique goods
> specific performance of personal services

Once you have identified the topics that you want to address, you can classify the problems presented in the list and can determine their proper relationships to one another.

b. Illustration: Everything in Its Place

When they were young, my two sons used a remarkably similar process when they cleaned their playroom. Scattered throughout the room were stuffed animals and dolls, fiction and nonfiction books, and toy dinosaurs and cars. They knew that the stuffed animals and dolls belonged on the window box, the dinosaurs belonged in the red toy bin, the cars belonged in a special box, and the books belonged on one of two shelves. Their nonfiction reference books, such as those on science and nature, belonged on a shelf in their bedroom closet. All other books were stored between bookends on top of a bedroom dresser. When putting away these belongings, they typically waded through the scattered objects, picking out all the objects within a single category or subcategory, such as all cars, and putting them in their proper place before gathering objects from another category or subcategory. The organizational structure of their activity could be represented in the following way:

> I. Proper Places for Dolls, Toys, and Books
>   A. Dolls and Stuffed Animals
>   {together as single category on window box}
>   B. Toys
>   1. Dinosaurs
>   {red toy bin}
>   2. Cars
>   {special box}

>   C. Books
>   1. Nonfiction Reference Books
>   {bedroom closet shelf}
>   2. All Other Children's Books
>   {between bookends on dresser}

c. Special Challenges of Organizing Course Materials

Of course, my children's chore was relatively simple. Their playthings were tangible, simple, and readily distinguished from one another. Moreover, my wife and I devised the categories and the corresponding storage areas.

As a law student, however, you must work with abstract principles and must devise your own categories and subcategories. Your casebook's table of contents may provide some hints on categories and organization, but you should not hesitate to depart from it. A casebook occasionally adopts an unusual organizational structure for pedagogic purposes, and you may prefer a more straightforward structure that translates more readily to a guide for solving problems.

Organizing an outline of legal points is not an exact science. The flexibility and uncertainty inherent in the analysis of much of the material that you encounter in the first year of law school make it impossible to identify a single "correct" method of organizing an outline of that material. Nonetheless, your diligent efforts leading to a reasonable outline will develop skills of organization that you can transfer directly to more formal legal documents such as briefs, memoranda, and contracts.

B. Content of the Outline

1. Identifying, Constructing, and Stating Rules

As a means of preparing to apply general legal rules to the facts of an exam problem, you should identify or even construct legal rules from the statutes and cases you have studied. This process does not compel an unduly simplistic and mechanical approach to the law. The legal rules are simply shorthand representations of more complex sets of information that you can explore in greater detail when you refer to the case law from which the rules are drawn.

On some topics, a legislature supplies a statutory rule or a court states a general rule derived from earlier case law. Even dictum from a judicial opinion may provide a reliable guide to a tentative statement of a general rule. Although you must identify the narrow holding of a decision to evaluate the effect of the case as precedent, you may safely look to dictum for aid in constructing a general rule that you can profitably apply in an examination.

In many instances, however, you will not find concise statements of general rules in statutes or in the holdings or dicta of judicial decisions. Instead, you must identify the cases that address issues related to the topic, and you must use techniques of synthesis, such as inductive reasoning, to construct a general rule from the individual cases. To use the example presented in Section II.B above, you might study the holdings in a series of decisions denying punitive damages in different kinds of contracts cases and construct a general rule that punitive damages are not available for breach of contract, even if none of the decisions stated such a rule of general application. Indeed, your synthesis at the outline stage may lead you to revise your earlier, more tentative generalizations about a series of cases.

2. Illustrating Rules with Examples

a. Case Summaries as Examples or Exceptions to a Rule

Regardless of the method that you use to identify a general legal rule, your statement of the rule should not stand alone. You should illustrate and give more definite shape to the rule by

1. summarizing the case law from which the rule was derived and
2. identifying competing rules or exceptions to the rule:

V. Punitive Damages
  A. Purpose and Measure
  • • • •
  B. Availability
    1. Torts . . . .
  • • • •
    2. Contracts—Courts generally do not award punitive damages for breach of contract.
      a. Example: In *White v. Benkowski,* CB at 12, the court affirmed a trial court's denial of punitive damages for breach of an agreement to supply water, even though the jury found that the breaching parties acted maliciously.
      b. Exception to Rule: In dictum, the *White* court suggested that it might retain a traditional exception allowing punitive damages for breach of a marriage agreement.
      c. Minority Approach for Malicious Breaches: A very few jurisdictions have followed the lead of *Jordan v. Ash,* CB at 16, which granted punitive damages for an employer's "malicious and oppressive" breach of an employment agreement, even though the employee had not proved all the elements of an independent tort.

The concise statement of the general rule in subsection B.2 of the outline above represents the kind of information that you must recall and express on a law school examination. To apply that rule to the facts of an exam question, however, you must have a more concrete understanding of the law than is reflected in the abstract statement of the general rule. For this, you must analyze individual cases, as illustrated in subsections a, b, and c in the above example.

Subsections a and b illustrate a student's understanding of the parameters of the rule in most jurisdictions: Pursuant to a traditional exception, some courts might still award punitive damages in the case of breach of a marriage agreement; otherwise, even a finding of malice on the part of the breaching party will not cause the court to depart from the general rule against punitive damages. Subsection c reflects the student's judgment that *Jordan* represents a minority approach: In a few jurisdictions, courts might be disposed to grant punitive damages for breach of any kind of contract, if the breach is accompanied by the kind of malicious intent sometimes associated with an egregious intentional tort. By identifying the factual context of *Jordan*, the student can remain sensitive to the possibility that this minority approach is limited to employment contracts or other contracts in which the parties have disparate bargaining power.

In adding case summaries to the outline, you should retain a basic structure that organizes the subject matter around legal rules and that subordinates the cases to illustrations of those rules. For example, a case that addresses distinct issues relating to the proper measure of compensatory damages and to the availability of punitive damages might appear in summarized form in two different places in the outline: (1) a summary of the court's first holding would illustrate a rule about compensatory damages, and (2) a summary of the second holding would illustrate a rule about punitive damages stated in a different section of the outline.

b. Adding Policy Analysis

A more sophisticated outline of the same material might incorporate a policy analysis of the rule and the cases that illustrate it, perhaps reflecting the student's evaluation, as well as her synthesis, of the cases:

---

2. Contracts—Courts generally do not award punitive damages for breach of contract.

   a. Possible Policy Justifications: A breach of a private contract may not injure community interests as much as would a tort or a crime. Indeed, in some instances a breach may benefit the community economically by permitting reallocation of the freed resources to more productive uses. In many cases, compensatory damages would permit this reallocation while making the victim of the breach whole, but the risk of liability for punitive damages would discourage the reallocation.

   b. Example: In *White v. Benkowski*, CB at 12, the court affirmed denial of punitive damages for even a malicious breach of a contract to supply water. This decision doesn't seem to further any important policy, however, because the supplier did not reallocate the water to a more urgent use.

   c. Exception: In dictum, the *White* court suggested that it might retain a traditional exception allowing punitive damages for breach of a marriage agreement, because such breaches often had led to "community resentment" in the nineteenth century cases that established this exception.

　　d.　Minority Approach: In *Jordan v. Ash*, CB at 16, the court approved puni-
　　　　tive damages for an employer's "malicious and oppressive" breach of
　　　　an employment agreement, even though the employee had not proved
　　　　all the elements of an independent tort. Deterrence through punitive
　　　　damages is appropriate in such cases, because the injurious conduct
　　　　is designed to harm others rather than to reallocate resources or serve
　　　　any other business needs.

　　The policy analysis may be suggested in the opinions themselves, may
be the topic of class discussion, or may be the product of your original
analysis. In this example, subsection c does more than simply identify possible limitations to the rule. It also implicitly raises questions about the continued viability of an aging exception that arguably is rooted in outdated
values. Similarly, subsection d does more than identify a minority approach
as a different kind of qualification to the general rule. In conjunction with
subsection b, it implicitly compares the merits of maintaining certainty in a
broad rule of general application (subsection b) with the case-specific fairness achieved by narrowly shaping rules so that they apply no further than
the reasons that support them (subsection d).

　　If time permits, you may wish to consult a treatise for clarification or
for ideas that enrich your outline. However, you will develop skills best by
preparing outlines from course materials and class notes with minimum reference to study aids and with only occasional reference to respected treatises
to help clear up areas of confusion.

c. Examples on Either Side of the Line Defined by the Rule

　　Often, you can best illustrate the parameters of a rule by comparing two
factually distinguishable, legally consistent cases that reach different results.
By identifying a set of facts that satisfies the legal rule and by contrasting
them with a set of facts that does not, the outline helps to bring concrete
meaning to an otherwise abstract rule.

　　To return to an earlier example, an outline of the consideration doctrine
in a Contracts course would address the topic of illusory promises, ones that
do not satisfy the consideration requirement because—even though they are
in promissory form—they leave the promisor free to perform or not at her
whim. The best way to form a concrete understanding of this concept is to
compare the facts of cases that fall on either side of this legal line:

　　　　I.　Consideration

　　　　　　• • • •

Issue and rule　　　　　　C.　Conditional and Illusory Promises—A con-
　　　　　　ditional promise may commit the promisor and sat-
　　　　　　isfy the consideration requirement if the event on
　　　　　　which the promisor's performance is conditioned is
　　　　　　not within his complete control. In contrast, if the
　　　　　　"promise" permits the promisor to perform or not
　　　　　　according to his unrestricted whim, it is illusory and
　　　　　　does not satisfy the consideration requirement.

1. In *Atco Corp. v. Johnson*, CB at 22, a purported promise to forbear from collecting a debt until "I want my money" left any and all forbearance to the promisor's complete discretion and thus stated no commitment at all.	**Facts that amount to an illusory promise and thus do not satisfy the consideration requirement**
2. *In Bonnie v. DeLaney*, CB at 25, a buyer's promise to purchase a house unless the buyer "cannot qualify" for a specified mortgage stated a commitment that satisfied the consideration requirement, because it conditioned the buyer's performance on market factors outside the buyer's control rather than on buyer's unrestricted desire to buy or not.	**Facts that state a nonillusory promise and thus satisfy the consideration requirement**

In this outline, subsections 1 and 2 give concrete meaning to the abstract rule stated in subsection C by providing an example of facts that fail to satisfy the rule stated in subsection C for consideration (because they describe an illusory promise) and then contrasting those with facts that satisfy the consideration rule.

Exercise 8-2

1. Outlining Exercise—Rules of the House

Imagine that parents, Gerald and Janice, are teaching their toddler, Debbie, good habits and behavior. Debbie can't fully understand abstract rules, so Gerald and Janice teach her through positive or negative feedback in specific situations. Debbie remembers the following experiences for which she received praise or admonishment:

The Case of the Hand in the Cookie Jar: Debbie reached into a cookie jar and helped herself to a cookie shortly before dinner. Janice and Gerald admonished Debbie that the cookie would spoil her appetite for dinner.

The Case of the Broken Vase: Debbie climbed onto a chair, reached a vase on a table top, and threw the vase to the floor, breaking it. Janice and Gerald sent Debbie to her room, admonishing her that she should not play with her parents' possessions.

The Case of the Chocolate Ice Cream: After dinner one night, Debbie asked for some chocolate ice cream. To her surprise, her parents served her a dish of ice cream, praising her for having finished her vegetables.

The Case of the Mistreated Teddy Bear: Anxious to test her parents' limits, Debbie climbed onto a chair with her favorite teddy bear and threw the teddy bear onto the living room carpet. Debbie's parents saw this event but had no reaction; they continued reading the newspaper and watching TV.

The Case of the Bouncing Ball: Emboldened by the teddy bear incident, Debbie brought out her favorite rubber ball and began kicking it around the

162   **Part IV. Stepping Stones to Legal Memoranda**

living room, causing it to bounce off the TV set and to narrowly miss Janice's glass of wine sitting on the coffee table. Janice flashed Debbie an angry glance, and Gerald sternly said, "Outside with that ball!"

Assignment: From these cases, derive at least two general rules governing Debbie's behavior in her home. Illustrate each of your rules with brief summaries that show what kinds of behavior either satisfy or violate the rules. If appropriate, draft an overview statement that captures the essence of all the rules and examples. When you have completed your outline, compare it with the sample outline toward the end of Chapter 9.

2. Outlining Exercise—Advertisements as Offers

Review the case briefs that you prepared for Exercise 7-1(3) in Chapter 7. Prepare an excerpt of a Contracts outline that addresses the question of whether a store's newspaper advertisement amounts to an offer. Derive a general legal rule from the two cases and use summaries of the cases as illustrations of the rule.

3. Outlining Exercise—Rules for Lina

Review Exercise 8-1. From the four cases, derive rules, or several elements of a single rule, that describe limitations that Katherine imposes on Lina's social activities. Prepare an outline of this topic, organizing the outline around the rules or elements of a rule. Illustrate each statement of a rule or element of a rule with a one-sentence summary of one of the cases or with an observation of your own.

4. Advanced Outlining Exercise—UCC § 2-207

Study the following provisions of a section of the Arizona Commercial Code, based on section 2-207 of the Uniform Commercial Code.[3] Try to determine the general issue addressed by each of the three subsections, and begin an outline organized around those three issues. Next, try to identify the rules addressed within each subsection and create subsections in your outline corresponding to those rules. Fill out your outline with statements of the statutory rules at ever increasing levels of specificity, organized in a logical fashion. If you are studying this section in your Contracts course, include the holdings of cases that interpret elements of the statute, taking care to explain how the facts of those cases satisfied, or failed to satisfy, a statutory element.

> **Arizona Revised Statutes section 47-2207.** Additional terms in acceptance or confirmation
>
> A.   A definite and seasonable expression of acceptance or a written confirmation which is sent within a reasonable time operates as an acceptance even though it states terms additional to or different from those offered or agreed upon, unless acceptance is expressly made conditional on assent to the additional or different terms.

---

3. The UCC uses different subsection lettering and numbering for section 2-207, with subsections (1), (2), and (3), and further subsections (a), (b), and (c) within section (2).

    B.   The additional terms are to be construed as proposals for addition to the contract. Between merchants such terms become part of the contract unless:

       1.   The offer expressly limits acceptance to the terms of the offer;

       2.   They materially alter it; or

       3.   Notification of objection to them has already been given or is given within a reasonable time after notice of them is received.

    C.   Conduct by both parties which recognizes the existence of a contract is sufficient to establish a contract for sale although the writings of the parties do not otherwise establish a contract. In such case the terms of the particular contract consist of those terms on which the writings of the parties agree, together with any supplementary terms incorporated under any other provisions of this title.

C. The Outline as a Study Tool

Although the process of preparing an outline is more valuable than the finished product, a thoughtful outline makes an excellent study tool. When reviewing for exams, you can put your notes aside and use the brief references to cases in the outline to trigger your memory about the more expansive case analysis that you performed earlier in the semester.

In the few hours before an exam, you may want to take a broader view of the course by skimming the legal rules stated in the major sections and subsections of your outline. The factual context provided by case summaries will easily come to mind if you have previously analyzed those cases, expressed the analysis in the outline, and read the entire outline once or twice after preparing it. Indeed, you may find it helpful to prepare a brief outline of the outline by writing down the major headings of the outline on a separate sheet of paper. From this list of headings, you might develop an even shorter checklist of issues most likely to be addressed in a final examination.

D. Flowcharts

In addition to outlining the course material, you might find that you can restate some of the rules in vivid and accessible fashion with a more graphic visual aid. One popular method is tracing the decision points in a legal rule in a flowchart. In a flowchart, you can use a series of boxes and arrows to show how a multifaceted rule leads from one decision point to another, with forks leading to conclusions or more questions, depending on the answer to a question stated in the previous box.

For example, consult the outline that you prepared in Exercise 8-2.4 above. How did you describe the issue addressed in each of the three subsections to section 47-2207? A flowchart at a high level of generality, like the one that follows, can show the basic relationship between these subsections without getting bogged down in the details of this complex statute:

This basic structure of section 47-2207, accessible from a glance at the flowchart, is a valuable starting point for your study of this section. But it is only a starting point because each of these subsections presents a number of puzzles that, taken together, would fill a very complicated flowchart. Accordingly, you might be content to limit your flowchart to the basic information above and to address the details of section 2-207 in your outline. On the other hand, if you find that flowcharts are especially helpful to your understanding of complex rules, you could attempt to develop a flowchart for each of the subsections, tracing the subissues, decision points, and rules of each.[4]

IV. Summary

To outline course material, follow these steps:

1. Analyze and synthesize by briefing and comparing the cases and by reflecting on class discussion.
2. Identify topics that you intend to address in the outline. You should identify significant general rules that are stated in the course materials or that you can construct from the course materials through a process of inductive reasoning.
3. State those rules in an organized fashion that displays the proper relationships between the rules.
4. Finally, illustrate the general rules with brief summaries of the cases from which the rules are derived, showing how particular facts satisfied or failed to satisfy the rule.

---

4. For more examples of creating flowcharts, including a sample flowchart for the first subsection of UCC § 2-207, see Charles R. Calleros, LAW SCHOOL EXAMS: PREPARING AND WRITING TO WIN 74-82 (2d ed. 2013).

Exercise 8-3

This chapter, along with previous ones, has introduced you to an integrated process of case analysis, case synthesis, and reorganization of information in an outline. The next chapter addresses flexible application of deductive reasoning in applying principles to new sets of facts, such as those in examination questions.

The following exercises introduce you to these processes on a level that should require no formal training or knowledge of special legal rules. Follow the directions, use your common sense, and express your answers in simple, concise language. For practice in outlining traditional course material, perform Assignment 2 in Appendix III.

1. Case Analysis

In each of the three cases below, try to derive a lesson or a rule from the case that would help guide the central character, Han Li, in his future actions regarding speed limits on streets and highways. State this point in a simple sentence or two, including a brief statement of the probable policy justifications for the rule. If you wish, you may also briefly describe special facts that help illustrate the rule. In the second and third cases, you may also consider commenting briefly on ways in which the case compares or contrasts with the preceding case or cases.

In this exercise, do not concern yourself with the question of whether Mr. Li obeyed or violated the speed limit. Instead, focus on the facts and policies that justify the establishment of different speed limits in different settings.

In the first case analysis below, the exercise is completed as an example.

a. The Case of the School Zone

Han Li recently immigrated to the United States, enrolled in a community college in Phoenix, Arizona, and obtained a driver's license. While driving throughout the state, he carefully surveyed his surroundings so that he could quickly learn the customs and rules of driving in the United States.

When approaching an elementary school on a two-lane residential street at 8:15 on Monday morning, Li noticed dozens of children laughing and running in the schoolyard, as well as a few children walking on the sidewalk toward the school. He also noticed a sign stating "15 mph when children are present." Before Li could slow down, however, a police officer pulled him over and cited him for driving 25 miles per hour.

Sample Statement of Lesson: The speed limit in an elementary school zone in a residential neighborhood is 15 mph when children are arriving or leaving, because the risk of children running into the road is heightened at that time and place. In this case, that risk was underscored by the presence of numerous children on the playground and sidewalk.

b. The Case of the Urban Freeway

Later that morning, Li entered the interstate freeway from the center of Phoenix. Near the center of the city, the divided freeway meandered through the city in gentle curves, varying in width from three to four lanes in each direction. It was heavily traveled, with cars and trucks frequently changing lanes and merging near the numerous freeway entrances and exits, some of which were only one mile from the next set of entrances and exits.

Li was traveling 65 miles per hour but slowed down when he noticed a sign stating "55 mph." He was not anxious to repeat his experience in the school zone.

Lesson?

c. The Case of the Rural Freeway

As Li proceeded south on the freeway toward Tucson, through less congested areas in adjacent cities, he noticed that the speed limit increased to 65 miles per hour. He soon began to pass through a stretch of more than 50 miles of rural, nonresidential desert, outside any city limits. The freeway was mostly straight and level, varying in width from two to three lanes in each direction. Traffic was light, and several consecutive sets of freeway entrances and exits were separated by 10 to 15 miles. Li noticed a sign posting a speed limit of 75 miles per hour, and he increased his speed accordingly.

Lesson?

2. Synthesis and Outlining

Use the three cases in section 1 of this exercise to generalize about legislative policy in setting speed limits on different roads. As an example of one approach, try the following:

First, think about the factors that seem to influence the setting of speed limits. Your stated policy justifications in each of the cases should help you here. Then, try to make a single statement that helps to explain all of the speed limits described in the cases. As an example, you might complete the following sentences:

Speed limits on streets and freeways range from 15 mph to 75 mph, depending on such factors as . . . . These factors reflect general policy concerns for . . . .

For this exercise, you should not concern yourself with the question of whether Li obeyed or violated the speed limits in each of the cases. To keep this exercise simple, focus your attention only on the speed limits and the justifications for them. Of course, quite apart from Li's obeying or violating the speed limits, the particular circumstances of each case will help you identify the justifications for the speed limits.

Once you have constructed your statement, illustrate it with a series of three examples. Each example should be a brief summary of the critical information in each of the three cases. The information is critical if it helps to illuminate the point that you make in your general statement.

For example, your series of illustrations could take the following form:

Speed limits on streets and freeways range from 15 mph to 75 mph, depending upon such factors as . . . . These factors reflect an overarching policy concern for . . . .

1. *Example* — In The Case of the School Zone, the speed limit in a residential elementary school zone is set at 15 mph while children are present, because . . . .
2. *Example* — In contrast, in The Case of the Rural Freeway . . . .
3. *Example* — In The Case of the Urban Freeway . . . .

---

3. Predicting the Outcome of a New Case

Just before reaching Tucson, Li exits the freeway and drives on a straight, level undivided highway through desert, with one lane in each direction. Side roads intersect the highway every few miles. The traffic is light, and the area is sparsely populated, but several homes border the highway over a ten-mile stretch.

One hundred yards ahead, a police officer sits in his car at a stop sign where a side road intersects the highway. Li is traveling 50 mph. He is eager to obey the speed limit but has forgotten to note the posted speed limit a few miles back.

In the face of uncertainty about the speed limit, Li prudently slows down as he approaches the officer. However, the incident stimulates his curiosity about the speed limit.

Place yourself in Li's position. Use your general statement in section 2 of this exercise as a guide for guessing the speed limit for the highway. Apply the factors that you derived from each of the previous cases to the facts of this new case. Then, reach some reasonable conclusion about the probable speed limit. Do not look for some magic number as the single correct answer. Simply make a reasonable estimate based on the other cases and support your estimate with good analysis of the policies and the facts.

Chapter 9

Essay Examinations

I. Overview—Perspective and General Format

The answer to a law school essay examination is generally similar to the discussion section of an office memorandum, which is addressed in detail in Chapters 11 and 12. When you reach those chapters, you should reflect on the parallels between an office memorandum and an essay examination answer. To better prepare you for the comparison, this chapter occasionally pauses to identify facets of examination answers that have counterparts in office memoranda and to point out the differences in styles appropriate to each document.[1]

---

1. For a more comprehensive discussion of law school exams, including objective questions such as multiple-choice questions, *see* Charles R. Calleros, LAW SCHOOL EXAMS: PREPARING AND WRITING TO WIN (2d ed. 2013).

A. Perspective

Most essay examinations ask for a balanced analysis of a problem with a direction such as the following: "Discuss the claims and defenses that the parties may reasonably assert. Be sure to discuss arguments on both sides of each issue." Like an actual office memorandum assignment, the exam problem may identify one of the parties as your client. Nonetheless, the exam presumably requests that you adopt an objective perspective rather than advocate only your client's claims and defenses. In addition to developing arguments for your own client, you must anticipate and demonstrate an understanding of the counterarguments that the opposing party likely will raise.

Indeed, many exam problems do not even identify one of the parties as your client. Your perspective then will be even more strictly neutral than it would be for an office memorandum, which at least anticipates advocacy on behalf of an identified client.

Finally, on rare occasions an exam may ask you to present only the claims and defenses of an identified client. If so, your answer should take the partisan approach of a brief to a court, but only if the exam includes clear directions to that effect.

B. General Format

As introduced in Chapter 6, an answer to an essay examination and the discussion section of an office memorandum typically share a general structure: After (1) identifying the *issue*, you should (2) summarize the applicable *legal rule* or rules, (3) *apply* the rule to the relevant *facts* to determine whether the facts satisfy the legal rule, and (4) state a reasonable *conclusion*.

Some of the more formal components of other legal documents are notably missing from a good exam answer. For example, professors normally do not require you to formally state all the issues at or near the beginning of your answer, as you would in an office memorandum or in some briefs. Even more important, you should never waste time drafting an introduction that separately restates all the facts of the problem. In all but the most unusual examinations, the problem will state the facts for you. Accordingly, your professor will test your ability to analyze groups of those facts in the context of specific issues, but not your ability to restate all the facts at the outset.

II. Elements of the Answer

A. Issues

1. Identifying Issues

Occasionally, a professor will identify examination issues by asking you to respond to specific questions, such as, "Did Seller make an offer to Buyer?" More commonly, the exam problem will end with a very general question about the rights and liabilities of the parties, and it will require you to identify the relevant issues.

To identify the issues, you must apply the skills and knowledge that you have acquired from briefing cases and outlining course material throughout the semester. By briefing countless cases, you have learned to sift through complicated fact patterns and to recognize the kinds of facts that have potential legal significance. Moreover, by briefing and synthesizing cases and by outlining the course material, you have armed yourself with a general knowledge of relevant legal rules and policies. By carefully studying the facts of the exam problem, you can now determine what claims and defenses the parties can reasonably assert and which elements of those claims and defenses are placed in doubt.

For example, suppose that an exam problem asks you to assume that the relevant jurisdiction has retained the common law definition of burglary, as in Chapter 6, Exercise 6-1. The problem describes Robert Glass opening the door of the cab of a VW bus just before dawn and reaching inside to steal stereo equipment lying on the driver's seat, which he spied through the window. It also states that the owner of the bus, Leova Rosales, is on a road trip and sleeping in the back of the vehicle, with curtains drawn between her and the cab of the bus. The problem also asks you to assume that theft of the stereo equipment would constitute felony larceny in the jurisdiction.

You know from your studies that the common law crime of burglary requires proof of the breaking and entering of a dwelling of another at night with the intent to commit a felony, and that a "breaking" only requires the opening of a barrier to entry, and not damage or destruction to it. Armed with this knowledge, you can see that the facts provide a nonfrivolous basis for prosecuting Robert Glass for common law burglary. For example, Robert's opening the closed cab door and reaching into the VW bus to steal the stereo equipment are almost certainly a "breaking and entering" with the "intent to commit a felony." These elements of the crime probably do not raise issues warranting substantial discussion. At most, you might briefly argue that Leova's leaving the door unlocked invited entry to an extent that negates a "breaking" in some jurisdictions; however, that argument is sufficiently weak that it doesn't warrant more than a brief mention if any mention at all.

Other elements of the crime, however, are in greater doubt. Even though Leova had drawn her curtains to permit her to sleep late, the moments "just before dawn," when the glow of an impending sunrise begin to appear on nearby hills, are only arguably "during the night." Moreover, the cab of Leova's bus is not clearly part of a "dwelling." Thus, whether Robert committed a burglary is subject to some debate and is a general issue in the problem.

Moreover, each element of the crime that is in doubt forms the basis of a subissue. For example, the element of "dwelling" not only helps to show that the general crime of burglary is in issue; It is itself a subissue that warrants full discussion in its own IRAC. Leova is in fact using the VW bus as her residence while she travels, as the place where she sleeps at night. The bus, however, almost certainly differs in character from the more conventional houses that satisfied the "dwelling" requirement in the common law cases that you have studied. Although Leova is temporarily using the bus as her sleeping quarters, the vehicle is arguably primarily a means of transportation; moreover, the cab is physically separated from the sleeping quarters. Because you can reasonably argue either side of this topic, whether the cab of Leova's bus is part of a "dwelling" for purposes of common law burglary is a subissue warranting discussion. Other elements of the crime and possible defenses may be placed in issue by the facts summarized above or by other facts in the problem.

2. Scope of Analysis

Because the process of identifying issues requires you to exercise judgment, you can never determine with complete certainty which questions your professor thinks are sufficiently clearly raised by the facts to warrant discussion. Moreover, some professors directly examine your ability to identify as many issues as possible, including those related to novel or particularly creative legal theories. When in doubt, therefore, you should identify and at least briefly discuss even marginal issues. If the professor expects some discussion of a marginal issue, you will earn valuable points for your brief discussion. On the other hand, if the professor disagrees that a particular matter warrants analysis, you will have minimized the lost time by having limited your discussion to a summary of the most basic points.

3. Expressing Your Identification of Issues

You need not state each of the issues and subissues of an examination problem in polished detail. However, your answer should leave no doubt about which issue you are analyzing in any passage in the answer. To guide your reader through your analysis, you can use the same techniques that help convey organization to the reader in the discussion section of an office memorandum. You should discuss major issues in separate sections and should precede each discussion with a section heading that generally identifies the issue analyzed in that section.

A section heading introducing an issue or subissue can be a word or phrase that refers to a claim, a defense, or one element of a claim or defense. Unless the question raises the possibility of claims of only one party against one other, section headings also should identify which party is bringing a claim against which other in each section.

For example, an examination problem might raise issues about various tort claims among three parties: Smith, Jones, and King. A student might display the general organization of his answer with section headings such as the following:

I. *Smith v. Jones*
  A. Battery
  • • • •
  B. Infliction of Emotional Distress
  • • • •
II. *Smith v. King*
  A. Negligence
  • • • •
  B. Strict Products Liability
  • • • •
III. *Jones v. Smith* — Defamation
  • • • •

In some cases, you may wish to illuminate the issue that is denoted by a section heading with an introductory sentence or two. Such an introduction might refer briefly to a potential argument of one of the parties, to facts that raise the issue, or to a preliminary legal conclusion that sets up the issue. For example, under section II.A in the example above, you might provide this orientation: "Smith may claim that King negligently hired Jones, proximately causing Smith's injuries at Jones's hands."

Alternatively, you can replace the word or phrase in the section heading with a question stated in a full sentence: "Is King liable to Smith for negligently hiring Jones, proximately causing Smith to suffer injuries at Jones's hands?" If you adopt this approach, however, remember that the professor reading your answer typically will not expect the precision and specificity appropriate for the formal statement of issues in a case brief, office memorandum, or brief to a court. Therefore, you should not waste valuable time trying to meet those standards in framing your issue in an exam answer.

If your analysis of an issue is lengthy or complex, you may want to use subsection headings to identify your discussions of subissues, with or without section numbers and letters. In the following example, each of four elements of the tort of intentional infliction of emotional distress is in issue and warrants discussion in a separate IRAC, each of which is identified with a subsection heading:

I. *Smith v. Jones*
  A. Battery
• • • •
  B. Intentional Infliction of Emotional Distress
    [overview of elements of claim]
    1. Extreme and Outrageous Conduct
• • • •
    2. Intent or Recklessness
• • • •
    3. Severe Emotional Distress
• • • •
    4. Causation
• • • •

In many cases, however, subtler guides to the reader may be sufficient to identify subissues, particularly when the subissues relate to elements of a single claim, such as a single tort or crime. You can separate your discussions of distinct subissues into separate paragraphs, and you can use a topic sentence to identify the subissue addressed in each paragraph:

Intentional Infliction of Emotional Distress:

[overview of elements of claim]

"Extreme and outrageous" conduct is limited to . . . . Viewed in isolation, Principal Jones's method of questioning Schoolboy Smith about illegal drugs . . . .

Reckless disregard for the risk of causing severe distress can be established through . . . . In this case, Principal Jones was aware . . . .

Severe emotional distress means more than . . . .

Principal Jones's conduct will be viewed as the legal cause of Schoolboy Smith's injuries if . . . .

In an office memorandum or a brief to a court, an introduction to your discussion or arguments may provide the reader with helpful orientation. This extra step, however, is a waste of time in most exams. Unless you have very good reason to compose a short introduction, you will use your time most efficiently by starting your answer with your identification and discussion of the first issue.

B. Legal Rule

1. Presentation of Legal Rules

At the broadest level, the statement of a legal rule may consist of a summary of the elements of a claim that a party in the examination problem may reasonably pursue:

Intentional Infliction of Emotional Distress:

Principal Jones may be liable to Schoolboy Smith for intentional infliction of emotional distress if he engaged in extreme and outrageous conduct that caused Smith severe emotional distress, and if Jones either intended to cause such distress or recklessly disregarded the near certainty of causing such distress.

If you divide the discussion of this claim into subsections or paragraphs to address separate subissues, you might state a subrule in the form of a definition or other illumination of one of the elements of the claim:

"Extreme and outrageous" conduct is limited to shocking conduct that is beyond all possible bounds of decency. The defendant's conduct is more likely to satisfy this standard if he occupies a position of power or authority over the plaintiff.

Some examination problems may raise questions about choice of law or the precise formulation of the applicable rule. For example, a problem in a Contracts examination may raise the question of whether the Uniform Commercial Code or the common law applies to a transaction.[2] Other examination problems may raise questions about the choice between traditional rules and progressive trends, or between majority rules and minority approaches. If you have time to discuss such problems, consider briefly discussing each of the competing rules. Then, in the fact analysis that follows, you can discuss the likelihood of success of a claim or defense under each legal rule.

2. Depth and Formality of Analysis of Legal Rules

When writing an office memorandum, you normally must discuss specific statutes and case law from a particular jurisdiction that apply to the dispute, and you must carefully cite to the authority on which you rely. Moreover, you often will present the in-depth case analysis and synthesis from which you derive a legal rule.

In contrast, most law school examinations will require you to discuss general legal principles rather than, for example, the law of a particular state. You ordinarily will not have time to describe the process of synthesizing cases from which you have derived legal rules. Instead, you may simply present the kind of concise statements of law that you have previously constructed for your outlines.

Moreover, some professors will not require you to cite to authority when you discuss legal rules in your examination answer, and some others will award extra points only for citation to particularly significant authority. You can discover your professor's preferences by discussing these matters in class before the examination or by reviewing model answers from the professor's previous examinations.

C. Fact Analysis—Application of Law to Facts

1. Presentation of Fact Analysis

In each section or subsection devoted to an issue or subissue, you should identify facts relevant to the issue and should briefly explain whether the facts satisfy the legal rule that you have summarized. In most cases, you will have identified a matter as an issue because the facts of the problem suggest uncertainty about whether a legal rule is satisfied. Therefore, you usually can find facts that support each side of the dispute, and you should take care to argue both sides:

---

2. "Unless the context otherwise requires," article 2 of the Uniform Commercial Code applies "to transactions in goods." U.C.C. § 2-102 (2011).

Intentional Infliction of Emotional Distress:

Principal Jones may be liable . . . .

Viewed in isolation, Principal Jones's method of questioning Schoolboy Smith about illegal drugs probably was not "extreme and outrageous" in itself, because Jones "addressed Smith politely" and "never raised his voice." On the other hand, Jones was inherently intimidating to Smith, a ten-year-old child, because of Jones's status as an adult and as the highest authority at the elementary school. Moreover, it was common knowledge in the school that Jones had suspended two other students that semester for forging false notes excusing absences. By asking Smith to empty his pockets and to reveal the contents of his desk and locker, Jones implicitly accused Smith of lying when Smith denied any involvement with illegal drugs. In light of Jones's position of authority, his request to search Smith may have been unusually shocking and intimidating, particularly because the request immediately followed Smith's sincere denials.

2. Depth and Formality of Fact Analysis

In an office memorandum, you will explore in depth the application of legal rules to facts by carefully comparing the facts and reasoning of previous cases to the facts of your own case. Through this process of analogizing and distinguishing precedent, you can thoroughly analyze the facts of your case to determine whether they satisfy the applicable legal rules.

In contrast, your professors will not necessarily expect you to describe particular cases studied in class and to expressly analogize them to, or distinguish them from, the dispute presented in an exam problem. If you have conscientiously briefed your cases throughout the semester, you will recall cases that help you to spot issues and to analyze the problem, and you may mentally draw direct distinctions and analogies. However, you will seldom have sufficient time to express those distinctions and analogies in thorough analysis of precedent in your examination answer. Instead, absent contrary instructions from your professor, you should directly explain how relevant facts support or undermine an argument that the requirements of a legal rule are satisfied.

D. The Conclusion

1. Taking a Position

Some professors will examine your ability to apply settled law to familiar facts to reach a certain "correct" conclusion on several issues. In such cases, you should use the IRAC method of organization to explain how the law and facts lead you to a single, correct answer.

More typically, however, professors will examine you on the kinds of issues that actually would be litigated, ones that do not have a certain answer because of uncertainty in the law or in the application of the law to novel facts. In such a case, the professor expects you to argue both sides of the dispute and will not require you to identify a single "correct" answer. Nonetheless, just as your supervising attorney will expect you to reach conclusions, in the form of predictions, even on close questions in an office memorandum, most law professors will expect you to state a conclusion for each issue that you discuss in an examination answer. On close questions, you can hedge the conclusion with qualifying terms, such as "probably." Furthermore, the professor may accept any of several reasonable positions as an acceptable conclusion. Still, she will expect some resolution of each issue and subissue:

Intentional Infliction of Emotional Distress:
    Principal Jones may be liable to Schoolboy Smith . . . .

Extreme Conduct—
[rule and fact analysis on this subissue]
    Principal Jones's questioning and request to search constituted extreme and outrageous conduct.

Subsidiary conclusion

Intent or Recklessness—
[rule and fact analysis on this subissue]
    Although Principal Jones may not have intended to inflict severe emotional distress, he probably acted recklessly.

Subsidiary conclusion

Severe Emotional Distress—
[rule and fact analysis on this subissue]
    Schoolboy Smith's transitory fear probably did not amount to severe emotional distress.

Subsidiary conclusion

Causation—
[rule and fact analysis on this subissue]
    Any fear that Schoolboy Smith suffered over the incident was directly caused by Principal Jones's reckless actions.

Subsidiary conclusion

Conclusion—
    Because Schoolboy Smith probably did not suffer extreme emotional distress, I conclude that Principal Jones is not liable for intentional infliction of emotional distress.

General conclusion

2. Comprehensive Conclusions

In an office memorandum, you should not only state conclusions at the end of your discussion of each issue and subissue, you should also summarize all your major conclusions and express your recommendations in a separate conclusion section.

In contrast, few law professors will expect you to summarize all previous major conclusions in a general summary of claims and defenses at the end of your answer to an exam problem. For example, in the illustration in the immediately preceding subsection, if the examination also raised issues of battery and false imprisonment, you would state a general conclusion for each of the three tort claims (battery, false imprisonment, and intentional infliction of emotional distress) as you completed your discussion of each claim, but you ordinarily would not be expected to end your discussion of the problem with a comprehensive restatement of your conclusions on all three claims. Such a consolidated restatement of conclusions will score few points on an examination unless it adds new information or enhances the clarity of the discussion that precedes it. In most cases, you will score more points by using the last few minutes allocated to a problem to look for additional issues or arguments that you might have missed rather than to summarize conclusions that you have already clearly communicated in your discussions of individual issues.

III. Techniques for Writing Exam Responses

A. Effective Use of Time

At the beginning of the examination, you should determine how much time you will allocate to each problem, and you should adhere to that schedule. Adequate discussions of all the problems in an examination typically will score more points than unusually thorough discussions of some of the problems at the cost of inadequate treatment of others. The same holds true for treatment of issues within a problem: An adequate discussion of all the major issues typically will score more points than an unusually thorough discussion of only half the issues. Thus, if an exam problem raises an unusual number of issues, the professor may expect only a superficial discussion of each.

Although law school examinations require quick thinking, uninterrupted concentration, and rapid writing, you should not begin writing prematurely. You are more likely to write sensible responses and to avoid wasted effort if you spend up to a quarter of the time allotted for each problem in mastering the assignment and in "prewriting."

B. Mastering the Assignment

You should read an exam problem once at a moderately quick pace to get a general picture of the events described, to classify the general nature of the probable claims and defenses, and to discover the particular question or questions posed by the professor, usually at the end of the problem. You should then read the problem at least once again, this time at a much more deliberate pace, to spot specific issues and to make marks or margin notes that highlight important facts.

C. Prewriting

A few students have such well-developed skills of organization, such good memories, and such powers of concentration that they can write their examination answers without first outlining their analyses. The rest of us, however, will benefit greatly if we devote a few minutes to analysis and outlining before beginning to write.

Do not waste time, however, by writing an overly detailed outline that largely duplicates your formal answer. Your outline on scratch paper should be nothing more than a few words or phrases referring to the issues that you intend to address and the significant facts relating to each of those issues. The outline becomes your primary vehicle for analysis and organization. Before you begin writing, you can use it to decide which issues you will address, what order of presentation is most logical or efficient, and what facts support each side of the dispute in each section:

Q1 —
  I. *Smith v. Jones*
    A. Battery—injurious contact, and no consent, but requisite intent? Jones stumbled but was already reaching
    B. Intent. Inflic. of Emot. Distress
      1. Extreme Conduct—Jones—polite, but great authority. Request to search suggests disbelief and possibility of discipline.
      2. Intent or Reckless
    • • • •
    C. Defamation
    • • • •

Unlike the exam's facts, the legal rules should not be new to you. Nonetheless, if the rules associated with an issue are unusually complex, or if you desire to discuss alternative legal theories, you may wish to include some reference to the law in the outline as well.

By constructing a quick outline, you can examine your analysis at a glance and can determine whether it makes sense. If the analysis appears to be faulty, incomplete, or illogically organized, you can easily change your plans at the outlining stage. You would find it much more difficult to change your approach after you had written half of your response.

Finally, after completing your outline, you should quickly scan the problem once again before beginning to write. Because you have fully analyzed the problem in the outline, you can now more effectively recognize the legal significance of facts in the problem. Facts that appeared to be insignificant in earlier readings may now reveal themselves to be material.

D. Writing the Answer

If you have prepared an outline, writing your answer should be a fairly mechanical process. Your task is simply to express in full sentences the ideas that are represented in your outline, taking care to cover all the elements of a complete answer: issue, rule of law, application of law to facts, and conclusion. Your outline provides a guide that will keep you on track even when you momentarily lose sight of the main issues because of nervousness or temporary devotion to the details of a subissue.

Because of the intense time pressures of most essay examinations, law professors do not expect polished writing or perfect organization, and you should not waste precious time thinking about the best possible way to express your ideas. Nonetheless, you will have an advantage if you have worked conscientiously in your legal writing class to develop the skills of organization and clear, concise writing for office memoranda that are addressed in Chapters 12 and 13 of this book. You will score more points by clearly expressing many relevant ideas than will students whose verbose and repetitious prose expresses fewer ideas in the same space or whose writing is so unclear that the professor simply cannot understand it.

If you discover near the end of an exam that you have insufficient time to complete your analysis in full prose, you should simply outline the remainder of your response in your examination answer booklet. Most professors will give more points for a clear overview of all the remaining issues than for a fuller development of only one of several remaining issues.

IV. Summary

To prepare for law school essay examinations,

1. brief and synthesize cases; and
2. prepare a course outline by further synthesizing cases, reorganizing materials to highlight legal principles, and illustrating the principles with summaries of the case briefs.

To write a good essay examination answer,

1. read and analyze each examination problem, taking care to allocate your time wisely;
2. quickly and briefly outline your response to a problem; and
3. express your response in a clear, well-organized fashion, taking care to discuss both sides of each issue within the framework of IRAC: Issue, Rule, Application to facts, and Conclusion.

Sample Synthesis, Outline, Essay Exam, and Answer

Below are study and exam materials that illustrate the process of studying law, from briefing cases to taking an exam. Because this example is taken from a family setting, the summary of cases is much less formal than a series of briefs of judicial opinions. With a bit of imagination, however, you can draw an analogy between these sample materials and those that you will prepare in law school.

Notice that the legal rules stated in the exam answer are taken directly from the student's outline, which the student has committed to memory. Moreover, the student's knowledge of the case illustrations in the outline helps the student engage in the fact analysis in the examination answer. Finally, one issue in the exam requires the student to develop new rules by extrapolating from the familiar rules and the policies that support them.

Case Summaries with Syntheses

The Case of the Hand in the Cookie Jar: Debbie reached into a cookie jar and helped herself to a cookie shortly before dinner. Janice and Gerald admonished Debbie that the cookie would spoil her appetite for dinner.

The Case of the Broken Vase: Debbie climbed onto a chair, reached a vase on a table top, and threw the vase to the floor, breaking it. Janice and Gerald sent Debbie to her room, admonishing her that she should not play with her parents' possessions.

The Case of the Chocolate Ice Cream: After dinner one night, Debbie asked for some chocolate ice cream. To her surprise, her parents served her a dish of ice cream, praising her for having finished her vegetables. Unlike in the cookie jar case, Debbie did not spoil her appetite by eating the ice cream.

The Case of the Mistreated Teddy Bear: Anxious to test her parents' limits one evening, Debbie climbed onto a chair with her favorite teddy bear and threw the teddy bear onto the living room carpet. Debbie's parents saw this event but had no reaction; they continued reading the newspaper and watching TV. Unlike in the broken vase case, Debbie's actions here did not jeopardize her parents' possessions.

The Case of the Bouncing Ball: Emboldened by the teddy bear incident, Debbie brought out her favorite rubber ball and began kicking it around the living room, causing it to bounce off the TV set and to narrowly miss Janice's glass of wine sitting on the coffee table. Janice flashed Debbie an angry glance, and Gerald sternly said, "Outside with that ball!" This is more similar to the broken vase case than to the teddy bear case, because Debbie's bouncing ball threatened to cause harm to her parents' television set and wine glass.

Outline

Rules for Debbie

I. Overview—Debbie's parents try to restrict Debbie's activities to those that are beneficial to her health and that protect her parents' possessions from harm.

II. Dietary Rules—Debbie is permitted to eat sweets, but only at times that won't spoil her appetite for more healthful foods.

   A. Example: In *The Case of the Chocolate Ice Cream*, Debbie's parents gladly served her ice cream after dinner, because she had eaten all her vegetables.

   B. Example: In *The Case of the Hand in the Cookie Jar*, Debbie was not permitted to eat a cookie shortly before dinner, because it would ruin her appetite for dinner.

III. Rules about Toys—Debbie is permitted to play only with her own toys and not in a way that will endanger her parents' possessions.

   A. Example: In *The Case of the Broken Vase*, Debbie was disciplined for breaking her parents' vase.

   B. Example: In *The Case of the Bouncing Ball*, Debbie was admonished for playing with her rubber ball in a way that endangered her parents' possessions, such as the TV set and wine glass.

   C. Example: In *The Case of the Mistreated Teddy Bear*, Debbie was permitted to play with her teddy bear, even by throwing it onto the floor, apparently because such conduct did not harm any of her parents' possessions.

Examination Problem

On Saturday morning, Debbie began coloring in her coloring book with a box of crayons. She soon expanded her artistic activity to drawing a multicolored mural on one of the walls of her room. Displeased with the quality of her drawing, Debbie broke each of her 24 crayons in half and threw them into her wastebasket. Indeed, she was so displeased with her artistry that she decided to wash her drawing off the wall. To that end, Debbie opened the cabinet under the kitchen sink and took a bottle of liquid drain cleaner, which she thought was a form of soap but was in fact a toxic chemical capable of burning her eyes and skin. At that moment, Debbie's parents intercepted her and discovered each of her activities during the day. Fully discuss whether Debbie has violated any rules of her house.

Examination Answer

I. Harm to Parents' Possessions   Issue[3]

    Debbie's parents permit her to use and even   Rule
abuse her own toys, but they do not allow Debbie
to harm their possessions.

    Debbie did not harm her parents' property   Application
by drawing in her coloring book. And she prob-
ably did not harm their property by breaking her
crayons, because those presumably were her own
toys. However, Debbie almost certainly violated
her parents' rules by drawing on her bedroom
wall. Although the wall was in her room, her parents probably view it as part of their possessions,
because they undoubtedly are responsible for
maintaining it. Debbie did not physically break the
surface of the wall as she might break a vase. However, a crayon drawing on the wall might require
vigorous scrubbing or even repainting. Therefore,
it probably represents actual harm to the wall.

    Debbie has violated her parents' rule against   Conclusion
harming their possessions.

II. Promotion of Debbie's Health and Protection   Issue
of Parents' Possessions

    In addition to prohibiting Debbie from harm-   Rule
ing their possessions, Debbie's parents forbid her
to eat sweets if they will spoil her appetite for more
healthful foods.

    Debbie has not tried to eat sweets at an inap-   Application
propriate time. However, she has endangered her
health by carrying a dangerous chemical, the drain
cleaner, with the intention of opening the bottle
and using the chemical to clean her wall. The policy behind the dietary rule is apparently to help
maintain Debbie's health. Therefore, Debbie's
parents likely would disapprove of other activities
that endanger her health, particularly activities that
would cause more serious and immediate harm
than simply eating unhealthful foods.

---

3. The margin labels are included in this sample to remind you that a complete legal
analysis should include four basic elements. Those labels should *not* appear in the margins of an
actual examination answer; some professors may be offended by such a mechanical approach.

Similarly, Debbie's parents may admonish her under an extension of their rule prohibiting harm to their possessions. Debbie is unlikely to do any harm to the drain cleaner. On the other hand, the drain cleaner is one of her parents' possessions rather than one of Debbie's toys. Moreover, if Debbie spilled the drain cleaner, she would waste it, and she might harm other possessions of her parents that came in contact with the chemical. Therefore, Debbie's parents are likely to disapprove of Debbie's taking the drain cleaner, out of concern for their possessions as well as concern for Debbie's safety.

Conclusion

Because the chemical could cause serious harm to Debbie and to her parents' possessions, I conclude that her parents will admonish her and will adopt a general rule prohibiting her from taking such bottles from the cabinet.

Sample Essay Answers

1. Sample Examination Answer

Read Sample Memorandum 1, which can be found near the end of Chapter 11. Imagine that an examination problem raises several issues, one of which is similar to the consideration issue discussed in that sample memorandum. The general structure of the discussion of that issue in the examination answer would be similar to that of the Discussion section of the sample memorandum. Nonetheless, even a thorough examination answer would be less formal than the memorandum. For example, the examination answer normally would omit citations and in-depth case analysis:

Q1

Lender v. Borrower

• • • •

Lender v. Guarantor

• • • •

Issue

Consideration—Illusory Promise:

The lender's promise to refrain from asserting his claim and demanding payment until he "needs the money" arguably is illusory, thus creating doubt about whether the guarantor's promise is enforceable.

An enforceable contract requires a bargained-for exchange in which a promisor exchanges his own promise for a return promise or performance. The requirement of an exchange is not satisfied if one party gives only an illusory promise, which does not commit the promisor to any future performance. Even if a promise leaves open the possibility that the promisor will escape obligation, however, the promise is valid if the promisor does not have complete control over the events on which the promisor's obligation is conditioned.

Rule

The lender's promise to forbear until he "needs" the money appears to condition the length of his forbearance on financial events that are at least partly outside his control: As long as his income and expenses created no need for the money, the lender had a commitment to forbear from demanding payment. In an effort to escape obligations, the guarantor could argue that the lender could create financial need at his whim by spending money, or that the word "need" refers to a subjective perception of deprivation that is inseparable from one's desires, which are subject to the promisor's unfettered discretion. More than "want," however, the word "need" normally is viewed as a matter that is subject to the influence of external events.

Application

Because the formality of the written agreement suggests that the parties must have intended to create binding obligations, a court probably would interpret the word "need" to impose objective restrictions on the lender's rights and conduct, thereby satisfying the consideration requirement and making the guarantor's promise enforceable.

Conclusion

2. Sample Examination Problem and Response

Examine the following contracts problem and response. Although the fact analysis is fairly simple, the internal organization is more complex than that in the sample answer above, because the issue of recovery under quasi-contract invites discussion of two subissues in separate paragraphs, each with its own subrule, fact analysis, and preliminary conclusion.

Problem

While jogging one morning, realtor Maria Reyes came upon the victim of an auto accident that had occurred a few minutes earlier. The victim was unconscious and bleeding profusely from a severed artery. Reyes saved the victim's life by flagging down a motorist and applying direct pressure to the severed artery during the ten-minute ride to the hospital. A paramedic would have charged $300 for providing a similar lifesaving technique. Reyes's clothes were covered with blood, but they washed clean. Reyes herself was shaken and exhausted for a few hours after the incident. Reyes later demanded compensation from the victim. Discuss the potential liability and remedies.

Sample Answer

Liability for Unjust Enrichment:[4]

The unconscious victim could not communicate a promise to pay Reyes. Therefore, Reyes cannot recover on the basis of contract or promissory estoppel.[5]

Reyes likely will bring an action in quasi-contract for restitution of the reasonable value of the benefit that she conferred on the victim. To recover on this theory, she must prove that she unjustly enriched the victim.[6]

Enrichment is a measurable benefit. Reyes enriched the victim by rendering tangible first-aid services and summoning help, thus saving the victim's life.[7]

Reyes must prove that it would be unjust for the victim to retain the benefits of the first-aid services without compensating Reyes for them. Reyes could prove this by showing that she had some relationship with the victim that led Reyes reasonably to expect compensation. However, the courts ordinarily presume that emergency services at the scene of an accident are provided gratuitously. Reyes could overcome that presumption if she could show that she acted in a professional capacity when rendering the services or that the services she rendered were unusually burdensome or hazardous.

Reyes cannot establish any expectation of compensation based on her profession: She is a realtor and is not in the business of charging for medical services. She might have a better chance of rebutting the presumption of gratuitous emergency services by showing that her services were so

---

4. This heading reflects the exam writer's decision to discuss issues of liability separately from those of remedies. Within the section addressing liability, the writer introduces and separately analyzes the elements of quasi-contract: (1) enrichment that is (2) unjust. She could have begun each of those analyses with a subsection heading, but good paragraphing appears to be a sufficient guide to organization within the two major sections, particularly because the facts raise no significant issue about enrichment.

5. This paragraph makes an introductory point about claims not in issue by stating the facts and conclusion and leaving the rules implicit. This paragraph could be omitted, but it might be good for an extra point or two because it explains how the student selected some issues for discussion and excluded others.

6. This paragraph identifies the main issue and states the applicable rule on the broadest, most general level.

7. This paragraph introduces a minor subissue, "enrichment," states the applicable rule, and reaches a conclusion on that subissue by applying the rule to the facts. Because this element of the claim is not seriously in doubt, it does not warrant fuller discussion. The brief discussion of this subissue serves primarily to introduce a more substantial issue in the next paragraph.

burdensome that she expected compensation. After all, she engaged in the physically demanding task of cradling an accident victim in a moving car for ten minutes while applying direct pressure to a severed artery. The physical and emotional distress of this event caused her to suffer exhaustion and distress for several hours. On the other hand, Reyes's actions posed little risk to her own safety, took relatively little time, and did not require special knowledge, skill, or training. Moreover, she likely would have felt distressed by the accident even if she had only witnessed the injury and had not acted to treat the victim.[8]

Although this is a close question, the facts suggest that Reyes could not reasonably have expected compensation for her emergency services. Therefore, I conclude that Reyes cannot recover.[9]

Remedies

Assuming that Reyes could prove a claim for quasi-contract, she would be entitled to restitution measured by the reasonable value of the benefit that she bestowed on the victim. The purpose of such relief would be to deny the unjust enrichment to the recipient of the benefit; therefore, whenever feasible, damages ought to be measured by the value that the recipient places on the benefit. If that is not feasible, a court may award damages based on the general market value of the benefit or, as a last resort, on the out-of-pocket costs incurred by the provider of the benefit.[10]

In this case, from the perspective of the victim, the value of the benefit bestowed by Reyes arguably is the value of the victim's life. A court would not use this value as the measure of the restitutionary relief, because it is relatively difficult to fix and because it is disproportionately greater than the effort expended by Reyes. Instead, the court probably would award the damages based on the general market value of Reyes's services. That measure is more nearly proportionate to Reyes's efforts, and it can easily be established by reference to the $300 fee that would have been charged by a paramedic. Alternatively, a court might award damages based on the actual costs incurred by Reyes, as measured by such things as inconvenience to Reyes and the cost of cleaning her jogging clothes. However, because the market-value remedy is more consistent with restitution, I conclude that a court would award $300 in damages if Reyes could establish a claim based on quasi-contract.[11]

---

8. The preceding paragraph identifies a subissue and states the law applicable to that subissue. This paragraph reaches a conclusion on that subissue by applying the law to the facts. Notice how this paragraph argues both sides of the facts on this close question.

9. This paragraph states a conclusion on the entire issue of liability. A student undoubtedly could have received equal credit for reaching the opposite conclusion, so long as the student discussed all the facts and arguments. Indeed, notice how the next section assumes the opposite conclusion, for purposes of raising the issue of remedies.

10. This paragraph discusses the legal rules for computing damages.

11. This paragraph reaches a conclusion on the question of damages by applying the legal standards to the facts.

Exercise 9-1

1. The Surfing Burglar

Review Exercise 6-1 in Chapter 6. Treat it as a closed-book examination question and write a response in essay form that identifies the issues, summarizes the law, applies the law to the facts relevant to each issue, and arrives at a conclusion on each issue. You may supplement the statements of law in Exercise 6-1 with any common law of burglary that you have studied in your Criminal Law course. Otherwise, base your analysis on the general legal rules provided in Exercise 6-1.

2. Rules for Lina

Review Exercises 8-1 and 8-2.3 in Chapter 8. Using your own outline or one supplied by your professor as a study aid prior to a closed-book test, or as an in-exam guide in an open-book test, draft an answer to the following essay question:

Question

On Friday night, Lina went to the football game with a date, Pat, and then to JJ's Pizza Parlor. Lina had earlier informed her mother of these plans. When Lina and Pat returned at 11:55 P.M., they parked in the driveway at Lina's house, within view of Lina's mother, who saw them through the living room window. While parked in the driveway, Lina and Pat talked and held hands for 20 minutes. After Pat kissed Lina goodbye and drove away, Lina entered her house at 12:15 A.M.

On Saturday afternoon, Lina plans to ask her mother whether Lina can go with friends to the high school basketball game to watch Lina's brother play in the first of more than two dozen games in the basketball season. This first game is being played in another city, so Lina will ride in the car of another family, which plans to go out for a snack after the game, and probably will not return Lina to her home until after midnight. Lina's mother plans to attend some home games during the season, but she does not plan to attend this first "away" game.

Fully discuss whether Lina's action on Friday and request on Saturday are consistent with her mother's rules regarding Lina's social activities. For every issue that you identify, summarize the rule that helps to resolve that issue, apply the rule to the relevant facts, and reach a conclusion. Whenever possible, discuss both sides of the question. Support your arguments with specific facts, and with policy considerations when feasible.

Part V

Predictive Analysis—The

Office Memorandum of Law

Chapters 10 through 14 discuss various stages of preparing an office memorandum of law, including researching the problem, organizing and drafting the memorandum, and citing to authority. In many first-semester legal writing programs, the office memorandum will be your primary vehicle for studying legal method and writing. Nonetheless, remember that the previous nine chapters have laid the foundation for this part of the book; you should not hesitate to review them when that would be helpful.

In an actual assignment in a law office, your first task in preparing an office memorandum will be to spend substantial time in a law library researching the law that applies to the issues raised in your assignment. Accordingly, the first chapter in Part V introduces basic research techniques and strategies.

On the other hand, many first-semester writing courses gradually introduce students to the challenges of preparing law office memoranda, initially assigning first a "closed-universe" problem, which includes the necessary legal materials. In such an assignment, students will not need to research the law, and they may even be prohibited by the assignment from supplementing the research supplied by the instructor.

If you begin with a closed-universe assignment, you can safely skip Chapter 10 until you are faced with a research assignment. Even so, you may want to begin thinking about the research process by glancing through Chapter 10 and contemplating how you might have used research tools to find the legal materials that your instructor supplied to you.

Once you have completed your study of Part V, you will be ready to perform one or more of the office memorandum assignments in Appendix IV.

Chapter 10

Introduction to the Law Library

I. Mastering the Assignment

The surest way to disappoint a supervising attorney is to misunderstand the assignment. Even a thoroughly researched and beautifully written memorandum will fall flat if it fails to address the matters that the supervisor wanted the associate to analyze.

Unfortunately, many supervising attorneys are too busy to communicate their assignments clearly and thoroughly. Even worse, most will not accept blame for confusion about the assignment. Instead, they expect you to assume responsibility for clarifying vague or confusing points. Consequently, you should not be shy about requesting additional information from the supervising attorney. Indeed, even at the risk of momentarily causing inconvenience to your supervising attorney, you should aggressively dig out the information that you need to master your assignment so that you can draft a memorandum that precisely meets the attorney's needs. On reading such a memorandum, the delighted supervising attorney will remember little about the minor inconvenience.

Confusion about the topics that your supervising attorney expects you to address may take various forms. In some cases, you may be unable to identify narrow, precise issues because the assignment is unavoidably general or abstract. Supervising attorneys occasionally request office memoranda on general, abstract questions of law, such as the likely scope and effect of a new statute. Although they are not yet working on any disputes relating to the assigned issues, they expect that the general legal analysis developed in such memoranda will help them counsel clients who are concerned about their rights or obligations under the new law. You can tailor such a memorandum to your supervisor's needs by requesting clarification on (1) the kinds of topics that your supervisor deems to be essential and (2) the kinds of disputes in which the firm's clients likely would become embroiled.

In many cases, abstraction in the assignment is unnecessary because the supervising attorney intends to use the legal analysis in the memorandum to help represent a client in an active, concrete dispute. In such a case, if your supervising attorney does not provide you with sufficient information to enable you to thoroughly understand the factual context, you should ask her for further factual details or for a convenient source of such information. By anticipating the application of legal standards to facts, you can frame the issues precisely and narrowly, and you can tailor the research and analysis to your supervisor's real needs. You may even wish to be present, if feasible, when the supervising attorney consults with the client, so that you can learn about the case firsthand.

Vagueness in an assignment often is attributable to precisely the analytic uncertainty on which the memorandum is intended to shed light. Therefore, after receiving the initial assignment but before writing the memorandum, you may benefit from secondary meetings with the supervising attorney. In some cases, your supervising attorney will not even attempt to identify issues but will instead supply the factual context and ask you to define and analyze the issues. In other cases, the supervisor may state the issues in general and preliminary form, expecting you to refine and supplement them. Even if the supervisor has no such expectation, you may be able to acquire information that allows you to focus the assigned issues more sharply. With a thorough knowledge of the factual context, you can clarify the essential issues as your research deepens your understanding of the legal standards.

As your research proceeds and your understanding of the issues sharpens, questions may arise about appropriate limits on the range of topics that you should address or about the depth to which the supervisor would like you to analyze a tangential issue. If so, you should consider whether the supervisor can conveniently give brief guidance on these questions before you begin writing. Although you should not become dependent on such guidance, neither should you give credence to a popular assumption that supervisors are universally hostile to such contacts. A good way to solicit guidance is to provide your supervisor with a skeleton outline of your preliminary research and request feedback.

II. Research Tools

A. Mastering Legal Research

Legal research is a skill best developed through experience. You will hone your research skills over the years by spending hours finding and reading books in a law library or on your computer. Reading this chapter will not substitute for hands-on training provided by your professor, law librarian, or representative from a commercial provider of computer research tools. Nonetheless, this introduction to research tools should prepare you for the necessary training and practice that awaits you.

Legal resources are increasingly available on the Internet, both on commercial web sites and on sites open to the public without fees. Consequently, you will conduct most of your legal research online. Basic skills in finding and using hard-copy resources in a law library, however, are still essential to the practice of law. When researching a legal issue, your goal should be to obtain a complete picture of the relevant law in an efficient, cost-effective manner. Although you can achieve this goal most often through computer-assisted research on the web, for some issues a physical, printed volume will provide an equally efficient or even superior research tool.

Moreover, even assuming that you will complete most research assignments entirely with web-based research tools, your initially working with bound volumes in the library should help you understand the nature of the authority that you are finding on the web. Accordingly, the following discussion introduces the topic of legal research with a description of resources and research tools in bound volumes. By looking up the described volumes in your law library, you can gain a concrete understanding of various kinds of resources and research tools in bound volumes. In turn, that experience will help you work with similar resources and tools available online.

B. Traditional Research Tools

As suggested in Chapters 3 and 4, most research assignments require research of primary law in state or federal constitutions, statutes, or judicial decisions. The judicial decisions establish case law, some of which develops common law principles and some of which interprets and applies constitutional or statutory provisions.

1. Statutes—Code Services

Most state and federal statutes are published in codes, in which statutory enactments are organized by subject matter. For example, the multivolume official United States Code reproduces the text of the United States Constitution, federal statutes enacted by Congress, and rules governing federal judicial proceedings, such as the Federal Rules of Civil Procedure and the Federal Rules of Evidence.

To illustrate, consider an issue that certainly will be governed by statutory law: the question of whether a crime's statute of limitations has run, thus barring prosecution of a fugitive who had evaded capture for many years. As suggested by the name "statute of limitations," the time limit for bringing a prosecution is set by the legislature.

If you are researching the statute of limitations for a federal crime, you will turn to the United States Code, which sets forth federal statutory law, organized by subject matter. By glancing at the spines of the volumes of the United States Code, you'll see that issues regarding "Crimes and Criminal Procedure" are codified in a volume designated as "Title 18." Within that volume is section 3290 (18 U.S.C. § 3290), which provides, "No statute of limitations shall extend to any person fleeing from justice." You might have found section 3290 by using the subject-matter index of the Code or seeing it cited in an article or a treatise that you consulted for background information.

Particularly useful as a research tool is an annotated code service, such as United States Code Annotated, United States Code Service, or any of the various annotated state code services. The annotated codebooks cite to related agency regulations and to law review articles analyzing the statute, and they briefly summarize judicial decisions that interpret the statute. The excerpts from the United States Code Annotated, for example, supplement the text of section 3290 with an indexed summary of cases in which the statute has been interpreted and applied. Under category 9, entitled "Constructive Flight," an annotation cites to and describes a holding of *United States v. Catino*, which appears in volume 735 of West's Federal Reporter 2d and which interprets the statutory phrase "fleeing from justice."

2. West's Case Reporters with Headnotes and Key Numbers

Using the citation in the annotated codebook as a guide, you can find the full text of the judicial decision that interprets the constitution, statute, or rule. Normally, you will find the decision in a multivolume service known as a "reporter" system, such as Federal Reports. In a reporter published by West, the text of the judicial decision is preceded by consecutively numbered "headnotes," which summarize critical points of law or applications of fact in the opinion. To help you find the portion of the text of the opinion that corresponds to a particular headnote, the West reporter inserts within the text a bracketed number that matches the corresponding headnote number. To facilitate further research, each headnote refers to an issue in the case with a "key number," which refers to a section of a West case digest that collects other cases addressing the same issue.

For example, West's presentation of *United States v. Catino*, begins with the case name, a brief overview, and then a list of West Headnotes that relate to the issues in the case. The actual opinion released by the court begins after a line identifying the authoring judge: "LUMBARD, Circuit Judge:". Then, after reviewing the facts and discussing preliminary points of law, the opinion states a rule about intent to flee, immediately after the numbers "4,

5" within brackets. The number "4" within the brackets corresponds to the fourth headnote preceding the opinion. That headnote not only summarizes the point about intent to flee stated in the opinion, it also assigns that point to a category that is designated as "Criminal Law 153."

3. West's Case Digests

The designation "Criminal Law 153" includes a picture of a key. "Criminal Law" is the "Digest Topic," and "153" is the "Key Number" corresponding to a subtopic within the Criminal Law topic. Together, they correspond to a subsection of the multivolume West's Federal Practice Digest 4th, which is essentially an enormous outline of federal case law, similar in form and design to the kind of course outline described in Chapter 8. Your library will have similar digests for state law, collecting decisions by state or region.

By pulling the appropriate volume on "Criminal Law" in West's Federal Practice Digest 4th and turning to section 153, you will find summaries of judicial decisions. There, you will see citations not only to *United States v. Catino*, but also to other cases addressing the same or similar issues. In addition to the citations, the digest often summarizes the point in each opinion that relates to the Key Number topic.

Of course, if you are researching a question governed exclusively by common law, you can bypass the legislative materials and focus your attention immediately on case law. Again, you might find a citation to a helpful case while studying a secondary authority, such as an article or treatise. Although such secondary authorities are not sources of primary law that directly bind any government official, they may help you understand the contours of a legal topic and find citations to cases that can act as a springboard for further research.

4. Legislative History

As discussed in Section II.B of Chapter 4, scholars and judges disagree on the manner and extent to which courts should consult legislative history as an aid in interpreting ambiguous statutory language. Controversial or not, however, legislative history finds its way into many briefs and judicial decisions.

Techniques for finding legislative history will vary, depending on the resources available in your library and the jurisdiction that produced the legislation. Historically, for example, many state legislatures have not published as much information about the legislative history of a bill as has been typical with federal legislation. In some states you may need to consult with the clerk of the state senate or house of representatives to obtain a legislative committee report or an audio tape or written transcript of committee proceedings or floor debates. On the other hand, a few states have long published legislative reports and proceedings in library resources similar to those available for federal legislative history. Moreover, such information is increasingly available on state legislative Internet sites. If you have any question about the status of state legislative history in your jurisdiction, ask your law librarian for guidance.

A number of research tools in bound volumes can help you find *federal* legislative history, especially for legislation enacted in recent decades. A few states have analogous resources for state legislation. A brief overview of some of these resources will get you started.

a. Codebooks

In Subsection 1 above, this chapter introduced you to one simple research tool for finding legislative history: codebooks. If you have already located a statute in a codebook, the codebook will provide the public law numbers of the legislation, the dates of legislative amendments, and citations to Statutes at Large, which will set forth the text of the legislation as it appeared at its original enactment or at a later stage of amendment.

If the codebook is annotated, it will refer as well to sources of pre-enactment legislative history, such as congressional committee reports. For example, following the text of a section of Title VII of the Civil Rights Act of 1964, 42 U.S.C.A. § 2000e-2, United States Code Annotated refers to Senate Report No. 88-872 and House Report No. 88-914, representing the findings, explanations, and recommendations of congressional committees prior to consideration of the Civil Rights Act of 1964. The annotated codebook states that these reports are published beginning on page 2355 of the 1964 United States Code Congressional and Administrative News (USCCAN), a set of bound volumes that you should have in your law library. The annotated codebook contains similar citations to a House Report and a Conference Report on the 1972 amendments to the Civil Rights Act, and to a House Report, an Interpretive Memorandum, and a Statement by the President on the 1991 amendments to the Civil Rights Act. Once again, these citations in the annotated codebook are to USCCAN, which selectively compiles useful documents and other proceedings regarding significant federal legislation enacted since 1945.

b. Congressional Information Service

For federal legislation enacted since 1970, a more complete legislative research tool is provided by the Congressional Information Service (CIS). Once you get the public law number of the statute in question from the CIS Index, a bound volume of CIS will set forth annotations briefly identifying the legislative history of the statute, such as congressional committee reports, legislative hearings, and floor debates. The annotation may also refer to an "Abstract" in yet another CIS volume, which will describe the legislative history in slightly greater detail, such as by listing the witnesses who testified at legislative hearings, or by providing a synopsis of committee reports. Finally, CIS provides the full text of the reports and hearings in microfiche form, separately stored in your library. CIS's electronic index, "LexisNexis Congressional," makes it an even more useful tool for researching legislative history.

c. Individual Compiled Legislative Histories

Of course, if a scholar has compiled and analyzed the legislative history of a particular statute, you may find the legislative history to be most accessible in that specific compilation. You can find such individual compilations through Nancy P. Johnson's SOURCES OF COMPILED LEGISLATIVE HISTORIES: A BIBLIOGRAPHY OF GOVERNMENT DOCUMENTS, PERIODICAL ARTICLES, AND BOOKS, 1ST CONGRESS—102ND CONGRESS (1996). For example, page B195 of this bibliography cites to resources relating to the Omnibus Trade and Competitiveness Act of 1988. One of the cited resources is a ten-volume legislative history of the Act, prepared by Bernard D. Reams, Jr., and Mary A. Nelson, and published in 1991. Johnson's bibliography notes that the ten-volume compilation includes congressional reports, hearings, and debates.

You should feel particularly lucky if you find such a compilation for legislation predating 1945, for which neither CIS nor USCCAN will provide legislative history. Researching the history of such early legislation is much more difficult, and you will benefit greatly from the work of any scholars who have already undertaken the task and published the fruits of their labors.

5. Research Tools for Administrative Regulations and Specialized Areas of Practice

A few other kinds of research tools are worth a brief mention, even though full exploration is beyond the scope of this chapter's brief introduction to legal research. You should be aware of research tools for agency regulations and some specialized areas of practice, and you should ask for assistance from your law librarian when researching these and other specialized topics.

A surprising proportion of our law consists of administrative rules and regulations issued by state and federal executive agencies that are legislatively authorized to assist in the implementation of statutory schemes. The National Labor Relations Board, for example, helps to interpret and enforce federal labor laws, in part by issuing rules and regulations.[1] For an introduction to research tools in administrative law, ask your librarian to show you the Code of Federal Regulations, popularly known by its abbreviation, C.F.R., which collects rules and regulations issued by federal administrative agencies.

Special research tools are also available for some specialized areas of practice, such as labor and employment law, tax law, bankruptcy law, Indian law, and international law, to name a few. Some of these areas are addressed by comprehensive looseleaf services in oversized binders that are frequently updated. You can find looseleaf services on the topic of labor and employment law, for example, that provide updated reports on relevant state and

---

1. *See* 29 U.S.C. §§ 153, 156 (2006); Am. Hosp. Ass'n v. NLRB, 499 U.S. 606, 609 (1991).

federal statutes; decisions of courts and arbitrators; and administrative rules, regulations, and adjudications.[2]

The Internet will be especially helpful when you search for primary sources, especially case law, from a foreign country on international law or on the domestic law of the foreign country. Two commercial and several free web services, discussed in the next section, will serve as illustrations of helpful sites.

C. Making the Most of Computer-Assisted Research

1. Online Resources

In a world increasingly geared to electronic information, computers may eventually render obsolete most of the bound volumes found in law libraries. A law office with limited library space can use computers to find the text of judicial decisions and statutes that are available on government web sites, university law library web sites, commercially available CD-ROMs, or electronic databases such as the latest versions of online computer research services from Bloomberg Law, LexisNexis, and Westlaw. You can best learn computer search techniques through hands-on training from your law school librarian or a Bloomberg, LexisNexis, or Westlaw representative.

Some free online services[3] are surprisingly comprehensive, either through comprehensive treatment of a specific topic or through more general coverage of national and global law. The Pace University Law School, for example, maintains a web site for the Institute of International Commercial Law,[4] which includes a wealth of resources about the United Nations Convention on Contracts for International Sales of Goods, including the text of this treaty in all its official languages, materials on its legislative history, scholarly articles commenting on the treaty, opinions of an official advisory board on the proper interpretation of the treaty, and the decisions of courts and arbitrators applying the treaty. Similarly, the LegiFrance web site[5] places at your fingertips English translations of French legislative codes, as well as French-language versions of those code provisions, constitutional provisions, and the decisions of French appellate courts. The Cornell University Law School maintains the Legal Information Institute,[6] a more general online source of state, federal, and global enacted law. Alternatively, commercial online services may charge access fees to a public library, which then

---

2. *E.g.*, LABOR RELATIONS REPORTER (BNA); CCH LABOR LAW REPORTER (CCH).

3. For a listing of free web sites, see, for example, Carole A. Levitt and Mark E. Rosch, THE CYBERSLEUTH'S GUIDE TO THE INTERNET: CONDUCTING EFFECTIVE FREE INVESTIGATIVE & LEGAL RESEARCH ON THE WEB (2009); Stacey L. Gordon, ONLINE LEGAL RESEARCH: A GUIDE TO LEGAL RESEARCH SERVICES AND OTHER INTERNET TOOLS 238-416 (2004). CALI, *The Law Student Guide to Free Legal Research on the Internet*, http://freelaw.classcaster.net/.

4. http://www.cisg.law.pace.edu.

5. http://legifrance.org.

6. http://www.law.cornell.edu.

can make some elements of the research tool available without charge to its users. Some attorneys even find that certain kinds of authority are efficiently retrieved with a simple Google search, or by the "Scholar" search engine within Google, at least if you know the name of the authority and are not beginning a general search.[7]

2. Using a Citation Service to Check Subsequent History

You must check the "subsequent history" of any judicial decision on which you rely in your analysis. This history reveals significant developments in the case law after the judicial decision was issued.

For this purpose, online computer citation services have effectively replaced *Shepard's* more traditional multivolume citation service. With a citation service, you should examine the "history" of a cited judicial decision to determine whether the decision has been affirmed, overruled, followed, distinguished, or questioned, or whether it has been accepted or rejected for future appellate review. WestlawNext, for example, uses different colored flags in the top left corner of its presentation of a judicial decision to alert the user to subsequent judicial activity that might undermine the binding or persuasive value of the decision.

Unwittingly relying on an overruled decision is a serious error of research and analysis that you should avoid at all costs. Conversely, you can cite to a decision with an extra sense of security if your search for subsequent history reveals that the decision has not been overruled or accepted for review.

3. Efficient Use of Both Online and Traditional Resources

To the extent that you use a computer research tool that charges a fee, you should develop a sense of the relative efficiency of different kinds of research tools in various kinds of searches. For example, even though the LexisNexis, Westlaw, and now Bloomberg computer research services have revolutionized legal research, they are not the exclusive answer to your research problems in this era of transition from bound volumes to electronic information.

You can still accomplish some research tasks with great efficiency in the stacks of bound volumes. As a student, you may be entitled to free access to computer research tools for law school assignments. Outside that academic context, however, your clients ultimately will pay for your access to these sites. You may inflate your bills to your clients if you spend precious time searching for and reading text on a fee-based online service that you could readily locate in a bound volume a few feet from your office.

Accordingly, to ensure cost-effective use of expensive computer research tools, you should also master the traditional library resources in bound volumes. As you supplement this knowledge with computer research skills, you will probably determine that some kinds of computer searches will be cost-

---

7. *See* http://scholar.google.com.

effective because they will significantly reduce your research time, freeing you for work on other cases and offsetting the computer research expense with fewer hours billed to the client. Conversely, you may find that you can accomplish other research tasks more effectively and inexpensively with bound volumes if traditional research tools address those topics efficiently and comprehensively. With some care and experience, you can acquire a sense of balance between traditional and computer-assisted research tools.

For example, some researchers find that a bound volume codebook is the most effective way to gain general familiarity with a statutory scheme in which several statutory sections operate together. With a bound volume, a researcher can easily flip pages to browse through several related sections to see how they work together and to determine which are relevant to the case at hand. After gaining familiarity with the statutory scheme, some researchers might then go online to find cases interpreting the statute in particular contexts. Similarly, a researcher might find the text and citation for a case through a free online service and then turn to a fee-based computer service to check the subsequent history of the case.

III. Research Strategy

Before setting your sights on specific primary authority in the library, you should acquire a general grasp of the fundamental principles of law relevant to your assignment so that you can more effectively identify issues and exclude unproductive lines of inquiry. A general survey course on the subject in law school should be sufficient to enable you to define issues and to delve immediately into specific, primary authority such as statutes or case law. If you have not taken a course on the subject matter of the assignment, you should consider beginning your research with a secondary source that provides general background information. As their labels suggest, primary authority within the relevant jurisdiction takes analytic precedence over secondary authority. Nonetheless, you will often find and use the primary authority more effectively if you first consult a secondary source, such as a reputable treatise, to enhance your understanding of the broad outlines of the subject.

Once you have begun to explore primary authority, you should look for relevant legislation before digging too deeply into case law. A single statute can diminish or even destroy the authoritative value of a whole line of case law that developed early common law doctrines or that interpreted previously effective legislation. Thus, you can avoid hours of marginally productive reading by immediately finding the latest applicable legislation.

Even when you know that a body of case law interprets currently effective legislation, you should turn first to the statute itself. The statutory language will provide valuable context for the case law that interprets the statute. Moreover, an annotated codebook may help you find interpretive case law that you missed with other case-finding tools. If you can find no judicial

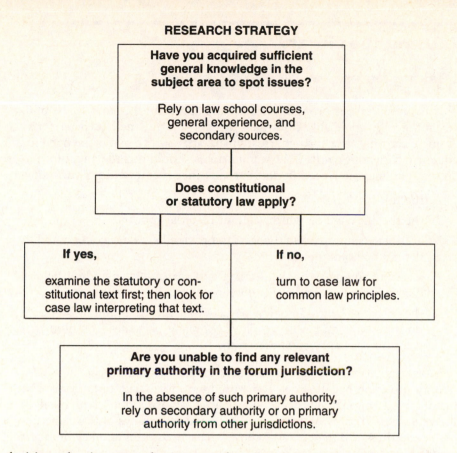

RESEARCH STRATEGY

Have you acquired sufficient general knowledge in the subject area to spot issues?

Rely on law school courses, general experience, and secondary sources.

Does constitutional or statutory law apply?

If yes,

examine the statutory or constitutional text first; then look for case law interpreting that text.

If no,

turn to case law for common law principles.

Are you unable to find any relevant primary authority in the forum jurisdiction?

In the absence of such primary authority, rely on secondary authority or on primary authority from other jurisdictions.

decisions that interpret the statutory language in question, you should look for helpful legislative history, if any.

Of course, if you find no statute or constitutional provision on point, you may safely turn to case law for applicable common law. In the absence of any relevant primary authority in the jurisdiction, you can rely on the persuasive authority provided by secondary sources or by primary authority from other jurisdictions.

Once you have identified the issues and the applicable law, consider scheduling a quick conversation with your assigning attorney, bringing along a preliminary outline of your analysis. In most cases, the assigning attorney will confirm that your research and preliminary analysis are addressing the client's needs, giving you the green light to express your analysis fully in a memorandum. Alternatively, your outline might prompt the assigning attorney to clear up a miscommunication about the nature of the assignment, allowing you to redirect your research before you have committed time and energy to the writing process. Or, he might ask you to adjust your focus, perhaps by asking you to omit an issue that another attorney is researching or by adding an issue that the assigning attorney believes might bear fruit, despite your overlooking or dismissing it. Early collaboration with your intended audience will help ensure that your final product will fully meet his needs.

IV. Using the Library

A. Taking Notes

You should take thorough notes on any authority that may be helpful. Even marginally applicable cases may warrant a note; their relevance may become clear only after further research and analysis. To avoid the need for frequent return trips to the library, your notes should include any information that you may later need in drafting the office memorandum, including

1. the full citation,

2. the specific page on which relevant material appears,

3. a sufficient summary of the facts to provide necessary context and to define the holding,

4. a careful summary of the holding and reasoning, including helpful dicta on any issues relevant to your research assignment, and

5. the verbatim language of any passage that you think might be worth quoting; you may want to photocopy any part of an opinion that warrants special or extended study.

Moreover, to facilitate further research, you should record data provided by the publisher designed to be used with formal research tools. For example, an opinion that is reproduced in a reporter published by West will begin with West "headnotes," each of which includes at least one key number. As discussed in Section B above, these headnotes and key numbers are worth recording in your notes, because they will help you find other cases on point. For example, the following library notes refer to a West key number:

Osterholt v. St. Charles Drilling Co., 500 F. Supp. 529 (E.D. Mo. 1980).
    pp. 530-32. Landowner sued drilling company for damages stemming from installation of defective well and water system. pp. 534-35—Judgment for P on K.
    p. 536 (Fraud 61)—punitive damages denied for alleged misrepresentation, because of absence of "aggravating circumstances" such as willful, wanton, reckless, or malicious conduct.
    Court refers to other case at 582 F.2d at 1087—should look this up.

In this example, the researcher is particularly interested in the passage on page 536 discussing punitive damages. The shorthand citation at the end of the notes refers to an opinion cited in *Osterholt* that the researcher will examine. The note "(Fraud 61)" refers to a West key number that will help the researcher use the West digest system to find other cases discussing the same issue. Indeed, that key number may lead to other cases reported in the West system that will supply the researcher with other West key numbers that are productive on the topic of punitive damages.

B. Library Courtesy

In light of the scarcity of resources in any law library, discourtesy in the library can lead to frustration and wasted time for all. Rather than pile three dozen books on a table for an afternoon's reading, you should take only one or two books off the shelves at a time, take notes, and immediately replace the books on the shelves. If you follow a methodical approach, you can efficiently exhaust the research possibilities with minimum duplication of effort.

V. Reorganization and Outlining

As summarized at the beginning of Chapter 8, the process of transforming library notes into a well-organized office memorandum is similar to that of summarizing and reorganizing case briefs in a student course outline. Both processes require you (1) to synthesize cases to arrive at general principles and (2) to classify cases to show which of them illustrates each principle. With this synthesis and reorganization, you can highlight ideas and illuminate them with illustrative cases, rather than simply present a laundry list of individual cases whose relationships to one another are unclear.

If you produce voluminous library notes for a complex assignment, you may wish to begin the process of reorganization by indexing your notes in the manner described at the beginning of Chapter 7. For example, a researcher has assigned a number to each authority summarized in the following library notes:

1. Statute of frauds—Ariz. Rev. Stat. Ann. § 44-101 (West 2002).

"No action shall be brought in any court in the following cases unless the promise or agreement upon which the action is brought . . . is in writing and signed by the party to be charged . . . 5. Upon an agreement which is not to be performed within one year from the making thereof."

2. *Tiffany Inc. v. W.M.K. Transit Mix, Inc.*, 16 Ariz. App. 415, 493 P.2d 1220 (1972).

416-17, P.2d at 1221-22—Tiffany prepared a bid to state agency to complete work on highway project; before bidding, it received oral price quote from Transit Mix for the supply of sealcoat chips for the project. Tiffany used that quote in its bid, the state awarded the bid to Tiffany, Transit refused to perform, Tiffany sues, and Transit raises statute of frauds as defense.

417-18, P.2d at 1222-23—UCC statute of frauds applies

a. 419-20, P.2d at 1224-25 [5-7] (Estoppel 52, 85, 99)—distinction between equitable and promissory estoppel: equitable—reliance on misrepresentation of fact; used as a "shield" or defense against a claim. Promissory—reliance on a promise; used as a defense or as basis for cause of action for damages.

b. 420, P.2d at 1225 [8, 9] (Estoppel 85)—If proved at trial, following facts would support application of promissory estoppel: Transit promised to supply sealcoat chips at certain price in the event that Tiffany got the main bid; Tiffany relied by using quote in its own bid; Transit should have foreseen that Tiffany would use its quote if it were the lowest.

420-21, P.2d at 1225-26 [10] (Frauds, stat. of 144)—nonetheless, statute of frauds bars enforcement of promise. Court recognizes estoppel to avoid statute if promisee relies on misrepresentation about requirements of statute (equitable estoppel?) or on promise to satisfy or not to rely on statute—but can't avoid statute by relying on other party's underlying oral promise to perform.

3. *Mac Enters. v. Del E. Webb Dev. Co.*, 132 Ariz. 331, 645 P.2d 1245 (Ct. App. 1982).

336, P.2d at 1250 [6] (Frauds, stat. of 144)—no estoppel to avoid statute of frauds, because Webb made no promise upon which Mac could reasonably rely.

4. *Kiely v. St. Germain*, 670 P.2d 764 (Colo. 1983) (en banc).

768-69—[7] (Frauds, stat. of 119(1))—good discussion of liberal Rest. 2d use of promissory estoppel to avoid statute of frauds and case law that prompted it—*Tiffany* cited as example of narrower approach.

. . . .

After analyzing the problem, the researcher then developed a rough outline to express a proposed organization for the office memorandum. As illustrated at the beginning of Chapter 8, the outline of the discussion section is organized around legal principles and identifies which authority supports and illustrates each principle:

III. Discussion

A. Applicability and Satisfaction of Statute of Frauds

Rules: requires writing signed by party to be charged if cannot be performed in 1 year [ARS § 44-101(5), #1]

Facts: K is for 2 years, and no writing at all

Conclusion: statute applies & is not satisfied

B. Estoppel to Avoid Statute

1. Misrep. or Promise about Statute's Requirements

Rules: equitable estoppel and promissory estoppel relating to requirements of statute [*Cress*, #6; and *Johnson*, #10, or *Tiffany*, #2a]

Facts: no representation or promise about statute's requirements

Conclusion: trad. forms of avoidance through estoppel not available

2. Reliance on Underlying Promise to Perform

Rules: Introduce liberal doctrine [Rest. 2d, #5, *Kiely*, #4]. Discuss whether AZ likely to adopt liberal rule [*Cf. Fremming*, #9, with *Tiffany*, #2b]—Some cases have assumed theory, but found elements not satisfied [*Trollope*, #8, and *Mac*,

#3] — Distinguish *Tiffany*? [*Wallach*, #13 and U.C.C. sections it cites; *Trollope*, #8, *Dean*, #7, and *Johnson*, #10]

Facts: Williams's actions probably constitute detrimental, foreseeable reliance

Conclusion: If AZ court adopts liberal view of avoidance of statute through promissory estoppel, facts probably support claim for damages.

Some authorities appear more than once and in different parts of the outline because those authorities contain information relevant to more than one topic or subtopic in the discussion. Each shorthand reference to an authority is followed by the index number to the place in the author's research notes where that authority is summarized. As illustrated at the beginning of Chapter 8, the index number helped the author quickly locate the authority in his notes when he drafted the memorandum.

You should avoid the temptation to include in your memorandum every idea and authority that you have encountered in the library. The outlining stage provides a good opportunity to exclude marginally relevant material as well as to reorganize and analyze. Once you are satisfied with the organization and analysis reflected in your outline, you can use the outline as a general guide when writing the memorandum.

VI. Summary

Before drafting an office memorandum, you should

1. master the assignment,
2. research and analyze the problem, and
3. reorganize your research notes into a rough outline of the discussion section of your memorandum.

In researching the problem, use secondary authority to help you identify issues and important lines of primary authority, but rely on applicable primary authority for your final analysis whenever it is available. In researching primary authority, look first for statutes or constitutional provisions that may apply, and then look for judicial decisions that interpret and apply the statute or constitution. Whether a judicial decision interprets statutory law or develops common law, check its subsequent history before relying on it.

If you need help identifying or locating the best research tool for your assignment, do not hesitate to ask your librarians for assistance. They have great expertise and will gladly take the time to share it with you. They can also refer you to books devoted entirely to legal research, including some that focus on researching the law of a particular state.[8]

The remaining chapters in Part V thoroughly explore the process of writing and organizing an office memorandum, as well as citing to legal

---

8. *E.g.*, Tamara S. Herrera, Arizona Legal Research (2d ed. 2013).

authority. The next chapter describes the general content of an office memorandum so that you can get a clearer idea of your goal. Once you have that goal in mind, you can better absorb the detailed information in the remaining three chapters regarding writing style, organization, and citation form.

Chapter 11

Content of the Office Memorandum of Law

I. Overview

A. Oral Report, E-Mail Memo, or Full Office Memorandum?

To save time and the client's money, an experienced attorney may draft a brief or an advice or demand letter directly from research notes, thus skipping the intermediate step of an office memorandum. Frequently, however, an office memorandum or other report will serve as an intermediate step. A more senior attorney may ask you to assist in a project by performing the research and preliminary analysis, which you then must convey to her in some manner. The nature and formality of your report will vary depending on her needs.

1. Oral Report

When you have completed a very limited research assignment, you may find that a quick oral report to the assigning attorney is the most efficient means to convey your analysis. For example, while she completes the first draft of a brief to a court, or while she prepares for contract or settlement negotiations, the assigning attorney may uncover an issue of law or fact that is not addressed by previous legal research or investigation of facts in the files. She may ask you to perform some quick supplementary research to clarify this matter while she is completing her task on a deadline. Or, based on her general knowledge of the law, she may be confident that she can advance an argument, but she asks you to find the latest cases on point to confirm and support her position.

After several hours of research and analysis, you can organize the essential points in rough notes, prepare a succinct presentation, meet with the assigning attorney at the appointed time, and state your findings in a concise and well-organized oral report. If the assigning attorney submitted a specific question to you, get to the point quickly: recall the issue posed to you and state the conclusion you have reached. Then explain your reasoning on the law and facts while supplying copies of the statutes and cases on which you rely. Fully disclose weaknesses in your client's position but recommend a strategy for overcoming those difficulties. Be prepared to describe your research methods and the sources you consulted, to help the assigning attorney determine whether further research might bear fruit.

When delivering an oral report to an assigning attorney, do not be intimidated by your audience's greater experience. If you have researched the issue competently, your knowledge of this specific topic may be superior to that of your assigning attorney. Although you should be courteous and deferential, you should state your findings directly, candidly, and with the confidence of one who has studied the issue carefully.

The assigning attorney likely will respond with some helpful ideas or incisive questions. Be prepared to brainstorm the issues thoroughly and creatively, using your initial analysis as a staging point and not as a constraint on the discussion. The assigning attorney may ask you to follow up with a brief e-mail note summarizing your findings.

2. Traditional Office Memorandum of Law

In other cases, particularly major disputes that are advancing through litigation, a client may have sufficient resources to justify your exhaustively researching a case and preparing a comprehensive written memorandum analyzing the law and facts on several issues that merit in-depth discussion. A typical office memorandum will include several sections, titled "Issues," "Brief Answers," "Facts," "Discussion," and "Conclusion." As explained below, these sections serve distinct, albeit overlapping, purposes.

Some assigning attorneys will ask you to deliver the legal memorandum in hard copy. Others will prefer an electronic word processing file of the memorandum, either e-mailed as an attachment or uploaded onto the firm's electronic case management system. If you deliver the memorandum as an attachment to an e-mail, you can provide an executive summary in the body of the e-mail, to provide the assigning attorney with an instantly accessible introduction to your memorandum.

3. Streamlined E-Mail Memo

Somewhere between these two extremes are limited research assignments that merit more than a quick oral report but for which you may be able to present a complete analysis in 1-3 pages of text in a streamlined format. A report this short could fit into the body of an e-mail and could easily be read on the screen of a small, handheld device, such as a smartphone.[1] The format for such an "e-mail memo" should remain flexible so that it can be adapted to suit the requirements of each assignment. For illustration, you might include the following elements in an e-mail memo assigned as a follow-up to a previously submitted office memorandum:

- an overview describing the limited issue or assignment addressed as a follow-up to a previous analysis, perhaps referring to the source of assumed or agreed facts in the previous memorandum,
- a brief answer to the follow-up issue or assignment,
- a concise but complete analysis of the law and its application to facts, and
- a recommendation.

On the other hand, if assigned to find three or four precedents from a specific state supporting a proposition, you might best present the fruits of your research in a list of case citations with a parenthetic explanation for each citation. You should be willing to select or create any format that efficiently achieves the purpose of the e-mail memo.

A streamlined e-mail memo merits special mention because it is sufficiently concise that you can easily copy its content into the body of the e-mail—regardless of whether you additionally attach it as a word processing file—so that the assigning attorney can easily gain access to the text through any hand-held electronic device with Internet access. Accordingly, this approach should normally be reserved for assignments that are quite limited in scope. If the assignment presents three or four substantial issues that require the application of unsettled or uncertain law to complex facts, you should forgo the efficiency and convenience of a short e-mail memo in the interest of presenting a thorough analysis in a full office memorandum format, which is better designed to help a reader navigate a complicated analysis. Such an analysis undoubtedly will require more than a few pages of text, making it unsuitable for presentation in the body of an e-mail message.

When an analysis is sufficiently short and simple to be conveyed in the body of an e-mail, you must write with the same precision and care that you would in a more traditional document. Don't let the e-mail format lull you into adopting the breezy style to which you are accustomed in personal e-mail and text messages. You should address your assigning attorney with

---

1. *See* Kristen Konrad Robbins-Tiscione, *From Snail Mail to E-Mail: The Traditional Legal Memorandum in the Twenty-First Century*, 58 J. LEGAL EDUC. 32 (2008) (reporting on survey of graduates of Georgetown University Law Center regarding the growing use of short and simplified office memos, which can be easily e-mailed).

the requisite formality and respect, carefully proofread the memo, and edit it to correct errors and to revise overly casual language or abbreviations. More generally, remember that e-mails are particularly easy to forward, sometimes beyond the intended recipients. Accordingly, take care to ensure that your e-mail memo would be suitable for critical reading by anyone in the law firm and perhaps outside that audience.

4. Pedagogic Focus on Traditional Office Memoranda

This chapter provides a comprehensive guide to the traditional office memorandum in full format. In many cases, such a document will best meet the needs of a client or lead attorney, perhaps because the issues in the dispute are too complicated for abbreviated treatment in the body of an e-mail message. Additionally, the more complete format of a traditional office memorandum may be helpful to the assigning attorney when she prepares a document in direct representation of the client, such as a brief to a court.

More important to the first-year law student, the full office memorandum is an indispensable tool for developing skills of analysis and articulation of facts and arguments. Once you have mastered the traditional office memorandum, you can easily adapt your presentation style to provide a more streamlined e-mail or oral report when less depth and formality will suffice and are welcomed by your assigning attorney.

After first exploring full, traditional legal memoranda in depth, this chapter ends with illustrations of the way in which a more limited report could be conveyed in the body of an e-mail message. Using e-mail to convey a short advice letter or demand letter is addressed in Chapters 24 and 25.

B. Traditional Office Memorandum: Audience, Purpose, and Perspective

1. Audience and Purpose

An office memorandum of law analyzes the law and the facts of a dispute, predicts an outcome, and recommends measures to assist the client. It is one of the most effective means through which you can directly help a more senior attorney represent a client. The assigning attorney may be preparing a more formal document such as a pleading or brief to a court, an advice letter to a client, or a demand letter to an opposing party. When preparing any of these documents, the supervising attorney may use the office memorandum as a source of information, or even as a partial rough draft. In other cases, the supervising attorney may use the information in an office memorandum to develop a tax strategy for a business client or a settlement strategy for negotiations on behalf of a litigation client. The careful statement of facts in an office memorandum also helps you to confirm the facts with the client, after providing the client with a copy of the memorandum or with an advice letter based on the memorandum.

2. Perspective

Unless an assigning attorney requests a memorandum that serves as the first draft of a brief, an office memorandum informs and predicts rather than advocates. To effectively represent the client, the assigning attorney must know both the weaknesses and the strengths of the client's claims and defenses. If you present a balanced analysis of the dispute in your office memorandum, you will enable your assigning attorney to focus his attention on his strongest arguments, to anticipate the counterarguments of the opposing party, and to develop an effective strategy. On the other hand, if you selectively bear only the good news to your assigning attorney, you will mislead him. Indeed, your skewed analysis may cause him embarrassment when further proceedings expose problems in his client's case—problems that he might have avoided or at least anticipated had the law firm confronted them at an earlier stage.

On the other hand, an office memorandum is not entirely neutral; in most cases, it anticipates advocacy on behalf of a client. Therefore, even though you explore arguments on both sides of a dispute in your memorandum, you should not convey a detached indifference to the outcome. Many experienced attorneys complain that student law clerks and recent graduates of law school tend to treat office memoranda as purely academic exercises and to abandon a client's cause too readily after identifying obstacles to the client's claims or defenses. To avoid such criticism, you should go beyond identifying weaknesses in a client's case; you should also present the best means of overcoming them. You must neither conceal such weaknesses nor surrender to despair over them. Instead, you should identify the best means to exploit the strengths of the client's case and suggest creative solutions to the problems raised by the weaknesses.

In sum, you should be zealous in your search for a winning argument for your client. However, if you believe that problems in your client's claim or defense are insurmountable, then you should candidly convey that conclusion to your assigning attorney.

II. Alternative Formats for a Traditional Office Memorandum

A. Tradition, Flexibility, and Adaptation

A full office memorandum will proceed in deliberate fashion through several stages of information and analysis, with some intentional overlapping of sections. Beyond that traditional structure, however, the format need not be static or inflexible; like alternative formats for student case briefs or streamlined e-mail memos, a number of formats for traditional office memoranda are popular.

If your law firm or assigning attorney expresses a strong preference for a particular format, you should respect that preference unless you have a compelling reason to employ an alternative format for an exceptional case. In the absence of a stated preference, you should choose a format that suits the needs of the particular assignment. The following are examples of three alternative formats for a traditional office memorandum:

Format A	Format B	Format C
I. Issue(s)	I. Overview	I. Issue(s)
II. Brief Answer(s)	II. Facts	II. Conclusion
III. Facts	III. Issue(s)	III. Facts
IV. Discussion	IV. Brief Answer(s)	IV. Discussion
V. Conclusion	V. Discussion	
	VI. Conclusion	

B. Format A: Effective for Multi-Issue Memoranda

1. Ordering the Elements to Aid Comprehension

Format A presents the issues first so that the reader of your memorandum can appreciate the legal significance of the facts when he reads them later in the memorandum. Once presented with the questions posed in the Issues section, however, the reader is anxious to learn the answers—or probable answers—to which your research and analysis point. Accordingly, prior to the statement of facts, the Brief Answers section provides a succinct preview of your conclusion on each issue:

Issue(s)
Brief Answer(s)
Facts
Discussion
Conclusion

2. Facts in Different Places to Perform Different Tasks

After the statement of all essential facts in the Facts section, the Discussion section of your memorandum analyzes each issue previously stated in the Issues section, usually in a separate IRAC and in a separate subsection for each issue. Within each such IRAC analysis, some of the facts will reappear, but only those that are relevant to *that issue* and thus can help you discuss whether the rules applicable to *that issue* are satisfied.

a. Example: Narration of All Essential Facts in Action for Breach of Contract

In a commercial contracts dispute, for example, your Facts section likely would present a chronological narrative of all essential facts, such as those describing (1) the formation of the contract between an owner and a contractor; (2) several complaints by the owner about the contractor's performance of the contract; (3) the unilateral termination of the contract by the dissatisfied owner; and (4) economic injuries suffered by the owner because of the allegedly substandard performance by the contractor, as well as economic injuries suffered by the contractor because of the owner's allegedly unjustified termination of the contract.

b. Example: Analysis of Facts Relevant to Each Issue in the Discussion Section

In turn, if one of the Discussion subsections addresses an issue relating to the owner's right to cancel the contract, your analysis in that subsection should summarize applicable rules about a contractor's "material breach," and it then should discuss whether the facts *relevant to that issue* support a conclusion that the contractor materially breached the contract and thus justified termination by the owner.[2] Those facts could include the extent and quality of the contractor's performance of obligations spelled out in the contract, as well as circumstances showing the extent to which the owner's interests could be protected by retaining a right to money damages without firing the contractor.[3]

A separate subsection in the Discussion section could address a remedies issue by summarizing rules defining the kinds of injuries that are legally recoverable for breach of contract, and then analyzing the facts relevant to *that issue*. The remedies subsection would include a discussion of whether specific economic losses suffered by the victim of breach satisfy the rules for inclusion in an award of damages for breach of contract. For example, if your fact analysis shows that the victim of breach could reasonably have avoided some of his economic losses, those losses would not be included in the category of legally recoverable damages.[4]

3. Conclusions in Different Places to Perform Different Tasks

Each such IRAC analysis in the Discussion section will end with your subsidiary conclusion for *that issue*, as previously previewed in the Brief Answers section. For example, you may conclude in one subsection of the Discussion that the contractor did not materially breach the contract, so that the owner committed a total breach by terminating the contract without justification. You may conclude in another subsection that some of the contractor's injuries are not recoverable as damages because the contractor reasonably could have avoided those losses even after the owner's breach.

To complete the circle, the Conclusion section will gather the conclusions for all the issues, comment on their collective legal significance to the dispute, and reach a recommendation about the actions that might be taken on behalf of the client.

---

2. *See, e.g.*, Walker & Co. v. Harrison, 347 Mich. 630, 81 N.W.2d 352 (1957) (lessee of commercial neon sign committed first material breach by unilaterally terminating contract when the lessor's failure to maintain the sign amounted to only a minor breach, rather than a material one).

3. *See id.*; RESTATEMENT (SECOND) OF CONTRACTS § 241 (1981) (listing factors relevant to determination of whether breach is material or only minor).

4. *See* RESTATEMENT (SECOND) OF CONTRACTS § 350(1) (1981).

Consequently, the reader is exposed to conclusions in three places: (1) in the Brief Answers, to provide a quick and early bottom line; (2) at the end of the analysis of each issue in the Discussion section, to provide closure to each such analysis; and (3) in a summation and synthesis of all subsidiary conclusions in the Conclusion section, to provide a comprehensive perspective and to establish premises for a recommendation. If you choose to state conclusions, rather than topics or issues, in the section headings in the Discussion section, then each conclusion could appear in four places in the memorandum.

4. Overlapping Sections are Like Actors Returning to Play Different but Complementary Roles

We might compare a traditional office memorandum to a play with several scenes in two acts. We can readily see that format A contemplates repeat performances of issues, facts, and conclusions, although in slightly different roles in various scenes or acts of the play.

In a very simple, single-issue dispute, these repeat performances might seem repetitive and inefficient, thus justifying a more streamlined format, perhaps conveyed in the body of an e-mail. In a more complex, multi-issue dispute, however, the more deliberate analysis and overlapping sections of format A will provide your assigning attorney with a helpful roadmap to the analysis and with an effective tool for client representation.

If you deliver such an office memorandum as an attachment to an e-mail, you could copy the final Conclusion section into the body of the e-mail. Your e-mail message would then provide a quick "executive summary" of the attached memorandum, easily accessible with any device that can gain access to the Internet.

C. Format B: For Especially Complex Cases

In rare cases, complex multiple transactions and confusing relationships between multiple parties may make statements of the issues incomprehensible to one who has not first read the facts. However, if the reader wades into the facts without first understanding at least the general nature of the issues, he will be robbed of the opportunity to read the facts with an appreciation for their legal significance.

Format B provides a special format to address this dilemma:

Overview
Facts
Issue(s)
Brief Answer(s)
Discussion
Conclusion

Ideally in a single paragraph, the brief Overview section describes the general nature of the dispute, identifies the nature of the issues in broad terms, and summarizes your assessment of the relative strength of the parties' positions. The Overview section remains concise because it avoids the temptation to prematurely delve into facts, issues, and conclusions in detail. Nonetheless, its quick glimpse of the full landscape enables the reader to appreciate the legal significance of the events narrated in the Facts section. In turn, both the Overview and Facts sections provide the reader with information that enables him to better comprehend the formal statement of the issues.

If you deliver your memorandum as an e-mail attachment, you could copy and paste the Overview section into the body of the e-mail, providing a particularly useful and readily accessible executive summary.

D. Format C: A Slightly Streamlined Approach for a Full Memorandum

Format C eliminates the Brief Answers section and replaces it with a Conclusion section, so that the Discussion section ends the memorandum:

Facts
Issue(s)
Conclusion
Discussion

Format C has the disadvantage of ending the memorandum on the final topic of discussion rather than in a Conclusion section that ties all the strands of the analysis together. It also forces the reader to assimilate a full conclusion and recommendation near the beginning of the memorandum without having first digested the analysis in the Discussion section. Nonetheless, some lawyers and law firms prefer format C because it reduces overlap and provides a bottom line and recommendation in the first few pages of the memorandum.

The potential drawbacks of format C are mitigated if the memorandum addresses a single issue, because the Discussion section would then present a single analysis, and the reader would not hunger at the end of the memorandum for a consolidated Conclusion section that synthesizes a number of earlier subsidiary conclusions. Indeed, if the law and relevant facts in a single-issue assignment are quite simple or limited in scope, the analysis might be suitable for presentation in the body of the e-mail, possibly in an even more streamlined format than format C. If the issue is more complicated and requires more than a few pages of analysis, then a fuller, more traditional memorandum is appropriate. Format C offers a middle ground by providing a slightly more streamlined format than does format A or B, allowing delivery either in the body of an e-mail or attached in a more formal and lengthy legal memorandum, depending on the scope and complexity of the analysis.

E. Flexibility and Adaptation

Unless your law firm or assigning attorney has requested a particular format, you should feel free to adapt a standard format to the needs of a particular assignment. Let's assume, for example, that an assignment raises a single issue and that you are content to state your straightforward answer to the issue only once in the memorandum, as in format C. If you nonetheless determined that the reader would not fully appreciate your recommended action until she has digested the analysis, you could create a new format to suit your purpose. The example below extracts the answer and recommendation from the Conclusion section, states the answer immediately after the Issue section, and returns the recommendation to the end of the memorandum:

Facts
Issue
Answer
Discussion
Recommendation

In any of these formats, an assigning attorney or law firm may ask you to add a short section summarizing your research or to place your research notes in the case file. If another member of the firm later wonders whether a particular source was consulted or a trail of research was fully explored, the research summary or research notes may help ensure that all helpful resources are brought to bear without wasteful duplication of efforts.

III. Elements of an Office Memorandum

The heading of a memorandum is simple and requires only brief discussion. The heading should identify the recipient of the memorandum; the author of the memorandum; the subject matter, stated in a manner that facilitates filing and later retrieval; and the date:

To: Susan Elias
From: James Nelson
Re: Enforceability of Julie Week's Promise to Act as Guarantor for Loan Obligation; File 14-127
Date: July 31, 2014

Some law offices may also include a line above "RE:" for identification of the means of delivering the memorandum, such as "Via: Printed Copy" or "Via: E-Mail Attachment."

The following subsections examine the more substantive elements of format A for an office memorandum: Issue(s), Brief Answer(s), Facts, Discussion, and Conclusion.

A. Issues—Identification and Expression

1. Review

Section III of Chapter 6 discusses the general process of identifying issues for analysis; Section II.B.2.a of Chapter 7 discusses the process of framing issues for statement in a case brief; and Section II.A of Chapter 9 discusses the process of identifying issues for discussion in an essay examination. These sections lay the foundation for identifying and framing issues in an office memorandum, and you should review them now.

Your task of identifying issues for analysis in an office memorandum is similar to that of identifying issues on a law school examination: You must have at least a general knowledge of the law governing the dispute so that you can recognize the legal problems raised by the facts. In many cases, courses that you have taken in law school will enable you to identify the general nature of the issues and to direct your research efforts; otherwise, a secondary source such as a good treatise may provide the necessary background information.

You should be prepared to revise your statement of the issues in the final stages of drafting. When you prepare a case brief for class discussion, you ordinarily cannot state with particularity the issues discussed in the judicial decision until you have completed your analysis of the entire opinion. Similarly, when preparing an office memorandum, you ordinarily cannot state with particularity the issues raised by the facts of the dispute until you have finished your research and have fully analyzed the problem. At that time, you must decide which elements of a claim or defense are sufficiently in doubt that they warrant identification and discussion as issues.

2. Example: Identifying Issues in a Title VII Suit

Title VII of the Civil Rights Act of 1964 imposes liability on employers for engaging in "unlawful employment practices," and it defines "employer" in part as "a person engaged in an industry affecting commerce."[5] Although engagement "in an industry affecting commerce" is always an element of employer liability, in most cases the facts known to all parties leave no doubt that the employer's activities satisfy the statutory rule under any reasonable interpretation. In such a case, the party charged with discrimination could not credibly dispute its status as an "employer" on grounds relating to commerce, and you should not identify that matter as an issue in your memorandum. At most, you might briefly state this conclusion in an introduction to the discussion of a substantial issue.

In the same case, however, unusual facts and uncertainty in the applicable legal standards might raise doubts about whether the employer has committed an "unlawful employment practice." Because the employee plausibly claims that the employer committed an unlawful employment practice, and

---

5. 42 U.S.C. §§ 2000e(b) (definition of "employer"), 2000e-2(a) (unlawful employer practices) (2006); *see also* §§ 2000e(g) and (h) (definitions of "commerce" and "industry affecting commerce").

because the employer plausibly denies it, the parties reasonably dispute that matter, and you should identify it as an issue for discussion.

3. Expressing Issues with Particularity

Once you have identified and analyzed issues for discussion in your memorandum, you should state them with the same specificity and attention to facts that would be appropriate in the statement of issues in a case brief prepared for class discussion. To review these techniques, you may want to return briefly to Section II.B.2 of Chapter 7.

For example, you should not state the issue in such general terms as "whether the employer committed an unlawful employment practice under Title VII of the Civil Rights Act of 1964." The author of the memorandum might be tempted to state such a general issue if he anticipates that other attorneys will consult the memorandum for general guidance when analyzing Title VII claims brought by other clients in different factual contexts. The author may fear that the other attorneys will fail to recognize the value of the memorandum as a general resource if the issue in the memorandum is so specific that it reveals the narrow factual context of the dispute, a context that differs from the ones confronted by the other attorneys. But this fear is misplaced. The other attorneys will recognize instantly that the memorandum in the file will likely set forth general standards about Title VII that will be useful in most Title VII claims, and they will be grateful for an issue statement that tips them off quickly about the ways in which their cases differ from the one analyzed in the memorandum.

Accordingly, after researching the law and analyzing the facts, you should more precisely identify the contours of the dispute likely to be raised by the parties:

Did Salerno create a hostile working environment for the complaining female employees by repeatedly asking them for dates, thus making Salerno liable for sex discrimination under Title VII by altering the female employees' terms or conditions of employment through unwelcome sexual advances?

If your question becomes tangled with excessively complex factual or legal details, you can make it simpler by leaving some of those details for the brief answer:

I. ISSUE

Did Salerno create a hostile working environment for the complaining female employees by repeatedly making unwelcome sexual advances, in violation of Title VII of the Civil Rights Act of 1964?

II. BRIEF ANSWER

Probably yes. Salerno allowed his male employees to work unmolested, but he repeatedly and aggressively asked three female employees for dates, long after the employees expressed their discomfort with the advances. In light of the intrusive and sexually charged manner in which Salerno made his requests, he probably created a hostile working environment for the employees. If so, he is liable under Title VII for engaging in sex discrimination that altered the employees' working conditions.

Section II.B.2.b of Chapter 7 discusses a similar technique: drafting a case brief so that the statements of issue and holding share the burden of expressing important details. Alternatively, legal writing expert Bryan Garner recommends that students and attorneys state the premises of an issue in separate sentences within the issue statement.[6] For example, you could state the Title VII issue in the following way:

I. ISSUE

Title VII imposes liability on an employer that discriminates on the basis of sex in a way that alters terms or conditions of employment. One way to alter employment conditions is by creating a hostile working environment for employees. In our case, the employer repeatedly directed sexually charged requests for dates to three female employees, even though the employees complained that the advances were unwelcome. The employer discriminated on the basis of sex because he allowed his male employees to work unmolested. Did the employer's discriminatory conduct also amount to a hostile working environment for the female employees sufficient to alter their conditions of employment?

This format for a multi-sentence issue statement may not meet with the approval of every assigning attorney, and it may not be perfectly consistent with some court rules governing the statement of issues in a brief. Still, when supervisors and court rules permit, you may want to experiment with this approach for particularly complex issues.

B. Brief Answer

Each brief answer should be a succinct response to the question presented in each issue. Unless the assigning attorney requests a detailed statement of your conclusions early in the memo, you should not use the brief answer to explore analytic justifications in great depth; the reader can more easily absorb a complex summary of the analysis after she has read the Discussion section of the memorandum. For example, the medical malpractice dispute discussed in Chapter 6 might raise the following issues and brief answers:

---

6. *See* Bryan A. Garner, THE WINNING BRIEF: 100 TIPS FOR PERSUASIVE BRIEFING IN TRIAL AND APPELLATE COURTS 92-97 (2d ed. 2004) ("Rule 12: Weave facts into your issues to make them concrete."); Bryan A. Garner, *The Deep Issue: A New Approach to Framing Legal Questions*, 5 SCRIBES J. LEGAL WRITING 1 (1994-95).

I. ISSUES

A. Does the phrase "any toxic material" in New Maine's strict liability statute encompass a generally safe anesthetic that produced a fatal reaction in a patient with a rare nerve disorder?

B. Is Humane Hospital liable to Souza's estate for negligent administration of the anesthetic?

1. Did Humane's anesthesiologist breach a duty of care by administering the anesthetic without assistance and by failing to monitor Souza's reactions to the anesthesia?

2. Did Souza's nerve disorder constitute a supervening cause that broke the chain of causation between the anesthesiologist's conduct and Souza's death?

II. BRIEF ANSWERS

A. Probably not. A restrictive interpretation is supported by the legislative history and by a general public policy in New Maine encouraging the provision of affordable medical services. The legislature probably did not intend the statutory phrase "toxic material" to include medically prescribed substances that ordinarily produce a beneficial result or otherwise facilitate medical treatment.

B. Probably yes.

1. Probably yes. Under generally accepted hospital procedures, at least two trained medical personnel must monitor the administration of anesthesia, with at least one person monitoring the patient's reactions. A jury likely will find that the anesthesiologist breached a duty of care to the patient by administering the anesthesia alone.

2. No. The jury likely will also find that the patient's nerve disorder was not a supervening cause and that the anesthesiologist's negligence proximately caused the patient's death.

C. Facts

Some new associates in a law firm regularly omit statements of facts in their legal memoranda. The associates often explain that a supervising attorney obviously knows the facts of an assigned case because she gave the facts to the associate in some oral or written form when she assigned the memorandum.

For several reasons, however, you should include at least a brief statement of facts in a legal memorandum unless your supervising attorney specifically authorizes you to omit it. The supervising attorney may have been familiar with the facts when she assigned the memorandum, but she may need a brief review to refresh her memory when she later reads your memorandum. Alternatively, she may simply want reassurance that you share her understanding of the facts. Furthermore, the memorandum should be a self-contained document that is helpful to any member of the firm who may be called on to take over the file, including an attorney who knows nothing about the case and does not have time to glean the facts from the file. Finally, a statement of the factual premises on which you based your legal analysis helps you focus your research and analysis, and it protects you from criticism if that analysis later becomes obsolete or misleading in light of newly discovered facts.

Your statement of facts should focus on material facts and background facts with attention to the considerations that you would apply in preparing a case brief for class. However, more so in an office memorandum than in a case brief, you can justify mentioning even a marginally significant fact. When briefing a case for class, you must rely on the court's summary of the facts as a complete record on which the court based its decision; moreover, you can test your analytic abilities by attempting to isolate the material facts and helpful background facts and by omitting the others. In contrast, when preparing an office memorandum at an early stage of a dispute, you know that the facts on which you rely for your analysis are incomplete. Subsequent proceedings may reveal other facts that support new claims, defenses, or arguments. As a consequence, previously known facts that appeared to be unimportant when you drafted the memorandum may take on new legal significance. In your statement of facts, therefore, you should recite all material facts in detail, and you should summarize any other information that either provides helpful background material or appears to have the potential to take on new significance as the litigation proceeds.

D. Discussion

1. Introducing Your Analysis

In the discussion section of your legal memorandum, you will express your complete legal analysis of each of the issues stated at the beginning of the memorandum. If your memorandum addresses a single issue that you have formally stated at or near the beginning of the memorandum, your discussion of the issue need not begin with any descriptive heading beyond the major section heading "Discussion." If you address multiple issues, however, you should separately analyze each issue under a descriptive section heading.

Some supervising attorneys may wish you to restate the issue in full or nearly full detail in the corresponding section heading of the discussion:

IV. DISCUSSION

A. Does the phrase "any toxic material" in New Maine's strict liability statute encompass a generally safe anesthetic that produced a fatal reaction in a patient with a rare nerve disorder?

• • • •

Other supervisors may prefer that you state your *conclusion* in the section heading because they want your memorandum to develop an argument that they can critique:

IV. DISCUSSION

A. New Maine's strict liability statute likely does not apply to a generally safe anesthetic that produced a fatal reaction in a patient with a rare nerve disorder.

• • • •

If your legal writing professor teaches such a format, she might substitute the acronym "CRAC" for IRAC in the Discussion section. Or your professor might invoke "CREAC" or "CRuPAC" to remind you that a legal rule that addresses a matter in controversy normally will require *explanation* or *proof*[7] of the rule, such as with case analysis or legislative history, rather than a simple summary in a sentence or two of "black-letter law."

This chapter on office memoranda, however, normally sets forth neutral, issue-oriented subject headings as illustrations. Accordingly, it adheres to the concise acronym IRAC, and Chapter 12 addresses the need to develop the content of a rule as a matter of "depth of analysis."

Indeed, if you adopt a neutral section heading, a topical word or phrase may be sufficient to remind the reader of an issue that is more specifically stated earlier in the memorandum. Moreover, the neutrality of such a heading helps to show that the author examined both sides of the law and the facts:

IV. DISCUSSION

A. Strict Liability for Use of Toxic Materials

• • • •

B. Negligence

• • • •

   1. Negligent Act

• • • •

   2. Proximate Cause

• • • •

Immediately after you identify an issue with a section heading, you may want to illuminate the issue in an introductory sentence or two that refers briefly to facts, arguments, or theories that help to explain the significance of the issue. For example, the following opening sentence expands on the section heading by explaining the significance of the theory of strict liability:

---

7. Richard K. Neumann, Jr., & Kristen Konrad Robbins-Tiscione, Legal Reasoning and Legal Writing § 12-2, at 145-47 (7th ed. 2013) (discussing rule proof and explanation and mentioning both "CREAC" and "CRuPAC"); *see* Linda H. Edwards, Legal Writing: Process, Analysis, and Organization 91-96 (5th ed. 2010) (introducing and discussing "rule explanation").

A. Strict Liability for Use of Toxic Materials

If a statute or the common law imposes strict liability for Souza's death, then Souza's estate can establish liability without proving negligence.

In some instances, the opening paragraph of a section may even draw subsidiary legal conclusions as a means of pinpointing the narrow question in dispute. For example, the following paragraph concludes that a proposed transaction would include a sale of goods. Coupled with other observations, that subsidiary conclusion leads to the primary issue of the section:

A. Choice of Law — UCC or Common Law

Whether Maldonado accepted Weinstein's offer depends in part on whether the common law of contracts or the Uniform Commercial Code (UCC) applies to the transaction. The UCC applies to "transactions in goods." U.C.C. § 2-102 (2011). Weinstein's offer to supply specifically identified, separately priced, movable plumbing parts clearly contemplates a sale of goods as part of the transaction. *See* U.C.C. § 2-105(1) (2011). His proposed transaction, however, also involves the service of installing the fixtures, raising a question about the applicability of the UCC to mixed transactions for both services and the sale of goods.

The UCC applies to such a mixed transaction only if . . . .

Of course, if an issue is adequately represented in a section heading and needs no further elaboration, the discussion can proceed immediately to an analysis of the legal standards:

A. Applicability and Satisfaction of the Statute of Frauds

The Arizona statute of frauds bars enforcement of "an agreement which is not to be performed within one year from the making thereof," unless it, "or some memorandum thereof, is in writing and signed by the party to be charged." Ariz. Rev. Stat. Ann. § 44-101(5) (2005) (copy of full text attached). . . .

2. Analyzing the Law and the Facts

After you have drafted the section heading and the optional elaboration of the issue, you ordinarily should follow the IRAC pattern of deductive reasoning developed in Chapter 6: For each issue or subissue, analyze the law and apply the law to the facts to reach a conclusion. The nature of the analysis in a discussion section obviously will vary with each issue. If the clearly applicable abstract legal rule is simple, you can present the rule and supporting authority directly and concisely, permitting you to direct most of your attention to fact analysis. Other issues may require a choice among competing rules or a clarification of the content of the applicable legal rule. If so, you may need to discuss the abstract legal rule in depth before applying it to the facts. Of course, determining the content of the rule and applying it to the facts are often related tasks: Your discussion of the question of whether particular facts satisfy the legal standard may help to clarify the content of a vague or uncertain rule.

a. Example: Statutory Analysis

Reproduced below is a portion of the discussion section of a sample office memorandum set in the fictitious state of New Maine, whose case law we will assume is published solely in the New Maine Reporter, abbreviated "N. Me." It analyzes the issue of statutory liability for administering anesthesia.

The statutory analysis in the passage focuses on defining the legal rule in a simple factual context, thus requiring relatively little independent fact analysis. In contrast, the memorandum must engage in original statutory analysis because no judicial decision has yet interpreted the statutory language in question. Accordingly, after refining the issue in an introduction, the author of the discussion presents the statutory analysis on three levels, in descending order of priority: the language of the statute, its legislative history (often difficult to find for state legislation, but easily accessible in published materials in this fictitious jurisdiction), and general policy considerations. In this example, the author has applied the law to the relevant facts at each level of the statutory analysis rather than in a single consolidated fact analysis at the end of the discussion; other means of organizing the discussion, however, are presented in the next chapter.

IV. DISCUSSION

A. Strict Liability for Use of Toxic Material

Introduction

If a statute or the common law imposes strict liability for Souza's death, then Souza's estate can establish liability without proving negligence. New Maine's common law doctrine of strict liability for injuries caused by ultrahazardous activities does not apply to noncriminal medical practices engaged in by licensed physicians. *Stanislaus v. Good Samaritan Hosp.*, 212 N. Me. 113, 115 (1989). New Maine has recently enacted a statute, however, that imposes strict liability for injuries stemming from the use of "any toxic material": "A commercial enterprise is liable for injuries proximately caused by its use of any toxic material, without regard to the degree of care exercised by the enterprise." 12 N. Me. Rev. Stat. Ann. § 242 (Supp. 2013) (effective Jan. 1, 2014). As a profit-making hospital, Humane presumably is a "commercial enterprise" within the meaning of the statute. It is less certain, however, that the anesthetic administered to Souza would qualify as a "toxic" material.

Narrow issue

The common meaning of the word "toxic" is "poisonous." *E.g.*, THE RANDOM HOUSE DICTIONARY OF THE ENGLISH LANGUAGE 1500 (unabridged) (1970). Souza's estate might plausibly argue that the anesthetic was a toxic material because it was poisonous to Souza, even though it would not have been poisonous to most others. The word "toxic," however, applies more naturally to substances that are universally harmful to humans, such as cyanide, DDT, or sulfuric acid. It strains the common meaning of "toxic" to apply it to an anesthetic that might occasionally be harmful to persons with unusual allergies or other extraordinary conditions.

Legislative history also supports a restrictive interpretation of the statutory term "any toxic material." The report of the New Maine Senate Committee on Health and Welfare suggests that the legislature was concerned only with the most deadly of substances:

> The purpose of this bill is to reallocate the cost of unavoidable accidents from victims to industry and its consumers, to discourage unnecessary use of deadly chemicals and other hazardous materials, and to encourage the development and use of substitute materials that are generally safe for human contact.

N. ME. COMM. ON HEALTH AND WELFARE, S. 78-112, 2d Sess., at 2 (2013). The anesthetic in this case is closer to the materials "generally safe for human contact" condoned by the legislature than it is to the "deadly chemicals and other hazardous materials" condemned by it.

Finally, general state policy appears to support an interpretation that excludes medically prescribed substances from the reach of the statute. The legislature and judiciary of New Maine have recognized a policy of limiting the liability of physicians to encourage the ready availability of affordable medical services. For example, under the New Maine "Good Samaritan" statute, physicians who provide certain emergency medical services are not liable for adverse consequences unless they engage in culpable conduct amounting to at least gross negligence. 12 N. Me. Rev. Stat. Ann. § 229 (2010). This protective policy is also reflected in the courts' refusal to extend common law strict liability for ultrahazardous activities to even experimental medical practices. *See Stanislaus*, 212 N. Me. at 115. The legislature presumably was aware of these laws when it enacted the toxic materials statute in 2013.

Analysis of statutory language

Preliminary fact analysis

Legislative history

Fact analysis

Policy analysis

Souza's estate may argue that the legislature intended to retreat from the protective policies of these laws by imposing strict liability on a limited segment of the activities of commercial medical practices. Absent more specific evidence of legislative intent to depart from existing legal policies, however, it is more likely that the legislature retained its protective attitude and assumed that the term "toxic material" would not include routinely prescribed medicines or anesthetics.

Fact analysis

In this case, the prescribed anesthetic, ethane, was not the safest available at the time of Souza's operation. Nonetheless, it is a frequently prescribed substance that produces beneficial results with only minor side effects in all but the most unusual cases.

Conclusion

The strict liability statute almost certainly does not apply to Souza's death.

b. Example: Established Common Law

In contrast to the previous example, the sample discussion below briefly summarizes noncontroversial legal standards and places greater emphasis on fact analysis. After illuminating the issue of negligence and summarizing general principles, the discussion separately addresses distinct subissues in different subsections. Within the first of those subsections, devoted to "negligent act," the author has consolidated the relatively simple legal standards in a single paragraph, leading to a single, uninterrupted line of fact analysis. She has divided the fact analysis itself into two paragraphs, presenting opposing factual arguments.

IV. DISCUSSION

A. Strict Liability for Use of Toxic Materials

• • • •

B. Negligence

Introduction

Assuming that Humane Hospital is not strictly liable for Souza's death, it may nonetheless be liable to Souza's estate if its agent caused the death through negligence. *See Kityama v. Mercy Hosp.*, 183 N. Me. 752, 759-60 (1974) (hospital liable for negligence of its nurse). An action for negligence requires proof of a negligent act or omission that proximately causes injury. *Baker v. Bruce*, 153 N. Me. 817, 820 (1967).

Narrow issues

In our case, the injury to Souza is obvious. In greater doubt are the elements of negligent act and proximate cause.

1. Negligent Act

A negligent act or omission consists of the breach of a duty of care owed to another. *Id*. at 821. A medical specialist owes a duty to patients to exercise at least the ordinary skill and care that is reasonable and customary nationwide in that medical specialty. *Kityama*, 183 N. Me. at 760. Furthermore, under the "thin-skulled plaintiff" rule, that duty of care encompasses the special care necessary to address increased risks created by a patient's unusual susceptibility to injury. *Id*. In this case, Humane's anesthesiologist, Unger, may have breached duties of care in her unassisted administration of general anesthesia in the face of Souza's known nerve condition.

Legal rules

Unger exercised care in determining Souza's disorder of the nervous system and in informing her of the risks presented by each of the most suitable anesthetics. Moreover, when administering the anesthetic selected by Souza, Unger took care to provide the prescribed dosage by monitoring the anesthetic intake gauge.

Fact analysis favoring Humane

However, Unger's intense concentration on the anesthetic intake gauge may have been an act of carelessness, rather than enhanced care, because it diverted Unger's attention from Souza and from equipment monitoring Souza's vital signs. Faced with Souza's known nerve disorder, Unger probably had a duty to follow the standard medical practice of summoning a nurse to assist her in administering the anesthesia. Had she done so, the team could have monitored both Souza's vital signs and the intake gauge, and a team member undoubtedly would have detected signs of distress at least 10 seconds before death, arguably enough time to cease anesthesia and take corrective measures.

Fact analysis favoring Souza's estate

On these facts, a jury could find that Unger was negligent in her administration of the anesthetic.

Conclusion

2. Proximate Cause

• • • •

In many cases, of course, an assignment calls for substantial analysis of both the law and the facts, because the parties are likely to dispute both the content of the law and its application to facts. The sample memoranda at the end of this chapter, for example, include examples of in-depth analysis and synthesis of case law, as well as opposing arguments regarding the application of the synthesized case law to facts.

E. The Conclusion

Even though the questions addressed in an office memorandum may be close, and even though your supervising attorney will not feel bound by your advice, she will expect you to take a position by stating your conclusions. A thorough memorandum will include both (1) a brief resolution of each issue within the part of the discussion section devoted to that issue, and (2) a more general summary of conclusions in a separate section at the end of the memorandum.

In the Conclusion section, you can summarize the individual conclusions that you have reached in the Discussion section of the memorandum. In addition, you may wish to summarize the analytic support for the conclusions in a depth that would have been inappropriate in the brief answers stated earlier.

You should not raise new legal arguments in the Conclusion section. However, you can and should use this section to express any strategic recommendations that your analysis inspires. For example, you may recommend that the law firm file a complaint, settle a weak case, investigate certain facts, or concentrate its efforts on a particular legal theory.

Although you may express more information in the Conclusion section than in the brief answers, your conclusion should nonetheless represent a selective summary of your analyses and recommendations. In a simple case, a few sentences may suffice; even moderately complex cases require no more than a few paragraphs.

For example, the following passage concisely synthesizes the conclusions previewed above in Section B as brief answers, and it adds strategic recommendations:

V. CONCLUSION

Summary of analyses

In light of legislative and judicial policies favoring limits on physicians' liability, the strict liability statute regulating toxic materials probably will not apply to the administration of anesthetic in this case. The courts will be even less likely to retreat from precedent by applying the common law doctrine of strict liability for ultrahazardous activities. A jury may find, however, that Humane's anesthesiologist was negligent in failing to summon assistance to administer the anesthesia or to monitor the patient closely. We can try to characterize Souza's nerve condition as a supervening cause, but *Rainbow Landscaping* will not be easy to distinguish.

Strategic recommendation

Because the risk of substantial liability is great, I recommend that we advise Humane to settle. Souza's estate may be willing to compromise; its negligence claim is not appropriate for summary disposition and thus is subject to the unpredictability of a jury.

IV. Summary

Choose a suitable format for your office memorandum, such as the following:

    I. Issues
   II. Brief Answers
 III. Facts
 IV. Discussion
   V. Conclusion

As you draft your office memoranda, remember your audience and purpose. Your goal is to inform a supervising attorney, who typically is preparing to represent a client. The supervisor usually needs an analysis that is balanced but that creatively explores means of overcoming obstacles to the client's claims or defenses. Be certain to cover the elements of IRAC in the discussion section of your memorandum: For each issue, or subissue, analyze the legal rule and apply the rule to the facts to reach a conclusion.

Samples

1. Sample 1: Office Memorandum 1

Imagine that an attorney from the fictitious state of Calzona drafted the following office memorandum using only authority from the Calzona Supreme Court. Study the memorandum and consider the questions that follow it.

Memorandum

To: Susan Elias
From: James Nelson
Re: Enforceability of Julie Week's Promise to Act as Guarantor
             for Her Cousin's Loan Obligation; File 14-127
Date: July 31, 2014

I. Issue

By stating that he would refrain from demanding payment from Borrower on a loan obligation until he "needs the money," did Lender state a promise that provided consideration for Guarantor's promise to pay the obligation in the event that Borrower failed to pay on demand?

II. Brief Answer

Probably yes. Although the Lender's promise arguably is illusory, it probably satisfies the consideration requirement by committing the Lender to a performance, subject only to economic events not entirely within the Lender's control.

III. Facts

One of our regular business clients, Julie Week (Guarantor), asserted the following facts in an interview.

On December 15, 2013, Guarantor's cousin, Don Caslin (Borrower), purchased two rare antique automobiles from a private owner, Thomas Beatty (Lender), for a total of $200,000. In a self-financing arrangement, Borrower paid $80,000 on delivery and agreed in writing to pay the remainder of the purchase price in 12 monthly installments of $10,000 each, beginning January 1, 2014.

From January to April 2014, Borrower paid Lender a total of $40,000 in monthly installments. In late April, however, Borrower suffered unusual losses in his private business, and he failed to pay the installments due on May 1 and June 1. After Lender threatened to sue for the return of the automobiles, Guarantor and Lender entered into a written agreement (the Guarantee Agreement) designed to give Borrower time to recover from his temporary financial difficulties. Dated June 6, 2014, the Guarantee Agreement refers to the agreement between Lender and Borrower as the "CREDIT/SALE AGREEMENT," and it contains the following statement of mutual obligations:

> 1. LENDER will refrain from asserting his claim against BORROWER and from demanding payment on the CREDIT/SALE AGREEMENT until LENDER needs the money.
> 2. In the event that BORROWER fails to pay all amounts due under the CREDIT/SALE AGREEMENT upon demand by LENDER, GUARANTOR will pay those amounts immediately and will pay further installments as they become due under the CREDIT/SALE AGREEMENT.

On July 1, 2014, Lender demanded payment from Borrower of sums due from May through July, but Borrower explained that he could not yet pay anything. On July 5, 2014, Lender demanded immediate payment of $30,000 from Guarantor; he also stated that he expects either Borrower or Guarantor to pay the remaining five installments as they become due on the first of each month. Borrower states that he will not be able to make further payments for at least the remainder of this year, and Guarantor hopes to avoid responsibility for the debt.

We do not yet have any evidence that Lender engaged in fraud during formation of the Guarantee Agreement or that he lacked a genuine "need" for the money in early July. You have asked me to analyze the question whether the Guarantee Contract is unenforceable on its face for lack of consideration.

IV. Discussion

Lender's promise to refrain from asserting his claim and demanding payment until he "needs the money" arguably is illusory. If so, Guarantor's promise is not supported by consideration and is unenforceable.

An enforceable contract requires consideration in the form of a bargained-for exchange in which a promisor exchanges his own promise for a return promise or performance. *Smith v. Newman*, 161 Calz. 443, 447, 667 P.2d 81, 85 (1984). The exchange can satisfy the consideration requirement even if one party's promise runs solely to the benefit of a third party rather than to the other party to the contract. *Id*. The requirement of an exchange, however, is not satisfied if one party gives only an illusory promise, which does not commit the promisor to any future performance. *Atco Corp. v. Johnson*, 155 Calz. 1211, 627 P.2d 781 (1980).

In *Atco Corp.*, the manager of an automobile repair shop purportedly promised to delay asserting a claim against the owner of an automobile for $900 in repairs. Specifically, he promised to forbear from asserting the claim "until I want the money." In exchange, a friend of the owner promised to act as guarantor of the owner's obligation. *Id*. at 1212, 627 P.2d at 782. The word "want" stated no legal commitment because it permitted the manager at his own discretion to refuse to perform any forbearance at all. Because the manager incurred no obligation, the guarantor's promise was gratuitous and unenforceable. *See id*. at 1213-14, 627 P.2d at 783-84.

On the other hand, even if a promise leaves open the possibility that the promisor will escape obligation, the promise is valid if the promisor does not have complete control over the events on which the promisor's obligation is conditioned. *Bonnie v. DeLaney*, 158 Calz. 212, 645 P.2d 887 (1982). In *Bonnie*, an agreement for the sale of a house provided that the buyer could cancel the agreement if the buyer "cannot qualify for a 30-year mortgage loan for 90% of the sales price" with any of several banks listed in the agreement. *Id*. at 213, 645 P.2d at 888. In enforcing the agreement against the seller, the court distinguished *Atco Corp.* on the ground that the word "cannot" referred to the buyer's ability to obtain a loan rather than to his desire. Because his ability to obtain a loan was partly controlled by events and decisions outside his control, the promises in the sale agreement were nonillusory and binding. *Id*. at 214-15, 645 P.2d at 889-90.

Despite the superficial similarity of guarantee agreements in both our case and *Atco. Corp.*, our client's case probably is more nearly analogous to *Bonnie*. Lender's promise to forbear until he "needs" the money appears to condition the length of his forbearance on financial events that are at least partly outside his control: As long as his income and expenses create no need for the money, Lender has a commitment to forbear from demanding payment.

To convince a court to draw an analogy to *Atco Corp.* rather than to *Bonnie*, we could argue that the word "need" refers to a subjective perception of deprivation that is inseparable from one's desires. Lender arguably can control his financial needs through his personal spending decisions, subject only to his own discretion.

Unfortunately for Guarantor, the analogy to *Bonnie* is stronger because financial need is normally viewed as a matter that is controlled at least partly by external factors. Lender's promise probably is not illusory.

V. Conclusion

The promises stated in the Guarantee Agreement appear to satisfy the consideration requirement, because Lender assumed a legal obligation by promising to refrain from asserting his claim and demanding payment until he "needs" the money. Unless we discover other serious defects in the Guarantee Agreement or Lender's performance of it, Guarantor appears to be obligated to pay, and her defenses will not be worth litigating. We should urge Guarantor to settle Lender's claim, and we should try to persuade Borrower to indemnify Guarantor and to assume responsibility for further payments, even if he must sell the cars or other property to generate funds.

Questions on Sample Memorandum 1

a. Did the substantive labels assigned to the parties serve as helpful reminders of the respective roles of the parties, or would you have retained the parties' last names as less distracting references?

b. Does the statement of facts include any facts that you would omit or summarize further? Does it omit any important facts to which the author likely had access?

c. Identify the parts of the "Discussion" section that illuminate the issue, discuss the legal standards, analyze the facts, and state a conclusion.

d. Do you agree with the author's analysis? Does it adequately explore both sides of the dispute? Is it too pessimistic?

2. Sample 2: E-Mail Memo 1

From: James Nelson
Sent: Wednesday, August 07, 2014 11:39 AM
To: Susan Elias
Subject: Follow-up on File 14-127: Consideration in Absence of Direct
   Benefit to Guarantor
Attachments [electronic copy of *Green v. Day*]

ASSIGNMENT:

This morning you asked me to:

(1) assume the facts as stated in my legal memorandum dated July 31 and

(2) determine whether Guarantor's promise to guarantee payment of Borrower's debt lacks consideration because Lender's "return" promise provided no benefit directly to Guarantor.

CONCLUSION and ANALYSIS:

The absence of a direct benefit from Lender to Guarantor does not undermine a finding of consideration. Lender's promise to delay collecting a debt from a third party, such as Borrower, can be exchanged for Guarantor's promise to Lender. *See Green v. Day*, 175 Calz. 32, 37, 865 P.2d 1204, 1209 (1993) (finding consideration in similar guarantee context). If Guarantor sought Lender's promise in exchange for her own, it is irrelevant whether she received a direct benefit from Lender's performance of the promise. *Id.* at 38, 865 P.2d at 1210 (citing to Restatement (Second) of Contracts §§ 71(2), 79 (1981)).

RECOMMENDATION:

On the facts currently known to us, Guarantor's best argument remains her claim that Lender's promise is illusory. As explained in the main memorandum, however, the claim of illusory promise is a relatively weak argument, because the phrase "until Lender needs the money" is not easily interpreted to leave Lender's performance to his unrestricted discretion. However, it may introduce enough uncertainty regarding consideration to convince Lender to compromise his claim against Guarantor in a reasonable settlement.

* * * *

Alternative Presentation of E-Mail Memo 1, with non-traditional spacing and paragraphing:

From: James Nelson
Sent: Wednesday, August 07, 2014 11:39 AM
To: Susan Elias
Subject: Follow-up on File 14-127: Consideration in Absence of Direct Benefit to Guarantor
Attachments [electronic copy of *Green v. Day*]

ASSIGNMENT

This morning you asked me to:

(1) assume the facts as stated in my legal memorandum dated July 31, and

(2) determine whether Guarantor's promise to guarantee payment of Borrower's debt lacks consideration because Lender's "return" promise provided no benefit directly to Guarantor.

ANALYSIS

The absence of a direct benefit from Lender to Guarantor does not undermine a finding of consideration:

* Lender's promise to delay collecting a debt from a third party, such as Borrower, can be exchanged for Guarantor's promise to Lender.

See Green v. Day, 175 Calz. 32, 37, 865 P.2d 1204, 1209 (1993) (finding consideration in similar guarantee context).

* If Guarantor sought Lender's promise in exchange for her own, it is irrelevant whether she received a direct benefit from Lender's performance of the promise.

Id. at 38, 865 P.2d at 1210 (citing to Restatement (Second) of Contracts §§ 71(2), 79 (1981)).

CONCLUSION AND RECOMMENDATION

The additional research does not change the conclusion of the September 16 memo:

* On the facts currently known to us, Guarantor's best argument remains her claim that Lender's promise is illusory.

* As explained in the main memorandum, however, the claim of illusory promise is a relatively weak argument, because the phrase "until Lender needs the money" is not easily interpreted to leave Lender's performance to his unrestricted discretion.

* However, it may introduce enough uncertainty regarding consideration to convince Lender to compromise his claim against Guarantor in a reasonable settlement.

3. Sample 3: Office Memorandum 2

The following memorandum, which is set in a fictitious jurisdiction, borrows from examples set forth in previous sections of this chapter addressing individual elements of a traditional office memorandum.

Memorandum

TO: James Clapton
FROM: Ginger Jackson
RE: Souza v. Humane; strict liability and negligence—File
           No. 14-63
DATE: September 9, 2014

I. Issues

A. Does the phrase "any toxic material" in New Maine's strict liability statute encompass a generally safe anesthetic that produced a fatal reaction in a patient with a rare nerve disorder?

B. Is Humane Hospital liable to Souza's estate for negligent administration of the anesthetic?

1. Did Humane's anesthesiologist breach a duty of care by administering the anesthetic without assistance and by failing to monitor Souza's reactions to anesthesia?

2. Did Souza's nerve disorder constitute a supervening cause that broke the chain of causation between the anesthesiologist's conduct and Souza's death?

II. Brief Answers

A. Probably not. A restrictive interpretation is supported by the legislative history and by a general public policy in New Maine encouraging the provision of affordable medical services. The legislature probably did not intend the statutory term "toxic material" to include medically prescribed substances that ordinarily produce a beneficial result or otherwise facilitate medical treatment.

B. Probably yes.

1. Probably yes. Under generally accepted hospital procedures, at least two trained medical personnel must monitor the administration of anesthesia, with at least one person monitoring the patient's reactions. A jury likely will find that the anesthesiologist breached a duty of care to the patient by administering the anesthesia alone.

2. No. The jury likely will also find that the patient's nerve disorder was not a supervening cause and that the anesthesiologist's negligence proximately caused the patient's death.

III. Facts

On February 17, 2014, our client, Humane Hospital, Inc. (Humane), admitted 22-year-old Teresa Souza to its facility in Greenville, New Maine, for surgery to correct a bone deformity in her foot. Souza's bone deformity was not life threatening, but it severely hampered her mobility. The planned surgery required general anesthesia.

Dr. Roberta Unger, an anesthesiologist for Humane, studied Souza's medical history and discovered that she suffered from a rare nerve disorder that slightly increased the risk that she would suffer an adverse reaction from anesthesia. Unger carefully informed Souza of the advantages and risks associated with each of the three safest and most effective general anesthetics. Souza decided to proceed with the operation and with the administration of general anesthesia. Unger and Souza ultimately agreed that Unger would administer ethane, a widely used and generally safe form of ether. Unger had initially recommended Forane, a potent muscle relaxant that maintains a stable heart rate. Souza, however, rejected Forane because of its greater cost.

At 10:00 A.M. on February 18, Souza was prepared for surgery. While the circulating nurse was occupied with another patient, and before the surgical team arrived, Unger began administering the prescribed anesthetic to Souza. Unger and Souza were alone in the room. Apparently because she was concerned that an overdose might trigger an adverse reaction, Unger concentrated intensely on the anesthetic intake gauge, which monitored the flow of anesthetic. As a consequence, she failed to watch either Souza or the equipment monitoring Souza's reactions. Approximately one minute after Unger began administering the anesthetic, the monitoring equipment sounded an alarm, as Souza's heart stopped beating. Efforts to revive her failed. According to computer records, the monitoring equipment reflected growing signs of distress in Souza beginning approximately 10 seconds before her death and before the alarm sounded.

An autopsy showed that the anesthetic combined with Souza's nerve disorder to trigger a reaction that caused cardiac arrest. Mary L. Richards, Ph.D., a professor at the University of New Maine School of Nursing, has told us that hospitals throughout the nation ordinarily require the anesthesiologist to be accompanied by a nurse during the administration of anesthesia. Both the nurse and the anesthesiologist are expected to continuously assess the patient's reaction to anesthesia by reading monitoring equipment and by observing the patient directly. Although she cannot be certain, Richards guesses that the fatal reaction was triggered largely by the final 10 seconds of Unger's administration of anesthesia.

Souza's estate has sued Humane in tort for wrongful death. It advances two theories of tort liability: (1) statutory strict liability for use of toxic materials and (2) negligence in the administration of the anesthetic.

IV. Discussion

A. Strict Liability for Use of Toxic Materials

If a statute or the common law imposes strict liability for Souza's death, then Souza's estate can establish liability without proving negligence. New Maine's common law doctrine of strict liability for injuries caused by ultrahazardous activities does not apply to noncriminal medical practices engaged in by licensed physicians. *Stanislaus v. Good Samaritan Hosp.*, 212 N. Me. 113, 115 (1989). New Maine has enacted a statute, however, that imposes strict liability for injuries stemming from the use of "any toxic material": "A commercial enterprise is liable for injuries proximately caused by its use of any toxic material, without regard to the degree of care exercised by the enterprise." 12 N. Me. Rev. Stat. Ann. § 242 (Supp. 2013) (effective Jan. 1, 2014).

The New Maine courts have not yet had an opportunity to interpret the strict liability statute in a published opinion. As a profit-making hospital, Humane presumably is a "commercial enterprise" within the meaning of the statute. It is less certain, however, that the anesthetic administered to Souza would qualify as a "toxic" material.

The common meaning of the word "toxic" is "poisonous." *E.g.*, THE RANDOM HOUSE DICTIONARY OF THE ENGLISH LANGUAGE 1500 (unabridged) (1970). Souza's estate might plausibly argue that the anesthetic was a toxic material because it was poisonous to Souza, even though it would not have been poisonous to most others. The word "toxic," however, applies more naturally to substances that are universally harmful to humans, such as cyanide, DDT, or sulfuric acid. It strains the common meaning of "toxic" to apply it to an anesthetic that might occasionally be harmful to persons with unusual allergies or other extraordinary conditions.

Legislative history also supports a restrictive interpretation of the statutory term "any toxic material." The report of the New Maine Senate Committee on Health and Welfare suggests that the legislature was concerned only with the most deadly of substances:

> The purpose of this bill is to reallocate the cost of unavoidable accidents from victims to industry and its consumers, to discourage unnecessary use of deadly chemicals and other hazardous materials, and to encourage the development and use of substitute materials that are generally safe for human contact.

N. ME. COMM. ON HEALTH AND WELFARE, S. 78-112, 2d Sess., at 2 (2013). The anesthetic in this case is closer to the materials "generally safe for human contact" condoned by the legislature than it is to the "deadly chemicals and other hazardous materials" condemned by it.

Finally, general state policy appears to support an interpretation that excludes medically prescribed substances from the reach of the statute. The legislature and judiciary of New Maine have recognized a policy of limiting the liability of physicians to encourage the ready availability of affordable medical services. For example, under the New Maine "Good Samaritan" statute, physicians who provide certain emergency medical services are not liable for adverse consequences unless they engage in culpable conduct amounting to at least gross negligence. 12 N. Me. Rev. Stat. § 229 (2010). This protective policy is also reflected in the courts' refusal to extend common law strict liability for ultrahazardous activities to even experimental medical practices. *See Stanislaus*, 212 N. Me. at 115. The legislature presumably was aware of these laws when it enacted the toxic materials statute in 2013.

Souza's estate may argue that the legislature intended to retreat from the protective policies of these laws by imposing strict liability on a limited segment of the activities of commercial medical practices. Absent more specific evidence of legislative intent to depart from existing legal policies, however, it is more likely that the legislature retained its protective attitude and assumed that the term "any toxic material" would not include routinely prescribed medicines or anesthetics.

In this case, the prescribed anesthetic, ethane, was not the safest available at the time of Souza's operation. Nonetheless, it is a frequently prescribed substance that produces beneficial results with only minor side effects in all but the most unusual cases. The strict liability statute probably does not apply to Souza's death.

B. Negligence

Assuming that Humane is not strictly liable for Souza's death, it may nonetheless be liable to Souza's estate if its agent caused the death through negligence. *See Kityama v. Mercy Hosp.*, 183 N. Me. 752, 759-60 (1974) (hospital liable for negligence of its nurse). An action for negligence requires proof of a negligent act or omission that proximately causes injury. *Baker v. Bruce*, 153 N. Me. 817, 820 (1967).

In our case, the injury to Souza is obvious. In greater doubt are the elements of negligent act and proximate cause.

1. Negligent Act

A negligent act or omission consists of the breach of a duty of care owed to another. *Id*. at 821. A medical specialist owes a duty to patients to exercise at least the ordinary skill and care that is reasonable and customary nationwide in that medical specialty. *Kityama*, 183 N. Me. at 760. Furthermore, under the "thin-skulled plaintiff" rule, that duty of care encompasses the special care necessary to address increased risks created by a patient's unusual susceptibility to injury. *Id*. In this case, Humane's anesthesiologist, Unger, may have breached duties of care in her unassisted administration of general anesthesia in the face of Souza's known nerve condition.

Unger exercised care in determining Souza's disorder of the nervous system and in informing her of the risks presented by each of the most suitable anesthetics. Moreover, when administering the anesthetic selected by Souza, Unger took care to provide the prescribed dosage by monitoring the anesthetic intake gauge.

On the other hand, Unger's intense concentration on the anesthetic intake gauge may have been an act of carelessness, rather than enhanced care, because it diverted Unger's attention from Souza and from the equipment monitoring Souza's vital signs. Faced with Souza's known nervous disorder, Unger probably had a duty to follow the standard medical practice of summoning a nurse to assist her in administering the anesthesia. Had she done so, the team could have monitored both Souza's vital signs and the intake gauge, and a team member undoubtedly would have detected signs of distress at least 10 seconds before death, arguably enough time to cease anesthesia and take corrective measures.

On these facts, a jury could find that Unger was negligent in her administration of the anesthetic.

2. Proximate Cause

Even if its agent was negligent, Humane will not be liable to Souza's estate unless the negligence proximately caused Souza's death. *See, e.g., Baker v. Bruce*, 153 N. Me. 817, 821 (1967). Proximate cause is a flexible doctrine that precludes liability if the relationship between negligence and an injury is so attenuated that it would be unfair to hold the negligent party responsible for the injury. *Id*. at 821-22.

In this case, Humane can argue that the signs of distress appearing for ten seconds on the monitoring equipment prior to the alarm would not have given even two observant medical workers sufficient time to reverse Souza's fatal reaction. If so, even careful administration of anesthesia would have resulted in death, suggesting that Souza's reaction was truly an unforeseeable accident rather than the proximate result of any negligent act. Unfortunately, the factual premise of this argument may be unsound: According to our own expert, cessation of the anesthesia at the first signs of distress could have prevented the fatal reaction. We may want to investigate this further with other experts.

As a fall-back position on proximate cause, Humane could try to characterize Souza's rare nerve condition as a supervening cause. Such an intervening cause may break the chain of causation between the negligence and the injury, particularly if the intervening event was unexpected. *See Safehouse Ins. Co. v. Rainbow Landscaping Co.*, 223 N. Me. 29, 31, 35 (1987) (dictum). Unfortunately, a court may be reluctant to analyze this issue within the framework of supervening cause. Under the more conventional approach, a court would simply apply the "thin-skulled plaintiff" rule to expand Unger's duty of care to encompass responsibility for increased risks of injury created by Souza's known nerve condition. However, if we can persuade the court to depart from the conventional approach and to analyze the increased risk within the less clearly applicable framework of supervening cause, we will gain the opportunity to develop an additional argument to avoid liability.

To develop a supervening-cause argument, we must distinguish *Rainbow Landscaping*, which liberally allocates the risks of some intervening causes to the tortfeasor. In *Rainbow Landscaping*, a landscaping company agreed in writing with a general contractor to install a sprinkler system in the yards surrounding a new house in its final stages of construction. The written contract specifically obligated the landscaper to perform its work "in a manner that does not interfere with the ongoing work of other subcontractors or deface their finished product." *Id*. at 32. On the day that the landscaper began its work, its employees knew that another subcontractor was painting the interior of the house. While welding a sprinkler pipe to a house water line, an employee of the landscaper ignited paint fumes that had accumulated in a room recently painted by the painting subcontractor. The resulting fire entirely destroyed the nearly completed house.

In a suit brought against the landscaper by the owner's insurer, the landscaper argued on its motion for a directed verdict that, even if the landscaper had acted negligently, the paint fumes constituted an intervening cause that precluded a finding of proximate cause. The trial court denied the motion, and the jury returned a verdict for the insurer. The New Maine Supreme Court affirmed. It held that the landscaper was responsible for the consequences of the combustion of paint fumes that it had triggered because its employee should have been aware of the paint fumes and the danger they posed. *Id*. at 35. In dictum, the court stated that it might have reached a different result had the landscaper reasonably failed to foresee that the welding could trigger such a blaze. *See id*.

We can try to distinguish our case from *Rainbow Landscaping* by arguing that the landscaper's agreement to accommodate the work of other subcontractors justified the finding that the landscaper should have known of the hazard. Under this reasoning, the agreement was critical to the allocation of responsibility to the landscaper for the consequences of igniting the paint. That contract has no direct counterpart in our case. Moreover, in light of New Maine's policy of limiting the liability of medical care providers, a court might be willing to apply the doctrine of proximate cause more stringently in a hospital setting than in a construction setting.

On the other hand, although Souza's adverse reaction to the anesthetic was not highly probable, it was certainly foreseeable as a possible consequence of Souza's known nerve condition. Indeed, Unger's intense concentration on the intake gauge shows that she indeed specifically anticipated such a reaction. The absence of a contract such as the one in *Rainbow Landscaping* might be viewed as a technical and immaterial distinction.

Therefore, even if we can persuade a court to analyze Souza's nerve condition within the framework of supervening cause, the court probably will not find the doctrine satisfied on the facts of this case. If Souza's estate can prove that Unger was negligent, it almost certainly can show proximate cause as well.

V. Conclusion

In light of legislative and judicial policies favoring limits on physicians' liability, the strict liability statute regulating toxic materials probably will not apply to the administration of the anesthetic in this case. The courts will be even less likely to retreat from precedent by applying the common law doctrine imposing strict liability for ultrahazardous activities. A jury may find, however, that Humane's anesthesiologist was negligent in failing to summon assistance for the administration of the anesthesia and to monitor Souza more closely. We can try to characterize Souza's nerve condition as a supervening cause, but *Rainbow Landscaping* will not be easy to distinguish.

Because the risk of substantial liability is great, I recommend that we advise Humane to settle. Souza's estate may be willing to compromise; its negligence claim is not appropriate for summary disposition and thus is subject to the unpredictability of a jury.

Questions on Office Memorandum 2

a. Distinguish between the statutory and common law claims discussed in Office Memorandum 2. How does the legal method differ in the analysis of each claim?

b. Review the statutory analysis in section IV.A of Office Memorandum 2. Its original analysis of language, legislative history, and policy is indispensable precisely because no court had yet interpreted the statute. Imagine instead that the author of the memorandum had found a New Maine case that discusses the applicability of the strict liability statute to a restaurant that sold raw oysters infected with the vibrio vulnificus bacteria. Most oysters naturally absorb this bacteria, and almost all persons who ingest the bacteria after eating raw oysters suffer no ill effects. However, in a tiny percentage of persons, particularly those with liver or kidney problems, the bacteria can lead to septicemia, which often results in death. In the New Maine case, *Spratt v. Shuck*, a man developed a bacterial infection and died after eating raw oysters served in a restaurant.[8]

Imagine that the New Maine Supreme Court examined the language, legislative history, and policy of the New Maine statute governing strict liability for toxic materials. Imagine further that it found that a raw oyster infected with the vibrio vulnificus bacteria is not a "toxic material" within

---

8. The facts for this fictitious case are inspired by those of Simeon v. Doe, 618 So. 2d 848 (La. 1993).

the meaning of the statute. Would the author of the memorandum discuss the issue of statutory liability in the same manner if a case like *Spratt v. Shuck* were available? Would he rely as heavily on his own analysis of language, legislative history, and policy? How would the analysis differ if it focused on case law such as *Spratt v. Shuck*?

c. Review the subsection discussing the element of proximate cause in a negligence action. Note how the author of the memorandum seeks to manipulate the analytic framework within which to address the legal consequences of Souza's unusual nerve condition. Is this a fair method of argument? Can it be used in other contexts? Most professors of Tort Law readily conclude that a court would analyze Souza's nerve condition within the "thin-skulled plaintiff" rule regarding the scope of duties and not within the framework of proximate cause. In that light, is the argument in the memorandum a welcome exercise in creative argument, or is it a misleading waste of time for the reader?

d. Notice the frequent use of the word "we" in the section on proximate cause. Should the author of a memorandum avoid using such first-person pronouns in a legal analysis? Are first-person pronouns appropriate when referring to the law firm's development of facts or legal theories? Are they better than passive voice or other abstractions?

4. Sample 4: E-Mail Memo 2

From: Ginger Jackson
Sent: Wednesday, November 13, 2013 3:19 PM
To: James Clapton
Subject: New Strict Liability Statute for use of Toxic Materials, as Applied to Anesthesia
Attachments [Word file of this e-mail memo]

I.   Overview: Background, Issue, and Conclusion

Our client, Humane Hospital ("Humane"), is concerned about recent legislation in New Maine. When it becomes effective January 1, 2014, it will impose strict liability for injuries caused by commercial use of toxic materials. Humane is particularly concerned about liability for careful administration of anesthesia to a patient who has an unexpected adverse reaction.

You asked me to address the following issue:

Does the phrase "any toxic material" in New Maine's strict liability statute encompass a generally safe anesthetic that produces a fatal reaction in a patient with a rare and previously undetected intolerance for the anesthetic?

Based on the statutory text, legislative history, and state policy, Humane can safely conclude that its administration of anesthesia will not trigger strict liability under the new statute.

II. Discussion

New Maine recently enacted a statute that imposes strict liability for injuries stemming from the use of "any toxic material": "A commercial enterprise is liable for injuries proximately caused by its use of any toxic material, without regard to the degree of care exercised by the enterprise." 12 N. Me. Rev. Stat. Ann. § 242 (Supp. 2013) (effective Jan. 1, 2014).

The common meaning of the word "toxic" is "poisonous." *E.g.*, THE RANDOM HOUSE DICTIONARY OF THE ENGLISH LANGUAGE 1500 (unabridged) (1970). A generally safe anesthetic conceivably could be viewed as a toxic material under this definition because it could produce a fatal reaction in some patients with a rare intolerance for the anesthetic. The word "toxic," however, applies more naturally to substances that are universally harmful to humans, such as cyanide, DDT, or sulfuric acid. It strains the common meaning of "toxic" to apply it to an anesthetic that might occasionally be harmful to persons with unusual allergies or other extraordinary conditions.

Legislative history also supports a restrictive interpretation of the statutory term "any toxic material." The report of the New Maine Senate Committee on Health and Welfare suggests that the legislature was concerned only with the most deadly of substances:

> The purpose of this bill is to reallocate the cost of unavoidable accidents from victims to industry and its consumers, to discourage unnecessary use of deadly chemicals and other hazardous materials, and to encourage the development and use of substitute materials that are generally safe for human contact.

N. ME. COMM. ON HEALTH AND WELFARE, S. 78-112, 2d Sess., at 2 (2013). The anesthetic in this case is closer to the materials "generally safe for human contact" condoned by the legislature than it is to the "deadly chemicals and other hazardous materials" condemned by it.

Finally, the legislature and judiciary of New Maine have recognized a policy of limiting the liability of physicians to encourage the ready availability of affordable medical services. For example, under the New Maine "Good Samaritan" statute, physicians who provide certain emergency medical services are not liable for adverse consequences unless they engage in culpable conduct amounting to at least gross negligence. 12 N. Me. Rev. Stat. § 229 (2010). This protective policy is also reflected in the courts' refusal to extend common law strict liability for ultrahazardous activities to even experimental medical practices. *See Stanislaus v. Good Samaritan Hosp.*, 212 N. Me. 113, 115 (1989). The legislature presumably was aware of these laws when it enacted the toxic materials statute in 2013. Absent evidence of legislative intent to depart from these legal policies, it is likely that the legislature retained its protective attitude toward the medical profession and assumed that the term "any toxic material" would not include routinely prescribed medicines or anesthetics.

III. Recommendation

The new statute almost certainly will not impose strict liability for injuries stemming from Humane's administration of generally safe medical procedures such as anesthesia. Thus, negligence will remain the only basis for tort liability stemming from Humane's delivery of medical services. Accordingly, we should advise Humane to avoid negligence by continuing to exercise the utmost care with patients, such as by informing patients of known risks, allowing the patient to choose between alternative treatments when appropriate, and refraining from administering an anesthetic to a patient with a known allergy or intolerance to that anesthetic.

We should monitor our state's case law, to determine whether we should update our analysis and advice in light of any judicial interpretations of the new statute.

Chapter 12

Organization of Office Memoranda and Briefs

One of the most important features of effective legal analysis and writing is good organization. Techniques of organization are also among the most difficult things to develop and to teach. With a few months of practice, however, you can steadily improve your skills. Regular outlining of course material in law school is an excellent way to build basic skills.

Although the focus of Part V is objective analysis in office memoranda, the techniques of organization described in this chapter apply directly to both office memoranda and legal briefs. Accordingly, this chapter uses examples from both memoranda and briefs. The following sections explore problems of organization on four different levels, progressing from broader problems of (1) format and (2) relationships among multiple issues, to narrower problems of (3) progression within sections and (4) effective paragraphing.

I. Format

Before drafting any legal document, you must select an appropriate format for the document. The format will determine the essential content of the document and the order in which you present the different parts of that content.

Rules of procedure and local court rules prescribe formats for appellate briefs. With somewhat less detail, they also prescribe or suggest formats for trial pleadings, motions, and briefs. You should take care to follow these rules, because they presumably reflect the court's views about effective content and administrative efficiency. If you depart from the prescribed format, you may irritate the judge or judges who must read the document. Indeed, you may even lead the judge or the clerk's office to reject the document for filing or to impose other sanctions.[1]

The most appropriate format for other documents, such as a contract or an office memorandum, is partly a matter of judgment or style for you or your law firm. For example, Section II of Chapter 11 outlines three different formats for a formal office memorandum; whether one is more appropriate to an assignment than another will depend on the complexity of the memorandum, the preferences of your assigning attorney, and your own personal style. Before beginning to write such a document, you should take a few moments to determine which format will best suit your audience, your personal style, and the purposes of the document.

II. Relationships Among Multiple Issues and Subissues

Your statement of the issues and your discussion or argument section of an office memorandum or legal brief should reflect the proper relationships among multiple issues and subissues. Good organization at this broad level requires a thorough understanding of the substantive analysis as well as attention to effective writing techniques. Therefore, if you experience unusual difficulty with this level of organization, you may wish to supplement your research before proceeding further. By reviewing basic principles in a secondary source, you can gain a broad perspective that will help you organize your material.

---

1. *See, e.g.*, N/S Corp. v. Liberty Mut. Ins. Co., 127 F.3d 1145 (9th Cir. 1997) (striking appellant's briefs and dismissing appeal, and citing to similar actions in other cases); Westinghouse Elec. Corp. v. NLRB, 809 F.2d 419, 424-25 (7th Cir. 1987) (imposing $1,000 penalty on counsel for evading federal rule limiting the number of pages of its opening brief).

A. Proper Relationships Among Topics

Stated most simply, the section headings of the discussion or argument section of a document should show which topics are distinct and independent, and which are subsets of a more general topic. The statement of the issues should show the same relationships. These relationships are a function of the elements of the legal claims or defenses in question.

For example, suppose that you are preparing an office memorandum to discuss the following theories of employer liability for the discharge of an employee: (1) violation of a promise expressed in the company policy manual to invoke specified hearing procedures before terminating any employee, (2) wrongful discharge for a reason that violates public policy, and (3) intentional infliction of emotional distress.

The following information about the legal content of these claims in one state will help you devise an appropriate organizational structure. The elements of a contract action for breach of promise in a policy manual are (1) a promise in the manual by the employer to restrict the circumstances justifying discharge of the employee; (2) a basis for enforcing the promise, such as incorporation of the manual into the employment contract; and (3) breach of the promise.[2] The elements of the tort of wrongful discharge of an at-will employee in violation of public policy are (1) discharge of the employee (2) for a reason that contravenes a legislative public policy.[3] Finally, the elements of the tort of intentional infliction of emotional distress are (1) extreme and outrageous conduct (2) that is taken with the intent to cause emotional distress or with reckless disregard for the possibility of those consequences and (3) that causes (4) severe emotional distress.[4]

Although organization of these topics is a matter of judgment rather than an exact science, most legal writers will agree that the following section headings of the discussion section of the memorandum leave room for improvement:

IV. DISCUSSION

    A. Wrongful Discharge—Violation of Public Policy or Breach of Promise in Employee Manual

    B. Intentional Infliction of Emotional Distress

        1. Remedies

First, section A inappropriately encompasses two distinct kinds of claims. True, both claims represent theories of liability in an emerging field known generically as "wrongful discharge." Under this state's law, however, wrongful discharge in violation of public policy is a tort whose elements have little

---

2. *See* ARIZ. REV. STAT. ANN. § 23-1501(2) (Supp. 2009); Leikvold v. Valley View Cmty. Hosp., 141 Ariz. 544, 688 P.2d 170 (1984) (common law predecessor to § 23-1501(2)).

3. *See* ARIZ. REV. STAT. ANN. § 23-1501(3)(b) (Supp. 2009); Wagenseller v. Scottsdale Mem'l Hosp., 147 Ariz. 370, 376-81, 710 P.2d 1025, 1031-36 (1985) (common law predecessor to § 23-1501(3)(b)).

4. *See, e.g.*, Watts v. Golden Age Nursing Home, 127 Ariz. 255, 619 P.2d 1032 (1980).

in common with those of a claim for breach of a contractual promise to restrict the circumstances of terminating the employment contract.

Second, section B inappropriately includes a single subsection on remedies. If remedies were the only topic in section B, a subsection designation would be unnecessary. On the other hand, if section B discusses a theory of liability as well as remedies, both subtopics should be represented in subsection headings if either is. Finally, if the topic of remedies encompasses all of the theories of liability, it should not be buried within a section that addresses only the theory of intentional infliction of emotional distress.

By applying principles discussed in Section III.A of Chapter 8, you could address these defects and adopt an improved organizational structure such as the following:

IV. DISCUSSION
    A. Breach of Contract
    B. Wrongful Discharge in Violation of Public Policy
    C. Intentional Infliction of Emotional Distress
    D. Remedies

Of course, this sample outline represents only one of many reasonable organizational structures for the memorandum in question. Other organizational structures may reflect different ways of presenting the analyses of remedies. For example, you might recognize that sections A through C present various theories of liability and could be consolidated in a section that is on the same level as the separate topic of remedies. Because the remedies for breach of contract are significantly different from those available for either of the tort claims, the section on remedies could discuss them separately:

IV. DISCUSSION
    A. Theories of Liability
        1. Breach of Contract
        2. Wrongful Discharge in Violation of Public Policy
        3. Intentional Infliction of Emotional Distress
    B. Remedies
        1. Contract
        2. Tort

Alternatively, you might decide to discuss remedies within each of the sections that introduces a theory of liability, rather than in a separate comprehensive section devoted to remedies. Under this organizational scheme, you might consolidate the two tort theories into a single section if you concluded that the remedies for each would be governed by the same tort principles. Depending on the depth of discussion in the memorandum, you could discuss remedies either in a paragraph at the end of each major section or, as shown below, in separate subsections.

IV. DISCUSSION
    A. Breach of Contract
        1. Breach of Promise in an Employee Manual
        2. Contract Remedies
    B. Tort
        1. Wrongful Discharge in Violation of Public Policy
        2. Intentional Infliction of Emotional Distress
        3. Tort Remedies

Each of these alternative approaches to organization properly displays relationships among topics in a logical manner. Whether one approach advances the purposes of the document better than another is a matter of judgment for the writer.

B. Order of Topics

1. Logical Organization in an Office Memorandum

In an office memorandum, you should organize your topics in a logical order that permits early topics to build a foundation for subsequent topics. The clearest example of this is a multiple-issue discussion in which some issues are "threshold issues" in the sense that the resolution of those issues affects the analysis of other issues. Logically, you should discuss the threshold issues before you discuss the issues that are dependent on the outcome of the threshold issues.

For example, suppose that Maya Tortilla Co. alleges that Bakeway Supermarkets (1) formed a contract with Maya; (2) breached its contractual obligations, at least under Maya's interpretation of the contract; (3) and is liable to Maya for $20,000 in damages. If Bakeway disputes each of these allegations, the parties have raised three entirely separate issues.

Logically, you should discuss issue #1 first because contract formation is a threshold issue: Bakeway did not assume any contractual obligations and consequent potential liability if it did not form a contract with Maya. Similarly, you should discuss issue #2 before issue #3 for two reasons. First, Bakeway is not liable in damages unless it breached. Second, to determine whether Bakeway breached, you must interpret the contract and define Bakeway's obligation; in turn, the scope of Bakeway's obligation will determine Maya's expectation interest, on which damages will be based.

2. Strategic Organization in a Brief

If you are drafting a brief rather than an office memorandum, you might organize your arguments differently, because strategic considerations may lead you to depart from a purely logical ordering of arguments. Like other people, judges are strongly influenced by first impressions. In many cases, the first argument in a brief influences the judge more strongly than later ones. Also, if pressed for time, a busy trial judge may find herself rushing through the last few pages of a pretrial motions brief before oral argument. Accordingly, if one of your arguments is much stronger than the others, you can exercise discretion to present it first in your brief, even though another issue is logically prior.

3. Discussing or Arguing the Full Range of Issues

Finally, you should apply all these considerations only to order your topics effectively, not to cut off discussion of any of the issues. In a close case, you cannot predict with certainty how a court will resolve a threshold issue. Accordingly, if a threshold issue raises a question sufficiently doubtful to warrant full discussion in an office memorandum or a brief, you should address all of the other substantial issues, even if you tentatively resolve the threshold issue in a way that logically would cut off discussion. In an office memorandum, for example, if you conclude that Bakeway probably did not breach the contract, you should nonetheless discuss the question of the amount of damages for which Bakeway will be liable if—contrary to your prediction—the judge or jury finds that Bakeway breached.

C. Technique

As illustrated in Section V of Chapter 10, the most efficient way to organize the topics of a memorandum or brief is to outline them in the prewriting stage: after you have researched and analyzed the problem but before you begin to write. Even when you are working under severe time pressure, you should take a few minutes to organize your notes, think deeply and creatively about the analysis, and explore the relationships between topics by comparing different outlines of the discussion or argument. You can much more easily modify your analytic approach and writing strategy at the prewriting stage than you can midway through the first draft.

If you did not prepare an outline before writing the first draft, and if the first draft appears hopelessly disorganized, you can still derive benefits from outlining techniques, albeit with less efficiency than at the prewriting stage. By writing out the section and subsection headings of your first draft in outline form, you can expose and evaluate the organization of your draft and improve the organization by modifying the outline.

Finally, once you have chosen an organizational structure, you should clearly communicate that structure to the reader with descriptive section and subsection headings that are at least roughly parallel to the structure of the statement of issues. In an answer to a law school examination, such headings may even take the place of more formal statements of the issues.

III. Progression Within Section or Subsection

Once you have divided your topics into separate sections, you are ready to organize the discussion or argument within each section. At the most general level, your analysis should follow the familiar "IRAC" pattern of deductive reasoning: After introducing the issue or argument with a heading and perhaps with a brief introduction in the text, you should discuss or argue the law, apply that law to the facts, and reach a conclusion.

Effective progression within a section also requires attention to one or more of four considerations:

1. hierarchy of authority,
2. progression from general to specific,
3. progression from fundamental to uncertain, and
4. separation or consolidation of logical discussions or arguments.

The first three of these considerations deal mainly with the development of legal standards. The fourth deals with methods of combining legal and factual analysis.

A. Hierarchy of Authority

In statutory analysis, the hierarchy of authority leads to a convention of organization. You should analyze, or at least present, the statutory language in question before analyzing cases that either interpret the statute or that discuss supplemental common law:

C. Commercial Impracticability

The Uniform Commercial Code (UCC) provides that, in limited circumstances, a seller's failure to deliver goods is not a breach of contract "if performance as agreed has been made impracticable by the occurrence of a contingency the non-occurrence of which was a basic assumption on which the contract was made." U.C.C. § 2-615(a) (2011). The UCC's use of the term "impracticable" suggests a more liberal standard for discharging obligations than the traditional common law standard of "impossibility of performance." *See Bjorn v. Borg* . . . .

The normal convention of starting with the statutory language will occasionally apply with less force in the analysis of some of the more commonly litigated provisions of a constitution. Because constitutional provisions are typically even more general than statutory provisions, the enormous body of case law interpreting a provision may take on a life of its own, overshadowing the text of the constitutional provision. Thus, you need not quote the language of the Fourth Amendment before asserting a well-established proposition about the need to obtain a warrant before searching a dwelling; reference to case law interpreting the Fourth Amendment in most cases will be sufficient. Nonetheless, you should begin the analysis by at least identifying the Fourth Amendment as the source of the restriction on searches. Moreover, some constitutional issues, like most issues of statutory interpretation, will be sufficiently novel to require attention to text, in which case you should begin the analysis with the language of the constitutional provision.

B. Progression from General to Specific

Reading a legal analysis or argument should be like viewing a large painting that covers a third of the wall of a museum exhibit room. As the viewer enters, he sees the general outlines of the whole painting, and he becomes curious about a few provocative parts of the whole. He then moves closer to the painting to separately examine each of these parts. Finally, when he steps back for a final view of the painting as a whole, he may now appreciate it more fully because of his prior exploration of some of the details.

Similarly, overlapping sections in a legal document can

1. provide an overview to the document,
2. separately explore important matters in some detail, and
3. conclude with a summary or with general insights that are easier to appreciate after the discussion of details.

On a broad level, a memorandum or brief performs these functions with (1) the statement of issues or other introduction, (2) the discussion or argument, and (3) the conclusion. On a narrower level, this kind of progression is often appropriate within a section of the discussion or argument.

For an example of progression within a section, suppose that the plaintiff in a tort action alleges that the defendant intentionally inflicted emotional distress. If the defendant, your client, contends that the facts in the record fail to satisfy two of the elements of that tort, your brief for the defendant might address each of those two elements separately, either in separate paragraphs or in separate subsections of the argument. If so, you can orient the reader by beginning with a paragraph that introduces each of the elements:

II.   ARGUMENT

A. Lew's Allegations in Count II Fail to State a Claim for Intentional Infliction of Emotional Distress.

General
overview

To establish a right to relief for intentional infliction of emotional distress, Lew must plead and prove that (1) Smith engaged in extreme and outrageous conduct (2) with the intent to cause severe emotional distress or with reckless disregard for the possibility of those consequences, and that (3) his actions caused Lew to suffer (4) severe emotional distress. *See Watts v. Golden Age Nursing Home,* 127 Ariz. 255, 619 P.2d 1032 (1980). Even assuming the truth of Lew's allegations about the manner in which Smith terminated Lew's employment contract, the complaint does not properly allege either the extreme conduct or the severe distress required for liability. Therefore, Lew has failed to state a claim for relief in Count II.

1. Smith's Alleged Conduct Was Not "Extreme and Outrageous."

Only the most deplorable and shocking conduct satisfies the narrow definition of "extreme and outrageous conduct." *Beers v. Bolton*, ... In *Beers*, ...

In this case, the complaint alleges only that Smith was a blunt manager who exercised his contractual privilege to fire Lew without advance notice and who stated his reasons for firing him with utmost candor. . . .

Specific argument

2. Lew's Alleged "Depression" Does Not Amount to Severe Emotional Distress.

Proof of severe emotional distress . . . .

The introduction in the first paragraph above not only provides an overview of the legal standards, it summarizes the overall argument of the section. That argument appears elsewhere as well: The brief (1) states it concisely in the heading for section A; (2) develops it in greater detail in each of the subsections; and (3) should repeat it in general terms at the end of section A, in a separate conclusion section at the end of the document, or both.

At a different level within a section, you might introduce a general principle in a topic sentence before exploring it in greater detail within the same paragraph:

Even if a promise leaves open the possibility that the promisor will escape obligation, however, the promise is valid if the promisor does not have complete control over the events on which the promisor's obligation is conditioned. *Bonnie v. DeLaney*, 158 Calz. 212, 645 P.2d 887 (1982). In *Bonnie*, an agreement for the sale of a house provided that the buyer could cancel the agreement if the buyer "cannot qualify for a 30-year mortgage loan for 90% of the sales price" with any of several banks listed in the agreement. *Id.* at 213, 645 P.2d at 888. In enforcing the agreement against the seller, the court distinguished *Atco Corp.* on the ground that the word "cannot" referred to the buyer's ability to obtain a loan rather than to his desire. Because his ability to obtain a loan was partly controlled by events and decisions outside his control, the promises in the sale agreement were nonillusory and binding. *See id.* at 214-15, 645 P.2d 889-90.

Topic sentence

Specific case analysis

In the preceding example, the opening sentence of the paragraph summarizes the general point that the *Bonnie* decision illustrates. That introduction prepares the reader for the detailed analysis of *Bonnie* that follows.

C. Progression from Fundamental to Complex

Some legal discussions or arguments may lend themselves to a related method of organization within a section or subsection: progression from fundamental or undisputed points to complex or disputed points. In some cases, the preliminary points may address matters that should not be disputed; they may simply provide helpful background information or establish legal premises to the main topic of discussion.

For example, the following passage from a brief provides background information about statutory policies. That information helps support the ultimate argument that a contractual provision attempting to fix damages for breach is not enforceable:

C. The Liquidated Damages Clause Is Void as a Penalty

Fundamental premises

The contract for the sale of the engine parts is a "transaction in goods" and thus is covered by the Uniform Commercial Code (UCC). U.C.C. §§ 2-102, 2-105 (2011). UCC remedies for breach of contract are designed to compensate the victim of the breach for the loss of the value of the expected performance. *See* U.C.C. § 1-305(a) (2001). They do not permit imposition of a penalty that is designed to discourage breach or to punish the breaching party. *See id.*

Transition to disputed point

Within limited parameters, the UCC permits parties to agree to fix damages for breach in advance by including a provision for "liquidated damages" in their sales contract. However, such damages must be limited to

> an amount which is reasonable in the light of the anticipated or actual harm caused by the breach, the difficulties of proof of loss, and the inconvenience or nonfeasibility of otherwise obtaining an adequate remedy. A term fixing unreasonably large liquidated damages is void as a penalty.

U.C.C. § 2-718(1) (2011). In this case, section 5.4 of the contract attempts to fix damages at an amount that is disproportionate to any anticipated or actual harm. Thus, it is an unenforceable penalty clause . . . .

The first paragraph of the preceding passage addresses fundamental matters of statutory policy that are technically not in issue because the opposing party will not dispute them. It provides a general orientation, however, that will help to place in perspective the argument relating to the hotly disputed question: Does the liquidated damages clause constitute an impermissible penalty under the UCC? True, each major section in a brief should begin with an unqualified statement of the argument. In this example, however, the short and plain section heading arguably meets that strategic requirement, paving the way for immediate establishment of premises that support a fuller statement of the argument.

D. Separation or Consolidation of Analyses

1. Overview—IRAC in Context

In analyzing an issue in a memorandum or a brief, you ordinarily should follow the general structure of the syllogism of deductive reasoning:

major premise—rule of law
minor premise—application of law to facts
conclusion

At the simplest level, you can analyze a topic in a single, undivided IRAC, or in a version of IRAC that begins with an argument or conclusion rather than a neutral reference to the issue. In other words, you would organize your analysis or argument around a syllogism presented in a single, undivided section of your Discussion or Argument:

A. Topic or Argument
   Introduction [if needed to illuminate the issue or argument]
   Legal Rule
   Application to Facts
   Conclusion

Many topics, however, are not so simple. If a topic is unusually complex, you might separately present the elements of a single syllogism in several subsections:

A. Topic or Argument
   Introduction
   1. Legal Rule
      a. Synthesis and In-Depth Analysis of Persuasive Authority
      b. In-Depth Policy Analysis
   2. Application to Facts
      a. Analysis of Facts Relating to First Transaction
      b. Analysis of Facts Relating to Second Transaction
   3. Conclusion

Conversely, if your main topic of discussion or argument encompasses closely related subtopics that do not warrant separation into formal subsections, you might exercise discretion to discuss more than one topic within an undivided section or subsection. If so, you can present your analysis in either of two ways. First, you can separate the topics into several smaller syllogisms within the section. Each syllogism would include its own legal and factual analyses, set forth in separate paragraphs:

A. Topic or Argument
    Introduction
    Legal Rule 1
    Application to Facts 1
    Conclusion 1
    Legal Rule 2
    Application to Facts 2
    Conclusion 2

Alternatively, you can consolidate the related topics into a single syllogism, a single IRAC with a consolidated statement of multiple rules and analysis of multiple facts:

A. Topic
    Introduction
    Legal Rules 1 & 2
    Application to Facts 1 & 2
    Conclusions

Most writers tend to react to these problems of organization on a subconscious, intuitive level. However, the decision to separate or consolidate is sufficiently important to warrant conscious analysis.

2. Single Syllogism in Undivided Section

At the broadest level, if a topic or argument is sufficiently important and discrete to warrant a separate section or subsection heading, you ordinarily should develop it completely and resolve it within that section or subsection. In the following excerpts from a brief, an advocate divides the arguments about two elements of a tort into subsections. In each of these subsections, the advocate analyzes an element in a single, complete syllogism. For example, in subsection A.1 below, she provides the facts and holding of case law to help define the legal element of "extreme and outrageous conduct," applies the law to the facts of her case relevant to that element, and states a conclusion about the sufficiency of the allegations relating to that element:

II. ARGUMENT

A. Lew's Allegations in Count II Fail to State a Claim for Intentional Infliction of Emotional Distress

To establish a right to relief . . . .

1. Smith's Alleged Conduct Was Not "Extreme and Outrageous"

Only the most deplorable and shocking conduct satisfies the narrow definition of "extreme and outrageous conduct." *See* . . . . Conduct that simply reflects normal social and economic adversities is not extreme or outrageous. *See, e.g., Frank v. Boswell,* . . . .

In *Frank*, a landlord's eviction notice did not reflect extreme and outrageous conduct, even though it was "rude and intimidating." *Id*. at 289. The court reasoned that . . . .

In this case, Lew's complaint alleges conduct that is even less extreme than the conduct in *Frank*. It alleges that Smith "fired Lew without severance pay and with full knowledge that Lew's family was facing a desperate financial crisis." Plaintiff's Second Amended Complaint ¶ 7. It further alleges that Smith communicated his decision in a "terse, unfriendly, and unsympathetic conversation, without advance notice." *Id*. at ¶ 8.

These allegations state only that Lew was the victim of his own economic distress and that Smith acted to protect the interests of his business. Although some business owners might take it upon themselves to offer personal counseling and financial aid to their employees or ex-employees, Smith has no legal duty to do so.

Thus, the complaint does not allege circumstances that could establish the requisite "extreme and outrageous conduct."

2. Lew's Alleged "Depression" Does Not Amount to Severe Emotional Distress

Proof of severe emotional distress . . . .

Annotations (right margin):

- Major argument
- First subargument
- General rules of law
- In-depth analysis of case law
- Facts of current dispute
- Analysis of facts
- Conclusion
- Second subargument

3. Separation of Elements of Single Syllogism into Multiple Subsections

In a particularly complex analysis, you might depart from the most basic organizational structure by developing only one element of a complete analysis within a section or subsection. For example, you could develop the legal rules in one section and analyze the facts in a separate section, perhaps even dividing the fact analysis into subsections:

A. Officer Bates Could Not Lawfully Arrest Jones Without Probable Cause to Believe That Jones Had Committed a Felony

Legal rules

Although a police officer may arrest a suspect without a warrant in some circumstances, he may not place a suspect under full custodial arrest without probable cause to believe that the suspect has committed a crime. *See* . . . . A police officer does not have probable cause unless . . . .

B. Officer Bates Did Not Have Probable Cause

Application to facts

At the suppression hearing, Officer Bates asserted that Jones matched the description of the burglar and that Jones volunteered incriminating statements. Whether taken separately or together, however, these factors did not create probable cause.

1. Jones Did Not Match the Description of the Burglar

First subset of facts

A written transcript of the radio report shows that Officer Bates received the following description of the burglary suspect: white male, six feet tall, 180 lbs., short brown hair, wearing a navy blue windbreaker . . . .

2. Jones's Statements Did Not Create Probable Cause

Second subset of facts

The combined testimony of Jones and Officer Bates creates a clear and consistent picture of their conversation on Washington Street . . . .

Under this approach, the discussion of the law appears primarily in section A of the brief, and section B addresses the fact analysis. It would not be uncommon, however, for the author of such a passage to refer briefly to legal authority within section B when helpful to support the fact analysis.

4. Multiple Syllogisms Within a Single, Undivided Section

Conversely, you may have occasion to present more than one complete analysis in a discrete section or subsection. If so, you can either (1) fully develop and resolve one syllogism before analyzing the next, or (2) combine the related legal rules of arguably distinct syllogisms and then apply them in combined form to all the relevant facts.

a. Separation of Multiple Syllogisms

Within an undivided section, you may occasionally address several closely related topics, none of which is sufficiently important and discrete to warrant further subdivision into subsections. In many such cases, you can develop these related topics separately within the section or subsection.

For example, you can completely develop and resolve an introductory analysis before moving on to the main topic, as in the following excerpt from a legal memorandum:

A. Option Contract Under UCC

In some circumstances, a merchant's promise to refrain from revoking an offer to buy or sell goods is enforceable even if gratuitous: | General statutory rules

> An offer by a merchant to buy or sell goods in a signed writing which by its terms gives assurance that it will be held open is not revocable, for lack of consideration . . . but any such term of assurance on a form supplied by the offeree must be separately signed by the offeror.

U.C.C. § 2-205 (2011).

"Merchant" includes "a person who deals in goods of the kind." U.C.C. § 2-104 (2011). Stillwell regularly sells computers as part of her wholesale office supply business. Therefore, she is a merchant of the goods that she offered to supply to Azoulay, and section 2-205 thus governs the revocability of her offer. | Complete syllogism on preliminary matter

A more difficult question is whether Stillwell "separately signed" the promise not to revoke contained in the form supplied by Azoulay, the offeree. The purpose of the statutory requirement for a separate signing is . . . . | Transition to main topic of discussion

The second paragraph of this example quickly resolves the question of merchant status in a complete syllogism, with a statement of the law, an analysis of the facts, and a conclusion. Because that issue is simple and noncontroversial, it does not warrant presentation in a separate subsection with its own heading. On the other hand, it is sufficiently independent from the analysis of the requirement for a separate signing that you should develop and resolve it in its own IRAC within a separate paragraph before analyzing other topics raised by the general standards in the first paragraph.

Some legal writers strain this form of separation when using it within a section that features in-depth case analyses of a series of cases. Rather than synthesize these cases and apply the synthesized law in consolidated form to the facts, the writer pauses briefly after each case analysis and applies the holding of that case to the relevant facts. Although this is a popular form of argument, it sometimes results in repetition and a rambling, piecemeal effect. You should not use it as a substitute for effective expression of synthesis of authority, as explored in Chapter 14, Section II.B.

b. Consolidation of Multiple Syllogisms

In other cases, you may prefer to combine closely related legal standards and apply them as a group to all the relevant facts. This approach is illustrated by the second and third paragraphs of the following excerpt of a brief:

II. ARGUMENT

A. Bennett Will Prove That Tippett Is Liable Under 42 U.S.C. § 1983 for Violating Bennett's Civil Rights.

General statutory rules

Federal law imposes civil liability on a person who acts under the color of state law to deprive another of a federal right:

> Every person who, under the color of any [state law or custom], subjects, or causes to be subjected, any citizen of the United States or other person within the jurisdiction thereof to the deprivation of any rights, privileges or immunities secured by the Constitution and laws, shall be liable to the party injured . . . .

42 U.S.C. § 1983 (2012).

Consolidated discussion of rules for three subarguments

A private party acts "under the color of state law" if he acts in concert with a state official acting in his official capacity. *See Dennis v. Sparks*, 449 U.S. 24, 27-29 (1980). State action denying a litigant a fair and impartial hearing in civil litigation constitutes a deprivation of due process under the Fourteenth Amendment. *See Catchpole v. Brannon*, 36 Cal. App. 4th 237, 245, 42 Cal. Rptr. 2d

440, 443 (Ct. App. 1995). Although section 1983 implicitly incorporates the common law doctrine of absolute immunity for judges, that immunity does not protect private parties who conspire with the judge. *See Dennis*, 449 U.S. at 29-32.

In this case, Bennett will prove all the elements of his claim under section 1983. First, the evidence will show that Tippett conspired with Judge Bell by bribing Judge Bell to rule against Bennett on his motion for a preliminary injunction; Tippett therefore acted under the color of state law. Second, Tippett's bribe denied Bennett an impartial hearing and therefore deprived Bennett of his federal right to due process. Finally, even though Tippett acted under the color of state law, he had no official state function and therefore does not enjoy the protection of any official immunity.

> Consolidated application of three rules to facts

Thus, the evidence will show that Tippett is liable to Bennett for violating Bennett's due process rights.

> Conclusion

c. Discretion to Separate or Consolidate

The decision to separate or consolidate legal analyses often is a matter of judgment on which reasonable writers can disagree. As a general rule, a more superficial treatment of the topics lends itself to consolidation, as in the example above. On the other hand, if you analyze closely related topics in greater depth, you could divide the same discussion of a brief into separate syllogisms that are fully developed and resolved in separate paragraphs within the section:

II. ARGUMENT

A. Bennett Will Prove That Tippett Is Liable Under 42 U.S.C. § 1983 for Violating Bennett's Civil Rights.

Federal law imposes civil liability on a person who acts under the color of state law to deprive another of a federal right:

> General statutory rules

> Every person who, under the color of any . . . .

42 U.S.C. § 1983 (2012). In this case, Bennett will prove all the elements of his claim under section 1983.

Full syllogism on first subargument

A private party acts "under the color of state law" if he acts in concert with a state official acting in his official capacity. *See Dennis v. Sparks*, 449 U.S. 24, 27-29 (1980). In *Dennis*, a state judge . . . . Similarly, the evidence in this case will show that Tippett conspired with Judge Bell by bribing Judge Bell to rule against Bennett on his motion for a preliminary injunction. Therefore, Tippett acted under the color of state law.

Full syllogism on second subargument

The Fourteenth Amendment's guarantee of due process in state proceedings is a federal substantive right, the deprivation of which is remediable under section 1983. *See generally Carey v. Piphus*, 435 U.S. 247 (1978). State conduct denying a litigant a fair and impartial hearing in civil litigation constitutes a deprivation of due process under the Fourteenth Amendment. *See Catchpole v. Brannon*, 36 Cal. App. 4th 237, 245, 42 Cal. Rptr. 2d 440, 443 (Ct. App. 1995). In this case, Tippett's bribing the judge directly affected the outcome of the hearing on Bennett's request for a preliminary injunction. Therefore, Tippett caused a deprivation of Bennett's right to due process.

Full syllogism on third subargument

Finally, Tippett is not immune from liability for money damages. Bennett agrees that state judges are absolutely immune from liability for damages for their judicial acts taken within their jurisdiction. *See Stump v. Sparkman*, 435 U.S. 349 (1978). However, such immunity does not extend to a private party who conspires with a state judge, even though by so conspiring the private party acts under the color of state law. *See Dennis*, 449 U.S. at 29-32 (1980). In this case, the record shows that Tippett was not performing an official function and has no official status as an officer of the court. He is a private party who therefore enjoys no official immunity.

General conclusion

Thus, the evidence will show that Tippett is liable to Bennett for violating Bennett's due process rights.

Of course, if the topics are truly independent and warrant extended discussion, you may wish to adopt the conventional approach of presenting each analysis in a separate subsection and under a separate heading:

II. ARGUMENT

A. Bennett Will Prove That Tippett Is Liable Under 42 U.S.C. § 1983 for Violating Bennett's Civil Rights.

Federal law imposes civil liability . . . . 42 U.S.C. § 1983 (2012). In this case, Bennett will prove all the elements of his claim under section 1983.	**General statutory rules**

1. Tippett Acted Under the Color of State Law.

A private party acts "under the color of state law" if he acts in concert . . . . In *Dennis*, ... In this case, the evidence will show that Tippett conspired with Judge Bell . . . . Therefore, Tippett acted under the color of state law.	**Full syllogism in several paragraphs within first subsection**

2. Tippett Denied Bennett Due Process.

The Fourteenth Amendment's guarantee of due process in state proceedings is a federal substantive right, ... In *Catchpole*, ... In this case, Bennett will prove that Tippett bribed Judge Bell to rule against Bennett on his motion for a preliminary injunction . . . . Therefore, Tippett violated Bennett's rights to due process.	**Full syllogism in several paragraphs within second subsection**

3. Tippett Is Not Immune from Suit.

Bennett agrees that	**Third subsection**

d. Separate Analysis of Adverse Authority in Responsive Brief

A special organizational structure is sometimes appropriate for responsive briefs. In the ordinary three-stage briefing procedure, the answering brief will respond directly to the opening brief, and the reply brief will respond to the answering brief. In responding to an argument in a preceding brief, you can affirmatively develop a legal theory and apply it to the facts, and then separately address authority on which the preceding brief relies. You should address each adverse authority and discredit or distinguish it, or argue that it should be overruled, or concede that it controls one issue and seek to prevail on other issues. You can use the same technique in an opening brief that anticipates a counterargument.

For example, in the following sample passage, the brief writer has affirmatively and confidently argued that Tippett denied Bennett due process under a mainstream legal theory. Only after completing that argument does he seek to persuade the judge to reject an approach based on *Parratt v. Taylor*, on which the opposing party relied in a previous motion:

II. ARGUMENT

A. Bennett Will Prove That Tippett Is Liable Under 42 U.S.C. § 1983 for Violating Bennett's Civil Rights.

1. Tippett Acted Under the Color of State Law.

• • • •

2. Tippett Denied Bennett Due Process.

Full syllogism in several paragraphs within second subargument

The Fourteenth Amendment's guarantee of due process in state proceedings is a federal . . . .

In *Catchpole*, ...

In this case, Bennett will prove that Tippett bribed Judge Bell to rule against Bennett on his motion for a preliminary injunction. . . . Therefore, Tippett violated Bennett's rights to due process.

Separate paragraphs distinguishing adverse authority

Tippett argued in the reply brief to his motion to dismiss that Bennett has an adequate remedy under state tort law and that section 1983 therefore affords him no relief, citing *Parratt v. Taylor*, 451 U.S. 527 (1981). *Parratt* is distinguishable . . . .

In this example, *Parratt v. Taylor* does not clearly address a distinct topic; instead, it helps define the limits of due process in certain contexts. Thus, in a neutral analysis, you might consolidate your discussion of *Parratt* with your discussion of other authorities that establish the legal rule, even though you ultimately distinguish *Parratt* from your case.

In a responsive brief, however, you can invite the judge to analyze your case initially without the distraction of distinguishable adverse authority. By delaying your analysis of the adverse case law in this manner, you are free to develop the initial argument strongly and positively, without the qualifications inherent in the subsequent discussion of adverse authority.

5. Summary

These examples have primarily illustrated two issues of organization: (1) whether to present topics in separate sections or within a single, undivided section and (2) whether to separate or consolidate analyses within a section. These issues illustrate the role of judgment in legal writing and particularly in developing organizational structures. Many problems of this nature have no single, clearly correct solution; your resolution will depend on the nature and the depth of the analyses or arguments and on your personal style preferences.

IV. Paragraphs

A. The Role of Paragraphs Within a Section

Just as descriptive headings and subheadings communicate the division of a discussion or argument into sections or subsections, good paragraphing helps to communicate the organizational structure within a section or subsection. For instance, the paragraphing in the following passage signals the transition from (1) an analysis of the statutory requirements of conduct "under the color of state law" to (2) an analysis of Fourteenth Amendment guarantees:

A private party acts "under the color of state law" if he acts in concert with a state official acting in his official capacity. *See Dennis v. Sparks*, 449 U.S. 24, 27-29 (1980). *In Dennis*, a state judge . . . . Similarly, the evidence in this case will show that Tippett conspired with Judge Bell	**Statute**
The Fourteenth Amendment's guarantee of due process in state proceedings is a federal substantive right	**Constitution**

The following presentation of the same arguments assumes a greater depth of analysis. Imagine that each of five topic sentences begins a new paragraph. The five topic sentences represented by the phrases and clauses in the following example signal the transitions between (1) general legal rules, (2) in-depth case analysis, (3) fact analysis, (4) conclusion, and (5) analysis of potentially adverse authority.

The Fourteenth Amendment's guarantee of due process in state proceedings is a federal substantive right . . . . *See Catchpole v. Brannon,*	**Law**
In *Catchpole,*	**Case analysis**
In this case, Bennett will prove	**Facts**
Thus, Tippett is liable to Bennett	**Conclusion**
Tippett has argued . . . , citing *Parratt v. Taylor*, 451 U.S. 527 (1981). *Parratt* is distinguishable	**Adverse authority**

B. Paragraph Content and Development

To say that each paragraph should present a single topic or idea over-simplifies the matter, for the appropriate scope of the subject matter of each paragraph may depend on the relationship between the paragraph and the remainder of the discussion. For example, the following analysis of merchant status is superficial, conclusory, and preliminary to the main topic for discussion. Accordingly, you could combine the legal standard, fact analysis, and conclusion of this subsidiary topic in a single paragraph:

"Merchant" includes "a person who deals in goods of the kind." U.C.C. § 2-104(1) (2011). Stillwell regularly sells computers as part of her wholesale office supply business. Therefore, she is a merchant of the goods that she offered to supply to Azoulay, and section 2-205 thus governs the revocability of her offer.

In contrast, the reader can most easily absorb the typically more thorough analysis of the main topic if you divide the statement of legal rules and the fact analysis of the main topic into at least two separate paragraphs. At the simplest level, each paragraph could correspond to one of the three elements of deductive reasoning. For example, after it explains the issue, the following sample exam answer analyzes a problem in three paragraphs that (1) summarize the applicable legal rules, (2) apply the rules to the facts, and (3) state a conclusion:

Legal rules

An enforceable contract requires a bargained-for exchange in which a promisor exchanges his own promise for a return promise or performance. The requirement of an exchange is not satisfied if one party gives only an illusory promise, which does not commit the promisor to any future performance. A promise is illusory if it leaves the promisor free to perform or not according to his unfettered whim or discretion, such as . . . .

Application to facts

Guarantor should argue that Lender's promise to forbear until he "needs" the money permits Lender to decide at his own whim and unfettered discretion when to demand payment, because he has some control of his own needs. However, that argument would prevail only if the word "need" refers to a subjective perception of deprivation that is inseparable from Lender's purely personal wants or desires. Lender can argue . . . .

Conclusion

Unfortunately for our client, Lender's promise in the guarantee agreement probably is not illusory, because the word "need" provides some substance to Lender's commitment to forbear. Therefore, Guarantor's promise probably is supported by consideration and is enforceable.

In more complex analyses, the development of legal standards alone may progress through several paragraphs, perhaps beginning with an overview of general standards in one paragraph, followed by two or more additional paragraphs, each of which explores a significant case or a policy argument. Similarly, the fact analysis may progress through several paragraphs, perhaps displaying different levels of fact analysis or different categories of facts. For example, the five paragraphs represented by the following phrases and clauses help to signal the transitions between (1) general legal standards, (2) in-depth case analysis, (3) identification of relevant facts, (4) analysis of those facts, and (5) conclusion:

A. Smith's Alleged Conduct Was Not "Extreme and Outrageous."

. . . Conduct that simply reflects normal social and economic adversities is not extreme or outrageous. *See, e.g., Frank v. Boswell,*	Law
In *Frank,*	Case analysis
In this case, Lew's complaint alleges conduct that is even less extreme than the conduct in *Frank.* . . .	Facts
These allegations state only that	Fact analysis
Thus, the complaint does not allege circumstances that could establish the requisite "extreme and outrageous conduct."	Conclusion

C. The Role of Sentences Within a Paragraph

A paragraph does not contain some magic number of sentences. The appropriate number of sentences depends in part on the relationship between the paragraph and the topics addressed in surrounding paragraphs.

Of course, if you find that you have set off a single sentence as a separate paragraph, you should always question whether the isolated sentence would better serve as the concluding sentence of the previous paragraph or the topic sentence of the next one. As illustrated by the concluding paragraph of the illustration above, just before section C, however, a single sentence may stand by itself as a separate paragraph if it completely addresses a discrete topic or if presentation in a separate paragraph achieves important goals of clarity or emphasis. If you adhere without exception to a rule against single-sentence paragraphs, you may find yourself composing an unnecessary, empty sentence to accompany an informative sentence that could have stood alone.

Whenever possible, your first sentence in a multiple-sentence paragraph should communicate your strategy by introducing the topic of the paragraph, expressing a transition, or both. For example, the first sentence in the following example signals the transition from the analysis of precedent to the identification of the relevant facts of the current dispute, and it provides an overview of the case comparison:

In this case, Lew's complaint alleges conduct that is even less extreme than the conduct in *Frank*. It alleges that Smith "fired Lew without severance pay and with full knowledge that Lew's family was facing a desperate financial crisis." Pl.'s Second Am. Compl. ¶ 7. It further alleges . . . .

In the preceding sample paragraph, the topic sentence introduces fact analysis. Similarly, you should use topic or transition sentences or paragraphs to introduce discussions of legal authority, such as statutes and case law. Section II of Chapter 14 thoroughly discusses and illustrates this critical element of legal writing.

After you have composed an effective topic sentence, you should organize other sentences within a paragraph to develop information in a logical, organized fashion. For example, the paragraph below is designed to define the limits of the scope of the Uniform Commercial Code and to raise a question about the applicability of the Code to a particular transaction. The awkward placement of the second and third sentences of the paragraph disrupts continuity by stating an intermediate conclusion before establishing its legal premise:

General issue

Application to facts

Legal premise

Specific issue

Whether Maldonado accepted Weinstein's offer depends in part on whether the common law of contracts or the Uniform Commercial Code (UCC) applies to the transaction. Weinstein's offer to supply specifically identified, separately priced, movable plumbing parts clearly contemplates a sale of goods as part of the transaction. *See* U.C.C. § 2-105(1) (2011). The UCC applies to "transactions in goods." U.C.C. § 2-102 (2011). His proposed transaction, however, also involves the service of installing the fixtures, raising a question about the applicability of the UCC to mixed transactions for both services and the sale of goods.

Reversing the order of the second and third sentences develops points in a more logical order and retains the coherence of transitions:

General issue

Legal premise

Application to facts

Specific issue

Whether Maldonado accepted Weinstein's offer depends in part on whether the common law of contracts or the Uniform Commercial Code (UCC) applies to the transaction. The UCC applies to "transactions in goods." U.C.C. § 2-102 (2011). Weinstein's offer to supply specifically identified, separately priced, movable plumbing parts clearly contemplates a sale of goods as part of the transaction. *See* U.C.C. § 2-105(1) (2011). His proposed transaction, however, also involves the service of installing the fixtures, raising a question about . . . .

Many different organizational approaches may help your reader efficiently assimilate information in a paragraph. Nonetheless, one simple technique is worth highlighting: You can lead a reader from familiar to new information in a paragraph by beginning each sentence with a previously established idea and linking it to a new idea. For example, the phrases in capital letters in the following passage represent new information, and the italicized phrases represent previously introduced information. In each sentence after the first one, previously introduced information is linked to a new idea.

An enforceable contract requires a bargained-for EXCHANGE in which a promisor exchanges his own promise for a return promise or performance. The requirement of an *exchange* is not satisfied if one party gives only an ILLUSORY PROMISE, which does not commit the promisor to any future performance. A *promise* is *illusory* if it leaves the promisor free to perform or not according to his unfettered whim or discretion, such as . . . .

This technique of consistently linking a familiar idea with a new one is only one of many approaches that you may use in developing a paragraph. You should always retain maximum flexibility to adapt your organizational approach to the particular characteristics of a passage. The final two chapters of Part V provide further guidance. They (1) continue to explore paragraphing and paragraph content in the context of presentation of authority and (2) address good organization of words and clauses within a sentence to enhance the clarity or persuasive force of the sentence.

V. Summary

When organizing the topics or arguments in an office memorandum or brief, you should

1. with few exceptions, discuss separate issues in separate sections or subsections;
2. arrange your sections and subsections so that they reflect the proper relationships among topics and subtopics; and
3. present your topics or arguments in a logical order, subject to considerations of strategy.

Within a section or subsection, you should

1. explain the legal rule,
2. apply the rule to the facts, and
3. reach a conclusion.

If the topic or argument within a section or subsection is governed by several closely related rules, you should exercise judgment to either

1. consolidate your statement of all the rules before applying them to all the relevant facts or
2. separately apply some preliminary legal rules to facts before progressing to other rules within the section or subsection.

When organizing material within a section or subsection, you should consider

1. the hierarchy of authority and
2. progression from general to specific and from fundamental to uncertain.

Chapter 13

Legal Writing Style in the
Office Memorandum

Chapter 1's introduction to writing style identified clarity and concision as the principal characteristics of effective legal writing. This chapter more comprehensively examines those topics, and Chapter 14 addresses special problems of citing to legal authority.

This chapter uses selected writing problems as vehicles for developing a method for legal writing. The method it promotes is a flexible approach that provides general guidance in any legal writing assignment. It seeks to show you that effective legal writing style to a great extent is analogous to the sound practices of legal method and analysis discussed in the preceding chapters. Accordingly, it invites you to treat rules and conventions of writing very much like legal rules: To use them well, you must understand their purposes and policies. For further practice in recognizing the policies underlying conventions of writing, perform the exercises in Appendix V.

Although this chapter primarily addresses writing style for office memoranda, most of the principles discussed apply equally to briefs, and some of

271

the examples are taken from briefs. Special techniques of persuasive writing are explored in Chapter 16.

I. Clarity

You cannot write clearly unless you first develop clear ideas. In many cases, muddled legal writing reflects an incomplete understanding of the substantive legal analysis and suggests the need for further research and reflection. Only when you have fully mastered your analysis can you clearly communicate the analysis to a comprehending reader.

Moreover, even writing that is clear on its face may in fact be *inaccurate* if you have recorded the wrong citation or statutory text, or failed to fully comprehend the holding or reasoning of a judicial opinion. Accordingly, the quality of your final written product obviously depends on the care with which you have performed early stages of the research and writing process.

Beyond sound and accurate analysis, an important element of clarity in any legal document is effective organization on all the levels discussed in Chapter 12. Other elements of clarity, discussed below, are simplicity, effective sentence structure, and precise word selection.

A. Simplicity and Plain English

For centuries, the public has complained about lawyers' fondness for legal jargon: stuffy, peculiar, archaic legal terminology. People have good reason to complain. For example, some lawyers still refuse to end a witness's sworn and notarized written statement with the perfectly descriptive word "signed." Instead, they insist on inserting the archaic phrase "Further affiant sayeth not."

Although the extent to which you stray from plain and simple terms is partly a matter of personal style, you should tend toward simplicity. If a simple, familiar word will clearly express your idea, your reader may find that a peculiar, complex, or unfamiliar word or phrase in its place is distracting or even unintelligible.

Moreover, simplicity in writing does not condemn you to expressing only simple ideas. Rather, it helps you to express even complex and abstract ideas in such clear, concrete, and simple terms that your reader easily grasps your ideas on first reading.

You can best appreciate the virtues of simplicity by recognizing the ultimate purpose of your document. A legal memorandum should efficiently communicate, and a brief should persuade. A document cannot perform either of these functions if the reader must pause at every sentence to ponder its meaning.

Unfortunately, unnecessary abstraction, complexity, and peculiarity found in some legal writing suggest that the writer's objective is to "sound like a lawyer" or to impress his supervising attorney or a judge with the breadth of his vocabulary. One judge describes the effect of such writing:

> [T]he use of legalese or "six-bit" college words may help convince your client that you are worth the hourly fee being charged, but it does not help win his case. Indeed, it actually interferes in your communication with the court when the judge is constantly shifting attention from the brief to either a Webster's, Black's Law, or a Latin-to-English dictionary. I know you received a high dollar education. Instead of trying to impress me with some high-brow vocabulary, use your education to figure out how to simplify what you are saying with plain language. After all, the simpler you make it, the easier it is for me to understand.[1]

Occasionally, a peculiar word or phrase earns its place in legal writing as a shorthand term for an unavoidably complex or unfamiliar concept. For example, Chapter 5 uses the term "stare decisis" to refer to a complex set of principles that help to define legal method in the United States. Although this Latin term is unfamiliar to most students entering law school, it qualifies as a useful "term of art" because it is widely accepted among trained lawyers as convenient shorthand for several related ideas whose collective meaning would otherwise require several sentences to convey. Surprisingly few forms of peculiar legal language, however, are justified as necessary terms of art. Therefore, you should critically evaluate any unusual language in your writing to ensure that it amounts to an informative term of art rather than distracting legal jargon.[2]

Legal jargon is particularly inappropriate in a document that is addressed to a layperson, who may be unfamiliar with even rudimentary legal terminology. When addressing such an audience, you should exercise special care to avoid unnecessary jargon, and you should explain in plain English the meanings of legal terms of art that other attorneys would easily recognize.

Exercise 13-1

A simple contract should (1) introduce the parties to the contract, (2) recite any background facts that explain the motivations of the parties and thus help to explain their bargain, (3) define the parties' rights and obligations by setting forth their mutual promises, and (4) signify each party's agreement to the terms of the contract.

The following contract is written in antiquated jargon. Parts of it are taken from the contract interpreted in *McMichael v. Price*, 58 P.2d 549 (Okla. 1936). Contract language from formbooks provided further inspiration.

Simplify all or part of the structure and language of the contract so that it expresses the terms of the parties' agreement in plain English. Feel free to use

---

1. Brian Quinn, *Dispelling Misconception*, 62 TEX. B.J. 890, 891 (1999).
2. *See* Richard C. Wydick, PLAIN ENGLISH FOR LAWYERS 57-60 (5th ed. 2005).

subject headings, section numbers, and paragraphing. Compare your revision with the sample contracts at the end of Chapter 23.

REQUIREMENTS CONTRACT

This contract for the purchase and sale of sand entered into on this, the _____ day of _____, by and between Sooner Sand Co., a general partnership of which Harley T. Price and W. M. McMichael are partners, hereinafter known as the party of the first part, and Bassi Distributing Co., a joint venture of Bassi Trucking Co. and Hardcore Rock & Gravel, Inc., hereinafter known as the party of the second part, Witnesseth:

Whereas, the party of the first part is engaged in the business of selling and shipping sand from Phoenix to various customers in the State of Arizona but has not developed markets outside of Arizona and desires to supply sand wholesale to a distributor with customers outside the state; and

Whereas, the party of the second part has an established business in Phoenix selling and shipping sand to various customers in several states outside Arizona, including California, Nevada, Utah, and Colorado, and desires a stable source of supply of sand for that business;

Now, therefore, in consideration of the mutual covenants herein contained, and other good and valuable consideration the receipt of which is hereby acknowledged, the parties hereby represent, warrant, affirm, promise, covenant, and agree that the said party of the first part will, upon receipt of periodic written orders submitted by the said party of the second part, furnish all of the sand which the said party of the second part requires for shipment to various and sundry points outside of the State of Arizona, for a period of five (5) years from the date hereinabove, said sand to be of a grade and quality at least equal in quality and comparable with the sand of various grades sold by other sand companies in the City of Phoenix, Arizona; furthermore, the said party of the second part agrees to pay as payment and compensation for said sand so furnished a sum per ton which represents sixty percent (60%) of the current market price per ton of concrete at the place of destination of said shipment.

In witness whereof, the said parties have hereunto set their hands and seals the day and year first above written.

_____

Sooner Sand Co.—Authorized Agent

_____

Bassi Distributing Co.—Authorized Agent

B. Sentence Structure

1. Structuring and Punctuating Long or Complex Sentences

Short, crisp sentences can be powerful:

Jenkins lived to tell his side of the story. Roberts did not.

On the other hand, a succession of very short sentences may sound stilted or may require empty or repetitive transitional phrases to link the sentences together:

It was 1:00 a.m. John left the party. He went home. He drove his BMW.

Moreover, long sentences that convey numerous thoughts in multiple clauses are not necessarily problematic; if punctuated and constructed sensibly, they may be clear and readable.

Unfortunately, however, legal writing often suffers from unnecessarily long and complex sentences that are poorly constructed. The readers of such sentences must assimilate too much information before pausing, and they often lose track of the proper relationships of the ideas expressed.

a. Closure Through Punctuation

You can use two devices to avoid or revise unmanageable sentences: closure and visual guides to structure.

Closure usually refers to punctuation that allows a reader to pause to assimilate one or more ideas before moving to the next. For example, the following passages illustrate three levels of closure. The first presents at least three distinct ideas in a single sentence punctuated only by commas:

Although punitive damages are designed to punish the wrongdoer rather than compensate the victim for actual injury, many courts will award punitive damages only if the plaintiff proves actual injury, and some of them may limit punitive damages to an amount that bears a reasonable relationship to the award of compensatory damages.

The sentence above is constructed reasonably well. However, the commas in the sentence invite only brief pauses between ideas, leaving the reader breathless if she is unfamiliar with the subject matter. Periods dividing the passage into three sentences encourage the reader to pause more substantially and to digest each idea before facing the next:

Punitive damages are designed to punish the wrongdoer rather than compensate the victim for actual injury. Nonetheless, many courts will award punitive damages only if the plaintiff proves actual injury. Moreover, some of those courts may limit punitive damages to an amount that bears a reasonable relationship to the award of compensatory damages.

If you desire to link the second and third ideas to one another more closely than to the first idea in the paragraph, you can replace the second period with a semicolon. The semicolon provides such a conceptual link with nearly the same level of closure as provided by a period:

Punitive damages are designed to punish the wrongdoer rather than compensate the victim for actual losses. Nonetheless, many courts will award punitive damages only if the plaintiff proves actual injury; moreover, some of those courts may limit punitive damages to an amount that bears a reasonable relationship to the award of compensatory damages.

In some passages, visual guides to the structure of a long sentence may effectively substitute for the closure provided by multiple short sentences. The following passages illustrate both techniques. The first sample passage takes advantage of closure by limiting each sentence to a single idea:

The evidence supports three critical factual conclusions. First, the marijuana, cocaine, and heroin all belonged to Carson and Klein. Second, Rivers was unaware of the presence of those drugs in the house when he entered the living room. Third, when Klein offered to sell the marijuana to Rivers, Rivers declined the offer and attempted to leave the house.

The closure is welcome in this example, because two of the factual conclusions set forth in separate sentences are sufficiently complex to require punctuation within those conclusions.

In the next sample passage, the series of conclusions in the first passage progresses through a single sentence without the disruption of substantial closure. It retains some of the qualities of closure by using numbers as the equivalent of road signs[3] to identify the end of one element of the series and the beginning of the next:

The evidence supports three critical factual conclusions: (1) the marijuana, cocaine, and heroin all belonged to Carson and Klein; (2) Rivers was unaware of the presence of those drugs in the house when he entered the living room; and (3) when Klein offered to sell the marijuana to Rivers, Rivers declined the offer and attempted to leave the house.

b. Repetition of Prepositions or Other Linking Words or Phrases

If the elements of the series are less complex, you can provide a subtler guide to sentence structure by repeating an introductory word or phrase, such as "that" in the following example:

Top Notch Co. is not liable on this contract theory unless Jackson can prove that the personnel manual was part of Jackson's employment contract, that the manual contained a promise of job security, and that Top Notch breached such a promise when it discharged Jackson for refusing to shave his beard.

---

3. *Cf. id.* at 45-46 (advocating listing of items on separate lines).

Some writers balk at using "that" in this manner. In some sentence structures, their point is well taken. For example, the word "that" is unnecessary in the following sentence:

I knew that he would come back.

Although the sentence above does not display any errors of grammar or syntax, a writer could exercise discretion to omit the word "that," thus adopting a more concise style with no appreciable loss of clarity:

I knew he would come back.

In other cases, however, the word "that," although unnecessary, may help the reader to distinguish quickly between two possible sentence structures. Consider, for example, the following sentences:

The court held two principles above all others.

The court held the defendant in custody without bail.[4]

The court held the defendant had not consented to the search.

In the first two sentences, the word "held" is used, at least figuratively, in the sense of possessing or retaining some thing, tangible or intangible. In those two sentences, the word "that" has no place; the writer could not insert it without adding other words. In the third sentence, however, the word "held" is used in a different sense and syntax. Like the word "said" or "concluded" in similar contexts, it introduces a holding or ruling of the court. In this context, a writer could exercise discretion to insert "that" after "held":

The court held that the defendant had not consented to the search.

Indeed, although not necessary, adding the word "that" in the final sample sentence helps the reader to avoid assuming the structure of the first two sample sentences and to instantly adopt the different structure of the third. Without the word "that" as a guide to the structure of the third sentence, the reader might momentarily assign the same meaning to "held" that it has in the first two sentences, relying later on context to dispel the confusion.

---

4. This sentence would be more precise if it stated that the court ordered the sheriff to hold the defendant without bail, but it suffices to illustrate the point under consideration.

Thus, one should not too quickly adopt an inflexible rule against insert-ing "that" in such contexts. The decision whether to employ such a guide to structure is a matter of judgment, style, and context.

c. Complex Series

Chapter 1 examined the serial comma rule and its relationship to the goal of clarity in writing. To ensure clarity in complex as well as simple contexts, adherents to the traditional approach consistently insert the final comma in any series of two or more things:

We braved high winds, driving rain, and flooded streets.

The elements of a series, however, need not be limited to simple nouns, such as "wind, rain, and streets." They may be verb phrases, such as "washed the car, mowed the lawn, and repaired the roof." They may even be inde-pendent clauses, each of which could stand alone as a complete sentence with a subject and verb.

Particularly troublesome is a multi-level series, in which the primary series is made up of two or more major elements, and at least one of those major elements incorporates its own subsidiary series of two or more sub-elements. For example, imagine that a sentence includes the following series of two major elements: The defendant (1) had left his car at the garage for maintenance and (2) lacked money for public transportation to another city. Now suppose that the first major element includes three subelements: The defendant (1) had left his car at the garage for (i) repairs, (ii) repainting, and (iii) other maintenance, and (2) . . . to another city. Unfortunately, many writers fail to distinguish between the major elements and the subelements within a major element:

The defendant had left his car at a garage for repairs, repainting, other mainte-nance, and lacked money for public transportation to another city.

The writer has punctuated this sentence as a single series with four ele-ments: "repairs," "repainting," "other maintenance," and "lacked money." The series is not parallel in structure because the first three elements are objects and the fourth is a verb with an object. Along with the content of the sentence, that lack of parallelism helps to reveal the intended sentence structure. If retained as a single sentence, the passage is best structured as a compound sentence with two independent clauses as the major elements and with a series of three subelements within the first major element:

The defendant had left his car at a garage for repairs, repainting, and other main-tenance, and he lacked money for public transportation to another city.

The seemingly minor revisions in the corrected sentence are significant. The addition of the conjunction "and" between the second and third element of the subsidiary series signals the end of that series. Moreover, the addition of the subject "he" in the second major element of the compound sentence transforms that element into an independent clause, parallel with the first major element.

d. Toward a Flexible, Policy-Oriented Approach to Punctuation

Many routine conventions of punctuation provide guides to sentence structure and should be applied flexibly to achieve that goal. For example, the insertion of a comma to separate independent clauses joined by a conjunction[5] is not arbitrary; it often avoids temporary confusion in sentence structure, as illustrated by the following unpunctuated sentence:

Coastal Bank breached its loan commitment to the owner and the contractor threatened to terminate its performance.

Halfway through the sentence, many readers assume that the conjunction "and" joins "owner" to "the contractor." Thus, on encountering "the contractor," those readers conclude for a fraction of a second that the bank owed its loan commitment to the contractor as well as to the owner. By the time they reach the verb "threatened," they realize from context that "the contractor" is the subject of a new independent clause rather than the second in a series of two objects of the prepositional phrase "to the." By that time, however, the ambiguity in sentence structure has caused readers to hesitate for a moment and perhaps even to regress by rereading part of the sentence. This momentary confusion may be even more pronounced in a more complicated compound sentence.

A comma inserted before the conjunction more instantly identifies "the contractor" as the beginning of a new independent clause:

Coastal Bank breached its loan commitment to the owner, and the contractor threatened to terminate its performance.

This example illustrates two general principles of style. First, the reader of a brief or memorandum may be able to glean the meaning of the first sample sentence from context; however, if multiplied many times in the course of a document, the additional labor and frequent instances of momentary confusion can leave the reader weary. Some conventions of punctuation or other matters of style may not be critical to the reader's ultimate comprehension, but they enhance the efficiency and ease with which the reader comprehends.

---

5. *See* William Strunk, Jr. & E. B. White, THE ELEMENTS OF STYLE 5 (5th ed. 2009).

Second, you should apply rules or conventions of writing style the way that you apply rules of law: Apply and extend them as far as necessary to vindicate their underlying purposes or policies, but no further. For example, the following compound sentence is perfectly readable without a comma separating the independent clauses:

The robber ran and the police gave chase.

Because this sentence is short and simple, the reader can recognize its structure at a glance, arguably making the comma unnecessary as a guide to structure.

You can avoid the comma question and raise others by placing a period after the first independent clause:

The robber ran. And the police gave chase.

This punctuation gives special emphasis to the action in each clause, but many writers recoil at the idea of beginning a sentence with the simple conjunction "and" or "but." Such usage is not grammatically incorrect; it is simply stylistically questionable in many cases. If the clauses are simple and short, they will normally flow more smoothly if combined in a single sentence with a conjunction in the middle of the sentence. On the other hand, if you want to divide the clauses into two sentences to emphasize each clause or to provide your reader with closure after a long clause, you probably will prefer a stronger transition word than "and" or "but." When writers decide to begin a sentence with a conjunction, most prefer to use a more substantial conjunctive adverb, such as "moreover," "furthermore," "in contrast," "however," or "nonetheless":

Mr. Blumquist survived the initial explosion. Nonetheless, he died a short time later of smoke inhalation.

Section III of Chapter 1 explains why you should reject an inflexible rule against starting sentences with the transition word "however." Signaling a change of direction at the beginning of a sentence may help you achieve an important objective in legal writing. And it should help you to minimize the need to begin a sentence with "and" or "but." But you should not conclude that the latter construction is universally incorrect. It will simply be a rare passage in legal writing that benefits from such construction. In this entire book, only a handful of sentences begin with "and" or "but." And the three in this paragraph are included primarily to underscore the theme of this subsection: Many rules of composition should be viewed as general guides to style rather than absolute prohibitions against unconventional usage.

A few more examples will further underscore this point. Consider, for example, the question of whether to insert a comma after a subordinate phrase or clause to separate it from the main clause that follows it:

After reviving the victim at the side of the pool{,} the paramedic transported her to the hospital emergency room.

Some writers, including this author, normally insert such a comma, even after a short and simple introductory phrase or clause. By analogy to the justification for the traditional serial comma rule, we reason that the comma almost never hurts and that it often provides a helpful guide to sentence structure, particularly if the introductory phrase or clause is long or complex.

Other writers, however, prefer to avoid unnecessary punctuation. They may prefer to insert a comma after an introductory phrase or clause only when necessary for clarity. Such an exercise of discretion is perfectly legitimate, although it requires the writer to determine the degree of complexity or length that would cause a reader to stumble in the absence of a comma.

For example, each of the following five sentences or excerpts begins with a subordinate word, phrase, or clause. The word or phrase beginning the main clause is printed in bold. In which of the examples would you insert a comma before the main clause?

  (i)   Later **he** mowed the lawn.

  (ii) In January 2011 **he** resolved to quit smoking.

 (iii) After she examined the patient **Dr. Ong** requested a conference with the chief surgeon.

 (iv) In light of Hart's conduct and his oral representations regarding the policy manual **the judge** ruled that . . . .

  (v) Although few courts have addressed the question of whether members of a city council enjoy the absolute immunity that protects state legislators **the policy** of protecting the legislative process from . . . .

As stated above, a writer could reasonably choose to insert a comma in each of the five examples. Others might exercise discretion to withhold further punctuation from example (i) and perhaps example (ii) because readers can recognize the simple structures of those examples at a glance. Even those inclined to preserve ink, however, should begin adding a comma at the level of complexity of example (iii) or (iv). The dependent clause at the beginning of example (iii) includes a subject, verb, and object. Moreover, the object, "the patient," might be confused with the subject of the main clause, "Dr. Ong," unless separated by a comma:

After she examined the patient, Dr. Ong requested a conference . . . .

In examples (iv) and (v), the introductory phrases or clauses are sufficiently long and complex that readers will appreciate a comma, because it invites them to pause to assimilate the information in the introduction before proceeding to the main clause.

A final example will serve to emphasize the role of style and judgment in punctuation and to illustrate the limits of inflexible rules. In the following sentence, a common convention of punctuation justifies each of the commas, at least when viewed in isolation:

The contract is written, signed, and dated, and, therefore, the statute of frauds does not apply.

The first two commas appropriately separate three elements of a series. The third comma appropriately separates the two independent clauses joined by the conjunction "and." The last two commas at least represent a defensible judgment that "therefore" is parenthetic and should be set apart from the rest of the clause with commas.

Nonetheless, most writers would be dissatisfied with the sentence, because the concentration of five commas within six words of text is distracting. In a flawed response, some writers might omit one or more commas without changing the structure of the sentence:

The contract is written, signed, and dated and, therefore the statute of frauds does not apply.

Although this revision is less cluttered, it incorrectly omits commas that served important functions.

An honest appraisal of the original sentence should reveal structural flaws. None of the five commas is incorrect; however, the sentence structure concentrates the commas in a manner that is stylistically displeasing. You can directly respond to this problem by changing the location of "therefore," thus decreasing the need for commas around it by lessening its parenthetic qualities:

The contract is written, signed, and dated, and the statute of frauds therefore does not apply.

Alternatively, you can replace one of the commas with a semicolon by omitting the conjunction "and" between the two independent clauses:

The contract is written, signed, and dated; therefore, the statute of frauds does not apply.

In sum, if you understand the policy justifications for conventions of punctuation, you can more confidently recall them, apply them, and even depart from them when the context justifies an unconventional approach. Conversely, even technically correct writing may display problems of style that invite you to exercise judgment and to consciously choose among alternative sentence structures.

Appendix V describes other common conventions of punctuation and asks you to analyze them.

Exercise 13-2

1. Care with Commas

Which of the following sentences requires further punctuation? Would you prefer to alter the structure of some of the sentences?

a. Two pieces of evidence link Jones to the crime: A witness observed Jones strike the victim with his fist and a glove recovered from the crime scene matches the one found in Jones's car.

b. The court dismissed the action and Romero appealed.

c. The judge dismissed the action because the limitations period had expired.

d. Because the limitations period had expired the court dismissed the action.

e. In some cases even perfectly relevant evidence should be excluded if it would seriously confuse the jury because the prejudicial effect of such evidence frequently outweighs its probative value.

f. The court rejected the defendant's argument that the action should be dismissed because the limitations period had expired reasoning that the plaintiff had established grounds for tolling the limitations period.

2. Closure and Road Signs

Redraft the following sentence to make it easier to read. Break it into multiple sentences or clauses, or use any other device to lead the reader gracefully through the ideas it expresses.

Plaintiff American Continental Can Co. brought this action against Defendants Conco Sheet Metal Co., Bassi Distributing Co., and Miller Trucking Co., alleging that Conco Sheet Metal Co. had sold it defective sheet metal, that Bassi Distributing Co. had fraudulently misrepresented the description and quality of Conco Sheet Metal Co.'s products, and that Miller Trucking Co. had negligently damaged sheet metal that it agreed to transport from the warehouse of Conco Sheet Metal Co. to the factory of American Continental Can Co., and requesting compensatory and punitive damages.

3. The Ambiguous Series

Identify the major elements of the series in the sentence set forth below. Where does the last element of the series begin? What different interpretations does the sentence permit? How would you use a comma to advance either interpretation over the other?

> In the event of default, the Lessee must vacate the premises, forfeit the security deposit and pay Lessor's actual damages or pay liquidated damages under section 12 of this Lease.

2. Concrete Verbs and Active Construction

a. Concrete Verbs

Lawyers often sacrifice vigor and clarity in their legal writing by employing vague and abstract verbs such as "involve," "exist," or "occur":

A modification to the contract occurred on July 1.

Even more frequently, lawyers drain the strength from verbs by building sentences around a form of the phrase "there is":

There was a modification to the contract on July 1.

The author of the preceding sentence has converted the active verb "modify" into the noun "modification," creating a need for the verb "was," a form of the relatively abstract and passive infinitive "to be." Unless you really intend to focus attention on the mere existence or absence of modification, you could improve this sentence by identifying the actors, abandoning the "be" verb, and focusing on the real action word in the sentence, "modify":

Nelson and Kubichek modified their contract on July 1.

In some cases, replacing abstract wording such as "there is" with a more concrete, active verb will enable you to add new meaning as well as vigor. For example, the following sentence abstractly comments on the absence of critical evidence:

There is no evidence in the record that Robert Emery intended to kill the bank teller.

A more concrete verb can emphasize the absence not only of direct evidence of intent but also of circumstantial evidence from which a factfinder might infer intent:

No evidence in the record even suggests that Robert Emery intended to kill the bank teller.

b. Active and Passive Construction

Avoidance of forms of "there is" in legal writing is simply a special branch of a more general preference for active voice in sentence structure. A clause in active voice presents its principal parts in the normal order of actor, verb, and object of the action, such as "curiosity killed the cat."

In contrast, the following sentence features three clauses in passive voice, each of which places the object before the verb and dispenses with the actor altogether:

The *Allen* doctrine has been criticized, but it continues to be applied because it has been approved in dictum.

The following revision identifies the actors associated with each verb, but it still uses passive voice throughout, as revealed by the inverted order of object, verb, and actor:

The *Allen* doctrine has been criticized by a few appellate judges, but it continues to be applied by trial judges because it has been approved in dictum by the Supreme Court.

Active voice is more informative than the minimalist passive structure in the first example above, and it more directly and concisely conveys all the information presented in the second example:

A few appellate judges have criticized the *Allen* doctrine, but trial judges continue to apply it because the Supreme Court has approved it in dictum.

The vigor of active construction can be especially useful in composing strong statements in persuasive writing. For example, the following sentence in passive voice fails to assign responsibility for the repair of the air conditioning:

The air conditioning was not repaired until 60 days after the tenant gave written notice of the defect.

In contrast, the next sentence uses active voice to identify the landlord as the responsible party and to characterize the landlord's inaction as a culpable omission:

The landlord neglected to repair the air conditioning until 60 days after the tenant gave written notice of the defect.

Although active voice generally is more direct, concise, or informative than passive voice, you may occasionally have reason to prefer passive voice. For example, you may use passive voice to deliberately omit reference to an actor or actors whose identities are unknown or unimportant:

The bridge was erected in 1923.

Even in this case, some writers so strongly prefer active voice that they refer to the actor or actors generically: "Workers built the bridge in 1923." Most writers, however, would reasonably adopt the passive construction to avoid diverting the reader's attention to unimportant information.

In some cases, you may be aware of the identity of the actor but use passive construction to avoid drawing attention to that identity. For example, a defense attorney might desire to emphasize mitigating factors in a crime while avoiding any reminder to the jury that her client stands accused of the wrongdoing:

The hostage was not harmed in any way.

Conversely, you may deliberately use passive voice to place unusual emphasis on the actor by placing the actor at the end of the sentence, as in the second of the following sentences:

The defense wants you to believe that Mr. Cass committed suicide by injecting himself with a lethal dose of heroin. To the contrary, the evidence shows that the heroin was injected by the defendant, Ms. Borden.

In some sentences, if you place the actor or actors at the beginning of the sentence, you will unduly delay introducing the verb:

Ms. Williams, the firm's top expert in tax law, and Mr. Scales, an eloquent oral advocate with 20 years of experience before the state appellate courts, argued the case.

With passive voice, you can introduce the simple verb and its object early in the sentence:

The case was argued by Ms. Williams, the firm's top expert in tax law, and by Mr. Scales, an eloquent oral advocate with 20 years of experience before the state appellate courts.

In summary, you should prefer vigorous, concrete verbs in active construction unless you have a specific purpose for a vague, abstract, or passive verb.

Exercise 13-3

1. Benefits of Active, Concrete Verbs

Replace the passive, abstract verbs in the following sentences with more active, concrete verbs.

a. There are only two Supreme Court decisions that address this issue.
b. It was argued by government counsel that the tax regulation was applicable to the land exchange.
c. The landlord was ordered by the court to achieve completion of the repairs within 30 days.
d. There was a conspiracy among four distributors to effect an immediate price increase.

2. Benefits of Passive Construction

By replacing the active verb with a passive verb, restructure the following sentence to minimize the number of words separating the subject, verb, and object and to emphasize the "clearly erroneous" standard.

Federal Rule of Civil Procedure 52(a)(6), which provides that a federal trial court's findings of fact in a nonjury trial "must not be set aside unless clearly erroneous," limits our review.

3. Effective Placement of Modifiers

For clarity, you should place a modifying word, phrase, or clause close to the part of the sentence that it modifies. On the other hand, to ensure a smooth flow in your writing, you should avoid interrupting important parts of a sentence with a lengthy modifier.

The following sample sentences illustrate how these principles relate to one another. If you patiently work through them, you will better appreciate how good writers make conscious choices between alternative sentence structures.

The subordinate clauses in the following sentence inconveniently delay introduction of the main clause:

Because the consumer fraud statute applies to misrepresentations in either the "advertisement or sale" of merchandise, and because the "sale" of merchandise normally is associated with the passing of title from the seller to the buyer, *see* U.C.C. § 2-106(1) (2011), the statute appears to apply to a seller's misrepresentations made during the delivery of merchandise under a preexisting contract.

You would only increase the reader's frustration by moving the subordinate clauses to the middle of the sentence, between the subject and the verb:

The consumer fraud statute, because it applies to . . . , and because the "sale" of merchandise normally is . . . , appears to apply to a seller's misrepresentations . . . .

You could reveal the information in the sentence more gracefully by starting with the main clause:

The consumer fraud statute appears to apply to a seller's misrepresentations made during the delivery of merchandise under a preexisting contract, because the statute applies to misrepresentations in either the "advertisement or sale" of merchandise, and because the "sale" of merchandise normally is associated with the passing of title from the seller to the buyer, *see* U.C.C. § 2-106(1) (2011).

In the context of this sample sentence, this structure does not produce the ambiguity or inappropriate sense of anticlimax that it produced in one of the revisions of the first sample sentence above.

Of course, this revised sentence is nonetheless too long and complex. You can solve all the problems in this passage simply by breaking it into shorter sentences, as recommended in the discussion of closure in Section I.B.1.a, above:

The consumer fraud statute applies to misrepresentations in either the "advertisement or sale" of merchandise. The "sale" of merchandise normally is associated with the passing of title from the seller to the buyer. *See* U.C.C. § 2-106(1) (2011). Therefore, the statute appears to apply to . . . .

Exercise 13-4

1. Precise Placement of Modifiers

Consider the different positions into which you could insert the word "only" in the following sentence: Officer Jones fired his gun three times at the suspect.

Which of the positions is most consistent with the information in each of the following?

    a. Officer Jones fired his gun three times, not five times as reported by a witness.

    b. Officer Jones fired his gun three times, but no other officer fired his gun more than once.

2. Modifying Clauses and Sentence Structure

Revise the following sentences. Which of several possible revisions do you prefer, and why?

    a. The trial judge, after reviewing the evidence and considering the arguments of the parties, ruled that the contraband was the product of an illegal search.

    b. Protesting that he had not finished his testimony, the bailiff escorted the witness from the courtroom.

4. Restrictive and Nonrestrictive Clauses

Most writers experience difficulty in identifying restrictive and nonrestrictive clauses and in choosing between the relative pronouns "that" and "which" once they have identified the clause. Most critical for clarity is your remembering to insert a comma before a nonrestrictive clause (and after the clause if it does not end the sentence) and to omit such a comma before a restrictive clause. If you wish to go beyond popular usage and satisfy purists in your circle, you will also remember to introduce a restrictive clause with the relative pronoun "that," saving "which" for nonrestrictive clauses. Both of these considerations are explained in detail below.

a. The Role of the Comma

To illustrate the distinction between restrictive and nonrestrictive clauses, imagine that you and a supervising attorney are standing next to a large conference table in a meeting room of your law firm. The conference table is the only table in the room, and eight chairs are placed around it. Your supervisor makes a statement that is reproduced below without internal punctuation:

This table *which we just purchased a year ago* is already showing signs of wear.

Now, imagine the inflection and timing of your supervisor's oral statement. She probably stressed the main clause: "This table is already showing signs of wear." On the other hand, you can imagine a change in tone when she interjected the italicized clause: "which we just purchased a year ago." You can imagine her pausing after "table" and "ago," lending a parenthetic quality to the information between the pauses.

The italicized clause is parenthetic because it is not needed to identify the subject, "this table." Your supervisor was clearly referring to objects in the room, and those objects include only one table. She has directed your attention to that unique object simply by referring to "this table." Her statement about the firm's recently purchasing the table helps to reinforce her point about the table's rapid deterioration, but that statement is not needed to identify the table and distinguish it from all others within the range of your perception. Thus, you could naturally treat the italicized clause as an "aside," an interruption of the main clause. The clause provides interesting additional information, but the rest of the sentence would stand alone coherently without it. The italicized clause is "nondefining" because it is not necessary to define the subject. Stated otherwise, it is "nonrestrictive" because it is not necessary to restrict the universe of tables to the conference table in this meeting room; the phrase "this table" had already accomplished that task.

In an oral statement, you would normally pause before and after such a nonrestrictive clause. In a written statement, you achieve the same effect by setting the clause apart with commas:

This table, which we just purchased a year ago, is already showing signs of wear.

Imagine now that your conversation turns to the eight chairs surrounding the conference table. You would undoubtedly experience confusion if your supervisor made the following statement without pointing to a particular chair:

The chair has several small holes in its upholstery.

The subject "the chair" is not sufficiently precise to identify the one chair among eight to which your supervisor is referring. She could avoid the confusion by adding a clause that directs your attention to a single chair. Each of the following revisions contains such a clause:

The chair *next to the potted cactus* has several small holes in its upholstery.

The chair *which sits next to the potted cactus* has several small holes in its upholstery.

The chair *that sits next to the potted cactus* has several small holes in its upholstery.

Regardless of which version your supervisor spoke, she did not pause before the italicized passage; instead, she plowed straight through the sentence at least until she had singled out one of the chairs. The italicized information is not parenthetic; rather than interrupting the main clause, it is a direct continuation of the subject, necessary to identify or to define the chair to which she is referring. In that sense, it is a "defining" or "restrictive" clause because it restricts the universe of eight chairs in the room to the single chair to which your supervisor intends to refer. Just as such a clause would not inspire a pause in an oral statement, it would not require commas in a written statement.

So far, your reaction to these examples is probably a resounding "Who cares?" The following sample sentences, however, illustrate that the distinction between a restrictive and a nonrestrictive clause occasionally materially affects the content of a sentence in legal writing. The construction of the first sample sentence suggests that all reckless driving constitutes a felony and that a new statute therefore applies to all reckless driving:

The new statute mandates a jail term for reckless driving, which constitutes a felony violation of the vehicle code.

The meaning of this sentence is conveyed partly by the comma, which suggests to the reader that the sentence would be perfectly sensible if it ended at "reckless driving" and that the clause following the comma simply adds parenthetic information. The clause following the comma is nonrestrictive, or nondefining, because it does not purport to identify a subset of the general category of things denoted by the term "reckless driving."

Even without any changes in wording, the next sample sentence suggests by the absence of a comma that only some forms of reckless driving rise to the level of a felony and that the statute applies only to those forms of reckless driving:

The new statute mandates a jail term for reckless driving which constitutes a felony violation of the vehicle code.

The absence of a comma invites the reader to rush to the end of the sentence to discover what kind of reckless driving is covered, suggesting that the sentence could not sensibly stop at the term "reckless driving." In this sentence, the clause following "reckless driving" is restrictive, or defining, because it identifies a subset of the things in the general category of reckless driving.

b. The Choice Between "That" and "Which"

Both sentences, however, use the relative pronoun "which" to introduce the restrictive or nonrestrictive clauses, leaving the burden of conveying the restrictive or nonrestrictive nature of the clause to the presence or absence of a comma. To partially relieve the comma of that heavy burden, careful writers—or at least the purists among them—use the relative pronoun "that" in a restrictive clause to emphasize the restrictive nature of the clause and to more clearly distinguish it from a nonrestrictive clause:

The new statute mandates a jail term for reckless driving that constitutes a felony violation of the vehicle code.

Similarly, in the earlier example of the chair with the holes in its upholstery, a sentence that uses a relative pronoun should use "that" rather than "which":

The chair that sits next to the potted cactus has several small holes in its upholstery.

Because many writers do not have a natural ear for the purist's use of "that," they tend to use "which" in both restrictive and nonrestrictive clauses. In fact, this practice is so widespread that some might characterize it as the popular approach. Nonetheless, many supervising attorneys will go "which hunting" when reviewing the work of associates.

In most cases, any ambiguity or uncertainty resulting from using "which" in a restrictive clause will be insignificant. For example, the difference in meaning between the following two sentences is insignificant to the analysis that the writer intends to convey:

The court applied a fairness test, which inquires whether a transaction was consummated through fair dealing and at a fair price.

The court applied a fairness test that inquires whether a transaction was consummated through fair dealing and at a fair price.

Because the sentence singles out one of many possible formulations of a test that incorporates considerations of fairness, the final clause probably should be restrictive, as in the second example. However, because emphasis of the restrictive nature of the clause is not necessary for analytic clarity, the following popular choice of words would be inoffensive:

The court applied a fairness test which inquires whether a transaction was consummated through fair dealing and at a fair price.

Moreover, returning to a previous example, a structural revision of the sentence may more clearly convey the intended meaning than use of restrictive or nonrestrictive clauses:

The new statute mandates a jail term for reckless driving, but only if it constitutes a felony violation of the vehicle code.

Nonetheless, when the choice between relative pronouns will affect clarity, you should follow the example of the United States Supreme Court, which carefully distinguished between restrictive and nonrestrictive clauses in the following excerpt from an opinion:

Although the Court of Appeals' construction of the Act and of Regulation Z is shared by three of the four other Courts of Appeals *that* have ruled on the question, this view, *which* is essentially a claim that the plain language of the statute and the regulation requires the result reached by the court below, has recently been challenged on several fronts.[6]

c. Procedural Labels

You may also raise questions about restrictive and nonrestrictive clauses when you join procedural labels, such as "plaintiff," to the names of parties to litigation. In that context, you need not worry about a choice between "that" and "which," but you may wonder whether you should insert a comma.

For example, if Robert Jones is one of three plaintiffs in an action, then a phrase that uses his name to define "plaintiff" is restrictive and should omit any comma:

Plaintiff Robert Jones moves for summary judgment . . . .

In this example, "Robert Jones" restricts the universe of "plaintiffs" to one of the three plaintiffs in the litigation.

In contrast, if Jones is the only plaintiff, you could treat a similar reference as nonrestrictive and include commas:

---

6. Anderson Bros. Ford v. Valencia, 452 U.S. 205, 211-12 (1981) (italics added).

Plaintiff, Robert Jones, moves for summary judgment . . . .

In this example, "Robert Jones" arguably supplies parenthetic information about a party who is already identified by the label "Plaintiff."

Alternatively, even if Jones is the only plaintiff, you could reasonably eliminate the commas by characterizing "Plaintiff" as a title that is joined with a name, as in "Dr. Long" or "Secretary-Treasurer Richard King":

Plaintiff Robert Jones . . . .

This is probably the least distracting stylistic option. However, you cannot adopt this usage of "plaintiff" as a title if you treat "plaintiff" as a common noun by preceding it with an article, such as "the." In that case, you must treat the party's name as a nonrestrictive modifier if he is the only plaintiff:

The plaintiff, Robert Jones, moves for summary judgment against the defendant, Cecelia Ynez.

Exercise 13-5

Relative Pronouns and Wealthy Relatives

Compare the following alternative provisions of a will:

I leave to my daughter my bank account that is in Western Savings.

I leave to my daughter my bank account, which is in Western Savings.

After drafting the will, but before death, the testator closed the bank account at Western Savings and used the funds from that account to open a new one at First Interstate Bank.[7] Which provision would most likely bequeath the First Interstate Bank account to the daughter?

---

7. The source of this problem is Rebecca W. Berch (now Chief Justice of the Arizona Supreme Court), *Words That/Which Cause Problems in Legal Writing*, 25 ARIZ. BAR BRIEFS No. 9 (1987).

C. Precision

1. Careful Expression of Analysis

Once you clearly understand the idea you want to communicate, you must select the words and phrases that precisely convey your intended meaning. As suggested in Chapter 1, achieving precision in writing may require you to subordinate other potential goals, such as entertaining your reader. For example, many writers believe that they will bore their readers if they repeatedly use a single word or phrase to refer to the same idea throughout a passage. They often address this concern by engaging in "elegant variation": using different words or phrases to refer to the same idea. However, any entertainment value of the variation will fail to justify the confusion that typically results.

For example, perhaps to elegantly vary their phrasing, many legal writers intermittently use "while" as a synonym for "although," and they use "when" or "where" as a synonym for "if." The following construction is common:

While the court declined to decide the issue of retroactivity in *Fleming,* its dictum in subsequent cases suggests that it has always assumed that the *Fleming* principle applies retroactively.

The primary meaning of "while" in this syntax is duration or simultaneity. But, of course, the writer does not mean that the court offered dictum in subsequent cases *at the same time* that it declined to decide the issue in a previous case. "Although" would more precisely convey the contrast or tension between the court's actions. In the context of the entire sentence, the less precise version does not cause serious confusion or inconvenience. By displaying care with details, however, the more precise wording strengthens the credibility of the writer on more substantive matters.

More substantial risks of confusion arise in the use of synonyms for "because." "Since" is particularly popular:

Since the employer invited the applicant to read the policy manual at the initial interview, the manual became part of their bargain.

Let's assume that the writer meant to say that the manual became part of the bargain *because* the employer introduced the manual into the negotiations, not simply that the manual became part of the bargain sometime after the initial interview. Although the multiple dictionary definitions of "since" typically include "because," the primary dictionary definition relates to time frame or sequence of events:

From then till now; in the interval; before this; before now; ago; after that time.—prep. Continuously from the time of; as, since yesterday; subsequent to; after.—conj. In the interval after the time when, as: I have been ill twice since I saw you last. Without interruption, from the time when; as, since we saw you last; because; seeing that; inasmuch as.[8]

Therefore, most readers fail to recognize "since" as a signal for a causal relationship when they first encounter it in a sentence such as the example above. Although the reader may later discover the intended meaning of "since" from context, that process may produce momentary hesitation or even regression in reading. The ambiguity is most serious when the sentence otherwise refers to a time frame:

Since Rabin breached the contract on January 1, 2008, the three-year limitations period expired before Smith filed suit on January 10, 2011.

This sentence will appear to some readers to make the marginally useful point that the limitations period expired after the breach of contract as well as before the filing of suit. The word "because" in place of "since" would more clearly convey the intended causal relationship: The breach of contract triggered the commencement of the running of the limitations period; therefore, the period expired before suit was filed.

You create an even greater risk of confusion if you replace "because" with "as," because causation is not a readily recognized connotation of "as":

Plaintiff is entitled to the equitable remedy of injunctive relief as his legal remedy is inadequate.

One popular dictionary does not even clearly list "because" as a definition for "as"; the closest it comes is listing "since" as a definition of "as" in its conjunctive form.[9] As explained above, even this reference to "since" is ambiguous.

In each of these three examples, "because" would more precisely and unambiguously convey the writer's intended meaning of causal relationship, because it has no other meaning.[10] Moreover, the word "because" is self-descriptive: The root word "cause" within it suggests its meaning.

2. Beyond Dogma

Popular use of synonyms for "because" illustrates the range of considerations that often influence nuances in writing style. Despite the precision that "because" permits, many writers depart from it in the interest of elegant variation, or they reject it altogether because they think that it has an unsophisticated ring to it. However, few readers demand variation or stimulation

---

8. NEW WEBSTER'S DICTIONARY 902 (encyclopedic ed. 1981).
9. *Id.* at 58.
10. *See id.* at 86.

from every word in a sentence. As with many other words—such as "the," "with," and "a"—the word "because" precisely and unobtrusively performs its function without diverting the reader's attention from more substantively important parts of the sentence.

The most interesting reason that writers give for substituting "since" or "as" for "because" is their recollection of an admonition in grade school never to begin a sentence with "because." Of course, if beginning a sentence with "because" offended some principle of syntax or other consideration of composition, replacing it at the beginning of the sentence with a synonym, and a poor one at that, would not cure the defect. In fact, some grade school teachers may have invented or repeated such a rule in reaction to students' early tendencies to write incomplete sentences, such as: "Because I missed the bus." Those teachers probably should have explained the requisite components of a complete sentence rather than place undeserved blame on the word "because."

Another defense of "as" and "since" as expressions of a causal relationship has greater merit. Some writers believe that "as" and "since" are not synonymous with "because" in that context but express slightly different shades of causation. Those writers reasonably use "because" to refer to a direct causal relationship and "since" or "as" to refer to a more attenuated relationship.[11] A style that carefully recognizes such a distinction arguably enhances precision. Unfortunately, few writers use "since" or "as" to connote a causal relationship in such a principled manner. Moreover, to a greater extent than in literary writing, legal writing tends to describe causal relationships that are sufficiently direct to justify use of "because" in place of the softer "since" or "as."

II. Concise Writing

When you concisely express clear and persuasive ideas in vivid, active, and precise prose, you can strive to convey the ideas with maximum efficiency and effect, as described by a character in Tom Stoppard's play, *The Real Thing*:

> Henry: . . . This thing here, which looks like a wooden club, is actually several pieces of particular wood cunningly put together in a certain way so that the whole thing is sprung, like a dance floor. It's for hitting cricket balls with. If you get it right, the cricket ball will travel two hundred yards in four seconds, and all you've done is give it a knock like knocking the top off a bottle of stout, and it makes a noise like a trout taking a fly . . . . (He clucks his tongue to make the noise.) What we're trying to do is to write

---

11. *See generally* William Strunk, Jr. & E. B. White, THE ELEMENTS OF STYLE 23-24 (5th ed. 2009) ("because" presented as concise replacement for the verbose phrase "the reason why is that," and "since" presented as primary replacement for "owing to the fact that"); E. B. White, THE SECOND TREE FROM THE CORNER 17 (1984) ("Parnell was not a playmate of mine, as he was a few years older . . . .").

cricket bats, so that when we throw up an idea and give it a little knock, it might . . . travel . . . .[12]

A legal document that effectively conveys its message in 10 pages is more like Henry's cricket bat than one that rambles on for 20 pages to convey the same message.

Still, you must not achieve brevity in your writing by omitting important ideas or sacrificing clarity of expression. You should strive first to express all important ideas in sufficient detail to successfully communicate or persuade. With that accomplished, you can streamline your writing by omitting extraneous ideas and expressing the important ones efficiently. Overworked supervisors and judges will thank you for it, as reflected in one state appellate judge's advice:

> First and foremost, more is not always better. . . .
> . . . .
> Conversely, avoid being overly "brief and concise." . . .
> In effect, you are being asked to strike a balance between too much and too little. Including needless matter poses the risk of distracting the court while being conclusory may result in the court holding the argument waived. Exercise your judgment with appropriate regard for the possible consequences when striking the balance.[13]

When you are satisfied that you have expressed all critical points and you have turned to the task of omitting needless matter, you should control the length of your document through content, form, and style. You can control content primarily through the scope and depth of analysis. You can achieve concise form and style through efficient organization, sentence structure, and phrasing.

A. Content: Scope and Depth of Analysis

"Scope of analysis" refers to the range of issues or topics that you address in your legal document. "Depth of analysis" refers to the level of detail with which you address a topic.

1. Scope of Analysis

The range of ideas that you address in your document can dramatically affect the document's length. In analyzing a problem, you need not develop every theory that you have encountered in the library. Instead, you can (1) thoroughly discuss the most important and clearly relevant topics, (2) exclude distracting tangents that are unlikely to affect the outcome of the dispute, and (3) determine whether to discuss topics between the two

---

12. Tom Stoppard, THE REAL THING 51 (1984).
13. Brian Quinn, *Dispelling Misconception*, 62 TEX. B.J. 890, 891 (1999).

extremes, perhaps in less detail than would be appropriate for a mainstream theory.

As discussed more fully in Section III.B of Chapter 6, you may find that you tend to apply different scopes of analysis to different kinds of documents. The scope of analysis ordinarily can be quite broad in your examination answers, because most of your professors will specifically test your ability to identify a wide range of issues. The scope of analysis should be much narrower in a brief, because briefs generally are most persuasive if they focus only on the strongest available arguments. The scope of analysis in a typical office memorandum is somewhere between the scope of analysis of an examination and that of a brief. An office memorandum should not fail to at least briefly discuss a theory or approach that may ultimately be helpful. On the other hand, to a greater extent than an examination answer, an office memorandum should focus on thorough development of the most helpful theories rather than on identification of every plausible approach.

2. Depth of Analysis

By properly balancing varying depths of analysis in the discussion or argument section of your memorandum or brief, you can make the document more concise and readable. For convenience, this book will use the terms "light analysis" and "in-depth analysis" to refer to the opposite extremes on the spectrum. You engage in light analysis when you simply state a proposition of law and cite to supporting authority. You engage in in-depth analysis when you analyze legal authority more thoroughly, such as by discussing the facts, holding, and reasoning of case law. You may also control the depth of analysis by choosing between (1) expressing a full deductive argument and (2) expressing an incomplete syllogism, leaving a premise of your deductive argument implicit.

a. Depth of Analysis of Legal Authority

Sample Memorandum 1 near the end of Chapter 11 provides an example of balance between light analysis and in-depth analysis of authority from the fictitious state of Calzona. The second paragraph of the discussion section briefly outlines fundamental principles, which provide helpful background information and which almost certainly will not be disputed by the parties. For this purpose, the author of the memorandum has used light analysis by simply stating propositions of law and citing to supporting authority:

An enforceable contract requires a bargained-for exchange in which a promisor exchanges his own promise for a return promise or performance. *Smith v. Newman*, 161 Calz. 443, 447, 667 P.2d 81, 85 (1984). The requirement of an exchange is not satisfied if one party gives only an illusory promise, which does not commit the promisor to any future performance. *Atco Corp. v. Johnson*, 155 Calz. 1211, 627 P.2d 781 (1980).

However, the memorandum also raises the more difficult issue of whether a particular promise made by a lender was illusory, an issue the parties obviously dispute. An adequate discussion of that issue requires a more thorough analysis of case law to determine which precedent is more nearly analogous to the facts of the current dispute. Such in-depth analysis explores the facts, holding, and reasoning of each significant case:

In-depth analysis of Atco

In *Atco Corp.*, the manager of an automobile repair shop promised to forbear "until I want the money" from asserting a claim against the owner of an automobile for $900 in repairs; in exchange, a friend of the owner promised to act as guarantor of the owner's obligation. *Id*. at 1212, 627 P.2d at 782. The word "want" stated no legal commitment, because it permitted the manager at his own discretion to refuse to perform any forbearance at all. Because the manager incurred no obligation, the guarantor's promise was gratuitous and unenforceable. *See id*. at 1213-14, 627 P.2d at 783-84.

In-depth analysis of Bonnie

On the other hand, even if a promise leaves open the possibility that the promisor will escape obligation, the promise is valid if the promisor does not have complete control over the events on which the promisor's obligation is conditioned. *See Bonnie v. DeLaney*, 158 Calz. 212, 645 P.2d 887 (1982). In *Bonnie*, an agreement for the sale of a house provided that the buyer could cancel the agreement if the buyer "cannot qualify for a 30-year mortgage loan for 90% of the sales price" with any of several banks listed in the agreement. *Id*. at 213, 645 P.2d at 888. In enforcing the agreement against the seller, the court distinguished *Atco Corp.* on the ground that the word "cannot" referred to the buyer's ability to obtain a loan rather than to his *desire*. Because his ability to obtain a loan was partly controlled by events and decisions outside his control, the promises in the sale agreement were nonillusory and binding. *See id*. at 214-15, 645 P.2d at 889-90.

The light analysis in the first sample paragraph in this subsection quickly establishes noncontroversial points without weighing the reader down with unnecessary detail. The more detailed analysis in the second and third sample paragraphs provides the reader with a fuller understanding of a specific legal doctrine, the illusory promise, thus creating a solid legal foundation for the fact analysis that will follow.

Sample Memorandum 2 near the end of Chapter 11 also displays a combination of light and in-depth analyses. Section IV.A of that sample memo presents an in-depth analysis of a new statute, including discussion of the statutory language, the legislative history, and the general policies reflected in other legislation and common law. In contrast, many of the settled principles of tort law explored in section IV.B of that sample memo were appropriately established with light analysis.

You must strike an effective balance between light and in-depth analyses to achieve the dual goals of clarity and concision. Unless the issue is extremely simple, if you use only light analysis to discuss a point in an office memorandum, you run the risk of defining the applicable legal principles with insufficient clarity to permit thoughtful fact analysis. Moreover, if you use only light analysis to argue a disputed point of law in a brief, you probably will fail to persuade. On the other hand, if you use in-depth analysis excessively, you may cause the reader to grow weary and to lose sight of the general legal theory while wandering endlessly among individual cases.

To help strike this balance, you can use citations with parenthetic explanations as a middle ground between light and in-depth analyses. For example, the following passage uses parenthetic explanations to explain how the cited authorities support the proposition for which they are cited:

In two other decisions, Arizona courts assumed that the statute of frauds is subject to mitigation to protect a party's reliance on the promise to perform, but they refused to apply the doctrine because the normal requirements of estoppel were not satisfied. *Trollope v. Koerner*, 106 Ariz. 10, 17-18, 470 P.2d 91, 98-99 (1970) (insufficient reliance); *Mac Enters. v. Del E. Webb Dev. Co.*, 132 Ariz. 331, 336, 645 P.2d 1245, 1250 (Ct. App. 1982) (no promise).

The brief reference to facts or holdings in the parentheses following the citations provides helpful information for the reader. A full paragraph of in-depth analysis of each case, on the other hand, is unnecessary and would distract from the fuller discussion of the cases that are more nearly on point.

b. Incomplete Syllogisms

So far, this section has discussed depth of analysis of legal principles. You may apply the same considerations to the complete deductive syllogism of major premise, minor premise, and conclusion. Normally, a memorandum or brief presents even a simple legal argument in a full syllogism with a discussion of the applicable legal rule, an application of the rule to the facts, and a conclusion:

Under the Uniform Commercial Code (UCC), the term "merchant" includes any person who "deals in goods of the kind." U.C.C. § 2-104(1) (2011). Wilson deals in used cars because he regularly buys and sells used cars as an adjunct to his car rental business. Therefore, he is a merchant of used cars under the UCC.

Alternatively, particularly if the argument is minor or tangential, you can present it in an incomplete syllogism, leaving the legal rule implicit:

Wilson is a "merchant" of used cars under the UCC because he regularly buys and sells used cars as an adjunct to his car rental business. *See* U.C.C. § 2-104(1) (2011).

A more detailed statement could mention the statutory definition, still without establishing the legal rule in a separate sentence:

Wilson is a "merchant" of used cars under the UCC because he regularly buys and sells used cars as an adjunct to his car rental business and thus "deals in goods of the kind." *See* U.C.C. § 2-104(1) (2011).

B. Form: Efficient Organization, Sentence Structure, and Phrasing

1. Organization and Repetition

By applying the principles of organization discussed in Chapter 12, you can write more concisely as well as more clearly. With good organization, you can eliminate unnecessary repetition and present ideas efficiently by building each subsection on the foundations laid in the previous ones.

You need not adopt an organizational framework that eliminates all repetition. Indeed, Chapter 11 explained how the format for a traditional office memorandum contemplates repetition of certain elements, like actors appearing in various scenes of a play, though performing slightly different roles each time they appear. This repetition or overlapping is not wasteful in a complicated analysis, particularly if you recognize the distinct purposes of the elements.

Nonetheless, needless repetition within such a framework may add pages without adding clarity. Good organization on all levels should minimize this problem.

2. Sentence Structure and Phrasing

You can often trace verbosity within a sentence to unnecessary repetition, loose verb structure, and expression of implicit information. In such sentences, the words expressing useful ideas are lost among words that convey marginally useful ideas or simply connect substantive ideas to one another.[14] In editing surplus words from your writing, however, you must not shave your writing so close that you sacrifice clarity.

---

14. One author recommends that writers maximize the ratio of "working words" to "glue words" in a sentence. *See* Richard C. Wydick, PLAIN ENGLISH FOR LAWYERS 7-10 (5th ed. 2005).

a. Repetition

As discussed in Subsection 1 above, some repetition is built into the general format of a legal document. Moreover, even at the level of words and phrases, carefully planned repetition may be justified on rare occasions as a guide to complex sentence structure or as a means of gaining unusual emphasis:

Jack Bailey has declared his guilt with his own actions. He declared his guilt when he fled the murder scene on the arrival of neighbors; he declared his guilt when he later tried to conceal the murder weapon; and he declared his guilt at trial by offering incredible and inconsistent testimony.

Repetition without purpose, however, merely adds words without contributing to the substance of a sentence. Even worse, it may cause the reader to wonder whether the repetitive words are intended to convey different ideas:

Section 24 of the lease is null, void, invalid, completely unenforceable, and of no legal force or effect whatsoever.

With a much shorter, cleaner sentence employing only one of the adjectives, you can precisely convey the intended meaning:

Section 24 of the lease is unenforceable.

On the other hand, even closely related terms are not repetitive if they convey meanings that are different in a way that is significant to the analysis. For example, state and federal statutes prohibit various kinds of discrimination based on "race, color, or national origin." Although the classes encompassed by these terms may overlap, they are not identical. Thus, an employer who discriminates against a dark-skinned African-American applicant in favor of a light-skinned African-American applicant arguably discriminates on the basis of color, even though not necessarily on the basis of race or national origin.[15]

b. Verb Structure

You will often add extra words to your sentences when you transform verbs into nouns or use verbs in the passive voice. For example, the author of the following clause added unnecessary bulk to his writing by transforming the verb "objected" into the noun "objection," and substituting "presented" as the verb:

---

15. *See generally* Walker v. Secretary of Treasury, I.R.S., 713 F. Supp. 403 (N.D. Ga. 1989).

Defense counsel presented an objection to the testimony.

You add further unnecessary bulk by using the passive voice, adding the words "was" and "by":

An objection to the testimony was presented by defense counsel.

If you employ the verb "objected" to express the action in active voice, you eliminate surplus words and lead the reader more directly to the main point:

Defense counsel objected to the testimony.

c. Implicit Information

Legal writers frequently express information that could remain implicit, by referring to procedure when defining a substantive legal principle:

If a party proves that a contract requires a performance that would violate a criminal statute, the court will strike down the contract as illegal and unenforceable.

Unless you intend to emphasize burdens of proof and court procedures, you can convey all the necessary information in fewer words by focusing exclusively on substance:

A contract is unenforceable if performance of its obligations would violate a criminal statute.

d. Tension Between Clarity and Concision

In your quest to eliminate surplus words, you should remain sensitive to the tension between clarity and concision, taking care to retain words and phrases that communicate important information. For example, the following sentences reflect each kind of verbosity cited at the beginning of this section:

Robert Jones, who is the plaintiff, brought this action against Mary Smith, the defendant. In this action, Jones filed a complaint that alleges that Smith committed a breach of the contract of employment between Smith and Jones.

You can combine these sentences into a single, much more concise sentence. At the margin, however, further revisions for concision may sacrifice important information, depending on your intended connotation and emphasis.

An initial revision reduces the number of words from 37 to 17, arguably without sacrificing clarity on any level:

Plaintiff Robert Jones brought this action against Defendant Mary Smith, alleging that Smith breached their employment contract.

Among other things, this revision eliminates the repetition of "this action," recognizes that the filing of a complaint is implicit in other phrases, uses "breached" as a direct verb, and replaces wordy clauses and phrases such as "who is the plaintiff" and "between Smith and Jones" with single but equally precise words.

By treating "Plaintiff" and "Defendant" as implicit, and by replacing "brought this action" with "sued," you can trim another five words from the sentence:

Robert Jones sued Mary Smith, alleging that Smith breached their employment contract.

This revision, however, may achieve concision at the expense of other considerations of style. To many readers, "sued" carries the negative connotation of harassing litigation; therefore, counsel for Jones might prefer the softer, though less concise, phrase "brought this action." Also, if you wish to refer to the parties subsequently only as "Plaintiff" and "Defendant" or only as "Jones" and "Smith," you may prefer to emphasize the relationship of each party's name with his or her procedural title by initially using the full phrases "Plaintiff Robert Jones," and "Defendant Mary Smith."

On the other hand, if you do not object to the last revision above, you could trim two more words from the sentence and achieve a more direct flow by eliminating the reference to "alleging":

Robert Jones sued Mary Smith for breaching their employment contract.

Sticklers for precision, however, might argue that you should use the preposition "for" to introduce a description of the requested relief rather than the ground for liability.

To summarize, revisions to achieve concise writing are matters of judgment that require sensitivity to considerations of emphasis, precision, connotation, and other elements of clarity.

Exercise 13-6

Rewrite the following sentence to make it more direct and concise.

The Federal Rules of Civil Procedure, Rule 26(c), provides that the issuance of protective orders to the effect that certain matters ought not to be inquired into in the course of discovery is within the authorization of the court.

III. Review and Revision

To polish your writing, you must critically review and revise early drafts. To do this well, you must approach writing analytically rather than purely intuitively: You must become sufficiently familiar with style problems that you can spot them in your own writing, even when the familiarity of your own prose tends to make you comfortable. You can best develop these editing skills by studying writing style in books or workshops, by reviewing and critiquing your own work and that of others, and by asking others to review and critique your writing.

Unfortunately, time pressures and limits on the client's resources will sometimes compel you to produce a final draft after only one or two opportunities for revision. The minimally acceptable level of review and revision is easily stated: At the very least, you must proofread your first draft and make necessary changes. Every judge has a horror story about an atrociously written brief, one that obviously was dictated and never proofread. No limitation on time or resources justifies such shoddy work.

The appropriate level of review and revision beyond the minimum is a matter of priorities and economics. A client with ample resources and with a great deal at stake in an important pretrial motion or appeal might expect its legal counsel to spare no expense in writing the best possible brief. You and your colleagues undoubtedly would begin work on the brief as early as possible, subject it to particularly critical review, and polish it through many drafts.

At the other end of the economic scale, in a modest case a firm might find it difficult to justify charging a client for a formal office memorandum prior to settlement negotiations. Instead, a supervising attorney might ask you to deliver your research and conclusions in an oral report or e-mail message. Even when a more formal document is appropriate, you will not serve your client well by piling up billable hours while subjecting a preliminary office memorandum or client letter to repeated scrutiny over half a dozen drafts. Such a document should be clear, complete, and concise, but limits on resources may preclude more than one or two rewrites. Moreover, even if you ordinarily avoid procrastination, you will occasionally be stuck with an emergency "rush job" that leaves you little time for revision.

Consequently, you should strive to produce the best possible written product on the first draft. You can do this by learning to avoid style problems common to your writing and by devoting appropriate attention to the pre-writing stage.

Ironically, to develop the ability to avoid common style problems on the first draft, you must identify and analyze your writing habits by initially devoting extra time and attention to your writing over many drafts. With the aid of a colleague or a writing manual, you will gradually become sufficiently conscious of your writing problems and their solutions that you can begin to avoid those problems on first draft, reducing the need for substantial editing.

For example, one summer associate in a major law firm learned from a writing consultant that he tended to overuse the passive, abstract verb form "there is." He resolved to use his word processing program to highlight this and related phrases in his first drafts, revise the highlighted passages on second drafts, and eventually become sufficiently sensitive to the problem to avoid it on first drafts.

You can further minimize the need for redrafting, and thus save time in the long run, by carefully formulating and organizing your analysis before beginning to write. You should prepare an outline of your document and consider discussing the outline with your assigning attorney or a peer. Once satisfied with the broad outline of your analysis, you can devote greater attention to the details when you begin writing or dictating.

One final note of caution: Word processing provides attorneys with the luxury of blocking and moving passages of text from one computer file to another, such as from a contract for one client to a similar contract for another client. Although this process can reduce the time needed to prepare the initial draft of the second document, it also underscores the need for careful proofreading and revision. The passage in the first document may be helpful as a starting point, but it may not be perfectly tailored to the transaction in the second document. Moreover, the imperfection may be sufficiently subtle to require special diligence in evaluating and revising initial drafts of the second document.

IV. Summary

Clarity and concision are the two most important goals in legal writing style. These two goals ordinarily are consistent and complementary. When they conflict, give priority to clarity. More specifically, to write clearly,

1. use simple, plain English unless a legal term of art will inform more than distract;
2. flexibly use effective sentence structure and punctuation, with adequate closure and guides to structure;

3. use concrete verbs in the active voice, unless passive construction serves a specific purpose;

4. distinguish between restrictive and nonrestrictive clauses when necessary for clarity; and

5. select the word or phrase that precisely conveys your meaning.

To write concisely,

1. maintain reasonable limitations on scope and depth of analysis; and

2. avoid verbosity by adopting efficient organization, sentence structure, and phrasing.

To polish your writing,

1. create the best possible product on first draft; and

2. revise and polish your document, with sensitivity to economic constraints.

Finally, avoid applying conventions of composition mechanically. Instead, adopt an approach to writing that is analogous to legal method: Strive to understand the purposes and policies of conventions of composition, and apply those conventions flexibly to satisfy the purposes and policies.

Chapter 14

Presenting, Quoting, and
Citing to Authority

When you assert your analysis or interpretation of the law in a memorandum or a brief, you must support your assertions with citations to legal authority, as illustrated in various examples in previous chapters. One manual on advocacy identifies two functions of citations: "(1) it tells the reader that your rule is supported by legal authority and is not merely a product of your imagination, and (2) it allows the reader to evaluate the persuasiveness of the authority you cited when deciding whether or not to accept your conclusion."[1] As explored in Section II.A.2 of Chapter 13, the manner in which you support your assertions of a legal rule will depend on the depth of analysis that is appropriate to the issue. For example, you might safely support a simple, noncontroversial assertion of law with a single citation to authority, while a less settled assertion might warrant several pages of analysis and synthesis of multiple authorities.

---

1. Bd. of Student Advisors, Harvard Law School, INTRODUCTION TO ADVOCACY: RESEARCH, WRITING, AND ARGUMENT 5 (Alisha Crovetto & Joshua Skoski, ed., 8th ed. 2013).

This chapter examines three elements of effective legal writing that you should keep in mind when you support your assertions of law with legal authority: (1) citing to authority in proper form, (2) presenting the law and citations effectively, and (3) quoting from legal authority effectively and sparingly. As with Chapter 13's discussion of legal writing style, this chapter occasionally refers to special techniques of advocacy, but it primarily addresses the balanced, nearly neutral analysis that is appropriate for an office memorandum. Techniques of advocacy are explored in greater detail in Parts VI through VIII.

I. Citation Form

You should cite to authority in a manner that clearly and concisely identifies the source of the authority and helps the reader find the authority in a library. These goals are met, occasionally in slightly different ways, by two popular guides to citation form: THE BLUEBOOK: A UNIFORM SYSTEM OF CITATION,[2] a citation manual published and distributed by the Harvard Law Review Association, and the ALWD CITATION MANUAL,[3] authored by the Association of Legal Writing Directors and Darby Dickerson.

Because this textbook was written and first published before the ALWD CITATION MANUAL was conceived, its citations in text and footnotes are set forth in BLUEBOOK form, except when it reproduces without substantial editing a brief or judicial opinion that uses a different citation form, or when the author consciously departs from BLUEBOOK format for reasons of personal taste, or when this section provides contrasting examples from the ALWD CITATION MANUAL.

The following subsections summarize a few of the more important citation rules of both the fifth edition of the ALWD CITATION MANUAL and the nineteenth edition of the BLUEBOOK. You should view the summaries below only as an overview and not as a substitute for careful study of your assigned citation manual. Keep in mind as well that your citation manual may be published in a newer edition before this textbook is revised to note the changes.

The sample citations in this section are for a legal memorandum or brief rather than a printed book or article. Accordingly, this section does not discuss or provide examples of special typefaces or citation forms that the

---

2. THE BLUEBOOK: A UNIFORM SYSTEM OF CITATION (Columbia Law Review Ass'n et al. eds., 19th ed. 2010) ("BLUEBOOK").

3. ALWD & Darby Dickerson, ALWD CITATION MANUAL: A PROFESSIONAL SYSTEM OF CITATION (5th ed. 2014) ("ALWD CITATION MANUAL"). The preceding citation is generally in the form required by the BLUEBOOK, to maintain consistency with the citations in the remainder of this textbook, most of which were composed before introduction of the ALWD CITATION MANUAL. As a matter of personal preference, however, this author departs from one BLUEBOOK rule by refraining from setting the author of a book in large and small capitals. The extent to which you may similarly substitute your carefully considered personal preferences for the form prescribed by a citation manual may depend on the requirements of your intended audience, whether it be a court, supervisor, or law school instructor.

BLUEBOOK reserves for more formal publications, such as for the footnotes in this book.

A. Constitutions, Codes, and Federal Regulations

Under either of the leading citation manuals, when citing to a specific constitutional provision that is currently in force, refer to the article or amendment number and, if appropriate, to a section number:[4]

U.S. Const. art. III, § 1.
U.S. Const. amend. XIV.
Ariz. Const. art. VI, § 1.

The first citation above refers to section 1 of article III of the United States Constitution. The second citation refers to the Fourteenth Amendment to that constitution. The third citation refers to section 1 of article VI of the Arizona Constitution.

A simple citation to a codified statute includes the volume or title number, code abbreviation, section number, and date of the code edition cited:[5]

42 U.S.C. § 1983 (2006).

The citation above refers to section 1983 in title 42 of the official United States Code, published in 2006. In some code systems, the title or volume number immediately precedes the section number, as in Ariz. Rev. Stat. Ann. § 47-2207 (West 2005), which refers to section 2207 in Title 47 of the Arizona Code.

If the code cited is not published under the supervision of government officials, both citation manuals generally require identification of the publisher in the parenthetic phrase that contains the year of publication. You should consult the appropriate appendix in each citation manual for examples from particular jurisdictions.[6]

Both the BLUEBOOK and the ALWD CITATION MANUAL mandate the year of publication as part of every full citation to a statute.[7] In practice,

---

4. ALWD CITATION MANUAL R. 13.2, at 104-106; BLUEBOOK R. 11, at 110. Following convention for citations within books, this book uses small and large capital letters when citing to constitutional provisions and court rules; the examples of citations to constitutional provisions in the text above, however, use regular font, which would be appropriate in a brief or office memorandum.

5. ALWD CITATION MANUAL R. 14.2, at 111-117; BLUEBOOK R. 12, at 111.

6. ALWD CITATION MANUAL app. 1; BLUEBOOK T.1, at 215-77.

7. ALWD CITATION MANUAL R. 14.2(f)(2), at 115; BLUEBOOK R. 12.3.2, at 115-16.

however, attorneys and courts frequently omit the year of publication unless it is significant or necessary to avoid confusion.

When citing to the *Code of Federal Regulations* (C.F.R.), however, attorneys should more conscientiously follow the manuals' mandate to specify the date of the most recent edition because the Code is frequently revised. For example, the ALWD CITATION MANUAL cites to a federal regulation by its title number, abbreviation for the code, section number, and date of edition cited:

48 C.F.R. § 53.246 (2009).[8]

BLUEBOOK format is consistent with the citation above.[9]

B. Published Case Law

This section discusses citations to judicial opinions that are selected by the authoring court for publication and thus clearly constitute case law with the force of precedent. Appellate courts also issue decisions that—although accessible to legal researchers—are not designated for official publication because they do not set forth new principles of law or novel applications of law to facts and therefore do not require the same care in drafting as would be devoted to a published opinion that breaks new ground. You should check local rules of court and case law within the jurisdiction to determine the purposes, if any, for which you may cite to unpublished court decisions in a brief within the jurisdiction.

1. Basic Citation Form

When citing to case law, specify the case name, the volume and page of the reporter, the court, and the year of decision:[10]

Bell v. United States, 349 U.S. 81 (1955).
Bundy v. Jackson, 641 F.2d 934 (D.C. Cir. 1981).
Wagenseller v. Scottsdale Mem'l Hosp., 147 Ariz. 370, 710 P.2d 1025 (1985).
Tucson Med. Ctr. v. Zoslow, 147 Ariz. 612, 712 P.2d 459 (Ct. App. 1985).

The first case cited above is a decision of the United States Supreme Court, found at page 81 of volume 349 of the official United States Reporter.

---

8. ALWD CITATION MANUAL R. 18.1, at 174.

9. BLUEBOOK R. 14.2, at 133-35.

10. ALWD CITATION MANUAL R. 12.1, at 60-61; BLUEBOOK R. 10, at 87. For the BLUEBOOK's position that case names are italicized or underscored in non-academic writing, see *id*. R. B1, at 3-4, R. B.4.1, at 7.

The second is a decision of the District of Columbia Circuit of the United States Court of Appeals, found at page 934 of volume 641 of the Federal Reporter, second series.

The third is a decision of the Arizona Supreme Court, found at page 370 of volume 147 of the official Arizona Reports, and also found at page 1025 of volume 710 of West's[11] unofficial regional Pacific Reporter, second series. Because a decision in the official Arizona Reports is assumed to be that of the Arizona Supreme Court unless otherwise designated, no further identification of the court is needed next to the date within the parentheses.[12]

In contrast, the fourth citation includes the notation "Ct. App." within the parentheses to identify the source of the authority as the Arizona Court of Appeals in BLUEBOOK form, as set forth in the BLUEBOOK's table of authorities in each state.[13] The full BLUEBOOK designation for that court, Ariz. Ct. App., is unnecessary next to the date in this example, because the reference to the official Arizona Reports in the parallel citation identifies the forum as an Arizona court. Reference to the department, district, or division of the authoring court, such as by adding "Div. 2" after "Ct. App." in the fourth citation above, is required by the citation manuals only if it is particularly relevant.[14]

2. Abbreviations of Case Names

The BLUEBOOK and ALWD CITATION MANUAL call for abbreviation of many words in case names in citations. For example, in the sample Arizona citations in subsection 1 above, the BLUEBOOK's table of abbreviations requires "*Memorial Hospital*" to be abbreviated to "*Mem'l Hosp.*" and "*Medical Center*" to be abbreviated to "*Med. Ctr.*"[15] The BLUEBOOK, however, does not permit abbreviation of "United States" when used as the name of a party.[16] In comparison, the ALWD CITATION MANUAL does not permit abbreviation of "United States" to "U.S." unless it is part of the name of a federal department, agency, or organization.[17]

3. Parallel Citations

Most case law appears in more than one published form. For example, the Arizona decisions cited above appear in both the official Arizona Reports

---

11. West Publishing merged with Thomson Legal Publishing in June 1996, producing West Group. Its parent company is now Thomson Reuters, and it typically goes by the simple name "West."

12. *See* BLUEBOOK R. 10.4(b), at 98; *see generally* ALWD CITATION MANUAL R. 12.6(a), at 82, R. 12.6(c)(1), at 82.

13. BLUEBOOK T.1, at 230.

14. ALWD CITATION MANUAL R. 12.6(c)(1), at 82; BLUEBOOK R. 10.4(b), at 98.

15. BLUEBOOK R. 10.2.2, at 94, T.6, at 430-31.

16. *Id.* R. 10.2.2, at 94-95. The BLUEBOOK, however, requires abbreviation of "United States" to "U.S." when it is part of the name of the institutional author of a book. *Id.* R. 15.1(d), at 139.

17. ALWD CITATION MANUAL R. 12.2(g), at 68.

and in the unofficial Pacific Reports, second series, published by West Publishing Company. The BLUEBOOK and ALWD CITATION MANUAL instruct you to use parallel citations in briefs if required by local court rules.[18] In the illustrations in Section I.B.1 above, the Arizona decisions are set forth in parallel citations, because Arizona rules for appellate briefs provide that "[c]itation of authorities shall be to the volume and page number of the official reports and also when possible to the unofficial reporters."[19]

In an office memorandum, or in a brief if parallel citation is not required by local rules, however, the ALWD CITATION MANUAL calls for citation to only one source, with a West reporter normally preferred over other print reporters[20] except in the case of decisions of the United States Supreme Court, for which citations to the official United States Reports are preferred.[21] Similarly, for office memoranda, the BLUEBOOK advises you to cite "the relevant regional reporter" and to the official public domain citation, if one is available.[22]

As a practical matter, however, you may want to include parallel citations in an office memorandum even though not required by citation manuals. If your memorandum will serve as the partial blueprint for a brief or other court filing that you or another attorney will later draft, and if the local court rules will require parallel citations in the future brief, then parallel citations in your office memorandum will be helpful to the author of the brief.

4. Subsequent History

Your case citation should include any significant subsequent history:[23]

Scott v. Sears, Roebuck & Co., 605 F. Supp. 1047 (N.D. Ill. 1985), *aff'd,* 798 F.2d 210 (7th Cir. 1986).

In the example above, the author of a memorandum has cited to a decision of the United States District Court for the Northern District of Illinois to support a proposition. She has noted in her citation that the United States Court of Appeals for the Seventh Circuit affirmed the district court's decision. We may assume that she cited primarily to the district court's opinion because it included some language or reasoning not expressed in the appellate court's opinion; otherwise, she could have cited directly to the appellate court's opinion to support her proposition.

According to both the BLUEBOOK and the ALWD CITATION MANUAL, a case citation need not include the denial of discretionary review, such as

---

18. *Id.* R. 12.4(c), at 79 (only if "required to do so by local rule"); BLUEBOOK R. 10.3.1(a), at 95 (cite to reporters, including parallel citations, "required by local rules").

19. ALWD CITATION MANUAL app. 2 (quoting ARIZ. R. CIV. APP. P. 13(a)(6)).

20. *Id.* R. 12.4(b)(2), at 77-78.

21. *Id.*

22. BLUEBOOK R. 10.3.1(b), at 95.

23. *See* ALWD CITATION MANUAL R. 12.8, at 85; BLUEBOOK R. 10.7, at 101.

the Supreme Court's denial of certiorari, from a decision that is at least two years old, unless the denial is "particularly relevant"[24] or "particularly important."[25] In practice, however, some attorneys routinely note all denials of certiorari in their citations.

5. Order of Authorities Within a String

You can string multiple citations in succession, separating them with semicolons:

Bundy v. Jackson, 641 F.2d 934 (D.C. Cir. 1981); *Barnes v. Costle*, 561 F.2d 983 (D.C. Cir. 1970); *Scott v. Sears, Roebuck & Co.*, 605 F. Supp. 1047 (N.D. Ill. 1985), *aff'd*, 798 F.2d 210 (7th Cir. 1986).

The BLUEBOOK and ALWD CITATION MANUAL list various kinds of authorities in hierarchical order, specifying the usual order of citation to different kinds of authority or to case law from different courts.[26] You should cite to cases decided by the same court in reverse chronological order.[27]

Both citation manuals, however, instruct authors to override the usual rules for ordering citations if more substantive criteria support giving priority to one or more authorities.[28] An author, for example, might cite to cases in descending order of strength of authority based on the breadth of their statements of helpful rules or based on the strength of factual analogy.

6. Specific Page Cites

When citing to a passage within a decision, cite to the specific page or pages on which the passage appears:[29]

Bundy v. Jackson, 641 F.2d 934, 936-37 (D.C. Cir. 1981).
Wagenseller v. Scottsdale Mem'l Hosp., 147 Ariz. 370, 380 n.5, 710 P.2d 1025, 1035 n.5 (1985).

In the first citation above, the cited passage appears on pages 936 to 937. In the second citation, the cited passage appears in footnote 5, which is found on page 380 of the Arizona Reports and on page 1035 of the Pacific

---

24. BLUEBOOK R. 10.7, at 101.

25. ALWD CITATION MANUAL R. 12.8(a), at 85, Sidebar 12.6, at 95, and Chart 12.2, at 76.

26. *Id.* R. 36, at 375-81; BLUEBOOK R. 1.4, at 56-59.

27. ALWD CITATION MANUAL R. 36.2(d), at 323; BLUEBOOK R. 1.4(d), at 57-58.

28. ALWD CITATION MANUAL R. 36.2, at 322; BLUEBOOK R. 1.4, at 56. This textbook follows this recommendation in more than one instance.

29. ALWD CITATION MANUAL R. 5.2(b), at 28, R. 12.5(b), at 92; BLUEBOOK R. 3.2(a), at 67, & 3.2(b), at 68.

Reporter. Alternatively, as discussed in Subsection 8.a below, you may cite to a specific paragraph in a public domain citation.

7. Short-Form Citation

If you have fully cited to a case in a brief or legal memorandum, you may refer to it within the same general discussion by a shortened case name, volume, reporter, and specific page cite:[30]

Bundy, 641 F.2d at 938.
Wagenseller, 147 Ariz. at 381, 710 P.2d at 1036.

You may use "*Id.*" in subsequent citations to a case first cited in a single source, if no other citations intervene:[31]

Bundy, 641 F.2d at 938. The court also held . . . discrimination. *Id.*

When using "*Id.*," add new specific page cites if appropriate:

Bundy, 641 F.2d at 938. The court also held . . . discrimination. *Id.* at 939.

You may also use "*Id.*" to refer to the first source in a parallel citation when citing to different pages in the sources:[32]

Wagenseller v. Scottsdale Mem'l Hosp., 147 Ariz. 370, 710 P.2d 1025 (1985). The court held that . . . policy. *Id.* at 381, 710 P.2d at 1036.

The ALWD CITATION MANUAL, however, reasons that each reporter in the parallel citation is a separate source, so it cautions you not to use "*Id.*" alone to refer to the same pages in an entire parallel citation,[33] as in the second "*id.*" in the following: ". . . policy. *Id.* at 381, 710 P.2d at 1036. The court reasoned that . . . statute. *Id.*" This is a fairly technical point, however, that is seldom honored in practice.

If the textual sentences after the initial citation refer to the case name, the short-form citation could omit the case name:

The *Wagenseller* court held that . . . policy. 147 Ariz. at 381, 710 P.2d at 1036.[34]

---

30. ALWD CITATION MANUAL R. 12.19(b), at 99–100; BLUEBOOK B5.2, at 18.
31. ALWD CITATION MANUAL R. 12.19(a), at 99; BLUEBOOK R. 4.1, at 72.
32. ALWD CITATION MANUAL R. 12.19(d), at 100; BLUEBOOK B4, at 14-15.
33. ALWD CITATION MANUAL R. 12.19(d), at 100.
34. *Id.* R. 12.19(c), at 116.

8. Citations to Alternative Sources of Case Law

a. Public Domain Citations

The citations for case law in Subsections 1 through 4 above are based on the publication of judicial opinions in bound reporter systems. The citations accordingly refer to specific volume and page numbers in those systems. The same case law, however, is increasingly available from electronic sources, such as CD-ROMs, online computer research services, or Internet sites. Partly to facilitate citation to decisions that may appear in a number of formats, some jurisdictions have adopted or proposed "public domain citation forms," also known as "universal," "vendor-neutral," or simply as "neutral" citation forms. Neutral citations allow the reader to locate a judicial opinion, as well as a paragraph within the opinion, in any case law reporter system, without reference to pagination in a bound volume.

Courts that adopt a public domain citation system[35] typically will sequentially number their opinions issued in a given year, and will sequentially number the paragraphs in each opinion. A neutral citation should include the following information at a minimum: case name, year of decision, abbreviation of authoring court, number assigned to the opinion, and parallel citation to a reporter or online source, if available, as in this example from the ALWD CITATION MANUAL:

Johnson v. Traynor, 1998 ND 115, 579 N.W.2d 184.[36]

If you wish to cite to a specific paragraph in the opinion, you should add the paragraph number, as in this example from the BLUEBOOK:

Beck v. Beck, 1999 ME 110, ¶ 6, 733 A.2d 981, 983.[37]

Although jurisdictions proposing or adopting neutral citation forms are currently in the minority, the movement is likely to gain momentum in light of endorsements by the American Bar Association (ABA) and the American Association of Law Libraries (AALL). The AALL publishes its own citation manual for vendor-neutral citations to cases, statutes, regulations, and other sources: Comm. on Citation Formats, Am. Ass'n of Law Libraries, UNIVERSAL CITATION GUIDE (1999). Of course, if the courts in your jurisdiction have adopted a particular format for neutral citations, you can safely adopt that format, and indeed must do so for court filings if mandated by local rules.

---

35. For a listing of courts with such citation systems, *see* ALWD CITATION MANUAL app. 2.

36. *Id.* R. 12.17, at 97-98.

37. BLUEBOOK R. 10.3.3, at 96-97 (adopting state's postal code to identify state's highest court); *see also* ALWD CITATION MANUAL R. 12.17, at 97-98 (presenting Wisconsin public domain citation followed by citations to two traditional reporter systems).

b. Bloomberg, Lexis, and Westlaw

Even if the relevant jurisdiction has not yet adopted a public domain citation system, you may occasionally need to cite to an electronic source for case law, or to a court's preliminary publication of its decision in an official "slip opinion," simply because the decision is so recent that it has not yet been published in a traditional reporter system.

For example, even before a decision appears in print in the paperback supplement to a West's regional reporter system, it may be available on the Bloomberg, LexisNexis, or Westlaw electronic databases, or in the court's own "slip opinions" published either in a printed hard copy or in electronic form at an Internet site. If so, you may wish to cite solely to one of these sources.

For example, the following citation in BLUEBOOK format refers to a decision of the United States Supreme Court as it appeared on the Bloomberg web site a few days after the opinion was released. It includes the case name, docket number, database citation (year, database, and document number), and the Court and date in parentheses:

United States v. Windsor, No. 12-1307, 2013 BL 169260 (U.S. June 26, 2013).

To the extent that the reference to the database clearly identifies the court, all or part of the court abbreviation may be omitted within the parentheses.[38]

To cite to a particular screen or page number within the case, insert an asterisk and the screen or page number after the database identifier, as in this example from the BLUEBOOK:

Albrecht v. Stanczek, No. 87 C 9535, 1991 U.S. Dist. LEXIS 5088, at *1, *3 (N.D. Ill. Apr. 15, 1991).[39]

For a subsequent short-form citation, you can use a shortened case name and omit the docket number, date, and specific court designation:

Albrecht, 1991 U.S. Dist. LEXIS 5088, at *2.[40]

The ALWD CITATION MANUAL is consistent with the illustrations above.[41]

---

38. ALWD CITATION MANUAL R. 12.13(b), at 94.

39. BLUEBOOK R. B4.1.4, at 11. This example is taken from the blue pages of the BLUEBOOK, which calls for underscoring or italicization of the case names for briefs, a style applied to all the examples in this chapter. The BLUEBOOK's white pages omit the italics in case names for books and articles, as illustrated in a similar citation, *id.* at R. 10.9(a)(ii), at 109.

40. *Id.* R. 10.9(a)(ii), at 109.

41. ALWD CITATION MANUAL R. 12.13(b), at 94.

c. Slip Opinions Issued by a Court

The BLUEBOOK presents the following example of a citation to a court's official slip opinion, this one from a jurisdiction that does not separately paginate each slip opinion, so that the slip opinion begins on page 3458 and contains a relevant passage on page 3465:

Charlesworth v. Mack, No. 90-567, slip op. 3458, 3465 (1st Cir. Jan. 19, 1991).[42]

The following would be an acceptable short-form citation:

Charlesworth, slip op. at 3466.[43]

If you are citing to the case generally, and not to a particular page number, you could omit the reference to the slip opinion page number:

Charlesworth v. Mack, No. 90-567 (1st Cir. Jan. 19, 1991).[44]

If you wish to cite to a particular page within the slip opinion, and the court's slip opinions are separately paginated so that each begins with page 1, you should refer only to the specific page within:

Charlesworth v. Mack, No. 90-345, slip op. at 6 (D. Mass. Dec. 4, 1990).[45]

The ALWD citation rules for slip opinions are generally consistent with the BLUEBOOK examples above.[46]

d. Direct Internet Citations

If a more conventional source is not readily available, cite to a case published on the Internet in the following format: the case name, docket number, an abbreviation for the court and the exact date within parentheses, the phrase "available at," and the web site's URL. The first example below is taken from the ALWD CITATION MANUAL, and the second is taken from the BLUEBOOK:

---

42. BLUEBOOK R. 10.8.1(b), at 105.

43. *See generally id.* R. 10.9(a), at 107-09 (presenting short-form citations for cases reported in reporters and electronic databases).

44. *See id.* R. 10.8.1(b), at 105.

45. *Id.* (presenting example that is similar but that is set in a different jurisdiction).

46. ALWD CITATION MANUAL R. 12.15, at 96, R. 12.19(f), at 101.

Menna v. Walmart, No. 08-2610 (N.Y. Sup. Ct. Suffolk Cnty. July 10, 2013), *available at* http://www.nycourts.gov/reporter/3dseries/2013/2013_51255.htm.[47]

Am. Mining Cong. V. U.S. Army Corps of Eng'rs, No. CIV A. 93-1754 SSH (D.D.C. Jan. 23, 1997), *available at* http://www.wetlands.com/fed/tulloch1.htm.[48]

C. Basic Citation Form for Books and Articles

The BLUEBOOK and the ALWD CITATION MANUAL advise you to cite to books or treatises by volume number (if any), the full name of the author, the title, the edition number if beyond the first edition, and the year of publication:[49]

Richard C. Wydick, *Plain English for Lawyers* (5th ed. 2005).[50]

The citation manuals additionally call for identification of the publisher, but only if the cited work is published by other than the original publisher.[51]

Under the rules of either citation manual, you should cite to articles in law journals by the full name of the author, title, volume and name of the journal, page number on which the article begins, and year of publication:[52]

Roscoe Pound, *Common Law and Legislation*, 21 Harv. L. Rev. 383 (1908).

For either kind of authority, if you refer to a specific passage within the authority, cite also to the specific page or pages on which the passage appears:[53]

Richard C. Wydick, *Plain English for Lawyers* 53–55 (5th ed. 2005).
Roscoe Pound, *Common Law and Legislation*, 21 Harv. L. Rev. 383, 387 (1908).

---

47. ALWD CITATION MANUAL R. 12.16, at 96-97. (recommending an Internet source only if no other source is available).

48. BLUEBOOK R. B.10.1.2, at 26 (recommending an Internet citation when "it will increase access to the source").

49. ALWD CITATION MANUAL R. 20.1, at 198; BLUEBOOK R. 15, at 138.

50. The typeface above is consistent with BLUEBOOK and ALWD CITATION MANUAL format for citation to a book in court documents or legal memoranda. ALWD CITATION MANUAL R. 20.1, at 198; BLUEBOOK R. B1, at 3-4, R. B8.1, at 23. The citation manuals call for a typeface of large and small capitals for the author and title of a book when cited in an article or book, such as this textbook. ALWD CITATION MANUAL R. 20.1(f), at 203; BLUEBOOK R. 15, at 138.

51. ALWD CITATION MANUAL R. 20.1(e)(3), at 202; BLUEBOOK R. 15.4(a), at 140-41.

52. ALWD CITATION MANUAL R. 21.2, at 215; BLUEBOOK R. 16, at 147.

53. ALWD CITATION MANUAL R. 20.1(d), at 200-201, R. 21.2(f), at 218; BLUEBOOK R. 15, at 129, R. 16, at 147.

D. Citation Within a Citation

If you support your proposition with authority that itself relies on other authority, you may express such reliance with a parenthetic explanation:[54]

Meritor Sav. Bank v. Vinson, 477 U.S. 57, 65 (1986) (quoting 29 C.F.R. § 1604.11(a)(3) (1985)). Moreover, the Court referred approvingly to . . . . *Id.* at 65-66 (describing holding of *Rogers v. EEOC*, 454 F.2d 234, 238 (5th Cir. 1971)).

To reverse the emphasis, you can cite first to the authority that above was viewed as parenthetic:[55]

29 C.F.R. § 1604.11(a)(3) (1985), *quoted in Meritor Sav. Bank v. Vinson*, 477 U.S. 57, 65 (1986).

E. Citation Signals

The following citation signals describe the relationship between the cited authority and either (1) the proposition for which it is cited or (2) other authority. In many of the sample citations below, a parenthetic explanation at the end of the citation supplements the signal by more specifically describing the relationship between the cited authority and the stated proposition or other authority. You may prefer to use parenthetic explanations even more liberally than suggested in the examples below. According to the BLUEBOOK, "[p]arenthetical information is recommended when the relevance of a cited authority might not otherwise be clear to the reader."[56]

1. No Signal

Use no signal to introduce a citation if the proposition for which authority is cited (1) quotes from the cited authority, (2) names the authority or otherwise refers to it, or (3) is directly supported by the authority, often because the proposition is a paraphrase or summary of a passage in the authority.[57] Each of these types of propositions is illustrated, in the order set forth above, in the following passage. The second and third citations use "*id.*" to refer to the previously cited authority, *Oncale*, but none of the citations begins with a citation signal:

Sexual harassment constitutes sex discrimination if "members of one sex are exposed to disadvantageous terms or conditions of employment to which members of the other sex are not exposed." *Oncale v. Sundowner Offshore Servs., Inc.,*

---

54. ALWD CITATION MANUAL R. 37.4(a), at 333; BLUEBOOK R. 1.6(c), at 61.
55. *See* ALWD CITATION MANUAL R. 37.4(b), at 334; BLUEBOOK R. 1.6, at 61.
56. BLUEBOOK R. 1.5, at 59.
57. ALWD CITATION MANUAL R. 35.2, at 314; BLUEBOOK R. 1.2(a), at 54.

523 U.S. 75, 80 (1998) (quoting *Harris v. Forklift Sys., Inc.*, 510 U.S. 17, 25 (Ginsburg, J., concurring)). The *Oncale* Court held that same-sex harassment could meet this standard and thus constitute sex discrimination under Title VII. *Id.* at 80, 82. Such discrimination, however, does not trigger liability under the statute unless it so degrades the working environment that it alters terms or conditions of employment. *Id.* at 78, 81.

2. "See"

Introduce a citation with "*see*" if the cited authority supports your proposition, but only indirectly, thus requiring the reader to infer an unstated logical link between the proposition and the authority.[58] For example, your proposition may not appear in the cited authority, but it may follow directly from it if you tailor the holding of the cited authority to the facts of your own case. In the following example, Gracy's, Inc., Bailey, and Johnson are nowhere mentioned in the cited authority, *Oncale*. Therefore, even though the *Oncale* decision clearly supports the proposition about Johnson's claim, it does so only indirectly: It requires the reader to infer that the proposition regarding Johnson's claim follows from the application of general principles in *Oncale* or from an analogy to *Oncale*'s application of general principles to the facts of *Oncale*'s claim:

Gracy's, Inc., will be liable for sex discrimination under Title VII if its general manager, Bailey, selectively harassed Johnson because of his sex and if the harassment was so severe or frequent that it altered Johnson's conditions of employment. *See Oncale v. Sundowner Offshore Servs., Inc.*, 523 U.S. 75, 78-82 (1998).

3. "Accord"

According to the BLUEBOOK, if a proposition quotes or names an authority, you should cite to the quoted or named authority without any signal, and you may then use "*accord*" to introduce citations to additional cases that directly support the proposition but are not named or quoted in the proposition:[59]

"The general rule is that a seller of real estate is under a duty to disclose those material facts which would not be discoverable by the buyer in the exercise of ordinary care and due diligence." *Isaacs v. Bishop*, 249 S.W.3d 100, 114 n.14 (Tex. App. 2008); *accord, Robbins v. Capozzi*, 100 S.W.3d 18, 24 (Tex. App. 2002); *Smith v. Nat'l Resort Cmtys., Inc.*, 585 S.W.2d 655, 658 (Tex. 1979).

---

58. BLUEBOOK R. 1.2(a), at 54; *see* ALWD CITATION MANUAL R. 35.3, at 314, Chart 35.1, at 315 (use "*see*" when authority "only implicitly supports the stated proposition").

59. BLUEBOOK R. 1.2(a), at 54.

You can also use "*accord*" to introduce authority from other jurisdictions that adopt the same rule as is stated by the authority to which you have just cited without any introductory signal:[60]

In Georgia, courts have recognized an affirmative duty to disclose materials facts during negotiation of the sale of residential housing. *Condon v. Kunse*, 208 Ga. App. 856, 858, 432 S.E.2d 266, 269 (1993); *accord, Hill v. Jones*, 151 Ariz. 81, 725 P.2d 1115 (Ct. App. 1986) (finding seller's duty to disclose termite damage in dwelling as a matter of common law); *Isaacs v. Bishop*, 249 S.W.3d 100, 114 n.14 (Tex. App. 2008) (citing to Texas cases that recognize the duty in both residential and commercial real estate transactions).

The ALWD CITATION MANUAL is in accord with this approach.[61]

4. "See Generally"

Use "*see generally*" to signify that the cited authority provides general background information related to the proposition for which the authority is cited:[62]

In Arizona, an employer may be liable in some circumstances for breach of a promise in a company policy manual. *See Leikvold v. Valley View Cmty. Hosp.*, 141 Ariz. 544, 546, 688 P.2d 170, 172 (1984); *see generally* Michael A. Di Sabatino, Annotation, *Modern Status of Rule that Employer May Discharge At-will Employee for Any Reason*, 12 A.L.R. 4th 544 (1982) (examining erosion of doctrine that employer may terminate without liability an employee hired for an indefinite period of time).

The annotation cited above does not provide direct support for the proposition about Arizona law, because the annotation predated the *Leikvold* case, which firmly established the Arizona law on point. Instead, the annotation provides general background information about a national trend of expanding employee rights under tort and contract law, background information that can give the reader a fuller understanding of the general topic raised in the proposition.

5. "Cf." and "Compare . . . with"

Use "*cf.*" to introduce an authority that supports the stated proposition by analogy or distinction, followed by parenthetic explanation:[63]

---

60. *Id.*
61. ALWD CITATION MANUAL R. 35.3, at 314, Chart 35.1, at 315.
62. *Id.*; BLUEBOOK R. 1.2(d), at 55.
63. ALWD CITATION MANUAL R. 35.3, at 314, Chart 35.1, at 315; BLUEBOOK R. 1.2(a), at 55.

The "Proposal to Purchase Real Estate" probably is not an offer to buy a lot within the subdivision, because it does not address terms of payment. *Cf. Craft v. Elder & Johnston Co.*, 38 N.E.2d 416 (Ohio Ct. App. 1941) (holding that a newspaper ad for indefinite quantity of sewing machines was only an invitation to negotiate); *Lefkowitz v. Great Minneapolis Surplus Store*, 86 N.W.2d 689 (Minn. 1957) (holding that a newspaper ad was an offer, but only because it was unusually specific and definite).

Neither of the authorities cited above directly supports your proposition about the real estate proposal, because the authorities address the specialized factual context of newspaper advertisements. Nonetheless, the first citation above supports the stated proposition by showing how analogous facts in the context of a newspaper advertisement supported the same result as the one proposed for a personalized real estate transaction. The second citation indirectly supports the stated proposition by explaining that a different result from the one proposed depended on materially different facts, also in the specialized context of a newspaper advertisement.

To directly compare these two different kinds of support, or to contrast different legal approaches, you can use "*Compare . . . with*," along with parenthetic explanations.[64] The following example compares two different kinds of support for a proposition:

A newspaper ad is an offer only if it is sufficiently complete and definite that it leaves no important terms open for further negotiation. *Compare Craft v. Elder & Johnston Co.*, 38 N.E.2d 416 (Ohio Ct. App. 1941) (newspaper ad for indefinite quantity of sewing machines was only an invitation to negotiate), *with Lefkowitz v. Great Minneapolis Surplus Store*, 86 N.W.2d 689 (Minn. 1957) (newspaper ad was an offer because it was unusually specific and definite).

6. "See also"

As an alternative to the signals discussed in Subsections 3 through 5 above, you may introduce additional supporting authority with "*see also*." The BLUEBOOK defines "*see also*" so that it arguably lies roughly between no signal, "*accord*," and "*see*," on the one hand, and "*cf.*" or "*see generally*" on the other:

Cited authority constitutes additional source material that supports the proposition. "See also" is commonly used to cite an authority supporting a proposition when authorities that state or directly support the proposition already have been cited or discussed. The use of a parenthetical explanation

---

64. ALWD CITATION MANUAL R. 35.3, at 314, Chart 35.1, at 315; BLUEBOOK R. 1.2(b), at 55.

of the source's relevance . . . following a citation introduced by "see also" is encouraged.[65]

According to the ALWD CITATION MANUAL,

[u]se [see also] to cite authority, in addition to that previously cited, that supports the proposition. This signal's support for a proposition is not as strong or direct as [no signal] or see. In addition, see also may be used when the cited authority supports a point, but is in some respect distinguishable from previously cited authorities.[66]

You likely will use the "*see also*" signal to introduce additional supporting authority that follows authority introduced with a "*see*" signal, or perhaps with no signal. You typically will use "*see also*" to introduce authority that supports your proposition less directly than does the authority preceding it, thus justifying a parenthetic explanation.

For example, suppose the first authority in a citation sentence is introduced with "*see*" because it clearly supports your proposition, but only indirectly, requiring some inference on the reader's part. You might introduce the second authority with "*see also*," rather than with no further signal, if the second authority states or supports your proposition, but not so clearly or obviously that you can dispense with a parenthetic explanation. Of course, in some contexts "*see generally*" or "*cf.*" would be appropriate to signify such an attenuated relationship between the authority and the proposition. Consequently, "*see also*" should be reserved for supporting authority that is not so far removed from the specific topic of your proposition that it provides only general background information, a level of support that is better signified by "*see generally*." Nor should you use "*see also*" to introduce authority that is so contextually different from your proposition that it supports the proposition only by analogy, a relationship better signified by "*cf.*"

For example, the first authority in the following passage, *Rite Realty, Inc. v. Simmons*, is introduced with "*see*" presumably because the court in *Rite Realty* found no offer on facts very similar to those of the "Proposal to Purchase Real Estate," which is the subject of the office memorandum or brief. In contrast, the second authority is introduced with "*see also*" because its more extreme facts moderate the degree of support it provides to the main proposition:

The "Proposal to Purchase Real Estate" probably is not an offer to buy a lot within the subdivision, because it does not address terms of payment. *See Rite Realty, Inc. v. Simmons*, . . . (1968); *see also Frost v. Baker*, . . . (finding no offer because document proposed to sell a working farm at a certain price without identifying the farm or its location within the county).

---

65. BLUEBOOK R. 1.2(a), at 54.
66. ALWD CITATION MANUAL R. 35.3, at 314, Chart 35.1, at 315.

In this example, *Frost v. Baker* requires parenthetic explanation, because the reader should be apprised of how its facts raised more obvious problems in finding an offer than does the "Proposal to Purchase Real Estate" in the case at hand.[67] Nonetheless, *Frost* provides more than general background information. Moreover, neither its reference to a proposal to sell rather than buy nor the more obvious indefiniteness in the terms of its proposal suggest that its support requires the reader to draw an analogy to find support. Accordingly, "*see also*" is a more appropriate introductory signal than "*see generally*" or "*cf.*"

Many writers more naturally and intuitively use "*see also*" in a slightly different context, suggested by the BLUEBOOK's statement that "*see also*" might follow the citation to an authority that has already been *discussed*. For example, if you have engaged in an in-depth discussion of a case and applied it to the facts to reach a conclusion, you might end your discussion with a "*see also*" citation to provide additional support, particularly if the additional support is somewhat less telling, perhaps because the facts are not as squarely on point or because the authoring court is less authoritative within the jurisdiction:

Officer Caruso's warrantless search of Kelly's motor home is squarely supported by the Supreme Court's decision in *California v. Carney*, 471 U.S. 386 (1985). In *Carney* . . . . Similarly, in this case, Kelly had parked his motor home at a parking strip along a state beach. . . . Thus, Officer Caruso needed only probable cause to search Kelly's motor home. *See id.; see also Wisconsin v. Snide* . . . (Wis. 1993) (upholding warrantless search of fishing boat with sleeping berths while it was docked lakeside and subject to administrative regulation of government authorities).

---

7. "But" and "Contra"

Introduce an authority that opposes your proposition with a new citation sentence beginning with "*but*," combined with another signal, such as "*see*" or "*cf.*," as in "*But see*" or "*But cf.*":[68]

The "Proposal to Purchase Real Estate" probably is not an offer to buy a lot within the subdivision, because it does not address terms of payment. *Cf. Craft v. Elder & Johnston Co.*, 38 N.E.2d 416 (Ohio Ct. App. 1941) (newspaper ad for indefinite quantity of sewing machines was only an invitation to negotiate). *But cf. Buntz v. Great Calzona Surplus Store*, 251 Calz. 188 (1957) (newspaper ad was an offer at a sale price even though the duration of the sale was left uncertain).

---

67. Of course, a parenthetic explanation following the citation to *Rite Realty* might be helpful as well. Still, in the example above, the need for a parenthetic explanation is much stronger in the second citation, reflecting its more attenuated relationship to the stated proposition.

68. ALWD CITATION MANUAL R. 35.3, at 314, Chart 35.1, at 315; BLUEBOOK R. 1.2(c), at 55.

In this example, the fictitious opinion in *Buntz* plays a different role than did the *Lefkowitz* case in Subsection 5 above. Although *Lefkowitz* reached a different result than stated in your proposition, its reasoning and materially different facts nonetheless supported your proposition by analogy. In contrast, *Buntz* opposes your proposition to some degree because it finds an offer despite an argument that an important term was missing from the ad; therefore, the negative signal "*But*" is appropriate. Because the author viewed the context in *Buntz* as only analogous to that of her case, and because the missing term in Buntz was different in character than the missing term in the present case, the author appropriately paired "*But*" with "*cf.*" in introducing *Buntz*. If an authority contradicted your proposition indirectly, requiring some inference but not analogy to a different context, you would introduce it with "*But see.*" If an authority directly contradicted your proposition, you would introduce it with "*Contra.*"[69]

8. "E.g."

Use "*e.g.,*" combined with another signal if necessary, to show that the cited authority is simply an example of numerous cases that might be cited to support the proposition:[70]

See, e.g., Dothard v. Rawlinson, 433 U.S. 321, 323-32 (1977) (height and weight requirement for prison guards).

Alternatively, you may cite to multiple authorities without the "*e.g.*" signal:

See Dothard v. Rawlinson, 433 U.S. 321, 323-32 (1977) (height and weight requirement for prison guards); *Griggs v. Duke Power Co.*, 401 U.S. 424 (1971) (high school diploma or intelligence test); *Blake v. City of L.A. Police Dep't*, 595 F.2d 1367 (9th Cir. 1979) (height and physical abilities test for police officers).

As a matter of style, however, you should avoid long string citations of multiple authorities unless you have good reason to cite to more than two or three strong, illustrative authorities. For example, to establish that six circuits of the United States Court of Appeals have agreed that the same ambiguous statute should be interpreted in a certain manner, you might reasonably cite to a decision in each of six circuits in a long string citation. In most other contexts, however, you can save your reader time and effort by citing to your best one, two, or three authorities and by preceding the

---

69. *See* ALWD CITATION MANUAL R. 35.3, at 314, Chart 35.1, at 315; BLUEBOOK R. 1.2(c), at 55.

70. BLUEBOOK R. 1.2(a), at 54; ALWD CITATION MANUAL R. 35.3, at 314, Chart 35.1, at 315.

g." signal to signify that numerous other authorities

Exercise 14-1

1. Editing Citations

Using the citation manual designated by your professor, correct the errors in the following citations.

a. Article III, Federal Constitution, sec. 1.

b. U.S. Code, section 1983, title 42 (1994).

c. *Crane Co. v. American Standard, Inc.*, C.A.2d, 1973, 490 F.2d 332 at 335 through 336.

d. *Michigan Sugar Co. v. Jebavy Sorenson Orchard Co.*, Mich. Ct. App., 1976, 239 N.W.2d 693, 66 Mich. App. 642. {cited in a brief to a Michigan court}.

2. Constructing Citations

Express the correct citation for the following authorities in a brief to a Connecticut court:

a. In 1980, the Connecticut Supreme Court issued a decision in *Cherwell-Ralli, Inc. v. Rytman Grain Co.* It appeared in volume 180 of the Connecticut Reporter, the official reporter for the Connecticut Supreme Court, beginning at page 714. It also appeared in volume 433 of the unofficial, regional Atlantic Reporter, second series, beginning at page 984.

b. You wish to cite in full to the decision described in paragraph *a* above at page 716 of the official reporter and page 986 of the unofficial reporter. After an additional sentence of text, you wish to cite to the same authority at page 715 of the official reporter and page 985 of the unofficial reporter. No other citation has intervened.

c. You wish to cite to the decision described in paragraph a above at page 717 of the official reporter and page 987 of the unofficial reporter. You last cited to this authority in the previous page of your document, as described in paragraph *b* above; since then, several citations to other authorities have intervened.

3. Selecting Citation Signals

In each excerpt below, select the appropriate citation signal, or mark an "x" to designate that no signal is appropriate.

a. At a minimum, due process requires a hearing before a disinterested, unbiased judge. ____ *Bracy v. Gramley* . . . . {*Bracy* directly states this proposition, although in slightly different words.}

b. At a minimum, due process requires a hearing "before a judge with no actual bias against the defendant or interest in the outcome of his particular case." ___ *Bracy v. Gramley* . . . . {*Bracy* is the source of the quote.}

c. Except in special circumstances, police officers must secure a warrant before searching a residence. ____ *Agnello v. United States* . . . ; ____ *California v. Carney* . . . (permitting warrantless search of a motor home because of its mobility and because of reduced expectation of privacy stemming from administrative regulation of all motor vehicles). Because no special circumstances justified a warrantless search in this case, the discovery of the marijuana was the product of an illegal search. ____ *Agnello v. United States* . . . {*Agnello* directly states the opening proposition, though in other words, and it is only the first of many Supreme Court decisions to directly affirm this proposition. *Carney* supports a different result in a limited context that shares some factual elements with those encompassed by the main proposition, but nonetheless is distinguishable from the fixed residence in *Agnello*. *Agnello* indirectly supports the second proposition, because—in the context of a different case, not involving the discovery of the marijuana in the present case—it stated that failure to obtain a warrant in similar circumstances could make a search illegal}.

II. Presenting Your Authority Effectively

A. Subordinating Your Citations

1. Citation Clauses and Sentences

Authors of law journal articles or treatises can gracefully insert case names at the beginning or in the middle of textual sentences, because they customarily drop the remainder of the citations to footnotes. Some attorneys and judges have advocated a similar style for office memoranda and briefs to courts.[71] According to current convention, however, most citations in briefs and in office memoranda remain in the text, raising issues about the best way to combine the citations with the propositions for which they are cited.

Occasionally, a citation to authority is so short that you can unobtrusively insert it into the middle of a sentence as a citation clause:

---

71. *See, e.g.*, William Glaberson, *Legal Citations on Trial in Innovation v. Tradition*, N.Y. TIMES, July 8, 2001, at A1 (footnote notation in title of article omitted).

Because the employer is potentially liable for punitive damages, 42 U.S.C. § 1981a(a)(1) (2006), we should seriously consider the plaintiff's offer to settle for reasonable compensatory damages.

Longer citations at the beginning or middle of a sentence in an office memorandum or brief, however, can divert attention from substantive ideas in the text of the sentence:

In *Tucson Med. Ctr. v. Zoslow*, 147 Ariz. 612, 614, 712 P.2d 459, 461 (Ct. App. 1985), the court held that, in the absence of an express restriction by contract or statute, a tenant generally has the unrestricted right to assign or sublet.

The passage above draws the reader's attention first to the authority, and only then to the proposition for which the authority is cited. Because the case citation has little independent significance in the example, you could improve this passage by moving the citation to a separate citation sentence, permitting you to reserve the main text for the ideas for which the authority is cited. If you do not wish to emphasize the identity of the authoring court, you can make the strongest substantive statement by presenting the legal proposition as an unqualified statement of truth that at least one court has incidentally discovered:

In the absence of an express restriction by contract or statute, a tenant generally has the unrestricted right to assign or sublet. *Tucson Med. Ctr. v. Zoslow*, 147 Ariz. 612, 614, 712 P.2d 459, 461 (Ct. App. 1985).

On the other hand, if the decisions of the authoring court are controlling on the court adjudicating the current dispute, you may want to identify the authoring court in the textual sentence, while continuing to subordinate the case name and the rest of the citation:

The Arizona Court of Appeals has held that, in the absence of an express restriction by contract or statute, a tenant generally has the unrestricted right to assign or sublet. *Tucson Med. Ctr. v. Zoslow*, 147 Ariz. 612, 614, 712 P.2d 459, 461 (Ct. App. 1985).

On rare occasions, you might appropriately retain a full citation to authority in a textual sentence if the citation itself has such great independent significance that it warrants such emphasis:

In *Brown v. Board of Education*, 347 U.S. 483 (1954), the Supreme Court unanimously held that state-sponsored racial segregation in public schools violates the equal protection guarantee of the Fourteenth Amendment.

In this example, the case name, the identity of the authoring court, and even the date of the decision all trigger recognition in most readers. Alternatively, some writers might refer to the instantly recognizable case name in the textual sentence, saving the remainder of the citation for a separate citation sentence:

In *Brown v. Board of Education*, the Supreme Court unanimously held that state-sponsored segregation in public schools violates the Equal Protection guarantee of the Fourteenth Amendment. 347 U.S. 483 (1954).

Because it separates the case name from its citation, however, this form is unconventional if it represents the initial citation to this authority in the memorandum or the brief. Therefore, it may not meet with the approval of every editor or supervising attorney.

2. In-Depth Case Analysis

You will have even greater reason to subordinate your citations when you present an in-depth case analysis. The following introduction to the analysis of a fictitious case not only inappropriately begins a textual sentence with a full citation, it also begins exploring the details of the case without first explaining generally why the case warrants in-depth analysis:

In *Bonnie v. DeLaney*, 158 Calz. 212, 645 P.2d 887 (1982), an agreement for the sale of a house provided that the buyer could cancel the agreement if the buyer "cannot qualify for a 30-year mortgage loan for 90% of the sales price" with any of several banks listed in the agreement. *Id.* at 213, 645 P.2d at 888. In enforcing the agreement against the seller, the court distinguished . . . .

The reader trudges through such a passage with little interest and at least moderate irritation, because he doesn't discover the point of the case until the end of the passage. A series of such paragraphs presenting a laundry list of cases can produce a rambling effect that causes the reader to lose track of the principles that the cases are meant to illustrate.

You can greatly improve the passage quoted above by introducing it with an overview of the point that the in-depth case analysis will illustrate:

On the other hand, even if a promise leaves open the possibility that the promisor will escape obligation, the promise is valid if the promisor does not have complete control over the events upon which the promisor's obligation is conditioned. *Bonnie v. DeLaney*, 158 Calz. 212, 645 P.2d 887 (1982). In *Bonnie,* an agreement for the sale of a house provided that the buyer could cancel the agreement if the buyer "cannot qualify for a 30-year mortgage loan for 90% of the sales price" with any of several banks listed in the agreement. *Id.* at 213, 645 P.2d at 888. In enforcing the agreement against the seller, the court distinguished . . . .

The preceding passage uses a topic sentence to summarize the point that the case analysis will illustrate. In more complex analyses, you might precede the case analysis with a paragraph that provides the appropriate overview in two or more sentences.

This method of presenting authority enables you to introduce the case citation in a separate citation sentence and to begin the in-depth case analysis with an unobtrusive, short-form reference to the case name:

. . . events upon which the promisor's obligation is conditioned. *Bonnie v. DeLaney*, 158 Calz. 212, 645 P.2d 887 (1982). In *Bonnie*, an agreement for the sale of a house provided . . . .

Moreover, if you intend to analyze several cases on the same issue, you can use the topic sentence or overview paragraph to help you to express your synthesis of the case law. As first discussed in Section II.B.7 of Chapter 7, which you may wish to review now, synthesis of authority is a critical component of legal method, warranting further exploration of writing techniques that effectively display synthesis.

B. Synthesis of Case Law

Many legal rules are the products of synthesis of two or more legal authorities. In an office memorandum or a brief, you should present such legal rules with clear guides to your synthesis rather than with isolated and unconnected analyses of the individual authorities.

1. Lack of Synthesis Burdens the Reader

For example, suppose that a section of an office memorandum analyzes the issue of whether a federal civil rights act addresses employment discrimination against a person because he is French-Canadian. The following sample passage presents a "laundry list" of case briefs. It is ineffective because it provides insufficient guidance to the author's synthesis, or perhaps because it betrays the author's failure to synthesize:

I. Racial Classifications Under Section 1981

General statutory rules

Section 1981 of title 42 of the United States Code provides in part as follows:

All persons within the jurisdiction of the United States shall have the same right in every State and Territory to make and enforce contracts . . . as is enjoyed by white citizens . . . .

In *Runyon v. McCrary*, 427 U.S. 160 (1976), African-American applicants to private, commercially operated, nonsectarian schools sued the schools through their parents. They alleged that the schools refused to admit them because of their race in violation of section 1981. A divided Supreme Court ruled that the school's discriminatory admissions policy violated the statute. It held that the statute applied to private contracts and that application of the statute to the school's admissions policy did not infringe upon the constitutional interests of the students or their parents in association, privacy, and parental control.

In-depth analysis without topic sentence to express an overview

In *McDonald v. Santa Fe Trail Transp. Co.*, 427 U.S. 273 (1976), white employees sued their employer and their union under section 1981 and Title VII of the Civil Rights Act of 1964. They alleged that their discharge for misappropriation of property was racially motivated because an African-American employee similarly charged was not dismissed. The Supreme Court acknowledged that the "immediate impetus" for the 1866 predecessor to section 1981 was "the necessity for further relief of the constitutionally emancipated former Negro slaves." *Id.* at 289. Nonetheless, on the strength of legislative history indicating that the bill would protect all races, the Supreme Court held that section 1981 imposes liability for discrimination aimed at any race, including whites. *Id.* at 289-96.

In-depth analysis without topic sentence to express overview or synthesis

In *St. Francis College v. Al-Khazraji*, 481 U.S. 604 (1987), a college professor of Arab ancestry sued his employer under section 1981 and other civil rights statutes. He alleged that the denial of his application for tenure was racially motivated because similarly situated Caucasians fared better in the tenure process. The trial court dismissed the section 1981 claim on the ground that it failed to state a claim of race discrimination because Arabs were not a race distinct from Caucasians. *See id.* at 606. The court of appeals reversed and remanded for further proceedings, and the Supreme Court affirmed the decision of the court of appeals.

In-depth analysis without topic sentence to express overview or synthesis

The Supreme Court held that scientific knowledge and cultural attitudes at the time of enactment of the 1866 and 1870 predecessors to section 1981 shaped the racial classifications addressed by

the statute. Legislative history and popular dictionary and encyclopedic sources of the era reflect the
view that groups with relatively narrowly defined
ancestral roots and ethnic characteristics, such as
"Germans," "Greeks," "Jews," and "Gypsies,"
represent distinct races. The Supreme Court concluded that Arabs would be viewed as a separate
race under those standards and that section 1981
therefore addresses discrimination based on Arab
ancestry. *See id*. at 610-13.

In our case . . . .

2. The Benefits of Expressing Your Synthesis

The preceding passage does not give adequate notice of the points or
issues that each case brief is intended to illustrate, nor does it explain how
the authorities relate to one another. The following passage provides a better guide to the author's synthesis. It uses a transition sentence or paragraph
to provide a preview of the point illustrated by each case brief and to explain
how each authority relates to previously analyzed authorities. The passage
below also flows more coherently because it limits its in-depth analysis to
the announced topic of the section and refers only tersely to other potential
problems in the scope of the statute.

I.   Racial Classifications Under Section 1981

**Introduction to
statutory language**

Federal civil rights legislation prohibits certain kinds of racial discrimination in contractual
relations:

Statutory language

> All persons within the jurisdiction of the
> United States shall have the same right
> in every State and Territory to make and
> enforce contracts . . . as is enjoyed by white
> citizens . . . .

42 U.S.C. § 1981 (2006).

**General guides from
case law interpreting
the statute**

As suggested by the statutory reference to
rights "enjoyed by white citizens," the "immediate
impetus" for the 1866 predecessor to section 1981
was "the necessity for further relief of the constitutionally emancipated former Negro slaves."
McDonald v. Santa Fe Trail Transp. Co., 427 U.S.
273, 289 (1976). Consequently, section 1981
applies most clearly to race discrimination against
African-Americans. *See, e.g., Runyon v. McCrary*,
427 U.S. 160 (1976).

Section 1981's prohibition of discrimination, however, extends beyond discrimination against African-Americans and applies more generally to discrimination based on any racial classification. *See McDonald*, 427 U.S. 273. In *McDonald*, white employees sued their employer and their union under section 1981 and Title VII of the Civil Rights Act of 1964. They alleged that their discharge for misappropriation of property was racially motivated because an African-American employee similarly charged was not dismissed. On the strength of legislative history indicating that the bill would protect all races, the Supreme Court held that section 1981 imposes liability for discrimination against members of any race, including whites. *See id*. at 289-96.

> Topic sentence introducing in-depth analysis of *McDonald*

McDonald did not attempt to identify all the racial classifications protected under section 1981. More recently, the Supreme Court held that the applicable classifications are not those recognized by many contemporary scientific theories, but are the narrower and more numerous classifications generally recognized when Congress enacted the predecessors to section 1981. *See St. Francis College v. Al-Khazraji*, 481 U.S. 604 (1987).

> Transition ¶ presenting (1) relationship of *McDonald* to *St. Francis* and (2) overview of *St. Francis*

In *St. Francis*, the Supreme Court reinstated the civil rights claims of a college professor of Arab ancestry who alleged that he was discriminatorily denied tenure because similarly situated Caucasians fared better in the tenure process. The Supreme Court held that scientific knowledge and cultural attitudes at the time of enactment of the 1866 and 1870 predecessors to section 1981 shaped the racial classifications addressed by the statute. Legislative history and popular dictionary and encyclopedic sources of the era reflect the view that groups with relatively narrowly defined ancestral roots and ethnic characteristics, such as "Germans," "Greeks," "Jews," and "Gypsies," represent distinct races. The Supreme Court concluded that Arabs would be viewed as a separate race under those standards and that section 1981 therefore addresses discrimination based on Arab ancestry. *See id*. at 610-13.

> In-depth analysis of *St. Francis*

In our case . . . .

3. Parallels to Effective Study Techniques

The two passages quoted above illustrate parallels between effective law school study techniques and techniques for preparing documents in a law office. The first passage resembles one of a series of only loosely connected case briefs, such as those you might prepare for class discussion. The case briefs contain useful information, but you can more effectively apply that information to an examination problem if you synthesize the cases and then reorganize them in a course outline. Moreover, as explained in Section III of Chapter 8, the outline will help you most if it emphasizes controlling principles and relegates the discussion of cases to the role of illustrating those principles.

In a law office, you will use a similar analytic process in presenting case law in a memorandum or brief. As illustrated in the second passage above, topic sentences or paragraphs introducing each case discussion emphasize principles and often act as transitions that convey case syntheses. The detailed discussion of each case simply illustrates a principle or qualification to a principle that you have already identified in a topic sentence. You should construct such a topic sentence or paragraph to introduce each in-depth case analysis. Your reader can then make her way through the series of individual case briefs without losing sight of the broader outlines of the analysis.

4. Consolidated Statement of Synthesis

In some analyses, you can state an overview of the complete synthesis in a single introductory sentence or paragraph rather than set it forth incrementally in the topic sentences of several paragraphs. For example, in a variation of a previous discussion of fictitious case law, the second paragraph of the following passage expresses the author's synthesis of two cases, both of which are immediately cited as support for the synthesis statement, followed by separate paragraphs analyzing each case in depth:

General rules

> An enforceable contract requires a bargained-for exchange in which a promisor exchanges his own promise for a return promise or performance. *Smith v. Newman*, 161 Calz. 443, 447, 667 P.2d 81, 84 (1984). The requirement of an exchange is not satisfied if one party gives only an illusory promise, which does not commit the promisor to any future performance. *Atco Corp. v. Johnson*, 155 Calz. 1211, 627 P.2d 781 (1980).

Synthesis derived from two cases

> Even a conditional promise, however, is valid if the promisor's duty to perform is not dependent solely on the promisor's desire to perform but instead can be triggered by external events over which the promisor does not have complete control. *Compare Bonnie v. DeLaney*, 158 Calz. 212,

213-15, 645 P.2d 887, 888-90 (1982) (buyer's obligation to purchase a house was not illusory because it was based on his ability to obtain a specified loan), *with Atco Corp.*, 155 Calz. at 1212-14, 627 P.2d at 782-84 (creditor's promise to delay demanding payment was illusory because it allowed him to make a demand as soon as he wanted the money).

Citation to the two cases, with parenthetic explanations

In *Bonnie,* an agreement for the sale of a house provided that the buyer could cancel the agreement if the buyer "cannot qualify for a 30-year mortgage loan for 90 percent of the sales price" with any of several banks . . . .

In-depth analysis of 1st case

In *Atco,* the manager of an automobile repair shop purportedly promised to delay asserting a claim against the owner of an automobile for $900 in repairs. Specifically, he promised to forbear from asserting the claim "until I want the money." In exchange, a friend of the owner promised to act as guarantor . . . . In contrast to the promise in *Bonnie,* . . . .

In-depth analysis of 2d case

III. Quotations

A. Using Quotations Selectively

If the interpretation or application of a statute or contract is disputed by the parties, the starting point of your analysis is the relevant language of the statute or contract. Accordingly, when presenting such an analysis in a memorandum or brief, you should quote the contractual provisions that must be interpreted or applied.

You should generally quote more sparingly from case law. Assigning attorneys and judges are primarily interested in your original synthesis of case law and your analysis of the facts within the legal framework. They are not impressed by your demonstrated ability to cut and paste lengthy passages written by others. If all or part of a judicial opinion is particularly significant to the analysis in an office memorandum, you need not clutter up your memorandum with lengthy quotation. You can simply attach a copy of the authority in hard copy or as an e-mail attachment.

Occasionally, a passage from case law is so clear, concise, powerful, and narrowly tailored to your dispute that paraphrasing cannot improve it. By quoting such a passage, you obviously will enhance the memorandum or brief. Indeed, this book has presented a few such paragraph-long quotations, often with extraneous words or phrases omitted, but only because they advance the discussion concisely and eloquently, as does this one:

[W]hen you do decide to quote authority in a brief or an office memorandum, you need not quote at epic length. Indeed, a sure way to induce
skimming is the back-to-back employment of two quotes of more than ten
lines each. . . . Select a short helpful quote, and show its application to your
case. Give enough to make your point but not so much as to sink your brief
from excess weight.[72]

More often, a long passage from case law will seem out of context if
quoted, perhaps because it clashes with your writing style or because its
relevant portions are unavoidably intermingled with distracting references
to points not relevant to your dispute. In such a case, you can help focus the
attention of your reader on important ideas, rather than on sudden shifts in
style or context, by stating the rule or analysis of a case in your own words.

This general admonition against excessive quotation probably applies
most strongly to appellate briefs. Although their workload is heavy, most
appellate judges or their law clerks have sufficient time to study the important
cases cited in appellate briefs. Moreover, appellate courts have the power to
overrule at least some of the precedent likely to be cited in the briefs. Consequently, appellate judges in particular tend to look for original analysis,
including policy analysis, rather than extensive quotation from authorities
that a judge or a law clerk can easily secure from the library.

In contrast, busy trial judges preparing for hearings on motions may not
have time to study carefully all the important cases cited in the briefs.[73] Additionally, they must follow, and cannot overrule, applicable appellate decisions within their jurisdiction. For both these reasons, some trial judges may
appreciate passages in briefs that quote arguably controlling holdings from
appellate case law. Even so, you should remember the recently quoted advice
to "select a short helpful quote" rather than quoting at "epic length."

Of course, when you do quote a source, you should not be so concerned
with brevity that you alter the meaning of the quoted source. Neither a
judge nor a supervising attorney will appreciate a brief or office memorandum that misleads the reader by concealing important information through
material omissions in quotations, or through quotations taken completely
out of context.[74]

B. Presenting and Introducing Quotations

1. Presenting Block Quotations

If you quote a substantial portion of any authority, you should set apart
the quoted passage in a single-spaced, indented block, without quotation

---

72. Noel Fidel, *Some Do's and Don'ts of Motion Writing*, ARIZ. B.J., Aug. 1983, at 9.

73. *Id.* at 10-11.

74. *See, e.g.*, Precision Specialty Metals, Inc. v. United States, 315 F.3d 1346 (Fed. Cir. 2003) (affirming reprimand against lawyer who gave a misleading impression of the law partly by replacing relevant information within a quotation with an ellipsis and by failing to cite and discuss an adverse case appearing in the quoted source).

marks other than those that appear within the original quoted text. This blocking technique helps the reader to distinguish the lengthy quotation from the original text. The BLUEBOOK citation manual calls for block quotation only if the quoted passage exceeds 49 words.[75] The ALWD CITATION MANUAL instructs you to block any quotation that exceeds 49 words, as well as any quotations of poetry or verse, regardless of length.[76] In the opinion of this author, however, the visual benefits of blocking are evident in shorter passages, and you should exercise discretion about whether to block any quotation that takes up all or part of at least three lines of text.

2. Using Substantive Introductions While Subordinating Citations

The principles stated in Section II above about subordinating citations and introducing case analyses with topic sentences apply equally to substantial quotations, especially block quotations. Unless the citation to a block quotation has independent significance, you should relegate it to the end of the quote by placing it at the left-hand margin on a new line below the block. You should also introduce the quoted passage with a thesis statement, a substantive overview that summarizes the point that you intend the passage to convey to the reader.

To start with a bad example, the following passage inappropriately introduces a block quotation of a statutory provision with a citation that has little independent significance. Moreover, the absence of a substantive introduction induced the writer to convey the point of the quote with distracting underlining:

Title 42 U.S.C. § 2000e-2(a)(1) provides:

It shall be an <u>unlawful</u> employment practice for an employer—
    (1) to fail or refuse to hire or to discharge any individual, or otherwise to discriminate against any individual with respect to his compensation, terms, conditions, or privileges of employment, because of such individual's race, color, religion, sex or national origin.

Using a substantive introduction, you could revise this passage to subordinate the citation, provide the reader with helpful orientation, and minimize the need for underlining as a means of emphasis:

Federal law prohibits sex discrimination in employment:

It shall be an unlawful employment practice for an employer—
    (1) to fail or refuse to hire or to discharge any individual, or otherwise to discriminate against any individual with respect to his compensation, terms,

75. BLUEBOOK R. 5.1(a), at 76.
76. ALWD CITATION MANUAL R. 38.3, at 336.

conditions, or privileges of employment, because of such individual's race, color, religion, sex or national origin.

42 U.S.C. § 2000e-2(a)(1) (2006) (Title VII § 703(a)(1)).

Alternatively, you may want to acknowledge that the title and name of the original legislative act in this example is familiar to most lawyers and therefore has independent significance. You can refer to the act in the introduction, while continuing to subordinate the code citation:

Title VII of the Civil Rights Act of 1964 makes it unlawful for an employer to engage in sex discrimination:

> It shall be an unlawful employment practice for an employer—
>   (1) to fail or refuse . . . .

42 U.S.C. § 2000e-2(a)(1) (2006) (Title VII § 703(a)(1)).

Finally, if you want to refer repeatedly to this section of the statute throughout your brief or memorandum, you can emphasize the section number within Title VII, which is more familiar to most lawyers than the code number, by referring to it in the introduction:

Section 703(a) of Title VII of the Civil Rights Act of 1964 makes it unlawful for an employer to engage in sex discrimination:

> It shall be an unlawful employment practice for an employer—
>   (1) to fail or refuse . . . .

42 U.S.C. § 2000e-2(a)(1) (2006). Section 703(a) identifies two principal elements of unlawful discrimination. . . .

In rare cases, you may find that an exceptionally long or complex passage should be quoted and cannot be cut to size with judicial editing. Particularly if the quotation addresses multiple themes, you can lead the reader through such material by breaking the quotation into parts and preceding each part with a substantive introduction:

Introduction to U.C.C. § 2-207(1)	Under the Uniform Commercial Code, a response to an offer may be an acceptance even though it varies the terms of the offer:
Text of U.C.C. § 2-207(1)	A definite and seasonable expression of acceptance or a written confirmation which is sent within a reasonable time operates as an acceptance even though it states terms additional to or different from those offered or agreed upon . . . .

U.C.C. § 2-207(1) (2011). However, a proviso to the same statute provides that the offeree may avoid acceptance and state a counteroffer if "acceptance is expressly made conditional on assent to the additional or different terms." *Id.*

> Proviso to
> U.C.C. § 2-207(1)

If the original offeree's response is an acceptance, the statute provides that some of the new terms in the acceptance may in some circumstances be added to the contract without the express assent of the original offeror:

> Introduction to
> U.C.C. § 2-207(2)

> The additional terms are to be construed as proposals for addition to the contract. Between merchants such terms become part of the contract unless:
>   (a) the offer expressly limits acceptance to the terms of the offer;
>   (b) they materially alter it; or
>   (c) notification of objection to them has already been given or is given within a reasonable time after notice of them is received.

> Text of
> U.C.C. § 2-207(2)

U.C.C. § 2-207(2) (2011).

3. Special Techniques for Advocacy

You can use a substantive introduction to a block quotation as effective preliminary advocacy in a brief. Your introduction will emphasize the point of the quote by presenting it in summary form.

Moreover, quotations from contracts, statutes, or case law often are reasonably subject to varying interpretations, and a substantive introduction can encourage the reader to interpret the quoted passage in a favorable manner. For example, the following passage from an employment contract lists several grounds for discharging an employee, but it doesn't expressly state whether the list is exclusive:

> XI. Ajax Co. reserves the right to discharge any employee who
>
>   1. fails to perform satisfactorily,
>   2. commits gross insubordination, or
>   3. commits a criminal act on the work site.

Assuming that an employee hired under this contract is employed for an indefinite term, the traditional common law at-will rule would permit the employer to discharge the employee for any reason if the contractual list of grounds for discharge is not intended to be exclusive. On the other hand, if the contract provision quoted above is interpreted to include an implicit promise by the employer to refrain from discharging an employee except for the listed reasons, then the contract would override the otherwise applicable common law rule.

When quoting this passage in the argument section of the brief for either the employer or a discharged employee, you will achieve the least impact with a stock introduction such as

---

Section XI of the Employment Contract provides, in relevant part, as follows:

Instead, as counsel for the discharged employee, you should use an argumentative introductory sentence to characterize the provision as a restriction on the employer's freedom to terminate the employment contract:

The Employment Contract expressly identifies only three grounds for discharge, all relating to poor performance or serious misconduct:

XI. Ajax Co. reserves the right to discharge any employee who

1. fails to perform satisfactorily,
2. commits gross insubordination, or
3. commits a criminal act on the work site.

Employment Contract § XI.

The parties intended this list to be the exclusive, because . . . .

Conversely, as counsel for the employer, you can use an argumentative introduction to characterize the provision as an affirmation of the employer's common law freedom to terminate:

No provision of the contract expressly limits Ajax Co.'s common law right to discharge any employee at Ajax's will. Indeed, the only provision addressing termination selects three particularly strong grounds for illustration and emphasis:

XI. Ajax Co. reserves the right to discharge any employee who

1. fails to perform satisfactorily,
2. commits gross insubordination, or
3. commits a criminal act on the work site.

Employment Contract § XI.

Nothing in the contract suggests that these listed grounds are exclusive. Instead, ...

You can always begin arguing for a favorable interpretation after neutrally presenting the quoted passage. However, the reader is more likely to adopt your proposed interpretation if a substantive introduction prepares him for the interpretation before he reads the quoted passage.

Exercise 14-2

Rewrite the following passage in an office memorandum to subordinate citations and to introduce the block quotation with a brief substantive overview. You may assume that the case names are not sufficiently independently significant to warrant emphasis in textual sentences.

DISCUSSION

A. Liability for Discrimination Under Section 1981

1. First Amendment Defense

Lilly Prep School has asserted in a letter to our client that it has a First Amendment right to teach and practice racial segregation in its classrooms. We expect it to raise this as a defense in any lawsuit that we file.

In *NAACP v. Alabama*, 357 U.S. 449 (1958), the Supreme Court recognized a First Amendment right "to engage in association for the advancement of beliefs and ideas." *Id.* at 460. In *Runyon v. McCrary*, 427 U.S. 160 (1976), however, the Court stated:

> From this principle it may be assumed that parents have a First Amendment right to send their children to educational institutions that promote the belief that racial segregation is desirable, and that the children have an equal right to attend such institutions. But it does not follow that the *practice* of excluding racial minorities from such institutions is also protected by the same principle.

Id. at 176.

IV. Summary

To present authority effectively,

1. subordinate citations, emphasize ideas, and express your syntheses in topic sentences or paragraphs;
2. use quotations selectively, subordinate the citations to the quotations, and introduce quotations with substantive overviews; and
3. use effective citation form and citation signals.

Part VI

Introduction to

Advocacy

Written advocacy is a special branch of legal method and writing that combines creative analysis, persuasive writing, and attention to local rules, special formats, and ethical considerations. Part VI provides an overview of advocacy at all stages of litigation, ending with an exercise that explores a motion to dismiss a complaint.

Parts VII and VIII examine written advocacy in the context of four other kinds of pleadings or briefs: (1) complaints and answers, (2) briefs on a motion for summary judgment, (3) briefs on a motion to exclude evidence, and (4) appellate briefs. Each of those chapters includes at least one full sample pleading or brief. By studying this chapter and some or all of the documents in the following chapters, you will develop a general grasp of the methods and purposes of brief writing, enabling you to prepare a brief for any stage of litigation.

Chapter 15

Advocacy: Overview and Ethics

I. Overview—Procedure and General Format

A. Procedure

In a typical dispute, you will advocate your client's case in various written documents through several stages of litigation. If correspondence between the parties fails to resolve the dispute in its early stages, the parties may commence formal litigation by filing pleadings, typically a complaint and an answer. Before trial, you might file or respond to "motions" that request the judge to take certain actions, such as to make advance rulings on the admissibility of evidence or to rule on the merits of some or all of the claims and defenses without a trial. During a trial with a jury, you may submit or respond to briefs that request the judge to instruct the jury on the law in a certain way or even to decide the case "as a matter of law" without the jury. At the outset of a trial without a jury, you may submit a trial brief that invites a judge or arbitrator to find certain facts and to apply your interpretation of the law to the facts to reach certain conclusions. Finally, if either party appeals the judgment of the trial court, you will draft one or more briefs to an appellate court, inviting the appellate court to either affirm or reverse the judgment of the court immediately below it.

Throughout these proceedings, the pleadings, motions, and appeals will follow similar briefing schedules:

1. The party seeking relief or seeking reversal of a lower court's judgment files a complaint, petition, or opening brief.

2. The opposing party responds with an answer, response, or answering brief.

3. Finally, the party who filed the petition or opening brief generally has the opportunity to file a reply brief that addresses points raised in the opposing party's answering brief or response. Under federal pleading rules, the drafter of a complaint will file an answer to any counterclaim contained in the defendant's answer;[1] otherwise, the drafter of a complaint or counterclaim will reply to the defendant's answer if the court orders a reply.[2]

B. Basic Formats for Briefs

The format of a complaint or answer, discussed in Chapter 18, differs significantly from that of a brief. Various pretrial, trial, and appellate briefs, however, have much in common. Each will include some statement of the background of the case, followed by an argument and a conclusion.

In some ways, an appellate brief may be more detailed and formal than a pretrial brief. By the time a case reaches an appellate court, the litigants have developed some record of the facts or factual allegations, and they have advanced the dispute through significant procedural steps. Accordingly, an appellate brief's description of the background of a case typically includes a formal statement of facts and a summary of the procedural history. On the other hand, when the parties litigate a pretrial motion, the facts may be sketchy and the procedural history brief. Consequently, many pretrial briefs combine the procedural history and statement of relevant facts in an "Introduction," "Background," or "Statement of Facts." As explored in Chapter 19, briefs on a motion for summary judgment are exceptional in their unusually formal pretrial presentation of facts.

An appellate brief may be more formal than a pretrial brief in other ways as well. For example, rules of procedure and local court rules typically require an appellate brief to include a table of contents, table of authorities, and formal statement of issues. These are customarily omitted from all but the most complex pretrial briefs.

---

1. FED. R. CIV. P. 7(a)(3).

2. FED. R. CIV. P. 7(a)(7); *see also id.* at Note on 2007 Amendment (referring both to a reply to an answer and to a reply to an answer to a counterclaim).

These differences, however, are relatively superficial in light of the universality of the heart of any brief: the argument. Unlike an office memorandum, your brief will not explore the strengths and weaknesses of both sides of the dispute. Instead, you will use the brief to advocate the legal and factual analysis that best supports the claims or defenses of your client.

This perspective of a brief is reflected not only in the subtler facets of writing style but also in fundamental elements of format such as section headings. Depending on the format adopted by a writer or a law firm, a section heading in the Discussion section of an office memorandum may state a conclusion, may restate the issue, or may use a neutral phrase or sentence that generally describes a topic of discussion and helps your reader recall an issue stated more formally at the beginning of the memorandum. In contrast, you will uniformly use "point headings" in the argument section of a brief to state the conclusions that you want the judge to adopt. In each point heading, you will assert a point in a complete sentence as a prelude to your full deductive argument on that issue.

Chapters 16 and 17 address these and other techniques of written and oral advocacy in greater depth. First, however, Section II introduces you to a few of the many ethical obligations that you assume as an advocate.

II. Good Faith, Reasonableness, and Full Disclosure

A. Assertion of Claims and Defenses

As an attorney, you owe a duty to your client to advocate her case vigorously.[3] In carrying out this duty, you will often argue for creative extension of existing law or for replacement of existing law with new rules.[4] Fundamental principles of professional responsibility, however, impose limits on your advocacy.[5] For example, Federal Rule of Civil Procedure 11 requires attorneys to certify that their written advocacy is supported by a reasonable investigation of the law and facts and is not advanced for an improper purpose:

(b) REPRESENTATIONS TO THE COURT. By presenting to the court a pleading, written motion, or other paper—whether by signing, filing, submitting, or later advocating it—an attorney or unrepresented party certifies that to the best of the person's knowledge, information, and belief, formed after an inquiry reasonable under the circumstances:

---

3. *See, e.g.*, MODEL CODE OF PROF'L RESPONSIBILITY EC 7-4 (2004); *id.* at Canon 7.

4. *See, e.g.*, Hunter v. Earthgrains Co. Bakery, 281 F.3d 144, 156 (4th Cir. 2002) (attorney was "plainly entitled (and probably obligated)" to argue that circuit precedent incorrectly applied Supreme Court precedent and should be overturned).

5. *See, e.g.*, MODEL RULES OF PROF'L CONDUCT R. (hereafter, "MODEL RULE") 3.3(a)(1) (2012) (proscribing knowingly false statements of material fact or law).

(1) it is not being presented for any improper purpose, such as to harass, cause unnecessary delay, or needlessly increase the cost of litigation;

(2) the claims, defenses, and other legal contentions are warranted by existing law or by a nonfrivolous argument for extending, modifying, or reversing existing law or for establishing new law;

(3) the factual contentions have evidentiary support or, if specifically so identified, will likely have evidentiary support after a reasonable opportunity for further investigation or discovery; and

(4) the denials of factual contentions are warranted on the evidence or, if specifically so identified, are reasonably based on belief or a lack of information.[6]

Rule 11 authorizes a judge to impose "an appropriate sanction on any attorney, law firm, or party that violated the rule or is responsible for the violation."[7] The sanction may include "nonmonetary directives; an order to pay a penalty into court; or, if imposed on motion and warranted for effective deterrence, an order directing payment to the movant of part or all of the reasonable attorneys' fees and other expenses directly resulting from the violation."[8]

Rule 11 also contains a "safe harbor" provision that permits a person responsible for a Rule 11 violation to escape sanctions by withdrawing the offending claim or defense within 21 days after receiving service of the motion for sanctions, or within another time set by the court.[9] As explored more fully in the following sections, however, perhaps the best guide to responsible advocacy is not the risk of sanctions but the desire shared by most advocates to maintain their reputations for candor and quality work.

B. Disclosure of Adverse Authority

As an advocate, you have no duty to argue your opponent's case or even to present a balanced analysis such as would be appropriate in an office memorandum. Nonetheless, every advocate is also an officer of the court[10] and owes a general duty of candor and fairness to the court and to other lawyers.[11] Within this framework, the American Bar Association (ABA) Model Rules of Professional Conduct specifically require every advocate to disclose significant authority adverse to the advocate's arguments:

A lawyer shall not knowingly:

. . . .

(2) fail to disclose to the tribunal legal authority in the controlling jurisdiction known to the lawyer to be directly adverse to the position of the client and not disclosed by opposing counsel.[12]

---

6. FED. R. CIV. P. 11(b).

7. FED. R. CIV. P. 11(c)(1).

8. FED. R. CIV. P. 11(c)(4).

9. FED. R. CIV. P. 11(c)(2).

10. *E.g.*, Ex parte Garland, 71 U.S. (4 Wall.) 333, 378 (1867), *cited in* ABA Formal Opinion 146 (1935).

11. MODEL RULE 3.3 (2012) (candor to court); ABA Formal Opinion 146 (1935).

12. MODEL RULE 3.3(a)(2) (2012).

As stated by Judge Posner, for example, "When there is apparently dispositive precedent, an appellant may urge its overruling or distinguishing or reserve a challenge to it for a petition for certiorari but may not simply ignore it."[13]

The scope of the duty stated in the Model Rules depends in large part on the interpretation of the phrase "directly adverse." However, the most sensible approach to disclosure is one that maintains your credibility as an advocate. If adverse authority within the forum jurisdiction is sufficiently analogous that the court would consider it in deciding a case, the judge or the judge's law clerk likely will discover the authority sometime before the end of the proceedings, even if it has escaped the notice of the opposing counsel. You can minimize the impact of such adverse authority by acknowledging it early in the proceedings and distinguishing or discrediting it.[14]

The reference to "controlling jurisdiction" in the disclosure rule appears to flatly exclude authority from outside the forum jurisdiction, even if it is squarely on point. In some circumstances, however, your desire to maintain credibility may be a better guide than a specific ethical rule. For example, if the question before the court is so novel that no authority within the forum jurisdiction addresses it, and if adverse authority from another jurisdiction would be particularly persuasive, then the court might expect you to disclose the nonbinding adverse authority and to squarely address it.

If an adverse authority does not meet these standards, you need not address it unless the other party relies on it or the court raises a question that encompasses it. In an opening brief, for example, you should not waste time by distinguishing marginally analogous adverse case law or by criticizing poorly reasoned persuasive authority on which the opposing counsel is unlikely to rely. Instead, you should concentrate on affirmatively presenting your own arguments and supporting authority, and you should attack only the most obvious adverse authority. Then, you can wait to see which authority the opposing counsel advances in the answering brief, and you can attack that adverse authority in your reply brief. Of course, if the court asks you about adverse precedent, you "should make such frank disclosure as the question seems to warrant,"[15] regardless of the scope of ethical duties or strategic considerations that might otherwise apply.

C. Misleading Legal Argument

The ABA Model Rules of Professional Conduct prohibit a lawyer from knowingly making "a false statement of fact or law to a tribunal."[16] However, a legal analysis will not amount to a false statement about the law unless it clearly falls outside the range of plausible interpretations of the legal authorities.

---

13. Gonzalez-Servin v. Ford Motor Co., 662 F.3d 931, 934 (7th Cir. 2011).
14. *See* Charles W. Wolfram, MODERN LEGAL ETHICS § 12.8, at 682 (1986).
15. ABA Formal Opinion 280 (1949).
16. MODEL RULE 3.3(a)(1) (2012).

For example, defining the holding of a judicial opinion and determining its effect as precedent is an exercise that produces disagreement among able jurists. Thus, as an advocate, you often have room to take an aggressive stance in identifying facts that appear to have been material to a decision and in characterizing the holding and reasoning of the decision.

As with other ethical questions, practical considerations of effective advocacy may provide the best guide to responsible conduct. Published precedent on which you rely is readily accessible to the opposing counsel and to the court. Careless or fraudulent analyses that cross the line separating creative advocacy from misrepresentation almost certainly will be brought to the court's attention. Few things can damage your credibility and effectiveness more than a reputation for stretching legal authority beyond the limits of plausible interpretation.

III. Summary

In shifting from neutral analysis to advocacy, you must adopt a suitable format for your document and make the transition from an objective writing style to a persuasive one, as explored in the following chapters. Take care to satisfy ethical duties in asserting claims and defenses, in disclosing adverse authority, and in representing the content of legal authority.[17]

---

17. For much more on ethics in legal writing in various contexts, *see* Melissa H. Weresh, LEGAL WRITING: ETHICAL AND PROFESSIONAL CONSIDERATIONS (2006).

Chapter 16

Developing Your Legal Arguments

By performing some or all of the exercises throughout Parts I through IV of this book, you have steadily developed your skills in spotting and analyzing legal issues and developing legal arguments. You now should be ready to select, organize, and express your legal arguments in a brief.

Your statements of issues, facts, and procedural history will vary greatly in style and content depending on the stage of the litigation at which you draft a legal document. Consequently, this book separately examines those elements of a pleading or a brief in Parts VII and VIII. Many techniques of advocacy, however, apply broadly to all kinds of briefs and are appropriately introduced in Part VI, Chapters 16 and 17. Specifically, this chapter examines methods of (1) organizing arguments, (2) introducing arguments, and (3) developing the elements of a deductive argument. Chapter 17 examines techniques of persuasive writing and oral argument.

I. Engaging the Reader with an Effective Theme

Before you begin writing, try to develop a theme for your brief, a thread that runs through the fabric of the brief from the Statement of Issues to the Conclusion. If possible, your theme should reflect some facet of the dispute that shows "that your client's position is not only legally correct but also equitably, ethically, and morally 'right.'"[1] Your best arguments are likely to be ones that not only are analytically sound but also that help you advance your underlying theme throughout your brief.

More specifically, experienced advocates often speak of developing a *theory* of the case, an analytic *framework* for the arguments, a *strategy* for trial or appeal, or a main *point, thrust, direction,* or *idea* that they want to convey to the judge. This process can help you decide which arguments to advance and which facts, case law, and policy arguments to emphasize in your brief so that a persuasive theme emerges.

In its simplest form, a theme may represent an appeal to common sense or justice that translates fairly directly into legal and factual arguments. For example, in litigation of a products liability suit, the injured plaintiff's brief might consistently advance a theme that highlights a dangerous defect in a product. In contrast, the defendant manufacturer's brief might consistently advance a theme that emphasizes the weakness of the causal link between the product's defect and the plaintiff's injuries. Although each brief may necessarily address matters that do not directly advance the theme, each authoring attorney should endeavor to bring the brief's theme to the fore in various parts of the brief, from the issue and fact statements to the argument.

Alternatively, the theme of a brief might encourage the court to embrace a particular judicial approach or philosophy that would pave the way for acceptance of one or more arguments. For example, various elements of the brief might emphasize that statutory language is unambiguous and should be interpreted according to the plain meaning of its text, rather than in a strained manner that relies heavily on legislative history or statutory purpose. Another brief might advance the theme that expansion of a common law doctrine would enmesh the court in hotly debated issues of social policy that would be best addressed by a democratically elected legislature.

A theme might also consist of a mood or perspective that forms a backdrop to the arguments. One attorney, for example, used the metaphor of a lawless frontier to convey a theme in a motion for summary judgment.[2] The motion challenged an arbitration decision interpreting a collective bargaining agreement, a decision to which a reviewing court would grant substantial deference.[3] Accordingly, the author of the brief bore the burden of showing that even a deferential standard of review imposed meaningful limits on the

---

1. Wiener, *supra* note 1, at 190.

2. The examples in this subsection were supplied in 2000 by Christopher Mason, an attorney with the Phoenix office of the law firm of Bryan Cave LLP.

3. *See* United Paperworkers Int'l Union v. Misco, Inc., 484 U.S. 29, 36-38 (1987).

arbitrator's interpretation and that the arbitrator had exceeded those limits as a matter of law.

Throughout the brief, the author argued those points with sound analysis of the law and facts and with traditional policy arguments. But the author of the brief wanted to create a mood as well, and the case itself invited the author to draw allusions to unrestrained frontier justice in the lawless Wild West: The workplace was a coal mine, and the arbitrator's last name was West. To introduce this theme, the first sentence of the argument suggested that failure to curb the arbitrator's discretion would render labor relations as chaotic and lawless as in some frontier outpost in the Wild West:

Despite the deference arbitrators are granted in reaching their decisions, one principle stands clear: the federal labor policy of promoting arbitration of industrial disputes does not create a lawless frontier where arbitrators are free to impose their own brand of "industrial justice."

The phrase "industrial justice" by itself is not pejorative, but the author linked it to an image of arbitrariness and lawlessness associated with untamed frontiers. The brief did not belabor this metaphor; however, it reminded readers of this image every time it named the arbitrator, West, and every time that it referred to West's "own brand of industrial justice." Finally, the author combined both these reminders with a new play on words at the beginning of the third subsection of the argument:

. . . Arbitrator West also shot holes through another provision of the [agreement], enforcing his own brand of "industrial justice."

In his response to the opposing party's cross-motion for summary judgment in the same case, this author argued that the arbitrator had refused to choose between two different plausible interpretations of the collective bargaining agreement and instead had compromised inappropriately by choosing an interpretation somewhere between the plausible meanings, arguably an interpretation that no language in the agreement supported. For this brief, the author developed a different theme, one that compared and then contrasted the arbitrator's interpretation with King Solomon's fabled solution:

Just as King Solomon threatened to do, the arbitrator in this dispute split the baby and imposed an irrational solution when a clear choice was required. Of course, once his threat produced the desired reaction, King Solomon ultimately revealed his wisdom by vacating his irrational decision. Here, the Court should likewise vacate Arbitrator West's irrational decision.

Using colorful metaphors or similes to create a theme is a matter of personal style and can never substitute for sound analysis of the law, facts, and social policies. You should never use a careless or distracting metaphor when a straightforward explanation would be clearer. A telling metaphor, however, may create an effective backdrop for the analysis, encouraging your reader to develop a gut reaction in favor of your client.

II. Organizing Your Arguments

As discussed in Section II of Chapter 12, you ordinarily should discuss or argue discrete issues in separate sections of your office memorandum or brief. Moreover, your section and subsection headings should show the proper relationships between your topics and subtopics. Beyond these considerations, you also must decide (1) which arguments to advance, (2) the order in which to present your arguments, and (3) the internal organization of each argument.

As you examine these matters in the following sections, reflect on the value of preparing an outline of the argument section of your brief before you begin writing it. The same techniques discussed in Chapter 8 for outlining course materials, and in Section V of Chapter 10 for outlining the discussion section of an office memorandum, will help you outline the argument section of your brief.

A. Selecting Arguments

1. Include Only Arguments That Earn a Place in Your Brief

As explained in Section III.B of Chapter 6, you should be more selective in choosing arguments to advance in a brief than in choosing issues to discuss in an essay examination or an office memorandum. For example, a federal appellate judge advises you to "[f]orce yourself to omit fringe issues and far-out theories; they will only dull the thrust of your appeal and obscure the potentially winning point."[4] A professor of trial practice and advocacy emphasizes that this

> means making choices. You throw out arguments that aren't plausible. You pick between the inconsistent legal theories. You cull out the weak points. You toss out whatever gets in the way. You discard what doesn't need to be said, even if it doesn't hurt.
>
> What's left is tight. Lean. Spare. It crackles with power because it's undiluted with stuff that doesn't matter.[5]

---

4. Hon. Jacques L. Wiener, Jr., *Ruminations from the Bench: Brief Writing and Oral Argument in the Fifth Circuit*, 70 TUL. L. REV. 187, 194 (1995).

5. James W. McElhaney, *The Art of Persuasive Legal Writing: Briefs Come Alive When Every Word Sings to the Reader*, A.B.A. J., Jan. 1996, at 76.

2. Consider Your Reader's Burdens

If you can envision two or more equally reasonable theories of your client's case, such as two competing legal frameworks within which to construct your arguments, you normally should choose the one that simplifies the judge's task. If your argument is so complicated that the judge has difficulty following it, the argument will not be persuasive; moreover, the judge will anticipate difficulty explaining a decision based on your arguments. Instead, opt for the approach that is easy to follow, easy to defend as consistent with precedent, and easy to explain in a ruling or opinion. If your brief contains straightforward passages that the judge could easily borrow and adapt for her written opinion, all the better.

B. Determining the Order of Your Arguments

Consider beginning your argument with a paragraph that states the theme of your brief or that provides an overview or roadmap to multiple arguments that follow. Such an overview paragraph would appear at the beginning of the Argument section of your brief, even before the subsection heading for the first of several arguments.

Of course, you cannot set forth an effective roadmap without first deciding on an effective ordering of your arguments. If your brief includes a formal statement of the issues, the organization of that statement should mirror the organization of your arguments. To determine the most appropriate order of arguments, you may need to balance neutral analytic considerations against strategic considerations. Moreover, in a responsive brief, you must decide whether to adopt or depart from the organizational structure of the opposing counsel's preceding brief.

1. Leading with Your Strongest Argument

As discussed in Section II.B of Chapter 12, neutral analytic considerations will lead you to argue threshold issues first and then to argue the issues that are dependent on the outcome of the threshold issues. Strategic considerations, however, may lead you to place your strongest argument first, even if that organization requires you to depart from a purely logical ordering of arguments.

The strategic considerations are based on the varying levels of emphasis associated with different parts of the argument section of the brief. Within a sentence, an idea generally will receive greater emphasis if placed at the beginning than if placed in the middle, but the place of greatest emphasis ordinarily is the end of the sentence. The same might be true of a short brief submitted to a judge who has plenty of time to study it. The first argument in such a brief would receive the emphasis associated with any initial encounter that makes a first impression. Ideas in the middle of the brief might capture slightly less attention, but they could help lay the foundation for a forceful climax. Presumably, the climactic argument would leave a lasting impression on the judge because it is the last argument that the judge would read.

Unfortunately, briefs are seldom brief, and judges often lack time to read them carefully. Indeed, a trial judge with a full pretrial motions calendar may have time only to skim through your motions brief before oral argument. Far from occupying the place of greatest emphasis, the end of your brief may not be read with the same care that the judge devoted to the beginning of the brief. Consequently, if one of your arguments is much stronger than the others, you can exercise discretion to present it before the others even though another issue is logically prior.

2. Special Considerations for Responsive Briefs

When you write a responsive brief, you might choose to adopt the preceding brief's organizational structure and methodically knock down each of your opponent's arguments. On the other hand, if you can more persuasively argue your case with a different organizational structure, you should not hesitate to depart from the structure adopted by your opponent.

For example, suppose that Maya Tortilla Co. has sued Bakeway Supermarkets, alleging that Bakeway (1) formed a contract with Maya; (2) breached its obligations, at least under Maya's interpretation of the contract; (3) and is liable to Maya for $40,000 in damages. Maya has filed a pretrial motion requesting the trial court to grant it summary judgment, which is judgment as a matter of law without a full trial on the facts. Maya has supported its motion with a preliminary showing of facts and with a brief that argues each of the issues in the order presented above. Bakeway can escape summary judgment on any issue by creating a genuine dispute of material fact on that issue, a dispute that must be resolved in a full trial.

As counsel for Bakeway, you could logically begin the argument of your answering brief with Maya's issue 1 because contract formation is a threshold issue: Bakeway did not assume any contractual obligations and consequent potential liability if it did not form a contract with Maya. Moreover, the opening brief begins with issue 1, and you could simplify your task by simply adopting the organizational structure of the opening brief.

However, suppose that you can most easily avoid summary judgment against Bakeway on issue 2. Although you cannot easily refute formation of a contract, you can point to admissible evidence of contract negotiations that supports Bakeway's interpretation of the contract. Moreover, under Bakeway's interpretation of the contract, Bakeway performed rather than breached the contract. Thus, you are confident that you can create a triable issue of fact about the meaning of the contract provision that states Bakeway's obligations. In those circumstances, you could reasonably begin your argument with issue 2, even though that organization departs from a purely logical ordering and from the structure of the opening brief. If you persuade the judge in your first argument that she should deny summary judgment on issue 2, she may then be more strongly disposed to order a trial on other issues as well.

Of course, a responsive brief should not fail to meet the arguments of the preceding brief "head-on, issue for issue, as they are posited."[6] Nonetheless, the responsive brief can do so on its own terms, within an organizational and analytic framework that places its arguments in the best light.

C. Internal Organization: Deductive Arguments

Once you decide the order of your arguments, you must adopt an effective scheme of internal organization for each argument. You should exercise the flexibility and creativity to adopt any method of internal organization and advocacy that will present your client's argument most effectively. Unless you have good reason to adopt some other approach, however, you should start with the elements and organization of a deductive argument.

"IRAC," which represents the form of deductive reasoning appropriate to an objective analysis in an office memorandum, is thoroughly discussed in Chapter 6. Moreover, Sections III and IV of Chapter 12 examine various techniques for organizing points within a deductive argument of a memorandum or a brief. Before writing your brief, you should review those passages.

The following section in this chapter emphasizes one difference between the deductive reasoning appropriate in the discussion section of an objective office memorandum and the deductive argument appropriate to a brief: An argument in a brief leads with the advocate's desired conclusion rather than with a neutral identification of an issue. Thus, each argument in a brief should include four major elements: Conclusion, Rule, Application of the legal rule to the facts, and Conclusion. The acronym "CRAC" may help you remember these elements.

Your writing professor may alternatively use a longer acronym, such as "CRuPAC, or "CREAC" to remind you to "prove" or "explain" your asserted rules to a skeptical reader.[7] This chapter, however, will adhere to the simpler acronym CRAC, while addressing the matter of explanation or proof of rules in its discussion of in-depth development of the law.

III. Introducing Legal Arguments

Judges read an enormous volume of material, and they appreciate concise writing that quickly gets to the point. In each of your arguments, you can satisfy this judicial demand with a well-crafted point heading, sometimes supplemented with an introductory paragraph.

---

6. Wiener, *supra* note 1, at 197.

7. Richard K. Neumann, Jr., & Kristen Konrad Robbins-Tiscione, LEGAL REASONING AND LEGAL WRITING § 12-2, at 145-47 (7th ed. 2013) (discussing rule proof and explanation and mentioning both "CREAC" and "CRuPAC"); *see* Linda H. Edwards, LEGAL WRITING: PROCESS, ANALYSIS, AND ORGANIZATION 91-96 (5th ed. 2010) (introducing and discussing "rule explanation").

A. Point Headings

For each issue in the argument section of your brief, you will discuss the law and apply the law to the facts to reach a conclusion. Before you begin your full argument, however, you will introduce it in an argumentative section heading, or "point heading." In each section or subsection that addresses a discrete issue, your point heading previews the conclusion.

Depending on the style adopted by the author, a section heading in an office memorandum may neutrally identify the issue addressed in that section. The section heading of an argument in a brief, however, always advocates a position by asserting a point and inviting the judge to reach a particular conclusion. It thus sets the tone for the full argument.

If a section or subsection of your argument develops a full deductive argument, its point heading should be tailored to the facts of your case, much like the statement of an issue and holding in a student case brief. Indeed, you may view your point headings as statements of the holdings in your case that you want the court to adopt:

II. ARGUMENT

    A. O'Gorman is not liable for medical costs associated with Wallace's heart failure, because O'Gorman's conduct did not proximately cause that injury.

    . . . .

    B. O'Gorman is not liable for punitive damages because he did not act with the requisite malicious intent or recklessness.

Because these point headings refer to the parties and incorporate important facts, they convey a clear, concrete point, even when read in isolation. The bold letters and the indentation help the point headings stand out on the page, providing conspicuous road signs for the reader.[8]

In some cases, as discussed in Section III.D.3 of Chapter 12, you may sometimes develop only one element of a deductive argument, such as an abstract legal principle, within a section or subsection. In such cases, of course, each point heading should be limited to stating a conclusion on the point developed in the section or subsection:

II. ARGUMENT

    A. O'Gorman is not liable for punitive damages because he lacked the requisite scienter.

        1. The jury may be permitted to award punitive damages only when the evidence is sufficient to permit a jury finding of malicious intent or recklessness.

---

8. For more tips on designing documents for legibility, *see* Ruth Anne Robbins, *Painting with Print: Incorporating Concepts of Typographic and Layout Design into the Text of Legal Writing Documents*, 2 J. ALWD 108 (Fall 2004).

. . . .

> **2. The evidence at trial will show that O'Gorman acted in a careful manner and certainly not with recklessness or malicious intent.**

The advantages of point headings are obvious in multiple-issue briefs, in which you must divide the argument into sections and subsections. Within the argument section of the brief, the point headings pop up periodically as road signs that signal an entrance to a new street or highway of your argument. Additionally, at least in an appellate brief, you will set forth your point headings together in the table of contents near the beginning of the brief, providing a quick summary of all your points and presenting a useful road map for the judge's journey through your brief.

Even in a single-issue brief, however, you should begin your argument with a point heading. It will simply stand alone in the argument section without any number or letter denoting division of the argument into sections:

III. ARGUMENT

> **The alleged agreement is unenforceable because it was not signed by the party against whom enforcement is sought.**
>
> The UCC statute of frauds requires . . . .

B. Introductory Paragraphs

Immediately after the point heading, but before discussing the legal authority, you might use an introductory sentence or paragraph to illuminate the issue and to expand on the point heading, or to place it within a larger context:

> **A. The alleged agreement is unenforceable under the UCC Statute of Frauds because it is not evidenced in a signed writing, as required for goods priced at more than $500.**
>
> Sun Printing Co. denies that it ever agreed to the contract alleged by Scott Paper Supply. This lawsuit presents precisely the kind of groundless contract claim that statutes of frauds are designed to bar by requiring a signed written contract as a requisite to enforcement.
>
> The Uniform Commercial Code statute of frauds generally bars . . . .

Such an introductory paragraph can be particularly helpful in a responsive brief. Rather than abstractly addressing the issues, an answering or reply brief should respond directly to each of the preceding brief's arguments.

Nonetheless, the response normally should begin by stating its counterargument affirmatively rather than by restating the opponent's argument.

The introductory paragraph following a point heading can set up your full response by adding more detail to the point heading, thus explaining generally why the opposing argument lacks merit, usually saving citation to authority for the more detailed discussion of law that follows:

A. Scott Paper Supply's timely confirmation of the agreement satisfied the UCC statute of frauds, because Sun Printing Co. failed to object to it.

The confirmation signed by Scott Paper Supply satisfied the statutory requirements of a signed writing. The UCC deems Sun Printing Co. to have implicitly adopted that confirmation, as though it had signed it, when Sun Printing Co. failed to object to the confirmation.

The UCC provides that . . . .

In rare cases, you may begin with a summary of your opponent's argument if that serves as an effective means of revealing the weaknesses in that argument and placing your own argument in a favorable light. When using this technique, you must immediately and convincingly refute your opponent's argument in the same breath with which you present his argument.

This technique works best, of course, if the opponent's argument sounds extreme even when presented on its own terms. If so, you can "set up" your opponent's argument for an easy response. Specifically, you should try to restate your opponent's argument fairly and accurately but in a way that fully reveals its weaknesses.

For example, suppose that your opponent's opening brief on appeal argues that the trial judge erred in denying injunctive relief, but it acknowledges the trial judge's broad discretion in such matters only in a vague passage buried in the middle of a lengthy section. In your answering brief, you will take greater pains to emphasize the discretionary nature of such relief. You might begin that emphasis not only in your point heading but also in an opening paragraph that summarizes your opponent's argument in a way that immediately reveals its weakness or the challenges it faces:

A. The trial court properly exercised its discretion to deny the extraordinary remedy of injunctive relief.

Redrock Co. bears the heavy burden of showing that Judge Norris abused her discretion by denying Redrock's demand for an injunction against further construction on the Big River Project. In fact, the record establishes a balance of equities that tip sharply against injunctive relief. Judge Norris's careful decision reflects a routine and proper exercise of discretion.

Injunctive relief is . . . .

IV. Developing the Deductive Argument

A. Arguing the Law

Chapter 6 and Chapters 12 through 15 have provided you with the legal method and the techniques of organization and writing with which you can construct an argument about the content of applicable law on a particular issue or subissue. An outline of these principles will illustrate the range of considerations that may enter into your strategic decisions when arguing the law within the argument portion of your brief.

1. Hierarchy of Authority

First, you must be sensitive to the hierarchy of authority. For example, suppose that (1) your client is not liable under state common law standards for actions that he took as an employer, but (2) a federal statute will impose liability if it applies to your client's business. If applicable, the statutory law will supersede the common law. Therefore, you must analyze the statute and determine whether you can argue either that it is unconstitutional or that it does not apply to your case. This statutory analysis might include arguments concerning the statutory language, the legislative history, the policy underlying the statute, or the limitations imposed by constitutional provisions.

For illustration, consider the first issue addressed in Sample 3: Office Memorandum 2 near the end of Chapter 11. It raises a question about the interpretation of a recently enacted, fictitious statute that created a form of liability beyond that recognized under the state's common law. Moreover, the statute is sufficiently new that no published judicial decision has yet interpreted the statutory term that is currently in dispute. One can imagine how the office memorandum's balanced analysis could be transformed into an argument on behalf of the defendant hospital:

> **A. Recently enacted New Maine legislation does not apply to a hospital's administration of general anesthesia.**
>
> A recently enacted statute of New Maine imposes strict liability on commercial enterprises for injuries caused by the use of "any toxic material." 12 N. Me. Rev. Stat. Ann. § 242 (Supp. 2013) (effective Jan. 1, 2014). Although the New Maine courts have not yet had an opportunity to interpret section 242 in a published opinion, the text and purpose of the statute establish that the anesthetic administered to Souza is not a "toxic material." This interpretation of the statute advances sound legal policies that support widespread availability of affordable medical care administered with due care.
>
> The common meaning of the word "toxic" is "poisonous." *E.g.*, THE RANDOM HOUSE DICTIONARY OF THE ENGLISH LANGUAGE 1500 (unabridged) (1970). "Toxic" thus applies most naturally to substances that are universally harmful to humans,

such as cyanide, DDT, or sulfuric acid. It strains the common meaning of "toxic" to apply it to an anesthetic that medical professionals use daily in surgeries that preserve the lives or improve the health of countless patients. A generally safe anesthetic is not transformed into a toxic substance simply because it may provoke an unusual reaction in a patient with a rare disorder; otherwise, wholesome cow's milk would be classified as poisonous or toxic simply because a small percentage of people may have a serious allergy to it.

Legislative history also supports a restrictive interpretation of the statutory term "any toxic material." The report of the New Maine Senate Committee . . . .

Finally, general state policy supports an interpretation that excludes medically prescribed substances from the reach of the statute. To encourage the availability of affordable medical services throughout the state, the legislature and judiciary of New Maine have recognized a policy of limiting the liability of physicians. For example, under the New Maine "Good Samaritan" statute . . . .

In this case, the prescribed anesthetic, ethane, is a frequently prescribed substance that produces beneficial results with only minor side effects in all but the most unusual cases. Souza's tragic reaction to ethane during her surgery is a product of her rare disorder, rather than any "toxic" characteristics of the ethane . . . .

2. Strength of Case Law as Precedent

Second, in analyzing case law, regardless of whether it interprets a statute or applies common law, you must appreciate the relative strength of different kinds of authorities. Case law from a higher court within the forum jurisdiction is potentially controlling on the facts of your case, and you must argue for a broader or narrower interpretation of its holding, depending on whether it supports or undermines your position. Case law from other jurisdictions may have persuasive value, but only in the absence of controlling law within the jurisdiction.

For example, in the following passage of an argument set in a fictitious jurisdiction and governed by common law, the counsel for Beatty, a lender, encourages the court to synthesize mandatory precedent in a favorable manner and to brush aside adverse persuasive authority from another jurisdiction:

Introduction to argument

Principles derived from a synthesis of the Calzona cases establish that Beatty's promise is not illusory. The consideration requirement therefore is satisfied, and Weeks's promise is enforceable.

In-depth analysis of favorable case law

Even if a promise leaves open the possibility that the promisor will escape obligation, the promise is not illusory if the promisor does not have complete control over the events on which the promisor's obligation is conditioned. *Bonnie v.*

DeLaney, 158 Calz. 212, 645 P.2d 887 (1982). In *Bonnie*, an agreement for the sale of a house provided that the buyer could cancel the agreement if the buyer "cannot qualify for a 30-year mortgage loan for 90% of the sales price" with any of several banks listed in the agreement. *Id.* at 213, 645 P.2d at 888. In enforcing the agreement against the seller, the court emphasized that the word "cannot" referred to the buyer's ability to obtain a loan rather than to his desire. Because his ability to obtain a loan was partly controlled by events and decisions outside his control, the promises in the sale agreement were nonillusory and binding. *See id.* at 214-15, 645 P.2d at 889-90.

The *Bonnie* court distinguished its earlier decision, *Atco Corp. v. Johnson*, 155 Calz. 1211, 627 P.2d 781 (1980). In *Atco Corp.*, the manager of an automobile repair shop promised to forbear "until I want the money" from asserting a claim against the owner of an automobile for $900 in repairs. In exchange, a friend of the owner promised to act as guarantor of the owner's obligation. *Id.* at 1212, 627 P.2d at 782. The word "want" stated no legal commitment because it permitted the manager at his own discretion to refuse to perform any forbearance at all. Because the manager did not incur even a conditional obligation, the guarantor's promise was gratuitous and unenforceable. *Id.* at 1213-14, 627 P.2d at 783-84.

> In-depth analysis of adverse case law

Together, these cases show that any limitation on the promisor's freedom will validate his promise. A promise is illusory only if it leaves the promisor complete control over his actions.

> Synthesis that emphasizes favorable case law

Under these controlling principles, the parties in this case each assumed valid obligations . . . .

> Application to facts

Thus, *Atco* is distinguishable from our case, and *Bonnie* is controlling.

Weeks attempts to salvage his flawed analogy to *Atco* by interpreting it in light of authority from New Maine. The New Maine cases, however, are not binding on this court and are inconsistent with the reasoning of the controlling authority in *Bonnie*. . . .

> Argument against application of nonbinding authority

In this example, counsel for Beatty placed her affirmative arguments in positions of priority before distinguishing or discrediting authority supporting counterarguments. She summarized her argument in the first paragraph.

In the second and third paragraphs, she synthesized local case law by reconciling two decisions with apparently contrasting holdings, starting with the supporting precedent. In the fourth paragraph, she concluded her synthesis with a form of inductive reasoning in which she derived a legal rule by generalizing from the two cases, emphasizing the supporting case law. In the fifth paragraph, as illustrated more fully in Section B below, counsel for Beatty applied this rule to the facts of her case, taking care to analogize the favorable precedent and to distinguish the adverse precedent. In the final paragraph, she protected this analysis by explaining why case law from another jurisdiction should not be used to interpret the local case law in a different manner.

The persuasive influence of authority from a lower court or from a court in another jurisdiction may be stronger in the absence of any applicable authority from the forum state. If persuasive authority undermines your client's position, you can try to distinguish it from the facts of your case or to discredit its reasoning as unworthy of adoption as the rule of law in the forum jurisdiction. Conversely, if persuasive authority supports your position, you should argue that its reasoning is sound and is consistent with the policy of the forum jurisdiction.

For example, in the following passage, in which fictitious case law has interpreted a fictitious federal statute in imaginary courts, an advocate attempts to persuade a court in the state of New Maine to adopt the reasoning of Calzona case law and to reject precedent from the jurisdictions of Floridia and the U.S. Court of Appeals for the Fifteenth Circuit:

In-depth analysis of favorable case law

The federal Food Quality Act (FQA) preempts more stringent state legislation seeking to ensure the quality and purity of food produced or sold in interstate commerce. *State v. Biggs*, 123 Calz. 56, 567 P.2d 765 (2009). In *Biggs,* state officials sought to enjoin the marketing and sale of fruits and vegetables advertised as "organic." The officials invoked a Calzona statute that set criteria for food labeled or advertised to be organic. *Id.* at 57, 567 P.2d at 766. The Calzona Supreme Court held that the FQA's provisions regarding organic produce were intended to be exclusive and to eliminate unreasonable restrictions on commerce. *Id.* at 58-60, 567 P.2d at 767-69. It therefore held that the FQA barred the state from prohibiting such regulation. *Id.* at 61, 567 P.2d at 770.

In reaching its decision, the California Supreme Court exhaustively analyzed the legislative history of the FQA. It noted that . . . .

Critical analysis of adverse case law

One other state court and one federal court had previously rejected the preemption argument adopted in *Biggs,* but each of them overlooked

the critical legislative history that *Biggs* so carefully analyzed. *Arzani v. Matlock*, 332 So. 2d 234
(Fldia. 2008); *Michigan v. Smedley*, 439 F.3d 166
(15th Cir. 2006).

For example, in *Arzani*, the court summarily
held that . . . .

The advocate obviously hopes that the preceding passage will persuade
the court to adopt the reasoning of *Biggs*. In the fact analysis, the advocate
can argue further that *Biggs* is analogous to the facts of her case and that the
rule of law it represents thus applies to those facts.

3. Depth of Analysis

In presenting your legal arguments and authority, you must exercise
firm control over depth of analysis, as introduced in Section IV.B.1 of Chapter 6 and discussed more thoroughly in Section II.A.2 of Chapter 13. You
should review those sections, which examine three different levels or depths
of analysis:

1. light analysis to present fundamental and undisputed propositions
   with direct statements of law and citation to authority,
2. direct statements of law and citation to authority with parenthetic
   explanations for a slightly deeper level of analysis, and
3. in-depth analysis of statutes or case law to explore policy and reasoning or to explain a rule by showing how precedent has applied the
   rule to facts in previous cases.

For example, the following introduction to an argument uses technique 2 above to quickly establish an undisputed point about federal law
before addressing state law claims in greater depth:

Because Comcon has always employed fewer than fifteen employees [Hart

SofF ¶ 1], Rembar has no claim against Hart under federal employment discrimi-

nation law. *See* 42 U.S.C. § 2000e(b) (2006) (defining employers covered by Title

VII of the Civil Rights Act of 1964).

A good brief typically will employ the full range of depths of analysis.
If a dispute reaches a court without a negotiated settlement, the issues are
presumably substantial and reasonably contested by both parties. Consequently, neither party will be able to prevail on crucial issues with conclusory
statements of the law and application to the facts. Instead, the brief likely
will advance in-depth arguments of the law, the facts, or both for all but
general background points.

Nonetheless, general legal background may set the context for your more specific legal analyses. Rather than jump too quickly to the details of a complex argument, you should first provide your reader with necessary foundational points, which often can be summarized quickly and succinctly.

In the following argument, for example, the author sets forth basic standards in "light analysis" before explaining an element of the legal rule by engaging in in-depth analysis of case law:

Hart is not liable for intentional infliction of emotional distress unless his conduct was so "extreme and outrageous" that it fell "within that quite narrow range" of conduct "at the very extreme edge of the spectrum." *Watts v. Golden Age Nursing Home*, 127 Ariz. 255, 258, 619 P.2d 1032, 1035 (1980). Moreover, "it is extremely rare to find conduct in the employment context that will rise to the level of outrageousness necessary to provide a basis for recovery for the tort of intentional infliction of emotional distress." *Mintz v. Bell Atl. Sys. Leasing Int'l, Inc.*, 183 Ariz. 550, 554, 905 P.2d 559, 563 (Ct. App. 1995) (quoting *Cox v. Keystone Carbon Co.*, 861 F.2d 390, 395 (3d Cir. 1988)).

In *Mintz*, an employee was hospitalized after suffering a nervous breakdown as the alleged result of gender discrimination in the workplace. The employer terminated her disability benefits, ordered her to return to work, and then—while the employee was again hospitalized after returning to work for one day—notified her of a reassignment of her duties by a letter delivered to the hospital. *Id.* at 552, 905 P.2d at 561. The Arizona Court of Appeals affirmed a finding that, as a matter of law, this alleged conduct was not extreme and outrageous, even assuming the employer had failed to promote the employee because of gender discrimination and assuming the employer knew that the employee was unusually susceptible to emotional distress. *Id.* at 553-54, 905 P.2d at 562-63.

In light of cases such as *Mintz*, a federal district court has characterized Arizona's standard for extreme and outrageous conduct as one requiring "extraordinary" conduct. *Tempesta v. Motorola, Inc.*, 92 F. Supp. 2d 973, 987 (D. Ariz. 1999). Applying *Mintz*, the *Tempesta* court granted summary judgment for the defendant employer on the employee's claim of intentional infliction of emotional distress, even after assuming the truth of the employee's allegations that he had suffered harassment and wrongful termination because of his sex. *Id.* at 986-87.

It is even clearer in this case that Hart did not engage in extreme and outrageous conduct. . . .

4. Elements or Factors in Legal Rules

As discussed in Chapter 6, Section VI.A, legal rules come in a variety of types. Some statutory or common law rules require proof of several mandatory elements. Failure to prove any one of the elements prevents satisfaction of the legal rule.

Other legal rules identify factors that a court should consider in determining whether the facts satisfy a general standard. The list of factors may not be exclusive, and the standard may be met without proof of every factor. Some legal rules, including many constitutional tests, contemplate the balancing of two or more competing factors or values.

The nature of a legal rule will influence your presentation and analysis of the rule. For example, the following argument introduces three mandatory elements of a tort and then presents separate arguments on each element. Each argument in a subsection then presents more detailed legal requirements for the element discussed in that subsection:

C. The undisputed facts show that Hart is not liable for intentional infliction of emotional distress.

The Arizona Supreme Court has adopted the Restatement test for intentional infliction of emotional distress, requiring proof of three elements: (1) extreme and outrageous conduct, (2) engaged in with intent to cause distress or with reckless disregard of the near certainty that distress will result, (3) causing severe emotional distress. *Watts v. Golden Age Nursing Home*, 127 Ariz. 255, 258, 619 P.2d 1032, 1035 (1980) (citing to the Restatement (Second) of Torts § 46 (1965)). Rembar cannot genuinely dispute that the facts fail to satisfy these elements.

1. Hart did not engage in extreme and outrageous conduct.

Conduct is not "extreme and outrageous" unless it is falls "within that quite narrow range" of conduct "at the very extreme edge of the spectrum." *Watts*, 127 Ariz. at 258, 619 P.2d at 1035. Moreover, "it is extremely rare to find conduct in the employment context that will rise to the level of outrageousness necessary to provide a basis for recovery for the tort of intentional infliction of emotional distress." *Mintz v. Bell Atl. Sys. Leasing Int'l, Inc.*, 183 Ariz. 550, 554, 905 P.2d 559, 563 (Ct. App. 1995) (quoting *Cox v. Keystone Carbon Co.*, 861 F.2d 390, 395 (3d Cir. 1988)).

In *Mintz*, an employee was hospitalized after suffering a nervous breakdown as the alleged result of gender discrimination in the workplace. . . .

In light of cases such as *Mintz*, a federal district court has characterized Arizona's standard for extreme and outrageous conduct as one requiring "extraordinary" conduct. *Tempesta v. Motorola, Inc.*, 92 F. Supp. 2d 973, 987 (D. Ariz. 1999). Applying *Mintz*, the *Tempesta* court granted summary judgment . . . .

In this case, the record on summary judgment will show that . . . .

2. Hart did not act with intent or reckless disregard.

. . . .

3. Rembar did not suffer severe emotional distress.

The following argument, in contrast, addresses material breach of contract, which permits the non-breaching party to cancel the contract. The concept of material breach is a standard for which several factors serve as guidelines. The argument rejects an assertion that every factor in the guidelines must be satisfied, and it argues that the preponderance of factors in favor of material breach outweigh a single factor supporting a finding of minor breach:

2. Tarasenko did not materially breach the contract.

In this jurisdiction, materiality of breach is not governed by a "single touchstone." Instead, the Michigan Supreme Court has drawn guidance from the six "influential" factors of section 275 of the Restatement (First) of Contracts:

> In determining the materiality of a failure fully to perform a promise the following circumstances are influential:
>
> (a) The extent to which the injured party will obtain the substantial benefit which he could have reasonably anticipated;
>
> (b) The extent to which the injured party may be adequately compensated in damages for lack of complete performance;
>
> (c) The extent to which the party failing to perform has already partly performed or made preparations for performance;
>
> (d) The greater or less hardship on the party failing to perform in terminating the contract;
>
> (e) The willful, negligent or innocent behavior of the party failing to perform;
>
> (f) The greater or less uncertainty that the party failing to perform will perform the remainder of the contract.

Walker & Co. v. Harrison, 347 Mich. 630, 635, 81 N.W.2d 352, 355 (1957) (quoting the Restatement (First) of Contracts § 275 (1932)).

In 1981, the second Restatement updated the relevant factors, providing a slightly modified guide to material breach, based on five "circumstances" that "are significant." Restatement (Second) of Contracts § 241 (1982). For example, the second Restatement refers to "standards of good faith and fair dealing" in place of the first Restatement's reference to "willful, negligent or innocent behavior." *Id.* at § 241(e). But the precise formulation of the Restatement's guidance is not significant. The Restatements characterize their factors only as "circumstances" that are "influential" or "significant." Moreover, the Court in *Walker* analyzed the facts of its case in a common sense fashion, without specifically relating facts of the case to every factor in the Restatement section that it had quoted. *Walker & Co.*, 347 Mich. at 636, 81 N.W.2d at 356 (adopting trial court's factual analysis and conclusion of no material breach).

Accordingly, Tarasenko misapplies the law in this state when she argues that her breach could not be material because her failure to fully perform was not the product of bad intentions or lack of care. Contrary to the premise of Tarasenko's argument, bad faith or other culpability is not a required element of material breach; instead, it is only one of "many factors" that are relevant. *Id.* at 635, 81 N.W.2d at 355 ("Many factors are involved."). This single factor in Tarasenko's favor is easily outweighed by the other relevant circumstances, which together strongly support a finding of material breach.

First, Jenkins received almost none of the benefit that he had expected . . . .

Second, ...

5. Presenting Your Authority

Finally, you must lead your reader through each of your arguments and support your assertions of law with supporting authority. Three techniques explored in Sections II and III of Chapter 14 are particularly important. You should

1. express your syntheses of authorities or other thesis statements in topic sentences or paragraphs;
2. unless the citations are independently significant, focus attention on your ideas and relegate citations to subordinate citation sentences; and
3. introduce quotations with substantive overviews that invite the judge to adopt your interpretation of the quoted material.

B. Analyzing the Facts

As discussed in greater detail in Chapter 22 in the context of appellate briefs, the opening statement of facts in a brief is most effective if it does not prematurely argue the law or the application of the law to the facts. In contrast, when you analyze the relevant facts in the argument section of a brief, you should explicitly reach a conclusion by relating the facts to the previously discussed legal rules. You may accomplish this by (1) directly applying the law to the facts or (2) using a form of inductive reasoning to analogize or distinguish precedent by comparing the facts and reasoning of the precedent to your own case.

To illustrate the first technique, suppose that you have established in your discussion of the law that a state police officer can be liable for punitive damages for recklessly depriving a citizen of her right to be free from arrest without probable cause. In the fact analysis of your argument, you could directly apply that rule of law to the facts by showing how the defendant police officer acted recklessly. In the following sample passage, the notations within brackets refer to pages of the trial court reporter's transcript on which critical testimony of witnesses is found.

Substantial evidence in the record supports the jury's finding that Officer Mullins acted with at least reckless disregard for Wong's clearly established Fourth Amendment rights. Mullins's actions show that even he did not believe that Wong fit the dispatcher's description of the robbery suspect. According to his own testimony, when he initially spotted Wong moments after receiving the robbery report, he passed by her and continued looking for the suspect. [RT at 324.] Only after failing to find a suspect who fit the dispatcher's description did he relocate Wong and summarily arrest her. [RT at 326.]

The jury could infer from these facts that Officer Mullins felt compelled to arrest somebody for the robbery and that he recklessly gambled that Wong might have been involved simply because of her general proximity to the robbery. This is precisely the kind of reckless disregard for constitutional rights that an award of punitive damages is designed to deter.

Alternatively, your discussion of the law may include in-depth case analysis and synthesis of arguably controlling, analogous, or distinguishable authority. If so, you may want to use the second technique of inductive reasoning to compare those cases directly to your dispute in your fact analysis:

Analogizing favorable case law on the facts	*Bonnie* is closely analogous to our case and thus supports the conclusion that Beatty's promise was not illusory. In both *Bonnie* and our case, the promised performance was conditioned on events not entirely within the control of the promisor. In *Bonnie* the buyer could escape his obligations only if market conditions rendered him *unable* to obtain a satisfactory mortgage loan. Similarly, in our case, Beatty could terminate his obligation to refrain from collecting on the debt only if economic conditions affected his income and expenses so as to create a need for the money.
Distinguishing adverse case law on the facts	Conversely, *Atco Corp.* is distinguishable from our case. The promisor in that case retained the freedom to escape all contractual obligations if, at his own discretion, he *wanted* to. In contrast, the Guarantee Agreement in this case did not permit Beatty to demand his money whenever he *wanted* it. Instead, ...

C. Conclusions

Immediately after your fact analysis in each argument of your brief, you should briefly repeat the conclusion that you previewed in the point heading for that section or subsection:

Scott Paper Supply timely objected to Sun Printing Co.'s written confirmation of the alleged agreement. Therefore, the confirmation does not satisfy the requirements of the statute of frauds.

Additionally, every brief should end with a formal conclusion section. Many attorneys squander this opportunity to summarize their analyses. The following boilerplate is typical:

III. CONCLUSION

For the foregoing reasons, Appellant respectfully requests this Court to reverse the judgment of the superior court.

Although this style is conventional, a more substantive conclusion ordinarily is more satisfying, particularly if the brief presents more than one argument.

A substantive conclusion need not take up much space. If your arguments are simple, your conclusion need only briefly and generally repeat the request for relief and the supporting grounds, as in this closing to a brief in support of a motion to exclude evidence before trial:

III. CONCLUSION

Under Rule 403, Powell is entitled to pretrial exclusion of all evidence of his membership in the Black Panther Party. The danger of confusion and the prejudicial effect of the evidence substantially outweigh its probative value, and the prejudice can be avoided only through exclusion of the evidence before trial.

In a more complex case, the conclusion might briefly summarize multiple arguments:

III. CONCLUSION

Yazzi's statement to the police officer is inadmissible on three grounds. First, it is not relevant to any issue in this suit. Second, even if it were relevant, it would be excludable because its prejudicial value substantially outweighs its probative value. Finally, it is inadmissible hearsay not falling within the exception for statements for purposes of medical treatment. This evidence should be excluded before trial to avoid exposing it to the jury and causing irremediable prejudice.

V. Summary

To effectively advocate your client's case in a written document,

1. organize your legal arguments in logical order, subject to overriding considerations of strategy;
2. introduce each of your arguments with an effective point heading and, if helpful, an introductory paragraph; and
3. present your analysis of the law, apply the law to the facts, and state the conclusion that you want the court to reach.>

The next chapter examines persuasive writing style, as well as oral argument.

Chapter 17

Expressing Your Advocacy: Persuasive Writing Style and Oral Argument

Persuasive brief writing begins with your developing a theme and selecting arguments, as discussed in Chapter 16. Additionally, depending on the nature of the brief and the procedural posture of the case, the brief frequently should include a fact statement that tells your client's story in a compelling fashion, which is discussed in Chapter 22. This chapter addresses persuasive style in presenting legal arguments.

I. Persuasive Writing Style

Supervising attorneys often complain that law students or recent graduates from law school do not use sufficiently strong language to write persuasively. Admittedly, advocacy calls for a writing style that departs from the more nearly neutral style appropriate for an office memorandum. Unfortunately, however, many supervising attorneys equate persuasive writing style with hyperbole, and they advise writers to pepper every sentence of a brief with exaggerated modifiers. Such a style may grab a judge's attention, but it does not often persuade. Judges recognize overstatement and tend to take everything in such a brief with an extra pinch of salt. Even worse, a writing style that is too obvious in its advocacy tends to divert the judge's attention from the substance of the argument and to focus it on the style itself.

The most persuasive writing style may be one that the judge hardly notices. It uses an engaging writing style that keeps the judge's attention riveted on the substance of the arguments, and it presents those arguments so reasonably and clearly as to give her the impression that the brief merely confirms her own independent conclusions. The most important element of such writing is good substantive analysis; a few extra hours of research and reflection may lead to an argument that is easily written in a persuasive manner. Beyond that, persuasive legal writing is distinguished by (1) strong, but not exaggerated, language and (2) effective emphasis through sentence structure, specificity, and vivid, concrete language.

A. Persuasive Language

1. The Adversarial Approach

To clearly communicate your legal analysis to a supervising attorney in an office memorandum, you must candidly reveal uncertainties in the law and weaknesses in your client's case. In contrast, a brief in the same litigation generally should not explore the weaknesses of a client's case except as necessary to satisfy ethical duties or maintain credibility. The adversary system ensures that opposing counsel will challenge your arguments.

Thus, in an office memorandum, you might candidly admit the weakness of the support for a client's argument, as with the following fictitious analysis of a client's preemption argument:

Only one state court has held that the federal Food Quality Act preempts more stringent state regulation. *State v. Biggs*, 123 Calz. 56, 567 P.2d 765 (2009). Two other courts have interpreted the Act to permit more stringent state controls that are consistent with its policy. *Arzani v. Matlock*, 332 So. 2d 234 (Fldia. 2008); *Michigan v. Smedley*, 439 F.3d 166 (15th Cir. 2006). To support our argument that federal law preempts the New Maine regulation of organic food labeling, we should emphasize the thorough reasoning of *Biggs* and try to discredit or distinguish *Arzani* and *Smedley*.

In *Biggs*, ...

In contrast, in a brief to the court in the same case, you must state your client's argument more positively, while acknowledging and attempting to distinguish or discredit the contrary authority:

The federal Food Quality Act preempts more stringent state regulations. *State v. Biggs*, 123 Calz. 56, 567 P.2d 765 (2009). In *Biggs*, state officials sought to prohibit . . . .

Two courts had previously rejected the preemption argument adopted in *Biggs*, but each of them overlooked the critical legislative history so carefully analyzed in *Biggs. See Arzani v. Matlock*, . . . ; *Michigan v. Smedley*, ... For example, in *Arzani* . . . .

The proposition for which *Biggs* is cited in the second example illustrates the power of the simple, unqualified statement:

The federal Food Quality Act preempts more stringent state regulation.

You should avoid unnecessary qualifiers that weaken arguments, such as the following introduction to the argument of your client, Mason:

Mason contends that the federal Food Quality Act preempts more stringent state regulation.

Because the argument section of your brief obviously comprises a series of legal contentions, specific introductions to that effect are superfluous. You may set up a response to your opponent's propositions by referring to them as "arguments" or "contentions," but such a characterization of your own conclusions or statements of law tends to weaken them.

2. Clichés that Weaken or Offend

Ironically, modifiers that are designed to reinforce a proposition sometimes sap the strength from an otherwise powerful statement. For example, comments such as "it is abundantly clear that" have little effect on the judge except to make him wonder whether the words were added to shore up a shaky proposition that in fact is subject to great debate. Along with other forms of exaggeration, clichés such as these tend to make the advocacy in the writing too obvious and distracting. A judge will accept your conclusions more readily if you offer persuasive arguments than if you invoke stock phrases that describe your arguments as persuasive.

The line between strong advocacy and overstatement is most delicate when referring directly to a matter within the court's discretionary power. For example, the word "should" in the following argument reflects lack of confidence in the argument:

This court should exclude evidence of Jenkins's subjective intentions regarding the lease.

On the other hand, a stronger verb suggests a presumptuous challenge to the power of the court:

This court must exclude evidence of Jenkins's subjective intentions regarding the lease.

On reading such an argument, the judge might be subconsciously inclined to demonstrate that she does indeed have the discretionary power to admit the evidence, the exercise of which would not likely be overturned on appeal. Restating the proposition in passive voice tends to soften and depersonalize the challenge:

Evidence of Jenkins's subjective intentions regarding the lease must be excluded.

Nonetheless, the challenge to the judge's power remains implicit in this construction. Perhaps the best statement is one that focuses directly on the character of the evidence rather than on the power of the judge:

Evidence of Jenkins's subjective intentions regarding the lease is inadmissible.

This proposition is strong and unqualified, yet it avoids expressing or directly implying a personal challenge to the judge.

3. Personal Attacks

Avoid personal attacks on opposing counsel. Although you may become exasperated with apparently unreasonable or offensive conduct by your opponent, judges do not appreciate being caught in a crossfire of personal insults. Unless misconduct by a party or his attorney is properly the subject of a motion, judges are far more interested in your response to the opposing counsel's arguments than in your personal opinion of your opponent's intelligence, research skills, or personality. Thus, you may safely characterize the opposing counsel's argument as internally inconsistent, but you should not comment that he is unable to write a coherent brief. Similarly, if your statement of the procedural history unemotionally records events that reflect the opposing counsel's bad faith, the judge will undoubtedly draw negative conclusions about his advocacy without any further comment from you.

A court's published reaction to a derogatory characterization of opposing counsel's argument is illuminating:

> There are good reasons not to call an opponent's argument "ridiculous," . . . . The reasons include civility; the near-certainty that overstatement will only push the reader away (especially when, as here, the hyperbole begins on page one of the brief); and that, even where the record supports an extreme modifier, "the better practice is usually to lay out the facts and let the court reach its own conclusions." *Big Dipper Entm't, L.L.C. v. City of Warren*, 641 F.3d 715, 719 (6th Cir. 2011).[1]

B. Sentence Structure

To preserve your credibility and ethical standards, you often must candidly acknowledge law that is adverse to your client's case and that you can neither discredit nor distinguish. You can minimize the resulting damage by using techniques of persuasive writing style to de-emphasize the adverse law and to focus attention on more helpful points.

One such technique consists of placing helpful information in the main clause and relegating adverse information to a dependent subordinate clause, a clause that cannot stand by itself as a complete sentence. For example, as counsel for the plaintiff in a contract action, you can de-emphasize the general rule against damages for emotional distress by disposing of it in an opening subordinate clause:

Although damages for emotional distress are not often awarded for breach of contract, Jones is entitled to such an award because of the exceptional nature of his case: The central purpose of his contract with Runyon Pet Cemetery was to alleviate his grief over the loss of his dog. *See generally* . . . .

You maintain credibility with this passage by facing, rather than evading, the general rule. Moreover, by placing the general rule in a subordinate clause, you invite the reader to give it only brief pause, as you might invite a guest at a restaurant to dine lightly on appetizers in anticipation of the main course.

Location of information within a sentence also affects emphasis. Generally, the end of a sentence conveys the greatest emphasis, the beginning of a sentence conveys secondary emphasis, and a parenthetic phrase or clause at a natural breaking point in the middle of the sentence conveys the least emphasis. For example, if you represent the defendant in the example above, you can emphasize the general rule by placing it at the end of the sentence:

---

1. Bennett v. State Farm Mut. Auto. Ins. Co., 731 F.3d 584, 584-85 (6th Cir. 2013).

In demanding an award of damages for emotional distress, Jones runs afoul of the general rule that such damages are not awarded for breach of contract.

Generally, you will emphasize the general rule least by placing it in a parenthetic clause at a natural breaking point in the middle of the sentence:

Jones is entitled to an award of damages for emotional distress in this exceptional case, even though such awards are rare in contract actions, because the central purpose of his contract with Runyon Pet Cemetery was to alleviate his grief over the loss of his dog.

This passage may be the best of the three for the plaintiff because it places favorable information in the positions of greatest emphasis.

Of course, if you are willing to sacrifice other style objectives, you can create unusual emphasis in the middle of the sentence with an abrupt, dramatic, or unnatural interruption of the sentence:

Jones unreasonably demands—while admitting that such damages generally are not awarded in contract actions—an award of damages for emotional distress.

Exercise 17-1

Foreclosure Falsities

In October 2010, in the wake of class action lawsuits and official investigations, some United States lending institutions suspended their home foreclosures nationwide to review their foreclosure procedures. Litigation challenging a home foreclosure in Maine revealed that GMAC, servicing a home loan for the Federal National Mortgage Association, had routinely engaged in a practice that the media soon dubbed "robo-signing": a "limited signing officer" would prepare hundreds of foreclosures each day, signing affidavits attesting that the requisites for foreclosure had been met even though the officer had not reviewed the relevant documents to confirm the assertions in the affidavits.

After discovering this practice in a deposition, a volunteer attorney for the homebuyer, Thomas Cox, persuaded the trial court in Maine to set aside its earlier partial summary judgment in favor of GMAC and to order GMAC to pay expenses associated with the deposition. Mr. Cox's brief included the following application of law to facts in his argument that the signing official (named in this exercise only as "S.O.") submitted his affidavit in bad faith, a legal prerequisite for an order of sanctions against GMAC:

> When [S.O.] says in an affidavit that he has personal knowledge of the facts stated in his affidavits, he doesn't. When he says that he has custody and control of the loan documents, he doesn't. When he says that he is attaching "a true and accurate" copy of a note or a mortgage, he has no idea if that is so, because he does not look at the exhibits. When he makes any other statement of fact, he has no idea if it is true. When the notary says that [S.O.] appeared before him or her, he didn't, and when the notary says that [S.O.] was sworn, he wasn't. The practice of GMAC Mortgage, LLC in submitting foreclosure affidavits such as this, knowing that they will be relied upon by a judge to enter an order taking away a family's home, must be seen as a quintessential definition of a summary judgment affidavit "presented in bad faith."[2]

1. Impact of the Facts

If you were the judge in this case, how would the preceding fact analysis affect your view of the case? If the case presented close legal issues or ones that permitted exercise of your discretion as the trial judge, would you be inclined to rule in favor of the homebuyer if any reasonable interpretation or application of the law permitted that result?

2. Analyzing the Presentation

Analyze the author's writing style. Explain how the style of presentation helps to maximize the persuasive effect of these compelling facts. Be specific in your description.

3. Persuasive Presentation in Other Styles

Can you rewrite the fact analysis in an alternative style of presentation, while still matching or exceeding the persuasive effect of the original? Describe the techniques of persuasive writing that you employ in your version.

II. Oral Argument to the Court

In many appeals and pretrial or trial motions, you will argue your client's case orally to the court after submitting your written brief. In most cases, your written brief will influence a judge more strongly than will your oral

---

2. The facts for this exercise are taken from court documents in Fed. Nat'l Mortg. Ass'n v. Bradbury, No. BR-OE-09-65 (9th Dist. Ct., ME), and from David Streitfeld, *From this House, a National Foreclosure Freeze*, N.Y. TIMES, Oct. 15, 2010, at A1. The quoted paragraph from Mr. Cox's brief omits a footnote that appeared in the brief after the third sentence of the paragraph. The author thanks Richard Neumann for bringing this example of persuasive writing to the attention of the legal writing community.

argument. Indeed, before oral argument, most judges read both parties' briefs and come to a tentative decision on the merits.

Nonetheless, oral argument is not yet a meaningless formality in our courts. It provides you with a final opportunity to emphasize critical points, respond to judges' questions, change the mind of a judge who had tentatively decided to rule in favor of the opposing party, or strongly influence a judge who has not formed a tentative opinion.

A. General Format

The typical oral argument follows a pattern similar to that of filing briefs: The advocate seeking relief or reversal of a judgment in a lower court argues first, the opposing advocate responds, and the first advocate has an opportunity for rebuttal. In some courts, the advocate arguing first must tell the court before she begins her argument whether she wishes to divide her time between opening argument and rebuttal.

Rebuttal is a powerful weapon. It provides the advocate who opens the oral argument with an opportunity to respond directly to the oral argument of the opponent. It also permits the advocate with the opening argument to have both the first and last word on the issues. Therefore, if you give the opening oral argument, you should always preserve the opportunity for rebuttal.

B. Formality and Demeanor

Appropriate courtroom attire is mandatory for any oral argument. For both men and women, this generally consists of a conservative, dark-colored suit. Beyond that, the level of formality of the proceedings will vary among courts.

For pretrial and trial motions, some state trial court judges hold oral arguments in their chambers rather than in the courtroom. After friendly, informal introductions, all are seated. As the judge listens from behind his desk, you and the opposing counsel will deliver your arguments while seated in office chairs.

Other trial judges and virtually all appellate panels of judges, however, conduct oral arguments with greater formality. In those courts, you deliver your oral argument from a lectern in the courtroom.

If you are uncertain about the customs in a court or the expectations of a particular judge, you can observe another attorney's oral argument before the judge, speak with a colleague who has practiced before the judge, or seek advice from the staff of the clerk's office or from the judge's personal law clerk. To consult with them, you can contact them by telephone or simply arrive early on the day of the argument.

Your demeanor in oral argument should be as formal as your attire. You should be confident and relaxed, but respectful of the judge, always addressing him or her as "Your Honor." If you disagree with a judge during the argument, you need not make him defensive by being disagreeable. For example, if he asks you whether your formulation of a legal rule will have certain adverse policy ramifications, you should answer the question confidently but without arrogantly suggesting that the question is silly.

Thus, you should *not* respond to a judge's question or assertion with a challenge to his analytic skills, such as the following:

No, your Honor, you are incorrect on that point.

Instead, you should answer the question without casting doubt on the questioner:

Your Honor, the Court can avoid those potential problems of line-drawing by stating its holding in this appeal narrowly. I suggest the following formulation: . . . .

In some cases, you may even want to validate the question before answering it:

That question has occupied the attention of a number of courts and scholars, your Honor. To answer it, I must review the rationale for the exclusionary rule.

C. Content of the Argument

1. Introduction of the Argument

In a formal courtroom argument, you should begin your presentation by introducing yourself and your representative capacity:

May it please the court, I am Terry Malloy. I represent Bakeway Stores, the appellant on this appeal and the defendant in the trial court.

The opening phrase, "May it please the court," oddly suggests that you hope that your name "pleases the court." However, it also signals respect to the court and a willingness to allow the judges to set the agenda for the dialogue through their questions and comments. Moreover, if a judge expects this traditional salutation, your departing from it may place the judge in an unreceptive mood. Accordingly, you probably should introduce yourself with this puzzling phrase unless you are confident that the judge or judges hearing your argument are comfortable with a more natural greeting, such as "Good morning, Your Honor."

After the personal introduction, you can capture a judge's attention with a brief characterization of the motion or appeal. If the facts are compelling, you can describe the general nature of the case in a sentence or two that conveys the theme of your argument. For example, suppose that a state is prosecuting an 18-year-old student for felony possession of illegal drugs on the premises of his high school. The attorney for the defendant student has filed a motion in the trial court to exclude evidence obtained in an allegedly illegal detention and search. He might introduce his oral argument at the suppression hearing with the following characterization of the case:

Your Honor, this motion concerns the reasonableness of a search by armed police officers who — acting solely on information about previous drug sales by a former student — rushed into a high school hallway with a barking police dog, ordered all fifteen high school students in the hallway to fall to their knees with hands behind their heads, and searched them, one-by-one. As the Supreme Court held in *Redding* . . . .

Of course, the prosecutor might respond with a very different characterization of the case:

Your Honor, the seizure of the crack cocaine in this case was the product of a thorough investigation in an ongoing effort by police and school administrators to protect all students from trafficking in illegal drugs at Richland High School.

2. Body of the Argument

a. General Strategy

Many courts impose a time limit on each oral argument. Although some courts of last resort may allow as long as 60 minutes for each side in a complex case, 15 to 30 minutes is more typical, and arguments on simple pretrial motions may be limited to an even shorter time. In most motions or appeals, you will not have time to address all the issues in the depth in which you explored them in your brief. Consequently, you should carefully study the arguments presented in both parties' briefs to determine the most effective strategy for oral argument.

Your strategy will differ depending on the circumstances of each case. In one appeal, for example, you may rely on multiple arguments that are both complex and interdependent. You may fear that, even with a well-organized brief to guide them, the judges may not fully appreciate how the arguments fit together to form the larger picture. You may thus decide to present an oral outline of all the arguments and their relationships, leaving the detail of each to your brief.

More often, you can identify an argument in your brief that you wish to emphasize. Perhaps it addresses a critically important threshold issue or is your strongest theory. In other cases, you may select an argument for oral presentation because it is the weakest link in your argumentative chain and needs extra support.

Whatever strategy you choose, you should communicate your intentions immediately after the introduction to your argument. For example, at a hearing to suppress evidence obtained in an allegedly illegal search, the prosecutor may try to justify the search on several grounds. Although she will introduce evidence at the hearing supporting each of the grounds and will advocate each ground in her brief, she might use her oral argument to focus on the determinative issue of consent to search. If so, she should reveal her plans to the court:

This hearing presents three major issues, all of which the briefs examine in detail. I will be happy to answer questions on any of the issues. However, I would like to focus my presentation on the issue of consent to search. If the facts show that the defendant consented to the detention and the search, this court need not address difficult legal issues such as those related to expectations of privacy on a high school campus.

b. Using the Facts

Many judges will advise oral advocates before argument that the judges are familiar with the facts of the case and that the advocates should proceed with their legal analyses. Even absent such an instruction, you ordinarily should not begin your argument with a lengthy recitation of the facts beyond a general characterization of the nature of the case. You might depart from this advice if the facts are particularly compelling and your legal arguments are not. In most cases, however, you will make better use of your limited time by arguing the law and applying the law to the facts without a separate introductory recitation of facts.

Whenever you rely on facts in an oral argument, be certain of the source of the facts. Be prepared to cite to the portion of the record that establishes the facts.

c. Responding to Questions

Questions from the bench constitute the most uncertain variable in oral argument. They ensure that oral advocacy in most cases is not a series of speeches but a dialogue, primarily between each advocate and the judges, and secondarily between the advocates as they respond to one another. Ironically, oral argument also permits judges on a panel to establish a coy dialogue between the judges, as they attempt to persuade each other with comments and questions ostensibly directed to the advocates.

You should genuinely welcome the opportunity to respond to questions. A judge's questions may reveal areas in which she has doubts, permitting you to directly influence her thinking on those points.

Occasionally, a judge will press you for a concession on your weakest among several alternative arguments. Your waiving the argument might be the most effective way to turn the judge's attention to your stronger arguments. However, you should not too quickly waive a major argument that you had earlier determined was sufficiently meritorious to warrant discussion in your brief. If you are arguing before a panel of judges, the other panel members may not share the doubts of the questioning judge; yet, if you expressly waive the controversial point during oral argument, none of the judges will take up that argument. Thus, even though it appears that you must waive the argument to preserve your credibility, you should first try to shift to a more productive topic of discussion after making a minor concession:

Your Honor, I prefer not to waive our argument that Todd has standing to establish unreasonable use of force based on the totality of the circumstances, including evidence showing how the entire police operation affected all of the students. I do concede, however, that unreasonable force is a secondary argument. Our principal argument on appeal is that the police violated the Fourth Amendment by detaining and searching Todd without even reasonable suspicion that any illegal activity was taking place.

Except when trying to avoid a waiver of an argument, you should not give the appearance of evading questions from the bench. Instead, you should confront and answer the questions directly. To answer judges' questions effectively, you must come to the argument thoroughly prepared. In particular, you should be ready to

- discuss the facts, holding, and reasoning of any case that you seek to rely on or to distinguish;
- cite to the record to identify the source of facts on which you rely; and
- discuss the policy implications of alternative holdings among which the court must choose.

An excellent method of preparing for the oral argument is to hold practice sessions with colleagues acting as judges. Your colleagues can provide constructive criticism and can help you anticipate the questions likely to be asked by the judges in the actual oral argument.

Even with excellent preparation, you may not always anticipate every question that a judge will ask you. If you cannot formulate a satisfactory answer to a truly unexpected and excessively challenging question, you probably will do better to acknowledge the difficulty of the question and to offer to address it in your rebuttal or in a supplementary brief than to simply bluff or brush the question aside.

Because you cannot always predict the number of questions from the bench, you must build maximum flexibility into your argument. You should be prepared to do either of the following or anything in between:

- present your arguments without interruption until your time elapses or you otherwise finish your argument; or
- present a brief introduction, respond without break to a series of questions that takes up all your allotted time, and request that the court permit you to end with a prepared conclusion no longer than a few sentences.

3. The Conclusion

You should end your argument on a compelling note, perhaps with a summary of your strongest points. A carefully planned conclusion will be particularly helpful if persistent questioning from the bench prevents you from covering all the points that you had planned to address in your oral argument. Faced with the impending expiration of your allotted time, you can fall back on the conclusion as a quick means of stating your points, if only in summary fashion.

D. Nervousness and Verbal Stumbling

All but the most experienced oral advocates feel some anxiety at the prospect of facing an inquisitive panel of judges in a public setting. If you feel such anxiety, you may be concerned that your nervousness will interfere with your speech patterns, causing your voice to shake or causing you to stumble over your words or to pause to collect your thoughts. You need not worry excessively about such problems for two reasons.

First, as long as the judge can understand you, the substance of your arguments and of your responses to questions will be more important than your charisma and stage presence. Some debate competitions may exalt form over substance: You may earn points if you can glibly respond to a judge's questions without pause, or lose points if you occasionally stumble over a difficult word. In actual oral arguments, however, a judge will be more concerned with establishing a genuine dialogue with you. She will not be uncomfortable with a few moments of silence from you; indeed, most judges will expect you to pause to think deeply before answering a particularly difficult question. Moreover, if you speak sufficiently slowly and clearly to make yourself understood, most judges will forgive you for the occasional verbal stumbling that nervousness may produce.

Second, you can minimize distracting imperfections in your delivery caused by nervousness. Perhaps the best way to bring such nervousness under control is to approach your oral argument with the confidence that comes from thorough preparation. If you have carefully prepared your analysis, mastered the facts and the record, anticipated questions, and rehearsed your argument before colleagues playing the role of inquisitive judges, you can confidently assume that you will bring an expertise to the courtroom that the judge will appreciate.

To deal with nervousness at the beginning of your argument, you can prepare a carefully worded introduction that you can commit to memory, so that you will not find yourself groping for words at the outset. Then, after you have warmed up your speaking voice, you can speak more flexibly from a rough outline of your main argument before closing with a carefully planned conclusion.

III. Summary

Effective advocacy requires sound analysis, sensible organization, and effective writing style. In addition to the matters examined in Chapter 16, you should adopt a persuasive writing style and carefully prepare an oral argument that strategically supplements your brief.

The following chapters examine further techniques of persuasive writing in the context of particular legal documents.

Exercise 17-2

Motion to Dismiss

Use the instructions below to draft a brief supporting or opposing a motion to dismiss a complaint.

Under Federal Rule of Civil Procedure 8(a)(2), a complaint must include "a short and plain statement of the claim showing that the pleader is entitled to relief." Under Rule 12(b)(6), a defendant may move to dismiss all or part of a complaint "for failure to state a claim upon which relief can be granted." Many states have adopted identical provisions in their state rules of civil procedure.

The imaginary state of Calzona has adopted the language of Rules 8(a)(2) and 12(b)(6) in a state rule of civil procedure, Calz. R. Civ. P. 8(a)(2), 12(b)(6) (2009). Unless your professor instructs otherwise, you may assume that the Calzona courts agree with the standards for evaluating the sufficiency of complaints that are set forth in *Greenwood v. Taft, Stettinius & Hollister*, 105 Ohio App. 3d 295, 297, 663 N.E.2d 1030, 1031 (Ohio Ct. App. 1995), or *McCurry v. Chevy Chase Bank, FSB*, 233 P.3d 861 (Wash. 2010) (for state procedure, rejecting new federal "plausibility" requirement).

Study Count I of the sample complaint in Appendix VI, Assignment 2, which alleges breach of a promise to marry. For purposes of this exercise, disregard

Count II of the complaint, and assume that Count I, in paragraphs I through XIII, constitutes the entire complaint. Research the law in your state, or in a state designated by your professor, to determine whether state law provides a claim for relief for such a breach, whether the designated state's law instead abandons or restricts such a claim, or whether the state's law has not yet addressed this question. As attorney for the defendant, James Clyde, determine whether you have good legal grounds to file a motion to dismiss the complaint for failure to state a claim, or at least to dismiss some of the complaint's requests for certain kinds of relief.

If you conclude that you can file a motion to dismiss in good faith, consider whether filing the motion represents a good expenditure of your client's resources. You might ask whether the motion has a good chance of succeeding, even assuming the truth of the allegations in the complaint.

If you conclude that filing a motion to dismiss represents sound strategy, prepare a motion using the following template, and with any further formatting required by your professor:

CALZONA SUPERIOR COURT
WARMS SPRINGS COUNTY

Georgia Anne TUCKER,
      Plaintiff,
 	
v.
 	
James CLYDE,
      Defendant.
	No. CIV-9X-79
	
	MOTION TO DISMISS
	
	(Oral argument requested)

Defendant, James Clyde, moves this Court to . . . . [State in plain language precisely what disposition you request. If you can do so in a simple clause or sentence, add a brief preview or summary of the general legal ground on which you base your request.]

                    [Signature of student representing Clyde]
                    [Name of student signing motion]
                    [Fictitious address of law firm]
                    Attorney for Defendant, James Clyde
                    [Date]

You should accompany the motion with a supporting brief. A brief in support of a motion was traditionally titled "Memorandum of Points and Authorities" and is now more commonly titled "Memorandum of Law." You may begin your brief with the following heading:

**MEMORANDUM OF LAW
IN SUPPORT OF MOTION TO DISMISS**

The body of your brief should include three parts:

I.   **Facts** [or "Introduction," or "Background," or "Statement of the Case"]

II. **Argument**

III. **Conclusion**

If the law in your designated state permits good faith argument on both sides of this issue, and if you are assigned to draft a brief opposing the motion, begin with a cover page that identifies the court, the parties, and the signing attorney in the same manner as in the motion. However, replace "Motion to Dismiss" with "Opposition to Defendant Clyde's Motion to Dismiss," and identify "Plaintiff, Georgia Anne Tucker" as the represented party. Below that, without stating a motion of your own, you can simply state the plaintiff's intent to oppose the motion, perhaps with a very brief reference to the nature of your argument. You can then begin your brief with the same heading as above, except with the phrase "IN OPPOSITION TO" in place of "IN SUPPORT OF."

Use the above format and the skills that you have acquired from Part VI to draft a short, simple brief supporting your motion, or one opposing the motion that you earlier submitted or that a classmate has submitted. In addition, be prepared to orally argue your position before an instructor or classmate posing as the trial judge.

For a similar exercise, complete Assignment 1 in Appendix VI.

Part VII

Pretrial Advocacy—

Pleadings and Motions

You might file different kinds of pleadings and briefs to a court from the inception of a lawsuit to its final disposition in a court of last resort. Part VI of this book ended with an exercise that introduced you to a motion to dismiss a complaint. This part of the book explores other kinds of pretrial pleadings and briefs with the aim of preparing you to initiate or respond to any form of written advocacy. Part VIII will examine appellate brief-writing.

The following three chapters introduce you to three kinds of pretrial written advocacy: pleadings, motions for summary judgment, and pretrial motions to exclude evidence. When combined with the motion to dismiss exercise at the end of Part VI, and with the discussion of appellate briefs in Part VIII, Part VII should provide you with the skills and confidence you need to perform any task of written advocacy.

Chapter 18

Pleadings

I. The Complaint

"A civil action is commenced by filing a complaint with the court."[1] Because a complaint is such a fundamental and significant document, law schools are increasingly offering students opportunities to draft complaints in legal writing or clinical courses. Still, when faced with the task of preparing a complaint, you may be tempted to turn to canned language in formbooks.

Forms may provide general guidance in some cases. In fact, many jurisdictions have officially authorized pleading forms for certain kinds of suits. Nonetheless, you will more quickly and thoroughly master pleading skills if you understand the components of a complaint well enough to draft one "from scratch." Your primary tools in such a task are the results of your

---

1. FED. R. CIV. P. 3.

investigation of facts and your knowledge of the applicable law. Beyond that, rules of procedure and local court rules provide the necessary guidance.

A. Format and Content

Local court rules on pleading often specify a standard caption that identifies the case and the nature of the document. For example, the Rules of Practice for the United States District Court for the District of Arizona specify the line spacing and precise location in the caption on the first page of a document for, among other things, the following information: (1) the name, address, e-mail address, state bar attorney number, telephone and fax number of the representing attorney, and the party represented; (2) the title of the court; (3) the names of the parties in a "title of the action"; (4) the docket number (or a space for it if the clerk has not yet assigned one); and (5) a designation of the nature of the document.[2]

More substantively, Federal Rule of Civil Procedure 8(a) requires a complaint to contain three elements:

(1) a short and plain statement of the grounds for the court's jurisdiction . . . ;

(2) a short and plain statement of the claim showing that the pleader is entitled to relief; and

(3) a demand for the relief sought, which may include relief in the alternative or different types of relief.

Each of these elements warrants further examination.

1. Jurisdictional Statement

The jurisdictional statement is particularly important in a complaint filed in federal court, because the subject matter jurisdiction of federal courts is limited to that authorized by Article III of the United States Constitution and by federal statutes.[3] Therefore, in the initial paragraphs of a complaint in federal court, you should allege facts establishing subject matter jurisdiction based on a federal question,[4] diversity of citizenship,[5] or a special statutory grant of jurisdiction.[6] Although the jurisdictional statement is sufficient if it alleges facts that support the court's exercise of jurisdiction,[7] federal pleaders customarily cite to the specific statutes that grant jurisdiction:

---

2. D. ARIZ. LRCIV. 7.1(a); *see also* FED. R. CIV. P. app. at Forms 1, 2 (caption and signature block, including e-mail address of attorney).

3. *See, e.g.,* Mayor v. Cooper, 73 U.S. (6 Wall.) 247, 252 (1868).

4. *See* 28 U.S.C. § 1331 (2006).

5. *Id.* § 1332.

6. *See, e.g.,* 42 U.S.C. § 2000e-5(f)(3) (2006) (granting jurisdiction of actions brought under Title VII of the Civil Rights Act of 1964).

7. Aguirre v. Auto. Teamsters, 633 F.2d 168, 174 (9th Cir. 1980).

3. This claim arises under Title VII of the Civil Rights Act of 1964; therefore, this court has subject matter jurisdiction under 42 U.S.C. § 2000e-5(f)(3) and 28 U.S.C. § 1331.[8]

Pleading subject matter jurisdiction is less important in state court than in federal court, because most state trial courts are courts of general jurisdiction. When state pleaders address subject matter jurisdiction at all, it is often with simple introductory allegations that the amount in controversy exceeds the amount reserved for state courts of limited jurisdiction. This is often coupled with a citation to the state constitutional or statutory provision that authorizes the court's exercise of general trial jurisdiction.

Nonetheless, many state rules of civil procedure have adopted all the elements of the governing federal rule of civil procedure, thus requiring some statement of "jurisdiction" in state court complaints. Because a special allegation of subject matter jurisdiction is less clearly necessary in a state court complaint, state pleaders often begin their complaints with allegations of *personal* jurisdiction over the defendants. Such statements typically introduce the parties and allege in fairly conclusory fashion that the defendant has engaged in conduct in the state out of which the claim arises or has otherwise established the requisite contacts with the state.

Some federal complaints also include allegations establishing that the court has personal jurisdiction over the defendant, even though the appendix of forms to the federal rules includes no such allegations in their samples.[9] Assuming that lack of personal jurisdiction is treated as an affirmative defense for pleading purposes, a complaint will not be insufficient for failure to affirmatively plead personal jurisdiction over the defendant.

2. Claim for Relief

Federal Rule of Civil Procedure 8(a)(2) omits any reference to "facts" in its requirement of a statement of the claim for relief. Nonetheless, "Rule 8(a)(2) envisages the statement of circumstances, occurrences, and events in support of the claim presented."[10] Most people would use the word "fact" to describe allegations of that nature. Similarly, this book will use "fact" in this context while attempting to avoid the historical confusion surrounding the term.

Thus, in the main body of the complaint, you will allege facts and conclusions of liability that establish entitlement to relief. This may require pre-

---

8. *See also* FED. R. CIV. P. app. at Form 7 (form allegations for federal question jurisdiction include both requisite fact allegations and citation to federal statute granting jurisdiction).

9. *See id.*

10. Advisory Committee on Rules for Civil Procedure, *Report of Proposed Amendments to the Rules of Civil Procedure for the United States District Courts* 18-19 (1955), *reprinted in* Richard H. Field, Benjamin Kaplan & Kevin M. Clermont, CIVIL PROCEDURE: MATERIALS FOR A BASIC COURSE 1151 (10th ed. 2010)

liminary legal research as well as a reasonable investigation of the facts, to help satisfy your ethical obligations under Rule 11.[11] Your knowledge of the law will enable you to identify legally significant facts, and your knowledge of the case will help you to determine what facts you can allege reasonably and in good faith.

To draft your claim for relief effectively, you must determine

1. the extent, if any, to which you should supplement fact allegations with references to the law;
2. the specific content of the fact allegations; and
3. the appropriate level of specificity of the allegations.

a. Allegations of Fact and Citations to Law

Your complaint normally should allege facts and ultimate conclusions establishing a claim for relief; you need not cite to supporting legal authority.[12] Thus, you need allege only two of the three elements of the syllogism of deductive reasoning:

[Major premise: Rule of Law]
Minor premise: Allegations of Fact
Conclusion: Allegation of Liability or Other Ultimate
                       Conclusion

A complaint with the minimum necessary elements will explicitly set forth the minor premise and the conclusion, and it will leave the major premise implicit.

For a simple example, a form complaint appended to the Federal Rules of Civil Procedure states a claim on a promissory note, alleging the subsidiary facts that the defendant has failed to pay money owed to the plaintiff on the note:

> 2. On <u>date,</u> the defendant executed and delivered a note promising to pay the plaintiff on <u>date</u> the sum of \$_____ with interest at the rate of ___ percent. A copy of the note [is attached as Exhibit A] [is summarized as follows: _____.]
> 3. The defendant has not paid the amount owed.[13]

These sample allegations do not explicitly state the major premise that a promise to pay money expressed in a written promissory note is enforceable under the common law of contracts or under some other legal author-

---

11. *See supra* Chapter 15, Section II.B (discussing ethical duties in filing documents with the court).

12. *E.g.,* Skinner v. Switzer, 131 S. Ct. 1289, 1296 (2011) ("a complaint need not pin plaintiff's claim for relief to a precise legal theory" or "provide an exposition of his legal argument"); Doss v. South Cent. Bell Tel. Co., 834 F.2d 421, 424-25 (5th Cir. 1987) (improper to dismiss complaint that pleaded improper legal theory if the allegations state a claim on any other legal theory).

13. FED. R. CIV. P. app. at Form 10, alternative allegation (a).

ity. Whether the alleged facts state a claim for relief under applicable legal authority can be addressed in subsequent proceedings, such as on a motion to dismiss.[14]

Thus, in practice, citation to specific legal authority is much less common in the claim for relief than in the jurisdictional statement. The only references to legal authority commonly found in claims for relief are descriptive headings that introduce counts with general legal theories of relief, such as "Negligence," "Wrongful Discharge," "Employment Discrimination," or "Breach of Contract."

Nonetheless, a pleader will sometimes cite to authority in the claim for relief for a strategic purpose. For example, in cases in which the plaintiff seeks a settlement at the outset of litigation, his attorney may briefly cite to authority in the complaint to demonstrate to the defendant that the claim is substantial and that further litigation is unlikely to reduce the risk of liability. In most cases, however, the attorney could achieve the same result with a demand letter that explains the merits of the claim. Such a letter could either precede or accompany the complaint.

In other cases, an attorney may cite to legal authority in the body of the complaint because the claim is admittedly novel and thus would not be readily recognized as meritorious on the basis of the factual allegations alone. The author of the complaint may hope that the citations will help the judge understand the advocate's legal theory and keep an open mind pending further proceedings.

When the allegations are unusually complex or the underlying legal theories novel or complex, some attorneys recommend a middle ground: Limit your allegations to factual matters but explain the nature of the claims and allegations in a short "Introduction" or "Overview" that precedes the specific factual allegations. In one or two paragraphs, you can help the reader see the whole forest before entering the confusing stands of trees by (1) briefly identifying any novel legal theories on which your claims depend, or (2) summarizing how numerous complicated transactions or other facts relate to one another, or both.[15]

b. Substance of Allegations

One writer has recommended that a claim for relief state the journalist's "five Ws": who, what, where, when, and why.[16]

Who—In some complaints, you will introduce the parties in the jurisdictional allegations. Otherwise, your statement of the claim for relief should identify them and their relationship to one another. It should also identify any other significant actors.

What, Where, When—The statement of the claim should describe the events that give rise to the claim. You should take care to allege all facts

---

14. *See* FED. R. CIV. P. 12(b)(6).

15. The author thanks Peter Friedman for sharing this idea.

16. Delmar Karlen, PROCEDURE BEFORE TRIAL IN A NUTSHELL 41-42 (1972).

or conclusions needed to support the request for relief. For example, you should support a request for specific performance with an allegation that the legal remedy of money damages is inadequate.

Why—You should allege any state of mind that is material to the claim or to the availability of special relief. For example, a request for punitive damages in a common law tort claim must be supported by an allegation of malice, willful misconduct, or at least recklessness, depending on the jurisdiction.

You need not allege all matters that may ultimately be in dispute; you need allege only the legal elements of your client's claim for relief, with sufficient factual allegations to make the claim plausible. Affirmative defenses must be pleaded in the answer,[17] and the complaint need not anticipate them. The federal rules list 18 affirmative defenses;[18] statutes and case law may help you define the burdens of pleading on other matters. In case of doubt, you should plead a matter as part of the claim for relief.

For example, suppose that the jurisdiction in which the complaint is filed recognizes a cause of action for intentional infliction of emotional distress on proof of four elements: (1) The defendant engaged in extreme and outrageous conduct (2) with the intent to cause severe emotional distress or with reckless disregard for the possibility of those consequences, and (3) the conduct caused the plaintiff to suffer (4) severe emotional distress.[19] After introductory allegations establishing personal jurisdiction and identifying Jansen as the plaintiff and Bostich as one of the defendants, the count for this claim should allege facts supporting each of the four elements of the prima facie case:

COUNT I

Infliction of Emotional Distress

Relationship of parties

3. Jansen worked on an assembly line at the Zydeco Radio factory under the direct supervision of Bostich. As Jansen's supervisor, Bostich had the authority to impose production quotas on Jansen and to impose discipline, including termination, for failure to meet quotas.

Conduct

4. From April 1 to June 10, 2014, Bostich engaged in the extreme and outrageous conduct of

---

17. FED. R. CIV. P. 8(c)(1). Rule 8(c)(1) formerly listed 19 affirmative defenses, FED. R. CIV. P. 8(c)(1) (2007), but the reference to "discharge in bankruptcy" was eliminated in 2010 to avoid confusion with a statute that addressed the effect of discharge, 11 U.S.C. § 524(a) (2006).

18. *Id.*

19. *See, e.g.*, Watts v. Golden Age Nursing Home, 619 P.2d 1032, 1035 (Ariz. 1980) (citing RESTATEMENT (SECOND) OF TORTS § 46).

imposing impossible production quotas on Jansen
and causing Jansen to believe that his job security
depended on his meeting the quotas.[20]

5. Bostich maliciously engaged in this conduct **State of mind**
for the purpose of causing Jansen to suffer severe
emotional distress. Alternatively, Bostich recklessly
disregarded the likelihood that Jansen would suffer
such distress.[21]

6. On June 10, 2010, as a direct result of Bos- **Causation and**
tich's conduct, Jansen suffered a complete nervous **severe distress**
breakdown requiring bed rest for three weeks and
extensive medical care.

7. Jansen continues to suffer insomnia, head- **Injuries**
aches, inability to concentrate at work, general
nervousness, and other emotional distress as a
result of Bostich's conduct. In an effort to address
these symptoms, Jansen has frequently consulted
a general physician and a psychological counselor,
incurring substantial medical expenses.

In contrast, even if the allegations raise some question of whether the
statute of limitations has expired, the complaint need not affirmatively allege
that the statute of limitations has not expired or has been tolled. Instead,
expiration of the statute of limitations is an affirmative defense that the
defendant has the burden of pleading.[22]

c. Specificity of Fact Allegations

The early, rigid common law forms of action largely disappeared in this
country in the nineteenth century with widespread enactment of versions of
the Field Code, named for David Dudley Field, which required complaints
to set forth a "statement of the facts constituting the cause of action, in ordinary and concise language."[23] In the twentieth century, the federal system
and most states replaced their versions of the Field Code with rules permitting pleadings that give the court and the opposing party more general

---

20. Whether the allegations of paragraphs 3 and 4 establish "extreme and outrageous
conduct" will depend on the law of that jurisdiction and could be litigated on a motion to
dismiss for failure to state a claim. *See, e.g.*, FED. R. CIV. P. 12(b)(6).

21. This allegation of scienter should suffice not only to satisfy the second element of the
tort but to support a request for punitive damages as well.

22. FED. R. CIV. P. 8(c).

23. *See* Richard L. Marcus, *The Puzzling Persistence of Pleading Practice*, 76 TEX. L. REV.
1749, 1753 & n.28 (1998) (discussing and quoting the Field Code).

notice of most claims and defenses.[24] Federal Rule of Civil Procedure 8(a)(2) requires the main portion of a complaint to include only a "short and plain statement of the claim showing that the pleader is entitled to relief." For the most part, revelation of specific factual and evidentiary details is left to the discovery and disclosure process, motions for summary judgment, and the pretrial conference.[25]

(i) Notice Pleading—Minimum Requirements

Of course, a bare allegation of liability or legal conclusions without any supporting factual context would be insufficient even under the relaxed "notice pleading" standards of the federal rules: Although Rule 8(a)(2) "does not require 'detailed factual allegations,'" it does require more than "'labels and conclusions,'" "'a formulaic recitation of the elements of a cause of action,'" "'naked assertion[s]' devoid of 'further factual enhancement,'"[26] or "conclusory statements without . . . factual context."[27]

The appropriate level of detail or generality of the factual context can be illustrated by a continuum that represents varying degrees of specificity in fact allegations. The continuum begins with allegations of legal conclusions based on underlying facts. It gains steadily in specificity until it presents specific evidence from which factual inferences can be drawn and on which factual conclusions can be based:

LEGAL CONCLUSION	FACTUAL CONCLUSION	SPECIFIC EVIDENCE
Negligence	D exceeded the speed limit, breaching duty of care	eyewitness estimate of speed and analysis of skid marks

As an example of extreme specificity, a complaint could state a claim for negligent operation of an automobile by alleging each bit of evidence with which the plaintiff hopes to prove negligence at trial:

3. . . . Jill Graham and Ben Cooper were standing at the corner of 7th Avenue and Washington Street in Smallville at noon and observed the defendant driving his automobile west on Washington Street past 7th Avenue and toward 8th Avenue. Each of them observed that the defendant was traveling at a substantially greater speed than all other cars proceeding normally in the same direction, passing them easily. An expert who examined skid marks at the accident scene

---

24. *See id.* at 753-54.

25. *See* FED. R. CIV. P. 16, 26-37, 56.

26. Ashcroft v. Iqbal, 129 S. Ct. 1937, 1949 (2009) (quoting Bell Atl. Corp. v. Twombly, 550 U.S. 544, 555, 557 (2007)).

27. *Id.* at 1954.

estimated that the defendant's automobile was traveling at 40-50 miles per hour when it entered the intersection of Washington Street and 8th Avenue. . . .

Nearer to the other extreme, the complaint could allege the ultimate legal conclusion of negligence, coupled with a brief description of factual context:

2. On January 1, 2014, at the intersection of Washington Street and 8th Avenue in Smallville, defendant negligently drove a motor vehicle against the plaintiff, striking her in the crosswalk.

3. As a result, ...

This second example is adapted from a sample form in the Federal Rules of Civil Procedure, with information about date and place replacing blanks in the form.[28] This example illustrates the apparent acceptability of surprisingly terse allegations on simple matters under federal notice pleading. It provides the defendant with general notice of the event that allegedly created legal liability, and the legal classification of the alleged wrongdoing (negligence), but little more.

(ii) Plausibility and Other Departures from Minimal Notice Pleading

Very few complaints, however, state the claim for relief in the exceedingly spare manner illustrated by the federal forms. The reasons for this are varied. Some states have retained rules that require greater specificity for complaints in state court than are traditionally required by the federal standards for notice pleading. Even under the federal rules, moreover, some kinds of matters must be alleged with greater specificity than is ordinarily required. Finally, as a matter of strategy and style, many advocates prefer to allege claims in greater detail than the minimum degree required by the applicable rules.

In states that retain the more fact-oriented pleading requirements of the Field Code, the appropriate level of specificity probably would lie somewhere in the middle of the continuum. For example, the complaint might allege that the defendant operated the car negligently by exceeding the speed limit, but it need not contain allegations of the specific evidence of speeding, such as the analysis of skid marks.[29]

---

28. FED. R. CIV. P. app. at Form 11 ¶¶ 2, 3; *see also* Swierkiewicz v. Sorema, 534 U.S. 506, 508 (2002) (under federal general notice pleading standards, a complaint need not "contain specific facts establishing a prima facie case of discrimination").

29. *See generally* Field et al., *supra* note 10, at 1148-49, 1152 (discussing Garcia v. Hilton Hotels Int'l, Inc., 97 F. Supp. 5 (D. P.R. 1951) and stating that a code pleader should not "plead his evidence").

Even the federal rules occasionally depart from the minimal demands of notice pleading. Rule 9(b), for example, provides that allegations of "fraud or mistake," must state the circumstances with particularity.[30]

Moreover, the federal rules governing pleading and motions to dismiss are subject to interpretation, and courts in some jurisdictions have developed a reputation for demanding greater specificity than might seem to be required by the plain language of the rules.[31] In 2007 and 2009, the U.S. Supreme Court joined this trend by requiring allegations in federal complaints to "state a claim to relief that is plausible on its face."[32] This new "plausibility" standard does not require allegations that establish the "probability" of liability,[33] nor does it transfer the more rigid particularity requirement of Rule 9(b) to Rule 8(a)(2).[34] On a motion to dismiss under Rule 12(b)(6), however, the plausibility requirement does direct a federal judge to use "experience and common sense" to determine whether the factual allegations permit a plausible inference of wrongdoing, rather than the "mere possibility" of wrongdoing.[35] For example, if the allegations of fact, assumed to be true, more readily permit an inference of innocent behavior than of wrongdoing, the complaint may be insufficient to resist dismissal under the plausibility standard.[36]

The plausibility requirement should not add significantly to the pleading burdens in a large percentage of cases. For one thing, states that have adopted notice pleading standards are not bound to adopt the plausibility requirement as an interpretation of their state versions of Rules 8(a)(2) and 12(b)(6).[37] For another, the addition of the plausibility requirement could be eliminated in the federal system by congressional legislation or by amendment of Rule 8(a)(2) or 12(b)(6) at the recommendation of the Judicial Conference.[38] Moreover, even when it does apply, the plausibility requirement should be easily satisfied in complaints that allege simple matters such

---

30. Fed. R. Civ. P. 9(b); *see also* Ziemba v. Cascade Int'l, Inc., 256 F.3d 1194, 1202 (11th Cir. 2001) (explaining purposes of Rule 9(b) but noting that it is not intended to abrogate the concept of notice pleading).

31. *See, e.g.*, Marcus, *supra* note 23, at 1774 ("courts sometimes construct dubious new pleading barriers," such as when they "apparently still strain to justify the application of [Rule 9(b)'s particularity requirements] outside their natural sphere"); Patricia M. Wald, *Summary Judgment at Sixty*, 76 Tex. L. Rev. 1897, 1941-42 (1998) (partly "fueled by the overloaded dockets of the last two decades," courts are increasingly using summary judgment to weed out marginal cases, and "appear to be requiring plaintiffs to plead facts with ever greater detail in order to survive motions to dismiss").

32. Ashcroft v. Iqbal, 556 U.S. 662, 678 (2009) (quoting Bell Atl. Corp. v. Twombly, 550 U.S. 544, 570 (2007)). *Iqbal* and *Twombly* effectively overrule Conley v. Gibson, 355 U.S. 41 (1957).

33. *Iqbal*, 556 U.S. at 678 (quoting *Twombly*, 550 U.S. at 556).

34. *Id.* at 686-87.

35. *Id.* at 678 (quoting or citing *Twombly*, 550 U.S. at 556, 557-58).

36. *Id.* at 678-80. The court will not assume the truth of allegations that amount to legal conclusions. *Id.* at 679-80.

37. *E.g.*, McCurry v. Chevy Chase Bank, FSB, 233 P.3d 861 (Wash. 2010) (rejecting plausibility requirement for the State of Washington's rules of procedure).

38. Bills to overturn *Iqbal* and *Twombly* were introduced in 2009. Notice Pleading Restoration Act of 2009, S. 1504, 111th Cong. (July 22, 2009); Open Access to Courts Act of 2009, H.R. 4115, 111th Cong. (Nov. 19, 2009).

as a breach of contract through delayed and substandard construction, or a shopkeeper's negligent failure to maintain safe premises by neglecting to clean up a spill. The new standard will more likely be a factor in claims perceived to be more speculative, such as those relying on general or circumstantial allegations to support an inference that independent entities acted in concert pursuant to a conspiracy or that a remote party directed the allegedly wrongful acts of others.[39]

(iii) Strategic Considerations

Once you have identified the minimum standards of specificity for allegations under applicable rules, you must determine whether to allege facts in substantially greater detail than is required. This determination may turn on your personal style and on strategic considerations peculiar to the case at hand.

Some attorneys will prefer to allege little more than is minimally required by the rules in each case. They may argue that unnecessarily complete and specific allegations could prematurely commit the plaintiff to a particular factual theory of the case, perhaps requiring amendment of the complaint after discovery is underway.

Some commentators, however, have argued for relatively complete and compelling narratives in complaints, to advance effective advocacy at the earliest stages of litigation.[40] For example, if a claim rests on clear and compelling facts that paint a vivid picture of injustice, strategic considerations may argue in favor of telling the client's story in greater detail than is required by applicable rules of procedure.[41] Alternatively, if a claim arises from complex events, detailed allegations may help the reader understand the relationships between multiple parties and numerous transactions.

In summary, once pleading rules have been satisfied, any additional specificity in your allegations is partly a matter of style and strategy. As long as you take care to allege facts supporting every element of your prima facie case, you can tailor the specificity of your allegations to your personal style and strategic needs. Even so, you should start with general allegations and add specificity only if you have good reason to do so. If excessively detailed allegations unnecessarily transform your pleading into a cumbersome tool

---

39. *E.g.*, Ashcroft v. Iqbal, 556 U.S. 662 (2009) (conclusory allegations that United States Attorney General condoned or shared the alleged discriminatory intent of lower-level F.B.I. agents); Bell Atl. Corp. v. Twombly, 550 U.S. 544 (2007) (allegations of parallel activity of firms was more consistent with innocent behavior than with a conspiracy in violation of antitrust laws); Moss v. U.S. Secret Serv., 572 F.3d 962 (9th Cir. 2009) (conclusory allegations that protestors were removed pursuant to a policy of the Secret Service to suppress anti-Bush message).

40. Elizabeth Fajans & Mary R. Falk, *Untold Stories: Restoring Narrative to Pleading Practice*, 15 Legal Writing: J. Legal Writing Inst. 3 (2009).

41. *See, e.g.*, Elizabeth Fajans, Mary R. Falk & Helene S. Shapo, Writing for Law Practice 37 (2004) (advocating for "artful pleading" rather than bare notice pleading, especially in cases with compelling stories, such as civil rights claims).

for its intended audiences, you may face a court that is receptive to a motion to strike your pleading.[42]

3. Request for Relief

Your complaint should end with a simple statement of the relief sought by your client. The main request for relief typically is for an injunction, an award of money damages, or both. Consult local rules to determine whether you must request a specific dollar amount for some kinds of damages and an unspecified amount for others.

Additionally, you should request an award of reasonable costs and attorneys' fees if your client has a legal basis for such an award. Finally, you can retain flexibility by closing the request for relief with a catch-all request for "other appropriate relief":

Jansen therefore requests judgment granting the following relief:

    1. an award of compensatory damages in an amount to be set at trial;

    2. an award of punitive damages in an amount to be set at trial;

    3. an award of reasonable costs and attorneys' fees; and

    4. such other relief as the court deems appropriate.

B. Style and Organization

1. Writing Style

Some of lawyers' stuffiest jargon can be found in antiquated pleadings:

Comes now the plaintiff before this honorable court and, through his attorneys, Jenkins, Brown, and Little, alleges, pleads, and avers as follows:

. . . .

3. That the defendant did employ said plaintiff as a designer of clothes . . . ;

4. That on July 6, 1927, said defendant did . . . ;

Wherefore, the plaintiff prays that this honorable court grant judgment . . . .

---

42. *See* Anserve Ins. Serv., Inc. v. Albrecht, 960 P.2d 1159, 1161 (Ariz. 1998) (en banc) ("Early on, the trial judge should have granted the motion to strike" a 269-page complaint.); McHenry v. Renne, 84 F.3d 1172, 1180 (9th Cir. 1996) (a complaint that was "written more as a press release, prolix in evidentiary detail, yet without simplicity, conciseness and clarity . . . fails to perform the essential functions of a complaint").

The federal rules reject jargon in favor of plain English: "Each allegation must be simple, concise, and direct. No technical form is required."[43] When stated in plain English, the allegations in the preceding example are unquestionably simpler and more concise:

Plaintiff alleges:

. . . .

3. The defendant employed the plaintiff as a designer of clothes. . . .

4. On July 6, 1927, the defendant . . . .

Plaintiff requests the following relief: . . . .

2. Organization

To facilitate analysis of the claims by the court and the parties, set forth the allegations of your complaint in consecutively numbered paragraphs. Separation of the statements of different claims for relief into separate counts may be permissible or required, depending on the circumstances.

If you have joined separate claims for relief based on different transactions or occurrences, federal rules require you to state the claims in separate counts "[i]f doing so would promote clarity."[44] Otherwise, presentation of allegations in separate counts appears to be discretionary.

Even if your client's claims arise out of a single transaction, separate counts may be helpful if you rely on distinct legal theories that are based on different fact allegations. For example, a consumer injured by a faulty electrical appliance may have a cause of action against the retailer on two legal theories: products liability in tort and breach of a contractual warranty. If you divide the allegations into separate counts, you can identify which fact allegations are material to each theory of relief. If some facts are common to both theories, one count can incorporate some of the allegations of the other:

COUNT I
Products Liability

4. On January 1, 2011, Green purchased a microwave oven from Retailer.

5. The microwave oven had an unreasonably dangerous defect. . . .

. . . .

---

43. FED. R. CIV. P. 8(d)(1). The Federal Rules of Civil Procedure were stylistically revised in 2007 to state the rules more concisely and in plain English. Therefore, much of the case law will refer to rules in their prior form, in slightly different language and organization of subsections.

44. FED. R. CIV. P. 10(b).

COUNT II
Breach of Warranty

8. Green realleges the allegations in paragraphs 4-7.

9. Babcock Appliance Center warranted the microwave oven to be free of defects. . . .

You must also exercise discretion to determine whether to follow each count with a separate request for relief or to consolidate them in a single request after presenting all counts. As with separation of theories into counts, separation of requests for relief to accompany different counts may be helpful if the available remedies vary with each count. For example, if punitive damages are available only on the products liability count and if attorneys' fees are available only on the count for breach of warranty, separate requests for relief after each count may facilitate subsequent analysis of the claims. On the other hand, if the requests for relief on different counts are identical, consolidation in a single request obviously avoids pointless repetition.

II. The Answer

To avoid judgment against him by default, the defendant must respond to a complaint by filing an answer or other appropriate response.[45] The defendant may move to dismiss the complaint on its face before filing an answer.[46] The answer must admit or deny each allegation of the complaint.[47] In addition, the answer may set forth any affirmative defenses,[48] assert counterclaims against the plaintiff,[49] or both. If the answer asserts a counterclaim, the original plaintiff must file an answer to the counterclaim.[50]

A. Admissions and Denials

If a defendant contests liability, he obviously is prepared to deny in good faith some of the material allegations of the complaint. On the other hand, nearly every complaint will contain some allegations that the defendant admits. Therefore, the typical answer will not generally deny all allegations of the complaint; instead, it will address each paragraph of the complaint and identify areas of dispute.[51] For example, an answer to the complaint

---

45. *See* FED. R. CIV. P. 12(a).
46. *See* FED. R. CIV. P. 12(b).
47. FED. R. CIV. P. 8(b)(1)(B).
48. *See* FED. R. CIV. P. 8(b)(1)(A), (c)(1).
49. *See* FED. R. CIV. P. 7(a), 8(a), (c)(2).
50. *See* FED. R. CIV. P. 7(a).
51. *See generally* FED. R. CIV. P. 8(b) (form of denials).

partially set forth earlier in this chapter might admit and deny allegations in the following manner:

ADMISSIONS AND DENIALS

1. Defendant Bostich admits the allegations in paragraphs 1-3 of Plaintiff Jansen's complaint.

2. Bostich denies the allegations in paragraph 4 of the complaint that he set impossible goals for Jansen and that he intimidated Jansen in his work. Bostich admits that he warned Jansen of the possibility of termination for failing to meet goals.

3. Bostich denies the allegations in paragraph 5 of the complaint.

4. Bostich has no information on which to form a belief in the truth of the allegations in paragraph 6 of the complaint, and he therefore denies them.

If the complaint is more than a few paragraphs long, it may help to match up the paragraphs of the complaint and answer, rather than admitting several paragraphs of allegations in the first paragraph of the answer:

1. Defendant Bostich admits the allegations in paragraph 1 of Plaintiff Jansen's complaint.

2. Defendant Bostich admits the allegations in paragraph 2 of the complaint.

3. Defendant Bostich admits the allegations in paragraph 3 of the complaint.

4. Bostich denies the allegations in paragraph 4 of the complaint that . . . .

One attorney even recommends that each paragraph of the answer restate or summarize the corresponding allegation of the complaint before admitting or denying it. The judge might be disposed to refer repeatedly to such a self-contained answer, rather than refer to the complaint, which would not include the defendant's denials.[52]

Conversely, you can consolidate your admissions and denials to maximum degree if you prefer the most concise possible answer:[53]

1. Defendant Bostich admits the allegations in paragraphs 1-3 of Plaintiff Jansen's complaint.

2. Bostich admits that he warned Jansen of the possibility of termination for failing to meet goals.

3. Bostich denies all other allegations.

---

52. Benjamin R. Norris, *Writing Pleadings*, ARIZ. ATT'Y, Dec. 2000, at 37.
53. *See* FED. R. CIV. P. 8(b)(3).

B. Affirmative Defenses

In a separate section of your answer, you should allege facts and conclusions supporting any affirmative defenses that your client, the defendant, may reasonably assert.[54] Even if the allegations of the complaint are true and are legally sufficient to state a claim for relief, a meritorious affirmative defense to the prima facie case will justify judgment for the defendant.

For example, in the litigation between Jansen and Bostich, suppose that the statute of limitations for tort actions in the jurisdiction is one year, that Jansen filed his complaint on June 9, 2011, and that Bostich last communicated a supervisory ultimatum to Jansen on June 6, 2010. Bostich may be prepared to argue that the statute of limitations has expired on the ground that Jansen's cause of action accrued at the latest on June 6, 2010, the date of Bostich's last act, rather than on June 10, 2010, the date of Jansen's nervous breakdown. If so, Bostich could assert this in fairly conclusory fashion as an affirmative defense:

AFFIRMATIVE DEFENSE

5. Bostich last exercised any supervisory control over Jansen on June 6, 2010. Therefore, Jansen's cause of action accrued more than one year before the filing of his complaint, and the statute of limitations bars his action.

C. Counterclaims

The defendant named in a complaint may himself wish to assert an independent claim for relief against the plaintiff. If so, the roles of the parties are reversed for purposes of the counterclaim, and the principles of pleading discussed in Section I above apply to the counterclaim.

For example, in the litigation between Jansen and Bostich, additional facts might support a claim against Jansen for battery:

COUNTERCLAIM
Battery

6. On the evening of July 16, 2010, Jansen struck Bostich over the head with a baseball bat as Bostich left the Zydeco Radio factory.

7. Jansen acted maliciously and for the specific purpose of causing serious injury to Bostich.

8. As a result of Jansen's malicious attack, Bostich lost consciousness, required treatment in a hospital emergency room, and suffered debilitating pain for 24 hours.

Therefore, Bostich requests the following relief: . . . .

---

54. *See* FED. R. CIV. P. 8(b)(1)(A), (c).

III. Summary

When drafting pleadings, follow the format prescribed by applicable rules. For example, federal rules require the drafter of a complaint to allege

1. jurisdiction,
2. a claim for relief, and
3. a demand for judgment.

In an answer, you

1. must admit or deny the allegations of the complaint, and
2. may also assert affirmative defenses or a counterclaim.

Generally, pleadings should allege ultimate conclusions and supporting facts but not legal standards. Although the claim for relief must plausibly allege all elements of the prima facie case, most allegations may be general and need not develop specific, evidentiary facts.

Exercise 18-1

Compare and critically evaluate the following three versions of a complaint in the same wrongful discharge action. Which level of specificity of allegations do you prefer? What other differences in style do the complaints reflect? Which styles do you prefer? Note that the line spacing of the sample complaints in this book do not conform with the line-spacing requirements of most local rules.

For further practice with pleadings, complete Assignments 2 through 4 in Appendix VI.

IN THE SUPERIOR COURT
MARICOPA COUNTY, ARIZONA

GEORGE BRYANT,
           Plaintiff,
 	
    v.
 	
MARIE JARDON, d.b.a.
Chez Marie,
           Defendant.
	No._____
	
	COMPLAINT

Plaintiff alleges:

COUNT 1

I

Plaintiff George Bryant is a resident of Phoenix, Arizona. Defendant Marie Jardon owns and operates Chez Marie, a restaurant located in Phoenix, Arizona.

II

Bryant worked for Jardon as a waiter at Chez Marie from August 16, 2012 to September 28, 2013.

III

At the time of his discharge on September 28, 2013, Bryant had an employment contract with Chez Marie that imposed substantive and procedural restrictions upon Jardon's right to terminate Bryant's employment.

IV

Acting through her agent, Mario Prieto, Jardon discharged Bryant on September 28, 2013, in breach of her employment contract with Bryant.

V

As a result of Jardon's breach of contract, Bryant has suffered lost wages and other incidental and consequential losses.

COUNT 2

VI

Bryant realleges and incorporates paragraphs I-V above.

VII

Acting through her agent, Jardon maliciously and unlawfully discharged Bryant for reasons that violate public policy, causing Bryant lost wages and other injuries.

Bryant therefore requests judgment granting the following relief:

1.   an order reinstating Bryant to his position as waiter at Chez Marie;

2.   an award of compensatory and punitive damages;

3.   an award of costs and attorneys' fees; and

4.   other appropriate relief.

Dated _____

                        by _____,

                        Thomas Sanchez

                        Simpson, Sanchez & Summers

                        303 North Central Avenue

                        Phoenix, Arizona 85002

                        (602) 229-1111

                        Bar No. 28371

                        Attorney for the plaintiff

ARIZONA SUPERIOR COURT
MARICOPA COUNTY

GEORGE BRYANT,
 	
    Plaintiff,
 	
  v.
 	
MARIE JARDON, d.b.a.
Chez Marie,
 	
    Defendant.
	No._____
	
	COMPLAINT

Plaintiff alleges:

1

BREACH OF PROMISE

1. Plaintiff George Bryant is a resident of Phoenix, Arizona. Defendant Marie Jardon owns and operates Chez Marie, a restaurant located in Phoenix, Arizona.

2. Bryant worked for Jardon as a waiter at Chez Marie from August 16, 2012 to September 28, 2013. Mario Prieto acted as the maître d' and supervisor of waiters at Chez Marie during Bryant's employment at Chez Marie. In all the events alleged below, Prieto acted on behalf of Jardon.

3. At the time of his discharge on September 28, 2013, Bryant had an employment contract with Chez Marie that included the terms of an "Employee Handbook."

4. The Employee Handbook contains promises of job security, including promises that (i) Jardon will not discharge any waiter except for inadequate performance and (ii) any waiter recommended for discharge has the right to meet with Jardon and Prieto to persuade them that the waiter should not be discharged. The Handbook also provides that Jardon will make the final determination in the event of disagreement between Prieto and Jardon on a discharge matter.

5. At all times during his employment at Chez Marie, Bryant performed his job in a manner that met the highest standards at Chez Marie. Despite the adequacy of Bryant's performance, Prieto discharged Bryant on September 28, 2013. Although Bryant immediately requested a meeting with Prieto and Jardon to discuss the discharge, both Prieto and Jardon refused to convene such a meeting.

6. As a result of Jardon's breach of promises in the Handbook, Bryant has suffered lost wages and other incidental and consequential losses.

7. Jardon's breach of promises in the Handbook constitutes a breach of her employment contract with Bryant. Moreover, Bryant foreseeably relied on promises in the Handbook, and Jardon's breach has created an injustice that can be avoided only by enforcing the promises.

II

WRONGFUL DISCHARGE

8. Bryant realleges and incorporates paragraphs 1-7 above.

9. In discharging Bryant, Prieto was motivated by malice, by an invidiously discriminatory animus, and by concerns unrelated to the successful operation of Chez Marie. Jardon's termination of Bryant's employment therefore violated public policy.

III

REQUEST FOR RELIEF

10. Bryant requests:

    i. an order reinstating Bryant to his position as waiter at Chez Marie;

    ii. an award of compensatory damages in an amount to be set at trial;

    iii. an award of punitive damages in an amount to be set at trial;

    iv. an award of costs and attorneys' fees; and

    v. such other relief as the court deems appropriate.

Dated _____

by _____,
Thomas Sanchez

. . . .

IN THE SUPERIOR COURT OF THE STATE OF ARIZONA
IN AND FOR THE COUNTY OF MARICOPA

GEORGE BRYANT,	No._____
Plaintiff,	
v.	
MARIE JARDON, d.b.a. Chez Marie, and	COMPLAINT
MARIO PRIETO,	(JURY TRIAL REQUESTED)
Defendants.	

Plaintiff George Bryant, by and through his attorneys, Simpson, Sanchez and Summers, alleges the following:

1. This is an action for injunctive relief and for compensatory damages exceeding $50,000. This court has original jurisdiction pursuant to the Arizona Constitution, Article 6, § 14(3).

2. Plaintiff is a resident of Phoenix, Arizona. Defendant Marie Jardon owns and operates Chez Marie, a restaurant located in Phoenix, Arizona. Defendant Mario Prieto acted as the maître d' and supervisor of waiters at Chez Marie during Bryant's employment at Chez Marie. All material events alleged below took place in Maricopa County.

I

FIRST CLAIM FOR RELIEF
(Breach of Contract)

3. Plaintiff worked for Defendants as a waiter at Chez Marie from August 16, 2012 to September 28, 2013. In all the events alleged below, Defendant Prieto acted on his own behalf as well as on behalf of Defendant Jardon.

4. On January 1, 2012, Defendants modified Plaintiff's employment contract to include promises of job security contained in the terms of an "Employee Handbook" and in oral assurances.

5. Among other things, the Employee Handbook contains the following promises of job security: (i) Defendants will not discharge any waiter except for inadequate performance and (ii) any waiter recommended for discharge has the right to meet with Defendants to persuade them that the waiter should not be discharged. The Handbook also provides that Defendant Jardon will make the final determination in the event of disagreement between Defendants on a discharge

matter. (Copy of text of excerpts of Handbook is attached and incorporated by this reference.)

6. At all times during his employment at Chez Marie, Plaintiff performed his job in a manner that met the highest standards at Chez Marie. Despite the adequacy of Plaintiff's performance, Defendants discharged Plaintiff on September 28, 2013. Although Plaintiff immediately requested a meeting with Defendants to discuss the discharge, Defendants refused to convene such a meeting.

7. As a result of Defendant's breach of contract, Plaintiff has suffered lost wages and other incidental and consequential losses.

THEREFORE, Plaintiff demands judgment granting the following relief:

    i. an order reinstating Plaintiff to his former position at Chez Marie;

    ii. an award of compensatory damages for all consequential and incidental losses;

    iii. an award of costs and attorneys' fees; and

    iv. such other relief as the court deems appropriate.

II
SECOND CLAIM FOR RELIEF
(Promissory Estoppel)

8. Plaintiff realleges paragraphs 1-7 above and incorporates them by this reference.

9. On January 1, 2012, Defendants gave Plaintiff promises of job security by making oral assurances and by distributing the Employee Handbook. Plaintiff relied to his detriment on those promises by performing extraordinary services and by forbearing from taking other job opportunities. That reliance was reasonably foreseeable by Defendants.

10. Defendants' termination of Bryant's employment on September 28, 2013 constituted a breach of their promises of job security and has created an injustice that can be avoided only by enforcing the promises.

THEREFORE, Plaintiff demands judgment granting the following relief:

    i. an order reinstating Plaintiff to his former position at Chez Marie;

    ii. an award of compensatory damages for all consequential and incidental losses;

    iii. an award of costs and attorneys' fees; and

    iv. such other relief as the court deems appropriate.

III
THIRD CLAIM FOR RELIEF
(Wrongful Discharge)

11. Plaintiff realleges paragraphs 1-10 above and incorporates them by this reference.

12. Defendants maliciously discharged Plaintiff because of his sexual orientation and because Plaintiff's exemplary performance made Defendant Prieto jealous. Those reasons for discharge reflect bad faith and violate the public policy of state laws.

THEREFORE, Plaintiff demands judgment granting the following relief:

   i.   an order reinstating Plaintiff to his position as waiter at Chez Marie;

   ii. an award of compensatory damages in an amount to be set at trial;

   iii. an award of punitive damages in an amount to be set at trial;

   iv. an award of costs and attorneys' fees; and

   v.   such other relief as the court deems appropriate.

Dated _____

                                   by _____,
                                   Thomas Sanchez

                                   . . . .

Chapter 19

Motion for Summary Judgment

I. Procedural Context

A pretrial motion for summary judgment is a popular means of determining whether the court should dispose of all or part of a dispute before the parties try the case to a jury. In most cases, you will have no difficulty alleging facts that state a claim for relief; therefore, your complaints will seldom be susceptible to attack for failure to state a claim. On the other hand, even if you allege a claim or defense in good faith, you may fail to gather substantial admissible evidence supporting the claim or defense. In such cases, the opposing party's motion for summary judgment exposes the absence of a triable issue of fact. It compels you to choose between making at least a preliminary showing of the evidence supporting your allegations or suffering adverse judgment before trial. In other cases, both parties concede the absence of any dispute of fact, stipulate to the facts, and use the motion for summary judgment to argue unsettled questions about the law and its application to the stipulated facts.

Summary judgment litigation often takes place only after each party has thoroughly investigated the case through the discovery and disclosure process.[1] Indeed, the trial judge may delay resolution of a motion for summary judgment if further discovery is needed to permit the nonmoving party to support its opposition. Nonetheless, if you successfully move for summary judgment, you will avoid the greater burdens of a full trial.

On the other hand, if the trial court denies your motion for summary judgment, your unsuccessful motion may hamper your ability to settle the case before trial. If the opposing counsel initially expected to settle the case, he may have only minimally prepared the case prior to summary judgment litigation. Your motion for summary judgment, however, will have forced your opponent to organize his facts and legal arguments. If the motion fails, he likely will be much more demanding in settlement negotiations for three reasons. First, the denial of the motion will strengthen his belief in the potential merits of his client's claims or defenses. Second, he will be more nearly prepared for trial after researching the law and gathering the facts to oppose your motion for summary judgment. Finally, his client will have invested significant resources in opposing the motion, expenditures that his client will likely incorporate into the client's new settlement position.[2] Consequently, you should not move for summary judgment unless you have a reasonable chance of success.

Summary judgment litigation provides you with a stimulating vehicle for developing brief-writing skills. You must remain constantly sensitive not only to the merits of the underlying claims or defenses but also to the standards for summary judgment. Moreover, the local rules of many courts prescribe a special format for summary judgment briefs, providing you a valuable opportunity to examine the role of procedural rules in written advocacy.

II. Standards for Summary Judgment

The federal rules authorize a court to grant summary judgment if the parties do not genuinely dispute any material facts and if the moving party is entitled to judgment as a matter of law.[3]

---

1. The federal procedures for discovery and disclosure are set forth in FEDERAL RULES OF CIVIL PROCEDURE 26-37.

2. *See, e.g.*, Raymond L. Ocampo, Jr., *Moving Violations*, CAL. LAW., Aug. 1984, at 47, 48.

3. *See* FED. R. CIV. P. 56(a). The citations and quotations in this chapter are based on amendments to Rule 56 became effective December 1, 2010. Because of the amendments, some of the new language and organization of subsections in Rule 56 depart from references to the rule in much of the case law, but judicial interpretations of prior statements of the rule should be compatible with the substance of the new rule. *See* Joseph Kimble, *Lessons in Drafting from the New Federal Rules of Civil Procedure*, 12 SCRIBES J. OF LEGAL WRITING 25 (2008-2009) (discussing project of redrafting federal rules for style only). Beyond the scope of this discussion are state standards for summary disposition that deviate from the federal rules. Many states follow the federal standards closely. *See, e.g.*, Orme Sch. v. Reeves, 802 P.2d 1000 (Ariz. 1990) (en banc) (interpreting Ariz. R. Civ. P. 56); *cf.* Aguilar v. Atl. Richfield Co.,

To illustrate the materiality requirement, let's imagine that the record on summary judgment establishes without dispute that a seller repudiated a binding sales contract with the buyer, compelling the buyer to purchase the goods from another supplier at a higher price. If the buyer moved for summary judgment on her contract claim against the seller, the repudiating seller could not successfully respond to the motion by establishing even a genuine dispute of fact about whether he had changed his mind and retracted his repudiation after the buyer had purchased the substitute goods. Under the governing Uniform Commercial Code, once the buyer had relied on the seller's repudiation by making a substitute purchase, the repudiation was final,[4] and the seller's attempted retraction would have no bearing on his liability. Thus, any dispute of fact about whether the seller in fact had attempted a late retraction would be immaterial to the buyer's contract claim and could not preclude summary judgment for the buyer on that claim.

The court does not resolve factual disputes on summary judgment. Nonetheless, to evaluate the genuineness of a purported factual dispute, the court may undertake a limited evaluation of the strength of the facts presented by the nonmoving party. A factual issue is not genuine if the nonmoving party's factual support is so trivial that "the record taken as a whole could not lead a rational trier of fact to find for the non-moving party."[5] In short, the nonmoving party "must do more than simply show . . . some metaphysical doubt as to the material facts."[6]

When moving for summary judgment, you may request summary judgment on one or more claims or defenses, or even on part of a claim or defense,[7] or to identify some uncontested material facts without granting any final judgment.[8] As the moving party, you have the initial burden of showing that the pretrial record supports judgment in your favor. If you move for summary judgment on the strength of a claim or defense on which you would have the burden of proof at trial, you must support your motion for summary judgment with admissible evidence tending to prove all the elements of the claim or defense.[9] You could make such a showing with deposition testimony, answers to interrogatories, admissions, or other information and documents obtained during discovery or disclosure, or with affidavits prepared specifically for the motion.[10]

---

24 P.3d 493, 512-14 (Cal. 2001) (amended California summary judgment rules are similar, though not identical to, federal standards).

4. *See* U.C.C. § 2-611(1) (2011).

5. Matsushita Elec. Indus. Co. v. Zenith Radio Corp., 475 U.S. 574, 587 (1986).

6. *Id*. at 586.

7. FED. R. CIV. P. 56(a).

8. *See* FED. R. CIV. P. 56(g) (permitting court to find the absence of material fact on an issue not resolved on summary judgment).

9. *See* Celotex Corp. v. Catrett, 477 U.S. 317, 331 (1986) (Brennan, J., dissenting); FED. R. CIV. P. 56(c)(1)(b), (c)(2) (allowing showing or objection that supporting evidence would not be admissible at trial).

10. *See generally* FED. R. CIV. P. 56(c)(1)(A), (c)(4).

As an alternative basis for summary judgment, you may demonstrate that the opposing party lacks factual support for an element of her claim or defense. If so, you need not affirmatively produce evidence tending to negate that element. Instead, you may satisfy your initial burden simply by reviewing the existing record and demonstrating that it contains no admissible evidence supporting the critical element.[11]

Once you have satisfactorily supported your motion, the opposing party can avoid summary judgment by establishing a genuine issue of material fact for trial. She may not rely on the allegations or denials in her own pleading but must point to the moving party's admissions or to facts in affidavits, deposition testimony, or other documentary evidence or fruits of discovery, unless she can show that the requisite information is not available to her.[12]

If the materials establish grounds for summary judgment, the federal rules state that the court "shall grant summary judgment,"[13] but some courts and commentators believe that the court nonetheless retains discretion to deny summary judgment and refer that matter to trial.[14]

III. Format for Summary Judgment Briefs—Overview

Rules of procedure, local court rules, and custom suggest that materials supporting a motion for summary judgment should include the following:

1. a motion requesting action by the court;
2. a statement of material facts;
3. affidavits, or other materials not already in the record, that support the fact statement and the motion; and
4. a supporting brief, sometimes referred to in court rules as a "memorandum of law" or, in less modern terms, a "memorandum of points and authorities."

The requirements for the response are similar except that the nonmoving party need not file a formal motion opposing the motion for summary judgment. Under typical local court rules, the nonmoving party's first page would resemble the motion but would identify itself as an "Opposition" or

---

11. *See* Celotex Corp. v. Catrett, 477 U.S. 317, 322-24 (1986) (majority opinion); *id.* at 329-31 (Brennan, J., dissenting); FED. R. CIV. P. 56(c)(1)(b), (c)(2).

12. *See* FED. R. CIV. P. 56(c)-(e); *see also* Southern Rambler Sales, Inc. v. Am. Motors Corp., 375 F.2d 932, 937 (5th Cir. 1967) ("Rule 56 [is] saying in effect, 'Meet these affidavit facts or judicially die.'").

13. FED. R. CIV. P. 56(a).

14. *See* Orme Sch. v. Reeves, 802 P.2d 1000, 1008 n.11 (Ariz. 1990) (en banc) (referring to the discretion to deny summary judgment as the "traditional rule"). Indeed, for a few years, the language of Rule 56 was amended to state that summary judgment "should be rendered" when the requirements were satisfied, FED. R. CIV. P. 56(c)(2) (2007), until the traditional term "shall" was restored in 2010.

"Response" to the motion, and could briefly introduce the supporting brief and other materials. The moving party's reply, if any, might consist of a brief that replies to the nonmoving parties' legal arguments and a fact statement that responds to additional facts asserted by the nonmoving party.

Some local rules describe parts of the required format in surprising detail. For example, local rules for some United States District Courts specify the information required on designated lines of the caption of the title page of each document filed in support of the motion.[15] The most interesting of the local rules addressing summary judgment, however, are those specifying formats for the statements of facts.

IV. Statements of Facts

Before the advent of local rules governing motions for summary judgment, briefs and supporting materials often failed to pinpoint areas of factual dispute. Often, counsel for the moving party summarized the materials supporting the motion in a general narrative fact statement, and counsel for the nonmoving party summarized supporting materials in a general counter-statement of the facts. Worse yet, in some cases, one or both advocates omitted any consolidated statement of the facts and simply referred to the record in fact analyses dispersed throughout the argument section of the brief.

To help trial judges identify the potential areas of factual dispute, many courts have enacted local rules specifying a methodical point/counter-point format for the statements of facts in motions for summary judgment. For example, the Arizona Rules of Civil Procedure require the moving party to state the facts in numbered paragraphs, similar to allegations in a complaint:

> Any party filing a motion for summary judgment shall set forth, separately from the memorandum of law, the specific facts relied upon in support of the motion. The facts shall be stated in concise numbered paragraphs.[16]

Unlike allegations in a complaint, this fact statement must include citations to supporting materials: "As to each fact, the statement shall refer to the specific portion of the record where the fact may be found."[17] If you represent the moving party, you could reasonably entitle this section "[Moving Party's] Statement of Material Facts."

Interpreting another court's local rules, one judge has stated that (1) a statement of material facts supporting a motion for summary judgment should "contain only factual allegations . . . limited to facts pertinent to the

---

15. *See, e.g.*, D. ARIZ. LRCIV. 7.1(a).

16. ARIZ. R. CIV. P. 56(c)(3). *See also* Malec v. Sanford, 191 F.R.D. 581, 583 (N.D. Ill. 2000) (quoting and interpreting Local Rule 56.1(a) for the United States District Court for the Northern District of Illinois, setting forth a similar format for the moving party's statement of material facts).

17. ARIZ. R. CIV. P. 56(c)(3).

outcome of the issues identified in the summary judgment motion," and (2) "the numbered paragraphs should be short," containing "only one or two individual allegations, thereby allowing easy response."[18]

The Arizona rules instruct the nonmoving party to respond to the moving party's statement of material facts by identifying areas of factual dispute in much the same way that an answer sets forth denials of allegations in a complaint:

> Any party opposing a motion for summary judgment shall file a statement in the form prescribed by this Rule, specifying those paragraphs in the moving party's statement of facts which are disputed, and also setting forth those facts which establish a genuine issue of material fact or otherwise preclude summary judgment in favor of the moving party.[19]

If you represent the nonmoving party, you might reasonably entitle this section "Response to [Moving Party's] Statement of Material Facts," or "[Nonmoving Party's] Statement of Material Facts," or even "[Nonmoving Party's] Statement of Undisputed and Disputed Material Facts" because you obviously hope that the court will rule that your documents establish a dispute with respect to at least some of the material facts.

Fact statements following this format provide the court with a clear guide to the parties' positions on summary judgment, because the nonmoving party must methodically respond to each factual assertion of the moving party, point by point, organized by numbered paragraphs.

This point/counterpoint format is not popular with all attorneys and in all fields of litigation, so your assigning attorney may prefer a less regimented format when permitted by local rules. Because the point/counterpoint format for fact statements is required by the local rules of many courts, however, and because it provides a systematic guide for the novice litigant, this chapter will adopt it for its instruction and examples.

For illustration, the following represents excerpts from the plaintiff's statement of facts on his motion for summary judgment in a suit alleging race discrimination in violation of federal law:

---

1. Defendant, Irma Barnes, owns and operates "Irma's Diner," a restaurant and bar located in Mesa, Arizona. Barnes employs more than 15 employees in this business. (Exh. D, Barnes Dep. at 3-4.)

2. Plaintiff, Michael Powell, is African American. He worked as the night manager of the bar at Irma's Diner from January 1, 2011 to June 17, 2011. (Exh. B, Personnel Record for Michael Powell.) . . . .

---

18. *Malec*, 191 F.R.D. at 583.

19. ARIZ. R. CIV. P. 56(c)(3). *See also Malec*, 191 F.R.D. at 583-84 (quoting and interpreting N.D. Ill. R. 56.1(b), setting forth a similar format for the opposing party's statement of undisputed and disputed facts). The Arizona rules also permit the nonmoving party to join with the moving party in stipulating to facts not in dispute. ARIZ. R. CIV. P. 56(c)(3).

3. . . . .

4. On June 17, 2011, Barnes confronted Powell about Powell's selection of a rhythm and blues band as musical entertainment for the bar. After using several racial slurs in the ensuing discussion, she fired Powell solely because of his race. (Exh. A, Powell Aff. ¶ 8.) . . . .

Barnes's response to the motion for summary judgment should specifically identify which portions of Powell's statement of facts she disputes. To highlight areas of dispute with maximum clarity, you probably should respond to each of the moving party's paragraphs with a corresponding, identically numbered paragraph:

1. Barnes does not dispute paragraph 1 of Powell's Statement of Facts.

2. Barnes does not dispute paragraph 2 of Powell's Statement of Facts.

3. Barnes does not dispute paragraph 3 of Powell's Statement of Facts.

4. Barnes does not dispute the assertions in paragraph 4 that Barnes fired Powell on June 17, 2011, after confronting Powell about his selection of musical entertainment. Barnes disputes that she used racial slurs or that race played any factor in her termination of Powell's employment. . . .

In addition, Barnes should identify the specific facts that reflect a genuine factual dispute on the material issue of Barnes's racial animus. Unless these facts appear in Powell's fact statement, Barnes normally would state them as "Additional Facts" in a separate section that follows her identification of areas of dispute:

STATEMENT OF UNDISPUTED AND DISPUTED FACTS

1. Barnes does not dispute . . . .

. . . .

4. Barnes does not dispute the assertions . . . musical entertainment. Barnes disputes . . . Powell's employment.

. . . .

ADDITIONAL FACTS

1. Barnes never used racial slurs in Powell's presence, and she fired Powell solely because he displayed insubordination in the face of direct instructions by Powell to replace the band Barnes had hired. (Plaintiff's Exh. D, Barnes Dep. at 24-25.)

Court rules should then permit the moving party to respond to the nonmoving party's statement of additional facts.[20]

Most court rules requiring separate fact statements for summary judgment can be interpreted to permit you to attach the statement of facts under the same title sheet that states the motion and covers the supporting brief, or that presents the opposition and supporting brief, as long as you set forth the statement of facts separately from the brief itself. Nonetheless, most attorneys prefer to file the formal statement of facts under a caption as a separate document.

V. Supporting Evidentiary Materials

You must support each assertion in your statement of facts with admitted alleged facts from the opposing party's pleading or with facts reflected in affidavits, materials generated through discovery and disclosure, or other evidence. Federal Rule of Civil Procedure 56 specifically provides that the affidavits must "be made on personal knowledge" and "set out facts that would be admissible in evidence."[21] Therefore, even though your opponent may overlook this matter,[22] your summary judgment materials should preliminarily establish the admissibility of (1) documents included in the summary judgment materials[23] or (2) the expected trial testimony represented in the materials, such as in affidavits or deposition testimony.[24]

For example, the following excerpt from an affidavit asserts the admissibility of other documents under the "business records" exception to the "hearsay rule" of evidence:[25]

---

20. *See Malec*, 191 F.R.D. at 584 (citing to N.D. Ill. R. 56.1(a)(3) (final unnumbered paragraph)).

21. FED. R. CIV. P. 56(c)(4); *see* Vandeventer v. Wabash Nat'l Corp., 867 F. Supp. 790, 798 (N.D. Ind. 1994) (rejecting and expressing displeasure with affidavit that was prepared by attorney and that did not reflect personal knowledge of party who signed affidavit).

22. *See, e.g.*, Catrett v. Johns-Manville Sales Corp., 826 F.2d 33, 37 (D.C. Cir. 1987) (regardless of whether letter qualified as a business records exception to the hearsay rule, trial court properly considered it on summary judgment because other party failed to object to its use).

23. *See* Andrews v. R.W. Hays Co., 998 P.2d 774 (2000) (court disregarded hearsay statements in affidavit because neither the affidavit nor other materials established exception to hearsay rule); *cf.* Olympic Ins. Co. v. H.D. Harrison, Inc., 418 F.2d 669, 670 (5th Cir. 1969) (document produced in ordinary course of business was sufficiently reliable to form basis for summary judgment).

24. *See Malec*, 191 F.R.D. at 585. ("[A]lthough the evidence supporting a factual contention need not be admissible itself, it must represent admissible evidence. For example, a deposition transcript is not usually admissible at trial but (obviously) may be used in support of summary judgment; . . . .").

25. *See* FED. R. EVID. 803(6).

5. The Payroll Action forms in Exhibits B and C are true copies of records that I prepared and kept in the course of my regularly conducted business activity, which includes maintaining such employment records as a uniform practice. Those forms include information within my own knowledge and information that my supervisor transmitted to me on matters within his knowledge.

Some attorneys separately file supporting affidavits and other evidence. If those materials are not voluminous, however, you can more conveniently and appropriately attach them to the formal statement of facts.

VI. The Motion

As with every document that you separately file with the trial court, you should begin your motion with a caption identifying the case and the nature of the document. In the motion itself, you should simply and clearly state your request for action and should briefly introduce the grounds supporting the request.

Unfortunately, many lawyers have developed a tradition of loading motions with abstract boilerplate that says almost nothing about the motion or the dispute:

Defendant, Sun Printing Co., by and through its undersigned attorneys, Jenkins, Powell, and Smith, P.C., hereby moves, pursuant to the Arizona Rules of Civil Procedure, Rule 56, for an order granting summary judgment against Plaintiff, Scott Paper Supply, on the grounds that there exists no genuine issue of material fact and that Defendant is entitled to summary judgment as a matter of law. This motion is supported by the attached memorandum of law, the Statement of Material Facts separately filed with this Court, and the documents and exhibits filed with this Court.

A judge learns almost nothing from such boilerplate. She does not need a superfluous reference to the legal representation; your identity as legal counsel is revealed in your signature at the end of the motion, and as well at the top of the cover page under the format prescribed by some local rules. In addition, the judge is well aware of the basic abstract standards for summary judgment;[26] repeating those standards in the motion adds nothing to her knowledge about your case.

---

26. *See* Noel Fidel, *Some Do's and Don'ts of Motion Writing*, ARIZ. B.J., Aug. 1983, at 8, 9 (advising legal writers to omit "canned" recitations of basic summary judgment standards).

The judge will read your motion with greater interest if you clearly and concisely state what relief your client wants and why he is entitled to it. In particular, you should convey new information to the court by tailoring the abstract standards to the facts:

Pursuant to Arizona Rule of Civil Procedure 56, the defendant, Sun Printing Co. ("Sun"), moves for summary judgment against the plaintiff, Scott Paper Supply ("Scott"). Sun is entitled to judgment under the UCC Statute of Frauds because Scott cannot genuinely dispute that the agreement alleged by Scott was for paper priced at more than $500 and was never reduced to writing.

This motion is supported by the attached memorandum of law, by the separately filed Statement of Undisputed Facts and accompanying exhibits, and by the record in this case.

By conveying the theme of the full argument, such a motion whets the judge's appetite for the supporting memorandum of law. An even crisper motion could state the first paragraph more concisely:

Defendant, Sun Printing Co., moves for summary judgment against Plaintiff, Scott Paper Supply. *See* Ariz. R. Civ. P. 56. Sun Printing Co. is entitled to judgment because the oral agreement alleged by Scott Paper Supply is unenforceable under the UCC Statute of Frauds as a matter of law. This motion is supported by . . . .

As terse as this passage may sound, it contains more useful information than the longer string of boilerplate in the first example.

When opposing a motion, you need not state a formal countermotion in the title page of your opposition materials. You may follow the caption immediately with your responsive brief. At the most, you might include a cover page with a brief statement of opposition parallel to the motion:

Plaintiff, Scott Paper Supply ("Scott"), opposes Defendant's motion for summary judgment. Defendant, Sun Printing Co. ("Sun"), is not entitled to judgment as a matter of law, because Scott's supporting materials show that Sun adopted Scott's written and signed confirmation of the agreement, thus satisfying the UCC Statute of Frauds under Ariz. Rev. Stat. Ann. § 47-2201(B) (2005). This opposition is supported by the attached memorandum of law, by the . . . .

VII. The Brief

Your brief, or legal memorandum, is your tool of persuasion. With it, you argue for a favorable interpretation of the law and analysis of the facts. A motions brief typically includes three sections:

1. an introduction,
2. an argument, and
3. a conclusion.

In a complex case, you should consider adding a formal statement of the issues at the beginning of your brief. Such a statement of issues would not be typical in a brief supporting or opposing a motion, but it could be helpful in unusual circumstances.

A. The Introduction

The first section of your supporting brief should summarize the facts, with the brief opposing summary judgment sometimes emphasizing material disputes of facts. In either party's brief, you might reasonably title this section "Introduction" or "Summary of Facts." In this introductory section, you can summarize the facts in a more concise and less formal manner than is possible in the separate, formal statement.

For each statement of a fact in this introduction, you should cite to a source—either to (1) the underlying evidentiary sources already in the record or added to the record in your summary judgment materials, or (2) paragraphs in your separately filed statement of facts, which in turn will cite to underlying evidentiary sources. Some courts prefer, or even require, the brief to cite only to paragraphs in the separately filed statement of facts.[27] When court rules or other judicial pronouncements do not specify a preference or requirement, you can exercise discretion to cite either to the original source or to your separately filed fact statement. If, for example, each of the fact statements in the Introduction is supported by a single underlying evidentiary source, such as an affidavit or deposition testimony, citation to that original source could be concise, informative, and helpful to the reader. On the other hand, if each of many fact statements is supported by several underlying sources, or if the citations to some underlying sources are quite lengthy, direct reference to those sources could impede the flow of the Introduction, and your reader will probably prefer more concise citations to the numbered paragraphs in your separately filed statement of facts.

In addition, you may use an introductory section to present a summary of your argument or a combination of facts, procedural history, and a summary of your argument. For example, you might begin your Introduction with a paragraph-long overview of your arguments or the issues in

---

27. *See, e.g., Malec*, 191 F.R.D. at 586.

the case, to provide a context for a summary of the facts in chronological order. Other passages of this book advise against premature legal argument in a statement of facts in other kinds of briefs, such as an appellate brief. However, this admonition applies with less force in the introduction to your summary judgment brief, because you will separately file a formal statement of facts for summary judgment.

Accordingly, the Introduction may be a suitable place to advance any theme that you have developed for your brief. Alternatively, you can express your theme or brief overview of your arguments in the first paragraph of your Argument section.

B. The Argument

Chapters 6 and 16 discuss techniques of legal argument. Indeed, some of the examples in Chapter 16 are taken from sample summary judgment briefs. This section addresses techniques of persuasion peculiar to summary judgment briefs.

Argument of purely legal questions can be crucial in some summary judgment litigation. If the court determines that material facts are not in dispute, or if the parties have stipulated to the absence of factual dispute, the court will decide whether a moving party is entitled to judgment as a matter of law.

Typically, however, the parties will also argue about the presence or absence of a genuine dispute of fact. In such a case, once you have established the law on an issue or subissue, you should thoroughly analyze the facts. As discussed in greater detail in the immediately preceding section, when you argue the facts, remember to cite to your formal, separately filed statement of facts or to the original evidentiary sources that are already in the record or are included in your supporting materials. The samples in this chapter suggest several ways to cite to either kind of source; unless local rules specify a particular format, any reasonable citation form is acceptable.

Also, remember to incorporate the standards for summary judgment into your argument. For example, if you are moving for summary judgment, you should not argue that the preponderance of the evidence shows that Sun Printing Co. objected to the contents of the confirmation within ten days after receipt. Such an argument gives the impression that you are inappropriately asking the judge to resolve a factual issue without a trial. Instead, your brief should refer to the "undisputed evidence" and the inferences that can be drawn from it, thus properly asserting the absence of a factual dispute.

Conversely, if you are opposing summary judgment, your brief should remind the judge periodically that nothing more than a genuine and material question of fact is needed to defeat summary judgment. In making this point, you should not simply reiterate the abstract standard; rather, you should identify issues of fact that make summary judgment inappropriate:

Scott Paper Supply's letter confirming the purchase agreement is dated September 1 (Exh. 2), and Scott's Distribution Manager personally mailed it that day (Exh. 3, Connor Aff. ¶ 3). Scott Paper Supply never received any objection to the terms of the confirmation. (*Id.* ¶ 4.) Moreover, Sun Printing Co. concedes that it has no record of making any such objection. (Exh. 4, Sun's Ans. to Scott's First Set of Inter., No. 23.)

Opposition facts

In direct opposition to Sun Printing Co.'s assertions, this evidence shows that Sun Printing Co. received the confirmation and failed to object to it. At the very least, this evidence raises a genuine dispute of fact that must be resolved at trial.

Dispute of fact

C. The Conclusion

You should end each section of the argument of your brief with a conclusion about the topic of that section, similar to the conclusion stated in the point heading that introduces the argument. Together, the point heading and the conclusion provide maximum emphasis in their positions as the first and last statements the judge reads within a section. Finally, as illustrated in Chapter 16, the entire brief should end with a section entitled "Conclusion" that encompasses all the arguments of the brief.

VIII. Summary

To prepare a motion for summary judgment,

1. draft a motion that requests summary judgment and briefly introduces the judge to the grounds for your motion;
2. prepare evidentiary materials that will support your statement of facts, if they are not already in the record;
3. draft a separate statement of facts that cites to the supporting materials; and
4. draft a supporting brief that
   a. summarizes the facts and procedural history,
   b. argues the law and facts relating to the issues, with attention to the standards for summary judgment, and
   c. states your conclusions.

When opposing a motion for summary judgment, you should prepare a brief and a separate statement of facts with supporting materials. To oppose a motion or to reply to an opposition brief, you need not file a separate motion. Instead, you should submit a brief that responds to the arguments presented in the preceding brief.

Study the following sample and think about the law and facts that you would need to respond successfully to it. For further practice with summary judgment, perform Assignments 5 and 6 in Appendix VI. Along with Assignment 2 in Appendix IV, Assignment 6 in Appendix VI presents evidence with which the plaintiff in the sample below can oppose the motion for summary judgment, partly by contesting the moving party's factual assertions.

Sample

ARIZONA SUPERIOR COURT

MARICOPA COUNTY

CHARLOTTE REMBAR, Plaintiff, v. ALEXANDER HART d.b.a. COMCON, Defendant.	No. C732431 Defendant Hart's Motion for Summary Judgment (Judge Wisdom)

Defendant Alexander Hart d.b.a. Comcon moves for summary judgment on all claims in this action. Under Arizona Rule of Civil Procedure 56, Hart is entitled to judgment as a matter of law because the undisputed facts show that Hart did not promise Rembar job security and did not discharge Rembar for an unlawful reason or in a wrongful manner.

This motion is supported by the attached Memorandum of Law, the separately filed Statement of Material Facts, and the entire record before the Court.

August 5, 2014

Lisa Hall
Kendricks, Hall, & Oats, P.C.
3310 Alma School Rd., Suite 200
Mesa, Arizona 85283
(480) 839-0365
Bar No. 0076089

MEMORANDUM OF LAW IN SUPPORT OF
MOTION FOR SUMMARY JUDGMENT

I. INTRODUCTION

As documented and set forth more fully in Defendant Hart's Statement of Material Facts ("Hart SofF"), Alexander Hart employed Charlotte Rembar as a computer systems consultant for Hart's sole proprietorship, Comcon. (Hart SofF ¶ 2.) Although Hart distributed an employment manual to Rembar, their employment contract permitted either party to terminate the contract at will. (Hart SofF ¶¶ 2-5.)

On November 1, 2013, Hart discharged Rembar because of her "negative attitude." (Hart SofF ¶¶ 7-8.) During her employment, Rembar often flirted with Hart, and Hart sometimes returned the flirtations; however, Hart and Rembar did not have a romantic relationship, and Hart never made any unwelcome advances toward Rembar. (Hart SofF ¶ 6.)

Rembar has asserted four claims for relief in her complaint: (1) breach of an alleged promise of job security, (2) sex discrimination in violation of the Arizona Civil Rights Act ("the ACRA"), (3) wrongful discharge in violation of public policy, and (4) intentional infliction of emotional distress. Because the record shows that Hart employed Rembar at will and that Hart discharged Rembar for a legitimate business reason and in a proper manner, Hart is entitled to judgment as a matter of law on all these claims.

II. ARGUMENT

A. Hart did not breach his employment contract with Rembar by discharging Rembar for her negative attitude.

"The employment relationship is severable at the pleasure of either the employee or the employer unless both the employee and the employer have signed a written contract to the contrary. . . ." Ariz. Rev. Stat. Ann. § 23-1501(2) (2005). In some circumstances, an employee manual can become part of the employment contract, and promises of job security in the manual can restrict the employer's freedom to terminate the contract. *See id.* Nonetheless, even assuming for purposes of summary judgment that Hart and Rembar's employment contract included the terms of the Comcon Policy Manual, Hart did not breach those terms for two reasons. First, neither the Policy Manual nor any other term of the contract imposed any restriction on Hart's freedom to terminate Rembar's employment. Second, even if the contract permitted Hart to fire Rembar only for unsatisfactory performance, her negative attitude created such grounds for discharge.

1. The Employment Contract Remained Terminable at Will.

Even assuming the Comcon Policy Manual was incorporated into the employment contract, the manual did not change the at-will nature of the contract because it did not contain requisite "provisions of job security." *Leikvold v. Valley View Cmty. Hosp.*, 141 Ariz. 544, 547, 688 P.2d 170, 173 (1984) (quoting *Pine River State Bank v. Mettille*, 333 N.W.2d 622, 628 (Minn. 1983)). Because the terms of the contract "are clear and unambiguous, the construction of the contract is a question of law for the court" and thus is appropriate for summary judgment. *Id.* at 548, 688 P.2d at 174.

Comcon hired Rembar for an indefinite term of employment, rather than for a fixed term. (Hart SofF ¶ 2.) The terms of Comcon's Policy Manual unambiguously left Hart free to terminate his contract with Rembar at his will. No provision of the Policy Manual purports to restrict the grounds for discharge of an employee. (Hart SofF ¶ 3.) Instead, the only provisions relating to termination affirmatively reserve Hart's right to discharge employees. (Hart SofF ¶¶ 4-5.) Because Rembar had worked at Comcon for more than 60 days, she was classified as a nonprobationary employee at the time of her discharge. (Hart SofF ¶¶ 2, 4-5.) Under the heading "Nonprobationary Employment," the Policy Manual especially emphasizes a particular ground for discharge: "Comcon reserves the right to terminate the employment of any employee who is not performing satisfactorily." (Hart SofF ¶ 5.) However, it does not state or even suggest that unsatisfactory performance is the exclusive ground for discharge. Absent such a stated restriction, Hart remains free under the general rule to terminate the contract for any reason or for no reason at all.

Hart's employment contract with Rembar was terminable at will.

2. Hart Validly Fired Rembar for Unsatisfactory Performance.

Even if the Policy Manual had identified unsatisfactory performance as the sole ground for discharging nonprobationary employees, Hart would not have breached such a provision.

Hart discharged Rembar because of her "negative attitude." (Hart SofF ¶¶ 7-8.) Because Rembar's position required her to work closely with clients, a pleasant personality and a positive attitude were indispensable qualities for satisfactory job performance. (Hart SofF ¶ 7.) Therefore, even assuming that the employment contract provided for limited job security, Hart did not breach the contract because the undisputed facts show that he discharged Rembar for unsatisfactory performance.

B. Hart did not engage in unlawful sex discrimination.

Because Comcon has always employed fewer than fifteen employees (Hart SofF ¶ 1), Rembar has no claim against Hart under federal employment discrimination law. *See* 42 U.S.C. § 2000e(b) (2006) (defining employers covered by Title VII of the Civil Rights Act of 1964). Comcon is a covered employer under the Arizona Civil Rights Act ("ACRA"), Ariz. Rev. Stat. Ann. § 41-1461(2) (2005); however, he did not violate its provisions.

The ACRA makes it an "unlawful employment practice for an employer: 1. To . . . discharge any individual or otherwise to discriminate against any individual with respect to his compensation, terms, conditions or privileges of employment because of such individual's . . . sex . . . ." Ariz. Rev. Stat. Ann. § 41-1463.B (2005). Rembar alleges that Hart discriminated against her by subjecting her to unwelcome sexual advances and discharging her in retaliation for her refusal to submit to the alleged advances. The record, however, contradicts these allegations.

Rembar's own frequent flirtations with Hart showed that she welcomed Hart's harmless flirtations and attentions. Hart never made advances that were not welcomed by Rembar, and he never conditioned benefits of employment on Rembar's acquiescing to his flirtations. (Hart SofF ¶ 6.) Most important, Rembar's discharge had nothing to do with any flirtations between Hart and Rembar; Hart discharged Rembar solely because of her unsatisfactory job performance. (Hart SofF ¶¶ 7-8.)

As a matter of law, Hart did not engage in sexually discriminatory conduct in violation of the ACRA.

C. Hart is not liable in tort for wrongfully discharging Rembar, because the Arizona Civil Rights Act provides the exclusive remedy for such alleged misconduct.

Before its statutory modification, the common law tort of wrongful discharge imposed liability for a violation of an important public policy reflected in the state's constitution, its statutes, or, in limited circumstances, its judicial decisions. *See Wagenseller v. Scottsdale Mem'l Hosp.*, 147 Ariz. 370, 378-79,

710 P.2d 1025, 1033-34 (1985). Rembar's complaint demands tort damages for common law wrongful discharge in violation of the public policies
reflected in the ACRA, a tort claim previously recognized in this state. *See*
Broomfield v. Lundell, 159 Ariz. 349, 767 P.2d 697 (Ct. App. 1988). Her
claim fails as a matter of law, however, both on the facts in this record and
through statutory preemption.

First, as stated in arguments A and B above, Hart did not engage in
sexual harassment or any other sexually discriminatory employment practice
that would violate the policies of the ACRA. Second, even if Rembar can
genuinely dispute those facts, her wrongful discharge claim is now governed
by the Arizona Employment Protection Act ("AEPA"), Ariz. Rev. Stat. Ann.
§ 23-1501 (Supp. 2009).

The AEPA provides that an employer may be liable for discharging
an employee "in violation of a statute of this state." Ariz. Rev. Stat. Ann.
§ 23-1501(3)(b) (Supp. 2009). If the violated statute provides its own civil
remedies, however, those remedies are exclusive; indeed, the AEPA lists the
ACRA as its first example of a source of such exclusive remedies:

> [T]he remedies provided to an employee for a violation of the stat-
> ute are the exclusive remedies for the violation of the statute or the
> public policy set forth in or arising out of the statute, including the
> following:
>   (i) The civil rights act prescribed in title 41, chapter 9.

Id.; *see also* Ariz. Rev. Stat. Ann. § 41-1481 (2005) (setting forth enforcement procedures and remedies for violations of the ACRA). Because Rembar
bases her wrongful discharge claim on alleged violations of the ACRA, her
remedy is limited to the relief available in the ACRA. *See Cronin v. Sheldon*,
195 Ariz. 531, 991 P.2d 231 (1999) (finding that the AEPA constitutionally
preempted the tort remedy recognized in *Broomfield*).

Accordingly, regardless of whether Rembar can establish a factual dispute about the reasons for her discharge, Hart is entitled to summary judgment on Rembar's tort claim of wrongful discharge.

D. Hart did not engage in extreme and outrageous conduct and therefore is not liable for infliction of emotional distress.

The AEPA would not preempt a claim of intentional infliction of emotional distress for an unlawfully discriminatory discharge. *Cronin*, 195 Ariz.
at 541, 991 P.2d at 241 (dictum). However, Hart is not liable for intentional infliction of emotional distress unless his conduct was so "extreme

436 Part VII. Pretrial Advocacy—Pleadings and Motions

and outrageous" that it fell "within that quite narrow range" of conduct "at the very extreme edge of the spectrum." *Watts v. Golden Age Nursing Home*, 127 Ariz. 255, 258, 619 P.2d 1032, 1035 (1980). As discussed above, Hart discharged Rembar for legitimate business reasons. (Hart SofF ¶¶ 7-8.) Moreover, Hart communicated his decision in a normal professional matter. (Hart SofF ¶ 8.) Because of its economic consequences, termination of employment is often an extremely distressing event for the discharged employee. However, discharge for business reasons is an economic fact of life and hardly amounts to a basis for tort liability.

Moreover, even if Rembar could establish a dispute of fact regarding the reason for her discharge, the dispute would not be material. "[I]t is extremely rare to find conduct in the employment context that will rise to the level of outrageousness necessary to provide a basis for recovery for the tort of intentional infliction of emotional distress." *Mintz v. Bell Atl. Sys. Leasing Int'l, Inc.*, 183 Ariz. 550, 554, 905 P.2d 559, 563 (Ct. App. 1995) (quoting *Cox v. Keystone Carbon Co.*, 861 F.2d 390, 395 (3d Cir. 1988)).

In *Mintz*, an employee was hospitalized after suffering a nervous breakdown as the alleged result of gender discrimination in the workplace. The employer terminated her disability benefits, ordered her to return to work, and then—while the employee was again hospitalized after returning to work for one day—notified her of a reassignment of her duties by a letter delivered to the hospital. *Id.* at 552, 905 P.2d at 561. The Arizona Court of Appeals affirmed a finding that, as a matter of law, this alleged conduct was not extreme and outrageous, even assuming the employer had failed to promote the employee because of gender discrimination and assuming the employer knew that the employee was unusually susceptible to emotional distress. *Id.* at 553-54, 905 P.2d at 562-63.

In light of cases such as *Mintz*, a federal district court has characterized Arizona's standard for extreme and outrageous conduct as one requiring "extraordinary" conduct. *Tempesta v. Motorola, Inc.*, 92 F. Supp. 2d 973, 987 (D. Ariz. 1999). Applying *Mintz*, the *Tempesta* court granted summary judgment for the defendant employer on the employee's claim of intentional infliction of emotional distress, even after assuming the truth of the employee's allegations that he had suffered harassment and wrongful termination because of his sex. *Id.* at 986-87.

It is even clearer in this case that Hart did not engage in extreme and outrageous conduct. Even if Rembar's allegations of mild sexual advances and retaliatory discharge were supported by the record, that conduct would not satisfy the demanding test of egregiousness applied in Arizona courts. As a matter of law, Hart is not liable for intentional infliction of emotional distress.

III. CONCLUSION

Rembar cannot genuinely dispute Hart's showing on the facts that Hart promised Rembar no job security, Hart discharged Rembar for poor performance, and Hart did not engage in sexual harassment. Therefore, Hart is entitled to summary judgment on all claims.

August 5, 2014

_____

Lisa Hall for
Kendricks, Hall, & Oats, P.C.
3310 Alma School Rd., Suite 200
Mesa, Arizona 85283

COPY OF THE FOREGOING MAILED
August 5, 2014 to:
Roberts and Cray
101 E. Washington St., Suite 600
Phoenix, Arizona 85001

ARIZONA SUPERIOR COURT
MARICOPA COUNTY

CHARLOTTE REMBAR, Plaintiff, v. ALEXANDER HART d.b.a. COMCON, Defendant.	No. C732431 Defendant Hart's Statement of Material Facts and Exhibits Supporting Motion for Summary Judgment (Judge Wisdom)

For purposes of summary judgment only, Defendant Alexander Hart d.b.a. Comcon presents the following material facts:

1. Alexander Hart is the sole owner and manager of Comcon, a firm that provides expert consulting on computer systems to businesses in the Phoenix metropolitan area. From January to November 2013, Comcon employed eight employees other than Hart himself; Comcon has never employed a greater number of employees before or since. [Hart Aff. ¶ 1 (Exh. D)].

2. Effective January 1, 2013, Hart hired Charlotte Rembar for the position of Comcon consultant at a salary of $5,000/month. [Dec. 30, 2012 Payroll Action (Exh. B)]. The only written record of Rembar's contract with Comcon is the Payroll Action form that states her date of hire and her salary. [Hart Aff. ¶ 2 (Exh. D)]. The term of Rembar's employment was left indefinite. [*Id.*].

3. At or before the time of Rembar's hiring, Alexander Hart gave Rembar a Policy Manual that summarizes many of the personnel procedures at Comcon. [Policy Manual (Exh. A)]. The Policy Manual includes one example of a ground for discharging a nonprobationary employee, but it does not explicitly limit Comcon's right to discharge an employee for any other reason. [*Id.* at § IV].

4. Under the heading *Probationary Employment*, section IV.A of the policy manual provides that "Each employee will work on probationary status during his or her first 60 days of employment. During this probationary period, Comcon reserves the right to terminate the employee for any reason or for no reason at all." [*Id.* at § IV.A].

5. Under the heading *Nonprobationary Employment*, section IV.B of the policy manual provides that "Comcon reserves the right to terminate the

employment of any employee who is not performing satisfactorily." [*Id.* at § IV.B].

6. From the beginning of her employment at Comcon, Rembar sought to attract Hart's attentions with casual flirtations, such as references to his appearance and suggestive smiles. Hart returned the flirtations in a similar manner, but no sexual relationship developed between them. Any flirtations directed by Hart toward Rembar were welcomed, and even invited, by her. Hart never demanded sexual favors from Rembar, and he never conditioned any benefits of employment on Rembar's submitting to a sexual demand or otherwise reacting to a flirtation. [Hart Aff. ¶ 3 (Exh. D)].

7. In the fall of 2013, Hart became dissatisfied with Rembar's performance. Specifically, she displayed a negative attitude in her work. Because Comcon consultants must work closely with their clients, a consultant with a negative attitude severely hampers Comcon's business relationships. [Hart Aff. ¶ 4 (Exh. D)].

8. Effective November 2, 2013, Hart terminated Rembar's employment because of her negative attitude. [Nov. 1, 2013 Payroll Action (Exh. C)]. Hart communicated the discharge to Rembar in a normal, professional manner. [Hart Aff. ¶ 4 (Exh. D)].

August 5, 2014

Lisa Hall
Kendricks, Hall, & Oats, P.C.
3310 Alma School Rd., Suite 200
Mesa, Arizona 85283
(480) 839-0365
Bar No. 0076089

Exhibit A

POLICY MANUAL
for Employees of Comcon

I. Introduction

The success of Comcon lies in its ability to recruit and retain the best employees available nationally. To promote a stable and productive workforce, Comcon provides attractive terms and conditions of employment, including those set forth in the following policies.

II. Salary

A. Initial Salary. . . .

B. Change in Salary. . . .

III. Holidays, Vacations, Sick Leave

A. Holidays. . . .

B. Personal Leave. . . .

IV. Termination

A. Probationary Employment

Each employee will work on probationary status during his or her first 60 days of employment. During this probationary period, Comcon reserves the right to terminate the employee for any reason or for no reason at all.

B. Nonprobationary Employment

Comcon reserves the right to terminate the employment of any employee who is not performing satisfactorily.

Exhibit B

PAYROLL ACTION

Nature of Action

___X___ New Hire   _____ Change in Pay ·_____ Termination

Previous Pay ___N.A._____

New Pay ___$5,000/mo._____

Effective Date ___Jan. 1, 2013_____

Reason for Change or Termination

Comments

Consultant

Date ___Dec. 30, 2012_____

Processed By ___Leslie West_____

Exhibit C

PAYROLL ACTION

Nature of Action

_____ New Hire   _____ Change in Pay   _X_ Termination

Previous Pay __*$5,000/mo.*_____

New Pay __*N.A.*_____

Effective Date __*Nov. 2, 2013*_____

Reason for Change or Termination

__*Negative Attitude*_____

Comments

Date __*Nov. 1, 2013*_____

Processed By __*Leslie West*_____

Exhibit D

AFFIDAVIT OF ALEXANDER HART
IN SUPPORT OF MOTION FOR SUMMARY JUDGMENT

Maricopa County, Arizona

Alexander Hart, under oath, swears to the following information from personal knowledge:

1. I am the sole owner and manager of Comcon, a firm that provides consulting services to businesses on the development and use of computer systems. From January to November 2013, I employed eight employees, the largest workforce that I have employed since I formed Comcon in 2008. Specifically, during that period I employed a secretary, an accountant, and six consultants.

2. Effective January 1, 2013, I hired Charlotte Rembar for the position of consultant. The Payroll Action form identified in this motion as Exhibit B is the only written record of Rembar's hiring and her terms of employment. Rembar and I understood at the time of hiring that her term of employment was indefinite. On or before the time of her hiring, I gave her a Comcon Policy Manual, which reaffirms that Rembar had no definite term of employment or guarantee of continued employment.

3. From the beginning of her employment at Comcon, Rembar sought to attract my attentions with casual flirtations such as suggestive smiles and compliments on my grooming and appearance. She made it clear that she welcomed reciprocation, and I often returned her flirtations with similar smiles and comments. Our personal relationship never advanced beyond these casual flirtations. Specifically, we never had a sexual relationship, and I never made any unwelcome sexual advances toward Rembar, nor did I ever condition any benefits of employment on Rembar's submitting to any sexual demands or otherwise reacting in any way to my flirtations.

4. Sometime in the fall of 2013, I began to notice that Rembar displayed a negative attitude about me, about herself, and about her work. I find it extremely important to maintain a workforce with positive attitudes and pleasant personalities, because the consultants work closely with clients, and our business thus depends on maintaining good personal relationships with clients. To ensure that we maintained those relationships, I discharged Rem-

bar effective November 2, 2013, to rid our workforce of her negativism. I communicated the discharge to Rembar in a normal, professional manner in an office meeting on November 1, 2013.

5. The Payroll Action forms in Exhibits B and C are true copies of records that were prepared and kept under my direction by my personal secretary, Leslie West, in the course of her regularly conducted business activity, which includes maintaining such employment records as a uniform practice. Those forms include information within Ms. West's own knowledge and information that I transmitted to her on matters within my knowledge. The Policy Manual in Exhibit A is a true copy of a manual that I drafted and printed in June 2009 and have since distributed to all employees.

I swear under oath that the foregoing is true:

_____   _____
Alexander Hart   Date

Chapter 20

Motion to Exclude Evidence

Before Trial

BLACK'S LAW DICTIONARY defines "in limine" as: "preliminary; presented to only the judge, before or during trial."[1] The typical motion in limine is a motion to exclude evidence before trial, or at least to require opposing counsel to raise the question of admissibility outside the presence of the jury if the trial is underway. Conversely, but much more rarely, an advocate may use it to move for admission of evidence before trial if she anticipates an objection to the evidence.[2]

Thus, in contrast to the typical motion for summary judgment, a motion to exclude evidence seeks to define the scope of the trial litigation rather than to dispose of the case before trial. It generally is simpler than a motion for summary judgment. If you can strip the mystery away from the popular Latin phrase, you should have little trouble supporting or opposing the motion.

---

1. BLACK'S LAW DICTIONARY 858 (9th ed. 2009).

2. *See* Hon. Robert E. Bacharach, *Motions in Limine in Oklahoma State and Federal Courts*, 24 OKLA. CITY U. L. REV. 112, 114 (1999).

I. Pretrial Exclusion of Evidence

The Federal Rules of Civil Procedure provide that "the admissibility of evidence" is appropriate for consideration and disposition in a pretrial conference.[3] Additionally, those rules and the Federal Rules of Evidence implicitly authorize a trial court to rule on pretrial motions to exclude evidence other than in pretrial conference, or they at least leave undisturbed the court's inherent power to do so.[4]

During trial, attorneys can and do object to evidence offered for admission.[5] However, pretrial rulings on complex, potentially prejudicial, or particularly significant evidentiary matters tend to improve the efficiency and quality of the trial proceedings.[6]

For example, suppose a visitor to your client's factory sues your client for injuries sustained at the factory. At trial, the plaintiff's counsel asks a defense witness in front of the jury to confirm that your client offered to pay the plaintiff's medical expenses. You can immediately object that the question seeks a response that may lead the jury to find liability on an improper ground.[7] In most jurisdictions, the judge will sustain your objection and will order the witness not to provide the solicited testimony.[8] However, the damage to your client's case may be irreparable if the question alone improperly influences the jury's deliberations, despite the court's admonishments to the jury to ignore it. You could have protected your client more effectively had you earlier persuaded the judge to exclude the evidence before trial and to order the parties and their attorneys to refrain from referring to the evidence in any way at trial.

Additionally, pretrial litigation of complex evidentiary matters permits more thorough written and oral argument by the parties and more considered deliberation by the court, all without disrupting an ongoing trial. Moreover, pretrial disposition of objections to particularly significant evidence gives the parties an opportunity to modify their trial strategies or to reassess their settlement positions.[9]

---

3. FED. R. CIV. P. 16(c)(2)(C).

4. *See generally* FED. R. EVID. 103(c) ("In jury cases, proceedings shall be conducted, to the extent practicable, so as to prevent inadmissible evidence from being suggested to the jury by any means, such as making statements or offers of proof or asking questions in the hearing of the jury."); Charles W. Gamble, *The Motion* In Limine: *A Pretrial Procedure That Has Come of Age*, 33 ALA. L. REV. 1, 2 & n.6 (1981).

5. *See* FED. R. EVID. 103(a) (unnumbered paragraph following subsections (1) & (2)) (referring to rulings "admitting or excluding evidence, either at or before trial").

6. *See* FED. R. CIV. P. 16(a) (stating objectives of pretrial conference).

7. *See* FED. R. EVID. 409, Advisory Comm. Note. Exclusion of such evidence also promotes a generally humanitarian policy of encouraging such assistance, regardless of liability. *Id.*

8. *See* FED. R. EVID. 409.

9. *See* Gamble, *supra* note 4, at 8-10.

II. Format

Unless local court rules specifically address motions in limine,[10] you should follow procedural rules governing motions generally.[11] Beyond that, the common format is a product of custom and common sense. As with any legal document, you can best support or oppose a motion to exclude evidence if you understand the purposes of your document and draft it accordingly.

III. The Motion

In a motion to exclude evidence, you should simply and clearly state the requested action and briefly summarize the grounds for the motion. In describing the relief requested, you probably should go beyond generally asking for exclusion of certain evidence. To ensure effective protection, you should describe the objectionable evidence as inclusively as possible and should request an order specifically prohibiting the opposing party from referring to the evidence:

The defendant, Axxon Corp., moves for a pretrial order excluding all evidence that Axxon Corp. offered to provide medical care and to pay the medical expenses of the plaintiff, Herb Taylor. The evidence is inadmissible under Federal Rule of Evidence 409.

Specifically, Axxon Corp. requests an order directing Taylor and his counsel (1) to refrain from referring to such an offer in any way in the presence of the jury during voir dire and all subsequent proceedings, and (2) to take all necessary steps to ensure that their witnesses avoid such references.

To oppose a motion to exclude evidence, you need not file a separate motion; you can simply file a brief that opposes the original motion. At the most, you might want to draft a cover page with a caption and a paragraph that parallels the motion in summarizing the ruling you seek and the supporting grounds:

---

10. *See, e.g.*, ARIZ. R. CIV. P. 7.2(b), (c) (specifying timing for motions in limine and disallowing reply briefs).

11. *See, e.g.*, D. ARIZ. LRCIV. 7.2(a)-(e) (specifying requirements for motions and for opening, answering, and reply briefs in this federal trial court); ARIZ. R. CIV. P. 7.1(a) (setting forth general requirements for motions in this state's trial practice).

Plaintiff Herb Taylor opposes Defendant Axxon Corp.'s motion to exclude evidence of Axxon Corp.'s offer to provide and pay for medical care. The evidence is admissible to show the extent of Taylor's injuries. The court should not exclude the evidence for this limited purpose.

IV. The Brief

A brief supporting or opposing a motion to exclude evidence, or any other motion, is often referred to as a "Memorandum of Law." When preparing a brief supporting a motion to exclude evidence, you ordinarily should follow the familiar pattern of Introduction, Argument, and Conclusion. The party opposing your motion should file a responsive brief that directly answers the arguments in your supporting brief. Similarly, if local rules permit a reply brief, you can rebut the counterarguments presented in the opposing brief.[12]

On a motion for summary judgment, you will address at least some of the claims or defenses of the litigation on their merits. In contrast, on a motion to exclude evidence, you will typically focus more narrowly on the admissibility of certain evidence. Consequently, in your supporting or opposing briefs, you should address the merits of claims or defenses only to the extent necessary to address some element of admissibility, such as relevance. This narrow focus affects the scope of the introduction and argument sections of the briefs.

A. The Introduction

In the introductory section of a brief supporting a motion to exclude evidence, you need not include a full statement of facts and procedural history. In light of the motion's focus on an evidentiary issue, your introduction need summarize only those portions of the facts and procedural history necessary to an understanding of that specific issue. You should accompany your motion with any necessary factual support for your assertions, such as affidavits or documents generated during discovery or prepared specifically for the motion. Additionally, you should cite to such attachments or to other parts of the record. Absent a local rule specifying a particular format, any reasonable citation form is acceptable; two examples are presented below. Finally, your introduction should explain why you expect the nonmoving party to attempt to introduce the evidence at trial and why the court should resolve the matter before trial, unless you choose to address those matters in the Argument section.

---

12. *Compare* D. Ariz. LRCiv. 7.2(b)-(d) (for all motions in this federal trial court, referring to the moving party's brief, the responsive memorandum, and the reply memorandum) *with* Ariz. R. Civ. P. 7.2(c) (disallowing reply briefs for motions in limine in this state's trial courts).

For example, the brief supporting the motion might begin with the following introductory points:

MEMORANDUM IN SUPPORT OF MOTION TO EXCLUDE EVIDENCE

I. Introduction

Herb Taylor, a sales representative for Corbin Heavy Equipment Co., brought this tort action against Axxon Corp. He alleges negligence in the maintenance of the Axxon manufacturing plant in Albuquerque, New Mexico.

Nature of the case

Specifically, Taylor alleges that, while touring the Axxon plant in January 2009 with Axxon General Manager Jerry Olshon, Taylor lost his footing, fell backwards, and struck his head against a forklift. [Compl. ¶¶ 3, 4.] According to Olshon's deposition testimony, as a humanitarian gesture, Olshon immediately offered on behalf of Axxon to provide transportation to the nearest hospital and to pay for Taylor's medical expenses. [Olshon Dep. 18.] Taylor later developed difficulties with his eyesight, which he alleges are the result of his accident at the Axxon plant. [Compl. ¶ 6.]

Facts

The critical issue in this case is whether Axxon negligently maintained its plant, causing Taylor to fall. Taylor's counsel has examined Olshon extensively during deposition about Olshon's offer to pay medical expenses, leading Axxon to believe that Taylor's counsel will attempt to introduce that evidence at trial.

Belief that evidence will be introduced

Evidence of Olshon's offer to pay medical expenses is inadmissible to establish Axxon's liability, and Axxon will not introduce it for other purposes. The evidence must be excluded before trial, because reference to it even in a question to a witness would indelibly and improperly influence the jury.

Need for pretrial exclusion

When opposing a motion, you should state any facts and procedural history that are material to your argument and that are not fairly stated in the opening brief:

I. Introduction

Plaintiff Taylor is prepared to prove that Defendant Axxon Corp.'s negligence proximately caused Taylor to lose nearly all sight in his right eye. Axxon apparently seeks to show that Taylor's

Issues for trial

Relevance of evidence on particular issue

injuries at the Axxon factory were slight and that Taylor's partial blindness must be unrelated. *See* Answer ¶ 6. Thus, the extent of Taylor's injuries at the factory is in issue.

Taylor plans to introduce Axxon Corp.'s offer to provide and pay for medical care as evidence that Axxon's agent at the scene of the accident determined Taylor's injuries to be serious. The evidence is admissible for this purpose and should not be excluded.

B. The Argument

The argument section of a motion to exclude evidence follows the same general pattern discussed in Chapters 6 and 16. Each section or subsection within the argument should state a contention in a point heading, analyze the law and the facts, and restate or summarize the contention in a conclusion.

1. Legal Rules

In the statement of legal standards in the opening brief supporting a motion to exclude evidence, you typically will focus on rules of evidence that restrict admissibility. If you prefer a thorough analysis, you may choose to develop the legal standards in some detail:

Even relevant evidence is inadmissible "if its probative value is substantially outweighed by the danger" that it will cause "unfair prejudice, confusion of the issues, or misleading the jury." Fed. R. Evid. 403. Evidence presents such a danger if it has "an undue tendency to suggest a decision on an improper basis, commonly, though not necessarily, an emotional one." *Id.*, Advisory Committee Note.

In this case, evidence of Powell's membership in the Black Panther Party more than 40 years ago has little, if any, probative value. . . .

On the other hand, the general standards for some of the more commonly invoked evidentiary rules are familiar to judges and attorneys. Therefore, you could exercise stylistic discretion to present those standards summarily, or even implicitly, and to move more quickly to the fact analysis:

Evidence of Powell's former membership in the Black Panther Party should be excluded because its probative value is substantially outweighed by its potential for confusion and unfair prejudice. *See* Fed. R. Evid. 403. The F.B.I. file report shows that Powell was a member of the Black Panther Party more than 40 years ago for the brief period of eight months. During that time, Powell participated in political rallies and peaceful protests against police brutality, and he met with other members in political strategy meetings. . . .

2. Application of Rules to Facts

As in any legal argument, the fact analysis should lead to a conclusion by relating the facts to the legal standard:

Purely political activities such as these have little or no probative value on the merits of Powell's position that he did nothing to provoke Officer Beatty's assault. As the record shows, when Powell was a member of the Black Panther Party for less than a year in 1970, he did not espouse violence or engage in any violent activities.	**Little relevance**
The primary effect of evidence of Powell's membership would be to inflame the passions of the jury. Despite the nonviolent role that Powell played as a member of the organization, many view the Black Panther Party as a radical organization that actively sought confrontation with established institutions such as police agencies. Some jurors undoubtedly would react emotionally to the controversial image of the Black Panthers.	**Unfair prejudice**
Moreover, some jurors may confuse the original Black Panther Party, a serious political movement, with an unrelated, less constructive, and more controversial "New Black Panthers Party." . . .	

The argument section of an opposing brief or a reply brief will contain similar elements, except that each will be narrowly tailored to respond directly to contentions advanced in the brief that preceded it.

C. The Conclusion

Chapter 16's discussion of conclusions includes examples from sample motions in limine. In summary, you should

1. end each argument in a brief with a conclusion on that argument, and
2. end the entire brief with a general summary of all the arguments and with your request for relief.

This sample sums up the theme of a brief that presented a single argument:

Part VII. Pretrial Advocacy—Pleadings and Motions

III. Conclusion

Officer Beatty is on trial in this civil suit. By offering evidence of Powell's membership in the Black Panther Party, Officer Beatty is inappropriately trying to turn the tables and put Powell on trial for his nonviolent political activities more than four decades ago. The evidence should be excluded because its minimal probative value, if any, is substantially outweighed by the danger of confusion and unfair prejudice.

V. Summary

To prepare a motion to exclude evidence before trial,

1. draft a motion that simply and clearly requests the court to exclude specified evidence and to prohibit the parties from referring to the evidence at trial;
2. draft a supporting brief that
   a. introduces the facts and procedural history relevant to the motion,
   b. argues the law and facts relating to the evidentiary issues, and
   c. states your conclusions; and
3. attach any documentary evidence or affidavits necessary to support your motion, or refer to evidence already in the record.

To oppose a motion to exclude evidence, or to reply to an opposition brief, you need not file a separate motion. Instead, you should submit a brief that responds to the arguments presented in the preceding brief.

For further practice with motions to exclude evidence, complete Assignment 6 in Appendix VI.

The following sample is taken from the files of an actual case, although it is reproduced here with lesser line spacing than in the original.

Sample

Deborah E. Driggs
State Bar No. 6081
David L. Keily
State Bar No. 12345
SACKS, TIERNEY, KASEN & KERRICK, P.A.
3300 North Central Avenue, Suite 2000
Phoenix, Arizona 85012-1576
Telephone: (602) 279-4900
Attorneys for Defendants Rayner

SUPERIOR COURT OF ARIZONA
MARICOPA COUNTY

AGUA FRIA SAND & ROCK, INC., an Arizona corporation, Plaintiff, v. Estate of DALE FAY RAYNER, Deceased; JACK RAYNER, JR., Personal Representative of the Estate of DALE FAY RAYNER, Deceased; Estate of JACK RAYNER, JR., Personal Representative of the Estate of JACK RAYNER, SR., Deceased; JACK RAYNER, JR., Defendants.	No. C-531100 MOTION IN LIMINE TO EXCLUDE TESTIMONY AS TO TRANSACTIONS WITH OR STATEMENTS BY JACK M. RAYNER, SR., AND DALE FAY RAYNER (Oral Argument Requested) (Hon. Gloria G. Ybarra)

Defendants Rayner move for an order excluding testimony by the plaintiff or its agents, or questions or statements by its counsel, about transactions with or statements by Jack M. Rayner, Sr., and Dale Fay Rayner. This motion is made pursuant to Arizona's Deadman's statute, Ariz. Rev. Stat. Ann. § 12-2251 (Supp. 1985), and is supported by the attached Memorandum of Points and Authorities.

DATED December 29, 1986.

By _____
Deborah E. Driggs
David L. Keily, for
SACKS, TIERNEY, KASEN & KERRICK, P.A.
Attorneys for Defendants

MEMORANDUM OF POINTS AND AUTHORITIES

I. FACTUAL BACKGROUND

Plaintiff Agua Fria Sand & Rock, Inc. (Agua Fria) brought this suit against defendants for fraud, breach of a duty of due care, and breach of a lease. Agua Fria was the assignee of a leasehold interest in certain real property owned by defendants. On this property, Agua Fria operated a sand and gravel mine. In February 1980, Agua Fria's plant and equipment were destroyed by a flood. After the flood, Agua Fria moved its operations to a new site on the property.

Agua Fria alleges that the defendants wrongfully evicted them from the new site. Although Agua Fria occupied the land as a tenant at will, it alleges that the defendants promised to execute and deliver a written lease for a term of 20 years.

The defendants deny that they had promised to execute and deliver a written lease for a term of 20 years to Agua Fria. They allege that Agua Fria was evicted because it had failed to make rental payments and to satisfy other lease obligations.

Jack M. Rayner, Sr., died on October 14, 1982. Dale Fay Rayner died on April 17, 1984. Jack M. Rayner, Jr., is the Personal Representative of the Estates of Jack M. Rayner, Sr., and Dale Fay Rayner. Agua Fria has sued Jack M. Rayner, Jr., in his capacity as Personal Representative of the estates of Jack M. Rayner, Sr., and Dale Fay Rayner.

Questions, argument, or testimony before the jury regarding alleged oral promises made by either testator will improperly influence the jury, even if objection at trial or related proceedings is sustained. Therefore, this Court should exclude all such references before trial.

II. ARGUMENT

The Arizona Deadman's Statute bars admission of testimony of transactions with, or statements by, Jack M. Rayner, Sr., and Dale Fay Rayner.

To reduce the danger of fraudulent testimony, the Arizona Deadman's statute restricts the admission of testimony about transactions with, or about statements made by, the testator in certain suits:

In an action by or against personal representatives, administrators, guardians or conservators in which judgment may be given for or against them as such, neither party shall be allowed to testify against the other as to any transaction with or statement by the testator, intestate or ward unless called to testify thereto by the opposite party, or required to testify thereto by the court. The provisions of this section shall extend to and include all actions by or against the heirs, devisees, legatees or legal representatives of a decedent arising out of any transaction with the decedent.

Ariz. Rev. Stat. Ann. § 12-2251 (Supp. 1985).

The statute clearly applies to this case. First, Agua Fria has filed suit against Jack M. Rayner, Jr., in his capacity as personal representative of the estates of Jack M. Rayner, Sr., and Dale Fay Rayner. Judgment may be granted for or against Jack M. Rayner, Jr., in his capacity as personal representative. Finally, Agua Fria plans to introduce evidence of an alleged oral agreement by the deceased, Jack M. Rayner, Sr., and Dale Fay Rayner, to execute a written lease with a term of 20 years.

The statute authorizes admission of testimony of transactions with or statements by the deceased if "required . . . by the court." Therefore, such admission ultimately lies within the discretion of the trial court. *Mahan v. First Nat'l Bank*, 139 Ariz. 138, 140, 677 P.2d 301, 303 (Ct. App. 1984). The trial court's determination to admit testimony of transactions with or statements by the decedent will be upheld only if (1) independent evidence corroborates the transaction with the decedent, and (2) an injustice will result if the testimony is rejected. *Id*.

Agua Fria has no independent evidence to support its claims that the deceased promised to execute and deliver a written lease of the premises for a term of 20 years. Instead, Agua Fria rests on the bald assertion that the deceased made such promises. This type of uncorroborated testimony is exactly what the statute was intended to proscribe.

Second, no injustice will result from exclusion of testimony of transactions with or statements by Jack M. Rayner, Sr., and Dale Fay Rayner. The exclusion will apply equally to both parties. Moreover, exclusion of the testimony comports strongly with public policy to render incompetent as witnesses persons who will gain from distortion of transactions with the decedent when death has rendered the decedent incapable of refuting these inaccuracies. *See Carrillo v. Taylor*, 81 Ariz. 14, 299 P.2d 188 (1956). The exclusion will simply preclude Plaintiff Agua Fria from making use of self-serving, uncorroborated declarations about what the deceased supposedly said. Agua Fria should not be able to manufacture lease obligations out of the alleged representations of those who are no longer able to refute them.

III. CONCLUSION

The objectionable testimony in this case is uncorroborated, and its exclusion will not result in an injustice. Therefore, this testimony should be excluded under the applicable Deadman's statute. To prevent evasion of the statute, this Court's order should apply broadly to comments or questions of counsel in front of the jury, as well as to testimony.

December 29, 1986.
SACKS, TIERNEY, KASEN & KERRICK, P.A.

Deborah E. Driggs
David L. Keily
3300 North Central Avenue
Phoenix, Arizona 85012-1576
Attorneys for Defendants

Part VIII

Appellate
Briefs

Writing appellate briefs differs from most pretrial brief writing in three respects. First, if you have fully tried your case before appeal, you will analyze the issues on appeal on a more complete factual record than was available during the litigation of pretrial motions. Second, in developing your arguments on appeal, you must consider standards of appellate review, which require varying levels of deference to trial court rulings and findings. Third, rules of procedure and local rules typically prescribe a more formal and detailed format for appellate briefs than for most pretrial or trial briefs.

Chapter 21

Standards of

Appellate Review

I. The Record on Appeal

Aside from physical exhibits and some kinds of documentary evidence admitted into court, the proceedings in the trial court are recorded in two records: the trial court clerk's record and the court reporter's transcript.[1] The trial history of a case can usually be most easily traced in the trial court clerk's record, which contains litigation documents filed with the trial court, from the initial pleadings to the notice of appeal. It also includes the written judgment of the court, along with orders reflecting the court's rulings on procedural and other preliminary matters. A docket sheet attached to the clerk's record contains a brief entry for each document in the record. This provides a convenient index to the record and a summary of the history of the litigation.

---

1. *E.g.*, FED. R. APP. P. 10(a).

The reporter's transcript is a record of all the statements made "on the record" in court during the litigation process. It includes oral arguments of the parties on motions, testimony of witnesses, rulings from the bench, and instructions to the jury.

Shortly after a disappointed litigant has filed notice of appeal from the judgment of the trial court, the parties on appeal designate the portions of the clerk's record and reporter's transcript that are necessary for the appeal.[2] In some circumstances, other original documents and physical exhibits admitted into evidence may also be forwarded to the appellate court.[3]

Before writing an appellate brief, you must master the record on appeal because the evidence and arguments presented to the trial court help to define the scope of the appellate court's inquiry. Indeed, when referring in your brief to testimony, arguments, rulings, or other portions of the trial history, you should carefully cite to the pages of the clerk's record or reporter's transcript that reflect that information. Although rules of procedure or local rules may specify a different citation form, common abbreviations for citation to, for example, page 134 of the clerk's record are "CR at 134," for "clerk's record." Page 383 of the reporter's transcript is commonly cited as "RT at 383" or "Trial Tr. at 383." If either record is bound in multiple volumes, you must also cite to the volume number in some reasonable fashion. For example, you might cite to page 115 of the third volume of the reporter's transcript as "III RT at 115" or "RT, vol. 3, at 115." In any of these citations, you can omit the "at," or replace it with an abbreviation for "page," depending on your style or applicable rules; for example, "CR 134," "RT p. 115"; or "RT, vol. 3, pg. 115." If separate records are not designated by volume numbers, include the date or other clarifying information. Finally, if the opening brief is accompanied by an appendix containing relevant parts of the record, appellate rules of procedure or local court rules may require citation to the appendix rather than to the underlying record.[4] One might cite to such an appendix in any of several reasonable ways, such as "Appendix p. 42," "Appendix at 42," or "App. 42."

II. Standards of Review in the Federal Courts

A. Overview

An appellate court will apply different standards of review to different kinds of trial court findings or rulings. For example, on a motion for summary judgment or a motion to dismiss an action for failure to state a claim, a trial court does not resolve any factual disputes; instead, it decides as a matter of law whether alleged or undisputed facts satisfy the applicable legal

---

2. *See, e.g.,* FED. R. APP. P. 10(b).

3. *See, e.g.,* FED. R. APP. P. 11(b)(2).

4. *E.g.,* FED. R. APP. P. 28(e).

standards. When reviewing a trial court's granting of such a motion, the appellate court will place itself in the position of the trial court and decide "*de novo*," without deference to the trial court's analysis, whether the moving party satisfied its burden on the motion.[5]

In contrast, a jury's verdict or a trial judge's findings of fact rendered after trial represent the fact finder's resolution of factual disputes. When reviewing such findings, an appellate court will restrict its review, deferring to some extent to the fact finder's resolution of conflicting evidence.

Thus, to effectively argue your case on appeal, you must consider the standard of review, or the degree to which the appellate court will defer to a finding or ruling made in the trial court. Indeed, the outcome of some appeals will depend directly on the standard of review that the appellate court chooses to apply.[6]

Appellate standards of review in the federal court system will serve as a starting point for your understanding standards that apply in a state court. Under the two most important standards—and subject to a "constitutional facts" exception discussed at the end of this chapter—an appellate court restricts its review of questions of fact but not of questions of law.

B. Restricted Appellate Review of Findings of Fact

1. Review of Jury Findings

The Seventh Amendment to the United States Constitution guarantees the right to a jury trial "in suits at common law," and it provides that "no fact tried by a jury shall be otherwise re-examined in any court of the United States, than according to the rules of the common law." Accordingly, a federal appellate court generally will uphold the factual findings of a jury in a civil case unless those findings are not supported by "any substantial evidence."[7] Federal statutes prescribe the same standard of review for the findings of some administrative agencies.[8]

Even though a different set of constitutional considerations applies, an appellate court will also restrict its review of a jury's findings of fact resulting

---

5. *See* Experimental Eng'g, Inc. v. United Techs. Corp., 614 F.2d 1244, 1246 (9th Cir. 1980) (reviewing dismissal of action for failure to state a claim); Heiniger v. City of Phoenix, 625 F.2d 842, 843-44 (9th Cir. 1980) (discussing standards of review for summary judgment).

6. *See, e.g.*, Chaline v. KCOH, Inc., 693 F.2d 477, 480 n.3 (5th Cir. 1982); Walsh v. Centeio, 692 F.2d 1239, 1241 (9th Cir. 1982).

7. *See, e.g.*, Aetna Life Ins. Co. v. Kepler, 116 F.2d 1, 4 & n.1 (8th Cir. 1941). Interestingly, a finding of negligence is not a pure finding of fact, because it requires the jury to define and apply a standard of care, resulting in a mixed conclusion of law and fact. For purposes of appellate review, however, such jury verdicts are treated as findings of fact. Appellate courts distinguish more finely between a trial judge's findings of fact and conclusions of law.

8. *See, e.g.*, 29 U.S.C. § 160(f) (2006) (appellate review of factual findings of the National Labor Relations Board); 5 U.S.C. § 706(2)(E) (2006) (judicial review of the factual findings of some administrative agency findings, as set forth in the Administrative Procedure Act); *In re* Gartside, 203 F.3d 1305 (Fed. Cir. 2000) (under the Administrative Procedure Act, "substantial evidence" standard of review applies to review of findings of fact of Patent and Trademark Office Board of Appeals).

in a criminal conviction. Specifically, rather than reweigh all the evidence, an appellate court may constitutionally uphold a criminal conviction if "the record evidence could reasonably support a finding of guilt beyond a reasonable doubt."[9]

The Seventh Amendment does not apply to state courts. Therefore, some states may permit broader appellate review of jury findings, particularly review of a jury's calculation of damages in a civil suit. New York, for example, has legislatively authorized its state appellate courts to overturn a jury's calculation of damages as excessive or inadequate if the jury award materially deviates from reasonable compensation. More typically, however, a state or federal trial court will set aside a jury's calculation of compensatory damages only if the damages are so excessive as to shock the conscience of the court, and an appellate court typically will overturn the trial court's determination on whether to set aside a jury award only if the trial court abused its discretion.[10]

2. Review of a Judge's Findings of Fact

In civil suits in which the parties have no constitutional or statutory right to a jury, or in suits in which the parties have waived their right to a jury, the trial judge will both find the facts and rule on the law. Under Federal Rule of Civil Procedure 52(a)(6), a federal court of appeals will not overturn the factual findings of a federal trial judge unless the findings are "clearly erroneous." Although Rule 52(a) applies only to civil proceedings and does not directly apply to a trial judge's factual findings on preliminary rulings in a criminal trial, some courts have adopted Rule 52(a)'s "clearly erroneous" standard by analogy for the criminal context.[11]

Under Rule 52(a)(1), a trial judge trying a case without a jury will divide his findings into findings of fact and conclusions of law. For example, he may state as a conclusion of law that a federal antidiscrimination statute requires proof of intent to discriminate, and he may state as a finding of fact that the evidence shows no discriminatory intent. On appeal, the appellate court could review without restriction the trial judge's interpretation of the statute to require proof of intent to discriminate; accordingly, it would reverse the trial court's conclusion on that question if it interpreted the statute differently. In contrast, the appellate court would not overturn the trial judge's factual finding of absence of discriminatory intent unless the record showed

---

9. Jackson v. Virginia, 443 U.S. 307, 318 (1979).

10. *See* Gasperini v. Ctr. for Humanities, Inc., 518 U.S. 415, 422 (1996) (comparing earlier judicial standards in New York courts to N.Y. CIV. PRAC. L. & R. § 5501(c) (McKinney 1995)). In *Gasperini*, the Court held that the Seventh Amendment is satisfied in a federal diversity action applying New York substantive law if the federal district court reviews the jury's award under the New York statutory standard and if the federal appellate court reviews the district court's determination only for abuse of discretion. *Id*. at 419, 432-39.

11. *See, e.g.*, Ornelas v. United States, 517 U.S. 690, 699 (1996) (in reviewing determinations of reasonable suspicion and probable cause in suppression hearing, appellate court reviews district court's findings of historical fact for clear error). Of course, the defendant has a right to a jury determination of the ultimate facts regarding criminal liability. *See* U.S. CONST. amend. VI.

that finding to be clearly erroneous,[12] even if the appellate judges might have found discriminatory intent had they been the initial fact finders.

One court has defined the clearly-erroneous standard of appellate review in a colorful manner that seems to require great deference to the trial court's findings of fact: "To be clearly erroneous, a decision must . . . strike us as wrong with the force of a five-week-old, unrefrigerated dead fish."[13] Under a more conventional measure of clear error, however, the reviewing court simply asks "whether 'on the entire evidence,' it is 'left with the definite and firm conviction that a mistake has been committed.'"[14] At least in theory, the clearly-erroneous standard permits slightly broader appellate review than does the substantial-evidence standard, which is typically applied to findings of juries and some administrative agencies:[15]

> Under the substantial-evidence standard, a reviewing court must uphold the findings of a jury or administrative agency if the record contains sufficient evidence to permit a reasonable person to make those findings. In contrast, the clearly-erroneous standard permits the reviewing court to review the entire record, and to overturn a finding of fact if it is convinced that the finding is clearly wrong, even though a reasonable person could have made the finding.[16]

An appellate court's deference to factual findings made in the trial court is supported by practical and policy considerations that recognize distinctions in the roles of trial and appellate courts. The fact finder in the trial court, either the judge or the jury, is generally in a better position than the appellate court to evaluate the evidence. This advantage is strongest when factual findings are based partly on the fact finder's evaluation of the credibility of witnesses: The mannerisms of the witness on the stand may be much more revealing than the cold print of the reporter's transcript. Accordingly, Rule 52(a)(6) specifically directs appellate courts to give "due regard to the trial court's opportunity to judge the witnesses' credibility."

Conversely, the trial court's advantage is weakest when factual findings are based largely on other evidence that is available in identical form to both the trial and appellate courts. Nonetheless, Rule 52(a)(6)'s restricted standard of review applies to "[f]indings of fact, whether based on oral or other evidence," suggesting that restrictions on appellate review must be at least

---

12. *See* Pullman-Standard v. Swint, 456 U.S. 273, 287-88 (1982).

13. Parts & Elec. Motors, Inc. v. Sterling Elec., Inc., 866 F.2d 228, 233 (7th Cir. 1988).

14. Easley v. Cromartie, 532 U.S. 234, 235 (2001) (quoting United States v. United States Gypsum Co., 333 U.S. 364, 395 (1948)).

15. *See, e.g.,* Dickinson v. Zurko, 527 U.S. 150, 162-64 (1999) (recognizing that the "clearly erroneous" standard allows for more searching review, but characterizing the difference as subtle, and observing that the choice between the two standards will not often determine the outcome); Loehr v. Offshore Logistics, Inc., 691 F.2d 758, 760-61 (5th Cir. 1982).

16. Charles R. Calleros, *Title VII and Rule 52(a): Standards of Appellate Review in Disparate Treatment Cases—Limiting the Reach of* Pullman-Standard v. Swint, 58 TUL. L. REV. 411 n.40 (1983) (citations omitted); *see also Zurko,* 527 U.S. at 162 (distinguishing between the "definite and firm conviction" required for clear error and the "reasonable mind" standard for the substantial evidence test).

partly based on policies other than a practical advantage enjoyed by the trial court.

In fact, restrictions on appellate review of findings of fact are independently justified by the importance of an appellate court's role in developing general principles of law relative to its role of correcting error in the judgment in a particular case. Admittedly, appellate courts should perform a limited "corrective" function by subjecting each trial judgment to some review for error and thus reducing the risk of injustice.[17] At least as important, however, is the appellate court's "institutional" function of "developing and declaring legal principles that will have application beyond the case that serves as the vehicle for expression of the principles."[18] This institutional function is strongest in the highest appellate court in a jurisdiction.[19] It emphasizes the development of a cohesive body of legal standards rather than the review of evidence supporting findings of fact.

C. Conclusions of Law: Mixed Conclusions of Fact and Law in a Nonjury Trial

In contrast to the restricted appellate review of findings of fact, appellate review of a trial judge's conclusions of law is unrestricted. The appellate court may freely correct the trial court's formulation of legal standards.[20]

Often, however, classifying a finding as more nearly one of law than of fact in a nonjury trial is a difficult task.[21] Without doubt, Rule 52(a)(6)'s clearly-erroneous standard applies to appellate review of a trial judge's findings of historical fact, such as findings about events and actions.[22] It also applies to review of "factual inferences" drawn by a trial court from "undisputed basic facts."[23] However, some trial court determinations fall between the two extremes of formulation of abstract legal standards and findings of historical fact or factual inference. For example, a trial judge's determination of whether the historical facts satisfy an abstract legal standard is a mixed finding of fact and law, which may contain elements of both factual inference and refinement of the legal standard.

1. Review of Discretionary Rulings

Appellate review of a narrow class of such mixed findings is restricted under a special standard of review. Specifically, an appellate court will severely

---

17. Calleros, *supra* note 16, at 421-22.

18. *Id.* at 420-21.

19. Indeed, under its "two-court rule," the United States Supreme Court will give particular deference to a finding of fact made by a trial judge and upheld on appeal in the intermediate court of appeals. *See, e.g.*, Rogers v. Lodge, 458 U.S. 613, 622-27 (1982).

20. *See* Pullman-Standard v. Swint, 456 U.S. 273, 287 (1982).

21. *See id.* at 288.

22. *See, e.g.*, Washington v. Watkins, 655 F.2d 1346, 1352 (5th Cir. 1981).

23. Commissioner v. Duberstein, 363 U.S. 278, 291 (1960) (citing United States v. United States Gypsum Co., 333 U.S. 364, 394 (1948)).

restrict its review of certain "discretionary" rulings of a trial judge, such as discovery and evidentiary rulings, the granting or denial of injunctive or declaratory relief, or the determination whether to grant a new trial. Assuming that the trial judge formulated the correct legal rule before applying it to the facts, the appellate court generally will not overturn such a mixed finding of the trial judge unless she abused her discretion.[24]

2. Mixed Findings as Predominantly Fact or Law

Most mixed findings, however, do not fall within this narrow class of discretionary rulings. Instead, for purposes of appellate standards of review, appellate courts must classify the findings under Rule 52(a) as findings of fact or conclusions of law. The proper means of accomplishing this classification is a matter of continuing debate.[25] However, the practical and policy considerations underlying restrictions on appellate review provide some guidance in the debate.

If a mixed question of fact and law requires the application of a simple, noncontroversial legal rule to complex historical facts, its resolution may primarily require the trial judge to refine her understanding of the facts rather than to engage in substantial legal reasoning. The trial judge is in the best position to make such a determination, and review of the resulting mixed finding requires exercise primarily of the appellate court's corrective function. Therefore, an appellate court should view the finding as more nearly a finding of factual inference than a conclusion of law, and it should restrict its review accordingly.

Consider, for example, a trial judge's ruling in one case that an employer's series of early retirement offers to employees did not amount to a "plan" subject to regulation under the federal Employee Retirement Income Security Act. The meaning of the statutory term "plan" adopted by the trial judge was a matter of law subject to unrestricted review; however, the mixed question of whether the early retirement offers satisfied the legal test for constituting a "plan" primarily required analysis of the factual characteristics of the offers. The appellate court thus treated this mixed question as "principally a question of fact," and it applied the restrictive "clearly erroneous" standard to its review of the trial judge's finding on that issue.[26]

---

24. *See, e.g.*, Gen. Elec. Co. v. Joiner, 522 U.S. 126 (1997) (district court's evidentiary rulings—including those on admission or exclusion of scientific evidence—are reviewed only for abuse of discretion); Browning-Ferris Indus. of Vt. v. Kelco Disposal, Inc., 492 U.S. 257, 279 (1989) (district court's decision whether to grant new trial or remittitur after jury award is reviewed for abuse of discretion), *cited with approval in* Gasperini v. Ctr. for Humanities, Inc., 518 U.S. 415, 435 (1996) (review of district court's decision whether to set aside jury award of damages in a diversity suit); Wilton v. Seven Falls Co., 515 U.S. 277, 289-90 (1995) (abuse of discretion standard for reviewing district court's decision whether to entertain a declaratory judgment action); Los Angeles Mem'l Coliseum Comm'n v. Nat'l Football League, 634 F.2d 1197, 1200 (9th Cir. 1980) (abuse of discretion standard for reviewing district court's decision whether to grant injunctive relief).

25. *See* Pullman-Standard v. Swint, 456 U.S. 273, 287 (1982).

26. Belanger v. Wyman-Gordon Co., 71 F.3d 451, 453-56 (1st Cir. 1995).

Conversely, if a mixed question of fact and law requires the application of complex, uncertain, or highly controversial legal standards to simple historical facts, the trial judge's resolution of the question may primarily reflect refinement of her understanding of the content of the legal rules. The appellate court is at least equally capable of making such a determination, and it will primarily exercise its institutional function on review. Therefore, an appellate court should view the finding as more nearly a conclusion of law than one of factual inference.[27]

Consider, for example, the question in one United States Supreme Court case of whether the government presented "clear, unequivocal and convincing" proof that a naturalized citizen had fraudulently procured his certificate of naturalization during World War II by falsely renouncing his allegiance to Nazi Germany and falsely swearing allegiance to the United States. The technical nature of the special standard of proof and the uncertainty and political sensitivity of the legal concept of "allegiance" made this mixed question primarily one of law. Therefore, the appellate courts could review the trial court's determination without restriction.[28]

3. Constitutional Facts Doctrine

Similarly, courts will freely review the mixed question of whether a jury award of punitive damages violates constitutional guarantees of due process[29] or whether particular speech falls within a category protected by the First Amendment.[30] Indeed, to safeguard constitutional guarantees of freedom of speech, courts have adopted a limited "constitutional facts" exception to the normally restricted review of findings of historical fact discussed above in Section II.B. In such cases, courts may examine the underlying record and freely review even some purely factual findings of a jury or trial court judge, if the facts are critical to the First Amendment analysis.[31] Even when freely reviewing findings of constitutional fact, however, the appellate court will defer to the fact finder's determinations of witness credibility.[32]

---

27. See generally United States v. McConney, 728 F.2d 1195, 1204 (9th Cir. 1984) (in a criminal case, adopting a "functional analysis that focuses on the nature of the inquiry required when we apply the relevant rule of law to the facts as established"); Calleros, supra note 16, at 425-32 (using different definitional framework to develop similar analysis).

28. Baumgartner v. United States, 322 U.S. 665 (1944).

29. Cooper Indus. v. Leatherman Tool Group, Inc., 532 U.S. 424 (2001).

30. See, e.g., Bose Corp. v. Consumers Union, 466 U.S. 485, 504-06 (1984).

31. Id. at 499-514 (freely reviewing district court's finding of actual malice in defamation case and referring to other cases and contexts, including independent review of the record in jury cases); see also id. at 515 (White, J., dissenting) (interpreting majority's analysis as applying to a pure question of fact); id. at 515 (Rehnquist, J., dissenting) (same); id. at 518 n.2 (Rehnquist, J., dissenting) (arguing that full independent review of constitutional facts found by state jury is less controversial than freely reviewing the careful, written findings of a district court judge); Adam Hoffman, Corralling Constitutional Fact: De Novo Fact Review in the Federal Appellate Courts, 50 DUKE L.J. 1427 (2001).

32. Bose, 466 U.S. at 499-500; Harte-Hanks Commc'ns, Inc. v. Connaughton, 491 U.S. 657, 688 (1989).

III. Summary

An appellate court will freely review a lower court's statement or formulation of a legal rule, without deference to the lower court's interpretation of the law. In contrast, an appellate court will substantially restrict its review of findings of fact in the trial court, with the precise standard of deference varying with the context. For the purpose of appellate review, a trial judge's application of law to facts will be treated in some courts either as a ruling of law or a finding of fact, depending on whether the trial court's analysis on that point is predominantly one of clarifying the legal rule in a factual context or one of drawing legally relevant factual inferences. Finally, an appellate court will restrict its review of a trial judge's exercise of discretion on certain kinds of issues.

The following chart summarizes widely adopted standards of appellate review for various kinds of trial rulings or findings. You should view the chart as only a starting point in your analysis of appellate review, because the precise standard of review in a particular context can vary between state and federal courts and between states.

TRIAL COURT DETERMINATION	APPELLATE STANDARD OF REVIEW
Finding of fact by jury and some administrative agencies	Affirmed if supported by substantial evidence
Finding of guilt by jury in criminal prosecution	Affirmed if rational basis or reasonable support in the evidence for a finding that prosecution met its burden of proof
Trial judge's exercise of discretion	Affirmed unless trial judge abused discretion
Trial judge's finding of fact	Affirmed unless clearly erroneous
Trial judge's ruling on the law or instructions on law to jury	Reviewed without restriction and rejected if appellate court disagrees on the merits
Trial judge's mixed finding of law and fact	Treated as finding of fact or conclusion of law, depending on whether legal or factual questions predominate

Chapter 22

The Brief—Effective Appellate Advocacy

I. Overview of Appellate Briefs: Formats and Filing

Rules of procedure and local court rules typically prescribe more formal and detailed formats for appellate briefs than for motions memoranda and other briefs. As the following examples illustrate, you must follow the latest version of applicable rules in the appropriate jurisdiction to ensure that the clerk's office of the court will accept your brief for filing.

A. Components of the Opening Brief

When you represent the "appellant" (bringing an appeal as a matter of right) or the "petitioner" (if you must petition the court to accept the case for discretionary review), you will file the opening brief, seeking reversal of the judgment below. At a minimum, typical rules will require this brief to include the following substantive components:

1. a statement of the issues raised on appeal;

2. a statement of the procedural history of the case (frequently entitled "Statement of the Case" or "Proceedings Below");

3. a statement of the facts relevant to issues raised on appeal;

4. an argument (often preceded by a summary of the argument, either as mandated by applicable rules or as a matter of the brief writer's discretion); and

5. a conclusion.

In addition, rules of procedure or court rules typically require other substantive and formal components such as a table of contents, an alphabetically arranged table of authorities, and statements of jurisdiction and of standards of review. For example, United States Supreme Court Rule 24.1 requires nine components in opening briefs to that court, along with a table of contents and a table of authorities in all but very short briefs:

Rule 24. Briefs on the Merits: In General

1. A brief on the merits for a petitioner or an appellant . . . shall contain in the order here indicated:

(a) The questions presented for review . . . .

(b) A list of all parties to the proceeding in the court whose judgment is under review . . . .

(c) If the brief exceeds 1,500 words, a table of contents and a table of cited authorities.

(d) Citations of the official and unofficial reports of the opinions and orders entered in the case by courts and administrative agencies. [This serves as a guide to the procedural history.]

(e) A concise statement of the basis for jurisdiction in this Court, including the statutory provisions and time factors on which jurisdiction rests.

(f) The constitutional provisions, treaties, statutes, ordinances, and regulations involved in the case, ...

(g) A concise statement of the case, setting out the facts material to the consideration of the questions presented, ...

(h) A summary of the argument, suitably paragraphed. . . .

(i) The argument, exhibiting clearly the points of fact and of law presented and citing the authorities and statutes relied on.

(j) A conclusion specifying with particularity the relief the party seeks.

For briefs filed with a United States Court of Appeals, Federal Rule of Appellate Procedure 28(a) specifies eight components for the appellant's opening brief, with two others required in certain circumstances. As amended in 2013, Rule 28(a)(6) now combines two previously separate components into a single "statement of the case," which includes both the procedural history and the statement of facts. Rule 28(a) now requires the following format for the opening brief:

Rule 28. Briefs

(a) Appellant's Brief. The appellant's brief must contain, under appropriate headings and in the order indicated:

(1) a corporate disclosure statement if required by Rule 26.1;

(2) a table of contents, with page references;

(3) a table of authorities — cases (alphabetically arranged), statutes, and other authorities — with references to the pages of the brief where they are cited;

(4) a jurisdictional statement, including:

(A) the basis for the district court's or agency's subject-matter jurisdiction, with citations to applicable statutory provisions and stating relevant facts establishing jurisdiction;

(B) the basis for the court of appeals' jurisdiction, with citations to applicable statutory provisions and stating relevant facts establishing jurisdiction;

(C) the filing dates establishing the timeliness of the appeal or petition for review; and

(D) an assertion that the appeal is from a final order or judgment that disposes of all parties' claims, or information establishing the court of appeals' jurisdiction on some other basis;

(5) a statement of the issues presented for review;

(6) a concise statement of the case setting out the facts relevant to the issues submitted for review, describing the relevant procedural history, and identifying the rulings presented for review, with appropriate references to the record (see Rule 28(e));

(7) a summary of the argument, which must contain a succinct, clear, and accurate statement of the arguments made in the body of the brief, and which must not merely repeat the argument headings;

(8) the argument, which must contain:

(A) appellant's contentions and the reasons for them, with citations to the authorities and parts of the record on which the appellant relies; and

(B) for each issue, a concise statement of the applicable standard of review (which may appear in the discussion of the issue or under a separate heading placed before the discussion of the issues);

(9) a short conclusion stating the precise relief sought; and

(10) the certificate of compliance, if [the brief satisfies length requirements through word or line count under Rule 32(a)(7), rather than through page limitations].

B. Components of Answering and Reply Briefs

If you represent the "appellee" or "respondent," the party seeking a ruling affirming the judgment of the court below, you must file an answering brief. In the United States Courts of Appeals, for example, Federal Rule of Appellate Procedure 28(b) provides that the appellee's answering brief should include all the components listed for the appellant's opening brief except for subsection (a)(9); however, the appellee may adopt the statements of jurisdiction, issues, case, facts, and standard of review presented in the appellant's brief if the appellee is satisfied with them.

According to subsection Rule 28(c), the appellant may respond to the appellee's answering brief with a reply brief, but the reply brief can dispense with most of the statements set forth in the appellant's opening brief. In addition to an argument responding to the answering brief, the reply brief need contain only a table of contents and a table of authorities, as well as the certificate of compliance if it satisfies length requirements through word or line count.

C. Formatting and Other Formal Requirements

Rules of procedure or local court rules typically specify additional formal requirements regarding such things as typeface, line spacing, margins, overall length, and the color of the cover sheets for the opening, answering, and reply briefs.[1]

The specified form for the information on the cover of an appellate brief varies in different jurisdictions. In some jurisdictions, the cover sheet includes the caption of the case in the same basic format as it appeared in trial pleadings and briefs, as illustrated by the sample briefs at the end of this chapter and Chapters 18 through 20. In other jurisdictions, including the United States Courts of Appeals, rules of procedure require the cover to include certain identifying information, which attorneys usually present on several widely spaced lines that are centered on the cover page.[2]

D. Filing the Brief in Hard Copy and Electronically

Court rules have traditionally contemplated that appellate advocates will provide multiple copies of briefs in "hard copy," printed or typewritten on paper. More recently, however, all federal courts and many state courts have adopted rules that permit or require parties to file briefs by electronic means, such as by uploading the brief onto the court's online case management system, and sometimes permitting hyperlinks that connect citations in the brief to cited authorities or passages in the record.[3] United States Supreme

---

1. *See, e.g.*, FED. R. APP. P. 32(a).
2. *See* FED. R. APP. P. 32(a)(2).
3. *See, e.g.*, FED. R. APP. P. 25(a)(2)(D) (authorizing federal courts of appeals to adopt local rules permitting electronic filing of briefs and other documents); 9TH CIR. R. 25-5 (requiring electronic filing of briefs by attorneys, with listed exceptions); 11TH CIR. R. 25-3,

Court rules require briefs submitted to that court to be filed both electronically and in hard copy.[4]

II. Statement of Issues

The art of stating issues in a student case brief or an office memorandum is discussed in detail in Section II.B.2 of Chapter 7 and Section III.A of Chapter 11. You should review those principles now as a starting point for drafting the statement of issues in your appellate brief. When drafting an issue statement in a brief, however, you should additionally strive to phrase the issue in a way that suggests a favorable response or otherwise serves to advocate your client's case.

A. Issue Statements as Preliminary Advocacy

Your statement of the issue can invite the court to apply an analytic framework or standard of review that best suits your client's arguments. Of course, you should develop that strategy primarily in the argument section of the brief. In addition, however, you can make the judge more receptive to your approach by initially exposing her to the theme of your brief in your statement of the issues.

For example, suppose that you represent an appellant who appeals from a trial judge's decision to deny a preliminary injunction. You know that the appellate court will overturn that decision only if the trial judge abused her discretion, provided that the trial judge applied the proper legal standards to the facts.[5] However, you believe that her ruling leaves some room for questions about the content of the legal rules governing injunctions that she applied to the facts. Accordingly, you might use the statement of the issue to invite the appellate court to find error in the trial judge's formulation of the legal rules, which formulation would be subject to unrestricted review, as discussed in Chapter 21:

In denying Surge Corp.'s request for a preliminary injunction, did the trial judge apply an incorrect legal rule by requiring a showing of likelihood of success on the merits, rather than using a "sliding-scale" test that would justify a prelimi-

---

31-5 (requiring electronic briefs in addition to paper briefs, usually uploaded onto the court's web site, but on CD-ROM if exemptions apply); 2D CIR. R. 25-1(c),(j) (mandating electronic filing unless exempt). The Second Circuit's rule requires that an initiating document be sent by e-mail, 2D CIR. R. 25-1(c)(2), and it allows briefs to contain hyperlinks to authority and to other filed documents, 2D CIR. R. 25-1(i).

4. U.S.S. CT. R. 25.

5. *See, e.g.*, Los Angeles Mem'l Coliseum Comm'n v. Nat'l Football League, 634 F.2d 1197, 1200 (9th Cir. 1980).

nary injunction upon a showing of especially great irreparable harm and at least substantial questions on the merits?

The opposing counsel may argue that the trial judge in fact applied a sliding-scale test and that the judge's balancing of the facts does not reflect an abuse of discretion under the most flexible of legal rules. Nonetheless, he might frame the issue so that it emphasizes the restricted standard of review of the ultimate ruling and refers only abstractly to potential questions about choices among legal rules:

Did the trial judge properly exercise her discretion to deny preliminary injunctive relief on the ground that Surge Corp. failed to make the requisite showing on the merits under applicable legal rules?

Of course, the nature of the opportunity to promote a favorable approach in the statement of the issue will vary with the circumstances of each appeal. For example, an appeal in a contract dispute might raise a purely legal question about whether the peculiar facts of an exceptional case justify a special exception to the general common law requirement of consideration for contract formation. If so, the parties might use their statements of the issue, as well as their arguments, to appeal either to the appellate judges' senses of fairness and justice or to their appreciation of the benefits of certainty in the law.

In those circumstances, if you represent the party who would benefit from an exception to the general rule, you might use the statement of the issue to promote the value of fairness by vividly and concretely emphasizing the peculiar facts of the case:

Does McGowin's moral obligation to perform his promise to pay Webb for past services give rise to a legal obligation in light of the serious physical injuries suffered by Webb and the immeasurable benefit he gave to McGowin in heroically saving McGowin's life?

This statement of the issue appeals to the appellate court's corrective function: reaching a just result on the unique facts of the particular case before it, even if that requires a departure from general principles.[6]

In contrast, if you represent the party who would benefit from application of the general rule, you would advance a different theme. Specifically, you might use the statement of the issue to promote the consideration rule in its abstract form or to emphasize the general policies supporting the rule:

---

6. *See generally* Webb v. McGowin, 168 So. 196, 199 (Ala. Ct. App. 1936) (Samford, J., concurring) (departing from "strict letter of the rule" in the interests of justice).

Did the trial court correctly reject a vague and uncertain "moral obligation" exception to the fundamental principle that a promise made in recognition of past services lacks consideration and therefore is unenforceable?

This issue appeals to the appellate court's institutional function: the wisdom of applying the rule in nearly every context, the importance of maintaining the vitality of a long-standing rule, and the need for certainty and predictability in the law.[7]

B. Credibility of the Advocate

In phrasing the statement of the issue to advocate an approach or a conclusion, you should not be so anxious to invite a favorable response that you state a false issue. For example, assume that you represent a criminal defendant who appeals from a state conviction for illegal possession of cocaine. The applicable criminal statute defines "possession" as contemporaneous intent and ability to exercise physical control over the substance. If the trial judge correctly instructed the jury on the applicable legal rules and definitions, you might still argue that substantial evidence did not support the jury finding of ability to exercise control over the cocaine. If so, the following statement of the issue would not effectively advance your client's cause:

Is proof of ability to control an illegal substance a requisite element of a conviction for illegal possession of that substance?

Under currently accepted legal definitions in the state, an appellate judge would readily agree that the question presented by this statement of the issue must be answered affirmatively. However, she would object that the question does not fairly characterize any genuine issue on appeal. Because the trial judge correctly instructed the jury on the applicable legal standards, your implicit attack on the completeness of the instructions would be futile. Instead, your issue statement must fairly address your client's true contention on appeal:

Is the jury's finding of Wade's ability to control the cocaine unsupported by the evidence in light of undisputed testimony that the officers found Wade standing outside the locked automobile containing the cocaine, without a key to the automobile?

---

7. *See generally* Mills v. Wyman, 3 Pick. 207 (Mass. 1825) (rejecting "moral obligation" exception in the interests of maintaining universal application of the consideration doctrine).

Thus, you must recognize limits on your efforts to invite a favorable response to a statement of the issue. Specifically, you must maintain credibility and must fairly link the statement of the issue to your genuine argument on appeal.

III. Statement of Procedural History

Rules of procedure or local court rules will specify whether you must state the procedural history in a separate section or combine it with the historical facts. If the rules require you to state the procedural history in a separate section, they typically designate the section as the "Statement of the Case." If the rules instead require you to combine the facts and procedural history, they typically designate the combined section as either the "Statement of the Case" or the "Statement of Facts." With either format, the essential elements of a statement of procedural history are brief descriptions of "the nature of the case, the course of proceedings, and the disposition below."[8]

In the opening paragraph of the statement of procedural history, you should introduce the parties and generally describe the claims and defenses that they presented in the trial court. Next, you should chronologically recite the portions of the trial history and the rulings of the court that are relevant to the issues on appeal, including the trial court's final judgment and the appellant's filing notice of appeal. In a brief to a second-level court of appeal, you should also summarize the ruling of the intermediate appellate court. As described in Section I above, court rules in some jurisdictions may require you to discuss additional matters.

Once you have identified parties as the appellant and the appellee in your brief, you would do well in any jurisdiction to follow federal appellate rules for referring to parties:

> References to Parties. In briefs and at oral argument, counsel should minimize use of the terms "appellant" and "appellee." To make briefs clear, counsel should use the parties' actual names or the designations used in the lower court or agency proceeding, or such descriptive terms as "the employee," "the injured person," "the taxpayer," "the ship," "the stevedore."[9]

IV. Statement of Facts

A. Telling a Compelling Story

The opening statement of facts in a brief can play a surprisingly important role in your advocacy. A persuasive statement of facts near the begin-

---

8. FED. R. APP. P. 28(a)(6).
9. FED. R. APP. P. 28(d).

ning of your brief may incline a judge to rule in favor of your client even before the judge has considered the legal analysis. If so, the judge may take advantage of the flexibility or uncertainty in the legal principles to reach the result that the facts have persuaded her to define as just, provided that she can do so without departing from clearly controlling precedent or otherwise upsetting the orderly development of a coherent body of law. A persuasive opening statement of facts will help make the judge receptive to the legal and factual analyses in the argument section of your brief.

As you can imagine, the appellant's statement of facts and the appellee's statement of facts should evoke very different reactions in the reader. Each brings the client's story to the fore while stating the facts accurately, fairly, and completely.

Good examples of fact statements appear in the opening and answering appellate briefs at the end of this chapter, taken from a case in which a shopper sued a department store and others for wrongfully detaining him after accusing him of shoplifting. The fact statement in each brief tells the story from a very different perspective than that advanced in the opposing brief. The brief for the shopper emphasizes facts that show how events unfolded from the shopper's perspective, detailing how he entered the store twice and made three separate purchases during those visits. The brief for the department store emphasizes facts that show how events unfolded within the perception of store employees, who were confused by the shopper's multiple purchases, some placed in the same shopping bag.

Each brief states the facts fairly, accurately, and completely, with citations to the record. Yet, each also succeeds in presenting the client's perspective in an engaging manner that holds the reader's attention. A simple trip to the store for farm tools unfolds as a drama, complete with the shopper's flirtation with a store employee, tough talk between the shopper and security guards, and a shoving match between the shopper and a police officer resulting in the shopper stumbling head first through a wall of the store's security room.

Not every case will present such dramatic events; consequently, it will not always be easy to present your facts in a way that "commands the reader's attention" and "compels the reader to keep reading."[10] Nonetheless, if you develop a good theme as discussed in Chapter 16, if you employ the techniques of persuasive writing style explored in Chapter 17, and if you emphasize facts that tell the story from your client's perspective, any case can lend itself to telling a compelling story.[11]

B. Constraints That Build Trust

To present the facts persuasively, you may be tempted to slant the record misleadingly in favor of your client's case or to introduce legal arguments and conclusions in the statement of facts. Neither technique will succeed.

10. Mark K. Osbeck, *What Is "Good Legal Writing" and Why Does It Matter?*, 4 DREXEL L. REV. 417 (2012).

11. For much more on telling your client's story, in both legal and factual argument, *see* Ruth Anne Robbins, Steve Johansen & Ken Chestek, YOUR CLIENT'S STORY (2013).

Conversely, if you combine persuasive themes and writing style with accuracy and completeness, judges likely to will turn to your statement of facts as a trustworthy reference.

1. Advocacy with Credibility

If you riddle your statement of facts with exaggerations or misleading omissions, you will simply diminish your credibility. Instead, your statement of facts should display your client in a favorable light while reflecting a concern for completeness and accuracy. If the judge is convinced that your statement is accurate and complete, he may repeatedly turn to it for a fair summary of the record, resulting in maximum exposure of the subtle advocacy of your statement.

Rather than omit unfavorable facts, you should place them in a context that minimizes their impact and that helps you emphasize favorable facts. In addition to the techniques of persuasive writing discussed in Chapter 17, you can use the organization of the entire fact statement to emphasize the favorable facts. Chronological order of facts may be the clearest and most logical; it is certainly the order most often recommended by judges. However, you can increase the impact of favorable events by describing them in the places of greatest emphasis: the beginning and end of the fact statement. If you can do so without unduly sacrificing clarity and continuity, you can justify departing from chronological order or at least supplementing a chronological statement with a second reference to a critical and favorable fact at the beginning or end.

You can also emphasize favorable facts by using specific, concrete descriptions and strong verbs in active voice. Conversely, you can lessen the impact of unfavorable facts by describing them in general, abstract terms.

For example, suppose that Samuel Hughes, convicted of first-degree murder, had sought at trial to mitigate the offense by showing that he was intoxicated at the time of the crime and therefore could not have premeditated the killing. On appeal, he hopes to persuade the court to interpret the statutory requirement of premeditation in a restrictive manner so that it will apply only to deliberation with a relatively clear mind.

As appellate counsel for Hughes, you could emphasize the intoxication, while referring to the murder with a light touch, even though you must concede that Hughes struck the fatal blow, as established by several eyewitnesses:

When he fatally injured the decedent, Samuel Hughes was staggering from the effects of a full pint of whiskey.

This statement refers to both the killing and the victim in abstract terms and in a subordinate clause. Moreover, it humanizes the defendant in the main clause by referring to him by name and describing his intoxication vividly.

Conversely, as the prosecutor on appeal, you could deemphasize Hughes's intoxication by referring to it generally, and you could emphasize his aggressive conduct by describing it in gruesome detail:

While under the influence of self-induced intoxication, the defendant murdered Grace Smith by bludgeoning her from behind with a baseball bat.

This statement relegates the defendant to anonymity by referring to him with a procedural label. In contrast, it names the victim, thus inviting the reader to recognize her as a person, rather than a statistic. Moreover, the description of the attack as one from behind tends to portray the victim as particularly sympathetic and defenseless. The statement not only refers to the defendant's impaired state of mind abstractly and in a subordinate phrase, it invites the reader to reject intoxication as a mitigating factor by characterizing it as self-induced. Finally, powerful verbs—"murdered" and "bludgeoning"—convey the horror of the assault.

Neither of these statements directly addresses the legal issue of statutory interpretation. Both are designed, however, to remind the judge of the concrete factual context in which the statute will apply in this case. Each statement portrays the event in a light that could make the judge more or less receptive to a restrictive interpretation of the statute.

2. Premature Legal Argument

If your fact statement crosses the line between presenting facts in a favorable light and prematurely introducing legal argument, you may undermine its effectiveness as a vehicle for making the judge receptive to your main argument. A judge knows that the legal argument of a brief will be one-sided, and he generally reserves judgment on legal conclusions until he has read both briefs. But he may be more willing to develop an immediate impression of the case from an apparently complete and accurate statement of facts.

For example, if the prosecutor's statement of facts specifically characterizes an act as premeditated, thus assuming a favorable interpretation of that statutory element, the judge may react defensively; he may warn himself that he should resist such a mixed conclusion of law and fact until he has thoroughly studied the arguments in both briefs. On the other hand, if the prosecutor's statement of facts vividly describes the convicted defendant as seething from a humiliating insult and then selecting a baseball bat as a weapon for retaliation after rejecting a cue stick as insufficiently weighty, the judge is invited to draw his own conclusion that the statutory element of premeditation does not require a restrictive interpretation to account for intoxication. Even if tentative or subconscious, that conclusion could predispose the judge at an early stage to accept the prosecutor's explicit legal arguments and conclusions in the argument section of the prosecutor's brief.

Conversely, when the judge reaches the argument section of the brief, he may resist arguments supporting conclusions that you had bluntly attempted to force on him in the statement of facts. He will be more comfortable with arguments that seem to confirm conclusions he had reached on his own after reading apparently nonargumentative facts.

3. Permissible Sources for the Facts

Your statement of facts on appeal is subject to two further limitations. First, except for matters within common knowledge or otherwise subject to judicial notice,[12] the appellate court and the litigants are constrained by the trial court record as the exclusive source of the facts of the dispute. In a fully tried case, those facts are reflected in testimony recorded in the reporter's transcript, in documentary evidence admitted at trial, and in any physical evidence admitted at trial and retained by the trial court clerk. If the trial court disposed of the case on the pleadings or on summary judgment, the facts are reflected in the allegations of the pleadings or in the preliminary presentation of evidence on the motion for summary judgment. Rules of procedure and local court rules will set forth the responsibilities of the parties, primarily the appellant, in forwarding all or part of the trial court record to the appellate court and in filing relevant portions in an appendix to the appellate briefs.[13]

Second, if findings of fact are made by a jury or by the trial court, those findings take on greater significance than the underlying record of testimony and other evidence because of the restricted appellate review of such findings, as discussed in Chapter 21. If the appellant wishes to challenge the findings of fact, the appellant should refer to the underlying record of evidence to support the challenge; however, the findings normally will stand unless they are clearly erroneous or unsupported by substantial evidence. If the appellant instead chooses to limit the attack to a challenge of the trial judge's formulation of legal standards or the judge's application of those standards to facts, the appellant must rely on the findings of fact, perhaps with supplementary references to illuminating evidence that is consistent with the findings. The appellee should focus on either the findings or the underlying evidence supporting the findings, depending on which response most appropriately meets the appellant's challenge. These strategic considerations are illustrated in Section V.D.1, below.

As discussed in Chapter 21, Section I, when you refer to facts or procedural history in any section of your appellate brief, you must cite to the source. Applicable rules may require you to cite directly to the underlying record on appeal or to an appendix that contains excerpts of the record.[14]

---

12. *See, e.g.*, FED. R. EVID. 201 and advisory committee note on subsection (f) (judicial notice of adjudicative facts in trial and on appeal); United States v. Pink, 315 U.S. 203, 216 (1942) (appellate judicial notice of record in other case); Ellie Margolis, *Beyond Brandeis: Exploring the Uses of Non-Legal Materials in Appellate Briefs*, 34 U.S.F.L. REV. 197 (2000) (arguing for effective use of nonlegal materials to establish "legislative facts" on appeal, as well as at trial).

13. *E.g.*, FED. R. APP. P. 10 (the record on appeal), 11 (forwarding the record), 30 (appendix to the briefs), 32(b) (form of appendix).

14. *E.g.*, FED. R. APP. P. 28(e), 30(c)(2); *see also* Han v. Stanford Univ., 210 F.3d 1038 (9th Cir. 2000) (appeal dismissed for failure to correct opening and reply briefs' omission of

C. Summary and Perspective

To ensure that your opening statement of facts increases the judge's receptivity to your main argument, you should

1. tell a compelling story from your client's perspective;
2. state the facts completely and accurately, drawn from permissible sources;
3. emphasize favorable facts and deemphasize unfavorable ones through sentence structure, varying levels of specificity and concreteness, and general organization; and
4. avoid premature argument.

V. The Argument

Earlier chapters and exercises have provided you with the basic information and skills you need to formulate, organize, and express your arguments in any brief. In summary, for each issue you should

1. state the conclusion you want the court to adopt in an argumentative point heading,
2. argue for a favorable interpretation of legal authority,
3. apply the legal rules to the facts, and
4. state the conclusion that you want the appellate court to reach.

This section will supplement the earlier chapters by examining some characteristics that are peculiar to appellate arguments.

A. Summary of Argument

Some rules of procedure and local court rules will require, or at least permit, appellate advocates to include a summary of the argument immediately before the main argument.[15] If applicable rules do not require a summary, you should include one in a separate section if your brief is sufficiently complex that an overview of your arguments will substantially enhance your reader's comprehension. If a summary in a separate section is neither required nor appropriate, you nonetheless should consider beginning your argument with an overview paragraph that outlines your arguments and conveys the theme of your brief.

If you do include a summary of argument in a separate section of your brief, you should place it under a section heading entitled "Summary of

---

citations to the record). For a guide to preparing an appellate appendix containing excerpts of the record on appeal, *see* Roger J. Miner, *Essay: Common Disorders of the Appendix and Their Treatment*, 3 J. App. Prac. & Process 39-54 (2001).

15. *E.g.*, Fed. R. App. P. 28(a)(7).

Argument." United States Supreme Court Rule 24.1(h) calls for a "clear and concise condensation of the argument made in the body of the brief," and it contemplates a multi-paragraph summary, because it states that the summary should be "suitably paragraphed."

The summary, however, should not stretch into several pages. A summary should do no more than briefly explain your major points in a few paragraphs, citing only to the most significant authorities. Along with the collection of point headings in your Table of Contents, the Summary of Argument can provide your reader with a general road map of her journey through your brief. If the summary delves into your argument in even moderate detail, however, it will make the main argument seem repetitive, to the irritation of your reader.

B. Standard of Review

Standards of appellate review are examined in detail in Chapter 21, and their significance to appellate strategy and argument is evident throughout the current chapter. Not surprisingly, the standard of review for each issue on appeal is a matter of great interest to the court as well as to the advocates. Consequently, even if applicable court rules do not require it, you should state the standard or standards of review, either in a separate section of the brief or at the outset of your argument for each issue on appeal. Your statement might be as simple as a single sentence, such as the following reference to unrestricted review: "This Court will engage in *de novo* review of the district court's summary judgment for the defendant. *See Heininger* . . . ."

Occasionally, the standard of review will be a matter of dispute between the parties; if so, you should devote a section of your argument to this topic, just as you develop other arguments in your brief. In an appeal by your client from a nonjury trial in federal court, for example, the parties might dispute whether the trial judge correctly classified a finding as one of law or fact. You might have reason to argue that a finding classified as a "finding of fact" should be treated instead as a mixed finding of law and fact in which questions about the boundaries of the legal rule predominate. If the appellate court agrees with your description of the finding, it might review the finding without restriction, as a question of law rather than as a finding of fact.

C. Arguing the Law—The Role of Policy Analysis

1. The Enhanced Role of Policy Analysis on Appeal

Appellate briefs differ in style from pretrial and trial briefs in part because they examine the underlying policies of legal standards to a greater extent. Depending on the procedural posture and other circumstances of a particular appeal, this difference in approach may be reflected in such factors as the restrictions on appellate review of factual findings, the appellate court's institutional function of developing a cohesive body of law, and the varying degrees to which stare decisis controls decisions at various levels of the court system.

Unless the appellant assumes the difficult burden of challenging factual findings made in the trial court, the appellate briefs likely will explore questions about the content of legal rules, either in the abstract or in the process of determining whether the accepted facts satisfy the rules. Because the appellate court can overrule its own precedents, it will consider policy arguments that favor or oppose extending, modifying, or overruling those precedents.

The institutional function of the appellate courts further encourages policy analysis in appellate brief writing. For two reasons, this effect is greatest in the highest court of a jurisdiction. First, unlike an intermediate court of appeals, the highest court is not bound by the precedent of any court within that jurisdiction.[16] Second, the highest courts in many jurisdictions will accept review of some kinds of lower court decisions only after a discretionary determination that appellate resolution would help develop a cohesive body of law or otherwise would significantly affect the outcome of many cases other than the one that serves as the vehicle for addressing the questions.

Thus, more often than in trial briefs, appellate advocates will allocate substantial portions of their arguments to the policies underlying legal rules and to the social and jurisprudential consequences of retaining or abandoning those rules. Moreover, these characteristics typically will be even more pronounced in a court of last resort than in an intermediate court of appeals.

For example, the following two passages are excerpts of arguments about the proper application of precedent of the state supreme court, the highest court in the state. The first argument could be addressed to the trial court or even to the intermediate court of appeals. Because neither court can overrule the state supreme court precedent, the argument focuses on the applicability of the precedent to the facts of the dispute:

B. The trial judge erred in instructing the jury that Bramwell could be liable for the tort of wrongful discharge if he discharged Kirkeide in "bad faith" rather than in violation of public policy.

The trial court's instruction on the tort of wrongful discharge fails to distinguish between conduct that violates a public policy and conduct that may strike the employee as unfair or unwarranted in the context of a particular employment relationship. This instruction permitted the jury to award damages against Bramwell for conduct that is not a tort in this state.

Introduction to argument

---

16. Of course, decisions of a state court of last resort on a question of federal law could be reviewed by the United States Supreme Court, and the state court would be bound by United States Supreme Court precedent on such questions.

**General legal
rule**

The New Maine Supreme Court has recently recognized a cause of action in tort for wrongful discharge. However, it carefully limited its holding to discharges that violate public policy:

> Thus, an employer is liable in tort for wrongful discharge if it discharges an employee for a reason that violates an important public policy of the state. Pronouncements of public policy will most often be found in our state's constitution and its legislation.

Blass v. Arcon Co., 337 N. Me. 771, 776 (1996).

In-depth case analysis

In *Blass*, the employer discharged a truck driver in retaliation for the driver's refusal to transport toxic wastes in unsafe containers. The employer was liable in tort for wrongful discharge because its conduct violated the policies of state environmental and occupational safety statutes. *See id.* at 777.

**Application
to facts**

In contrast to *Blass*, Bramwell's discharge of Kirkeide in this case did not violate any public policy. At most, Bramwell acted hastily and exercised poor business judgment, but not in a way that implicates public policy. Yet, the trial court's instruction permitted the jury to impose liability . . . .

In the preceding illustration, the *Blass* decision did not need to address whether a discharge can be tortious for reasons other than a violation of public policy; therefore, it does not preclude future extensions of the new tort of wrongful discharge. Nonetheless, the brief writer has reasonably assumed that a trial court or intermediate court of appeals would not readily extend a newly recognized tort beyond the terms of the Supreme Court's holding. Thus, the brief writer concentrates on explaining the holding of the *Blass* decision and distinguishing it.

In contrast, the following passage is addressed to the New Maine Supreme Court, the mythical author of the *Blass* decision. Because that court can overrule, limit, or extend its own precedent, the argument spends more time on policy analysis. Specifically, it argues that, as a matter of policy, the court should not broaden the tort of wrongful discharge beyond the holding of the *Blass* decision.

B. The trial judge erred in instructing the jury that Bramwell could be liable . . . .

**Introduction to
argument**

The trial court's instruction on the tort of wrongful discharge fails to distinguish between conduct that violates a public policy and conduct that . . . .

Although this Court has recently recognized a cause of action in tort for wrongful discharge, it carefully limited its holding to discharges that violate public policy:

    Thus, an employer is liable . . . .

Blass v. Arcon Co., 337 N. Me. 771, 776 (1996).

In *Blass*, the employer discharged a truck driver in retaliation for the driver's refusal to transport toxic wastes in unsafe containers. . . .

This court should reject Kirkeide's invitation to extend the tort of wrongful discharge beyond the holding of *Blass*. This state has long promoted the policy of freedom of contract, permitting contracting parties to shape their own rights and obligations. *See, e.g.*, *Snell v. Abundes*, 128 N. Me. 217, 221 (1970). Even if limited to violations of public policy, the tort of wrongful discharge effectively limits the parties' freedom to create a contract that is terminable at the will of either party. Any further restriction on the freedom to contract would require courts to review nearly every contested business decision that affects the tenure of an employee. To preserve freedom of contract and to conserve judicial resources, this Court should narrowly tailor the tort of wrongful discharge to impose liability only for discharges that offend the values of society as a whole, and not for employment decisions that merely reflect a failed relationship between two private parties.

In our case, the trial court's instruction, approved by the court of appeals, extended the tort of wrongful discharge beyond the holding of *Blass*. By permitting an award of damages for a "bad-faith" discharge, ...

*Side annotations:*

General legal rule

In-depth case analysis

Policy analysis

Application to facts

2. The Persuasive Value of Warning About Negative Consequences

Of course, an advocate should always explain to a judicial panel why the holding desired by the advocate is consistent with precedent, logical analysis, and sound policy. But advocates should not overlook the persuasive power of combining this positive argument with a negative story about the undesirable consequences of the holding sought by the opposing party.

Judges normally are relatively cautious creatures. When creating precedent, they are sensitive to the risk of taking the law on a path that will be difficult to traverse in future cases, or one that may lead to an undesirable destination. Accordingly, an advocate frequently can dissuade a judge from adopting a particular holding by describing the difficulties of applying the resulting rule to other factual contexts, or by explaining how the holding could lead to an absurd result if logically extended. In this fashion, the advocate can make the judge more receptive to the holding sought by the advocate's client. Indeed, a negative argument against an adverse holding may pack even more persuasive punch than the advocate's positive description of the virtues of the holding desired by the advocate.

For example, in the immediately preceding sample passage (ending with subsection 1 above), the writer warns that expansion of the tort of wrongful discharge would launch the judiciary on a path of inappropriately assessing whether every challenged discharge is consistent with sound business practices. Such a path not only would erode the established policy of freedom of contract, it also would divert judicial resources from matters more appropriately assigned to the judiciary.

In a different case, an advocate for the plaintiff might warn of the future repercussions of a holding that fails to recognize a claim on the plaintiff's facts. The advocate might explain that the plaintiff's case is not an isolated one and that a negative holding will lead to numerous injustices:

Defendant correctly points out that this court has not yet based a finding of substantive unconscionability solely on price disparity. Nonetheless, such a finding represents a natural extension of existing precedent and is necessary to vindicate important policies favoring consumer protection. Failing to find unconscionability in grossly inflated and unfair pricing would leave countless consumers at the mercy of unscrupulous vendors, many of them highly trained and experienced in high-pressure sales tactics.

D. Arguing the Law and the Facts

1. Strategic Choices

The appellant will seek to overturn unfavorable findings or conclusions of the trial court. As explained in Section V.B above, the appellant will benefit from unrestricted appellate review of conclusions of law. Moreover, the appellate court is not bound by the trial court's characterization of a finding as one of fact or law. Accordingly, if you represent the appellant, you should try to characterize unfavorable mixed findings of fact and law in a nonjury trial as conclusions of law, which are reviewable on appeal without restriction. In a jury trial, on the other hand, a jury's mixed finding of fact and law normally will be treated as a finding of fact for purposes of restricted appellate review.

If an unfavorable finding is undeniably one of fact, you must make some strategic choices among alternative approaches on appeal. As counsel for the appellant, you must decide whether to challenge the unfavorable finding of fact under a restricted standard of review, argue that the trial court applied the wrong legal rule to the facts, or both.

For example, suppose the plaintiff in a federal civil rights suit successfully sought compensatory and punitive damages against your client, a police officer, for false arrest in violation of the Fourth Amendment. At trial, the judge gave the following instructions to the jury over your objection:

If you find that Officer Mullins arrested Ms. Wong without probable cause, you must find that Officer Mullins violated Ms. Wong's clearly established constitutional rights, and you must award Ms. Wong compensatory damages in the amount of her actual injuries. Furthermore, if you find that Officer Mullins was grossly and inexcusably careless with regard to Ms. Wong's constitutional rights, you may exercise discretion to award Ms. Wong punitive damages in an amount that will punish Officer Mullins and discourage him and others from similar violations.

Applying these instructions to the facts, the jury found Officer Mullins liable and awarded Ms. Wong $5,000 in compensatory damages and $25,000 in punitive damages. The trial court also awarded Ms. Wong her reasonable attorneys' fees.

Your client, Officer Mullins, has appealed. As one of your arguments on appeal, you wish to challenge the award of punitive damages, which is necessarily premised on a jury finding that Officer Mullins was "grossly and inexcusably careless." You can attack the award in either or both of two ways.

First, to take advantage of unrestricted appellate review of matters of law, you can try to persuade the appellate court that the trial judge incorrectly instructed the jury on the law:

A. Officer Mullins is entitled to a new trial because the trial judge erroneously instructed the jury that it could award punitive damages for conduct less culpable than reckless disregard for constitutional rights.

The United States Supreme Court has established a recklessness standard for punitive damages in federal civil rights actions:

> We hold that a jury may be permitted to assess punitive damages in an action under § 1983 when the defendant's conduct is shown to be motivated by evil motive or

General legal rule

intent, or when it involves reckless or callous indifference to the federally protected rights of others.

Smith v. Wade, 461 U.S. 30, 56 (1983).

Related legal rules

A standard based on reckless misconduct or callous indifference requires a greater showing of culpability than simple negligence. *See Johnson v. Lundell* . . . . In *Johnson* . . . .

Policy analysis

The extraordinary nature of punitive damages justifies close scrutiny of the trial judge's instructions to ensure that they recognize even fine distinctions in culpability. Otherwise . . . .

Application to facts: the instruction

In this case, the trial court instructed the jury that it could award punitive damages if it found that Officer Mullins was "grossly and inexcusably careless." (III R.T. 52.) This instruction did not adequately convey the requisite standard: reckless or callous disregard of constitutional rights.

Further analysis of instruction

Even when coupled with the adjective "grossly," the word "careless" connotes only a breach of duty rising to the level of negligence. . . .

Conclusion

The trial court improperly instructed the jury on the standard for punitive damages. Officer Mullins is entitled to a new trial so that the jury may apply the proper legal standard to the facts.

Alternatively, if you are prepared to labor against a restricted standard of review, you can try to persuade the appellate court to overturn the jury's implicit finding that Officer Mullins was "grossly and inexcusably careless." Under this approach, you must review the underlying evidence, such as the testimony at trial, and explain why the jury's finding is not supported by substantial evidence:

B. Alternatively, this court should vacate the award of punitive damages because substantial evidence does not support the jury's finding that Officer Mullins acted with the requisite culpability to justify punitive damages.

Introduction to argument

Even if the trial court's instructions adequately conveyed the culpability required for an award of punitive damages, the jury did not properly find such culpability on the part of Officer Mullins. At most, the evidence supports the conclusion that Officer Mullins made a reasonable mistake in judgment in chaotic circumstances. Therefore, the trial judge erred in denying Mullins's Motion for Judgment Notwithstanding the Verdict on the issue of punitive damages, and this Court should overturn the jury's award of punitive damages.

This Court may overturn a finding of the jury if the finding is unsupported by substantial evidence in the record so that no reasonable juror could have made the finding on the evidence. *See* . . . . This substantial-evidence standard permits appellate courts to review jury findings to guard against verdicts based on bias, passion, or incompetence. *See* . . . . To satisfy the purposes of such review, this court should scrutinize the record for . . . .

Rules governing review of jury's findings

Officer Mullins's uncontradicted testimony establishes the reasonableness of his actions. He testified that the report over his squad car radio identified the robbery suspect only as a young man of slight build with dark, shoulder-length hair. (II RT at 335-36.) One block from the robbery site, Officer Mullins spotted Ms. Wong walking at a very brisk pace away from the robbery site. *Id.* at 336. He initially passed her by because he was looking for a male suspect. *Id.* at 337. However, when he found no other suspects in the vicinity, he realized that Ms. Wong fit the description of the robbery suspect except for her gender. *Id.* at 339. He remembered that Ms. Wong was wearing jeans and a sweatshirt, and he realized that an agitated witness might have been mistaken about her gender. *Id.* at 339-40. Consequently, he turned his squad car around, found Ms. Wong again, and stopped her for questioning. *Id.* at 340.

Examination of facts: the testimony

Other testimony supports Officer Mullins's version of the events. Ms. Wong herself testified that she had been walking at an unusually brisk pace. (I RT at 327.) She also admitted that she had trouble answering Officer Mullins's questions. *Id.* at 331. Although in her testimony Ms. Wong offered innocent explanations for her hurried pace and her inability to communicate effectively with Officer Mullins, *id.* at 360, nothing in the record shows that these explanations were apparent to Officer Mullins at the time of the arrest. . . .

In sum, the evidence leads inescapably to one conclusion: In his eagerness to fulfill his duties as a police officer, Officer Mullins mistakenly arrested the wrong person, but he did not recklessly

Analysis of testimony: permissible inferences

disregard anyone's constitutional rights in doing so. Quite the contrary, he took steps at several stages to safeguard Ms. Wong's rights.

The record simply does not contain substantial evidence supporting the jury's finding of sufficient culpability to justify an award of punitive damages. Apparently, the jurors misunderstood or ignored the trial court's instructions and based their verdict on irrelevant factors.

Conclusion

For these reasons, this Court should overturn the jury's award of punitive damages. The evidence does not support this extraordinary award.

Counsel for the appellee can respond to either of these arguments directly. In response to the first sample argument, for example, she can argue either that (1) the law permits an award of punitive damages for culpability less than recklessness, perhaps because "callous indifference" denotes a lower standard that equates to gross and inexcusable carelessness, or (2) the trial judge's instructions adequately conveyed the requisite standard of recklessness. In response to the second sample argument, she can (1) emphasize the restricted standard of appellate review, (2) describe evidence in the record that supports a jury finding of recklessness or callous indifference, and (3) explain why that evidence should be viewed as "substantial."

2. Varieties of Fact Analysis

As illustrated in the preceding subsection, the appropriate nature and depth of fact analysis on appeal will depend in part on two factors: (a) the nature of the appellant's challenge to the trial court's judgment, and (b) the procedural posture of the case when the trial court disposed of it.

a. Nature of Appellant's Challenge

For an example of the first factor, suppose that you represent the appellant and that you choose to challenge not the jury's findings of fact but only the trial judge's instructions on the law, as in the first sample passage in Subsection 1 above. Your arguments on such a challenge will often focus on the law and include only modest fact analysis. Specifically, after your arguments on the law, your application of the law to the facts could include no more than a comparison of the correct legal rule to the actual instruction and a statement about the need for a new trial with proper instructions to the jury:

In this case, the trial court instructed the jury that it could award punitive damages if it found that Officer Mullins was "grossly and inexcusably careless." (III R.T. 52.) This instruction did not adequately convey . . . .

. . . Officer Mullins is entitled to a new trial so that the jury may apply the proper legal standard to the facts.

In contrast, detailed fact analysis will be mandatory if the appellant challenges the findings of fact of the trial judge or jury, as did the appellant in the sample briefs at the end of this chapter. As illustrated in the second sample passage in Subsection 1 above, the parties then must review the record and argue whether the evidence supports the finding of fact under the applicable standard of review:

Officer Mullins's uncontradicted testimony establishes the reasonableness of his actions. He testified that the report over his squad car radio . . . .

Other testimony supports Officer Mullins's version of the events. Ms. Wong herself testified that she had been walking at an unusually brisk pace. (I RT at 327.) She also admitted . . . .

In sum, the evidence leads inescapably to one conclusion: . . . .

The record simply does not contain substantial evidence supporting the jury's finding of sufficient culpability to justify an award of punitive damages. . . .

b. Procedural Posture

Your fact analysis may also vary with the second factor: the procedural posture of the case at the time of trial disposition. Specifically, dispositions at different pretrial and trial stages will lead to appellate analyses of different kinds of facts.

For example, suppose that the trial court dismissed the action for failure of the complaint to state a claim for relief. On appeal, you can argue the law, but you will have no findings of fact or even underlying evidence in the record to which to apply the law. Instead, you must argue whether the factual allegations of the complaint state a claim for relief under the correct interpretation of the law.

On appeal from summary judgment, on the other hand, you ordinarily will have a record of preliminary showings of fact with documents, affidavits, and other discovery materials. Therefore, you can argue whether the evidentiary materials submitted by both parties created a genuine issue of fact for trial under the applicable law.

Finally, the record will include formally introduced evidence if either party has appealed from the trial judge's denial of a motion for a directed verdict or for a judgment notwithstanding the verdict after presentation of the evidence in a jury trial. Moreover, on appeal from judgment after a full trial, the record will include both the evidence and the findings of the judge or jury. As explored above, the record in either case may provide a fertile source for fact analysis, depending on the appellant's strategic choices and the nature of her challenge to the ruling or judgment in the trial court.

VI. The Conclusion

The discussion in Section III.C of Chapter 16 about the conclusion section of a brief applies with full force to appellate briefs. At the least, your conclusion must briefly restate the action that your client requests the appellate court to take. In a complex case, your conclusion may also include a brief summary and synthesis of the arguments presented in your brief.

VII. Summary

When preparing an appellate brief, you should

1. follow rules of procedure and local court rules governing format,
2. state the issues and facts in a manner that invites a favorable conclusion but that maintains credibility and accuracy, and
3. argue the case with attention to the law, the facts, and policy considerations.

Exercise 22-1

In addition to responding to the appellant's arguments on appeal, an appellee may file its own "cross-appeal" to affirmatively challenge aspects of a lower court's decision. The following appellate briefs are the Opening Brief, Answering Brief, and Reply Brief on a cross-appeal filed by the appellee of the main appeal. The briefs reproduced below appear in their original form, with the exception of corrections of minor typographical errors, the reduction of line spacing, the deletion of some references to the main appeal, and the omission of a procedural issue and a portion of the arguments on punitive damages.

The briefs depart in many ways from the citation form and writing style recommended in this book, perhaps illustrating that a variety of styles can effectively communicate or persuade. As you read these briefs, consider what changes you would make to conform the writing to your own style, and consider the following questions.

1. Statements of the Case

Study the procedural history traced in the statements of the case in the opening brief and the answering brief. Identify the trial court rulings challenged by each party. Is it clear why both Koepnick and Sears were dissatisfied, resulting in cross-appeals? What standard did the trial court apply in reaching its decision on the point appealed from on the cross-appeal? What standard of review should the appellate court apply?

2. Statements of Fact

Study the statements of fact in the opening and answering briefs. Could you identify the author of each statement if you read no other parts of the briefs? Does each fact statement successfully present an apparently complete and neutral summary of the facts while placing the advocate's client in the best possible light?

Consider the points of conflict between the two fact statements. In what instances is the apparent conflict simply a reflection of each advocate using techniques of writing style to emphasize some facts and deemphasize others? In what instances is the conflict rooted in genuine disagreement about the factual conclusions that find support in the record? What is the legal significance on appeal of conflicting evidence in the record on a material point, given the procedural posture of this case?

3. Statements of Issues

Study the statements of the issues in the opening and answering briefs. Does each advocate successfully phrase each issue in a way that invites a favorable response for his client? Does either state a false issue that easily invites a favorable response but that does not fairly identify the real issue on appeal?

4. Arguments

Study the arguments in all three briefs. How important is fact analysis to the arguments in each brief? Would the brief allocate more time to discussion of legal rules if the appellant were appealing from the trial court's rejection of a novel legal theory of recovery? Would the main point headings be easier to read if they did not capitalize the first letter of nearly every word in each heading?

5. Responsive Arguments

Does the answering brief effectively respond to the opening brief? Does the reply brief effectively respond to the answering brief?

6. Writing Style

How would you change the writing style or presentation of authority in any of the briefs? Explain the reasons for your editing.

7. Format

How well do the briefs conform to the following formats for appellate briefs that were prescribed by the version of the Arizona Rules of Civil Appellate Procedure in effect when the briefs were filed? (But note that the line spacing is less than typically required by court rules, to reduce the space occupied by the sample briefs in this book.)

Rule 13. Briefs

13(a) Brief of the Appellant. The brief of the appellant shall concisely and clearly set forth under appropriate headings and in the order here indicated:

1. A table of contents with page references.
2. A table of citations, which shall alphabetically arrange and index the cases, statutes and other authorities cited, with references to the pages of the brief on which they are cited.
3. A statement of the case, indicating briefly the basis of the appellate court's jurisdiction, the nature of the case, the course of the proceedings and the disposition in the court below.
4. A statement of facts relevant to the issues presented for review, with appropriate references to the record . . . .
5. A statement of the issues presented for review . . . .
6. An argument, which shall contain the contentions of the appellant with respect to the issues presented, and the reasons therefor, with citations to the authorities, statutes and parts of the record relied on. The argument may include a summary . . . .
7. A short conclusion stating the precise relief sought.
8. An appendix if desired.

13(b) Brief of the Appellee. The brief of the appellee shall conform to the requirements of the preceding subdivision, except that a statement of the case, a statement of the facts or a statement of the issues need not be included unless the appellee finds the statements of the appellant to be insufficient or incorrect.

13(c) Reply Brief. The appellant may file a reply brief, but it shall be confined strictly to rebuttal of points urged in the appellee's brief. No further briefs may be filed except as provided in Rule 13(e) or by leave of court. . . .

13(e) Briefs in Cases Involving Cross-Appeals. A party who files a cross-appeal may combine in one brief his brief as appellee and his brief as cross-appellant. If the appellant wishes to file a further brief, he may combine in one brief his reply brief as appellant and his brief as cross-appellee. The cross-appellant may file a reply brief on the issues of the cross-appeal.

Fred Cole
Roger W. Perry
Gust, Rosenfeld, Divelbess & Henderson
3300 Valley Bank Center
Phoenix, Arizona 85073
Attorneys for Defendant-Appellee/Cross-Appellant

IN THE COURT OF APPEALS
STATE OF ARIZONA

Division One

MAX KOEPNICK,	
Plaintiff-Appellant	1 CA-CIV 9147
Cross-Appellee,	MARICOPA County Superior Court
v.	No. C-502081
SEARS, ROEBUCK & COMPANY,	
Defendant-Appellee	
Cross-Appellant.	

OPENING BRIEF ON CROSS-APPEAL

TABLE OF CONTENTS

TABLE OF AUTHORITIES

APPELLEE'S OPENING BRIEF ON CROSS-APPEAL

STATEMENT OF THE CASE

Plaintiff-appellant Max Koepnick ("Koepnick") commenced this action by filing a complaint on December 5, 1983 (C.T. at 1). The defendants named in the complaint were defendant-appellee Sears, Roebuck & Company ("Sears") and the City of Mesa ("Mesa"). The complaint set forth claims in six counts, which were all alleged to have arisen out of an incident that occurred at the Sears store at Fiesta Mall in Mesa, Arizona on December 6, 1982. Sears was named as defendant in only four of the counts. These were Count One for false arrest, Count Four for trespass to chattel, Count Five for invasion of privacy and Count Six for malicious prosecution. Mesa was named as defendant in Count Two for false arrest and Count Three for assault and battery. Mesa was also named as a co-defendant with Sears in Counts Five and Six.

Prior to trial, Mesa moved for summary judgment on Count Two for false arrest (C.T. at 55). The court granted Mesa's motion on that count based on the court's determination that probable cause existed for Mesa to detain Koepnick (Minute entry dated January 9, 1986).

Trial to a jury on the other counts of Koepnick's complaint commenced on January 10, 1986. At the close of Koepnick's case-in-brief, Sears moved for a directed verdict on all counts asserted against it (7R.T. at 13). Plaintiff stipulated to the dismissal of Count Six for malicious prosecution against Sears, and the court granted Sears a directed verdict on Count Four for invasion of privacy (Minute entry dated January 21, 1986). Mesa made a similar motion and was granted directed verdicts on Count Two for false arrest, Count Five for invasion of privacy, Count Six for malicious prosecution, and all plaintiff's claims for punitive damages (Minute entry dated January 21, 1986).

At the close of evidence, Sears and Mesa again moved for directed verdicts on all the remaining claims against them. These motions were denied (8R.T. at 84-92). The remaining claims were submitted to the jury. The jury returned verdicts against Sears for $25,000.00 in compensatory damages and $500,000.00 in punitive damages on Count One for false arrest and $100.00 in compensatory damages and $25,000.00 punitive damages on Count Four for trespass to chattel (9R.T. at 101-03). The jury also returned verdicts against Mesa for $50,000.00 on Count Three for assault and battery and $100.00 on Count Four for trespass to chattel (9R.T. at 101-03). Judgment was entered on the verdicts on February 25, 1986 (C.T. at 97; Appendix A).

Sears filed motions for judgment notwithstanding the verdicts and for a new trial on Counts One and Four on March 11, 1986 (C.T. at 100). Mesa filed a motion for a new trial on March 11, 1986 (C.T. at 101) and a motion for judgment notwithstanding the verdict or, in the alternative, for a new trial and for remittitur on

March 12, 1986 (C.T. at 104). An amended motion for judgment notwithstanding the verdicts and for new trial was filed by Sears on April 16, 1986 (C.T. at 113).

A hearing on the post-trial motions was held on April 17, 1986. Upon consideration of the motions, the court granted Sears' and Mesa's motions for judgment N.O.V.[17] on Count Four for trespass to chattel and granted Sears' motion for new trial on Count One for false arrest. The court granted judgment N.O.V. for defendants on the trespass to chattel claim as Koepnick failed to present evidence that the alleged trespass caused any damage or injury, which is an essential element of an actionable claim. The court granted a new trial on the false arrest claim as the court determined that reasonable cause to detain Koepnick existed as a matter of law and that, therefore, it had erred in instructing the jury on the issue of reasonable cause (Minute entry dated May 14, 1986; Appendix B).

A second hearing occurred on June 24, 1986, pertaining to further post-trial motions, and the court clarified its minute entry of May 14, 1986 (Minute entry dated June 27, 1986; Appendix C). (The trial court's attempt at clarification did not completely succeed in that the minute entry repeatedly refers to the "assault" claim when the court actually means to refer to the false arrest claim.) The final order setting forth the court's disposition of the post-trial motions, including the granting of judgment on Count Four for trespass to chattel and the granting of Sears' motion for new trial on Count One for false arrest, was entered July 23, 1986 (C.T. at 125; Appendix D).

Koepnick filed a notice of appeal on July 24, 1986, with respect to the trial court's order granting Sears' motion for judgment notwithstanding the verdict on Count Four for trespass to chattel and for a new trial on Count One for false arrest (C.T. at 124). Sears filed a notice of cross-appeal with respect to the portions of the judgment dated February 24, 1986, granting judgment in favor of Koepnick and the portions of the order dated July 18, 1986, denying Sears' motion for judgment notwithstanding the verdict on Count One for false arrest and conditionally denying defendant Sears' motion for new trial on Count Four for trespass to chattel (C.T. at 128). No appeal was taken by either Koepnick or Mesa with respect to the adjudications of the claims asserted by Koepnick against Mesa. Accordingly, Mesa is not a party to this appeal.

The parties stipulated to waiving the posting of cost bonds on the appeals. This court has jurisdiction of the appeal and cross-appeal pursuant to A.R.S. §12-1201 B and F.

---

17. [Author's note: "N.O.V." is an abbreviation for the Latin term *non obstante veredicto*, which means "notwithstanding the verdict," the phrase used earlier in the Statement of the Case. A judgment notwithstanding the verdict refers to a ruling by the judge that the jury's verdict on an issue is not supported by the evidence presented at trial and should be replaced by the court's contrary judgment on that issue.]

STATEMENT OF FACTS

On December 6, 1982, Koepnick drove to the Sears store located at Fiesta Mall to get some screwdrivers (4R.T. at 145-47). He arrived at approximately 5 p.m. (4R.T. at 145). Once in the store, he was assisted by Mara Thomas, a sales clerk in the hardware department (4R.T. at 147; 8R.T. at 36). After Koepnick selected the tools he wanted, Thomas carried them to the cash register (4R.T. at 148). Koepnick was waited on at the cash register by Bruce Rosenhan, another sales clerk, who rang up the tools for Koepnick (4R.T. at 150-51; 7R.T. at 88). These tools consisted of a set of screwdrivers, a wrench set, a nut-driver set, an open-end wrench set and a set of pliers (7R.T. at 88-89; Ex. 11). Koepnick asked Rosenhan for an itemized receipt (4R.T. at 151; 7R.T. at 88). Rosenhan bagged Koepnick's purchases, stapling the bag closed with the receipts on the outside (4R.T. at 151; 7R.T. at 89). Koepnick left the cash register area (4R.T. at 171; 7R.T. at 89).

After waiting on Koepnick, Rosenhan went out to work on the sales floor (7R.T. at 90). Rosenhan saw Koepnick again in the hardware department approximately 15 minutes after he had waited on him (7R.T. at 90-91). Koepnick came over to where he and Thomas were in the back of the department (7R.T. at 90). Rosenhan saw Koepnick speak to Thomas and pull a large wrench out of the shopping bag Rosenhan had earlier stapled closed (7R.T. at 91). At that time, Koepnick's bag was open and there were no receipts in view on it (7R.T. at 91). Rosenhan realized that the wrench Koepnick pulled out of the bag was not one of the wrenches from the sets that he sold to Koepnick (7R.T. at 91). When Rosenhan finished with the customer he was helping, he asked Thomas if Koepnick put the wrench back in his bag and whether she had sold it to him (7R.T. at 92). Thomas told him that Koepnick put it back in his bag and that she had not sold that wrench to him or had anything to do with it (7R.T. at 92). Rosenhan asked all the other employees present in the department whether they had sold that particular wrench to Koepnick and learned that none of them had either (7R.T. at 92).

Rosenhan went to the front register and used the phone to call security (7R.T. at 92). He spoke with Steve Lessard, one of the security agents on duty at that time in the store (4R.T. at 77). It was approximately 5:35 to 5:40 when Lessard received the call from Rosenhan (4R.T. at 83). He informed Lessard that he believed that there was a customer in the store who was a shoplifter (4R.T. at 77). Lessard told him to meet in the sewing machine department, which is located next to hardware (4R.T. at 77-78). When Rosenhan and Lessard met, Rosenhan explained what had occurred with the purchase of the tools and the subsequent incident of the large wrench being observed in the bag (7R.T. at 93; 4R.T. at 78-79). Lessard radioed to Dave Pollock, another security agent on duty at Sears, and requested that he come and assist him (4R.T. at 79).

When Pollock arrived, Lessard explained what he had learned from Rosenhan and asked him to watch Koepnick while he spoke with the other employees (4R.T.

at 79-80). Lessard went around the hardware department and spoke with each of the employees present there (4R.T. at 80). Among the employees he spoke with was Mara Thomas, who informed Lessard of her contacts with Koepnick and confirmed the fact that she did not sell or help Koepnick with the large wrench he had in his bag (4R.T. at 80-81; 8R.T. at 41).

After Lessard had spoken with all of the employees in the hardware department and confirmed that none of them sold the wrench in question, he observed Koepnick in the socket aisle (4R.T. at 82). Koepnick picked out some sockets and then put the bag he was carrying down at the cash register (4R.T. at 82). Koepnick went back to the socket aisle and picked up another socket (4R.T. at 82). While Koepnick was away from the cash register area, Lessard instructed Pollock to go by the shopping bag and confirm that the large wrench in question was still in it (4R.T. at 82). When Pollock went over to the bag, he observed that the bag was pulled open and the wrench was inside (7R.T. at 41). No receipts were seen in or on the bag by Pollock (7R.T. at 41, 84). Pollock reported back to Lessard and told him what he saw (7R.T. at 41).

Lessard and Pollock observed as Koepnick returned to the cash register and purchased some sockets (7R.T. at 42; 4R.T. at 82-83). As Koepnick began to leave the store, Lessard went to the clerk at the cash register and asked what items had been purchased, verifying that Koepnick had not paid for the crescent wrench in question at that time (7R.T. at 83-84). Lessard and Pollock followed Koepnick out of the store (4R.T. at 84). At no time did either observe Koepnick take any receipts off the shopping bag he was carrying (4R.T. at 84). As they followed Koepnick out of the store, they discussed the information they had and decided to stop Koepnick with respect to the large wrench in question (4R.T. at 84).

Koepnick estimated that it was approximately 6:15 P.M. when he exited the east door of the store (5R.T. at 72). Lessard approached Koepnick as he walked into the parking lot area approximately 20 to 25 feet from the door of the store (4R.T. at 87). Koepnick refused to stop when Lessard first spoke to him (5R.T. at 178; 4R.T. at 87-88). Koepnick testified that Lessard then came around in front of him, pulled the wrench in question out of the bag and told him that he did not have a receipt for it (4R.T. at 178). Koepnick was also told he was under arrest for shoplifting (4R.T. at 178). Both Koepnick and Lessard testified that Koepnick was shown identification by Lessard, although Koepnick testified that he did not see it clearly (4R.T. at 179-80; 4R.T. at 87-88). Koepnick did not show a receipt for the wrench when Lessard stopped him (4R.T. at 91; 5R.T. at 63).

Koepnick initially refused to return to the store with Lessard and Pollock (4R.T. at 179). Koepnick was informed that he had to return to the store with them (4R.T. at 180). After some further discussion, Koepnick was escorted up to the security office in the Sears store (4R.T. at 179-81; 5R.T. at 70-72). He was not handcuffed or physically injured in any way by the Sears employees (5R.T. at 70,

72). Once in the security office, Koepnick was instructed to sit down to wait for the police to arrive (4R.T. at 183).

In the security office, Lessard examined the shopping bag Koepnick had been carrying and found receipts for the purchase of the sockets (4R.T. at 94; 5R.T. at 72-73). No other receipts were found in or on the bag (4R.T. at 95). Although Koepnick had the receipts for his other purchases in his front shirt pocket, he never attempted to show them to the Sears employees (5R.T. at 63, 66). While waiting for the police to arrive, Koepnick asked if he could get a drink of water or go down to his truck, but those requests were refused (4R.T. at 183).

While Pollock watched Koepnick, Lessard continued his investigation and began to prepare his report of the incident (4R.T. at 97-98). Lessard telephoned the hardware department and spoke to Kim Miller, the hardware department manager. Lessard called the hardware department as he needed the stock number for the wrench in question (8R.T. at 72). He also wanted to have the audit tape on the cash register checked as there were no receipts in the shopping bag for the tool sets that Rosenhan had told him he had rung up for Koepnick (8R.T. at 72).

Officer Michael Campbell of the Mesa Police Department arrived at 6:30 P.M., approximately 15 minutes after Koepnick had been brought to the security office (6R.T. at 67; 4R.T. at 186). Campbell and Lessard stepped across the hall to permit Lessard to inform the officer as to what he had observed (4R.T. at 186; 4R.T. at 101-102). As Lessard was talking with Officer Campbell, Koepnick attempted to walk out of the security office (4R.T. at 187; 4R.T. at 58). Officer Campbell came out into the hallway and met Koepnick at the door to the security office (4R.T. at 187; 4R.T. at 59). Koepnick and Officer Campbell became involved in an altercation, resulting in Koepnick striking his head against the back wall of the security office (4R.T. at 187-88; 4R.T. at 60-64). After that occurred, Officer Campbell was able to handcuff Koepnick (6R.T. at 96-98).

Officer Campbell had made the decision to arrest Koepnick when the altercation started (6R.T. at 93). While he was being handcuffed by Officer Campbell, Koepnick took the receipts that had been in his shirt pocket and stuffed them inside his shirt (4R.T. at 189; 6R.T. at 96-97). Once Koepnick was handcuffed, Officer Campbell removed the receipts he had observed Koepnick stuffing inside his shirt (4R.T. at 66; 6R.T. at 100). The receipts that were found on Koepnick were examined and matched to the various tools Koepnick had in his shopping bag (4R.T. at 191; 4R.T. at 68).

During the altercation, Officer Campbell had instructed Pollock to use his radio to call for assistance (6R.T. at 98). Sergeant Reynolds and Officer Gates came to the Sears security office in response to the request (6R.T. at 108).

Lessard learned after the altercation that another sales clerk, Jeff Ward, had also been working in the hardware department that day (4R.T. at 103-104). Ward, however, had left the sales floor before Rosenhan observed Koepnick with the wrench in the shopping bag and called Lessard down to investigate the situation (8R.T. at 9-10). When Ward later returned to the hardware department, Miller informed him of the call from Lessard and that security had some questions about whether a customer paid for a certain wrench (8R.T. at 110). Ward told Miller that he had rung up such a wrench for a customer (8R.T. at 11). Miller took Ward up to the security office (8R.T. at 11). They arrived about the time the altercation occurred between Koepnick and Officer Campbell (4R.T. at 103; 8R.T. at 12).

Once Lessard became aware of Ward's contact with Koepnick, he interviewed Ward (4R.T. at 104). Ward stated that he had first observed Koepnick as Koepnick walked up to the cash register and pulled the receipt off a shopping bag that was lying on the counter (4R.T. at 104; 8R.T. at 6). Ward asked him if that was his package and Koepnick said it was (4R.T. at 104; 8R.T. at 6). Koepnick had a large combination wrench and a smaller set of wrenches with him to purchase (4R.T. at 104; 8R.T. at 6). Ward rang these items up, and Koepnick paid for them (4R.T. at 104). Ward then bagged these wrenches in a smaller brown bag, which Koepnick placed inside the larger shopping bag he already had (4R.T. at 104; 8R.T. at 104; 8R.T. at 8). Koepnick then placed the receipts Ward had prepared for the wrenches in his shirt pocket and left (8R.T. at 8). Ward did not see Koepnick again on the sales floor that night (8R.T. at 9). After Ward finished ringing up the other customers at the cash register, he left the sales floor (8R.T. at 9, 24). Ward told Lessard he had been on a break (4R.T. at 72). Ward could not recall at trial exactly where he went when he left the sales floor (8R.T. at 9).

After questioning Ward, Lessard discussed with the police officers the possibility that Koepnick had taken the wrench he purchased from Ward out to his truck and brought the shopping bag back in and put another wrench in it (4R.T. at 69-70). Lessard was familiar with this method of shoplifting through his work as a security agent (4R.T. at 105). The information Lessard had that caused him to believe that this was a possibility was (1) Ward's statement that he had bagged the large wrench in a separate brown bag that was not present in the large shopping bag Koepnick had when he was stopped, (2) Rosenhan's statement that there was a period of 15 minutes from the time he last saw Koepnick after his first purchase until he saw him again in the hardware department with the wrench, and (3) Koepnick's actions in not exhibiting the receipts for his purchases when he was detained (4R.T. at 105-06, 111).

The police officers made the decision to search Koepnick's truck (6R.T. at 101-02; 6R.T. at 128). Officer Campbell testified that he asked Koepnick for permission to search the truck and Koepnick consented (6R.T. at 130). Koepnick testified that he consented to the search only on the condition that he be allowed to go with them (4R.T. at 194). Lessard accompanied Officer Gates down to Koepnick's truck (4R.T. at 107). Officer Gates opened the vehicle and Lessard assisted him in looking in the truck (4R.T. at 107). No Sears merchandise was found (4R.T. at 107). The search of the truck lasted about two minutes (4R.T. at 72-73). Nothing was taken or damaged in the search (4R.T. at 110-11, 197).

Once Officer Gates and Lessard returned to the security office, the police officers discussed what action they would take (4R.T. at 197-98). Sergeant Reynolds made the decision to cite Koepnick for disorderly conduct for his actions in striking Officer Campbell (6R.T. at 130). After Koepnick received the citation, he was released by the Mesa Police Department (4R.T. at 198).

ISSUES PRESENTED

1. Did the trial court err in denying Sears' motion for judgment notwithstanding the verdict on the claim for false arrest when the evidence is insufficient to support a finding by the jury that plaintiff was detained by Sears in an unreasonable manner or for an unreasonable length of time?

2. Did the trial court err in denying Sears' motion for judgment notwithstanding the verdict on the punitive damage claims where the evidence fails to establish a *prima facie* case for such damages?

ARGUMENT

I. Sears' Motion for Judgment Notwithstanding the Verdict on the Claim for False Arrest Should Have Been Granted by the Trial Court.

A. Applicable Standard of Review.

The standard of review for determining the appropriateness of the granting of a judgment N.O.V. is whether the evidence is sufficient that reasonable men could discern facts to support the verdict. *Rancho Pescado, Inc. v. Northwestern Mutual Life Insurance Co.*, 140 Ariz. 174, 680 P.2d 1235 (App. 1984). In reviewing a judgment N.O.V., the appellate court views the evidence most favorably to sustaining the verdict. *Lerner v. Brettschneider*, 123 Ariz. 152, 598 P.2d 515 (App. 1979). When the evidence is insufficient to meet the burden of proof to establish the claim, entry of judgment N.O.V. is proper. *Rancho Pescado, Inc. v. Northwestern Mutual Life Insurance Co.*, 140 Ariz. at 186, 680 P.2d at 1247; *Lerner v. Brettschneider*, 123 Ariz. at 155, 598 P.2d at 518.

B. There Was Insufficient Evidence to Justify Any Finding of Liability on the Claim of False Arrest.

A.R.S. §13-1805C sets forth the statutory shopkeeper's privilege for detaining a suspected shoplifter. A detention is deemed privileged under this statute if it is made with reasonable cause for a proper purpose and done in a reasonable manner and for reasonable time. *Gortarez v. Smitty's Super Valu, Inc.*, 140 Ariz. 97, 680 P.2d 807 (1984). The undisputed evidence established the existence of all the elements necessary for this privilege. Therefore, Sears' motion for judgment notwithstanding the verdict on plaintiff's claim of false arrest should have been granted by the trial court.

1. Reasonable Cause.

The existence of reasonable cause and the reasonableness of the detention, both as to time and manner, are for the court to decide as a matter of law where there is no conflict in the evidence. *Id.* at 104. The trial court determined as a matter of law that reasonable cause did exist for plaintiff's detention in granting of the motion for new trial. The propriety of that decision is discussed in Section I.E of Sears' response brief, which is incorporated herein by reference to avoid duplication.

The remaining elements of A.R.S. §13-1805C that must be established for the privilege to exist are (1) a proper purpose for the detention, (2) the reasonableness of the time of the detention, and (3) the reasonableness of the manner of the detention. *Id. Gortarez*, 140 Ariz. at 104.

2. Proper Purpose.

A.R.S. §13-1805C sets forth two purposes for which a privileged detention may be made under the statute. They are (1) questioning the subject, or (2) summoning a law enforcement officer. Given Koepnick's testimony at trial, which must be accepted for the purposes of deciding a motion for judgment N.O.V., there is plainly a dispute in the evidence as to what questioning, if any, occurred during Sears' detention of him. Koepnick's testimony was that he was not questioned at all (4R.T. at 184-85). There is, however, no question about the existence of the alternative purpose authorized by the statute for Koepnick's detention—summoning a law enforcement officer. It is undisputed that the Mesa Police Department was contacted by Sears and requested to respond to where plaintiff was being detained (Opening brief, p. 8). Thus, this element of the privilege is unquestionably present in this case.

3. The Length of Detention.

The reasonableness of the length of Koepnick's detention is also undisputedly established by the evidence. There is no evidence in the record that creates any issue of fact as to the reasonableness of the length of Sears' detention of Koepnick. The undisputed evidence is that plaintiff was taken to the Sears security office and the police called without any undue delay on the part of Sears. No evidence of anything to the contrary is present in the record. Upon Officer Campbell's arrival, Lessard immediately began to explain the situation to him. Even before he could even finish, the altercation between Koepnick and Officer Campbell occurred. At that time, Koepnick was placed under arrest by Officer Campbell independently of any shoplifting and taken into the custody of the Mesa Police. From that point on plaintiff was no longer in Sears' custody.

These facts are undisputed. There is nothing in the evidence which would permit the jury to conclude that the length of Koepnick's detention by Sears for the express statutory purpose of summoning a law enforcement officer was unreasonable. Indeed, there was no way Sears could make Koepnick's detention for that purpose any shorter. The length of that detention was determined by the amount of time it took the Mesa Police to respond to the Sears store. This is something that Sears had no control over; in any event, there is no evidence to permit a jury to find that the actual amount of time it took the officer to respond was in any way unreasonable. Accordingly, the trial court should have determined that the length of Koepnick's detention by Sears was reasonable as a matter of law.

4. *The Manner of Detention.*

Neither is there any evidence in the record that creates any issue of fact as to the reasonableness of the manner of Koepnick's detention by Sears. The evidence is again undisputed that Koepnick was stopped by Lessard, escorted up to the Sears security office and detained there until the police arrived. The Arizona Supreme Court in *Gortarez* stated that reasonable force may be used to detain a suspected shoplifter. 140 Ariz. at 104, 680 P.2d at 814. There is no evidence that any unreasonable force was ever used on plaintiff by Sears employees. Sears employees never struck or fought with Koepnick (5R.T. at 70-72). They did not even handcuff or search him (4R.T. at 96; 5R.T. at 70). Koepnick confirmed in his testimony that he was not physically injured in any manner by Sears employees (5R.T. at 72). In short, there is absolutely no evidence to indicate that the manner of plaintiff's detention by Sears was unreasonable.

As indicated above, the reasonableness of the detention, both as to time and manner, is one for the court to decide as a matter of law where there is no conflict of the evidence. *Id.* As there was no conflicting evidence presented at trial as to these elements that would support a finding that the manner and length of Sears' detention of Koepnick was unreasonable, the trial court should have determined that the detention was reasonable as a matter of law and not submitted any issue of this claim to the jury. Accordingly, Sears' motion for judgment notwithstanding the verdict on the claim of false arrest should have been granted by the trial court.

II. Sears' Motion for Judgment Notwithstanding the Verdict on the Claims of Punitive Damages Should Have Been Granted by the Trial Court.

A. The Applicable Standard.

The Arizona Supreme Court has recently modified the standard for determining whether there has been a *prima facie* showing permitting the assessment of punitive damages. The decisions discussing and applying this new standard include *Filasky v. Preferred Risk Mutual Insurance Co.*, No. CV-86-0237-T (filed

March 2, 1987); *Gurule v. Illinois Mutual Life and Casualty Co.*, No. CV-86-0488-PR (filed March 2, 1987); *Rawlings v. Apodaca*, 151 Ariz. 149, 726 P.2d 565 (1986); and *Linthicum v. National Life Insurance Co.*, 150 Ariz. 326, 723 P.2d 675 (1986). The portion of the *Linthicum* decision setting forth the new standard is quoted at length in Section IV.B of Appellee's response brief, which is incorporated herein by reference to avoid duplication.

Although the trial court denied Sears' motion for judgment N.O.V. with respect to punitive damages before the Supreme Court announced the more stringent standard in *Linthicum v. National Life Insurance Co.*, that standard applies to cases upon appellate review. *See, e.g., Hawkins v. Allstate Insurance Co.*, No. CV-86-0010-PR (filed February 26, 1987) (applying standard announced in *Linthicum* to trial court's pre-*Linthicum* ruling on motion for judgment notwithstanding the verdict).

Under the new standard, plaintiffs are not automatically entitled to an instruction on punitive damages upon the showing of a *prima facie* intentional tort. To recover punitive damages, something more is required over and above the "mere commission of a tort." *Rawlings v. Apodaca*, 151 Ariz. at 162, 726 P.2d at 587. There must be a showing of either an intent to injure the plaintiff or a conscious pursuit of a course of conduct knowing that it creates a substantial risk of significant harm to others. *Linthicum v. Nationwide Life Insurance Co.*, 150 Ariz. at 330, 723 P.2d at 679. The requirement of this "something more" or "evil mind" is to assure that punitive damages are awarded only where the purposes of deterrence are furthered. *Gurule v. Illinois Mutual Life and Casualty Co.*, slip op. at 3. The punishment resulting from punitive damage is appropriate only where there is "some element of outrage similar to that usually found in crime." *Rawlings v. Apodaca*, 151 Ariz. at 161, 726 P.2d at 578, *quoting* Restatement (Second) of Torts, §908, comment b (1979).

B. The Evidence Fails to Show a *Prima Facie* Case for Punitive Damages with Respect to the Claim of False Arrest.

As discussed in Section I.B of this cross-appeal brief, the evidence in the record is insufficient to make out a *prima facie* case of false arrest, let alone rise to the level necessary to permit the assessment of punitive damages. There is absolutely no evidence that suggests that Sears intended to injure Koepnick or that it consciously pursued a course of conduct knowing that it created a substantial risk of tremendous harm to him. As the trial court determined, the facts are uncontradicted that Lessard actually and reasonably believed that when Koepnick left the store he had merchandise for which he had not paid. Acting on that reasonable belief, Lessard stopped Koepnick . . . .

. . . .

C. The Evidence Fails to Establish a _Prima Facie_ Case for Punitive Damages with Respect to the Claim of Trespass to Chattel.

. . . .

CONCLUSION

The trial court was correct in finding that reasonable cause existed as matter of law for Sears' detention of Koepnick. The court erred, however, in ruling that there was sufficient evidence to submit to the jury the issues of the reasonableness of the time and manner of the detention. Accordingly, the trial court's order of July 23, 1986 should be reversed to the extent that it provides for a new trial on these issues. The trial court should be instructed to enter judgment notwithstanding the verdict in favor of Sears on the false arrest claim.

The evidence was also insufficient to submit the issue of punitive damages to the jury on either of the claims of false arrest or trespass to chattel. Accordingly, Sears is entitled to judgment notwithstanding the verdict on the issue of punitive damages as well.

Respectfully submitted this 13th day of April, 1987.

GUST, ROSENFELD, DIVELBESS & HENDERSON

By _____

    Fred Cole

    Roger W. Perry

    Attorneys for Defendant-Appellee/Cross-Appellant

Thomas J. Quarelli, Esq.
1832 E. Thomas Road
Phoenix, Arizona 85016
William J. Monahan, P.C.
340 E. Palm Lane, Suite 130
Phoenix, Arizona 85004
Paul G. Ulrich, P.C.
3030 N. Central, Suite 310
Phoenix, Arizona 85012
Attorneys for Plaintiff-Appellant/Cross-Appellee

IN THE COURT OF APPEALS
STATE OF ARIZONA
DIVISION ONE

MAX KOEPNICK,	
Plaintiff-Appellant	No. CA-CIV 9147
Cross-Appellee,	MARICOPA County Superior Court
v.	No. C-502081
SEARS, ROEBUCK & COMPANY,	
Defendant-Appellee	
Cross-Appellant.	

APPELLANT'S CROSS-APPEAL ANSWERING BRIEF

TABLE OF CONTENTS

TABLE OF AUTHORITIES

APPELLANT'S CROSS-APPEAL ANSWERING BRIEF

STATEMENT OF THE CASE

On December 5, 1983, Plaintiff/cross-appellee Max Koepnick sued Defendant/cross-appellant Sears, Roebuck & Co. ("Sears") and the City of Mesa ("Mesa") for false arrest, assault, trespass to chattel (by further detaining him while searching his truck), invasion of his right of privacy and malicious prosecution. These claims all arose out of Koepnick's arrest for alleged shoplifting on December 6, 1982 (Appendix A, C.T. at 1). The counts in Koepnick's complaint alleging invasion of privacy against both defendants and alleging malicious prosecution, false arrest and punitive damages against Mesa were all disposed of by directed verdicts (Appendix B, C.T. at 97). Those issues are not involved in this appeal.

The remaining portions of Koepnick's complaint were tried to a jury on January 13-22, 1986. The jury awarded Koepnick $25,000 in compensatory damages and $500,000 in punitive damages against Sears for false arrest. It awarded him $100 in compensatory damages against both Sears and Mesa and $25,000 in punitive damages against Sears for trespass to Koepnick's personal property. The jury also awarded Koepnick $50,000 in compensatory damages against Mesa for assault (9R.T. at 101-03). Judgment was entered against both defendants pursuant to those jury verdicts on February 25, 1986 (Appendix B, C.T. at 97).

On March 11, 1986, Sears filed motions for judgment notwithstanding the verdicts and for new trial (C.T. at 100). Mesa also filed a motion for a new trial on March 11, 1986 (C.T. at 101). Mesa then also moved for judgment notwithstanding the verdict and, in the alternative, for new trial and for remittitur on March 12, 1986 (C.T. at 104). Sears thereafter filed an amended motion for judgment notwithstanding the verdicts and for new trial on April 16, 1986 (C.T. at 113). Koepnick filed responses to Mesa's and Sears' motions on March 20 and 25, 1986, respectively (C.T. at 107, 108, 109). Both Sears and Mesa filed reply memoranda in support of their respective motions on April 16, 1986 (C.T. at 114, 115).

On May 14, 1986, the trial court entered the following minute orders: (1) granting Sears' motion for new trial on Koepnick's false arrest claim; (2) granting Sears' and Mesa's motions for judgment N.O.V. with respect to Koepnick's claim of trespass to personal property; and (3) denying Mesa's motion for new trial or for judgment N.O.V. with respect to Koepnick's assault claim. On June 27, 1986, the trial court clarified its May 14, 1986 minute order by denying Sears' motion for judgment N.O.V. on Koepnick's false arrest claim to the extent it granted Sears' motion for a new trial concerning that issue. Having granted a new trial on Koepnick's false arrest claim, the trial court also vacated his judgment against Sears for punitive damages. A formal written order incorporating all those rulings and directing that it be entered as a final judgment was filed on July 23, 1986 (C.T. at 124).

On July 24, 1986, Koepnick filed a notice of appeal only from the portions of the trial court's order granting Sears' motion for new trial on his false arrest claim and for judgment N.O.V. on his claim of trespass to chattel (C.T. at 124). The portion of the litigation involving Mesa has been settled. Mesa is therefore not a party to this appeal and has not filed a cross-appeal. Sears filed a notice of cross-appeal with respect to other portions of the judgment on August 5, 1986 (C.T. at 128). The parties have stipulated that the cost bonds for their respective appeals are waived. This Court has jurisdiction concerning this appeal pursuant to A.R.S. §12-2101(F)(1).

STATEMENT OF FACTS

I. Koepnick and His Purchases.

Max Koepnick was a manager, foreman, and mechanic for a large Queen Creek farming operation whose assets exceed $2,500,000 (4R.T. at 145, 6R.T. at 21). His lawsuit resulted from his detention and arrest for shoplifting while he was purchasing tools for the farm at the Sears store in Fiesta Mall, Mesa, Arizona, on December 6, 1982 (4R.T. at 145-47). Koepnick paid cash for those tools and had the receipts for all of them in his possession when he was arrested, including the receipt for a 1 5/16 open-end crescent wrench. That wrench was the precipitating cause of his arrest.

Koepnick drove to Sears in the farm pickup truck he used for business purposes (4R.T. at 145-46). He entered the store at approximately 5:00 P.M. (4R.T. at 145, 5T 68). Business in the Sears store happened to be slow at that particular time (3R.T. at 13). Koepnick proceeded to the hardware department. He first purchased a five-wrench set, a nut-driver, an open-end wrench set, a plier set, and a set of screwdrivers (Ex. 11). Bruce Rosenhan, Sears hardware department manager, rang up those purchases on a cash register and stapled portions of the Sears seven-part handwritten receipt used at customers' requests for cash purchases to the outside of the bag (4R.T. at 149, 173). Sears' policy was to staple the register receipt and the original of the seven-part receipt to the outside of the bag (3R.T. at 22, 4R.T. at 45). The customer's purchases were also recorded automatically on the cash register tape (3R.T. at 18-19). The other six copies of the handwritten receipt may have been placed in a trash can on one of the shelves below the cash register (3R.T. at 21).

Koepnick then left his purchases at the cash register counter to look for a wrench (4R.T. at 151). During this time he flirted with a salesperson, Mara Thomas, who showed him various tools. Ms. Thomas then escorted him to the register where he purchased a 1 5/16 open-end crescent wrench. Sales clerk Jeff Ward made this sale. At that time, Ward prepared another handwritten seven-part form, since this sale was also for cash (8R.T. at 8-9, Ex. 12). As had occurred with Koepnick's first purchases, the crescent wrench was bagged and stapled together with the receipt. This bag was placed inside the first, with the wrench handle sticking out (4R.T. at 173). At trial, Koepnick denied the wrench was ever put into a separate brown bag (4R.T. at 173, 174). He also testified all the receipts were stapled onto the original bag (4R.T. at 17). Jeff Ward then left the hardware department to take a break (3R.T. at 12, 8R.T. at 9).

Koepnick picked up the bag from the register counter and started to leave. However, he then remembered he needed some spark plug sockets (4R.T. at 174). He therefore went back to the register, set the bag down and proceeded to look for the sockets (4R.T. at 175).

During this time, manager Rosenhan contacted Sears security guards Steve Lessard and Dave Pollock, who began observing Koepnick. Lessard spoke with all four hardware department employees then on the floor about whether there was a receipt for the open-end crescent wrench (3R.T. at 9). None could remember ringing it up. However, Lessard failed to ask those employees if anyone else was then on a break (id.). He simply assumed those four employees were the only ones on duty (3R.T. at 10-11). Moreover, no one checked either the register tape or the receipts tray behind the counter (3R.T. at 34). Doing so would have confirmed that Koepnick had in fact paid for the crescent wrench, since the cash register tape could have been checked against the wrench's stock number (3R.T. at 19-20). Lessard also admitted at trial that he also could have searched for the six discarded copies of Koepnick's three sets of receipts that were probably in the trash container below the cash register (3R.T. at 21-22).

Meanwhile, Lessard had Pollack walk past the bag on the counter to confirm visually that the wrench in the bag was a Sears product (3R.T. at 28). Pollack could see a price tag sticker on the end of the wrench. However, although the stapled receipts on the bag were also in plain view, they were not checked against the merchandise (4R.T. at 175). Lessard himself admitted that Pollack had an "easy view" of the receipts (3R.T. at 29-30).

Lessard himself also saw the bag on the counter. However, he did not notice the handwritten receipts and cash register tape stapled to the top of the bag (3R.T. at 27). He also testified at trial he could not dispute testimony that the register receipts and handwritten receipts were stapled to the top of the bag (id.). He "didn't recall" whether anyone bothered to look for those receipts on the bag before Koepnick was stopped, although he conceded that it would have been a "fairly reasonable thing to do" (3R.T. at 30).

While this "investigation" was occurring, Koepnick located and purchased the sockets, returned to the register counter, picked up his bag from the counter, tore off all the receipts, placed them in his shirt pocket and left the store. Lessard and Pollack followed him (4R.T. at 177). Lessard estimated that he had between 20 and 25 minutes to make his investigation before he stopped Koepnick outside the store (3R.T. at 14). He even had time to discuss with Pollack that they had "done a thorough investigation" (3R.T. at 34).

II. Koepnick's Detention, Arrest, Assault, and Eventual Release.

Koepnick placed the time and location of his stop and arrest by Lessard and Pollack at 6:15 P.M., in a dark, dimly lighted area of the Sears parking lot (5R.T. at 72). Koepnick's version of the facts was that in that dimly lighted area two punks accosted him, yelled "Hey," and positioned themselves on each side of him (4R.T. at 178). They then jerked the wrench out of the bag stating, "You don't have a receipt, do you?" (4R.T. at 180-81).

Koepnick thought he was being hustled. He asked who his captors were. Their response was, "We're security guards." (4R.T. at 179). Koepnick asked them to "prove it." In response, one of the guards flashed his badge (*id.*). However, Koepnick could not see it clearly (4R.T. at 179-80). Koepnick was then told that he was going with the guards and that he was under arrest for shoplifting (4R.T. at 180).

Koepnick was escorted to an upstairs security room, denied a drink of water, and seated, with no inquiry as to whether he had a receipt for the wrench (4R.T. at 180). The Mesa police were called. When Koepnick attempted to enter the hallway to obtain a drink of water, he and Officer Campbell (who was wearing a bulletproof vest) got into a pushing match. As a result, Koepnick fell or was thrown head first through the wall of the security room, causing him to incur neck and other injuries (4R.T. at 60-64).

Koepnick was then handcuffed. While he was recovering from the blow to his head, the Mesa police and the Sears security staff verified every item he had purchased against every receipt on the table of the security room (4R.T. at 68). Lessard had also verified with Jeff Ward that Koepnick had in fact purchased the crescent wrench. The bag which supposedly contained the wrench had already been accounted for in the security office. However, despite all of Koepnick's purchases being fully accounted for, the Mesa police continued to detain him at Sears' insistence while Lessard conducted a non-consensual, unescorted search of his truck, looking for an alleged "brown bag" (4R.T. at 71). Koepnick had approximately $1,200-1,400 in cash and all of his business records in the truck (4R.T. at 197). The search, which required approximately 15 to 20 minutes, proved fruitless (4R.T. at 197-98). During this time, Koepnick remained under detention. Had Lessard not decided to search Koepnick's truck, Koepnick would simply have been cited immediately for disorderly conduct and then released (6R.T. at 115). Instead, after the search, Koepnick was then freed of his handcuffs and cited for disorderly conduct (4R.T. at 198). He was finally permitted to leave the Sears security room at about 7:00 P.M. (4R.T. at 199).

ISSUES PRESENTED

1. Did the trial court properly deny Sears' motion for judgment notwithstanding the verdict on Koepnick's false arrest claim where the evidence, viewed most favorably to him, was disputed as to each element of the statutory shopkeeper's privilege, A.R.S. §13-1805(C)?

2. Did the trial court properly deny Sears' motion for judgment notwithstanding the verdict on Koepnick's false arrest punitive damage claim where the evidence presented reasonably established a *prima facie* case for such damages?

3. Was the evidence supporting punitive damages as to Koepnick's trespass to chattel claim sufficient to submit that issue to the jury as well?

ARGUMENT

I. The Trial Court Properly Denied Sears' Motion for Judgment Notwithstanding the Verdict with Respect to Koepnick's False Arrest Claim.

A. The Applicable Standards of Review.

In reviewing the trial court's denial of a motion for judgment notwithstanding the verdict, the appellate court will review the evidence to determine whether it was of sufficient character that reasonable minds could differ as to inferences to be drawn from the facts. *Adroit Supply Co. v. Electric Mutual Liability Insurance Co.*, 112 Ariz. 385, 542 P.2d 810 (1975); *Marcal Limited Partnership v. Title Insurance Co. of Minnesota*, 150 Ariz. 191, 722 P.2d 359 (App. 1986). In doing so, this Court will view the evidence in the light most favorable to sustaining the verdict. It then must review the evidence to determine whether the evidence would permit a reasonable person to reach the challenged verdict. *Maxwell v. Aetna Life Insurance Co.*, 143 Ariz. 205, 693 P.2d 348 (App. 1984).

When the sufficiency of evidence to sustain the jury's verdicts is questioned on appeal, every conflict in the evidence and every reasonable inference therefrom will be resolved in favor of sustaining the verdict and judgment. *See McNelis v. Bruce*, 90 Ariz. 261, 367 P.2d 625 (1961). On appeal, a reviewing court must take the evidence in the light most favorable to upholding the jury's verdict. *Miller v. Schafer*, 102 Ariz. 457, 432 P.2d 585 (1967). Applying these standards to the evidence in this record, Koepnick submits the trial court properly denied Sears' motion for directed verdict with respect to his false arrest claim.

B. Requirements to Sustain the Statutory Shopkeeper's Privilege.

A.R.S. §13-1805(C) provides that a merchant "with reasonable cause may detain on the premises in a reasonable manner and for a reasonable time any person suspected of shoplifting . . . for questioning or summoning a law enforcement officer." The statute thus states four elements, all of which must be established to sustain the shopkeeper's privilege: (1) reasonable cause for detention; (2) reasonable manner for detention; (3) reasonable time; and (4) proper purpose (for questioning or summoning a law enforcement officer). Koepnick submits that a directed verdict in Sears' favor with respect to his false arrest claim would not be justified unless the evidence satisfied the applicable standard of review previously stated with respect to all four elements required to establish the statutory privilege. Viewing the evidence most favorably to Koepnick, this record simply does not permit that conclusion.

Each of the elements of Sears' defense also required Sears to prove the affirmative of the issue. *E.g.*, *Black, Robertshaw, Frederick, Copple & Wright, P.C. v. United States*, 130 Ariz. 110, 634 P.2d 298 (App. 1981); *Yeazell v. Copins*, 98 Ariz. 109, 402 P.2d 541 (App. 1965). Unless Sears could persuade a jury by a preponderance of the evidence and reasonable inferences therefrom that each statutory element had been satisfied, Sears thus could not prevail.

1. Reasonable Cause.

Given the facts and reasonable inferences therefrom most favorable to Koepnick, he was clearly entitled to have the reasonable cause issue submitted to the jury. In the first place, Lessard testified he had 20 to 25 minutes to make an investigation before Koepnick left the Sears store and stated that he had made a thorough investigation. He therefore did not have to make a "snap" decision based on incomplete evidence to detain someone who might be hurriedly leaving. Koepnick testified that all of the handwritten receipts for the tools he bought were stapled to the outside of his shopping bag in plain view. However, neither Lessard nor Pollack ever attempted to read them to determine whether the open-end crescent wrench was listed. Lessard was also unable to dispute Koepnick's testimony in this regard, and admitted that looking at the receipts would have been a reasonable thing to do.

Lessard also failed to make the basic inquiry whether there were other hardware department employees then on duty other than the four he interviewed. The possibility that another employee might have been on a break was certainly a reasonable one to be explored. The security guards also never looked for the extra copies of the seven-part receipt, although they might well have been found either in the receipts tray behind the counter or in a trash container on one of the shelves below the cash register. No one ever checked the register tape which would have shown the stock number for the open-end wrench Koepnick had paid for. Given all these deficiencies in the security guards' investigation, there was certainly a reasonable basis for disputing Sears' position that it had reasonable cause to detain Koepnick. Moreover, pursuant to A.R.S. §13-1805(d), "reasonable cause" is a defense to a false arrest claim. Sears therefore had the burden of proving the affirmative of this issue. *E.g.*, *Black, Robertshaw, Frederick, Copple & Wright,*

P.C. v. United States, 130 Ariz. 110, 634 P.2d 298 (App. 1981); *Yeazell v. Copins*, 98 Ariz. 109, 402 P.2d 541 (1965). Unless it could persuade a jury by a preponderance of the evidence and reasonable inferences therefrom that the nature and extent of its investigation was appropriate under the circumstances, Sears could not prevail. Given all the deficiencies in the security guards' investigation and in view of the relatively lengthy time available for them to pursue the simple additional inquiries that could have been made, the trial court could not properly remove the "reasonable cause" issue from the jury in Sears' favor.

2. Proper Purpose.

Sears' Cross-Appeal Opening Brief at p. 3 concedes there was a factual dispute concerning what questioning, if any, occurred during Sears' detention of Koepnick. The statutory purpose of "questioning the subject" was thus admittedly not satisfied for purposes of obtaining a directed verdict. The other possible proper purpose permitted by A.R.S. §13-1805(C) for privileged detention is "summoning a law enforcement officer." Koepnick acknowledges that Sears did contact the Mesa Police Department, but only after he was detained by Sears employees. He was not necessarily detained for that purpose. Moreover, after Officer Campbell's investigation, the officer testified he would simply have cited Koepnick immediately for disorderly conduct and then let him go (6R.T. at 115). Instead, Lessard, Sears employee, insisted that Sears search Koepnick's truck even after all the receipts for his purchases had been accounted for (6R.T. at 101, 102). Koepnick remained in detention for at least 15 to 20 minutes more while Lessard and Officer Gates searched his truck (4R.T. at 197). His handcuffs were not removed until this search had been completed (4R.T. at 197). Koepnick submits that this continuation of his detention was improper because it was motivated by Lessard's desire to search his truck, not for any legitimate reasons connected with the police officers' investigation. There was therefore an issue presented as to whether a proper purpose existed throughout the entire period of time in which Koepnick was detained.

3. Length of Detention.

Koepnick contends that the length of his detention was reasonable only until the Sears employees and Mesa police officers had completed their investigation. Once that occurred, Koepnick should have been released immediately. Instead, he was then detained for an additional 15 to 20 minutes at Lessard's request so Lessard could search his truck. Although Koepnick technically may have been in the police officers' custody during that additional period of time, the evidence clearly established that this additional period of detention would not have occurred but for Lessard's request. Under these circumstances, there is also a factual issue as to the propriety of the length of time Koepnick was detained so far as Sears is concerned.

4. *Manner of Detention.*

Factual disputes were also presented as to the manner in which Koepnick was detained by Sears. To begin with, he was accosted by Lessard and Pollack in an accusatory manner. Koepnick testified they stated, "You don't have a receipt, do you?" (4R.T. at 180-81) rather than asking to see a receipt. Then, although Koepnick responded that he had a receipt, he was nevertheless detained for shoplifting without further questioning on that subject. Koepnick submits the manner of his initial detention was thus improper for that reason.

Koepnick was then escorted to an upstairs security room where he was denied a drink of water and seated with no inquiry as to whether he had a receipt for the wrench (4R.T. at 180). When Koepnick entered the hallway to obtain a drink of water, he and Officer Campbell got into a pushing match which resulted in Koepnick falling or being thrown head first through the wall of the security room, causing him to incur neck and other injuries (4R.T. at 60-64). Koepnick was then handcuffed. However, had Koepnick been offered a drink of water and had the proper inquiries been made by Sears employees initially, his injuries arguably would not have occurred.

Koepnick submits these facts all raise factual issues as to whether the manner of his detention was reasonable. Based on these facts, a jury could reasonably have found that Sears security guards did not handle his detention in a reasonable manner.

II. The Trial Court Properly Denied Sears' Motion for Judgment Notwithstanding the Verdict as to Koepnick's Punitive Damages Based on his False Arrest Claims.

A. The Applicable Standards of Review.

The recent Arizona appellate decisions modifying the standard for determining whether there has been a *prima facie* showing permitting the assessment of punitive damages do not necessarily require that all prior jury verdicts awarding such damages be reversed. For example, *Filasky v. Preferred Risk Mutual Insurance Co.*, 152 Ariz. 591, 734 P.2d 76 (1987), instead recognizes that "a jury's decision to award punitive damages should be affirmed if any reasonable evidence exists to support it." *Gurule v. Illinois Mutual Life and Casualty Co.*, 152 Ariz. 600, 734 P.2d 85 (1987), also states that the appellate court must review the facts in a light most favorable to the party obtaining a punitive damage award and affirm the jury's verdict if a reasonable juror could conclude that the defendant either intended to violate his rights or consciously pursued a course of conduct knowing that it created a substantial risk of doing so. 734 P.2d at 88.

Of the various recent decisions, both *Hawkins v. Allstate Insurance Co.*, 152 Ariz. 490, 733 P.2d 1072 (1987), and this Court's Opinion in *Carter-Glogau*

520 Part VIII. Appellate Briefs

Laboratories, Inc. v. Construction, Production & Maintenance Labors Local 383, (1 CA-CIV 8107, 8128 filed October 30, 1986, *review denied*, May 12, 1987), have affirmed punitive damages awards where the evidence presented met the standards stated in *Linthicum v. Nationwide Life Insurance Co.*, 150 Ariz. 326, 723 P.2d 675 (1986). *Rawlings v. Apodaca*, 151 Ariz. 149, 726 P.2d 565 (1986), also remanded for further proceedings as to punitive damages where it was uncertain whether the trial judge had applied the appropriate standards.

According to *Gurule, supra*, the "evil mind" required for punitive damages may be satisfied by "defendant's conscious and deliberate disregard of the interests and rights of others." 152 Ariz. at 602, 734 P.2d at 87. It may also be established by defendant's expressed statements or inferred from his expressions, conduct or objectives. *Id.* If a defendant conducts himself in an outrageous or egregiously improper manner, the inference is permitted that he intended to injure or consciously disregarded the substantial risk that his conduct would cause significant harm. The "evil mind" may also be inferred if a defendant "deliberately continued his actions despite the inevitable or highly probable harm that would follow." *Id.*

B. Applying These Standards, the Evidence Demonstrated a *Prima Facie* Case for Punitive Damages with Respect to Koepnick's False Arrest Claim.

Numerous deficiencies in Sears' investigation support a jury's finding that its employees acted with conscious and deliberate disregard of Koepnick's rights and interests. The "bottom line" of Lessard's investigation at the time Koepnick left the Sears store was that he and Pollack "felt we had done a thorough enough investigation for us to ask [Koepnick] if he had a receipt for the wrench" (3R.T. at 35). Significantly, Lessard himself apparently did not then believe he had sufficient cause to detain Koepnick for shoplifting at that time without further questioning. Yet Lessard and Pollack accosted Koepnick in a hostile and threatening manner in a dark corner of the parking lot and accused him of not having a receipt, instead of asking in a more normal manner whether he had a receipt. Then, even though Koepnick told Lessard and Pollack in response to their accusations that he did have a receipt, he was ordered under arrest for shoplifting without further discussion or inquiry (4R.T. at 178-81). These facts clearly could support a reasonable conclusion that Sears employees had the required "evil mind" in making their initial decision to detain Koepnick without adequate investigation or proper inquiry concerning whether he in fact had the receipts they should be seeking. . . .

C. The Evidence Supporting Koepnick's Punitive Damages with Respect to His Trespass to Chattel Claim Was Sufficient to Submit That Issue to the Jury as Well.

        . . . .

CONCLUSION

For all the foregoing reasons, the trial court properly denied Sears' motions for judgment notwithstanding the verdict as to Koepnick's claim for false arrest, for punitive damages with respect to the false arrest, and for punitive damages with respect to Koepnick's trespass to chattels claim. The trial court's rulings concerning the issues properly before this Court should therefore be affirmed.

DATED this day 11th of May, 1987.

Respectfully submitted,
THOMAS J. QUARELLI, ESQ.
WILLIAM J. MONAHAN, P.C.

By _____
William J. Monahan
and
PAUL G. ULRICH, P.C.

By _____
Paul G. Ulrich
Attorneys for Appellant
Cross-Appellee

Fred Cole
Roger W. Perry
Gust, Rosenfeld, Divelbess & Henderson
3300 Valley Bank Center
Phoenix, Arizona 85073
Attorneys for Defendant-Appellee/Cross-Appellant

IN THE COURT OF APPEALS
STATE OF ARIZONA
DIVISION ONE

MAX KOEPNICK,	
Plaintiff-Appellant	1 CA-CIV 9147
Cross-Appellee,	MARICOPA County Superior Court
v.	No. C-502081
SEARS, ROEBUCK & COMPANY,	
Defendant-Appellee	
Cross-Appellant.	

APPELLEE'S REPLY BRIEF ON CROSS-APPEAL

TABLE OF CONTENTS

TABLE OF AUTHORITIES

ARGUMENT

I. Sears Is Entitled to Judgment Notwithstanding the Verdict on the False Arrest Claim.

Koepnick fails to demonstrate any valid issue of fact that would preclude the granting of judgment in favor of Sears on the false arrest count. All four of the necessary elements for a privileged detention under A.R.S. §13-1805 C are undisputedly established in the record. On the element of reasonable cause, the trial court, after hearing all the evidence, determined that reasonable cause existed for Koepnick's detention. This ruling was a proper exercise of the trial court's discretion and is fully justified by the evidence. There is no basis for this court to reverse the trial court's determination on this issue. To avoid duplication, Sears incorporates all its proper arguments on this issue by this reference.

The evidence also undisputedly establishes a proper purpose for Koepnick's detention pursuant to the statute. It is uncontroverted that Sears detained Koepnick to summon the Mesa police concerning the suspected shoplifting. Indeed, Koepnick never made any claim or offered any jury instruction with respect to some other purpose for his detention by Sears. For Koepnick to now make the bald, totally unsupported statement in his response brief that "He was not necessarily detained for that purpose" is ridiculous (Cross-appeal answering brief, p. 5). Koepnick does not even suggest any other purpose in support of this statement. As for the period of time after the police arrived, the evidence is also undisputed that Koepnick was legitimately in the Mesa police department's custody, not Sears'. Probable cause existed for the police to detain Koepnick during this period, and Sears had no control over whether or how Koepnick was kept in detention by the police.

There is also no dispute concerning the reasonableness of the length of time Sears detained Koepnick. Koepnick concedes that the length of his detention in Sears' custody until the police arrived and investigated was reasonable (Cross-appeal answering brief, p. 6). As stated above, from that point on, Koepnick was in the Mesa police department's custody, not Sears'. Koepnick was under arrest for his altercation with Officer Campbell. Prior to trial, the trial court ruled that probable cause existed for the Mesa police department's detention of Koepnick during that period for the alleged assault on Officer Campbell. (*See* Minute entry dated January 9, 1986.) Koepnick has never raised any issue or objection with respect to that ruling.

Although Koepnick repeatedly states that Steve Lessard "requested" his continued detention by the Mesa police department during this period, such statements have no support in the record. Koepnick fails even to cite to the record when making such assertions of "fact." (*See, e.g.,* cross-appeal answering brief, p. 6.) The uncontroverted evidence is that Lessard simply told the police the information and knowledge he had in his possession (4R.T. at 105-06). This information included the fact that the bag Jeff Ward stated he had wrapped the wrench in before placing it in the larger shopping bag was missing (4R.T. at 104-05). Contrary to Koepnick's statements in his briefs, that bag was never accounted for in the security office (4R.T. at 104-05). It was the police officers who made the decision to search Koepnick's truck (6R.T. at 128). Lessard had no control over whether Koepnick was detained or released by the police during that period (8R.T. at 59-60).

Finally, the element of the reasonableness of the manner of Sears' detention of Koepnick is also undisputedly established by the record. Koepnick's arguments in trying to explain why Sears' detention of him should be viewed as unreasonable are nothing less than frivolous. Koepnick's first argument revolves around the fact that, according to Koepnick's testimony, Lessard approached him and said, "You don't have a receipt, do you?" rather than asking to see his receipt. Even accepting all of Koepnick's testimony as true, as we must on this appeal, there is still no evidence of any abusive conduct that would rise to the level of a tortiously unreasonable specific manner of detention. If the court were to accept Koepnick's argument, potential liability would exist any time a subject stopped pursuant to A.R.S. §13-1805 did not like the manner in which he was addressed. It is inconceivable that the legislature intended such a result when referring to a "reasonable manner" of detention in A.R.S. §13-1805 C. Much more substantial conduct is required for liability to exist for false arrest.

Koepnick further argues that the manner of his detention was unreasonable in that he should have been questioned by Sears. A.R.S. §13-1805 C, however, indicates that store personnel are not required to question a subject; they can simply detain for the purpose of summoning a law enforcement officer to handle the investigation.

Finally, Koepnick stretches so far as to attempt to attribute the injuries he received in his altercation with Officer Campbell in the hallway to the fact that the Sears employees declined to give him a drink of water. Koepnick's need for such a nonsensical argument makes readily apparent the total lack of any factual basis for any claim that Sears detained Koepnick unreasonably. The undisputed facts show that Koepnick was simply stopped outside the store and then taken to the security office to await the arrival of the police. According to even Koepnick's testimony, he was not physically or verbally abused by the Sears employees. As such, there is no evidence that would warrant submitting this issue to the jury.

As all the elements for a privileged detention under A.R.S. §13-1805 C are undisputedly established in the record, Sears is entitled to have judgment entered in its favor on the false arrest claim.

II. Sears Is Entitled to Judgment Notwithstanding the Verdicts on the Punitive Damage Claims.

As Koepnick acknowledges in citing *Filasky v. Preferred Risk Mutual Insurance Co.*, 152 Ariz. 591, 734 P.2d 76 (1987), and *Gurule v. Illinois Mutual Life and Casualty Co.*, 152 Ariz. 600, 734 P.2d 85 (1987) (en banc), a punitive damage award will only be sustained on appeal when there is reasonable evidence to support it. In discussing the nature of an act necessary to permit punitive damages, the Arizona Supreme Court observed that "[p]unishment is an appropriate objective in a civil case only if the defendant's conduct or motive involves 'some element of outrage similar to that usually found in a crime.'" *Gurule*, 734 P.2d at 86 (quoting *Rawlings v. Apodaca*, 151 Ariz. 149, 162, 726 P.2d 565, 578 (1986)).

Where a trial court submits the issue of punitive damages to the jury on slight and inconclusive evidence of such conduct, an appellate court may correct the error. *Filasky*, 734 P.2d at 84. In both *Filasky* and *Gurule*, the Supreme Court found that the evidence did not measure up to the requisite standard and reversed the awards of punitive damages. The same conclusion should be reached in this appeal.

A. The False Arrest Claim.

Koepnick attempts to support the punitive damage award on the false arrest claim based on alleged "deficiencies" in the initial investigation and Lessard's alleged "request" that the Mesa police officers continue to detain Koepnick while his truck was searched. Both of these arguments ignore the uncontroverted facts in the record and fail to demonstrate a level of conduct sufficient to justify an award of punitive damages. First, Koepnick's assertion that the investigation by Lessard was inadequate and unreasonable is belied by the trial court's ultimate determination that reasonable cause existed for Sears' detention of Koepnick. Inherent in the trial court's ruling that reasonable cause existed for Koepnick's detention is the determination that the pre-stop investigation conducted by Lessard was reasonable. If the facts and investigation relied on by Sears were unreasonable, reasonable cause could not exist for the detention. It would be completely illogical for the same evidence that the trial court found to establish reasonable cause for the detention to also be deemed sufficient to support an award of punitive damages for the same detention.

. . . .

B. The Trespass to Chattel Claim.

. . . .

CONCLUSION

The trial court properly granted Sears' judgment notwithstanding the verdict on the claim of trespass to chattel. The trial court erred, however, in not doing the same on the claim of false arrest. There are no issues of fact present to justify submitting this claim to the jury. This court should therefore reverse the trial court's ruling that denied Sears' motion for judgment N.O.V. on this count.

Furthermore, there was no evidence to justify the submission of the claims for punitive damages on either of the two counts submitted to the jury. Thus, regardless of the ultimate decisions on the trespass to chattel and false arrest counts, Sears is entitled to have the trial court instructed to grant it judgment N.O.V. on the punitive damage claims.

Respectfully submitted this 8th day of June, 1987.

GUST, ROSENFELD, DIVELBESS & HENDERSON

By _____
   Fred Cole
   Roger W. Perry
   Attorneys for Defendant-Appellee/Cross-Appellant

Part IX

Writing to Parties: Contracts and Correspondence

Parts V through VIII examined advocacy to a court and written communication between members of a law firm. As a practicing attorney, however, you will communicate not only with judges and other attorneys but also with your clients and other parties.

For example, you may draft a written contract that the parties adopt as the final and complete expression of their negotiated agreement. If your client later complains that the other party has breached the contract, you may draft an "advice letter" to your client, advising her of her legal rights and recommending certain action. Depending on your client's assessment of her options, you might then send a "demand letter" to the opposing party, demanding that he take certain action to satisfy your client's claims.

Part IX examines contracts and letters as examples of drafting directed to parties. It does not proceed on the premise that your immediate audience will invariably be the parties themselves. On the contrary, if you know that the opposing party is represented by counsel, you will ordinarily address your contract proposal or your demand letter to the opposing counsel. Similarly, if you or your law firm is the outside counsel for a corporation, you may address your advice letter to the corporation's in-house counsel. Nonetheless, more so than with office memoranda and briefs, contracts and letters are directed ultimately to the parties themselves.

Contracts and letters may be useful at various stages of litigation. For example, a contract may lead to a dispute, or it may express the parties' agreement to settle a dispute that has already proceeded through pretrial, trial, or even appellate litigation. Similarly, although you will often draft advice and demand letters at the earliest stages of litigation, you may use them at any stage of the litigation that raises new questions or that creates a new opportunity to state your demands.

Chapter 23

Contracts

I. Basic Approaches

With some limitations, parties can privately shape their legal rights and obligations by exchanging enforceable promises in a contract. Each party's promises impose contractual duties on that party and create contractual rights in the other.

The authors of one contracts casebook believe that the contractual promise is the greatest human invention, even greater than the wheel, the lever, and the pulley:

> [F]or it is the promise that breaks the ultimate physical restraint. It permits us to live a bit of the future today. When two or more employ the tool of promise in concert, they create a unique social engine—the *bargain*.[1]

---

1. Daniel W. Fessler & Pierre R. Loiseaux, CONTRACTS, MORALITY, ECONOMICS AND THE MARKETPLACE (CASES AND MATERIALS) 1 (1982).

Although this claim may provoke some debate about the relative merits of the promise and the pulley, none will dispute that enforceable contracts are indispensable to modern commerce.

As with pleadings, you can readily find forms for contracts in a form-book or in a dusty file cabinet of a law office. However, many such forms are as antiquated as the parody of a contract presented in Exercise 13-1 near the beginning of Chapter 13. You will produce a much better contract if you throw away the outdated forms, understand the purposes of each section of a contract, and express the agreement of the parties in plain, simple, clear English.

On the other hand, you need not reinvent the wheel with every contract. Some law firms produce high-quality form contracts for common transactions. For example, some firms have created a series of provisions for real estate contracts and maintain them in computer files. An attorney assigned to a real estate transaction can (1) browse through available provisions, (2) select the paragraphs that are best suited to the current transaction, (3) create a document with the selected paragraphs, and (4) tailor the document to the particular facts and requirements of the current transaction. Such a system can be highly successful if its users ensure that the forms are well written and if they avoid complacency in tailoring the forms to particular transactions.

For contracts that do not lend themselves to a computerized form system, you should feel comfortable drafting "from scratch" without reliance on an antiquated form. You can draft with confidence if you understand the fundamental components of a contract.

II. Fundamental Components

A. General Format

A written contract should always contain the following provisions:

1. an introduction identifying the parties to the transaction,
2. a section describing the rights and obligations of the parties, and
3. signature lines showing the parties' agreement to the terms of the contract.

A contract may also include:

1. a statement of "recitals," which describes the background of the transaction and the parties' reasons for entering into the contract,
2. a glossary of defined terms, or
3. a section of miscellaneous provisions addressing such topics as termination or modification of the contract, the relationship of the contract to other transactions, or the parties' choice of law or forum in the event of a dispute.

B. Introduction to the Contract

In the first lines after the title of a contract, you should identify the parties as simply and clearly as possible. If more than two parties join in the transaction, or if at least one of the parties is a complex entity, you should set the parties' names apart from each other on the page.

For example, you can start with a descriptive section heading and use paragraphing to separate the parties' names:

I.   PARTIES

The parties to this contract for the purchase and sale of sand are:

1. SOONER SAND CO., a general partnership consisting of Harley T. Price and W. M. McMichael, general partners, and

2. BASSI DISTRIBUTING CO., a joint venture of Bassi Trucking Co. and Hardcore Rock & Gravel, Inc.

If you use this format for the introduction, you can refer to the parties throughout the contract by the formal names of their business entities: SOONER SAND CO. and BASSI DISTRIBUTING CO. Alternatively, you can assign descriptive labels to the parties, such as Seller and Buyer:

1. Sooner Sand Co. ("Seller"), a general . . . .

2. Bassi Distributing Co. ("Buyer"), a joint . . . .

Many drafters also like to assign a label to the contract itself and to include the date of the agreement in the introductory sentence:

This contract for the purchase and sale of sand (the "Agreement") is entered into on May 1, 2006, by the following parties:

C. Recitals

Although not essential to an enforceable contract, a statement of the factual background of the transaction, popularly known as a statement of "recitals," can help a neutral party interpret the contract if the parties dispute its meaning. Recitals can even help establish consideration for the contract by showing the parties' reciprocal inducements or by providing a basis for implying obligations. For example, in the celebrated contracts case *Wood v. Lucy, Lady Duff-Gordon*,[2] Justice Cardozo of the New York Court of Appeals relied partly on the recitals of a written contract to imply an

---

2. 118 N.E. 214 (N.Y. 1917).

obligation by an exclusive agent to use reasonable efforts, thus satisfying the consideration requirement.

Recitals in an outdated contract are easy enough to spot. Each recital of a background fact appears in a clause beginning with the word "whereas" and is strung together with other recitals in a single, unmanageably long run-on sentence. To provide better guidance to your reader, you should (1) introduce the recitals with a section heading, such as "Recitals" or "Background" and (2) state your recitals in conventional sentences within numbered paragraphs:

II. RECITALS

1. Seller is engaged in the business of selling and shipping sand from Phoenix to various customers in the State of Arizona but has not developed markets outside of Arizona. Seller desires to supply sand wholesale to a distributor with customers outside the state.

2. Buyer has an established business . . . .

When used in a traditional manner, recitals state only the background of the transaction and the motivations of the parties, not the actual obligations that the parties have assumed by their agreement and have stated with special precision in a different section of the written contract. Drafters of some contracts, however, have expressly incorporated their Recitals section into their statement of mutual rights and obligations, either by reference or by making it a subsection of a portion of the contract devoted to mutual promises. In doing so, the drafter hopes to legally bind the parties to the recitals, making the recitals the equivalent of warranties of the stated facts.

D. Statement of Reciprocal Promises

The heart of any contract is the parties' statement of their reciprocal promises. Those promises define the parties' mutual rights and obligations, which form the consideration for the agreement.

1. Introductory Clause; Recital of Consideration

Perhaps in an excess of caution, many drafters still begin their statements of reciprocal promises with outdated recitals of consideration such as the following:

NOW, THEREFORE, in consideration of the mutual covenants herein contained, and other good and valuable consideration the receipt of which is hereby acknowledged, the parties hereby agree . . . .

Aside from displaying an antiquated writing style, in most cases the reference to "the receipt" of "other . . . consideration" is simply false and is an exceedingly poor way to establish consideration. Expressing a promise in a signed writing raises a presumption of consideration in some states,[3] but a recital of consideration has no additional legal effect under the majority rule.[4]

Especially antiquated is the reference to "good and valuable" consideration. Centuries ago, conventional consideration with economic value—such as money, goods, or services—was known as "valuable consideration," and a familial or other personal relationship with the other party was viewed as "good consideration" for a promise to that party, but the latter form of consideration has long been abandoned by the common law.[5]

Under modern theory, the consideration in a typical contract consists of the parties' mutual promises, exchanged for one another with reciprocal inducement.[6] Rather than pompously recite the existence of consideration, you should simply state the mutual promises under a descriptive section heading and a simple introductory clause that refers to the promises as "mutual" or "reciprocal," or otherwise as part of a "bargained-for exchange":

III. MUTUAL RIGHTS AND OBLIGATIONS

Seller and Buyer agree to the following exchange of reciprocal promises:

1. *Supply.* For a period of five years from the date of formation of this contract, Seller will supply Buyer with all the sand that Buyer requires. . . .

2. *Delivery.* . . .

3. *Quality.* . . .

4. *Price.* For each ton of sand delivered, Buyer will pay Seller a sum equal to . . . .

Some drafters are tempted to begin each statement of an obligation with a phrase such as "Seller promises to supply" or "Seller agrees to supply." The reference to "promises" or "agrees," however, is unnecessary. If you begin your section with an appropriate heading, such as "Mutual Rights and Obligations" or "Mutual Promises," and if you follow immediately with an umbrella statement such as "Seller and Buyer agree to the following bargained-for exchange:" you need not repeatedly invoke the word "agree" in each statement of a promise. Moreover, to state a promise, you need not use the word "promise." If preceded by the appropriate section heading and umbrella statement, words such as "will" and "must" in the statements of

---

3. *See, e.g.,* CAL. CIV. C. § 1614 (West 1982).

4. *See* John D. Calamari & Joseph M. Perillo, CALAMARI AND PERILLO ON CONTRACTS § 4.6 at 158 n.3 & accompanying text (6th ed. 2009).

5. *See* Eugen Bucher, ENGLAND AND THE CONTINENT: DISTINGUISHING THE PECULIARITIES OF THE ENGLISH COMMON LAW OF CONTRACT 54 (Tony Weir, trans., 2009).

6. *See* RESTATEMENT (SECOND) OF CONTRACTS § 71 (1981).

obligation will appropriately convey a party's intent to commit to a future performance:

IV. MUTUAL RIGHTS AND OBLIGATIONS

The parties agree to the following exchange of mutual promises:

1. Bank will approve a construction loan application submitted by Contractor, if the application satisfies the following requirements: . . . .

On the other hand, the permissive term "may" would denote the granting of a discretionary power or authority under the contract:

---

12. If Tenant commits a major default as defined in Section 11, Landlord may demand acceleration of the remaining rent pursuant to Section 13 or may demand liquidated damages pursuant to Section 14, at its option.

Other authors and drafters advocate use of "shall," "must," "may," and "will" to serve different roles in expressing, respectively: mandatory duties, predicates to asserting contractual rights, authorizations of discretionary action, and predictions of future events. If you find that employing such terms help you differentiate between different kinds of contract terms, you will find support in sample contracts and in drafting books that explore drafting challenges in greater depth than is possible in this chapter.[7] If you employ terms consistently, and if you accurately and precisely express your meaning, you likely can achieve your drafting goals with any of several approaches.

2. Precision in Drafting

a. Simplicity; Terms of Art

The terms of the exchange are a matter of negotiation between the parties. If you represent your client in the negotiations, you can participate in shaping the substance of the bargain. As part of that process, you may draft proposed contract provisions to serve as offers or counteroffers to the other party. In other cases, your client may ask you to prepare a formal written document expressing a bargain that the parties have previously negotiated. In either case, one of your primary tasks as drafter of the final document is to express the parties' negotiated rights and obligations as precisely as possible to reduce the risk of misunderstanding and costly disputes during performance of the contract.

To draft precisely, you should take advantage of helpful terms of art but avoid unnecessary jargon. For example, the provisions below refer to the buyer's "requirements," a legal term of art that has special meaning

---

7. *See, e.g.*, Tina L. Stark, DRAFTING CONTRACTS: HOW AND WHY LAWYERS DO WHAT THEY DO (2007).

and legal consequences under the Uniform Commercial Code.[8] Otherwise, however, the provisions contain plain, simple English:

1. *Supply.* For a period of five years from the date of formation of this contract, Seller will supply Buyer with all the sand that Buyer requires for Buyer's business of selling and shipping sand to customers outside the State of Arizona.

2. *Delivery.* Buyer may order sand as Buyer's requirements arise by sending a written purchase order to Seller. . . .

Some legal terms are not necessarily terms of art but may be generally helpful and inoffensive. In the following passage, for example, the seller makes a special kind of promise by "warranting" the quality of the goods:

3. *Quality.* Seller warrants that the quality of the sand that is delivered to Buyer will be at least equal to that of sand of corresponding grades sold by other sand companies in the City of Phoenix, Arizona.

The word "warrants" in this passage is not a necessary term of art under the Uniform Commercial Code. The seller would assume the same legal obligation by simply promising that

Seller will deliver to Buyer sand of a quality that is at least equal . . . .[9]

Nonetheless, drafters typically and reasonably use the term "warrants" or "warranty" to draw attention to the special nature of a promise that goods or services will meet certain standards.

Similarly, many drafters use special phrases to draw attention to statements of "conditions," which qualify or limit contractual duties. In a standard insurance contract, for example, the insured will assume an absolute obligation to pay premiums to the insurer, but the insurer will pay money to the insured only if the insured suffers a loss of the type covered by the insurance contract. You could introduce the insurer's conditional promise with the simple word "if":

If Insured suffers a covered loss as defined in section VI above, the insurer will reimburse the insured for . . . .

Many insurers, however, like to emphasize the conditional nature of their promises with special phrases, such as "on the condition that" or "in the event that":

---

8. U.C.C. § 2-306(1) (2011).
9. *See* U.C.C. § 2-313(1)(a), (2) (2011).

In the event that Insured suffers a covered loss as defined in section VI above, the insurer . . . .

b. Deliberate Imprecision

Occasionally, precision is neither feasible nor desirable. In some cases, for example, the parties may have failed to reach precise agreement on some difficult issue, even though they are ready to go forward with their general transaction. If so, you may be forced to express their imperfect agreement on the difficult issue in terms that are sufficiently imprecise to encompass the range of interpretations that describes their divergent positions.

For example, the buyer of factory equipment may demand during negotiations that the seller agree to repair or replace defective parts within 10 days after receiving notice of the defect. The seller might counteroffer to repair or replace defective parts within 45 days after receiving notice of the defect. If the parties cannot agree on a time period measured by a specific number of days, they might instead agree on the vague language "within a reasonable time in light of all the circumstances," realizing that they might not share the same interpretation of that language in particular applications.

Language such as this may save the deal if negotiations are stalled on a contentious issue. Moreover, if performance of the contract proceeds smoothly, the parties may never test their divergent interpretations of the language. On the other hand, if adverse circumstances place a strain on performance, the lack of perfect agreement on the precise meaning of the provision may erupt into a serious dispute. Thus, during the negotiation of such a deal, you must help your client weigh the benefits of reaching general agreement against the risks of subsequent disputes over the meaning of vague language.

3. Merger Clauses and Parol Evidence

As an example of a typical miscellaneous provision, a "merger clause" states that the written contract is the exclusive statement of the parties' agreement. If the other party subsequently asserts that the total agreement includes rights and obligations not expressed in the written contract, you can refer to the merger clause and seek to exclude evidence of the alleged unwritten obligations under the "parol evidence rule." With some exceptions, the common law parol evidence rule views the final and complete written agreement as the exclusive statement of the terms of the parties' agreement, thus excluding prior written notes or testimony about prior oral statements if offered to alter or add to the written terms.

A typical merger clause refers only generally to the subject matter of the agreement:

XXV. *Prior Agreements Superseded*—This written contract constitutes the parties' complete and exclusive statement of their agreement on the subject matter covered by this contract, and it supersedes all previous agreements, promises, or representations regarding that subject matter.

Unfortunately, such a clause does not eliminate the risk of litigation of a common question under the parol evidence rule: Does an alleged additional agreement address topics within the subject matter of the main written contract so that the main contract supersedes it, or does the additional agreement address unrelated topics so that it can stand separately as an independent, enforceable contract?[10]

For example, suppose that on July 1 the parties signed a written contract for the lease of restaurant space with a fully equipped kitchen. The lessee later asserted that the lessor also orally agreed on June 28 to sell dining tables and chairs to the lessee at the spectacularly low price of $450. The lessor denies the oral agreement. He also points to the merger clause and argues that, assuming he did tentatively agree on June 28 to sell the dining furniture, such an agreement was simply part of continuing negotiations that the parties abandoned and superseded in their July 1 agreement.

However, to successfully invoke the merger clause to exclude evidence of the oral agreement, the lessor must demonstrate that the alleged agreement to sell dining furniture falls within the subject matter of the July 1 contract; otherwise, the alleged June 28 agreement can stand outside the field occupied exclusively by the July 1 contract. Unfortunately, the merger clause cannot help the lessor much because it fails to define the subject matter of the contract.

If you intend a written contract to broadly supersede prior agreements or promises on related transactions, you must describe the subject matter of your contract expansively so that the merger clause can have the intended effect. If you anticipate particular problems stemming from failed negotiations on collateral matters, you can address those matters explicitly:

XXV. *Prior Agreements Superseded*—This written contract constitutes the parties' complete and exclusive statement of their agreement on all matters relating to the lease of the Scottsdale premises, the operation of a restaurant on those premises, and the furnishings and equipment needed for the operation. This contract supersedes all previous or contemporaneous agreements, promises, or representations regarding that subject matter.

This merger clause expresses the parties' intent to abandon any prior agreement for the sale of restaurant furnishings or equipment and to replace it with the terms of the lease agreement.

E. Signature Line

You may end your contract with any reasonable means of presenting the parties' signatures as evidence of their agreement to the terms of the contract. You do not need to invoke formalistic jargon such as: "In witness whereof, the said parties have hereunto set their hands and seals the day and year first above written."

---

10. *See, e.g.*, Gianni v. R. Russell & Co., Inc., 126 A. 791 (Pa. 1924).

Instead, you may simply precede the signature lines with the single word "Signed." At most, you might introduce the signatures with a clause such as, "The undersigned parties agree to these terms."

If you have not already dated the contract at the beginning, you can include a space for the date next to each party's signature. The latest date on a signature line will correspond to one party's acceptance of the other party's offer and normally will identify the date of contract formation.

III. Summary

To draft a simple contract, you should

1. identify the parties in an introductory provision,
2. recite the background facts, if helpful,
3. state the reciprocal promises of the parties as precisely as possible, and
4. provide signature lines as a means for the parties to express their assent to the terms of the contract.

Exercise 23-1

1. Sample Requirements Contract

Study the following contract. Compare it with the antiquated version presented in Exercise 13-1, near the beginning of Chapter 13, and with your revision of that contract.

REQUIREMENTS CONTRACT

I. PARTIES

The parties to this contract for the purchase and sale of sand are:

1. Sooner Sand Co. ("Seller"), a general partnership consisting of the general partners Harley T. Price and W. M. McMichael, and

2. Bassi Distributing Co. ("Buyer"), a joint venture of Bassi Trucking Co. and Hardcore Rock & Gravel, Inc.

II. RECITALS

1. Seller is engaged in the business of selling and shipping sand from Phoenix to various customers in the State of Arizona but has not developed markets outside of Arizona. Seller desires to supply sand wholesale to a distributor with customers outside the state.

2. Buyer has an established business in Phoenix selling and shipping sand to various customers in several states outside Arizona, including California, Nevada, Utah, and Colorado. Buyer desires a stable source of supply of sand for that business.

III. MUTUAL RIGHTS AND OBLIGATIONS

Seller and Buyer agree to the following bargained-for exchange:

1. *Supply.* For a period of 5 years from the date of formation of this contract, Seller will supply Buyer with all the sand that Buyer requires for Buyer's business of selling and shipping sand to customers outside the State of Arizona.

2. *Delivery.* Buyer will order sand as Buyer's requirements arise by sending a written purchase order to Seller. On receipt of such a purchase order, Seller will deliver the ordered sand within 10 days to Buyer's facility at 1531 Range Road in Glendale, Arizona.

3. *Quality.* Seller warrants that the quality of the sand that is delivered to Buyer will be at least equal to that of sand of corresponding grades sold by other sand companies in the City of Phoenix, Arizona.

4. *Price.* For each ton of sand delivered, Buyer will pay Seller a sum equal to 60% of the market price per ton of concrete in the City of Phoenix at the time of Seller's delivery to Buyer.

5. *Term of Payment.* Seller may give an invoice to Buyer for sand on or after Seller delivers the sand to Buyer. Buyer will pay the full amount of such an invoice within 30 days of its receipt of the invoice.

Signed:

_____   _____

SELLER—Authorized Agent for Sooner Sand Co.   Date

_____   _____

BUYER—Authorized Agent for Bassi Distributing Co.   Date

2. Format for More Complex Agreement

a. Compare the following outline of a sample contract with the sample contract in Problem 1 above. The sample below displays an alternative introductory section, and it contemplates more complex provisions that must be subdivided into more numerous subsections.

b. In section 4.2 of the contract, draft a merger clause that identifies your document as the complete and exclusive statement of the parties' agreement. In particular, be certain to supersede prior failed negotiations in which Seller proposed to lease trucks to Buyer for the transportation of the sand to other states.

REQUIREMENTS CONTRACT

This contract for the purchase and sale of sand (the Agreement) is entered into on _____ by the following parties:

1. Seller—Sooner Sand Co., a general partnership consisting of Harley T. Price and W. M. McMichael, general partners, and

2. Buyer—Bassi Distributing Co., a joint venture of Bassi Trucking Co. and Hard-core Rock & Gravel, Inc.

RECITALS

1. Seller is engaged . . . .

2. Buyer has an established . . . .

MUTUAL RIGHTS AND OBLIGATIONS

Seller and Buyer agree to the following bargained-for exchange:

Article I – Definitions

1.1 *Grades of sand*—. . . .

1.2 *Market price*—. . . .

Article II – Supply of Sand

2.1 *Quantity*—. . . .

2.2 *Quality*—. . . .

2.3 *Delivery*—. . . .

Article III – Payment

3.1 *Price*—. . . .

3.2 *Terms of Payment*—. . . .

Article IV – Miscellaneous Provisions

4.1 *No Oral Modification*—. . . .

4.2 *Prior Negotiations Superseded*—. . . .

4.3 *Mandatory Arbitration of Disputes*—. . . .

Signed

_____   _____

Chapter 24

Advice Letters

As counselor and advocate, you will draft many kinds of letters to your client or to others on your client's behalf. Two of the most important are advice letters and demand letters. These letters are closely related to two kinds of documents examined in previous chapters: office memoranda and briefs. Like an office memorandum, an advice letter communicates a balanced legal analysis of a dispute or proposed action, predicts an outcome, and recommends a course of action. In contrast, a demand letter is like a brief in that it advocates a position and usually requests the addressee to take specific action. This chapter examines advice letters; Chapter 25 examines demand letters.[1]

---

1. Many of the ideas in Chapters 24 and 25 are taken with permission from lecture materials prepared by Frank M. Placenti and Mark Hileman, shortly before submission of the first edition of this book in 1989, when they worked for the Phoenix law firm Streich, Lang, Weeks & Cardon, P.A., which has since merged with the law firm of Quarles & Brady.

I. Advice Letters Distinguished from Opinion Letters

Many attorneys and commentators use the term "opinion letter" to refer to any letter addressed to a client that offers a legal analysis, opinion, or recommendation. Within this general class of letters, however, are two important subcategories, each of which warrants a narrowly descriptive label. The term "opinion letter" best describes highly specialized letters that provide clients with formal opinions on certain kinds of legal questions. The term "advice letter" accurately describes the far more common kind of letter in which you will more generally analyze a legal problem and advise your client about the relative merits of alternative courses of action.

More specifically, an opinion letter is a formal document that expresses your opinion, or that of your law firm, that a specified act is legally valid. For example, you might issue to a corporate client your formal opinion that the corporation has validly issued certain stock under applicable laws and under the articles and bylaws of the corporation. Because the client will significantly rely on such an opinion, the standards for an opinion letter are high, and its format is fairly rigid.

In contrast, in an advice letter, you will communicate your analysis of a legal problem to a client in much the same way that you would use an office memorandum to communicate the analysis to a supervising attorney. Even if you cannot definitively resolve the legal issues in the analysis, you can evaluate the relative merits of the parties' claims and defenses, estimate the probability of success on the merits, and recommend a course of action or describe alternative courses of action. You can thus provide your client with valuable advice short of giving a definite opinion of the legality of certain actions.

In many law firms, only designated attorneys are authorized to issue formal opinion letters on behalf of the firm. Moreover, those attorneys tend to follow carefully developed forms when drafting their opinion letters, leaving little room for flexibility in format or creativity in analysis. Further examination of opinion letters is beyond the scope of this book. Instead, this chapter will explore the more common advice letter.

II. Purpose, Audience, and Writing Style

The writing style that you adopt for a document is partly a function of your intended audience and the purpose of your document. When you draft an office memorandum, you can easily identify your audience and purpose: You will communicate a balanced legal analysis to an experienced attorney. When you draft an advice letter, however, your audience and purpose may be less clear.

For example, the legal experience and general sophistication of your audience may vary greatly from one letter to the next. One client may be new to his business, have no legal training, and have learned English only after recently arriving from a foreign country. Another client may be a sophisticated, experienced businesswoman with at least a rudimentary knowledge of the laws that affect her business. Still another client may be a corporation with an in-house counsel to whom you will direct your advice letter. Obviously, you should adapt your writing style to suit the experience and legal training of your audience. In a letter to the legally inexperienced client described above, you should take particular care to use plain, simple English and to avoid legal jargon. In letters to more experienced and legally knowledgeable clients, you can safely use more sophisticated language and legal terminology. In each case, however, your goal is the same: to communicate clearly, not to impress the reader with the breadth of your legal vocabulary.

In some cases, your client may wish to share your advice letter with customers, partners, or other attorneys. If so, you should draft the letter with the needs of the secondary audience in mind. For example, if your law firm's client is a corporate manager, she may intend to discuss your advice letter with the corporation's separate, in-house counsel. If so, you may want to provide a full explanation of your underlying legal analysis or even attach a copy of the formal office memorandum on which the advice letter is based.

III. Format

You should adopt any format that suits your audience and the purpose of your advice letter. As a starting point, you can follow the basic elements of a reasonable format for an office memorandum:

Issues
Brief Answers
Facts
Discussion
Conclusion

With this format, your advice letter would

1. restate the questions that your client posed to you,
2. briefly summarize your conclusions,
3. state the facts on which your analysis is based,
4. summarize your analysis of the law and the facts, and
5. state your conclusions and your strategic recommendations.

If your advice letter is simple and brief, you need not use formal section headings to display the transitions between elements of your format. Instead, you can simply use sensible paragraphing to lead the reader from one element to the next. Indeed, some clients prefer to receive short advice letters in the body of an e-mail message, easily accessible to a client who is on the move.

On the other hand, if your letter is long and complex, you should use section headings, just as you would in an office memorandum or a brief. You need not use precisely the same format headings as you would for an office memorandum. One attorney used the following primary headings in an advice letter to introduce the issues, brief answers, facts, discussion, and conclusion:

Issues Addressed

Executive Summary of Conclusions

Background

Analysis (divided into subsections)

Recommendations

IV. Introduction and Statement of Issues

Immediately after the address and before the salutation of your advice letter, you should concisely state the general subject matter of the letter:

Clay Franks
Vice-President, Construction
GRT Developers
1212 Central Ave., Suite 2201
Boomtown, Calzona 81717

RE: TRI Corp.'s possible breach of contract on the Westcourt project.

Dear Mr. Franks,

Then, in the first paragraph after the salutation, you should refer to your client's inquiry on this subject matter and state the issues that your letter addresses.

In some cases, your client will pose a general question that asks for strategic advice rather than legal conclusions: "Should we fire TRI and sue it for breach of contract?" If so, you may want to inform your client of the legal issues on which your strategic advice will depend:

Dear Mr. Franks,

You have asked us to advise you whether you should fire TRI from the Westcourt project and sue it for breach of contract. In formulating our advice on this matter, we have analyzed the following questions:

(1) Did TRI breach the construction contract by using Cohoes pipe rather than the Reading pipe called for in the architect's plans?

(2) If so, was TRI's breach "material," thus permitting you to cancel the construction contract and fire TRI from the project?

(3) If TRI has breached the contract, to what remedies is GRT entitled?

If you decide to introduce the primary parts of your letter with formal section headings, you could begin with "Issues":

Dear Mr. Franks,

You have asked us to advise you whether you should fire TRI from the Westcourt project and sue it for breach of contract.

I.   Issues
In formulating our advice on this matter, we have analyzed the following questions:
     A. Did TRI breach the construction contract by using Cohoes pipe rather than the Reading pipe called for in the architect's plans?
     B. If so, was TRI's breach "material," thus . . . .
     C. If TRI has breached . . . .

V. Brief Answers

Some attorneys will discourage you from summarizing your conclusions in brief answers near the beginning of your advice letter. They fear that your client will fail to appreciate or will even misinterpret your conclusions if he has not read your full analysis first. Like a supervising attorney reading an office memorandum, however, a client reading an advice letter is anxious to reach the bottom line. You should not withhold it from him out of some misplaced concern that he is not ready to face it. Moreover, mindful that he has paid for the entire letter, the client is nearly certain to read beyond the brief answers and to appreciate your full analysis. Thus, unless the letter is very short, or unless exceptional circumstances compel you to lay unusual groundwork before revealing an unfavorable conclusion,[2] you should satisfy your client's curiosity early in the letter.

If you use a simple format without section headings, you may briefly summarize your conclusions in a sentence or two immediately following your statement of the issues in the opening paragraph:

---

2. *See* Henry Weihofen, Legal Writing Style 178, 199 (2d ed. 1980).

Dear Ms. Price,

You have asked us whether you would be liable for damages if you discharged your head chef in retaliation for his testifying against you in a hearing of the state Food and Beverage Commission. As discussed more fully below, we conclude that such a discharge would not constitute a breach of your employment contract, but it would render you liable under the state tort law of "wrongful discharge."

In a more complex letter, you could state your brief answers under some appropriate heading, such as "Brief Answers" or "Summary of Conclusions":

Dear Mr. Franks,

You have asked us to advise you whether you should fire TRI from the Westcourt project and sue it for breach of contract.

I.   Issues
In formulating our advice on this matter, we have analyzed the following questions:
A. Did TRI breach the construction contract by using Cohoes pipe rather than the Reading pipe called for in the architect's plans?
B. If so, was TRI's breach "material," thus permitting you to cancel the construction contract and fire TRI from the project?
C. If TRI has breached the contract, to what remedies is GRT entitled?

II.   Summary of Conclusions
A. TRI breached the construction contract, because the architect's plans clearly call for Reading pipe and do not permit substitutes.
B. TRI's breach almost certainly is not material, because Cohoes pipe is nearly identical to Reading pipe in all important specifications. Therefore, you cannot cancel the contract.
C. GRT is entitled to the difference between the value of the Reading pipe and that of the Cohoes pipe, a difference that appears to be insubstantial.

In addition to providing these answers to the specific legal issues that you have formulated, you might add a sentence to your overview paragraph that summarizes your response to the client's general strategic question:

Dear Mr. Franks,

You have asked us to advise you whether you should fire TRI from the Westcourt project and sue it for breach of contract. In this letter, we summarize our legal analysis and advise you not to fire TRI or withhold its payments.

VI. Facts

In every advice letter, you should state the facts on which your analysis is based. By making a record of the factual premises of your analysis, you can protect yourself against criticism or liability if subsequently discovered facts render your legal analysis obsolete. Indeed, if your client has supplied you with the facts, you may want to disclaim responsibility for any fact investigation:

III. Facts

The advice in this letter is premised on the following facts, which you have supplied and which we have not yet independently investigated. If the following facts prove to be incomplete or incorrect, you should not rely on the advice in this letter without first consulting us.

VII. Legal Analysis

In the body of your letter, you should reach a conclusion on each issue by applying the relevant law to the facts. In a letter to a corporate client's in-house counsel or to a sophisticated client who has some legal knowledge, you can develop your legal analysis and cite to authority in much the same way that you would in an office memorandum. Other clients, however, will have little use for your in-depth analysis of authority. They would rather read a simplified summary of your legal analysis, and they are willing to assume that your underlying research and analysis has been thorough.

Thus, even if you have more fully expressed your analysis in another document, you may want to simplify the discussion in your advice letter. For example, as an initial reaction to a client's inquiry, you often will draft a full office memorandum addressed to a supervising attorney. The memorandum will then serve as a basis for formulating advice to the client. In the advice letter, however, you need not analyze the legal authority with the same depth and formality that you found useful in the memorandum. Instead, you can more simply and briefly convey your analysis of each issue by (1) abstractly summarizing the law with little or no citation to authority, (2) identifying the relevant facts, and (3) stating your conclusion:

Under state tort law, you are liable for damages if you discharge an employee for a reason that violates public policy. Legislation of this state establishes public policies of maintaining health standards in restaurants and encouraging witnesses to testify fully and truthfully at state administrative hearings. Therefore, if you discharge Chef Boyardi in retaliation for his testifying about violations of hygiene standards in your restaurant, you will be liable for violation of public policy.

In some cases, you can even leave the legal rule implicit by simply stating a conclusion, after identifying the facts on which it is based:

> Your contract with Chef Boyardi does not commit the parties to a definite term of employment, and it does not restrict your right to terminate the contract. Therefore, under state contract law, you can discharge Chef Boyardi at any time and for any reason without breaching the contract.

If your client has some legal training or expects to share your letter with another attorney, you may want to analyze authority to an extent that approaches the depth of analysis in your office memorandum. Alternatively, you can summarize your analysis in the letter and simply attach the office memorandum on which the advice in your letter is based. In this way, the client can rely primarily on the more accessible information in the letter, but he also has access to your more thorough and formal memorandum if the need for it arises.

Some clients may even prefer to receive short and simple advice letters in the body of an e-mail message, to which they can easily gain access with a laptop computer or handheld device while on the move. If a longer and more formal legal document would be helpful as well, you can attach it to the e-mail message.

VIII. Conclusion; Strategic Recommendations

In a final paragraph or section of your advice letter, you should summarize your subsidiary conclusions and offer your ultimate advice. If your client's legal rights and obligations are unclear, do not hesitate to convey the uncertainty with words and phrases such as "probably," or "although the question is close, TRI probably committed a material because" or "although our client has some chance of success on her claim, we likely cannot prove . . . ." Even so, you should reach a conclusion, even if only a qualified one:

> Although the question is a close one, the noncompetition agreement probably is unreasonable in scope and therefore unenforceable as a violation of public policy. In particular, the geographic scope of the restrictions likely exceeds the area in which Exco has business interests now or in the foreseeable future. I recommend . . . .

Your ultimate advice likely will be strategic, such as a recommendation to file a lawsuit, communicate a settlement offer, or refrain from discharging an employee. If the ultimate decision for the client is essentially a business decision, such as whether to purchase property for development, you should outline the legal consequences of the purchase but leave the actual business decision to the client. On the other hand, if the ultimate decision is more clearly tied to the legal merits of a claim or defense, such as whether to settle a legal dispute, you can more strongly recommend a particular course of action.

Nonetheless, in all cases, you should invite the client to make the final decision. For example, when advising a client to settle, you should recommend a range of settlement offers within which your client can exercise some judgment to choose a particular position or to reject settlement altogether.

IX. Summary

In an advice letter, you should

1. use plain English whenever possible,
2. adapt your format and depth of legal analysis to your audience and your purpose,
3. restate the questions that your client has posed to you and identify the legal issues that they encompass,
4. briefly answer the issues,
5. state the facts on which your analysis and advice are premised,
6. discuss the law and apply the law to the facts to reach a conclusion for each issue, and
7. summarize your subsidiary conclusions and state your advice.

Exercise 24-1

1. Advice Letter Without Section Headings

The following advice letter is addressed to a restaurant owner with no legal training. The author has used only paragraphing to signal the transition from one element of the letter to the next, and he has not cited to authority.

a. Identify the purpose or purposes of each paragraph in the letter.

b. At its current length and format, would the letter be suitable for delivery in the body of an e-mail message if the client has easy access to the Internet?

c. Research the problem and rewrite the letter so that it conveys additional information to a client with legal training. Specifically, cite to authority and briefly analyze the authority. If appropriate, divide the expanded letter into sections with section headings.

August 1, 2014
Leona Price
Hep Crepe Restaurant
123 Washington St.
Spinach Village, New Maine 10307

RE: Liability for terminating Chef Boyardi's employment

Dear Ms. Price,

You have asked us whether you would be liable for damages if you discharged your head chef in retaliation for his testifying against you in a hearing of the state Food and Beverage Commission. As discussed more fully below, we conclude that such a discharge would not constitute a breach of your employment contract, but it would render you liable under the state tort law of "wrongful discharge."

Our analysis is premised on the following facts, as you have supplied them. The state Food and Beverage Commission has recently held hearings on violations of state health and hygiene regulations at various restaurants within the Village. The Commission requested your head chef, Anthony Boyardi, to testify at the hearings. Under examination by Commissioners, Chef Boyardi testified that employees have failed to control rat and insect infestations at Hep Crepe, resulting in continuing violations of state regulations. Because you view Chef Boyardi's act of testifying as disloyal conduct, you wish to fire him.

Your contract with Chef Boyardi does not commit the parties to a definite term of employment, and it does not restrict your right to terminate the contract. Therefore, under state contract law, you can discharge Chef Boyardi at any time and for any reason without breaching the contract.

Under state tort law, however, you will be liable for damages if you discharge an employee for a reason that violates public policy, regardless of whether the discharge would constitute a breach of contract. Legislation of this state establishes public policies of maintaining health standards in restaurants and encouraging witnesses to testify fully and truthfully at state administrative hearings. Therefore, if you discharge Chef Boyardi in retaliation for testifying at the administrative hearings, you will be liable for violation of public policy. Your liability will include damages designed to compensate Chef Boyardi for his losses and may extend to additional damages designed to punish you for your intentional misconduct.

In conclusion, if you discharge Chef Boyardi in retaliation for his testimony, he will have a valid claim against you for damages. We advise you not to discharge him unless you are prepared to justify the discharge on other grounds. We recommend that you address the infestations in your restaurant, repair your relationship with Chef Boyardi, and capitalize on the continued popularity of your restaurant.

If you have any questions on this matter, please call me at (898) 123-4567.

Sincerely,

_____

Robert Linzer
for Avila and Celaya, P.C.
222 N. 3d St.
Spinach Village, New Maine 10307

2. Advice Letter with Section Headings

a. Compare the following letter with the one above. Describe each way in which the letters differ in style and format.

b. Assume in the letter below that your client, Clay Franks, is an Anglo-American with racist tendencies and that the opposing party's representative, Cal Dunlap, is African-American. Do those facts affect your analysis of the problem? Does the letter below adequately address the problems potentially caused by your client's racism without unduly offending him? Should you be worried about offending him?

c. The letter below is addressed to a client who has at least a basic knowledge of the law relating to performance and breach of construction contracts. Rewrite the letter so that it is appropriate for a client who has no legal training or knowledge. Specifically, summarize your analysis without citing to specific authority. If appropriate, eliminate the section headings and guide your reader through the simpler letter with good paragraphing and transition sentences.

Marcia Todd
Todd, Brown & King
1212 Central Ave., Suite 401
Boomtown, Calzona 81717
July 5, 2014

Clay Franks
Vice-President, Construction
GRT Developers
1212 Central Ave., Suite 2201
Boomtown, Calzona 81717

RE: TRI Corp.'s possible breach of contract on the Westcourt project

Dear Mr. Franks,

You have asked us to advise you whether you should fire TRI from the Westcourt project and sue it for breach of contract. In this letter, we summarize our legal analysis and advise you not to fire TRI or withhold its payments.

I. ISSUES

In formulating our advice on this matter, we have analyzed the following questions:

A. Did TRI breach the construction contract by using Cohoes pipe rather than the Reading pipe called for in the architect's plans?

B. If so, was TRI's breach "material," thus permitting you to cancel the construction contract and fire TRI from the project?

C. If TRI has breached the contract, to what remedies is GRT entitled?

II. SUMMARY OF CONCLUSIONS

A. TRI breached the construction contract, because the architect's plans clearly call for Reading pipe and do not permit substitutes.

B. TRI's breach almost certainly is not material, because Cohoes pipe is nearly identical to Reading pipe in all important specifications. Therefore, you cannot cancel the contract.

C. GRT is entitled to the difference between the value of the Reading pipe and that of the Cohoes pipe, a difference that appears to be insubstantial.

III. FACTS

The advice in this letter is premised on the following facts, which you have supplied. We have not yet independently investigated the facts. If the following facts prove to be incomplete or incorrect, you should not rely on the advice in this letter without first consulting us.

GRT Developers is constructing a shopping center at the southwest corner of 27th Ave. and Marconi Way in Boomtown. As Vice-President of the Construction Division, you have hired TRI to install the plumbing system. GRT's contract with TRI incorporates the architect's plans, which you first transmitted to TRI in a letter soliciting its bid on the project. Those plans clearly call for the plumbing subcontractor to use Reading brand pipe for all plumbing: "All pipes in the plumbing system must be Reading pipe, in the sizes and grades specified in these plans, and no other brand pipe."

From the beginning, you have had difficulty working with TRI's foreman, Cal Dunlap. When TRI had completed about half of the plumbing on the project, you discovered that TRI had installed Cohoes brand pipe rather than Reading pipe. In a heated conversation with Dunlap, you demanded that TRI remove the Cohoes pipe, install Reading pipe, and compensate GRT for the resulting delay in construction. Dunlap agreed to install Reading pipe in the remainder of the plumbing, but he refused to replace the previously installed pipe. You now want to know whether you can fire TRI if Dunlap does not meet your demands.

Your own engineers have concluded that Cohoes pipe is equal to Reading pipe in durability and other relevant specifications. You do not know why the architect required Reading pipe, but you know that his brother-in-law is a sales manager for Reading Manufacturing Co.

IV. ANALYSIS

If TRI has breached the construction contract, GRT may sue it for all foreseeable damages caused by the breach, provided that GRT can prove the damages with reasonable certainty. *See Johnson v. Coombs Constr. Co.*, 345 Calz. 2d 331, 334 (1979). However, you may not fire TRI from the project unless TRI's breach is so substantial that a court would characterize it as "material," rather than "minor." *Lehman Brothers, Inc. v. Steenhook Enters.*, 401 Calz. 2d 112, 115 (1985). If a breach is only minor, you may not terminate the contract; instead, you must permit TRI to complete its performance, while reserving GRT's claim for damages resulting from its minor breach. *See id.* If you terminate the construction contract for only a minor breach, GRT will itself be guilty of the first material breach and will be liable to TRI for damages. *See id.*

A. *Breach of Contract*

The construction contract plainly requires TRI to use Reading pipe and no other. TRI has admitted that it used Cohoes pipe in approximately half of the plumbing. Therefore, TRI has breached the contract, and it is liable to GRT for foreseeable damages that GRT can prove with reasonable certainty.

B. *Materiality of Breach*

TRI's breach is material if it is so substantial that it either (1) robs GRT of the primary benefit that it expected from the contract, or (2) demonstrates that TRI is not competent to perform the work and therefore should not be allowed to continue. *See id.* at 116. Stated conversely, the breach is minor if TRI is competent to complete the contract and GRT can be fully compensated for its losses by an award of money damages that is small in proportion to the value of the entire contract. *See id.*

In this case, TRI's breach probably is not material under either branch of the test of materiality. First, GRT's primary benefit from the plumbing contract presumably is high-quality durable plumbing. Cohoes pipe is equal to Reading pipe in durability and other relevant specifications. The architect apparently required Reading pipe for personal reasons and not because it is superior to Cohoes pipe. Therefore, unless GRT has some special need for Reading pipe, it will get its primary benefit from the contract even though half of the plumbing consists of Cohoes pipe.

Second, although TRI's use of Cohoes pipe shows that Dunlap departed from the architect's plans, we have no evidence that he has failed to follow more important specifications of the plans or that his crews have performed poorly in the actual installation. Dunlap probably knows that Cohoes pipe is equal to Reading pipe, and he may have decided not to take that architect's requirement seriously. Therefore, the events do not suggest that TRI is incompetent to perform Dunlap's promise to complete the installation of plumbing with Reading pipe.

In summary, a court likely would infer that your unhappiness with TRI stems more from your personal dislike for Dunlap than from problems caused by TRI's use of Cohoes pipe. Therefore, a court almost certainly will find that TRI's breach is not material.

C. Remedies

Assuming TRI's breach was only minor, you have no right to fire TRI from the project. Instead, you must permit TRI to complete its performance, and you may demand that it compensate GRT for any damages that result from its minor breach. If you are reasonably certain about the breach and the extent of damages, you may collect the damages yourself by withholding an appropriate amount of payments that GRT otherwise would owe to TRI. *See Johnson*, 345 Calz. 2d at 335. On the other hand, if you wrongfully withhold a substantial portion of TRI's payments above any amount that it owes GRT for breach, GRT may itself be liable for breach. *See id.*

Unfortunately, without further evidence that the choice between Reading pipe and Cohoes pipe will affect the value of your project in any way, you will have difficulty proving any damages. Therefore, we advise you not to withhold any payments owed to TRI.

V. CONCLUSION

Although TRI has breached its contract with GRT, the breach almost certainly is not material, and it probably did not cause any recoverable damages. In these circumstances, if you fire TRI from the project, GRT will be liable to

TRI for breach of contract. Indeed, even withholding TRI's payments to cover damages caused by its breach is risky, because we have difficulty identifying any such damages.

We recommend that you work in a cooperative fashion with Dunlap to ensure the best possible performance of TRI's remaining duties under the contract. In the meantime, you may want GRT's engineers to determine what damages, if any, the installation of Cohoes pipe has caused. If you find any damages, we will be happy to advise you about the best possible means of demanding compensation from TRI.

Please do not hesitate to call me if you have any questions about this matter. My direct line is (111) 232-3232.

Sincerely,

_____

Marcia Todd
for Todd, Brown & King

Chapter 25

Demand Letters

I. Purposes of a Demand Letter

With a demand letter, you may seek to achieve one or more of three goals. First, you may seek to persuade another party to take or cease some action. For example, you may send a demand letter to your client's commercial tenant in an office building, demanding that he stop entering into unauthorized subleases and that he pay past due rent.

Second, you may seek to revoke a waiver of rights to permit your client to assert those rights in the future. For example, even though your client's lease agreement clearly requires payment of rent on the first of each month, your client may have implicitly waived her right to demand timely payment by frequently accepting late rent payments over the previous year without complaint. If so, you can help your client reassert her rights by sending a demand letter that (1) revokes any implied consent, (2) demands prompt payment of rent strictly according to the contract for the remainder of the lease, and (3) warns of your client's resolve to pursue legal remedies for future breaches of the lease.

Third, you may seek to obtain information or concessions from the opposing party to help your client assert rights in the future. In such a letter, you do not really expect the opposing party to accede to your client's demand; rather, you hope to provoke a reaction that you can use to your client's advantage. For example, suppose that your client orally agreed to purchase goods from a supplier for a total price of $10,000, but the supplier has balked at performing. You know that your client will have trouble enforcing the oral agreement, because the Uniform Commercial Code generally requires such agreements to be evidenced in a writing signed by the party against whom enforcement is sought.[1] You might nonetheless send a letter to the supplier setting forth the terms of the oral agreement and demanding performance pursuant to those terms. In so doing, you may hold out little hope that the supplier will immediately perform as promised; instead, you hope that the supplier will either (1) respond by repeating its decision not to perform but admitting that it had entered into the oral agreement or (2) fail to respond within ten days of receiving the letter, thus implicitly adopting your letter's description of the agreement.[2] Either reaction to the demand letter will satisfy the Uniform Commercial Code's requirement that the oral agreement be evidenced by a signed writing, thus enabling your client to assert a contract claim.[3]

II. Audience, Tone, and Writing Style

The audience for your demand letter is the opposing party, his attorney, or both. Your purpose is to persuade the other party to take or cease some action or to otherwise modify her relationship to your client. In addition to establishing the legal and factual soundness of your client's claim, you will seek to convince the other party that acquiescence to your demand is a more positive outcome than the alternatives, such as litigation.

Of course, you should adopt a tone that will most likely achieve your goals. Your task is complicated, however, by the multiplicity of audiences and goals. For example, although your primary audience is the opposing party, his attorney, or both, your own client is an important secondary audience. Even if you think that a conciliatory tone will achieve the best results with the opposing party, your client may make it clear that she has hired you to take the strongest possible stance and to intimidate the opposing party. On the other hand, the community as a whole is a possible tertiary audience, because the opposing party may seek to gain public support by airing the dispute in the news media. If a particularly strident passage in your demand letter is published, adverse public reaction may hinder your client's ability or

---

1. *See* U.C.C. § 2-201(1) (2011).
2. *See* U.C.C. § 2-201(2) (2011).
3. *See* U.C.C. § 2-201(1), (2) (2011).

willingness to assert her claims. Thus, you should adopt a tone that is firm but not nasty.

Indeed, because a demand letter frequently is the first step in a process of negotiation, one author believes that the letter should "prime" the recipient in a positive manner, to encourage compromise and settlement.[4] Under that view, you might adopt a more collaborative approach if the value of your client's claim is uncertain so that you seek a cooperative process of mutual compromise. On the other hand, if your client's claim is quite certain on the merits and in amount, you might be less interested in compromise and more determined in the manner in which you assert your client's demand for payment or other action that is clearly due.

Aside from tone, your style should be straightforward, businesslike, and professional. As is true in a brief, the most persuasive style in a demand letter is one that the reader does not notice, one that focuses the reader's attention on your demands, your justifications, and the consequences of his failure to satisfy the demands. Thus, you should write in plain English and avoid legal jargon or florid, distracting prose.

III. Format

You may adopt any reasonable format that will achieve the goals of your demand letter. At a minimum, your demand letter should include

1. an introductory sentence or overview paragraph,
2. a statement of the legal and factual support for your demands, and
3. a specific statement of the demands and the consequences of the opposing party's failure to satisfy the demands.

You need not divide a simple demand letter into sections; good paragraphing will suffice. If you divide a long or complex demand letter into sections, you should use whatever section headings suit the purposes of your letter.

IV. Overview

Immediately below the address and before the salutation of your demand letter, you should identify the general subject matter of the letter:

---

4. Carrie Sperling, *Priming Legal Negotiations Through Written Demands*, 60 CATH. U. L. REV. 107 (2010).

Arnold G. Hooper
Hooper Construction Co.
General Contractor
4094 Industrial Way
Fairbanks, New Maine 10713

RE: Damages for Delay in Completion of the Office Bldg. on Center St.

Dear Mr. Hooper,

In the first paragraph of your demand letter, you should provide any introductory information necessary to orient your reader. If this is your initial correspondence to the addressee, your opening paragraph should identify your representative capacity. Beyond that, the opening paragraph can provide such information as a general description of the relationships of the parties and an overview of your client's demands.

For example, the following opening sentence states the author's representative capacity and captures the reader's attention with a demand and the threat of a lawsuit:

Dear Mr. Hooper,

Our client, Dawn Development, Inc., has directed us to prepare legal proceedings against you if you delay further in paying the liquidated damages owed under the Center St. construction contract.

In contrast, the following opening paragraph in a settlement proposal develops the background and purpose of the letter more deliberately, and it introduces the demand for payment in a more conciliatory fashion:

RE: *Araiza v. Udave*

Mr. Phillips,

I met last Wednesday night with my clients, the plaintiffs in the suit against Max and Josephine Udave. All the plaintiffs are keen to press their claims. Nonetheless, they have agreed to make the following settlement offer: They will withdraw their suit if Max and Josephine Udave pay them a total of $10,000, conditioned on actual payment by noon on June 30, 2014. In light of my following evaluation of the case, I think you will find this offer to be quite reasonable.

V. Factual and Legal Basis for the Demands

A. Stating Your Legal Premises

Your explanation of the factual and legal justification for your client's demands may take many forms. In a routine collection letter, you can simply state the amount that is past due under an identified loan agreement, installment contract, or liquidated damages clause. In such a demand letter, the opposing party ordinarily will not dispute the general enforceability of such contracts, and you need not discuss the legal principles that make contractual obligations enforceable:

As you have conceded in correspondence with our client, your firm completed construction on the Center St. office building 22 days beyond the deadline in the Construction Contract dated September 8, 2013 (attached). This delay has caused Dawn Development to suffer damages, which you and Dawn Development reasonably estimated at the time of contracting would be $1,000 for each day of delay in completion. Accordingly, pursuant to the liquidated damages clause in section 15 of the contract, you are liable to Dawn Development for liquidated damages of $22,000. Our client has informally requested payment of these damages on several occasions, but has not received a satisfactory response from you.

In other cases, the fact or amount of the opposing party's liability may be more doubtful, prompting you to explain more thoroughly the legal basis for your client's demands. Such an explanation—at least if directed to the opposing party's attorney—may look very much like the legal analysis and application to facts in a brief. For example, the following passage justifies a demand for consequential damages stemming from a breach of contract:

In addition, the plaintiffs will be entitled to foreseeable consequential damages stemming from the breach. *See Southern Ariz. Sch. for Boys, Inc. v. Chery*, 119 Ariz. 277, 280, 580 P.2d 738, 741 (1978). Those will include the plaintiffs' expenditures on specialized accessories that were suitable only for the wedding and that some plaintiffs were unable to use. *See A.R.A. Mfg. Co. v. Pierce*, 86 Ariz. 136, 142, 341 P.2d 928, 932 (1959) (victim of breach entitled to award of damages for wasted promotional expenditures). Those members of the wedding party who could not fully participate in the wedding, the sole event for which the specialized gowns were ordered, can also recover damages for that lost opportunity. *See, e.g., Mieske v. Bartell Drug Co.*, 593 P.2d 1308 (Wash. 1979) (in UCC case, upholding award of $7,500 for emotional value associated with contracting parties' loss of home movies of significant events). Indeed, the opportunity to participate in the wedding formed the basis for the contracts for the gowns.

All of these losses are itemized in Count I of the complaint. They total approximately $20,000. Because the plaintiffs will certainly prove a breach of contract and will establish at least some of their alleged damages, they will also be entitled to an award of attorney's fees, which could add thousands more to the total recovery.

B. Audience

The appropriate level of formality of your legal analysis will depend on the sophistication of your audience. If you address your demand letter to the opposing party's attorney, or if you are certain that the opposing party will consult an attorney, you can reasonably cite to legal authority, as in the immediately preceding example. On the other hand, if the opposing party does not have legal training or legal representation, then you should express your arguments in terms that the party can understand. If you try to intimidate the opposing party with formal citations to authority, you might simply confuse or antagonize rather than persuade.

For example, the following excerpt of a demand letter to an insurance company's subrogation analyst assumes that the analyst has a sophisticated knowledge of business practices but has no formal legal training. The excerpt refers to three legal concepts: waiver, offer, and the "mailbox rule" governing the timing of acceptance. The author of the letter has tried to use these concepts in a persuasive manner without diverting the reader's attention to distracting citations:

Even if Mr. Upton's premium had arrived after expiration of the grace period, his rights were preserved in the conversation between him and Diane Campbell, assistant to Dee Boston, on March 12. In that conversation, Ms. Campbell notified Mr. Upton that his claim would be covered but that she would delay processing his claim until he paid his late premium. Mr. Upton stated over the phone that he would mail his premium. In effect, Ms. Campbell waived any condition to coverage that would require Mr. Upton to deliver the premium to her within the grace period. She thus made the date of her receipt of the premium relevant only to the matter of processing his claim. Alternatively, Ms. Campbell may have communicated a new offer of coverage that invited Mr. Upton's return promise to pay the premium. If so, Mr. Upton accepted the offer either over the phone or, under the "mailbox rule," when he placed his premium in the mailbox.

C. Avoiding Concessions, Admissions, and Waiver

A demand letter is not the proper place to make concessions or admissions that may come back to haunt you later. Therefore, if you choose to adopt a conciliatory tone, do so in a way that does not preclude you from taking a stronger position in the future. For example, suppose that your client demands compensation on the basis of a strong contract claim and a weak tort claim. To maintain credibility and to avoid antagonizing the opposing party, you might invoke only the contract claim to justify your client's demands in a demand letter. If so, you should remain silent about the weaker tort claim or refer to it only vaguely. If you affirmatively concede the weakness of that claim in writing, you may hinder your ability to pursue it later if newly discovered facts enhance its potential merit.

You should also avoid ambiguous conciliatory language that might grant unintended rights to the opposing party. For example, in a letter demanding payment of a liquidated sum owed, you should exercise caution before explicitly stating that the amount is negotiable. Such a statement is unnecessary because the opposing party is well aware of the possibility of negotiating a settlement that compromises the amount owed. Moreover, your statement of willingness to negotiate might be construed as an offer or promise to negotiate in good faith, to which the opposing party can bind you by accepting the offer or relying on the promise. To keep all your options open, state your demands in an uncompromising manner, even though you may be willing to compromise if the opposing party offers a reasonable settlement.

VI. Demands and Threats

You should not send a demand letter unless your client has a well-defined goal that you can formulate into a straightforward demand to the opposing party. Moreover, to maximize the chances of achieving that goal, you must provide the opposing party with an incentive to satisfy your client's demand. If the opposing party is fair-minded and your demand is just, your persuasive presentation of the legal and factual bases for the demand may help induce him to satisfy the demand. In most cases, however, you can provide the greatest incentive to the opposing party by threatening to take actions that would be more costly for the opposing party than satisfying the demand.

Thus, you must clearly state both your client's demand and the actions your client will take if the opposing party rejects the demand. To ensure prompt action, you should set a specific date by which the opposing party must satisfy your client's demand or suffer the adverse consequences of the threatened action.

If the relief to which your client is entitled is uncertain, your unstated objective may simply be to initiate settlement negotiations. More specifically, you may desire to induce your opponent to advance the first realistic settlement offer, which might reveal something about her evaluation of the case or her client's interests. If so, your demand letter might state the maximum possible liability and threaten formal action unless the opposing party takes action to reach a settlement.

In other cases, your client may seek payment of a certain sum of money. For example, if your client is demanding the payment of amounts past due on a loan, installment contract, or liquidated damages clause, you should

- state the precise payment that your client demands;
- set a date by which the opposing party must deliver the payment to a particular address;

- depending on the circumstances, threaten to sue on the contract or take other appropriate legal action if the demand is not satisfied; and

- take care to satisfy any statutory or common law duties that apply to your transaction. For example, some attorneys or law firms may qualify as debt collectors subject to the provisions of the federal Fair Debt Collection Practices Act,[5] which will require some kinds of demand letters to disclose certain information and to refrain from making certain kinds of threats,[6] as illustrated in the final paragraph of the illustration immediately below.

The following excerpt from a loan collection letter illustrates the clarity, specificity, and directness for which you should strive. Notice that it identifies the risk of increased liability if legal proceedings are commenced: interest, costs, and attorneys' fees.

If you desire to avoid legal proceedings, you must submit $22,000 on or before August 4, 2014, in cash, cashier's check, or certified funds made payable to Dawn Development, Inc. You must mail or deliver the payment directly to:

Dawn Development, Inc.
Suite 11000, Financial Plaza
1901 South Alma School Road
Fairbanks, New Maine 10701
Attention: Kathy Growl

Take notice that time is of the essence. If Dawn Development has not received the above amount on or before August 4, 2014, it will immediately commence legal proceedings to collect the liquidated damages with interest, costs, and attorneys' fees.

. . . .

Unless you notify this office within 30 days after receiving this notice that you dispute the validity of any portion of this debt, this office will assume that this debt is valid. If you dispute the debt in a written notification sent to this office within 30 days from receiving this notice, this office will obtain verification of the debt or obtain a copy of a judgment and mail you a copy of the judgment or verification. If you submit a request to this office in writing within 30 days after receiving this notice, this office will provide you with the name and address of the original creditor, if different from the current creditor.[7]

---

5. 15 U.S.C. §§ 1692-1692(o) (2006).

6. For a helpful discussion of the Act's requirements, *see* Scott J. Burnham, *What Attorneys Should Know About the Fair Debt Collection Practices Act, or, the 2 Do's and the 200 Don'ts of Debt Collection*, 59 MONT. L. REV. 179 (2000).

7. With minor changes, this paragraph quotes from one recommended by author Scott Burnham as offering language that would satisfy some disclosure requirements of the Fair Debt Collection Practices Act. *Id*. at 190. It might be included, in an excess of caution, as boilerplate language in all demand letters that seek payment of money, even if its terms do not always apply.

To avoid any dispute about the opposing party's receipt of your demand letter, you should normally send the demand letter by registered mail or through a reputable delivery service that offers easy tracing of the letter. If same-day delivery is necessary for some reason, then you can consider hand delivery, faxing, or even attaching the letter to an e-mail. A fax or e-mail, however, is not likely to convey the sense of gravity and formality of an original letter delivered in hard copy.[8]

Finally, to preserve your credibility in future correspondence, you must confirm that your client is willing and able to back up its threats with action if your demand is not satisfied. As stated by one author, "Don't poke the bear unless you are ready for a fight."[9]

VII. Summary

In a demand letter, you should

- use plain English whenever possible;
- adapt your format and depth of legal analysis to your audience and your purpose;
- use an introductory sentence or paragraph to identify your representative capacity, provide an overview of the purpose of your letter, or orient the reader in some other fashion;
- state the legal and factual bases for your demand;
- state your demands, including the time and place for satisfaction of the demands, and threaten to take action if the demands are not met; and
- stay abreast of common law and statutory regulation of demands in your transaction, and comply with the law in your communications.

---

8. *See* Bret Rappaport, *A Shot Across the Bow: How to Write an Effective Demand Letter*, 5 J. ALWD 32, 48 (2008).

9. *Id.* at 36.

Exercise 25-1

1. Collection Letter

Study the following collection letter and explain the purpose or purposes of each paragraph.

Scott L. Short
Stanley, Leeds & Cardon
100 W. Central Ave., Suite 2100
Fairbanks, New Maine 10701
July 21, 2014

CERTIFIED MAIL
RETURN RECEIPT REQUESTED
Arnold G. Hooper
Hooper Construction Co.
4094 Industrial Way
Fairbanks, New Maine 10713

RE: Damages for Delay in Completion of the Office Bldg. on Center St.

Dear Mr. Hooper,

Our client, Dawn Development, Inc., has directed us to prepare legal proceedings against you if you delay further in paying the liquidated damages owed under the Center St. construction contract.

As you have conceded in correspondence with our client, your firm completed construction on the Center St. office building 22 days beyond the deadline in the Construction Contract dated September 8, 2013 (attached). This delay has caused Dawn Development to suffer damages, which you and Dawn Development reasonably estimated at the time of contracting would be $1,000 for each day of delay in completion. Accordingly, pursuant to the liquidated damages clause in section 15 of the contract, you are liable to Dawn Development for liquidated damages of $22,000. Our client has informally requested payment of these damages on several occasions, but has not received a satisfactory response from you.

If you desire to avoid legal proceedings, you must submit $22,000 on or before August 4, 2014, in cash, cashier's check, or certified funds made payable to Dawn Development, Inc. You must mail or deliver the payment directly to:

Dawn Development, Inc.
Suite 11000, Financial Plaza
1901 South Alma School Road
Fairbanks, New Maine 10701
Attention: Kathy Growl

Take notice that time is of the essence. If Dawn Development has not received the above amount on or before August 4, 2014, it will immediately commence legal proceedings to collect the liquidated damages with interest, costs, and attorneys' fees.

Sincerely,

_____

Scott L. Short
Stanley, Leeds & Cardon

Notice: Unless you notify this office within 30 days after receiving this notice that you dispute the validity of any portion of this debt, this office will assume that this debt is valid. If you dispute the debt in a written notification sent to this office within 30 days from receiving this notice, this office will obtain verification of the debt or obtain a copy of a judgment and mail you a copy of the judgment or verification. If you submit a request to this office in writing within 30 days after receiving this notice, this office will provide you with the name and address of the original creditor, if different from the current creditor.

2. The Bad Example

Study the following collection letter and explain why it is less effective than the letter in Problem 1 above. Identify and describe each defect.

Green and Gain
120 West Washington
Phoenix, AZ 85003
April 1, 2014

Mr. and Mrs. Joe Smith
5555 North 55th Street
Phoenix, AZ 85055

RE: Delinquent Loan #9-1403726-841

Dear Borrower:

We are counsel of record for the Bank of Phoenix (hereinafter referred to as "the Bank"). Our client has informed us that you are behind in your home loan payments, and has asked that we write you on its behalf to request that you take some action to bring your loans current. We understand that you presently are approximately $2,500.00 behind in your payments.

Over the past several months, the few loan payments you have actually made have been consistently late. While the Bank was happy to take whatever it could get from you, it would prefer that you try to make payments on time. If you are having difficulty making your payments, the Bank would be happy to consider and, if reasonable, would agree to an extension of your loan, a modification of its terms, or a second loan to see you through whatever difficulties you may be experiencing. If you desire to pursue this offer, please call your loan officer or some other authorized representative of the Bank.

Please be advised, however, that the Bank has no intention of waiting forever for you to make good on your commitments. Frankly, in our experience the Bank has very little patience with deadbeat borrowers such as you appear to be. The Bank has ruined the credit of thousands of borrowers who, like you, did not take their obligations seriously. Hundreds more have been forced into bankruptcy. Moreover, the Bank is a large, powerful institution which can afford to hire big law firms such as this one, against which the average debtor has little chance of prevailing.

We spoke to your attorney about this matter over the phone this morning but found him to be uncooperative. We sincerely hope that you adopt a more constructive attitude and pay up.

The Bank therefore suggests that you make arrangements to bring the aforementioned loan current by paying the amount hereinbefore stated or making such other arrangements as you and said Bank may subsequently agree upon.

Sincerely,

_____

Bob Jenkins
Green & Gain

3. Settlement Letter

a. The settlement letter below is addressed to the opposing party's attorney in response to preliminary settlement discussions. It was written several months after suit was filed and shortly before a scheduled arbitration hearing. Explain the purpose or purposes of each paragraph. Precisely what does the letter demand? What action does the author of the letter threaten to take if the demand is not met?

b. Rewrite the letter so that it is appropriate for an unrepresented opposing party who has no legal training or knowledge. Summarize your analysis without citing to specific authority.

Charles Rehnquist, Esq.
333 S. Central Ave.
Phoenix, Arizona 85001
(602) 849-0101
June 2, 2014

Robert M. Phillips, Esq.
Kim, Phillips, Burley & Stewart
3301 E. Bethany Home Road, Suite B-111
Phoenix, Arizona 85012

RE: *Araiza v. Udave*

Mr. Phillips,

I met last Wednesday night with my clients, the plaintiffs in the suit against Max and Josephine Udave. All the plaintiffs are anxious to press their claims. Nonetheless, they have agreed to make the following settlement offer: They will withdraw their suit if Max and Josephine Udave pay them a total of $10,000, conditioned upon payment by noon on June 30, 2014. In light of my following evaluation of the case, I think you will find this offer to be quite reasonable.

I have no doubts about our ability to prove the claim for breach of contract. Indeed, your early correspondence and the defendants' answers to the complaint and interrogatories admit that Josephine failed to perform as promised. Even if she had acted in good faith and with best efforts, that would be no excuse for breach of the contract. Therefore, the defendants have essentially admitted to their breach of contract. The direct loss in value is easily computed: the difference between the value of each gown as promised ($900 each by your own correspondence) minus the value of the dress as delivered (we can prove that some are total losses).

In addition, the plaintiffs will be entitled to foreseeable consequential damages stemming from the breach. *See S. Ariz. Sch. for Boys, Inc. v. Chery*, 119 Ariz. 277, 280, 580 P.2d 738, 741 (1978). Those will include the plaintiffs' expenditures on specialized accessories that were suitable only for the wedding and that some plaintiffs were unable to use. *See A.R.A. Mfg. Co. v. Pierce*, 86 Ariz. 136, 142, 341 P.2d 928, 932 (1959) (victim of breach entitled to award of damages for wasted promotional expenditures). Those members of the wedding party who could not fully participate in the wedding, the sole event for which the specialized gowns were ordered, can also recover damages for that lost opportunity. *See, e.g., Mieske v. Bartell Drug Co.*, 593 P.2d 1308 (Wash. 1979) (in UCC case, upholding award of $7,500 for emotional value associated with contracting parties' loss of home movies of significant events). Indeed, the opportunity to participate in the wedding formed the basis for the contracts for the gowns.

All of these losses are itemized in Count I of the complaint. They total approximately $20,000. Because the plaintiffs will certainly prove a breach of contract and will establish at least some of their alleged damages, they will also be entitled to an award of attorneys' fees, which could add thousands more to the total recovery.

Josephine's own theory of the case is that she breached the contract because she lost the ruffles. Coupled with her failure to warn the plaintiffs to obtain gowns from an alternative source, those facts should easily support the negligence claim in Count II. That claim provides even stronger support than Count I for an award of general compensatory damages, including damages for emotional distress.

Also solid are the claims for promissory fraud and consumer fraud in Counts III and IV. The consumer fraud statute prohibits use of deception, fraud, false promises, or suppression of material fact with intent that others rely, in connection with the sale of any merchandise. A.R.S. § 44-1522. "Merchandise" includes services. A.R.S. § 44-1521(5). Like the common law tort of promissory fraud, a claim under the consumer fraud statute will support an award of punitive damages. *See Schmidt v. Am. Leasco*, 139 Ariz. 509, 512, 679 P.2d 532, 535 (Ct. App. 1983). We should have little trouble proving a claim under either theory: The plaintiffs will offer abundant and vivid testimony describing the way in which Max and Josephine deliberately misrepresented that many of the gowns would be ready on time, thus inducing many of the plaintiffs to wait until the last minute and beyond, when in fact Max and Josephine knew that the gowns could not possibly be completed on time. In light of the recklessness or malicious intent associated with such actions, these claims potentially could add thousands of dollars in punitive damages to the compensatory damages detailed in Count I.

In sum, the plaintiffs are angry and confident. They are anxious to go to an arbitration hearing, and they are ready to enforce their judgment by attaching the Udaves' property. Indeed, I experienced some difficulty getting them to agree to propose this settlement offer. I can assure you that it is not a bargaining posture; it represents their current bottom line, before they have incurred significant legal fees. Despite their passionate views on this matter, however, they have compromised their full claims substantially. The $10,000 figure represents 50% of the compensatory damages for Count I, without costs or attorney's fees, and without any punitive damages.

This offer remains open until noon, June 15. Please call or write to me before then if your clients wish to settle.

Sincerely,

_____

Charles Rehnquist, Esq.

4. Response to Demand Letter: Demand for Withdrawal of Claim

The following letter responds to a demand letter from an attorney for Framer Insurance Co. addressed to Michael Upton. Mr. Upton caused an automobile accident, resulting in injuries to Eileen Bradley, who was insured by Framer. Framer paid Ms. Bradley's claim for $10,000 in losses and medical expenses arising out of the accident. Framer then demanded that Mr. Upton reimburse Framer for Framer's payment to Ms. Bradley. Mr. Upton, however, claimed that he had liability insurance from Framer and that Framer thus was obligated to assume the cost of his liability to Ms. Bradley. The primary matter of dispute between Framer and Mr. Upton was whether Mr. Upton had validly renewed his insurance contract with Framer despite Framer's assertion that it received his late premium payment only after expiration of the policy's grace period.

a. Although it responds to a demand letter, the letter below is itself a demand letter, albeit a subtle one. What does it demand? What action does it implicitly threaten if the demand is not met? Should the author have stated the demand and threat more strongly?

b. Who is the audience for this letter? Assuming that Marilyn Branscomb is not a lawyer, would she likely consult with Framer's attorney, Jon Drake, before deciding whether to drop Framer's claim against Mr. Upton? If so, should the author have advanced a more formal legal analysis with citation to authority?

Charles Rehnquist, Esq.
333 S. Central Ave.
Phoenix, Arizona 85001
(602) 849-0101
January 28, 2014

Marilyn Branscomb
Subrogation Analyst for Framer Insurance
P.O. Box 3108
Mesa, Calzona 89211
Policy No. 881347 94

Dear Ms. Branscomb,

I represent Michael Upton in his claim for coverage under the above policy. I write in response to Jon C. Drake's letter dated January 7 to Michael Upton, in which Mr. Drake requests Mr. Upton to indemnify Framer for Framer's payment of claims to Eileen Bradley. I address this letter to you because Mr. Drake directed Mr. Upton to contact you. I'm sure that everyone hopes to resolve this matter before either party must incur the enormous legal expenses associated with litigation.

Mr. Upton is unwilling to pay the claim because he claims liability coverage under his policy and thus expects Framer to satisfy Ms. Bradley's claims. Mr. Upton recognizes that his insurance policy requires actual receipt of a late premium before expiration of the grace period. Even so, Mr. Upton is certain that the post office in fact delivered his premium within the three days remaining in the grace period, and he doubts Framer's claim that it received the premium a full week after it was posted five miles away. A jury would have the same doubts. Once Mr. Upton proves to a jury with his testimony and that of a witness that he posted the letter three days before expiration of the grace period, the jury will not likely believe that the letter took longer than the standard one to three days for delivery.

Mr. Upton is confident of his ability to prove his version of events before a jury, particularly in light of his previously communicated willingness to submit to a lie detector test. Of course, if litigation or other inquiry reveals that anyone within the Framer organization sought in bad faith to deny Mr. Upton coverage by covering up the facts, the resulting issues would transcend the relatively small dispute now before us. Thus, you should consider the possibility of a counterclaim to any claim that Framer might consider pursuing against Mr. Upton.

In sum, Mr. Upton is prepared to prove that he owes Framer nothing because Framer had a contractual duty to provide him insurance coverage for his liability to Ms. Bradley stemming from the March 12 accident. If Framer drops its claim, Mr. Upton will be happy to cease any further inquiry into possible claims he might have against Framer based on bad faith or other misconduct that Framer may have engaged in.

Sincerely,

_____

Charles Rehnquist, Esq.

cc: Jon C. Drake

Appendices

In a legal method and writing course, you can best master a challenging writing assignment by preparing for and accomplishing your task in at least three separate steps. First, you should acquire information about the topic of your assignment by reading assigned portions of a descriptive text, such as the main text of this book, and by attending classes in which an instructor lectures and leads class discussion. Second, you must become an active participant in the educational process by analyzing assigned problems and preparing legal documents, such as case briefs, office memoranda, and briefs. Third, you should welcome constructive criticism from instructors or peers, and you should thoughtfully react to their editorial comments by deciding which have merit and by revising your draft accordingly.

Along with the exercises in the main text, these Appendices provide you with the problems and other materials you need for the second step of the educational process: your active participation in research, analysis, and writing. The exercises in the main text are suitable for class discussion or for in-class writing exercises. They include policy questions, invitations to critique sample documents, an essay examination, and composition problems.

The Appendices include "problems" that are similar to the "exercises" in the main text: They provide further opportunities to think about and discuss fundamental questions of legal method and writing. Although an instructor could make these problems the subjects of formal writing assignments, they are primarily designed for individual review or for class discussion.

The "assignments" in the Appendices on the other hand, are take-home assignments requiring formal written documents. They ask you to analyze a problem and draft a document such as an office memorandum or a pretrial brief. Many of the assignments requiring formal documents provide all necessary materials and require no supplementary research. Others, particularly the more complex ones, provide you with little or no authority and require you to perform all necessary research in the library.

The assignments that require research will inspire different analyses depending on when you perform them and what authorities have been issued at that time. For example, statutes or judicial decisions issued after the publication of this book might radically alter the nature of the issues originally intended to be raised. Similarly, one of the office memorandum assignments is set in the state in which your law school is located. Because your analysis of the problem in that assignment will depend on the law of your particular state, the assignment may be more interesting in some law schools than in others. For all these reasons, your instructor may perform some "fine tuning" of some of the assignments by modifying the facts or otherwise adjusting the problems to avoid unintended difficulties raised by intervening laws or the laws of a particular state.

Appendix I

Introduction to the Legal System:

Problems for Part II of the Main Text

Problem 1. Sources and Limits of Lawmaking Powers

Examine each government action described in the sections below. Which represents a legitimate exercise of legislative, judicial, or executive authority?

a. The Flag-Bashing Bill

The First Amendment to the United States Constitution provides in part that "Congress shall make no law . . . abridging the freedom of speech, or of the press." Shortly before July 4, however, Congress sought to override the First Amendment by restricting speech critical of the American flag. Offended by a wave of public criticism of the American flag and the values for which it stands, Congress enacted the "Flag-Bashing Bill," which the president signed into law. Section 1 of that statute makes it an "unlawful publication practice for any person to publish any oral or written statement critical of the flag of the United States of America." Section 2 provides for fines of up to $5,000 for each violation of the statute.

Section 3 of the statute created the Flag Protection Commission (FPC), a federal agency, and granted it powers to investigate violations of the statute, to hold hearings on alleged violations, to impose fines for violations, and to issue rules and regulations to aid in its investigative and enforcement activities. Section 4 of the statute grants jurisdiction to the United States Courts of Appeals to review the FPC's actions, subject to further appeal to the United States Supreme Court.

b. The FPC Flexes Its Muscle

As the chief officer of the executive branch of the United States government, the president appointed several staunch flag enthusiasts to the FPC. Without delay, the FPC issued rules and regulations that, among other things, (1) describe procedures for FPC hearings, (2) authorize FPC hearing officers to impose fines of $1,000 to $10,000 for various kinds of violations of the Flag-Bashing Bill, and (3) define the statutory phrase "unlawful publication practice" to include any public criticism of the flag or the president's wardrobe.

c. Judicial Review

In the FPC's first major hearing, an FPC hearing officer found that a Washington, D.C., newspaper publisher had violated the Flag-Bashing Bill by publishing a critical commentary entitled "The Stars and Stripes—Do the Colors Clash?" The hearing officer fined the publisher $2,000. The publisher appealed to the United States Court of Appeals for the District of Columbia Circuit.

On appeal, the court of appeals overturned the hearing officer's decision. Contrary to the plain language, legislative history, and clear purpose of the Flag-Bashing Bill, the court found that the bill prohibited only oral criticism of the president's foreign trade policies.

The FPC appealed to the United States Supreme Court. The Supreme Court upheld the court of appeals' overturning of the hearing officer's decision, but on different grounds. The Supreme Court concluded that (1) the FPC had validly issued the rules and regulations on which the hearing officer had relied in this case, and (2) the hearing officer's findings and imposition of a fine were consistent with a proper interpretation of the Flag-Bashing Bill. However, the Supreme Court held that the statute was unenforceable because it violated the First Amendment to the United States Constitution.

Problem 2. Developing the Common Law and Interpreting Statutes That Modify the Common Law

In each of the sections below, fully explain the reasons for your conclusions. Express each step of your analysis.

a. Survival of the Fittest and the Common Law

If you have not already done so, perform Exercise 1-1 at the end of Chapter 1 in the main text. If you have already performed that exercise, review that exercise and your response to it.

b. The Justification of Self-Preservation

Assume that your court responded to *State v. Blight* by adopting the following common law rule and by remanding to the trial court for a new trial with jury instructions consistent with the new rule:

> A defendant is justified in killing another human being if the defendant is reasonably certain at the time of the killing that the killing is necessary to preserve his own life and that failure to kill the other will result in the death of both.

Do you support the rule? Apply this rule to the facts of *State v. Blight*. Should the jury acquit if instructed to apply this rule? Explain your answer in detail.

c. Mercy Killing and the Criminal Code

One hundred years after *State v. Blight*, your state has largely replaced the common law crimes with a comprehensive criminal code: a collection of statutes that defines criminal conduct and penalties, incorporating some common law principles and modifying or rejecting others. Section 101 of the criminal code defines the crime of murder as "the killing of another human being without justification." Section 101.A provides that "premeditated murder" constitutes first-degree murder, which carries a maximum penalty of life in prison. Section 101.G, enacted just last year, provides that "a desire to ease the suffering of a terminally ill person is not justification for ending the person's life prematurely." A state legislative committee report explained the purpose of the bill that later was codified as section 101.G:

> This bill makes it clear that euthanasia, popularly known as "mercy-killing," is not "justified" under § 101 of our criminal code and therefore is not excluded from our definition of murder. With this bill, the state declares its policies to promote the use of life-sustaining measures and to preserve the life of even a terminally ill patient for as long as possible, in the hope that a cure for the illness may be found before the patient dies. The physical and emotional suffering of terminally ill patients should be relieved through counseling and the prescription of pain-relieving drugs rather than the termination of life-sustaining medical equipment or treatment. Thus, even well-meaning friends or relatives who "pull the plug" on a terminally ill patient may be charged under our murder statute.

(1) Blight *Revisited*

Review Subsections a and b above. If facts identical to those of *State v. Blight* were presented to a jury today, should the jury convict the defendant of first-degree murder under the criminal code? How should the trial judge instruct the jury? If the state appellate courts have not yet interpreted section 101's reference to "justification," should the trial judge attempt to define that term for the jury? On what would it base its definition? Suppose that Blight has argued that the trial judge should not instruct the jury according to section 101.G, on the ground that section 101.G does not apply to his case. How should the trial court rule and why?

(2) The Pact

Emma Padilla was losing her battle against cancer. Although she continued to receive chemotherapy, it made her quite ill and offered her almost no hope of remission. Preferring to live her final days in familiar surroundings, she arranged for full-time nursing care in her home. She often spoke to her nurses about her desire to die and about her wish that no one prolong her life with heroic lifesaving measures.

One evening, Padilla suffered a seizure; her heart stopped beating, and she ceased breathing. Her night nurse, Jim Murrow, rushed to Padilla's side to administer cardiopulmonary resuscitation and to hook up a portable respirator and other lifesaving equipment. He stopped short, however, remembering Padilla's wish to die naturally. Murrow allowed Padilla to die, notified the hospital that had been treating Padilla with chemotherapy, and admitted to several colleagues that he had honored Padilla's wishes that he refrain from prolonging her life.

Is Murrow guilty of murder under sections 101 and 101.G of the criminal code? Fully analyze the law and the facts, taking care to advance arguments for both the defense and the prosecution.

Appendix II

Legal Method and Analysis:

Problems for Part III of the Main Text

Problem 1. Analogy, Distinction, and Precedent

Read the materials for Office Memorandum Assignment 1 in Appendix IV. The only two Arizona cases provided in the materials, *Henderson* and *Fogleman*, deny any award of damages for emotional distress. The only case in your materials that approves of such an award for breach of contract is *Browning*, an early decision from another jurisdiction. Fully explain how you could distinguish the facts of *Henderson* and *Fogleman* from Araiza's case, and explain how you could analogize the facts of her case to those of *Browning*. Further explain how dicta in *Henderson* and *Fogleman* support an analogy to *Browning*.

Problem 2. Legal Policy and Application to Facts

Cheryl Watkins, an expert pilot, retained Flight Ready, a private aircraft service, to maintain her single-engine private plane based at Palm City Airport in Calzona. While flying from Palm City to a nearby town on a business trip, Watkins noticed that the passenger door of the cabin had sprung partially open. She knew that the partially open door would reduce the stability of the aircraft under certain conditions and that flying for more than a few minutes with the door open would be distracting, if not hazardous. She rejected the idea of making an emergency landing on the busy highway below or on the desert dotted with massive saguaro cacti. Instead, Watkins leaned across the passenger's seat to close the passenger door, even though her instructor had twice warned her never to do so. As Cheryl reached for the passenger door, the plane abruptly rolled to the right and spiraled into a sharp dive. Watkins was not in position to take control of the aircraft, and it crashed into the desert seconds later, killing Watkins instantly. A tape recorder found in the wreckage had recorded Watkins's comments during the emergency, allowing investigators to reconstruct the events.

In a wrongful death action brought by Watkins's survivors in Calzona, the jury answered several specific questions called "special interrogatories," submitted to it by the court. Specifically, the jury found that personnel for Flight Ready had negligently repaired a latch on the passenger door of Watkins's aircraft, which door had previously stuck in the closed position. The negligent repair caused the door to spring open during the flight. The jury also found that the partially open door had reduced the stability of the aircraft, causing it to roll and dive when Watkins shifted her position in the aircraft. Finally, the jury found that had Watkins remained in the pilot's seat, she likely could have maintained control of the plane and either reached her destination without mishap or survived an emergency landing on the desert. Following an instruction based on the doctrine of "contributory negligence," the jury denied Watkins's survivors any recovery.

Under the traditional common law doctrine of contributory negligence, a victim of a tort is precluded from recovering damages from the tortfeasor if the victim negligently contributed to her own injuries. At the time of trial, Calzona courts still applied the doctrine of contributory negligence as a defense in a tort action brought either by the victim or by her survivors. Accordingly, the trial court had rejected a jury instruction proposed by counsel for the plaintiffs that would have permitted the jury to apply the doctrine of "pure comparative negligence." Under the proposed instruction, Watkins's own negligence would not preclude the plaintiffs from all recovery; instead, their recovery would simply be diminished in proportion to which Watkins's own negligence contributed to her death.

In class discussion or a written essay, respond to the following questions:

a. In the process of developing its common law, should the Calzona Supreme Court abandon its contributory negligence doctrine by adopting a pure comparative negligence scheme? Discuss the policy arguments supporting both sides of this issue.

b. As a legislator, would you support proposed legislation that would create a modified comparative fault system in which a plaintiff would receive the benefits of comparative negligence if she is no more than 50 percent at fault but would recover nothing if she is more than 50 percent at fault? State your reasons for your support or opposition.

c. How would either a pure or a modified comparative negligence standard likely apply to the facts on remand?

Appendix III

Assignment 1. Case Brief with Synthesis

Exercise 7-1(1, 2) in Chapter 7 of the main text includes excerpts and a sample case brief of *White v. Benkowski*. Review those materials now. Then read the following excerpt from the appellate opinion in *McKibben v. Mohawk Oil Co., Ltd.*, and prepare a case brief for a contracts class that includes a synthesis of this case with *White v. Benkowski*.

McKIBBEN V. MOHAWK OIL COMPANY, LTD.
Supreme Court of Alaska 667 P.2d 1223 (Alaska 1983)

BURKE, Chief Justice.

Plaintiffs Harley McKibben, Adolph Vetter, and Roudolph Vetter are the owners of the Christina mining claim located near Fairbanks. On December 2, 1977, plaintiffs entered into a mining lease agreement with Joseph Taylor and Paul Rice, giving Taylor and Rice the right to mine the land in a workmanlike manner until March 15, 1978. The lease also provided that the plaintiffs would receive forty-five percent of the value of all ores and minerals mined and extracted from the claims after deducting smelting and refining costs. Taylor and Rice would bear the entire costs of mining and milling the ore.

Taylor and Rice assigned their interest in the lease to Tri-Con Mining, Inc. [Tri-Con] with plaintiffs' consent. Plaintiffs and Tri-Con entered into an addendum of the lease, which provided that whenever the lessee's ore shipments had a specified low assayed value, plaintiffs' royalty interest would be reduced to ten percent. Soon after Tri-Con began mining the Christina claim, Tri-Con entered into a joint venture with Mohawk Oil and Gas, Inc. [Mohawk Inc.], a wholly owned subsidiary of Mohawk Oil Company, Ltd. [Mohawk Ltd.]. With only two weeks remaining in the term of the lease, Tri-Con and Mohawk Inc. engaged in a bulk mining program during which some 12,000 to 15,000 tons of ore were mined from the property and shipped to the nearby Fox Mill. Tri-Con and Mohawk Inc. processed and milled approximately 6,000 tons of the stockpiled ore. The percentage recovery of precious metals from the ore was extremely low. . . .

On March 21, 1980, plaintiffs filed a complaint against Tri-Con, Mohawk Ltd., and Mohawk Inc. First and second amended complaints were filed on September 18, 1980. As amended, the complaint alleges that defendants breached the lease; committed waste and conversion; engaged in unworkmanlike mining; and intentionally diluted the ore. Plaintiffs also requested punitive damages for the "purposeful and outrageous conduct" committed by defendants.

Defendants subsequently moved for partial summary judgment to dismiss plaintiffs' claims for intentional dilution, unworkmanlike mining, punitive damages, and waste. . . . [T]he superior court . . . denied defendants' motion to dismiss plaintiffs' claims for waste, intentional dilution, and unworkmanlike mining, but dismissed plaintiffs' punitive damages claim.

. . . .

VII. PUNITIVE DAMAGES

In their complaint, plaintiffs requested punitive damages for the defendants' purposeful and outrageous conduct, which apparently consisted of intentionally diluting the ore. Defendants moved for summary judgment on the punitive damages claim on the ground that punitive damages are not available in Alaska for a breach of contract. The motion was granted by the superior court.

In *Lull v. Wick Construction Co.*, 614 P.2d 321, 325-26 (Alaska 1980), we stated that it was an open question whether punitive damages may be awarded in a contract action, and noted that some states permit punitive damages when the breach is maliciously or grossly reckless or when the conduct associated with the breach also constitutes an independent tort. We refused to decide the issue in *Lull* because the breach in that case was neither malicious nor tortious in character. *Lull*, 614 P.2d at 326. However, in the case at bar, plaintiffs' claim that defendants intentionally diluted the ore is clearly tortious in character, since the alleged act is the basis of plaintiffs' claim for conversion. . . . Thus, the issue is now squarely before us.

According to the Restatement, punitive damages are recoverable for a breach of contract if the conduct constituting the breach is also a tort for which punitive damages are recoverable. *See* Restatement (Second) of Contracts §355 (1981). We now adopt this view[1] because it furthers our policy of allowing punitive damages for certain tortious acts. *See Bridges v. Alaska Housing Authority*, 375 P.2d 696, 702 (Alaska 1962). Since defendants' alleged conduct also constituted a tort for which punitive damages might have been recoverable, the superior court erred in dismissing plaintiffs' punitive damages claim.

Accordingly, the judgment below is affirmed in part, reversed in part, and remanded for proceedings consistent with this opinion.

Assignment 2. Course Outline

Imagine that you have studied the doctrine of quasi-contract in your contracts class and that you are ready to summarize your case briefs and to express your understanding of the subject in outline form. Further imagine that the notes reproduced below represent your briefs of principal and note cases on the topic. To prepare your outline, classify the holdings of the cases according to topic and subtopic, synthesize the holdings to arrive at an understanding of general legal rules, and develop a logical organization of the rules or problem areas. Then, summarize your ideas about them in outline form, using summaries of your case briefs as illustrations of legal rules.

Boswell v. Weldon (Texarkana S. Ct. 1958), CB 201
Issues and Holdings:

I. Did a bank employee enrich an accident victim by rendering nonprofessional but competent first aid that nonetheless failed to save the victim's life? Yes.

II. Was the enrichment unjust even though the bank employee did not expect compensation at the time that he rendered aid? No; judgment for Defendant Estate affirmed.

Facts:

Bank robbers shot and critically wounded Boswell, a security guard. Weldon, a bank loan officer, attempted to stop the guard's bleeding and to revive him with CPR. The loan officer had no medical training other than a single CPR class sponsored by the bank for all employees. He had never charged for first-aid services and had never expected to. Although he rendered competent first aid, the guard died of his wounds before an ambulance could arrive.

---

1. We do not now reach the issue of whether punitive damages are recoverable for a breach of contract, if the conduct constituting the breach is malicious but not tortious in character.

Procedural History:

The loan officer sued the guard's estate for compensation for the emergency first-aid services. The trial court granted the estate's motion for summary judgment on the grounds that (1) the loan officer provided no benefit to the security guard, and (2) any benefit provided by the loan officer to the guard did not unjustly enrich the guard. The loan officer appealed, and the state's only appellate court affirmed.

Reasoning on Each Issue:

I. Quasi-contract permits recovery on proof of unjust enrichment. Summary judgment cannot be based on lack of enrichment, because the record raises a genuine fact dispute about whether the loan officer transferred an actual benefit with measurable value to the guard. Even though the guard died, a jury could find that he received services with a market value that increased his chances of surviving.

II. On the undisputed facts, the loan officer could not reasonably have expected compensation at the time he rendered the emergency services. He is presumed to have rendered them gratuitously, and no facts rebut that presumption. Therefore, as a matter of law, it was not unjust for the guard and his estate to retain the benefit of the loan officer's services without compensating the loan officer.

Evaluation:

I find it odd to recognize enrichment in a person who dies soon after services are rendered. However, I agree with the ultimate disposition—it is reasonable to presume that emergency services would be rendered without expectation of compensation in a case such as this.

Cutter v. Noble (Texarkana S. Ct. 1982), CB 205
Issues and Holdings:

I. Was it unjust for the victim of an auto accident to retain emergency lifesaving medical services from a physician without compensating the physician? Yes.

II. Did the trial court correctly instruct the jury that it must award compensation based on the results of the emergency services, as valued by someone in the position of the recipient? No.

Facts:

The victim of an automobile accident lay in the street near the office of a physician who engaged in the general practice of medicine. Alerted by a witness to the accident, the physician ran to the accident site with medical instruments, and she stabilized the unconscious victim until an ambulance could transport the victim to a hospital. The victim fully recovered. He almost certainly would have died had not the physician rendered emergency aid before arrival of the ambulance. The physician sent a bill of $300 to the victim, which the victim refused to pay.

Procedural History:

The physician sued the victim on the theory of quasi-contract. After a trial before a jury, the victim moved for a directed verdict on the ground that no reasonable juror could find that the enrichment was unjust. The trial court denied the motion and instructed the jury that, if it found unjust enrichment, it could award the physician the full value of the benefit received by the victim. The jury awarded the physician $500,000. The victim appealed, and the appellate court reversed.

Reasoning on Each Issue:

I. Because the physician ordinarily charged for such services, and because the services she rendered were nontrivial, a reasonable jury could find that the physician reasonably expected compensation when she rendered the services. Therefore, the question of whether the enrichment was unjust was properly before the jury.

II. Full restitution of the benefit received by the victim would be disproportionately high if measured by the value of the life saved. To put practical limits on such awards more consistent with the quasi-contractual basis for relief, the trial court should have specifically instructed the jury that the benefit in such a case is measured by the general market price of the medical services rendered, or by some other measure that incorporates the physician's costs plus reasonable profit.

Evaluation:

I agree with the results on both issues, but some of the language of the second holding is analytically unsatisfying. If measured by the physician's costs, the interest protected is more like reliance than restitution.

Valenzuela v. Rose (Calzona S. Ct. 1942), CB 209
Issue and Holdings:

When a house painter enriched a homeowner by painting the owner's newly constructed house pursuant to a contract between the painter and the general contractor, was it unjust for the owner to retain the benefits of the paint job without compensating the painter for it? No.

Facts:

The owner, Rose, hired a general contractor to build a custom home, but the owner omitted painting from the tasks covered by their contract because a friend of the owner, Tierney, had separately agreed to paint the interior and exterior at a bargain price. The general contractor months later mistakenly hired Valenzuela to paint the interior and exterior of the owner's new house. When Valenzuela completed the painting according to his contract with the general contractor, the owner reminded the general contractor that painting was omitted from their contract, and the owner refused to pay either the general contractor or Valenzuela for the painting. In turn, the general contractor refused to pay Valenzuela for the work.

Procedural History:

Valenzuela sued the owner in quasi-contract for the reasonable value of the paint job. On the owner's challenge to the sufficiency of the complaint, the trial court dismissed the action. Valenzuela appealed, and the intermediate court of appeals affirmed. Here, the Supreme Court also affirmed.

Reasoning:

In contracting with Valenzuela, the general contractor acted independently and not as the agent of the owner. At the time of painting, the painter expected compensation from the general contractor, not from the owner. The court sympathizes with the painter's fear that local contractors would exclude the painter from bid lists if he sued the general contractor. Nonetheless, the painter's proper remedy is against the general contractor for breach of their contract. Given the posture of the case, it was not unjust for the owner to retain the benefit of the painting without paying the painter for it.

Evaluation:

It seems unfair that the owner is permitted to enjoy this windfall; perhaps the owner ought to pay the painter the same bargain rate that the owner's friend had agreed to charge, even if that would be less than the normal market rate. Also, I wonder whether the general contractor could recover against the owner if the general contractor were liable to the painter. If so, why not permit the painter to sue the owner directly and bypass the general contractor?

Note Cases, CB 213-214:

1. *Cirankowitz v. Pastorini* (New Maine Ct. App. 1957). On facts similar to those of *Valenzuela v. Rose*, the court permitted a carpenter's suit against the owner, because the general contractor with whom the carpenter contracted had declared bankruptcy by the time of suit.

2. *Firello v. Combs* (W. Dakansas Ct. App. 1975). While the owner of a new structure solicited bids directly from painters, an unemployed painter painted the exterior of the structure without the prior knowledge of the owner and demanded that the owner pay him the amount of the lowest bid that the owner received from other painters for the job. Although the paint job was exactly as the owner specified in the job solicitation, the owner refused to pay. The court affirmed dismissal of the painter's action against the owner, ruling that the owner was not unjustly enriched.

3. *Spencer's Distributing Co. v. Hometown Appliances* (New Maine S. Ct. 1981). A distributor sent 10 microwave ovens to a retailer that had not ordered the ovens. The court held that the retailer was unjustly enriched, because the distributor had sent the microwave ovens under a reasonable mistake to which the retailer had contributed. The distributor was entitled to restitution of the value of the benefit bestowed upon the retailer measured by the wholesale price at which the retailer normally could buy such ovens rather than by the retail price at which it sold them to the public or the relatively high wholesale price that the distributor usually offered to retailers.

Appendix IV

Office Memoranda: Assignments for Part V of the Main Text

The two assignments below vary in their complexity and in the extent to which they require research in your law library. The first assignment presents a single issue for analysis. Assignment 2 presents one or more issues for analysis, some of which you might divide into subissues. To some extent, precisely which and how many issues you discuss in Assignment 2 is a matter of judgment.

The first assignment is a "closed universe" problem: All the necessary authority is provided at the end of the assignment. In contrast, Assignment 2 is an "open library" problem: You must conduct your own research in the law library to find authorities that will help you analyze the problems. Of course, your instructor can modify these problems by (1) asking you to conduct research to supplement the materials provided to you in Assignment 1, or (2) providing you with some or all of the authorities that you will need for Assignment 2.

The page numbers within the opinions in the original reporters appear in brackets in the reproductions of the opinions at the end of Assignment 1. Some of the opinions cite to other authorities in a form other than the citation form recommended in Chapter 14 of this book. When you cite to any authority, adopt the citation form recommended in Chapter 14 or recommended by your instructor, rather than other forms reflected in some of the opinions.

Assignment 1 is set in Arizona, so that the Arizona case law is mandatory authority. Your professor will choose the jurisdiction in which Assignment 2 is set.

Assignment 1. Office Memorandum
Single Issue
Jurisdiction: Arizona
Closed Universe

You are an associate in a firm that represents 15 young women and their mothers. They complain that a seamstress intentionally breached a contract to provide gowns for their use in a Quinceañera ceremony in Phoenix, Arizona.

A Quinceañera ceremony is a traditional "coming out" party for a woman on her fifteenth birthday. It is celebrated in many Hispanic communities throughout the world. The celebration consists of a Catholic mass, followed by a formal reception that includes a dinner and dance. The celebrant, known as the "Quinceañera," traditionally wears a gown that is nearly as formal and ornate as a wedding gown. She is attended by relatives, by godmothers and godfathers, and by 14 maids of honor. The maids of honor are typically peers and close friends of the Quinceañera. The maids traditionally wear fancy gowns that match each other either in color or pattern. Along with their male attendants, they participate in both the mass and the reception.

Your primary client, Trina Araiza, turned 15 last July 10. She and her 14 chosen maids of honor hired Ramona Udave to sew gowns of a particular pattern for the Quinceañera celebration. Trina's mother, Cristina, negotiated the contract with Udave. Because the Quinceañera and her maids of honor were minors, their parents cosigned the contract to ensure enforceability. On March 15, the Quinceañera participants provided Udave with material for the gowns and met with Udave so that she could take measurements. On May 5, Udave met with each participant for final fittings. At that meeting, each gown was only partially sewn, was partially held together with pins, and was not wearable.

Throughout May and June, Udave repeatedly assured all the participants that she was making normal progress on the gowns and that the gowns would be ready on time. In early July, Udave represented that she was putting the finishing touches on the gowns and that they would all be ready by the morning of the Quinceañera. Although some of the participants were anxious to see the gowns, Udave said that she never let her clients see her work until the last stitch was in place.

On the morning of the Quinceañera celebration, the participants arrived at Udave's shop to pick up their gowns. Udave repeatedly assured each of them that her gown was minutes away from completion and that each one should wait for the gown in the front room of Udave's shop. Udave kept the participants waiting for varying periods of time, some beyond 1:00 P.M., the time for commencement of the mass. Araiza herself received her gown at 12:30 P.M.. At that time, she was nearly ill with anxiety. She dressed quickly and arrived at the site of the mass by 1:10 P.M. Her maids of honor, however, were still waiting for their gowns and therefore could not yet participate in the formal procession that begins the mass. By 1:30 P.M. five of the maids of honor had arrived with their gowns. Although the gowns were unfinished and looked terrible, Araiza and her five maids of honor walked in the procession and began the mass. Araiza was emotionally distraught during the mass, partly because of the absence of two maids of honor who were designated to recite prayers with her; those maids of honor were still waiting at Udave's tailoring shop on Udave's representations that their gowns were nearly complete.

In fact, the remaining gowns were in the same condition as they had been during the March fitting, and Udave never completed them. Although Udave continued to represent that the gowns were nearly completed, the remaining Quinceañera participants left her shop shortly after the mass and attended the reception in casual or semi-formal clothes. Although they participated in the traditional reception procession and waltz, they felt humiliated because of their inappropriate attire.

Araiza and the maids of honor suffered embarrassment and other forms of emotional distress as a result of Udave's actions. Based on information they acquired after the Quinceañera ceremony, they are convinced that Udave intentionally ruined the Quinceañera because of her friendship with a bitter rival of the Araiza family.

Your supervising attorney, Daniel Adams, intends to explore various potential claims, including breach of contract, fraud, and negligence. He wants you to assume that he can establish only the contract claim, and he wants you to analyze the question whether the Quinceañera and her maids of honor can recover damages for emotional distress on their claims for breach of their collective contract with Udave. He knows that they can recover damages for other kinds of losses stemming from the breach, but he thinks that the damages for emotional distress may be problematic.

Using only the following research materials, prepare an office memorandum, five to seven pages in length, discussing this question. In reciting the facts of this dispute, summarize only the facts material to your analysis. You may assume that the Quinceañera and her maids of honor are parties to an enforceable contract and that any dispute regarding the contract will be governed by Arizona law. Because Mr. Adams intends to use your memorandum to help him prepare a brief that he will submit to an Arizona tribunal, he wants you to use parallel citations when citing to either of the two Arizona decisions. To help you find your way through those decisions, internal page numbers for the official Arizona Reports are noted in bold in brackets, and internal page numbers for the Pacific Reporter are noted in italics in brackets. When citing to the Alabama decision, you may cite only to the regional reporter.

Research Materials

CONTRACTS
E. Allan Farnsworth
(4th ed. 2004)

§12.17 Other Limitations, Including Emotional Disturbance. . . .

[**pg. 810**] A limitation more firmly rooted in tradition generally denies recovery for emotional disturbance (or "mental distress") resulting from breach of contract, even if the limitations of unforeseeability and uncertainty can be overcome. . . . Whatever the basis of the limitation, courts have not applied it inflexibly. Some courts have looked to the nature of the contract and made exceptions, as under the Restatement Second rule, when serious emotional disturbance was a particularly likely result of the breach.

FARMERS INSURANCE EXCHANGE V. HENDERSON
82 Ariz. 335, 313 P.2d 404 (1957) (Arizona Supreme Court)

[**pg. 337**, *pg. 405*] WINDES, Justice.

The appellant, Farmers Insurance Exchange, issued to appellee, George Henderson, a public liability insurance policy insuring him against claims for death or bodily injury and property damage resulting from the operation of Henderson's car. The limit of the policy for death or bodily injury was $5,000 for one person and $10,000 for one accident and $5,000 for property damage. There was a collision between the Henderson car when operated by his employee, one Whitehead, and an automobile operated by Charles Breesman. Three actions were filed for damages resulting from the accident. One action was by . . . Breesman against Henderson and Whitehead. This . . . action was tried in the superior court. The present case is a suit by Henderson against the company for damages claimed to have resulted from the failure to settle the Breesman claim for an amount within its policy limits when opportunity was presented for such settlement. This failure caused Henderson and his wife to lose their business, because they were forced to sell the business to pay for liability in excess of their liability insurance limits. A jury trial resulted in a verdict and judgment against the company in the sum of $45,000. The company appeals. The appellant will be referred to as the company and individuals by name.

The principal questions presented for solution are the extent of the obligations of the insurer to the insured to settle within the policy limits a claim against the insured and, if liability is established, the correct measure of the insured's damages.

. . . .

[**pg. 342**, *pg. 408*] On the question of damages Henderson submitted and the court gave instructions that if the jury found the company breached its contract, it could assess damages for the following items: loss of the property as a going business and interest from time of loss, humiliation, pain and suffering, attorney fees incurred by Henderson, loss of earnings, expenses of seeking employment [*pg. 409*] including traveling expenses to that end, and his loss of business reputation and credit. Over the company's objection evidence on these items was admitted. Except as to the value of the business as a going concern and interest thereon from the time of its sale, the court erred in the admission of evidence and giving instructions on the foregoing items of damages.

The wrong involved is causing the destruction or conversion of insured's business property in satisfaction of the [**pg. 343**] company's obligation. The court correctly instructed that as a general rule the damages for the loss or destruction or conversion of a going business is its value at the time and place of destruction with interest. This is in accord with the pronouncements of this court. Jones v. Stanley, 27 Ariz. 381, 233 P. 598. The humiliation, mental pain, suffering and anguish incurred by the Hendersons was the direct result of the pecuniary loss suffered. If it is to be considered a breach of contract, to recover for these items the contract must be of such a nature that its breach would cause mental suffering for reasons other than the pecuniary loss. Restatement of Law, Contracts, section 341 . . . .

[**pg. 344**, *pg. 409*] The judgment is reversed with instructions for a new trial on the entire case as to all issues.

FOGLEMAN V. PERUVIAN ASSOCIATES
127 Ariz. 504, 622 P.2d 63 (Ct. App. 1980)

[**pg. 505**, *pg. 64*] HATHAWAY, Chief Judge.

In August of 1973, appellants were residents of Tucson, Arizona, and Mr. Fogleman was employed as a welder at a copper mine near Tucson. Appellees offered him employment at a mine operated by appellees at Quajone, Peru, and he accepted. The contract of employment was dated September 24, 1973, and was for a two-year period, employing Mr. Fogleman as welding supervisor at $1,700 per month plus housing allowance and other benefits.

Appellees terminated Fogleman's employment on March 8, 1974. Appellants brought this action alleging wrongful termination of the employment contract and seeking damages. After trial to the court, without a jury, judgment was entered in favor of appellants in the amount of $14,989.33, plus costs, together with interest commencing on the date of judgment. The trial court entered findings of fact and conclusions of law.

On appeal, appellants contend that they were entitled to an award of consequential general damages. . . .

[**pg. 506**, *pg. 65*] Appellants first contend that the trial court erred in not awarding consequential general damages because the evidence and findings support such an award. Specifically, the court found that appellees could terminate appellants' employment contract only for cause and that they did not have cause. This breach caused appellants economic loss of $14,989.33. In finding of fact number 10, the court found:

> 10. The wrongful conduct of the Defendants S.P.C.C., Fluor Utah and Peruvian Associates also caused Plaintiffs to suffer general damages, including emotional distress, anxiety, embarrassment, humiliation and other items listed on page 14 of Plaintiffs' Post-Trial Memorandum.

The court refused to award consequential damages, perceiving the rule to be that such damages are not allowed in a breach of contract action, and so stated in conclusion of law number 15.

Appellants argue that consequential damages are allowable in a breach of contract action and that appellees' wrongful conduct was both a breach of contract and a tort, therefore such damages were allowable. The trial court's first finding of fact stated that the action was for breach of contract. . . . We do not have before us an appeal from a tort action, and appellants' citations for the proposition that damages for mental anguish are allowable in actions which sound both in contract and in tort, are not applicable. The appropriate measure of damages for an employee who has been wrongfully discharged is the unpaid balance of the salary less the sums earned during the remainder of the contract period. . . .

In *Browning v. Fies*, 4 Ala. App. 580, 58 So. 931 (1912), cited by appellants, a special situation was presented where the plaintiff had hired a carriage to transport him to church for his wedding. The defendant was aware of the reasons and the time frame for performance and that the failure of performance would, under the circumstances, expose plaintiff to particular consequences, alluded to by the court and for which the plaintiff was allowed damages. This case is inapplicable to the facts herein. . . .

[**pg. 507**, *pg. 66*] Affirmed as modified.

BROWNING V. FIES
58 So. 931 (Ala. Ct. App. 1912)

[**pg. 932**] Appeal from City Court of Birmingham; Chas. A. Senn, Judge.

PELHAM, J. This is a suit for damages for the breach of a contract entered into between the appellant, who was the plaintiff below, and the appellees. Under the terms of the contract, the defendants, for the consideration of $5 paid to them by the plaintiff, agreed to furnish a carriage and team for the special purpose of carrying the plaintiff, his friends, and relatives from the home of the plaintiff near Rising Station to a church in Birmingham, Ala., a distance of about three miles, at which church the plaintiff on this particular occasion was to be married. The damages claimed and sought to be recovered were for the actual financial loss arising out of a breach of the contract, and damages for mental suffering, physical pain, humiliation, mortification, etc.

[The defendants] filed two motions to strike from each count of the complaint as amended the averments as to the plaintiff's having suffered great mental anguish, humiliation, distress, etc., on the ground that such allegations did not set up matters constituting proper elements for the recovery of damages. The defendants also separately moved to strike from each count of the complaint any claims for damages based on delay in reaching the place appointed for the marriage ceremony, for being compelled to ride to the church in a public street car, and for physical and mental pain and suffering, for humiliation, etc., etc., in consequence thereof, on the grounds that such damages were speculative, too remote, and not recoverable in an action of this nature. The court granted the defendants' motion to strike from the complaint these elements as claims of damage as to each count, and the plaintiff reserved exceptions to the court's ruling. On the pleadings as thus framed, the issues were tried before a jury. . . .

The evidence without conflict showed that the plaintiff, on the day of the evening upon which he was to be married, went to the defendants' place of business in Birmingham, Ala., and entered into a contract with the defendants, who were engaged in conducting a public livery business, to furnish the plaintiff, for the use of himself, friends, and family, a carriage and team which was to be sent to the plaintiff's residence at or near Rising Station at 7:30 o'clock P.M. on that day to carry plaintiff and his wedding party to the church in Birmingham, three miles distant, where the plaintiff was to be married at 8 o'clock on that evening. The defendants made a charge of $5 for this specified use of the carriage and team, which amount was paid to the defendants by the plaintiff, who at the time of making the contract informed the defendants of the purpose [**pg. 933**] for which the same was to be used and the hour appointed for the ceremony, and the defendants agreed and contracted to furnish the carriage and team to be used by the plaintiff for this specific purpose. It was also shown without conflict in the evidence that the defendants made default and breached the contract and failed to send the carriage at the time and place as they contracted to do, and no excuse whatever was offered upon the part of the defendants for having failed to perform the contract. The plaintiff, on account of the defendants' breach of the contract, was compelled, in order to reach the church where his prospective bride and friends were awaiting his coming, to resort to a public street car in which plaintiff and his family and friends, at the expenditure of 30 cents for street car fare, attended the wedding appareled in "dress" or "evening" clothes. The plaintiff and the lady members of his family, unsuitably attired for riding in a street car and for walking along the public streets, had to walk for several squares from the place necessary to leave the car line in going to the church, and the wedding ceremony was delayed for 45 or 50 minutes on account of the failure of the plaintiff to reach the church on time. During this period of delay, the bride, family, minister, and friends in attendance at the church were kept waiting upon the delayed arrival of the prospective groom.

On the trial the plaintiff offered in varying forms questions to elicit evidence going to show that he suffered mental and physical pain, mortification, and humiliation, but on objection of the defendants he was not allowed to make such proof or to show any elements of damage of this nature. At the instance of the defendants, the court gave the following charge in writing to the jury: "If the jury believe the evidence, they can only find a verdict for the plaintiff for $5.30 with interest thereon from the 26th day of April, 1906." The plaintiff requested charges in writing, which were refused by the court, to the effect that the plaintiff was entitled to recover for any mental suffering and physical pain caused as a proximate consequence of the defendants' breach of the contract. The jury returned a verdict for plaintiff for $6.55, and, from the judgment entered on this verdict, the plaintiff prosecutes this appeal.

The main contention of appellant is that the court was in error in its ruling on the pleading and on the evidence, and its rulings on the charges in refusing to allow mental suffering and physical pain as an element of recoverable damages for breach of the contract.

The plaintiff's special or ulterior purpose in making the contract was disclosed at the time it was entered into and thereby became incorporated into it and thus afforded a substantial basis for the assessment of special damages. The special circumstances having been known and assented to by each of the contracting parties, each is deemed to have contracted with reference to them, and the party who breaches the contract may be justly held to make good to the other whatever damages, general or special, he has sustained which are the reasonable and natural consequences of the breach under the known circumstances with reference to which the parties acted in making the contract.

When a contract is entered into under special circumstances within the knowledge of both parties, the natural and proximate consequences of a breach of which will entail special damages upon the party not in default, the larger amount of damages may be recovered as having been in the contemplation of both parties. [Citation omitted.] This was also the English rule and the rule at common law. Damages recoverable for the breach of a contract are measured, not only by the actual loss sustained that naturally results as the ordinary consequence of the breach, but extend to consequences which may, under the circumstances of entering into the contract, be presumed to have been in the contemplation of both parties as the probable result of a breach. [Citation omitted.] And, if the special circumstances are communicated, they become an element of the contract. [Citation omitted.]

But are damages for mental suffering an element of the special damages recoverable? "Injury to the feelings—mental harassment—is an element of actual damages. 'Wounding a man's feelings is as much an element of actual damages as breaking his limb.' *Head v. Georgia Pac.*, 79 Ga. 358 [7 S.E. 217, 11 Am. St. Rep. 434]." *Birmingham Water Wks. Co. v. Martini*, 2 Ala. App. 652, 56 So. 833.

The right to recover special damages for mental anguish growing out of a breach of contract to send and deliver a telegram, as said in the recent case of *W. U. Tel. Co. v. Cleveland*, 169 Ala. 131, 135, 53 So. 80, 82, "has been settled in this court," citing the cases sustaining this proposition.

If damages for mental suffering are actual damages and recoverable as compensatory damages when proximately resulting from a breach of the contract, because of the nature of a telegram and the relationship disclosed bringing this consequence of the breach within the contemplation of the parties, as was held in *W. U. Tel. Co. v. Haley*, 143 Ala. 586, 39 So. 386, we cannot perceive under what rule or by what sound reason such *actual* damages can be excluded as a proper measure of recovery in connection with the pecuniary loss sustained in any case where they flow naturally and as a direct consequence from the infraction [**pg. 934**] of a contract entered into under special circumstances known to both parties, and with reference to which they contracted. . . .

This court has also held [citation omitted] that, for a breach of contract for transportation, a woman may recover for mental distress and worry due to having been prevented and delayed in securing stateroom accommodations while on her bridal trip.

In this particular case, considering the subject matter of the contract, the special purpose and exceptional use to which plaintiff intended to put the carriage, which was communicated and well known to the defendants, and with reference to which they contracted, it would seem that it was in the reasonable contemplation of the parties when the contract was entered into under the special known circumstances, that the immediate effect and proximate result ensuing from a breach of the contract by the defendants would cause the plaintiff inconvenience, annoyance, mental harassment, or distress, and make him to suffer physical delay with the attendant discomfort, as well as mental pain in consequence thereof. Certainly it is but common knowledge that some distress of mind must be the natural and proximate consequence of being delayed and not having proper conveyance to meet an appointment of such delicate nature.

The plaintiff by proper averments claimed damages in different counts of the complaint for physical discomfort in consequence of being delayed and not having proper conveyance to meet the special and particular appointment (undoubtedly of great moment to him), and for mental distress attendant upon and suffered in consequence of these physical inconveniences, delay, etc. The court was in error in not submitting these questions to the jury as a proper element of recoverable damages, and in limiting the recovery to the actual financial loss sustained.

A detailed discussion of the various assignments of error is unnecessary. The main proposition involved in each of all of them goes to the question we have considered and determined in what has been said.

Reversed and remanded.

Assignment 2. Office Memorandum
Multiple Issues
Jurisdiction: State in which your law school
is located, or as dictated by your instructor
Open Library

You are an associate with the law firm of Roberts and Cray. Partner Susan Cray asks you to prepare an office memorandum analyzing the claims of Charlotte Rembar, a potential client. The following is a transcript of your interview with Rembar. Fill in "20ZZ" with the current year, "20YY" with the year before the current year, and "20XX" with the year before "20YY." Alternatively, you can use the dates provided in the sample motion for summary judgment at the end of Chapter 19.

Associate: I understand that you have a problem with your employer.

Rembar: My ex-employer—he fired me November 20YY; that's my problem.

Associate: Did he tell you why he fired you?

Rembar: It was pretty obvious—he cut me off because I wouldn't go to bed with him.

Associate: Start from the beginning. Tell me about your job and your employer.

Rembar: I worked for Alexander Hart. He owns Comcon, a local computer consulting firm; they help businesses determine the best computer system for their needs, and they create custom computer programs for them. Alex is a real genius, and he hires the best consultants to work for them, so his business is booming. I started working there January 1; 20YY.

Associate: What was your position with the firm?

Rembar: I was one of his consultants; I designed computer systems and developed programs. I graduated from Stanford with honors in May 20XX with a degree in computer programming; this was my first decent job in the computer industry.

Associate: How many of you work at the firm?

Rembar: Alex works in the field himself as a consultant, and he had six of us working also as consultants. Other than that, he's got a secretary and a part-time accountant.

Associate: Is that his full work force? Has it ever been bigger?

Rembar: As far as I know, that work force represented substantial expansion for him from previous years; his firm has never been bigger.

Associate: Tell me about your termination.

Rembar: Well, Alex had an eye for me since the day he hired me. He was always flirting and asking me out on dates. I always thought of some polite excuse not to go out with him; I didn't want to offend him, but I don't like him that much, and I didn't think it would be good for our working relationship to get involved in dating. It started getting worse last fall, and near the end of October, 20YY, he called me into his office at the end of the day and flatly propositioned me. I refused, and he fired me.

Associate: Precisely what did he say, and how did you respond?

Rembar: First he asked me how I liked my job and my pay; I said I liked it fine. Then he said that he was in love with me and that he wanted me to go home with him that night and sleep with him and that I wouldn't regret it if I did. I didn't know what to say—I was so shocked. I think I just stood there with a stupid expression on my face for a few seconds; then I told him I had to go to a Halloween party, and I ran out of his office.

Associate: Did he fire you then?

Rembar: Not at that meeting. I was so distressed, I could hardly eat or sleep the whole weekend. I was worried about how we were going to maintain a decent working relationship if he was infatuated with me. I decided to talk to him about it the next morning, but I never got a chance. When I arrived at work, Alex called me into his office and told me that he didn't need my services any longer and that I had one week to clean out my office. I was literally speechless. I just walked out to my car and cried and cursed him. I got my last paycheck a week later.

Associate: Were you upset for a long time?

Rembar: Oh yes. I had trouble sleeping for a month. I was so nervous and depressed that I couldn't attend normal social functions. And I felt guilty—and stupid. I thought that I could have avoided all this if I had been more assertive in the beginning and told Alex more clearly that I wasn't interested. I started seeing a doctor and a counselor so that I could cope with it. I guess you've probably handled bigger problems than this, but I felt like my world was coming apart. This was my dream job—I was making $5,000 a month doing work that I love. When Alex fired me, I didn't know how I would ever explain it to other employers in job interviews. Luckily, I told the truth to the personnel manager at IBM, and she believed me. I started working there at the same salary in early January, 20ZZ.

Associate: How was your performance at Comcon?

Rembar: Great. I was the newest consultant, but I was better than two or three of the more experienced ones.

Associate: Did Alex ever praise your work, either orally or in writing?

Rembar: Sure. In my first month, he said I was learning fast. And in August, he complimented me on a particularly good job I did with one account. But he never put anything like that in writing.

Associate: Did he ever complain about your work, either orally or in writing?

Rembar: Never.

Associate: Do you want your job back at Comcon?

Rembar: No. I'm happy at IBM, and I don't want to ever work for that worm again. But I went through a lot of pain, and I think he owes me something for it.

Associate: Did you have a written contract of employment with Comcon?

Rembar: No, we just orally agreed that I would provide the consulting services for a starting salary of $60,000 a year. But he gave me a little policy manual to look at when I interviewed for the job. I've got a copy of it right here.

Associate: Did he say anything when he gave it to you?

Rembar: Yeah, he said that he believed in treating his consultants like professionals and that he could offer me better benefits and working conditions than I would get at the bigger firms. He encouraged me to read the policy manual to confirm that. He obviously wanted to give the appearance of a class operation so that he could attract the best consultants; he made a lot of money off of us.

Associate: I think that's all I need. I don't have authority to take your case; I'll have to report to the partners and get a decision from them. I'll get back to you by the end of the month. If we don't take the case, I'll help steer you toward some other attorneys who may be interested. In the meantime, read this explanation of our fee system and call me if you have any questions.

POLICY MANUAL
for Employees of Comcon

I. Introduction

The success of Comcon lies in its ability to recruit and retain the best employees available nationally. To promote a stable and productive workforce, Comcon provides attractive terms and conditions of employment, including those set forth in the following policies.

II. Salary

A. Initial Salary. . . .

B. Change in Salary. . . .

III. Holidays, Vacations, Sick Leave

A. Holidays. . . .

B. Personal Leave. . . .

IV. Termination

A. Probationary Employment
Each employee will work on probationary status during his or her first 60 days of employment. During this probationary period, Comcon reserves the right to terminate the employee for any reason or for no reason at all.

B. Nonprobationary Employment
Comcon reserves the right to terminate the employment of any employee who is not performing satisfactorily.

Appendix V

Problem 1. Conventions of Punctuation: Policy and Style

Described below are several conventions for use of commas, semicolons, and colons.[1] For each convention of usage,

1. describe the policies of composition that support the rule; alternatively, critique the rule or comment on it;

2. explain what practical problems may arise if the rule is ignored;

3. determine whether the rule should be viewed as sufficiently flexible to permit exceptions when adherence to the rule is not necessary to satisfy important policies or to avoid significant problems; and

4. consider alternatives to the approach described in the rule.

If helpful, illustrate your points with examples.

---

[1]. For further examples, *see* William Strunk, Jr., & E. B. White, THE ELEMENTS OF STYLE 1-9 (5th ed. 2009).

a. Independent Clauses

An independent clause is a clause with a subject and verb, structured so that it could stand alone as a complete sentence. You should separate independent clauses either with a period, thus creating two sentences, or with the following punctuation:

(1) In the absence of a conjunction, use a semicolon, not a comma:

The roughest American team sport is football; basketball and baseball are comparatively gentle.

(2) Use a comma if the second independent clause begins with a coordinating conjunction, such as *and, but, yet, for, so, or, nor:*

For two weeks after the earthquake, the tap water in Sarah's house was contaminated, but potable water was available in plastic containers at a nearby Red Cross outpost.

(3) Use a semicolon if the second independent clause begins with a conjunctive adverb, sometimes called an adverbial connective, such as *therefore, however, moreover, consequently, accordingly, nevertheless, thus.* Follow the connective with a comma:

Basketball is not intended to be a contact sport; nonetheless, basketball players often deliver crushing blows to one another without incurring penalties.

For two weeks after the earthquake, the tap water in Sarah's house was contaminated; however, potable water was available in plastic containers at a nearby Red Cross outpost.

(4) Multiple verbs of the same subject do not create independent clauses and therefore should not be separated with a comma:

Joanie dribbled the ball past a defender and drove to the basket.

b. Lists or Illuminations

After an independent clause, use a colon to introduce a list or illumination of the first clause:

A claim under the due process clause requires proof of three elements: a protectable interest, deprivation of the interest by a state official, and the state's failure to afford procedural protections appropriate in the circumstances.

When the clause following the colon is independent, you may exercise discretion to begin it with a capital letter:

Judge Crowder looked forward to oral argument: He learned much from well-prepared advocates, and he took a perverse pleasure in grilling those who were ill-prepared.

c. Parenthetic Words, Phrases, or Clauses

Use a comma or commas to set off parenthetic words or phrases and nonrestrictive clauses:

One disgruntled patron in the back row, however, complained bitterly about the acoustics of the concert hall.

Carlos Nakai, the flutist and leader of the band, had composed the finale while visiting the Yucatan peninsula.

The audience stood and cheered for Carlos Nakai, who had composed the finale while visiting the Yucatan peninsula.

The court held that, in light of the predominance of service activities, Article 2 of the UCC did not apply to the transaction.

Problem 2. Prehistoric Prohibitions

The following questionable clichés of composition are outdated; indeed, some never rose to the level of an accepted rule. Nonetheless, they still have currency among some editors. If you accept any of these "rules," justify it according to the directions in Problem 1 above. If you reject a rule or would limit it significantly, explain the reasons for your more flexible approach.

1. Never start a sentence with "because," "however," "and," or "but."
2. Never split an infinitive, as in "to severely limit his use of water."
3. Do not insert a comma between the last two elements of a series of three or more elements joined by a conjunction, as in "red, white, and blue."

Appendix VI

Pleadings and Briefs: Assignments for

Parts VI-VIII of the Main Text

Assignment 1. Format—Trial Brief

Review Office Memorandum Assignment 1 in Appendix IV. Assume that (1) you have filed a complaint on behalf of the plaintiffs against Ramona Udave, and (2) the trial court has assigned the case to mandatory arbitration because of the relatively low amount in controversy.

The arbitrator has set the case for a hearing, but she is concerned about your claim for damages for emotional distress based on breach of contract. She has asked you to write a trial brief explaining why the plaintiffs would be entitled to such relief under the facts that you intend to prove at the hearing. She has specifically asked both parties to limit their briefs to that issue.

Without referring to a sample trial brief, draft the document requested by the arbitrator, and argue your clients' case persuasively. You are limited to the authorities reproduced in the office memorandum assignment. You may begin with the caption on the next page; otherwise, use any reasonable format that satisfies the purpose of the document and the needs of your audience. Although you may never have seen a trial brief before, have confidence in your common sense.

ARIZONA SUPERIOR COURT
MARICOPA COUNTY

Trina ARAIZA, et al.,
         Plaintiff,
   v.
 Ramona UDAVE,
         Defendant.
	No. CIV-9X-1279
	
	 OPENING TRIAL BRIEF
	
	 Before Elena Long,
	 Arbitrator

In response to the Arbitrator's request for briefing on Plaintiffs' request for damages for emotional distress, Plaintiffs submit this Trial Brief.

_____
Date

                             _____
                             [Your Name, below your signature]
                             [Your address and phone number]

OPENING TRIAL BRIEF
• • • •

Assignment 2. Revision of Sample Complaint

Critically evaluate the following complaint for substance and style. In this actual complaint, the names of the parties and attorneys have been changed, and the text is single-spaced to conserve space in this book.

a. Specificity of Allegations

Identify the fact allegations that are especially detailed and redraft them to achieve greater generality. What are the advantages and disadvantages of each version?

b. Simplicity

Discard clichés or jargon in the sample complaint and replace them with simple, plain English.

c. Request for Relief

Each count in the sample complaint includes a request for punitive damages, as well as compensatory damages. Would a court be likely to instruct a jury that it could award punitive damages on the first count, for breach of contract? What tort, if any, does the second count allege?

IN THE SUPERIOR COURT OF
THE STATE OF ARIZONA
IN AND FOR THE COUNTY OF MARICOPA

Georgia Anne TUCKER, 　　　　　　Plaintiff, 　　v. James CLYDE, 　　　　　　Defendant.	No. CIV-9X-79 C O M P L A I N T (Breach of Promise; Tort)

Plaintiff alleges:

I

This is an action for money damages exceeding $1,000.

II

Plaintiff is a resident of Cushing, Oklahoma. Defendant is a resident of Morris, Oklahoma. Defendant has caused an act to occur in Maricopa County, Arizona, out of which this cause of action arises.

COUNT ONE
(Breach of Promise)

III

At all relevant times, both Plaintiff and Defendant were over the age of 18 years, and in all respects capable of entering into a marriage contract.

IV

Plaintiff and Defendant were introduced and became acquainted with each other in September 1983. On or about December 8, 1983, Defendant proposed marriage to Plaintiff, and Plaintiff accepted. On January 17, 1984, the proposal and acceptance of marriage were reaffirmed when Defendant purchased a diamond engagement ring for Plaintiff.

V

Plaintiff and Defendant discussed their marriage agreement from time to time and on a great many occasions too numerous to mention herein. In the course of these discussions, Plaintiff and Defendant confirmed plans to be married in Hawaii on March 10, 1984.

VI

In January and February of 1984, Plaintiff and Defendant came to Phoenix, Arizona, for the purpose of locating and purchasing a home for their future marital residence. Defendant purchased a house located at 6052 East Cortez Drive, Scottsdale, Arizona. In addition, in preparation for the marriage, Defendant opened bank accounts, charge accounts, and utility service accounts in the names of James Clyde and Georgia Anne Clyde.

VII

At the insistence of Defendant and in reliance on the agreement to marry, Plaintiff gave up a profitable business as a hair stylist in Cushing, Oklahoma; borrowed and spent the sum of $12,000.00 to refurbish her residence in order to facilitate its sale; listed her residence for sale with a real estate agency; leased her residence to Defendant's son; withdrew her children from school; and moved her household possessions and her children from Cushing, Oklahoma, to Scottsdale, Arizona, at great expense and inconvenience.

VIII

On March 1, 1984, after having moved to Scottsdale, Arizona, Defendant presented to Plaintiff a prenuptial agreement that, among other things, listed the State of Arizona as the domicile of the parties and that provided for execution of the agreement in Maricopa County, Arizona. Plaintiff refused to sign the prenuptial agreement as written; however, despite Plaintiff's refusal to sign the prenuptial agreement, Defendant again renewed his promise to marry Plaintiff.

IX

On March 8, 1984, Defendant, Plaintiff, and three of Plaintiff's four children flew to Hawaii for the purpose of consummating the marriage, which was scheduled for March 10, 1984.

X

At approximately 8:00 A.M. on the morning of March 9, 1984, Defendant informed Plaintiff that he would not go through with the wedding. Since that date, Defendant has refused to carry out his promise to marry Plaintiff.

XI

On March 9, 1984, Defendant, Plaintiff, and Plaintiff's three children returned to Scottsdale, Arizona, where Defendant left Plaintiff and her three children in the house that was to have been the marital residence. On March 22, 1984, Defendant demanded that Plaintiff and her three children vacate the Scottsdale residence; for lack of other accommodations, Plaintiff was forced to return to Cushing, Oklahoma.

XII

By reason of Defendant's breach of promise to marry, Plaintiff has been deprived of Defendant's support and care for herself and her children, and of the commensurate standard of living that she would have enjoyed had the marriage been consummated. In addition to the foregoing, Plaintiff has suffered, and will continue to suffer, the following damages: a loss of past and future income as the result of Defendant's insistence that she give up her business; economic loss as the result of monies expended for refurbishing her residence in preparation for sale; economic loss resulting from the move from Cushing, Oklahoma, to Scottsdale, Arizona, and from Scottsdale, Arizona, back to Cushing, Oklahoma; and mental pain and anguish, wounded pride, mortification, humiliation, shame, and disgrace, which has directly impaired Plaintiff's health.

XIII

Defendant's actions in breaching his promise to marry were intentional or taken with reckless disregard for the rights of Plaintiff.

Plaintiff therefore requests judgment as follows:

1. past and future lost income in an amount to be determined at trial;
2. out-of-pocket expenses in an amount to be determined at trial, but not less than $12,000;
3. mental pain and anguish in an amount to be determined at trial, but not less than $10,000;
4. other compensatory damages in an amount to be determined at trial;
5. reasonable attorney's fees;
6. punitive damages in an amount to be determined at trial; and
7. such other and further relief as the Court deems just and proper.

COUNT TWO
(Tort)

XIV

Plaintiff realleges and incorporates into this count paragraphs I through XIII.

XV

Defendant stated to friends, relatives, and acquaintances of Plaintiff that Plaintiff and Defendant were engaged, that Plaintiff and Defendant were moving to Scottsdale, Arizona, and that Plaintiff and Defendant would be married on March 10, 1984.

XVI

After Defendant informed Plaintiff that he would not go through with the marriage, Defendant promised Plaintiff that he would provide her with the financial means to relocate wherever she desired so that she would not have to return to Cushing, Oklahoma, where she would experience the humiliation, shame, disgrace, pain, and anguish of explaining Defendant's failure to fulfill his marriage promise.

XVII

Defendant, after making the above-described promise to Plaintiff, forced Plaintiff to move out of the residence located in Scottsdale, Arizona, and refused to provide any financial assistance except transportation expenses to Cushing, Oklahoma.

XVIII

Defendant's actions in providing only transportation expenses for Plaintiff's return to Cushing, Oklahoma, were extreme and outrageous, were intentional, and were done with full knowledge of the emotional consequences to Plaintiff.

XIX

Plaintiff has suffered grievous mental pain, anguish, mortification, humiliation, shame, and disgrace; Plaintiff's mental and physical health has been impaired.

Plaintiff therefore prays for judgment as follows:

1. compensatory damages in an amount to be determined at trial, but not less than $12,000;
2. punitive damages in an amount to be determined at trial; and
3. such other and further relief as the Court deems just and proper in the premises.

Dated May 21, 1984   TICKER, STRANGER & NEAR

By _____
      James R. Near
      Joseph A. Hammer
      900 East Camelback Road
      Scottsdale, AZ 85281
      Attorneys for Plaintiff

Assignment 3. Drafting an Answer

Review the sample complaint in Assignment 2 above or the revised version prepared by you or by a classmate. The defendant, James Clyde, is prepared to prove that Georgia Anne Tucker repudiated the marriage agreement when she refused to sign a written prenuptial agreement, that he never renewed his promise after Tucker's repudiation, that Tucker called off the wedding, and that he suffered severe disappointment as a result. Draft an answer on behalf of Clyde.

Assignment 4. Drafting a Complaint

Review Office Memorandum Assignment 2 at the end of Appendix IV. Based on the analysis in your office memorandum, determine what claims you could allege in good faith, and draft a complaint for an action in state court on behalf of Charlotte Rembar. You may assume that both parties agree Ms. Rembar has received notice of right to sue by the appropriate state agency under Ariz. Rev. Stat. Ann. § 1481.D, or a similar statute in the jurisdiction in which your professor sets your assignment. You may also assume that your complaint meets all applicable limitations periods for any claim that you allege.

Assignment 5. Motion for Summary Judgment

Review (1) Office Memorandum Assignment 2 in Appendix IV, (2) Assignment 4 above, and (3) the sample motion for summary judgment at the end of Chapter 19 of the main text. Do you agree with the decision of Hart's attorney to concede for purposes of summary judgment that the employee manual stated terms of Rembar's employment contract with Comcon?

Now imagine that the second sentence in Section I of the Comcon Policy Manual (Exhibit A of the materials supporting the motion) instead stated the following: "To promote a stable and productive workforce, Comcon endeavors to provide attractive terms and conditions of employment, as reflected in the following policies." On these terms, would you still concede for purposes of summary judgment that the employee manual stated terms of Rembar's employment contract? Add a section to the argument of Hart's memorandum in support of his motion for summary judgment, arguing that the employee manual did not state contract terms under the statutory standard but instead set forth Comcon's current polices, to which it was not contractually bound.

Assignment 6. Opposition to Motion for Summary Judgment

Review (1) Office Memorandum Assignment 2 in Appendix IV, (2) Assignment 4 above, and (3) the sample motion for summary judgment at the end of Chapter 19 of the main text.

Prepare materials opposing Hart's motion for summary judgment, or opposing a similar motion on Hart's behalf supplied by your instructor.

In preparing your opposition, you may assume the following premises or developments:

a. Your firm filed a complaint alleging four claims for relief: (1) breach of a promise of job security, (2) violation of the Arizona Civil Rights Act, (3) wrongful discharge in violation of public policy, and (4) infliction of emotional distress. In his answer, Hart denied that Rembar's contract contained any provisions for job security and denied the allegations of sexual harassment. He alleged that he discharged Rembar for poor performance.

b. Rembar stands by the information she provided in the initial interview, set forth in Appendix IV, and she is willing to swear to it in an affidavit. Your independent fact investigation has revealed some corroborating evidence from Leslie West, Alex Hart's secretary during Charlotte Rembar's tenure at Comcon. In a recent interview, West revealed that she and Rembar developed a close friendship and that she was distressed to learn of Rembar's discharge. After Rembar filed suit, Hart became irritable and unpleasant to work for; West voluntarily quit her job at the end of the year after Rembar's discharge. She has offered to support Rembar with trial testimony and statements in an affidavit. The following is an excerpt from your interview of West:

> *West:* That was on Halloween last fall, 2013. I saw Charlotte leave the office in tears at quitting time. The following workday, in the afternoon, Mr. Hart told me to process the paperwork to terminate Charlotte's payroll at the end of the week. When I said that I had thought Charlotte was one of his best consultants, he said, "Her consulting isn't my problem—it's her stuck-up attitude." I asked him what I should put down on the paperwork as the reason for her termination, and he said something like, "I don't care what you put—just say that she has a negative attitude."

c. Through discovery requests, you have obtained copies of the contents of Rembar's employment file at Comcon. The file includes only a few insignificant notes and the two payroll action forms attached to Hart's motion for summary judgment.

d. In responding to the Motion for Summary Judgment, you may assume that both parties agree that Ms. Rembar has received notice of right to sue by the appropriate state agency under Ariz. Rev. Stat. Ann. § 1481.D, or a similar statute in the jurisdiction in which your professor sets your assignment, and you need not address that issue. You may also assume that your complaint met all applicable limitations periods for any claim that you alleged.

Assignment 7. Motion to Exclude Evidence

Review Office Memorandum Assignment 2 in Appendix IV and Assignments 4 and 6 above. Assume that you have successfully opposed Hart's motion for summary judgment and that the trial judge has scheduled a pretrial conference.

You are concerned about some embarrassing evidence that Hart has obtained through the discovery process. While a freshman at Stanford University, Rembar posed nude for a two-page spread in *Hustle and Bustle*, an adult magazine; some of the poses would strike the average juror as lewd and tasteless. Rembar explained that she posed for the pictures on a dare and that she didn't realize until later how lewd and revealing they would be. She regrets her decision to pose, and she insists that the pictures do not reflect her current personality or style of relating to friends or colleagues.

Hart probably learned of the magazine spread through one of Rembar's freshman college classmates or instructors. In a discovery request, Hart requested confirmation of the event, along with a copy of the out-of-print magazine. Pursuant to your state's counterpart to Federal Rule of Civil Procedure 26(c), you objected to the request on the ground that the information requested would be inadmissible at trial and that its production would result in annoyance, embarrassment, and oppression. The trial judge, however, compelled discovery on the ground that the information sought, whether or not admissible itself, might lead to the discovery of evidence relating to a claim or defense. *See* FED. R. CIV. P. 26(b)(1); *Kidwiler v. Progressive Paloverde Ins. Co.*, 192 F.R.D. 193, 199 (N.D. W. Va. 2000).

You now seek an advance ruling barring any reference to the magazine spread at trial. Draft a motion to exclude the evidence before trial.

INDEX